# History of Nazi Holocaust and Genocide (1941–1945)

Editor
**Loree Vallejo**

*Scribbles*

Year of Publication 2018

ISBN : 9789352979714

Book Published by

# *Scribbles*

*(An Imprint of Alpha Editions)*

email - alphaedis@gmail.com

Produced by: PediaPress GmbH
Limburg an der Lahn
Germany
http://pediapress.com/

The content within this book was generated collaboratively by volunteers. Please be advised that nothing found here has necessarily been reviewed by people with the expertise required to provide you with complete, accurate or reliable information. Some information in this book may be misleading or simply wrong. Alpha Editions and PediaPress does not guarantee the validity of the information found here. If you need specific advice (for example, medical, legal, financial, or risk management) please seek a professional who is licensed or knowledgeable in that area.

Sources, licenses and contributors of the articles and images are listed in the section entitled "References". Parts of the books may be licensed under the GNU Free Documentation License. A copy of this license is included in the section entitled "GNU Free Documentation License"

The views and characters expressed in the book are those of the contributors and his/her imagination and do not represent the views of the Publisher.

# Contents

**Articles**     **1**
   Introduction . . . . . . . . . . . . . . . . . . . . . . . . . . . . 1

**Names of the Holocaust**     **3**
   Names of the Holocaust . . . . . . . . . . . . . . . . . . . . . . . 3

**List of Nazi concentration camps**     **11**

**Nazi human experimentation**     **13**
   Nazi human experimentation . . . . . . . . . . . . . . . . . . . . 13

**Aktion T4**     **25**
   Aktion T4 . . . . . . . . . . . . . . . . . . . . . . . . . . . . . . 25
   Life unworthy of life . . . . . . . . . . . . . . . . . . . . . . . . 61
   Kristallnacht . . . . . . . . . . . . . . . . . . . . . . . . . . . . . 64

**The holocaust**     **87**
   The Holocaust in Poland . . . . . . . . . . . . . . . . . . . . . . 87
   Jewish ghettos in German-occupied Poland . . . . . . . . . . . . 120
   The Holocaust in Norway . . . . . . . . . . . . . . . . . . . . . . 137
   The Holocaust in Belgium . . . . . . . . . . . . . . . . . . . . . 162
   The Holocaust in Luxembourg . . . . . . . . . . . . . . . . . . . 176
   The Holocaust in France . . . . . . . . . . . . . . . . . . . . . . 178
   The Holocaust in Serbia . . . . . . . . . . . . . . . . . . . . . . 187
   The Holocaust in the Independent State of Croatia . . . . . . . . 194
   Jews of Libya during the Holocaust . . . . . . . . . . . . . . . . 207

**Concentration and labor camps**    **217**

  Nazi concentration camps . . . . . . . . . . . . . . . . . . . . 217

  List of Nazi concentration camps . . . . . . . . . . . . . . . . 231

  Extermination through labour . . . . . . . . . . . . . . . . . . 238

  Nazi ghettos . . . . . . . . . . . . . . . . . . . . . . . . . . . 253

  The Holocaust in Ukraine . . . . . . . . . . . . . . . . . . . . 258

  The Holocaust in Lithuania . . . . . . . . . . . . . . . . . . . 265

  The Holocaust in Latvia . . . . . . . . . . . . . . . . . . . . . 277

  The Holocaust in Estonia . . . . . . . . . . . . . . . . . . . . 296

  The Holocaust in Belarus . . . . . . . . . . . . . . . . . . . . 308

  The Holocaust in Russia . . . . . . . . . . . . . . . . . . . . . 320

**Death squads**    **329**

  Einsatzgruppen . . . . . . . . . . . . . . . . . . . . . . . . . . 329

  Final Solution . . . . . . . . . . . . . . . . . . . . . . . . . . 357

**Flow of information about the mass murder**    **377**

  The Black Book of Polish Jewry . . . . . . . . . . . . . . . . . 377

  The Polish White Book . . . . . . . . . . . . . . . . . . . . . 380

  The Black Book of Poland . . . . . . . . . . . . . . . . . . . . 383

  Raczyński's Note . . . . . . . . . . . . . . . . . . . . . . . . . 385

  Witold's Report . . . . . . . . . . . . . . . . . . . . . . . . . . 391

**Death marches**    **397**

  Death marches (Holocaust) . . . . . . . . . . . . . . . . . . . 397

**Victims and death toll**    **405**

  Holocaust victims . . . . . . . . . . . . . . . . . . . . . . . . . 405

  Responsibility for the Holocaust . . . . . . . . . . . . . . . . 425

  List of major perpetrators of the Holocaust . . . . . . . . . . 481

  Aftermath of the Holocaust . . . . . . . . . . . . . . . . . . . 493

# Appendix 501

References . . . . . . . . . . . . . . . . . . . . . . . . . . . 501

Article Sources and Contributors . . . . . . . . . . . . . . . . . . 557

Image Sources, Licenses and Contributors . . . . . . . . . . . . 560

# Article Licenses 567

# Index 569

# Introduction

The Holocaust, also referred to as the Shoah, was a genocide during World War II in which Nazi Germany, aided by its collaborators, systematically murdered some six million European Jews, around two-thirds of the Jewish population of Europe, between 1941 and 1945. Jews were targeted for extermination as part of a larger event involving the persecution and murder of other groups, including in particular the Roma and "incurably sick", as well as ethnic Poles and other Slavs, Soviet citizens, Soviet prisoners of war, political opponents, gay men and Jehovah's Witnesses, resulting in up to 17 million deaths overall. Germany implemented the persecution in stages. Following Adolf Hitler's rise to power in 1933, the government passed laws to exclude Jews from civil society, most prominently the Nuremberg Laws in 1935. Starting in 1933, the Nazis built a network of concentration camps in Germany for political opponents and people deemed "undesirable". After the invasion of Poland in 1939, the regime set up ghettos to segregate Jews. Over 42,000 camps, ghettos, and other detention sites were established. The deportation of Jews to the ghettos culminated in the policy of extermination the Nazis called the "Final Solution to the Jewish Question", discussed by senior Nazi officials at the Wannsee Conference in Berlin in January 1942. As German forces captured territories in the East, all anti-Jewish measures were radicalized. Under the coordination of the SS, with directions from the highest leadership of the Nazi Party, killings were committed within Germany itself, throughout German-occupied Europe, and across all territories controlled by the Axis powers. Paramilitary death squads called Einsatzgruppen in cooperation with Wehrmacht police battalions and local collaborators murdered around 1.3 million Jews in mass shootings between 1941 and 1945. By mid-1942, victims were being deported from the ghettos in sealed freight trains to extermination camps where, if they survived the journey, they were killed in gas chambers. The killing continued until the end of World War II in Europe in May 1945.

# Names of the Holocaust

## Names of the Holocaust

**Names of the Holocaust** vary based on context. "The Holocaust" is the name commonly applied in English since the mid-1940s to the systematic extermination of 6 million Jews by Nazi Germany during World War II. The term is also used more broadly to include the Nazis' systematic murder of millions of people in other groups, including ethnic Poles, the Romani, Soviet civilians, Soviet prisoners of war, people with disabilities, gay men, and political and religious opponents,[1] which would bring the total number of Holocaust victims to between 11 million and 17 million people.[2] In Judaism, **Shoah** (שואה), meaning "calamity" in Hebrew, became the standard term for the 20th-century *Holocaust*[3] (see Yom HaShoah). This is because 'Holocaust' connotes a sacrifice, and Jewish leaders argue there was no sacrifice.

## Names

### The Holocaust

The word "holocaust" originally derived from the Greek word *holokauston*, meaning "a completely (*holos*) burnt (*kaustos*) sacrificial offering," or "a burnt sacrifice offered to a god." In Greek and Roman pagan rites, gods of the earth and underworld received dark animals, which were offered by night and burnt in full. The word "holocaust" was later adopted in Greek translations of the Torah to refer to the olah,[4] standard communal and individual sacrificial burnt offerings that Jews were required[5] to make in the times of the Beit HaMikdash (Temple in Jerusalem). In its Latin form, *holocaustum*, the term was first used with specific reference to a massacre of Jewish people by the chroniclers Roger of Howden[6] and Richard of Devizes in England in the 1190s.

The earliest use of the word *holocaust* to denote a massacre recorded by the *Oxford English Dictionary* dates from 1833 when the journalist Leitch Ritchie, describing the wars of the medieval French monarch Louis VII, wrote that he "once made a holocaust of thirteen hundred persons in a church", a massacre by fire of the inhabitants of Vitry-le-François in 1142. As this occurred in a church, it could be seen as a religious offering. The English poet John Milton had used the word to denote a conflagration in his 1671 poem *Samson Agonistes,* in which the massacre was clearly divinely dedicated. The word gradually developed to mean a massacre thereon, taking on a secular connotation.[7,8]

In the early twentieth century, possibly the first to use the term was journalist Melville Chater in 1925, to describe the burning and sacking of Smyrne in 1922.[9,10] Winston Churchill used it in 1929 (Tatz, 2003), and other contemporaneous writers used it before World War II to describe the Armenian Genocide of World War I.[11,12] The Armenian Genocide is referenced in the title of a 1922 poem "The Holocaust" (published as a booklet) and the 1923 book "The Smyrna Holocaust" deals with arson and massacre of Armenians.[13] Before the Second World War, the possibility of another war was referred to as "another holocaust" (that is, a repeat of the First World War). With reference to the events of the war, writers in English from 1945 used the term in relation to events such as the fire-bombing of Dresden or Hiroshima, or the effects of a nuclear war, although from the 1950s onwards, it was increasingly used in English to refer to the Nazi genocide of the European Jews (or Judeocide).

By the late 1950s, documents translated from Hebrew sometimes used the word "Holocaust" to translate "Shoah", as the Judeocide. This use can be found as early as May 23, 1943, in *The New York Times,* on page E6, in an article by Julian Meltzer, referring to feelings in Palestine about Jewish immigration of refugees from "the Nazi holocaust."

One significant early use was in a 1958 recollection by Leslie Hardman, the first Jewish British Army Chaplain to enter Bergen-Belsen concentration camp in April 1945, where he ministered to survivors and supervised the burial of about 20,000 victims,

> *Towards me came what seemed to be the remnants of a holocaust – a staggering mass of blackened skin and bones, held together somehow with filthy rags. 'My God, the dead walk', I cried aloud, but I did not recognise my voice... [peering] at the double star, the emblem of Jewry on my tunic - one poor creature touched and then stroked the badge of my faith, and finding that it was real murmured, 'Rabbiner, Rabbiner'.*[14]

By the late 1960s, the term was starting to be used in this sense without qualification. Nora Levin's 1968 book *The Holocaust: The Destruction of European Jewry, 1933-1945* explains the meaning in its subtitle, but uses the unmoderated phrase "The Holocaust". An article called "Moral Trauma and the Holocaust" was published in the *New York Times* on February 12, 1968.[15] However, it was not until the late 1970s that the Nazi genocide became the generally accepted conventional meaning of the word, when used unqualified and with a capital letter, a usage that also spread to other languages for the same period.[16] The 1978 television miniseries titled "Holocaust" and starring Meryl Streep is often cited as the principal contributor to establishing the current usage in the wider culture.[17] "Holocaust" was selected as the Association for the German Language's Word of the Year in 1979, reflecting increased public consciousness of the term.

The Hebrew word *Shoah* is preferred by some people due to the supposed theologically and historically unacceptable nature of the word "holocaust".[18] The American historian Walter Laqueur (whose parents died in the Holocaust) has argued that the term "Holocaust" is a "singularly inappropriate" term for the genocide of the Jews as it implies a "burnt offering" to God.[19] Laqueur wrote, "It was not the intention of the Nazis to make a sacrifice of this kind and the position of the Jews was not that of a ritual victim". The British historian Geoff Eley wrote in a 1982 essay entitled "Holocaust History" that he thought the term Holocaust implies "a certain mystification, an insistence on the uniquely Jewish character of the experience".

The term became increasingly widespread as a synonym for "genocide" in the last decades of the 20th century to refer to mass murders in the form "X holocaust" (e.g. "Rwandan holocaust"). Examples are Rwanda, the Ukraine under Stalin, and the actions of the Khmer Rouge in Cambodia.

In order to suggest comparison with Nazi murders other historical events have also been labeled "Holocausts", for example the oppression of lower caste groups in India ("Sudra Holocaust") or the slave trade ("African Holocaust").

**Use of the term for non-Jewish victims of the Nazis**

While the terms *Shoah* and *Final Solution* always refer to the fate of the Jews during the Nazi rule, the term *Holocaust* is sometimes used in a wider sense to describe other genocides of the Nazi and other regimes.

The *Columbia Encyclopedia* defines *"Holocaust"* as "name given to the period of persecution and extermination of European Jews by Nazi Germany".[20] The Compact Oxford English Dictionary[21] and *Microsoft Encarta*[22] give similar definitions. The *Encyclopædia Britannica* defines "Holocaust" as "the systematic state-sponsored killing of six million Jewish men, women and children, and millions of others by Nazi Germany and its collaborators during World War II",[23] although the article goes on to say, "The Nazis also singled out the Roma (Gypsies). They were the only other group that the Nazis systematically killed in gas chambers alongside the Jews."

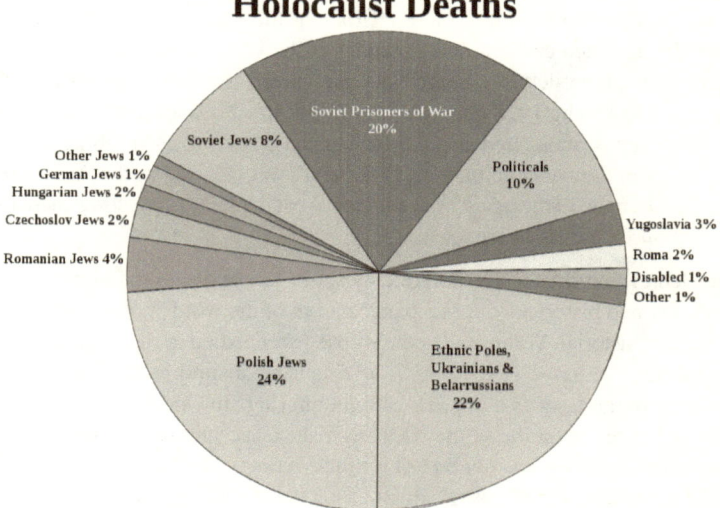

**Figure 1:** *Rough approximation of Holocaust deaths according to a broad definition that includes non-Jews, such as Romani, Slavs, Soviet POWs and political opponents (click image for more details).*

Scholars are divided on whether the term Holocaust should be applied to all victims of Nazi mass murder, with some using it synonymously with *Shoah* or "Final Solution of the Jewish Question", and others including the killing of Romani peoples, Poles, the deaths of Soviet prisoners of war, Slavs, homosexual men, Jehovah's Witnesses, the disabled, and political opponents.[24]

Czechoslovak–Israeli historian Yehuda Bauer, stated: "Let us be clear: ... Shoah, Churban, Judeocide, whatever we call it, is the name we give to the attempted planned total physical annihilation of the Jewish people, and its partial perpetration with the murder of most of the Jews of Europe." He also contends that the Holocaust should include only Jews because it was the intent of the Nazis to exterminate all Jews, while the other groups were not to be totally annihilated.[25] Inclusion of non-Jewish victims of the Nazis in the Holocaust is objected to by many persons including, and by organizations such as Yad Vashem, an Israeli state institution in Jerusalem established in 1953 to commemorate the victims of the Holocaust. They say that the word was originally meant to describe the extermination of the Jews, and that the Jewish Holocaust was a crime on such a scale, and of such totality and specificity, as the culmination of the long history of European antisemitism, that it should not be subsumed into a general category with the other crimes of the Nazis.[26]

Nobel laureate and Jewish Holocaust survivor Elie Wiesel, does consider other groups, besides the Jews, as Holocaust victims, declaring to President Jimmy Carter, "Not all the victims of the Holocaust were Jews, but all Jews were victims," when he asked his support for a national Holocaust museum in Washington.

British historian Michael Burleigh and German historian Wolfgang Wippermann maintain that although all Jews were victims, the Holocaust transcended the confines of the Jewish community – other people shared the tragic fate of victimhood.[27] Hungarian former Minister for Roma Affairs László Teleki applies the term *Holocaust* to both the murder of Jews and Romani peoples by the Nazis. In *The Columbia Guide to the Holocaust*, American historians Donald Niewyk and Francis Nicosia use the term to include Jews, Gypsies and the disabled.[28] American historian Dennis Reinhartz has claimed that Gypsies were the main victims of genocide in Croatia and Serbia during the Second World War, and has called this "the Balkan Holocaust 1941-1945".[29]

## Final Solution

The "Final Solution to the Jewish Question" (German: *Endlösung der Judenfrage*) was the Nazis' own term, recorded in the minutes of the Wannsee Conference on 20 January 1942, and translated into English for the Nuremberg Trials in 1945. Before the word "Holocaust" became normative this phrase was also used by writers in English. For example, in William Shirer's *The Rise and Fall of the Third Reich*, the genocide is described as "The Final Solution" (in quotation marks; the word "Holocaust" is not mentioned).[30] In both English and German, "Final Solution" has been widely used as an alternative to "Holocaust".[31] Whereas the term "Holocaust" is now often used to include all casualties of the Nazi death camps and murder squads, the "Final Solution" refers exclusively to "the attempt to annihilate the Jewish people," as defined at the site of the United States Holocaust Memorial Museum. For a time after World War II, German historians also used the term *Völkermord* ("genocide"), or in full, *der Völkermord an den Juden* ("the genocide of the Jewish people"), while the prevalent term in Germany today is either *Holocaust* or increasingly *Shoah*.

## Shoah

The biblical word *Shoah* (שואה), also spelled *Shoa* and *Sho'ah*, meaning "calamity" in Hebrew (and also used to refer to "destruction" since the Middle Ages), became the standard Hebrew term for the 20th-century *Holocaust* as early as the early 1940s.[3] In recent literature it is specifically prefixed with **Ha** ("The" in Hebrew) when referring to Nazi mass-murders, for the same reason that "holocaust" becomes *"The* Holocaust". It may be spelled *Ha-Shoah* or *HaShoah*, as in Yom HaShoah, the annual Jewish "Holocaust and Heroism Remembrance Day".

*Shoah* had earlier been used in the context of the Nazis as a translation of "catastrophe". For example, in 1934, when Chaim Weizmann told the Zionist Action Committee that Hitler's rise to power was an "unvorhergesehene Katastrophe, etwa ein neuer Weltkrieg" ("an unforeseen catastrophe, comparable to another world war"), the Hebrew press translated *Katastrophe* as *Shoah*.[32] In the spring of 1942, the Jerusalem historian BenZion Dinur (Dinaburg) used *Shoah* in a book published by the United Aid Committee for the Jews in Poland to describe the extermination of Europe's Jews, calling it a "catastrophe" that symbolized the unique situation of the Jewish people.[33,34] The word *Shoah* was chosen in Israel to describe the Holocaust, the term institutionalized by the Knesset on April 12, 1951, when it established *Yom Ha-Shoah Ve Mered Ha-Getaot*, the national day of remembrance. In the 1950s, Yad Vashem, the Israel "Holocaust Martyrs' and Heroes' Remembrance Authority" was routinely translating this into English as "the Disaster". At that time, *holocaust* was often used to mean the conflagration of much of humanity in a nuclear war.[35] Since then, Yad Vashem has changed its practice; the word "Holocaust", usually now capitalized, has come to refer principally to the genocide of the European Jews.[36] The Israeli historian Saul Friedländer wrote in 1987 of "the growing centrality of the *Shoah* for Jewish communities in the Diaspora" and that "The *Shoah* is almost becoming a symbol of identification, for better or for worse, whether because of the weakening of the bond of religion or because of the lesser salience of Zionism and Israel as an identification element". The British historian Richard J. Evans wrote in 1989 that the term Holocaust was unsuitable, and should not be used.

## Khurban and destruction

"**khurbn eyrope** *(אײראפע חורבן)*, *is the term for the Holocaust in Yiddish. The term uses the word 'Khurbn' of Hebrew origin (Hebrew: חרבן; Hebrew pronunciation: 'Khur'ban') which means "Destruction", and translates as "Destruction of Europe". The word "Khur'ban/'Khurbn" is also used for the destruction of both the First and the Second Temple in both Hebrew and Yiddish. Max Kaufmann's early (1947) history of the genocide in Latvia was called* Khurbn Lettland, *that is,* The Destruction of the Jews of Latvia.[37] *Published later, Raul Hilberg's most important work was* The Destruction of the European Jews.[38]

## Porajmos

The *Porajmos* (also *Porrajmos*) literally "Devouring", or *Samudaripen* ("Mass killing") is a term adopted by the Romani historian Ian Hancock to describe attempts by the Nazis to exterminate most of the Romani peoples of Europe. The phenomenon has been little studied.

# List of Nazi concentration camps

# Nazi human experimentation

## Nazi human experimentation

<indicator name="pp-default"> 🔒 </indicator>

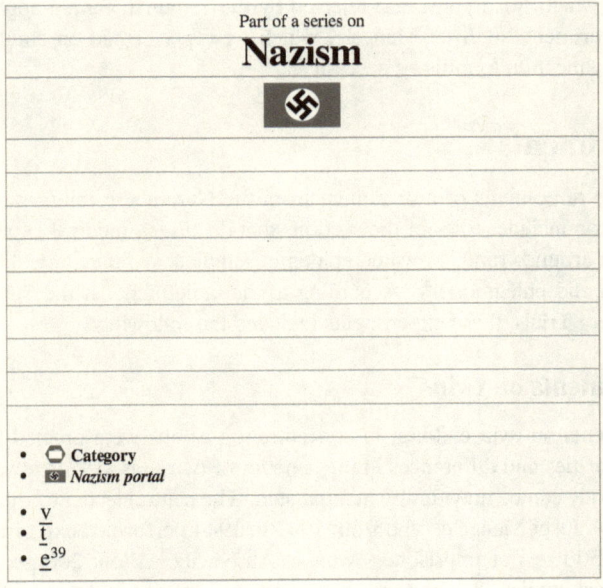

**Nazi human experimentation** was a series of medical experiments on large numbers of prisoners, including children, by Nazi Germany in its concentration camps in the early to mid 1940s, during World War II and the Holocaust. Chief target populations included Romani, Sinti, ethnic Poles, Soviet POWs, disabled Germans, and Jews from across Europe.

Nazi physicians and their assistants forced prisoners into participating; they did not willingly volunteer and no consent was given for the procedures. Typically, the experiments resulted in death, trauma, disfigurement or permanent disability, and as such are considered examples of medical torture.

At Auschwitz and other camps, under the direction of Eduard Wirths, selected inmates were subjected to various hazardous experiments that were designed to help German military personnel in combat situations, develop new weapons, aid in the recovery of military personnel who had been injured, and to advance the Nazi racial ideology. Aribert Heim conducted similar medical experiments at Mauthausen.

After the war, these crimes were tried at what became known as the Doctors' Trial, and revulsion at the abuses perpetrated led to the development of the Nuremberg Code of medical ethics. The Nazi physicians in the Doctors' Trial argued that military necessity justified their torturous experiments, and compared their victims to collateral damage from Allied bombings. But this defense, which was in any case rejected by the Tribunal, cannot apply to the twin experiments of Josef Mengele, which were performed on children and had no connection to military necessity.

# Experiments

The table of contents of a document from the Nuremberg military tribunals prosecution includes titles of the sections that document medical experiments revolving around: food, seawater, epidemic jaundice, sulfanilamide, blood coagulation and phlegmone.[40] According to the indictments at the Subsequent Nuremberg Trials, these experiments included the following:

## Experiments on twins

Experiments on twin children in concentration camps were created to show the similarities and differences in the genetics of twins, as well as to see if the human body can be unnaturally manipulated. The central leader of the experiments was Josef Mengele, who from 1943 to 1944 performed experiments on nearly 1,500 sets of imprisoned twins at Auschwitz. About 200 people survived these studies.[41] The twins were arranged by age and sex and kept in barracks between experiments, which ranged from injection of different dyes into the eyes of twins to see whether it would change their color to sewing twins together in attempts to create conjoined twins. Often times, one twin would be forced to undergo experimentation, while the other was kept as a control. If the experimentation reached the point of death, the second twin would be brought in to be killed at the same time. Doctors would then look at the effects of experimentation and compare both bodies.[42]

## Bone, muscle, and nerve transplantation experiments

From about September 1942 to about December 1943 experiments were conducted at the Ravensbrück concentration camp, for the benefit of the German Armed Forces, to study bone, muscle, and nerve regeneration, and bone transplantation from one person to another. Sections of bones, muscles, and nerves were removed from the subjects without use of anesthesia. As a result of these operations, many victims suffered intense agony, mutilation, and permanent disability.

On August 12, 1946 a survivor named Jadwiga Kamińska gave a deposition about her time at Ravensbrück concentration camp and describes how she was operated on twice. Both operations involved one of her legs and although she never describes having any knowledge as to what exactly the procedure was, she explains that both times she was in extreme pain and developed a fever post surgery. Yet she was given little to no care. Kamińska describes being told that she had been operated on simply because she was a "young girl and a Polish patriot". She describes how her leg oozed pus for months after the operations.[43]

Prisoners were also experimented on by having their bone marrow injected with bacteria to study the effectiveness of new drugs being developed for use in the battle fields. Many prisoners left the camps with disfigurement that would last the rest of their lives.

## Head injury experiments

In mid-1942 in Baranowicze, occupied Poland, experiments were conducted in a small building behind the private home occupied by a known Nazi SD Security Service officer, in which "a young boy of eleven or twelve [was] strapped to a chair so he could not move. Above him was a mechanized hammer that every few seconds came down upon his head." The boy was driven insane from the torture.[44]

## Freezing experiments

In 1941, the *Luftwaffe* conducted experiments with the intent of discovering means to prevent and treat hypothermia. There were 360 to 400 experiments and 280 to 300 victims indicating some victims suffered more than one experiment.

## "Exitus" (death) table compiled by Sigmund Rascher

| Attempt no. | Water temperature | Body temperature when removed from the water | Body temperature at death | Time in water | Time of death |
|---|---|---|---|---|---|
| 5 | 5.2 °C (41.4 °F) | 27.7 °C (81.9 °F) | 27.7 °C (81.9 °F) | 66' | 66' |
| 13 | 6 °C (43 °F) | 29.2 °C (84.6 °F) | 29.2 °C (84.6 °F) | 80' | 87' |
| 14 | 4 °C (39 °F) | 27.8 °C (82.0 °F) | 27.5 °C (81.5 °F) | 95' | |
| 16 | 4 °C (39 °F) | 28.7 °C (83.7 °F) | 26 °C (79 °F) | 60' | 74' |
| 23 | 4.5 °C (40.1 °F) | 27.8 °C (82.0 °F) | 25.7 °C (78.3 °F) | 57' | 65' |
| 25 | 4.6 °C (40.3 °F) | 27.8 °C (82.0 °F) | 26.6 °C (79.9 °F) | 51' | 65' |
| | 4.2 °C (39.6 °F) | 26.7 °C (80.1 °F) | 25.9 °C (78.6 °F) | 53' | 53' |

Another study placed prisoners naked in the open air for several hours with temperatures as low as –6 °C (21 °F). Besides studying the physical effects of cold exposure, the experimenters also assessed different methods of rewarming survivors.[45] "One assistant later testified that some victims were thrown into boiling water for rewarming."

Beginning in August 1942, at the Dachau camp, prisoners were forced to sit in tanks of freezing water for up to 3 hours. After subjects were frozen, they then underwent different methods for rewarming. Many subjects died in this process.

The freezing/hypothermia experiments were conducted for the Nazi high command to simulate the conditions the armies suffered on the Eastern Front, as the German forces were ill-prepared for the cold weather they encountered. Many experiments were conducted on captured Russian troops; the Nazis wondered whether their genetics gave them superior resistance to cold. The principal locales were Dachau and Auschwitz. Sigmund Rascher, an SS doctor based at Dachau, reported directly to Reichsführer-SS Heinrich Himmler and publicised the results of his freezing experiments at the 1942 medical conference entitled "Medical Problems Arising from Sea and Winter". In a letter from September 10, 1942, Rascher describes an experiment on intense cooling performed in Dachau where people were dressed in fighter pilot uniforms and submerged in freezing water. Rascher had some of the victims completely underwater and others only submerged up to the head.[46] Approximately 100 people are reported to have died as a result of these experiments.[47]

## Malaria experiments

From about February 1942 to about April 1945, experiments were conducted at the Dachau concentration camp in order to investigate immunization for treatment of malaria. Healthy inmates were infected by mosquitoes or by injections of extracts of the mucous glands of female mosquitoes. After contracting the disease, the subjects were treated with various drugs to test their relative efficiency. Over 1,200 people were used in these experiments and more than half died as a result. Other test subjects were left with permanent disabilities.

## Immunization experiments

At the German concentration camps of Sachsenhausen, Dachau, Natzweiler, Buchenwald, and Neuengamme, scientists tested immunization compounds and serums for the prevention and treatment of contagious diseases, including malaria, typhus, tuberculosis, typhoid fever, yellow fever, and infectious hepatitis.

## Epidemic jaundice

From June 1943 till January 1945 at the concentration camps, Sachsenhausen and Natzweiler, experimentation with epidemic jaundice was conducted. The test subjects were injected with the disease in order to discover new inoculations for the condition. These tests were conducted for the benefit of the German Armed Forces. Many suffered great pain in these experiments.

## Mustard gas experiments

At various times between September 1939 and April 1945, many experiments were conducted at Sachsenhausen, Natzweiler, and other camps to investigate the most effective treatment of wounds caused by mustard gas. Test subjects were deliberately exposed to mustard gas and other vesicants (e.g. Lewisite) which inflicted severe chemical burns. The victims' wounds were then tested to find the most effective treatment for the mustard gas burns.

## Sulfonamide experiments

From about July 1942 to about September 1943, experiments to investigate the effectiveness of sulfonamide, a synthetic antimicrobial agent, were conducted at Ravensbrück.[48] Wounds inflicted on the subjects were infected with bacteria such as *Streptococcus*, *Clostridium perfringens* (a major causative agent in gas gangrene) and *Clostridium tetani*, the causative agent in tetanus. Circulation of blood was interrupted by tying off blood vessels at both ends of the wound to create a condition similar to that of a battlefield wound. Infection was aggravated by forcing wood shavings and ground glass into the wounds. The infection was treated with sulfonamide and other drugs to determine their effectiveness.

## Sea water experiments

From about July 1944 to about September 1944, experiments were conducted at the Dachau concentration camp to study various methods of making sea water drinkable. These victims were subject to deprivation of all food and only given the filtered sea water. At one point, a group of roughly 90 Roma were deprived of food and given nothing but sea water to drink by Dr. Hans Eppinger, leaving them gravely injured. They were so dehydrated that others observed them licking freshly mopped floors in an attempt to get drinkable water.

A Holocaust survivor named Joseph Tschofenig wrote a statement on these seawater experiments at Dachau. Tschofenig explained how while working at the medical experimentation stations he gained insight into some of the experiments that were performed on prisoners, namely those where they were forced to drink salt water. Tschofenig also described how victims of the experiments had trouble eating and would desperately seek out any source of water including old floor rags. Tschofenig was responsible for using the X-ray machine in the infirmary and describes how even though he had insight into what was going on he was powerless to stop it. He gives the example of a patient in the infirmary who was sent to the gas chambers by Dr. Sigmund Rascher simply because he witnessed one of the low-pressure experiments.[49]

## Sterilization and fertility experiments

The Law for the Prevention of Genetically Defective Progeny was passed on 14 July 1933, which legalized the involuntary sterilization of persons with diseases claimed to be hereditary: weak-mindedness, schizophrenia, alcohol abuse, insanity, blindness, deafness, and physical deformities. The law was used to encourage growth of the Aryan race through the sterilization of persons who fell under the quota of being genetically defective.[50] 1% of citizens between the age of 17 to 24 had been sterilized within 2 years of the law passing. Within 4 years, 300,000 patients had been sterilized.[51] From about March 1941 to about January 1945, sterilization experiments were conducted at Auschwitz, Ravensbrück, and other places by Dr. Carl Clauberg. The purpose of these experiments was to develop a method of sterilization which would be suitable for sterilizing millions of people with a minimum of time and effort. The targets for sterilization included Jewish and Roma populations. These experiments were conducted by means of X-ray, surgery and various drugs. Thousands of victims were sterilized. Aside from its experimentation, the Nazi government sterilized around 400,000 people as part of its compulsory sterilization program. One survivor, who underwent experimentation at Auschwitz, said that the experimentation she endured caused, "fainting from severe pain for a year and a half." Years later she went to a doctor and discovered that her uterus had become one comparable to that of a 4-year-old.

Intravenous injections of solutions speculated to contain iodine and silver nitrate were successful, but had unwanted side effects such as vaginal bleeding, severe abdominal pain, and cervical cancer. Therefore, radiation treatment became the favored choice of sterilization. Specific amounts of exposure to radiation destroyed a person's ability to produce ova or sperm, sometimes administered through deception. Many suffered severe radiation burns.

M.D. William E. Seidelman, a professor from the University of Toronto, in collaboration with Dr. Howard Israel of Columbia University published a report on an investigation on the Medical experimentation performed in Austria under the Nazi Regime. In that report he mentions a Doctor Hermann Stieve, who used the war to experiment on live humans. Dr. Stieve specifically focused on the reproductive system of women. He would tell women their execution date in advance, and he would evaluate how their psychological distress would affect their menstruation cycles. After they were murdered, he would dissect and examine their reproductive organs. Some of the women were even raped after they were told the date when they would be killed, so that Dr. Stieve could study the path of sperm through their reproductive system.[52]

## Experiments with poison

Somewhere between December 1943 and October 1944, experiments were conducted at Buchenwald to investigate the effect of various poisons. The poisons were secretly administered to experimental subjects in their food. The victims died as a result of the poison or were killed immediately in order to permit autopsies. In September 1944, experimental subjects were shot with poisonous bullets, suffered torture and often died.

## Incendiary bomb experiments

From around November 1943 to around January 1944, experiments were conducted at Buchenwald to test the effect of various pharmaceutical preparations on phosphorus burns. These burns were inflicted on prisoners using phosphorus material extracted from incendiary bombs.

## High altitude experiments

In early 1942, prisoners at Dachau concentration camp were used by Sigmund Rascher in experiments to aid German pilots who had to eject at high altitudes. A low-pressure chamber containing these prisoners was used to simulate conditions at altitudes of up to 20,000 m (66,000 ft). It was rumored that Rascher performed vivisections on the brains of victims who survived the initial experiment. Of the 200 subjects, 80 died outright, and the others were executed. In a letter from April 5, 1942 between Dr. Sigmund Rascher and Heinrich Himmler, Rascher explains the results of a low-pressure experiment that was performed on people at Dachau Concentration camp in which the victim was suffocated while Rascher and another unnamed doctor took note of his reactions. The person was described as 37 years old and in good health before being murdered. Rascher described the victim's actions as he began to lose oxygen and timed the changes in behavior. The 37 year old began to wiggle his head at 4 minutes, a minute later Rascher observed that he was suffering from cramps before falling unconscious. He describes how the victim then lay unconscious, breathing only 3 times per minute, until he stopped breathing 30 minutes after being deprived of oxygen. The victim then turned blue and began foaming at the mouth. An autopsy followed an hour later.[53]

In a letter from Heinrich Himmler to Dr. Sigmund Rascher on April 13, 1942, Himmler ordered Rascher to continue the high altitude experiments and to continue experimenting on prisoners condemned to death and to "determine whether these men could be recalled to life". If a victim could be successfully resuscitated, Himmler ordered that he be pardoned to "concentration camp for life".[54]

## Blood coagulation experiments

Sigmund Rascher experimented with the effects of *Polygal*, a substance made from beet and apple pectin, which aided blood clotting. He predicted that the preventive use of Polygal tablets would reduce bleeding from gunshot wounds sustained during combat or during surgery. Subjects were given a Polygal tablet, and shot through the neck or chest, or their limbs amputated without anaesthesia. Rascher published an article on his experience of using Polygal, without detailing the nature of the human trials and also set up a company to manufacture the substance, staffed by prisoners.[55]

# Aftermath

Other documented transcriptions from Heinrich Himmler include phrases such as "These researches... can be performed by us with particular efficiency because I personally assumed the responsibility for supplying asocial individuals and criminals who deserve only to die from concentration camps for these experiments."[56] Many of the subjects died as a result of the experiments conducted by the Nazis, while many others were executed after the tests were completed to study the effects *post mortem*. Those who survived were often left mutilated, suffering permanent disability, weakened bodies, and mental distress. On 19 August 1947, the doctors captured by Allied forces were put on trial in *USA vs. Karl Brandt et al.*, commonly known as the Doctors' Trial. At the trial, several of the doctors argued in their defense that there was no international law regarding medical experimentation.Wikipedia:Citation needed Some doctors also claimed that they had been doing the world a favor. A SS doctor was quoted saying that "Jews were the festering appendix in the body of Europe." He then went on to argue he was doing the world a favor by eliminating them.

The issue of informed consent had previously been controversial in German medicine in 1900, when Dr. Albert Neisser infected patients (mainly prostitutes) with syphilis without their consent. Despite Neisser's support from most of the academic community, public opinion, led by psychiatrist Albert Moll, was against Neisser. While Neisser went on to be fined by the Royal Disciplinary Court, Moll developed "a legally based, positivistic contract theory of the patient-doctor relationship" that was not adopted into German law. Eventually, the minister for religious, educational, and medical affairs issued a directive stating that medical interventions other than for diagnosis, healing, and immunization were excluded under all circumstances if "the human subject was a minor or not competent for other reasons", or if the subject had not given his or her "unambiguous consent" after a "proper explanation of the possible negative consequences" of the intervention, though this was not legally binding.

In response, Drs. Leo Alexander and Andrew Conway Ivy drafted a ten-point memorandum entitled *Permissible Medical Experiment* that went on to be known as the Nuremberg Code. The code calls for such standards as voluntary consent of patients, avoidance of unnecessary pain and suffering, and that there must be a belief that the experimentation will not end in death or disability. The Code was not cited in any of the findings against the defendants and never made it into either German or American medical law. This code comes from the Nuremberg Trials where the most heinous of Nazi leaders were put on trial for their war crimes. To this day, the Nuremberg Code remains a major stepping stone for medical experimentation.

## Modern ethical issues

Frederik Pohl said in a 1963 editorial in *Galaxy Science Fiction* that despite their cruelty the Nazi experiments produced no useful results; "it was not science and it was not medicine". If the "Herr Doktors" had, he wrote, murdered pregnant women to study their ovaries the crimes would have advanced embryology, but the earliest stages of prenatal development were first observed in Boston in 1942 "without either torture or killing".

The results of the Dachau freezing experiments have been used in some modern research into the treatment of hypothermia, with at least 45 publications having referenced the experiments since the Second World War. This, together with the recent use of data from Nazi research into the effects of phosgene gas, has proven controversial and presents an ethical dilemma for modern physicians who do not agree with the methods used to obtain this data. Some object on an ethical basis, and others have rejected Nazi research purely on scientific grounds, pointing out methodological inconsistencies. In an often-cited review of the Dachau hypothermia experiments, Berger states that the study has "all the ingredients of a scientific fraud" and that the data "cannot advance science or save human lives."

Controversy has also risen from the use of results of biological warfare testing done by the Imperial Japanese Army's Unit 731. The results from Unit 731 were kept classified by the United States until the majority of doctors involved were given pardons.

# Further reading

- Annas, George J. (1992). *The Nazi Doctors and the Nuremberg Code: Human Rights in Human Experimentation*[57]. Oxford University Press. ISBN 0195101065.<templatestyles src="Module:Citation/CS1/styles.css"></templatestyles>
- Baumslag, N. (2005). *Murderous Medicine: Nazi Doctors, Human Experimentation, and Typhus*. Praeger Publishers. <templatestyles src="Module:Citation/CS1/styles.css" />ISBN 0-275-98312-9
- Michalczyk, J. (Dir.) (1997). *In The Shadow Of The Reich: Nazi Medicine*. First Run Features. (video)
- Nyiszli, M. (2011). "3". *Auschwitz: A Doctor's Eyewitness Account*. New York: Arcade Publishing.<templatestyles src="Module:Citation/CS1/styles.css"></templatestyles>
- Rees, L. (2005). *Auschwitz: A New History*. Public Affairs. <templatestyles src="Module:Citation/CS1/styles.css" />ISBN 1-58648-357-9

- Weindling, P.J. (2005). *Nazi Medicine and the Nuremberg Trials: From Medical War Crimes to Informed Consent*. Palgrave Macmillan. <templatestyles src="Module:Citation/CS1/styles.css" />ISBN 1-4039-3911-X
- USAF School of Aerospace Medicine (1950). *German Aviation Medicine, World War II*[58]. United States Air Force.<templatestyles src="Module:Citation/CS1/styles.css"></templatestyles>

# External links

- The Infamous Medical Experiments[59] from Holocaust Survivors and Remembrance Project: "Forget You Not"
- United States Holocaust Memorial Museum – Online Exhibition: Doctors Trial[60]
- United States Holocaust Memorial Museum – Online Exhibition: Deadly Medicine: Creating the Master Race[61]
- United States Holocaust Memorial Museum – Library Bibliography: Medical Experiments[62]
- Jewish Virtual Library: Medical Experiments Table of Contents[63]

## Controversy regarding use of findings

- Campell, Robert. "Citations of shame; scientists are still trading on Nazi atrocities.", *New Scientist*, 28 February 1985, 105(1445), p. 31.[64][65]
- " Citing Nazi 'Research': To Do So Without Condemnation Is Not Defensible[66]"
- " On the Ethics of Citing Nazi Research[67]"
- " Remembering the Holocaust, Part 2[68]"
- " The Ethics Of Using Medical Data From Nazi Experiments[69]"

# Aktion T4

## Aktion T4

| Aktion T4 | |
|---|---|
| Hitler's order for *Aktion T4* | |
| Also known as | T4 Program |
| Location | German-occupied Europe |
| Date | September 1939 – 1945 |
| Incident type | Forced euthanasia |
| Perpetrators | SS |
| Participants | Psychiatric hospitals |
| Victims | 275,000–300,000[70] |

*Aktion T4* (German, pronounced [akˈtsi̯oːn teː fiːɐ]) was a postwar name for mass murder through involuntary euthanasia in Nazi Germany.[71,72]</ref> The name T4 is an abbreviation of *Tiergartenstraße 4*, a street address of the Chancellery department set up in the spring of 1940, in the Berlin borough of Tiergarten, which recruited and paid personnel associated with T4.[73,74,75,76]</ref> Certain German physicians were authorized to select patients "deemed incurably sick, after most critical medical examination" and then administer to them a "mercy death" (*Gnadentod*).[77] In October 1939 Adolf Hitler signed a "euthanasia note" backdated to 1 September 1939 which authorized his physician Karl Brandt and *Reichsleiter* Philipp Bouhler to implement the programme.

The killings took place from September 1939 until the end of the war in 1945; from 275,000 to 300,000 people were killed at extermination centres in psychiatric hospitals in Germany and Austria, occupied Poland and the Protectorate of Bohemia and Moravia (now the Czech Republic).[78,79,80] The number of victims was originally recorded as 70,273 but this number has been increased by the discovery of victims listed in the archives of former East Germany.[81] About half of those killed were taken from church-run asylums, often with the approval of the Protestant or Catholic authorities of the institutions.[82,83] The Holy See announced on 2 December 1940 that the policy was contrary to the natural and positive Divine law and that "the direct killing of an innocent person because of mental or physical defects is not allowed" but the declaration was not upheld by some Catholic authorities in Germany. In the summer of 1941, protests were led in Germany by Bishop von Galen, whose intervention led to "the strongest, most explicit and most widespread protest movement against any policy since the beginning of the Third Reich", according to Richard J. Evans.[84]

Several reasons have been suggested for the programme, including eugenics, compassion, reducing suffering, racial hygiene, economy and pressure on the welfare budget.[85,86] Physicians in German and Austrian asylums continued many of the practices of *Aktion T4* until the defeat of Germany in 1945, in spite of its official cessation.[87] The informal continuation of the policy led to 93,521 "beds emptied" by the end of 1941.[88,89,90]Wikipedia:Citing sources[88]</ref>[91]</ref> Technology developed under *Aktion T4* was taken over by the medical division of the Reich Interior Ministry, particularly the use of lethal gas to kill large numbers of people, along with the personnel who had participated in the development of the technology and later participated in Operation Reinhard.[92]

The technology and personnel developed were instrumental in implementing the Holocaust.[93] The programme was authorized by Hitler but the killings have since come to be viewed as murders in Germany. The number of people killed was about 200,000 in Germany and Austria, with about 100,000 victims in other European countries.[94]

**Figure 2:** *This poster (from around 1938) reads: "60,000 Reichsmark is what this person suffering from a hereditary defect costs the People's community during his lifetime. Fellow citizen, that is your money too. Read '[A] New People', the monthly magazine of the Bureau for Race Politics of the NSDAP."*

## Background

At the beginning of the twentieth century, the sterilisation of people carrying what were considered to be hereditary defects and in some cases those exhibiting what was thought to be hereditary "antisocial" behaviour, was a respectable field of medicine. Canada, Denmark, Switzerland and the US had passed laws enabling coerced sterilisation. Studies conducted in the 1920s ranked Germany as a country that was unusually reluctant to introduce sterilisation legislation.[95] In his book *Mein Kampf* (1924), Hitler wrote that one day racial hygiene "will appear as a deed greater than the most victorious wars of our present bourgeois era".[96]Wikipedia:Manual of Style/Dates and numbers#Chronological items[97]

In July 1933 "Law for the Prevention of Hereditarily Diseased Offspring" prescribed compulsory sterilisation for people with conditions thought to be hereditary, such as schizophrenia, epilepsy, Huntington's chorea and "imbecility". Sterilisation was also legalised for chronic alcoholism and other forms of social deviance. The law was administered by the Interior Ministry under Wilhelm Frick through special Hereditary Health Courts (*Erbgesundheitsgerichte*), which examined the inmates of nursing homes, asylums, prisons, aged-care homes and special schools, to select those to be sterilised.[98] It is estimated that 360,000 people were sterilised under this law between 1933 and 1939.

The policy and research agenda of racial hygiene and eugenics were promoted by Emil Kraepelin.[99] The eugenic sterilization of persons diagnosed with (and viewed as predisposed to) schizophrenia was advocated by Eugen Bleuler, who presumed racial deterioration because of "mental and physical cripples" in his *Textbook of Psychiatry*,

<templatestyles src="Template:Quote/styles.css"/>

> *The more severely burdened should not propagate themselves... If we do nothing but make mental and physical cripples capable of propagating themselves, and the healthy stocks have to limit the number of their children because so much has to be done for the maintenance of others, if natural selection is generally suppressed, then unless we will get new measures our race must rapidly deteriorate.*[100,101,102]

Within the Nazi administration, the idea of including in the program people with physical disabilities had to be expressed carefully, given that one of the most powerful figures of the regime, Joseph Goebbels, had a deformed right leg.[103] </ref> After 1937 the acute shortage of labour in Germany arising from rearmament, meant that anyone capable of work was deemed to be "useful" and thus exempted from the law and the rate of sterilisation declined.[104] The term "Aktion T4" is a post-war coining; contemporary German terms included *Euthanasie* (euthanasia) and *Gnadentod* (merciful death).[105] The T4 programme stemmed from the Nazi Party policy of "racial hygiene", a belief that the German people needed to be cleansed of racial enemies, which included anyone confined to a mental health facility and people with simple physical disabilities.[106]

## Implementation

Karl Brandt, personal doctor to Hitler and Hans Lammers, the head of the Reich Chancellery, testified after the war that Hitler had told them as early as 1933—when the sterilisation law was passed—that he favoured the killing of the incurably ill but recognised that public opinion would not accept this.[107] In 1935, Hitler told the Leader of Reich Doctors, Gerhard Wagner, that the question could not be taken up in peacetime, "Such a problem could be more smoothly and easily carried out in war". He wrote that he intended to "radically

**Figure 3:** *NSDAP Reichsleiter Philipp Bouhler, Head of the T4 programme*

solve" the problem of the mental asylums in such an event.[107] *Aktion T4* began with a "trial" case in late 1938. Hitler instructed Brandt to evaluate a family's petition for the "mercy killing" of their son who was blind, had physical and developmental disabilities.[108,109]</ref> The child, born near Leipzig and eventually identified as Gerhard Kretschmar, was killed in July 1939.[110,111] Hitler instructed Brandt to proceed in the same manner in all similar cases.[112]

On 18 August 1939, three weeks after the killing of the boy, the *Reich Committee for the Scientific Registering of Hereditary and Congenital Illnesses* was established. It was to register sick children or newborns identified as defective. The secret killing of infants began in 1939 and increased after the war started; by 1941 more than 5,000 children had been killed.[113,114] Hitler was in favour of killing those whom he judged to be *lebensunwertes Leben* (Life unworthy of life). In a 1939 conference with Leonardo Conti, Reich Health Leader and state secretary for health in the Interior Ministry and Hans Lammers, Chief of the Reich Chancellery—a few months before the "euthanasia" decree—Hitler gave as examples the mentally ill who he said could only be "bedded on sawdust or sand" because they "perpetually dirtied themselves" and "put their own excrement into their mouths". This issue, according to the Nazi regime, assumed new urgency in wartime.[115]

After the invasion of Poland, Hermann Pfannmüller said

**Figure 4:** *Karl Brandt, Hitler's personal doctor and organiser of Aktion T4*

<templatestyles src="Template:Quote/styles.css"/>
> *Für mich ist die Vorstellung untragbar, dass beste, blühende Jugend an der Front ihr Leben lassen muss, damit verblichene Asoziale und unverantwortliche Antisoziale ein gesichertes Dasein haben. (It is unbearable to me that the flower of our youth must lose their lives at the front, while that feeble-minded and asocial element can have a secure existence in the asylum.)*[116]

Pfannmüller advocated killing by a gradual decrease of food, which he believed was more merciful than poison injections.[117,118]

The German eugenics movement had an extreme wing even before the Nazis came to power. As early as 1920, Alfred Hoche and Karl Binding advocated killing people whose lives were "unworthy of life" (*lebensunwertes Leben*). Darwinism was interpreted by them as justification of the demand for "beneficial" genes and eradication of the "harmful" ones. Robert Lifton wrote, "The argument went that the best young men died in war, causing a loss to the *Volk* of the best available genes. The genes of those who did not fight (the worst genes) then proliferated freely, accelerating biological and cultural degeneration".[119] The advocacy of eugenics in Germany gained ground after 1930, when the Depression was used to excuse cuts in funding to state mental hospitals, creating squalor and overcrowding.[120]

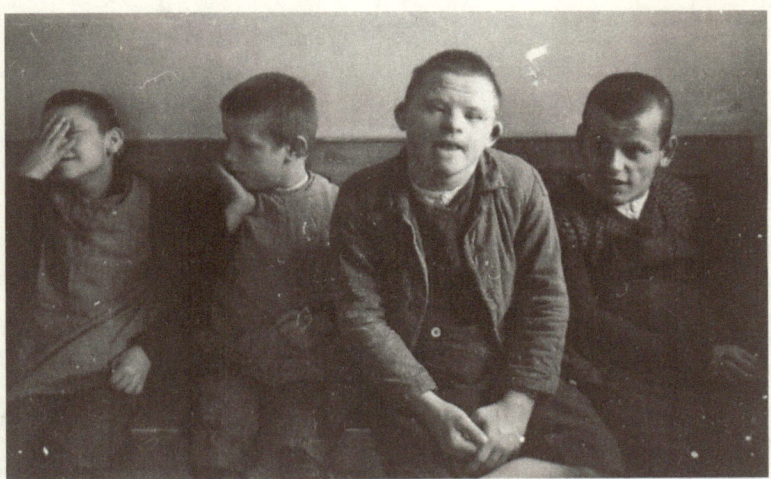

**Figure 5:** *Schönbrunn Psychiatric Hospital, 1934*
*(Photo by SS photographer Friedrich Franz Bauer)*

Many German eugenicists were nationalists and antisemites, who embraced the Nazi regime with enthusiasm. Many were appointed to positions in the Health Ministry and German research institutes. Their ideas were gradually adopted by the majority of the German medical profession, from which Jewish and communist doctors were soon purged.[121] During the 1930s the Nazi Party had carried out a campaign of propaganda in favour of euthanasia. The National Socialist Racial and Political Office (NSRPA) produced leaflets, posters and short films to be shown in cinemas, pointing out to Germans the cost of maintaining asylums for the incurably ill and insane. These films included *The Inheritance* (*Das Erbe*, 1935), *The Victim of the Past* (*Opfer der Vergangenheit*, 1937), which was given a major première in Berlin and was shown in all German cinemas, and *I Accuse* (*Ich klage an*, 1941), which was based on a novel by Hellmuth Unger, a consultant for "child euthanasia".[122]

# Killing of children

In mid-1939 Hitler authorized the creation of the Reich Committee for the Scientific Registering of Serious Hereditary and Congenital Illnesses (*Reichsausschuss zur wissenschaftlichen Erfassung erb- und anlagebedingter schwerer Leiden*), headed by Dr. Karl Brandt, his physician, and administered by Herbert Linden of the Interior Ministry as well as SS-*Oberführer* Viktor Brack. Brandt and Bouhler were authorized to approve applications to kill children in

**Figure 6:** *Viktor Brack, organiser of the T4 Programme*

relevant circumstances,[123,124] though Bouhler left the details to subordinates such as Brack and SA-*Oberführer* Werner Blankenburg.[125]

Extermination centres were established at six existing psychiatric hospitals: Bernburg, Brandenburg, Grafeneck, Hadamar, Hartheim, and Sonnenstein.[106,126] One thousand children under the age of 17 were killed at the institutions Am Spiegelgrund and Gugging in Austria.[127,128] They played a crucial role in developments leading to the Holocaust.[106] As a related aspect of the "medical" and scientific basis of this programme, the Nazi doctors took thousands of brains from 'euthanasia' victims for research.[129]

From August 1939, the Interior Ministry registered children with disabilities, requiring doctors and midwives to report all cases of newborns with severe disabilities; the 'guardian' consent element soon disappeared. Those to be killed were identified as "all children under three years of age in whom any of the following 'serious hereditary diseases' were 'suspected': idiocy and Down syndrome (especially when associated with blindness and deafness); microcephaly; hydrocephaly; malformations of all kinds, especially of limbs, head, and spinal column; and paralysis, including spastic conditions".[130] The reports were assessed by a panel of medical experts, of whom three were required to give their approval before a child could be killed.[131]</ref>

The Ministry used deceit when dealing with parents or guardians, particularly in Catholic areas, where parents were generally uncooperative. Parents were told that their children were being sent to "Special Sections", where they would receive improved treatment.[132] The children sent to these centres were kept for "assessment" for a few weeks and then killed by injection of toxic chemicals, typically phenol; their deaths were recorded as "pneumonia". Autopsies were usually performed and brain samples were taken to be used for "medical research". Post mortem examinations apparently helped to ease the consciences of many of those involved, giving them the feeling that there was a genuine medical purpose to the killings.[133] The most notorious of these institutions in Austria was Am Spiegelgrund, where from 1940 to 1945, 789 children were killed by lethal injection, gas poisoning and physical abuse. Children's brains were preserved in jars of formaldehyde and stored in the basement of the clinic and in the private collection of Heinrich Gross, one of the institution's directors, until 2001.[128]

When the Second World War began in September 1939, less rigorous standards of assessment and a quicker approval process were adopted. Older children and adolescents were included and the conditions covered came to include

<templatestyles src="Template:Quote/styles.css"/>

> ... *various borderline or limited impairments in children of different ages, culminating in the killing of those designated as juvenile delinquents. Jewish children could be placed in the net primarily because they were Jewish; and at one of the institutions, a special department was set up for 'minor Jewish-Aryan half-breeds'.*
>
> —Lifton[134]

More pressure was placed on parents to agree to their children being sent away. Many parents suspected what was happening, especially when it became apparent that institutions for children with disabilities were being systematically cleared of their charges and refused consent. The parents were warned that they could lose custody of all their children and if that did not suffice, the parents could be threatened with call-up for 'labour duty'.[135] By 1941, more than 5,000 children had been killed.[114,136]</ref> The last child to be killed under *Aktion T4* was Richard Jenne on 29 May 1945 in the children's ward of the Kaufbeuren-Irsee state hospital in Bavaria, Germany, more than three weeks after U.S. Army troops had occupied the town.[137,138]

**Figure 7:** *SS-Gruppenführer Leonardo Conti*

# Killing of adults

## Invasion of Poland

Brandt and Bouhler developed plans to expand the programme of euthanasia to adults. In July 1939 they held a meeting attended by Conti and Professor Werner Heyde, head of the SS medical department. This meeting agreed to arrange a national register of all institutionalised people with mental illnesses or physical disabilities. The first adults with disabilities to be killed en masse by the Nazi regime were Poles. After the invasion on 1 September 1939, adults with disabilities were shot by the SS men of *Einsatzkommando* 16, *Selbstschutz* and EK-*Einmann* under the command of SS-*Sturmbannführer* Rudolf Tröger, with overall command by Reinhard Heydrich, during the genocidal Operation Tannenberg.[139,140]</ref> All hospitals and mental asylums of the Wartheland were emptied. The region was incorporated into Germany and earmarked for resettlement by *Volksdeutsche* following the German conquest of Poland.[141] In the Danzig (now Gdańsk) area, some 7,000 Polish patients of various institutions were shot and 10,000 were killed in the Gdynia area. Similar measures were taken in other areas of Poland destined for incorporation into Germany.[142] The first experiments with the gassing of patients were conducted in October 1939 at Fort VII in Posen (occupied Poznań), where hundreds of prisoners were killed by means of carbon monoxide poisoning, in

**Figure 8:** *Bunker No. 17 in artillery wall of Fort VII in Poznań, used as improvised gas chamber for early experiments*

an improvised gas chamber developed by Dr Albert Widmann, chief chemist of the German Criminal Police (Kripo). In December 1939, *Reichsführer-SS* Heinrich Himmler witnessed one of these gassings, ensuring that this invention would later be put to much wider uses.[143]

The idea of killing adult mental patients soon spread from occupied Poland to adjoining areas of Germany, probably because Nazi Party and SS officers in these areas were most familiar with what was happening in Poland. These were also the areas where Germans wounded from the Polish campaign were expected to be accommodated, which created a demand for hospital space. The *Gauleiter* of Pomerania, Franz Schwede-Coburg, sent 1,400 patients from five Pomeranian hospitals to undisclosed locations in occupied Poland, where they were shot. The *Gauleiter* of East Prussia, Erich Koch, had 1,600 patients killed out of sight. More than 8,000 Germans were killed in this initial wave of killings carried out on the orders of local officials, although Himmler certainly knew and approved of them.[114,144]

The legal basis for the programme was a 1939 letter from Hitler, not a formal "Führer's decree" with the force of law. Hitler bypassed Conti, the Health Minister and his department, who might have raised questions about the legality of the programme and entrusted it to Bouhler and Brandt.[145,146]</ref>

<templatestyles src="Template:Quote/styles.css"/>

> *Reich Leader Bouhler and Dr. Brandt are entrusted with the responsibility of extending the authority of physicians, to be designated by name, so that patients who, after a most critical diagnosis, on the basis of human judgment [menschlichem Ermessen], are considered incurable, can be granted mercy death [Gnadentod].*
>
> —*Adolf Hitler, 1 September 1939*[105,145]

The killings were administered by Viktor Brack and his staff from *Tiergartenstraße* 4, disguised as the "Charitable Foundation for Cure and Institutional Care" offices which served as the front and was supervised by Bouhler and Brandt.[147,148] The officials in charge included Dr Herbert Linden, who had been involved in the child killing programme; Dr Ernst-Robert Grawitz, chief physician of the SS; and August Becker, an SS chemist. The officials selected the doctors who were to carry out the operational part of the programme; based on political reliability as long-term Nazis, professional reputation and sympathy for radical eugenics. The list included physicians who had proved their worth in the child-killing programme, such as Unger, Heinze and Hermann Pfannmüller. The recruits were mostly psychiatrists, notably Professor Carl Schneider of Heidelberg, Professor Max de Crinis of Berlin and Professor Paul Nitsche from the Sonnenstein state institution. Heyde became the operational leader of the programme, succeeded later by Nitsche.[149]

## Listing of targets from hospital records

In early October, all hospitals, nursing homes, old-age homes and sanatoria were required to report all patients who had been institutionalised for five years or more, who had been committed as "criminally insane", who were of "non-Aryan race" or who had been diagnosed with any on a list of conditions. The conditions included schizophrenia, epilepsy, Huntington's chorea, advanced syphilis, senile dementia, paralysis, encephalitis and "terminal neurological conditions generally". Many doctors and administrators assumed that the reports were to identify inmates who were capable of being drafted for "labour service" and tended to overstate the degree of incapacity of their patients, to protect them from labour conscription. When some institutions refused to co-operate, teams of T4 doctors (or Nazi medical students) visited and compiled the lists, sometimes in a haphazard and ideologically motivated way.[150] During 1940, all Jewish patients were removed from institutions and killed.[151,152,153,154]</ref>

As with child inmates, adults were assessed by a panel of experts, working at the *Tiergartenstraße* offices. The experts were required to make their judgements on the reports, not medical histories or examinations. Sometimes they

**Figure 9:** *Hartheim Euthanasia Centre, where over 18,000 people were killed.*

dealt with hundreds of reports at a time. On each they marked a **+** (death), a **-** (life), or occasionally a **?** meaning that they were unable to decide. Three "death" verdicts condemned the person and as with reviews of children, the process became less rigorous, the range of conditions considered "unsustainable" grew broader and zealous Nazis further down the chain of command increasingly made decisions on their own initiative.[155]

# Gassing

The first gassings in Germany proper took place in January 1940 at the Brandenburg Euthanasia Centre. The operation was headed by Brack, who said "the needle belongs in the hand of the doctor."[156] Bottled pure carbon monoxide gas was used. At trials, Brandt described the process as a "major advance in medical history".[157] Once the efficacy of the method was confirmed, it became standardised, and instituted at a number of centres across Germany under the supervision of Widmann, Becker, and Christian Wirth – a Kripo officer who later played a prominent role in the extermination of the Jews as commandant of newly built death camps in occupied Poland. In addition to Brandenburg, the killing centres included Grafeneck Castle in Baden-Württemberg (10,824 dead), Schloss Hartheim near Linz in Austria (over 18,000 dead), Sonnenstein Euthanasia Centre in Saxony (15,000 dead), Bernburg Euthanasia Centre in

**Figure 10:** *Bishop Jan Maria Michał Kowalski, killed at Hartheim Euthanasia Centre.*

Saxony-Anhalt and Hadamar Euthanasia Centre in Hesse (14,494 dead). The same facilities were also used to kill mentally sound prisoners transferred from concentration camps in Germany, Austria and occupied parts of Poland.

Condemned patients were transferred from their institutions to newly built centres in the T4 Charitable Ambulance buses, called the Community Patients Transports Service. They were run by teams of SS men wearing white coats, to give it an air of medical care.[158] To prevent the families and doctors of the patients from tracing them, the patients were often first sent to transit centres in major hospitals, where they were supposedly assessed. They were moved again to *special treatment (Sonderbehandlung)* centres. Families were sent letters explaining that owing to wartime regulations, it was not possible for them to visit relatives in these centres. Most of these patients were killed within 24 hours of arriving at the centres, and their bodies cremated.[159] For every person killed, a death certificate was prepared, giving a false but plausible cause of death. This was sent to the family along with an urn of ashes (random ashes, since the victims were cremated *en masse*). The preparation of thousands of falsified death certificates took up most of the working day of the doctors who operated the centres.[160]

During 1940, the centres at Brandenburg, Grafeneck and Hartheim killed nearly 10,000 people each, while another 6,000 were killed at Sonnenstein.

In all, about 35,000 people were killed in T4 operations that year. Operations at Brandenburg and Grafeneck were wound up at the end of the year, partly because the areas they served had been cleared and partly because of public opposition. In 1941, however, the centres at Bernburg and Sonnenstein increased their operations, while Hartheim (where Wirth and Franz Stangl were successively commandants) continued as before. As a result, another 35,000 people were killed before August 1941, when the T4 programme was officially shut down by Hitler. Even after that date, however, the centres continued to be used to kill concentration camp inmates: eventually some 20,000 people in this category were killed.[161]</ref>

In 1971, Gitta Sereny conducted a series of interviews with Stangl, who was in prison in Düsseldorf after having been convicted of co-responsibility for killing 900,000 people as commandant of the Sobibor and Treblinka extermination camps in Poland. Stangl gave Sereny a detailed account of the operations of the T4 programme based on his time as commandant of the killing facility at the Hartheim institute.[162] He described how the inmates of various asylums were removed and transported by bus to Hartheim. Some were in no mental state to know what was happening to them, but many were perfectly sane, and for them various forms of deception were used. They were told they were at a special clinic where they would receive improved treatment, and were given a brief medical examination on arrival. They were induced to enter what appeared to be a shower block, where they were gassed with carbon monoxide (the ruse was also used at extermination camps).[162]

## Number of euthanasia victims

The SS functionaries and hospital staff associated with *Aktion T4* in the German Reich were paid from the central office at *Tiergartenstrasse* 4 in Berlin from the spring of 1940. The SS and police from *SS-Sonderkommando Lange* responsible for murdering the majority of patients in the annexed territories of Poland since October 1939, took their salaries from the normal police fund, supervised by the administration of the newly formed *Wartheland* district; the programme in Germany and occupied Poland was overseen by Heinrich Himmler.[163] Before 2013, it was believed that 70,000 persons were murdered in the euthanasia programme, but the German Federal Archives reported that research in the archives of former East Germany indicated that the number of victims in Germany and Austria from 1939 to 1945 was about 200,000 persons and that another 100,000 persons were victims in other European countries. In the German T4 centres there was at least the semblance of legality in keeping records and writing letters. In Polish psychiatric hospitals no one was left behind. Killings were inflicted using gas-vans, sealed army bunkers and machine guns; families were not informed about the murdered relatives and the empty wards were handed over to the SS.[163]

**Victims of *Aktion T4* (official data from 1985), 1940 – September 1941**[164]

| T4 Center | Operation timetable | | Number of victims | | |
|---|---|---|---|---|---|
| | From | Until (officially and unofficially) | 1940 | 1941 | Total |
| Grafeneck | 20 January 1940 | December 1940 | 9,839 | — | 9,839 |
| Brandenburg | 8 February 1940 | October 1940 | 9,772 | — | 9,772 |
| Bernburg | 21 November 1940 | 30 July 1943 | — | 8,601 | 8,601 |
| Hartheim | 6 May 1940 | December 1944 | 9,670 | 8,599 | 18,269 |
| Sonnenstein | June 1940 | September 1942 | 5,943 | 7,777 | 13,720 |
| Hadamar | January 1941 | 31 July 1942 | — | 10,072 | 10,072 |
| | | Total by year[164] | 35,224 | 35,049 | **70,273** |

| Territories of occupied Poland[163] | | | |
|---|---|---|---|
| Hospital | Region | Extermination of mentally ill | Number of victims |
| Owińska | Warthegau | October 1939 | 1,100 |
| Kościan | Warthegau | November 1939 – March 1940[165] | (2,750) 3,282 |
| Świecie | Danzig-West Prussia | October–November 1939[166] | 1,350 |
| Kocborowo | Danzig-West Prussia | 22 Sep 1939 – Jan 1940 (1941–44)[165] | (1,692) 2,562 |
| Dziekanka | Warthegau | 7 Dec 1939 – 12 Jan 1940 (July 1941)[165] | (1,043) 1,201 |
| Chełm | General Government | 12 January 1940 | 440 |
| Warta | Warthegau | 31 March 1940 (16 June 1941)[165] | (499) 581 |
| Działdowo | Ostpreussen | 21 May – 8 July 1940 | 1,858 |
| Kochanówka | Warthegau | 13 March 1940 – August 1941 | *(minimum of)* 850 |
| Helenówek (et al.) | Warthegau | 1940–1941 | 2,200–2,300 |
| Lubliniec | Oberschlesien | November 1941 | *(children)* 194 |
| Choroszcz | Bezirk Bialystok | August 1941 | 700 |
| Rybnik | Bezirk Kattowitz | 1940–1945[165] | 2,000 |
| | | Total by number[165] | *c.* **16,153** |

## Technology and personnel transfer to death camps

After the official end of the euthanasia programme in 1941, most of the personnel and high-ranking officials, as well as gassing technology and the techniques used to deceive victims, were transferred under the jurisdiction of the national medical division of the Reich Interior Ministry. Further gassing experiments with the use of mobile gas chambers (*Einsatzwagen*) were conducted at Soldau concentration camp by Herbert Lange following Operation Barbarossa. Lange was appointed commander of the Chełmno extermination camp in December 1941. He was given three gas vans by the *RSHA*, converted by the Gaubschat GmbH in Berlin[167] and before February 1942, killed 3,830 Polish Jews and around 4,000 Romani, under the guise of "resettlement".[168] After the Wannsee conference, implementation of gassing technology was accelerated by Heydrich. Beginning in the spring of 1942, three killing factories were built secretly in east-central Poland. The *SS* officers responsible for the earlier *Aktion T4*, including Wirth, Stangl and Irmfried Eberl, had important roles in the implementation of the "Final Solution" for the next two years.[93,169]</ref> The first killing centre equipped with stationary gas chambers modelled on technology developed under *Aktion T4* was established at Bełżec in the General Government territory of occupied Poland; the decision preceded the Wannsee Conference of January 1942 by three months.[170]

## Opposition

In January 1939, Brack commissioned a paper from Professor of Moral Theology at the University of Paderborn, Joseph Mayer, on the likely reactions of the churches in the event of a state euthanasia programme being instituted. Mayer – a longstanding euthanasia advocate – reported that the churches would not oppose such a programme if it was seen to be in the national interest. Brack showed this paper to Hitler in July, and it may have increased his confidence that the "euthanasia" programme would be acceptable to German public opinion.[124] Notably, when Sereny interviewed Mayer shortly before his death in 1967, he denied that he formally condoned the killing of people with disabilities but no copies of this paper are known to survive.[171]

There were those who opposed the T4 programme within the bureaucracy. Lothar Kreyssig, a district judge and member of the Confessing Church, wrote to Gürtner protesting that the action was illegal since no law or formal decree from Hitler had authorised it. Gürtner replied, "If you cannot recognise the will of the Führer as a source of law, then you cannot remain a judge", and had Kreyssig dismissed.[120] Hitler had a fixed policy of not issuing written instructions for policies relating to what could later be condemned by international community, but made an exception when he provided Bouhler and

**Figure 11:** *Gas chamber in Hadamar*

Brack with written authority for the T4 programme in his confidential letter of October 1939 in order to overcome opposition within the German state bureaucracy. Hitler told Bouhler that, "the Führer's Chancellery must under no circumstances be seen to be active in this matter."[147] The Justice Minister, Franz Gürtner, had to be shown Hitler's letter in August 1940 to gain his cooperation.[148]

## Exposure

In the towns where the killing centres were located, many people saw the inmates arrive in buses, saw the smoke from the crematoria chimneys and noticed that the buses were returning empty. In Hadamar, ashes containing human hair rained down on the town. The T4 programme was no secret. Despite the strictest orders, some of the staff at the killing centres talked about what was going on. In some cases families could tell that the causes of death in certificates were false, e.g. when a patient was claimed to have died of appendicitis, even though his appendix had been surgically removed some years earlier. In other cases, several families in the same town would receive death certificates on the same day.[172] In May 1941, the Frankfurt County Court wrote to Gürtner describing scenes in Hadamar where children shouted in the streets that people were being taken away in buses to be gassed.[173]

**Figure 12:** *Hans Gerhard Creutzfeldt in 1920*

During 1940, rumours of what was taking place spread and many Germans withdrew their relatives from asylums and sanatoria to care for them at home, often with great expense and difficulty. In some places doctors and psychiatrists co-operated with families to have patients discharged or if the families could afford it, transferred them to private clinics beyond the reach of T4. Other doctors "re-diagnosed" patients so that they no longer met the T4 criteria, which risked exposure when Nazi zealots from Berlin conducted inspections. In Kiel, Professor Hans Gerhard Creutzfeldt managed to save nearly all of his patients.[174] Lifton listed a handful of psychiatrists and administrators who opposed the killings; many doctors collaborated, either through ignorance, agreement with Nazi eugenicist policies or fear of the regime.[174]

Protest letters were sent to the Reich Chancellery and the Ministry of Justice, some from Nazi Party members. The first open protest against the removal of people from asylums took place at Absberg in Franconia in February 1941 and others followed. The SD report on the incident at Absberg noted that "the removal of residents from the Ottilien Home has caused a great deal of unpleasantness" and described large crowds of Catholic townspeople, among them Party members, protesting against the action.[175] Similar petitions and protests occurred throughout Austria as rumors spread of mass killings at the Hartheim Euthanasia Centre and of mysterious deaths at the children's clinic, *Am Spiegelgrund* in Vienna. Anna Wödl, a nurse and mother of child with a disability, vehemently petitioned to Hermann Linden at the Reich Ministry of the Interior in Berlin to prevent her son, Alfred, from being transferred from Gugging, where he lived and which also became a euthanasia center. Wödl failed and Alfred was sent to Am Spiegelgrund, where he was killed on 22 February 1941. His brain was preserved in formaldehyde for "research" and stored in the clinic for sixty years.[176]

## Church protests

The Lutheran theologian Friedrich von Bodelschwingh (director of the Bethel Institution for Epilepsy at Bielefeld) and Pastor Paul-Gerhard Braune (director of the Hoffnungstal Institution near Berlin) protested. Bodelschwingh negotiated directly with Brandt and indirectly with Hermann Göring, whose cousin was a prominent psychiatrist. Braune had meetings with Justice Minister Gürtner, who was always dubious about the legality of the programme. Gürtner later wrote a strongly worded letter to Hitler protesting against it; Hitler did not read it but was told about it by Lammers.[177] Bishop Theophil Wurm, presiding the Evangelical-Lutheran Church in Württemberg, wrote to Interior Minister Frick in March 1940 and the same month a confidential report from the *Sicherheitsdienst* (SD) in Austria, warned that the killing programme must be implemented with stealth "in order to avoid a probable backlash of public opinion during the war".[178] On 4 December 1940, Reinhold Sautter, the Supreme Church Councillor of the Württemberg State Church, complained to the Nazi Ministerial Councillor Eugen Stähle for the murders in Grafeneck Castle. Stahle said "The fifth commandment Thou shalt not kill, is no commandment of God but a Jewish invention".[179]

Bishop Heinrich Wienken of Berlin, a leading member of the Caritas Association, was selected by the Fulda episcopal synod to represent the views of the Catholic Church in meetings with T4 operatives. In 2008, Michael Burleigh wrote

<templatestyles src="Template:Quote/styles.css"/>

> *Wienken seems to have gone partially native in the sense that he gradually abandoned an absolute stance based on the Fifth Commandment in favour of winning limited concessions regarding the restriction of killing to 'complete idiots', access to the sacraments and the exclusion of ill Roman Catholic priests from these policies.*[180]

Despite a decree issued by the Vatican on 2 December 1940 stating that the T4 policy was "against natural and positive Divine law" and that "The direct killing of an innocent person because of mental or physical defects is not allowed", the Catholic Church hierarchy in Germany decided to take no further action. Incensed by the Nazi appropriation of Church property in Münster to

**Figure 13:** *August von Galen*

accommodate people made homeless by an air raid, in July and August 1941 the Bishop of Münster, August von Galen, gave four sermons criticizing the Nazis for arresting Jesuits, confiscating church property and for the euthanasia program.[181,182] Galen sent the text to Hitler by telegram, calling on

<templatestyles src="Template:Quote/styles.css"/>

> ... *the Führer to defend the people against the Gestapo. It is a terrible, unjust and catastrophic thing when man opposes his will to the will of God ... We are talking about men and women, our compatriots, our brothers and sisters. Poor unproductive people if you wish, but does this mean that they have lost their right to live?*[183]

Galen's sermons were not reported in the German press but were circulated illegally as leaflets. The text was dropped by the Royal Air Force over German troops.[83,184] In 2009, Richard J. Evans wrote that "This was the strongest, most explicit and most widespread protest movement against any policy since the beginning of the Third Reich".[84] Local Nazis asked for Galen to be arrested but Goebbels told Hitler that such action would provoke a revolt in Westphalia and Hitler decided to wait until after the war to take revenge.[185,83]

In 1986, Lifton wrote, "Nazi leaders faced the prospect of either having to imprison prominent, highly admired clergymen and other protesters – a course with consequences in terms of adverse public reaction they greatly feared – or

**Figure 14:** *A plaque set in the pavement at No 4 Tiergartenstraße commemorates the victims of the Nazi euthanasia programme.*

**Figure 15:** *Commemorative plaque on wall on bunker No. 17 in Fort VII.*

else end the programme".[186] Evans considered it "at least possible, even indeed probable" that the T4 programme would have continued beyond Hitler's initial quota of 70,000 deaths but for the public reaction to Galen's sermon.[187] Burleigh called assumptions that the sermon affected Hitler's decision to suspend the T4 program "wishful thinking" and noted that the various Church hierarchies did not complain after the transfer of T4 personnel to *Aktion Reinhard*.[188] Henry Friedlander wrote that it was not the criticism from the Church but rather the loss of secrecy and "general popular disquiet about the way euthanasia was implemented" that caused the killing to be suspended.[189]

Galen had detailed knowledge of the euthanasia program by July 1940 but did not speak out until almost a year after Protestants had begun to protest. In 2002, Beth A. Griech-Polelle wrote that,

<templatestyles src="Template:Quote/styles.css"/>

*Worried lest they be classified as outsiders or internal enemies, they waited for Protestants, that is the "true Germans", to risk a confrontation with the government first. If the Protestants were able to be critical of a Nazi policy, then Catholics could function as "good" Germans and yet be critical too.*[190]

On 29 June 1943, Pope Pius XII issued the encyclical *Mystici corporis Christi*, in which he condemned the fact that "physically deformed people, mentally disturbed people and hereditarily ill people have at times been robbed of their lives" in Germany. Following this, in September 1943, a bold but ineffectual condemnation was read by bishops from pulpits across Germany, denouncing the killing of "the innocent and defenceless mentally handicapped and mentally ill, the incurably infirm and fatally wounded, innocent hostages and disarmed prisoners of war and criminal offenders, people of a foreign race or descent".[191]

## Suspension of T4 killings

On 24 August 1941, Hitler ordered the suspension of the T4 killings. After the invasion of the Soviet Union in June, many T4 personnel were transferred to the east to begin work on the final solution to the Jewish question. The projected death total for the T4 program of 70,000 deaths had been reached by August 1941.[192] The termination of the T4 programme did not end the killing of people with disabilities; from the end of 1941, the killing of adults and children continued less systematically to the end of the war on the local initiative of institute directors and party leaders. After the bombing of Hamburg in July 1943, occupants of old age homes were killed. In the post-war trial of Dr. Hilda Wernicke, Berlin, August, 1946, testimony was given that "500 old, broken women" who had survived the bombing of Stettin in June 1944 were euthanized at the Meseritz-Oberwalde Asylum.[193] The Hartheim, Bernberg, Sonnenstein and Hardamar centres continued in use as "wild euthanasia" centres to kill people sent from all over Germany, until 1945.[192] The methods were lethal injection or starvation, those employed before use of gas chambers.[194] By the end of 1941, about 100,000 people had been killed in the T4 programme.[195] From mid-1941, concentration camp prisoners too feeble or too much trouble to keep alive were murdered after a cursory psychiatric examination under Action 14f13.[196]

# Post-war

## Doctors' trial

After the war a series of trials was held in connection with the Nazi euthanasia programme at various places including: Dresden, Frankfurt, Graz, Nuremberg and Tübingen. In December 1946 an American military tribunal (commonly called the Doctors' trial) prosecuted 23 doctors and administrators for their roles in war crimes and crimes against humanity. These crimes included the systematic killing of those deemed "unworthy of life", including people with mental disabilities, the people who were institutionalized mentally ill, and people with physical impairments. After 140 days of proceedings, including the testimony of 85 witnesses and the submission of 1,500 documents, in August 1947 the court pronounced 16 of the defendants guilty. Seven were sentenced to death and executed on 2 June 1948, including Brandt and Brack.

The indictment read in part: <templatestyles src="Template:Quote/styles.css"/>

> *14. Between September 1939 and April 1945 the defendants Karl Brandt, Blome, Brack, and Hoven unlawfully, wilfully, and knowingly committed crimes against humanity, as defined by Article II of Control Council Law No. 10, in that they were principals in, accessories to, ordered, abetted, took a consenting part in, and were connected with plans and enterprises involving the execution of the so called "euthanasia" program of the German Reich, in the course of which the defendants herein murdered hundreds of thousands of human beings, including German civilians, as well as civilians of other nations. The particulars concerning such murders are set forth in paragraph 9 of count two of this indictment and are incorporated herein by reference.*
> 
> *—International Military Tribunal*[197]

Earlier, in 1945, American forces tried seven staff members of the Hadamar killing centre for the killing of Soviet and Polish nationals, which was within

**Figure 16:** *Aktion T4 marker (2009) in Berlin*

their jurisdiction under international law, as these were the citizens of wartime allies. (Hadamar was within the American Zone of Occupation in Germany. This was before the Allied resolution of December 1945, to prosecute individuals for "crimes against humanity" for such mass atrocities.) Alfons Klein, Karl Ruoff and Wilhelm Willig were sentenced to death and executed; the other four were given long prison sentences.[198] In 1946, newly reconstructed German courts tried members of the Hadamar staff for the murders of nearly 15,000 German citizens at the facility. Adolf Wahlmann and Irmgard Huber, the chief physician and the head nurse, were convicted.

## Other perpetrators

- August Becker, initially sentenced to three years after the war, in 1960 was tried again and sentenced to ten years in prison. He was released early due to ill health and died in 1967.
- Werner Blankenburg lived under an alias and died in 1957.[199]
- Philipp Bouhler committed suicide in captivity, May 1945.[199]
- Werner Catel was cleared by a denazification board after World War II and was head of pediatrics at the University of Kiel. He retired early after his role in the T4 program was exposed but continued to support the killing of children with mental and physical disabilities.
- Leonardo Conti hanged himself in captivity, 6 October 1945.[200]

- Dr. Ernst-Robert Grawitz killed himself shortly before the fall of Berlin in April 1945.[201]
- Dr. Herbert Linden committed suicide in 1945. Overseers of the program were initially Herbert Linden and Werner Heyde. Linden was later replaced by Hermann Paul Nitsche.
- Dr. Fritz Cropp d. 6 April 1984, Bremen. A Nazi official in Oldenburg, Cropp was appointed the country medical officer of health in 1933. In 1935 he transferred to Berlin, where he worked as a ministerial adviser in the Division IV (health care and people care) in the Ministry of the Interior. In 1939, he became Assistant Director; Cropp was involved in the Nazi "euthanasia" *Aktion T4* in 1940. He was Herbert Linden's superior and was responsible for patient transfers.[202]
- Dr. Werner Heyde[196] after escaping detection for 18 years, killed himself in 1964 before being brought to trial.
- Dr. Heinrich Gross was tried twice. One sentence was overturned and the charges in the second trial in 2000 were dropped as a result of his dementia; he died in 2005.
- Lorenz Hackenholt vanished in 1945.[203]
- Erich Koch served time in prison from 1950 to his death in 1986.[204]
- Erwin Lambert died in 1976.[203]
- Dr. Friedrich Mennecke died in 1947 while awaiting trial.
- Philipp, Landgrave of Hesse, the governor of Hesse-Nassau, was tried in 1947 at Hadamar for his role in *Aktion T4* but was sentenced only to two years' "time served"; he died in 1980.
- Paul Nitsche was tried and executed by an East German court in 1948.
- Professor Carl Schneider hanged himself in his prison cell in 1946, while awaiting trial.
- Franz Schwede was sentenced to 10 years in prison in 1948 and was released in 1956; he died in 1960.
- Dr. Ernst Illing was the director of the Vienna Psychiatric-Neurological Clinic for Children Am Spielgrund, where he killed about 200 children; sentenced to death on 18 July 1946.[205]
- Dr. Marianne Türk was a doctor at Vienna Psychiatric-Neurological Clinic for Children Am Spielgrund where, with Ernst Illing, she killed 200 children. She was sentenced to 10 years prison on 18 July 1946.[205]

The Ministry for State Security of East Germany stored around 30,000 files of *Aktion T4* in their archives. Those files became available to the public only after the German Reunification in 1990, leading to a new wave of research on these wartime crimes.[206]

**Figure 17:** *Aktion T4 memorial at Tiergartenstraße 4, Berlin*

# Memorials

The German national memorial to the people with disabilities murdered by the Nazis was dedicated in 2014 in Berlin. It is located in the pavement of a site next to the Tiergarten park, the location of the former villa at Tiergartenstrasse 4 in Berlin, where more than 60 Nazi bureaucrats and doctors worked in secret under the "T4" program to organize the mass murder of sanatorium and psychiatric hospital patients deemed unworthy to live.

# References

<templatestyles src="Template:Refbegin/styles.css" />

### Books

- Adams, Mark B. (1990). *The Wellborn Science: Eugenics in Germany, France, Brazil and Russia*. Monographs on the History and Philosophy of Biology. New York: Oxford University Press. ISBN 978-0-19-505361-6.<templatestyles src="Module:Citation/CS1/styles.css"></templatestyles>
- Aly, Gotz; Chroust, Peter (1994). *Cleansing the Fatherland [Contributions to National Socialist Health and Social Policy]*. Trans. Journal: Beiträge zur Nationalsozialistischen

Gesundheits- und Sozial- politik. Baltimore, MD: Johns Hopkins University Press. ISBN 978-0-8018-4775-2.<templatestyles src="Module:Citation/CS1/styles.css"></templatestyles>
- Annas, George J.; Grodin, Michael A. (1992). *The Nazi Doctors and the Nuremberg Code: Human Rights in Human Experimentation.* Oxford University Press. ISBN 978-0-19-977226-1.<templatestyles src="Module:Citation/CS1/styles.css"></templatestyles>
- Berenbaum, Michael; Peck, Abraham J. (2002). *The Holocaust and History: The Known, the Unknown, the Disputed and the Re-examined.* Bloomington, IN: Indiana University Press. ISBN 978-0-253-21529-1.<templatestyles src="Module:Citation/CS1/styles.css"></templatestyles>
- Bialas, Wolfgang; Fritze, Lothar (2015). *Nazi Ideology and Ethics.* Newcastle: Cambridge Scholars. ISBN 978-1-4438-5881-6.<templatestyles src="Module:Citation/CS1/styles.css"></templatestyles>
- Bleuler, E. (1924). *Textbook of Psychiatry [Lehrbuch der Psychiatrie].* trans. A. A. Brill. New York: Macmillan. OCLC 3755976[207].<templatestyles src="Module:Citation/CS1/styles.css"></templatestyles>
- Browning, Christopher (2005). *The Origins of the Final Solution: The Evolution of Nazi Jewish Policy, September 1939 – March 1942.* Arrow. ISBN 978-0-8032-5979-9.<templatestyles src="Module:Citation/CS1/styles.css"></templatestyles>
- Burleigh, Michael (1995). *Death and Deliverance: 'Euthanasia' in Germany 1900–1945.* New York: Verlag Klemm & Oelschläger. ISBN 978-0-521-47769-7.<templatestyles src="Module:Citation/CS1/styles.css"></templatestyles>
- Burleigh, Michael (2000). "Psychiatry, German Society and the Nazi "Euthanasia" Programme". In Bartov, Omer. *The Holocaust Origins, Implementation, Aftermath.* London: Routledge. ISBN 978-0-415-15036-1.<templatestyles src="Module:Citation/CS1/styles.css"></templatestyles>
- Cina, Stephen J.; Perper, Joshua A. (2010). *When Doctors Kill: Who, Why, and How* (online ed.). New York: Copernicus Books. ISBN 978-1-4419-1369-2.<templatestyles src="Module:Citation/CS1/styles.css"></templatestyles>
- Ericksen, Robert P. (2012). *Complicity in the Holocaust: Churches and Universities in Nazi Germany* (online ed.). Cambridge: Cambridge University Press. doi: 10.1017/CBO9781139059602[208]. ISBN 978-1-280-87907-4.<templatestyles src="Module:Citation/CS1/styles.css"></templatestyles>

- Evans, Suzanne E. (2004). *Forgotten Crimes: The Holocaust and People with Disabilities*. Chicago, IL: Ivan R. Dee. ISBN 978-1-56663-565-3.<templatestyles src="Module:Citation/CS1/styles.css"></templatestyles>
- Evans, Richard J. (2005). *The Third Reich in Power*. London: Allen Lane. ISBN 978-0-7139-9649-4.<templatestyles src="Module:Citation/CS1/styles.css"></templatestyles>
- Evans, Richard J. (2009). *The Third Reich at War*. New York City: Penguin. ISBN 978-1-59420-206-3.<templatestyles src="Module:Citation/CS1/styles.css"></templatestyles>
- Friedlander, Henry (1995). *The Origins of Nazi Genocide: From Euthanasia to the Final Solution*. Chapel Hill, NC: University of North Carolina Press. ISBN 978-0-8078-2208-1.<templatestyles src="Module:Citation/CS1/styles.css"></templatestyles>
- Friedlander, Henry (1 September 1997). *The Origins of Nazi Genocide: From Euthanasia to the Final Solution*[209]. Chapel Hill, NC: University of North Carolina Press. ISBN 978-0-8078-4675-9.<templatestyles src="Module:Citation/CS1/styles.css"></templatestyles>
- Friedman, Jonathan C. (2011). *The Routledge History of the Holocaust*. London: Routledge. ISBN 978-0-203-83744-3.<templatestyles src="Module:Citation/CS1/styles.css"></templatestyles>
- Griech-Polelle, Beth A. (2002). *Bishop von Galen: German Catholicism and National Socialism*. New Haven, CT: Yale University Press. ISBN 978-0-300-13197-0.<templatestyles src="Module:Citation/CS1/styles.css"></templatestyles>
- Hansen, Randall; King, Desmond S. (2013). *Sterilized by the State: Eugenics, Race and the Population Scare in Twentieth-Century North America* (Cambridge Books Online ed.). New York: Cambridge University Press. doi: 10.1017/CBO9781139507554[210]. ISBN 978-1-139-50755-4.<templatestyles src="Module:Citation/CS1/styles.css"></templatestyles>
- Hilberg, R. (2003). *The Destruction of the European Jews*. **III** (3rd ed.). New Haven, CT: Yale University Press. ISBN 978-0-300-09557-9.<templatestyles src="Module:Citation/CS1/styles.css"></templatestyles>
- Hitler, A. *Mein Kampf* [*My Struggle*] (in German).<templatestyles src="Module:Citation/CS1/styles.css"></templatestyles>
- Joniec, Jarosław (2016). *Historia Niemieckiego Obozu Zagłady w Bełżcu*[211] [*History of the Belzec Extermination Camp*] (in Polish). Lublin: Muzeum - Miejsce Pamięci w Bełżcu (National Bełżec Museum & Monument of Martyrology). ISBN 978-83-62816-27-9.<templatestyles src="Module:Citation/CS1/styles.css"></templatestyles>

- Joseph, Jay (2004). *The Gene Illusion: Genetic Research in Psychiatry and Psychology under the Microscope*. New York: Algora Publishing. ISBN 978-0-87586-344-3.
- Kershaw, Ian (2000). *Hitler: 1936–1945 Nemesis*. **II**. New York: Norton. ISBN 978-0-393-32252-1.
- Klee, Ernst (1983). *Euthanasie im NS-Staat. Die Vernichtung lebensunwerten Lebens* [*Euthanasia in the NS State: The Destruction of Life Unworthy of Life*] (in German). Frankfurt am Main: Fischer Taschenbuch Verlag. ISBN 978-3-596-24326-6.
- Klee, Ernst (1985). *Dokumente zur Euthanasie* [*Documents on Euthanasia*] (in German). Frankfurt am Main: Fischer Taschenbuch Verlag. ISBN 978-3-596-24327-3.
- Lifton, R. J. (1986). *The Nazi Doctors: Medical Killing and the Psychology of Genocide*[212]. New York: Basic Books. ISBN 978-0-465-04904-2. Archived from the original[213] on 3 September 2006.
- Lifton, R. J. (2000). *The Nazi Doctors: Medical Killing and the Psychology of Genocide*. New York: Basic Books. ISBN 978-0-465-04905-9.
- Longerich, P. (2010). *Holocaust: The Nazi Persecution and Murder of the Jews*. Oxford: Oxford University Press. ISBN 978-0-19-280436-5.
- Miller, Michael (2006). *Leaders of the SS and German Police*. **I**. San Jose, CA: R. James Bender. ISBN 978-93-297-0037-2.
- Padfield, Peter (1990). *Himmler: Reichsführer-SS*. London: Macmillan. ISBN 978-0-333-40437-9.
- Proctor, Robert N. (1988). *Racial Hygiene: Medicine under the Nazis*. Cambridge, MA: Harvard College. ISBN 978-0-674-74578-0.
- Read, J. (2004). "Genetics, Eugenics and Mass Murder". In Read, J.; Mosher, R. L.; Bentall, R. P. *Models of Madness: Psychological, Social and Biological Approaches to Schizophrenia*. ISPD book. Hove, East Sussex: Brunner-Routledge. ISBN 978-1-58391-905-7.

- *Ringelblum Archives of the Holocaust: Introduction*[214] (PDF). Warsaw: Wydawnictwa Uniwersytetu Warszawskiego. 2013. Retrieved 12 March 2017.
- Ryan, Donna F.; Schuchman, John S. (2002). *Racial Hygiene: Deaf People in Hitler's Europe*. Patricia Heberer, "Targetting the Unfit". Washington, D.C.: Gallaudet University Press. ISBN 978-1-56368-132-5.
- Schmidt, Ulf (2007). *Karl Brandt: The Nazi Doctor*. London: Hambledon Continuum. ISBN 978-1-84725-031-5.
- Schmitt, Gerhard (1965). *Selektion in der Heilanstalt 1939–1945* [*Selection in the Sanatorium 1939–1945*]. Stuttgart: Evangelisches Verlagsanstalt. OCLC 923376286[215].
- Schmuhl, Hans-Walter (1987). *Rassenhygiene, Nationalsozialismus, Euthanasie: Von der Verhütung zur Vernichtung "lebensunwerten Lebens", 1890–1945* [*Racial Hygiene, National Socialism, Euthanasia: From Prevention to Destruction of Life Unworthy of Life 1890–1945*]. Kritische Studien zur Geschichtswissenschaft (in German). **75**. simultaneous PhD University of Bielefeld, Bielefeld 1986 as *Die Synthese von Arzt und Henker*. Göttingen: Vandenhoeck & Ruprecht. ISBN 978-3-525-35737-8.
- Sereny, Gitta (1983). *Into that Darkness: An Examination of Conscience*. New York, NY: Vintage Books. ISBN 978-0-394-71035-8.
- Shirer, William L. (1960). *The Rise and Fall of the Third Reich*. New York: Simon and Schuster. ISBN 978-0-449-21977-5.
- Taylor, T. (1949). *Trials of War Criminals before the Nuernberg Military Tribunals: Under Control Council Law no. 10, Nuernberg, October 1946 – April 1949*[216] (transcription) (United States Holocaust Museum ed.). Washington, DC: U.S. Government Printing Office. OCLC 504102502[217]. Archived from the original[218] on 4 May 2006.
- Totten, Samuel; Parsons, William S. (2009). *Century of Genocide: Critical Essays and Eyewitness Accounts* (3rd ed.). New York: Routledge. ISBN 978-0-415-99084-4.

src="Module:Citation/CS1/styles.css"></templatestyles>
- Weindling, Paul Julian (2006). *Nazi Medicine and the Nuremberg Trials: From Medical War Crimes to Informed Consent*. Basingstoke: Palgrave Macmillan. ISBN 978-0-230-50700-5.<templatestyles src="Module:Citation/CS1/styles.css"></templatestyles>

## Conferences

- Baader, Gerhard (2009). *Psychiatrie im Nationalsozialismus zwischen ökonomischer Rationalität und Patientenmord*[219] [*Psychiatry in National Socialism: Between Economic Rationality and Patient Murder*] (PDF). Geschichte der Psychiatrie: Nationalsocialismus und Holocaust Gedächtnis und Gegenwart (PDF). geschichtederpsychiatrie.at. Retrieved 12 March 2017.<templatestyles src="Module:Citation/CS1/styles.css"></templatestyles>

## Journals

- Breggin, Peter (1993). "Psychiatry's Role in the Holocaust"[220] (PDF). *International Journal of Risk & Safety in Medicine*. **4** (2). doi: 10.3233/JRS-1993-4204[221]. PMID 23511221[222] – via PDF file direct download, 4.07 MB.<templatestyles src="Module:Citation/CS1/styles.css"></templatestyles>
- Burleigh, Michael (2008). "Between Enthusiasm, Compliance and Protest: The Churches, Eugenics and the Nazi 'Euthanasia' Programme". *Contemporary European History*. **3** (03): 253–264. doi: 10.1017/S0960777300000886[223]. ISSN 0960-7773[224].<templatestyles src="Module:Citation/CS1/styles.css"></templatestyles>
- Engstrom, E. J.; Weber, M. M.; Burgmair, W. (October 2006). "Emil Wilhelm Magnus Georg Kraepelin (1856–1926)". *The American Journal of Psychiatry*. British Library Serials. **163** (10). doi: 10.1176/appi.ajp.163.10.1710[225]. ISSN 0002-953X[226]. PMID 17012678[227].<templatestyles src="Module:Citation/CS1/styles.css"></templatestyles>
- Sandner, Peter (July 1999). "Die "Euthanasie"-Akten im Bundesarchiv. Zur Geschichte eines lange verschollenen Bestandes"[228] [The 'Euthanasia' Files in the Federal Archives. On the History of a Long Lost Existence] (PDF). *Vierteljahrschefte für Zeitgeschichte – Institut für Zeitgeschichte*. Munich. **47** (3): 385–400. ISSN 0042-5702[229].<templatestyles src="Module:Citation/CS1/styles.css"></templatestyles>
- Semków, Piotr (September 2006). "Kolebka"[230] [Cradle] (PDF). *IPN Bulletin*. Warsaw: Institute of National Remembrance (IPN Gdańsk) (8–9 (67–68)). 42–50 44–51/152. ISSN 1641-9561[231]. Retrieved 8 November 2015 – via direct download: 3.44 MB.<templatestyles src="Module:Citation/CS1/styles.css"></templatestyles>

- Fuller Torrey, Edwin; Yolken, Robert (January 2010). "Psychiatric Genocide: Nazi Attempts to Eradicate Schizophrenia"[232]. *Schizophrenia Bulletin*. Oxford University Press (The Maryland Psychiatric Research Center and Schizophrenia International Research Society). **36** (1): 26–32. doi: 10.1093/schbul/sbp097[233]. ISSN 0586-7614[234]. PMC 2800142[232]. PMID 19759092[235].<templatestyles src="Module:Citation/CS1/styles.css"></templatestyles>

**Newspapers**

- Buttlar, H. (1 October 2003). "Nazi-"Euthanasie" Forscher öffnen Inventar des Schreckens"[236] [Nazi 'Euthanasia' Researchers open Inventory of Horror]. *Der Spiegel* (online ed.). Hamburg. ISSN 0038-7452[237]. Retrieved 12 March 2017.<templatestyles src="Module:Citation/CS1/styles.css"></templatestyles>
- "Nazis Killed Hundreds at Austrian Mental Hospital"[238]. *The Local AB*. no oclc. 25 November 2014. Retrieved 16 February 2017.<templatestyles src="Module:Citation/CS1/styles.css"></templatestyles>

**Websites**

- Beer, Mathias (2015). "Die Entwicklung der Gaswagen beim Mord an den Juden"[239] [The Development of the Gas-Van in the Murdering of the Jews]. *The Final Solution*. Vierteljahrshefte für Zeitgeschichte. Munich: Jewish Virtual Library. pp. 403–417. ISSN 0042-5702[229]. Retrieved 12 March 2017.<templatestyles src="Module:Citation/CS1/styles.css"></templatestyles>
- Burleigh, Michael; Wippermann, Wolfang (2014). "Nazi Racial Science"[240]. Washington, D.C.: United States Holocaust Memorial Museum. Retrieved 12 March 2017.<templatestyles src="Module:Citation/CS1/styles.css"></templatestyles>
- Hojan, Artur; Munro, Cameron (2015). "Overview of Nazi 'Euthanasia' Programme"[241]. *The Central Office at Tiergartenstrasse 4 in Berlin*. The Tiergartenstrasse 4 Association. *Further information:* Kaminsky, Uwe (2014), "Mercy Killing and Economism"[242] [in:] Bialas, Wolfgang; Fritze, Lothar (ed.), *Nazi Ideology and Ethics*. pp. 263–265. Cambridge Scholars Publishing, <templatestyles src="Module:Citation/CS1/styles.css" />ISBN 1-4438-5422-0 <templatestyles src="Module:Citation/CS1/styles.css" />OCLC 875635606[243]. "Once emptied, the Polish institutions were almost exclusively turned over to the SS"[p. 265]. Retrieved 18 November 2017.<templatestyles src="Module:Citation/CS1/styles.css"></templatestyles>
- Hojan, Artur; Munro, Cameron (28 February 2013). "Nazi Euthanasia Programme in Occupied Poland 1939–1945"[244].

- Berlin, Kleisthaus: Tiergartenstrasse 4.<templatestyles src="Module:Citation/CS1/styles.css"></templatestyles>
- Jaroszewski, Zdzisław (1993). "German extermination of psychiatric patients in Poland 1939-1945"[245]. *Zaglada psychicznie chorych w Polsce 1939–1945 by Zdzisław Jaroszewski, ed., [Extermination of psychiatric hospital' patients in Poland 1939–1945].* PWN, Warsaw. Project InPosterum 2011. OCLC 68651789[246].<templatestyles src="Module:Citation/CS1/styles.css"></templatestyles>
- Wiadomości (6 December 2013). "Hospital director and 1,350 patients killed including children. Commemoration of murder victims"[247] [Zabili dyrektora szpitala psychiatrycznego w Świeciu oraz około 1350 pacjentów, także dzieci. Miasto upamiętni ten mord]. *Gazeta Pomorska.* Archived[248] from the original on 17 November 2017.<templatestyles src="Module:Citation/CS1/styles.css"></templatestyles>
- WNSP Świecie (2013). "History of Świecie Hospital"[249] [Historia szpitala w Świeciu]. Regional State Hospital: *Wojewódzki Szpital dla Nerwowo i Psychicznie Chorych, Samorząd Województwa Kujawsko-Pomorskiego.* Archived[250] from the original on 17 November 2017.<templatestyles src="Module:Citation/CS1/styles.css"></templatestyles>
- "Psychiatrzy w obronie pacjentów"[251]. Niedziela, Tygodnik Katolicki. 4 February 2013. Archived[252] from the original on 17 November 2017.<templatestyles src="Module:Citation/CS1/styles.css"></templatestyles>
- Kaelber, Lutz (29 August 2015). "Am Spiegelgrund"[253]. *University of Vermont.* Retrieved 12 March 2017.<templatestyles src="Module:Citation/CS1/styles.css"></templatestyles>
- "Quellen zur Geschichte der "Euthanasie"-Verbrechen 1939–1945 in deutschen und österreichischen Archiven"[254] [Sources on the History of the 'Euthanasia' Crime 1939–1945 in German and Austrian Archives] (PDF) (in German). Berlin: Bundesarchiv. Retrieved 3 March 2018.<templatestyles src="Module:Citation/CS1/styles.css"></templatestyles>
- "The Memorial Page of Nazi Euthanasia Programs"[255]. *Germany National Memorial.* Retrieved 12 March 2017.<templatestyles src="Module:Citation/CS1/styles.css"></templatestyles>
- "United States of America v. Alfons Klein et al"[256] (PDF). Captured German Records. National Archives and Records Administration. 1980. 12-449, 000-12-31. Retrieved 12 March 2017.<templatestyles src="Module:Citation/CS1/styles.css"></templatestyles>

# Further reading

**Books**

- Bachrach, Susan D; Kuntz, Dieter (2004). *Deadly Medicine: Creating the Master Race*. United States Holocaust Memorial Museum Washington D.C.: University of North Carolina Press, Chapel Hill, NC. ISBN 978-0-8078-2916-5.<templatestyles src="Module:Citation/CS1/styles.css"></templatestyles>
- Benzenhöfer, Udo (2010). *Euthanasia in Germany Before and During the Third Reich*. Münster/Ulm: Verlag Klemm & Oelschläger. ISBN 978-3-86281-001-7.<templatestyles src="Module:Citation/CS1/styles.css"></templatestyles>
- Binding, K.; Hoche, A. (1920). *Die Freigabe der Vernichtung lebensunwerten Lebens: Ihr Mass u. ihre Form* [*The Release of the Destruction of Life Unworthy of Life: Their Mass and Shape*]. Leipzig: Meiner. OCLC 72022317[257].<templatestyles src="Module:Citation/CS1/styles.css"></templatestyles>
- Burleigh, M.; Wippermann, W. (1991). *The Racial State: Germany 1933–1945*. Cambridge: Cambridge University Press. ISBN 978-0-521-39114-6.<templatestyles src="Module:Citation/CS1/styles.css"></templatestyles>
- Burleigh, M. (1997). *Ethics and Extermination: Reflections on Nazi Genocide*. Part II. Cambridge: Cambridge University Press. pp. 113–152. ISBN 978-0-521-58211-7.<templatestyles src="Module:Citation/CS1/styles.css"></templatestyles>
- Burleigh, M. (2001) [2000]. "Medicalized Mass Murder". *The Third Reich: A New History* (pbk. Pan ed.). London: Macmillan. pp. 382–404. ISBN 978-0-330-48757-3.<templatestyles src="Module:Citation/CS1/styles.css"></templatestyles>
- Friedlander, Henry (1995). *The Origins of Nazi Genocide. From Euthanasia to the Final Solution*. Chapel Hill: University of North Carolina Press. ISBN 978-0-8078-2208-1.<templatestyles src="Module:Citation/CS1/styles.css"></templatestyles>
- Klee, Ernst (1986). *Was sie taten. Was sie wurden: Ärzte, Juristen und andere Beteiligte am Kranken- oder Judenmord* [*What They Did. What They Became: Doctors, Lawyers and other Partners in the Murder of the Ill and Jews*] (in German). Frankfurt am Main: Fischer Taschenbuch. ISBN 978-3-596-24364-8.<templatestyles src="Module:Citation/CS1/styles.css"></templatestyles>
- Klee, Ernst; Cropp, Fritz (2005). *Das Personenlexikon zum Dritten Reich. Wer war was vor und nach 1945.*

Fischer Taschenbücher. Frankfurt am Main: Fischer-Taschenbuch-Verlag. ISBN 978-3-596-16048-8.<templatestyles src="Module:Citation/CS1/styles.css"></templatestyles>
- Ley, Astrid; Hinz-Wessels, Annette (eds.). *The "Euthanasia Institution" of Brandenburg an der Havel: Murder of the Ill and Handicapped during National Socialism*. Schriftenreihe der Stiftung Brandenburgische Gedenkstätten. **35**. Berlin: Metropol. ISBN 978-3-86331-086-8.<templatestyles src="Module:Citation/CS1/styles.css"></templatestyles>
- Werthman, Fredric (1967). *A Sign for Cain*. New York: Macmillan. ISBN 978-0-02-625970-5.<templatestyles src="Module:Citation/CS1/styles.css"></templatestyles>

**Journals**

- Ost, Suzanne (April 2006). "Doctors and Nurses of Death: A Case Study of Eugenically Motivated Killing under the Nazi 'Euthanasia' Programme". *The Liverpool Law Review*. **27** (1): 5–30. doi: 10.1007/s10991-005-5345-2[258]. ISSN 0144-932X[259]. PMID 17340766[260].<templatestyles src="Module:Citation/CS1/styles.css"></templatestyles>

**Websites**

- Webb, Chris (2009). "Otwock & the Zofiowka Sanatorium: A Refuge from Hell"[261]. *Holocaust Research Project*. Holocaust Education & Archive Research Team. Archived from the original[262] on 11 July 2011 – via Internet Archive.<templatestyles src="Module:Citation/CS1/styles.css"></templatestyles>

# External links

 Wikimedia Commons has media related to *Action T4*.

- Website with photo of Philipp Bouhler and facsimile of Hitler's letter to Bouhler and Brandt authorising the T4 programme[263]
- United States Holocaust Memorial Museum Final Solutions: Murderous Racial Hygiene 1939–1945[264]
- United States Holocaust Memorial Museum Euthanasia programme[265]
- Nazis euthanasia files made public by the BMJ/British Medical Association: files relating to the 200,000 euthanasia crimes[266]

# Life unworthy of life

> Part of a series on
> **The Holocaust**
>
> Jews on selection ramp at Auschwitz, May 1944
>
> - v
> - t
> - e[267]

The phrase **"life unworthy of life"** (in German: *"Lebensunwertes Leben"*) was a Nazi designation for the segments of the populace which, according to the Nazi regime of the time, had no right to live. Those individuals were targeted to be euthanized by the state, usually through the compulsion or deception of their caretakers. The term included people with serious medical problems and those considered grossly inferior according to the racial policy of Nazi Germany. This concept formed an important component of the ideology of Nazism and eventually helped lead to the Holocaust.[268] It is similar to but more restrictive than the concept of *"Untermensch"*, subhumans, as not all "subhumans" were considered unworthy of life (Slavs, for instance, were deemed useful for slave labor).

The euthanasia program was officially adopted in 1939 and came through the personal decision of Adolf Hitler. It grew in extent and scope from Action T4 ending officially in 1941 when public protests stopped the program, through the Action 14f13 against concentration camp inmates. The euthanasia of people with disabilities continued more discreetly until the end of World War II. The methods used initially at German hospitals such as lethal injections and bottled gas poisoning were expanded to form the basis for the creation of extermination camps where the gas chambers were built from scratch to conduct the extermination of the Jews, Poles, and Romani.[269,270]

# History

The expression first appeared in print via the title of a 1920 book, *Die Freigabe der Vernichtung Lebensunwerten Lebens* (*Allowing the Destruction of Life Unworthy of Life*) by two professors, the jurist Karl Binding (retired from the University of Leipzig) and psychiatrist Alfred Hoche from the University of Freiburg.[271] According to Hoche, some living people who were brain damaged, intellectually disabled, autistic (though not recognized as such at the time), and psychiatrically ill were "mentally dead", "human ballast" and "empty shells of human beings". Hoche felt killing such people was useful. Some people were simply considered disposable.[272] Later the killing was extended to people considered 'racially impure' or 'racially inferior' according to Nazi thinking.

The concept culminated in Nazi extermination camps, instituted to systematically kill those who were unworthy to live according to Nazi ideologists. It also justified various human experimentation and eugenics programs, as well as Nazi racial policies.

# Development of the concept

According to the author of *Medical Killing and the Psychology of Genocide* psychiatrist Robert Jay Lifton, the policy went through a number of iterations and modifications: <templatestyles src="Template:Quote/styles.css"/>

> *Of the five identifiable steps by which the Nazis carried out the principle of "life unworthy of life," coercive sterilization was the first. There followed the killing of "impaired" children in hospitals; and then the killing of "impaired" adults, mostly collected from mental hospitals, in centers especially equipped with carbon monoxide gas. This project was extended (in the same killing centers) to "impaired" inmates of concentration and extermination camps and, finally, to mass killings in the extermination camps themselves.*

**Figure 18:** *This poster (from around 1938) reads: "60,000 Reichsmark is what this person suffering from a hereditary defect costs the People's community during his lifetime. Fellow citizen, that is your money too. Read '[A] New People', the monthly magazine of the Bureau for Race Politics of the NSDAP."*

## External links

- "Life Unworthy of Life" and other Medical Killing Programmes[273] by Dr. Stuart D. Stein, University of the West of England
- Contemporary English translation of "Allowing the Destruction of Life Unworthy of life"[274] by Dr. Cristina Modak
- German text online of Die Freigabe der Vernichtung lebensunwerten Lebens[275]

# Kristallnacht

| Kristallnacht | |
|---|---|
| Part of the Holocaust | |
| The interior of the Fasanenstrasse Synagogue in Berlin after *Kristallnacht* | |
| Location | Nazi Germany (then including Austria and Sudetenland) Free City of Danzig |
| Date | 9–10 November 1938<br>12–13 November (in Danzig) |
| Target | Jews |
| Attack type | Pogrom, looting, arson, mass murder, state terrorism |
| Deaths | 91+ |

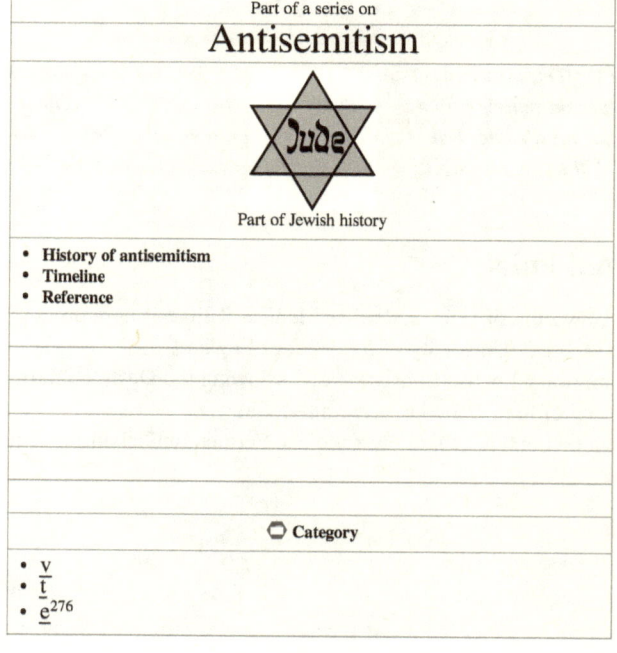

| Part of a series on |
|---|
| **Antisemitism** |
| Part of Jewish history |
| • History of antisemitism<br>• Timeline<br>• Reference |
| |
| |
| |
| |
| ○ Category |
| • v<br>• t<br>• e[276] |

*Kristallnacht* (German pronunciation: [kʁɪsˈtalnaχt]; lit. "Crystal Night") or *Reichskristallnacht* (German: [ˌʁaɪçs.kʁɪsˈtalnaχt] ( listen)), also referred to as the **Night of Broken Glass**, *Reichspogromnacht* [ˌʁaɪçs.poˈɡʁoːmnaχt] or simply *Pogromnacht* [poˈɡʁoːmnaχt] ( listen), and *Novemberpogrome* [noˈvɛmbɐpoɡʁoːmə] ( listen) (Yiddish: נאַכט קרישטאָל *krishtol nakht*), was a pogrom against Jews throughout Nazi Germany on 9–10 November 1938, carried out by SA paramilitary forces and German civilians. The German authorities looked on without intervening.[277,278] The name *Kristallnacht* comes from the shards of broken glass that littered the streets after the windows of Jewish-owned stores, buildings, and synagogues were smashed.

Estimates of the number of fatalities caused by the pogrom have varied. Early reports estimated that 91 Jews were murdered during the attacks.[279] Modern analysis of German scholarly sources by historians such as Sir Richard Evans puts the number much higher. When deaths from post-arrest maltreatment and subsequent suicides are included, the death toll climbs into the hundreds. Additionally, 30,000 Jewish men were arrested and incarcerated in concentration camps.

Jewish homes, hospitals, and schools were ransacked, as the attackers demolished buildings with sledgehammers. The rioters destroyed 267 synagogues throughout Germany, Austria, and the Sudetenland, and over 7,000 Jewish businesses were either destroyed or damaged.[280] The British historian Martin Gilbert wrote that no event in the history of German Jews between 1933 and 1945 was so widely reported as it was happening, and the accounts from the foreign journalists working in Germany sent shock waves around the world. The British newspaper *The Times* wrote at the time: "No foreign propagandist bent upon blackening Germany before the world could outdo the tale of burnings and beatings, of blackguardly assaults on defenseless and innocent people, which disgraced that country yesterday."[281]

The attacks were retaliation for the assassination of the Nazi German diplomat Ernst vom Rath by Herschel Grynszpan, a seventeen-year-old German-born Polish Jew living in Paris. *Kristallnacht* was followed by additional economic and political persecution of Jews, and it is viewed by historians as part of Nazi Germany's broader racial policy, and the beginning of the Final Solution and The Holocaust.

# Background

### Early Nazi persecutions

In the 1920s, most German Jews were fully integrated into German society as German citizens. They served in the German army and navy and contributed to every field of German business, science and culture.[282] Conditions for the Jews began to change after the appointment of Adolf Hitler (the Austrian-born leader of the National Socialist German Workers' Party) as Chancellor of Germany on 30 January 1933, and the Enabling Act (23 March 1933) assumption of power by Hitler after the Reichstag fire of 27 February 1933. From its inception, Hitler's régime moved quickly to introduce anti-Jewish policies. Nazi propaganda singled out the 500,000 Jews in Germany, who accounted for only 0.86% of the overall population, as an enemy within who were responsible for Germany's defeat in the First World War and for its subsequent economic disasters, such as the 1920s hyperinflation and Wall Street Crash Great Depression. Beginning in 1933, the German government enacted a series of anti-Jewish laws restricting the rights of German Jews to earn a living, to enjoy full citizenship and to gain education, including the *Law for the Restoration of the Professional Civil Service* of 7 April 1933, which forbade Jews to work in the civil service. The subsequent 1935 Nuremberg Laws stripped German Jews of their citizenship and forbade Jews to marry non-Jewish Germans.

These laws resulted in the exclusion of Jews from German social and political life. Many sought asylum abroad; hundreds of thousands emigrated, but as Chaim Weizmann wrote in 1936, "The world seemed to be divided into two parts—those places where the Jews could not live and those where they could not enter."[283] The international Évian Conference on 6 July 1938 addressed the issue of Jewish and Gypsy immigration to other countries. By the time the conference took place, more than 250,000 Jews had fled Germany and Austria, which had been annexed by Germany in March 1938; more than 300,000 German and Austrian Jews continued to seek refuge and asylum from oppression. As the number of Jews and Gypsies wanting to leave increased, the restrictions against them grew, with many countries tightening their rules for admission. By 1938, Germany "had entered a new radical phase in anti-Semitic activity".[284] Some historians believe that the Nazi government had been contemplating a planned outbreak of violence against the Jews and were waiting for an appropriate provocation; there is evidence of this planning dating to 1937.[285] In a 1997 interview, the German historian Hans Mommsen claimed that a major motive for the pogrom was the desire of the *Gauleiters* of the NSDAP to seize Jewish property and businesses. Mommsen stated:

> *The need for money by the party organization stemmed from the fact that Franz Xaver Schwarz, the party treasurer, kept the local and regional organizations of the party short of money. In the fall of 1938, the increased pressure on Jewish property nourished the party's ambition, especially since Hjalmar Schacht had been ousted as Reich minister for economics. This, however, was only one aspect of the origin of the November 1938 pogrom. The Polish government threatened to extradite all Jews who were Polish citizens but would stay in Germany, thus creating a burden of responsibility on the German side. The immediate reaction by the Gestapo was to push the Polish Jews—16,000 persons—over the borderline, but this measure failed due to the stubbornness of the Polish customs officers. The loss of prestige as a result of this abortive operation called for some*

**Figure 19:** *Polish Jews expelled from Germany in late October 1938*

*sort of compensation. Thus, the overreaction to Herschel Grynszpan's attempt against the diplomat Ernst vom Rath came into being and led to the November pogrom. The background of the pogrom was signified by a sharp cleavage of interests between the different agencies of party and state. While the Nazi party was interested in improving its financial strength on the regional and local level by taking over Jewish property, Hermann Göring, in charge of the Four-Year Plan, hoped to acquire access to foreign currency in order to pay for the import of urgently-needed raw material. Heydrich and Himmler were interested in fostering Jewish emigration.*

The Zionist leadership in the British Mandate of Palestine wrote in February 1938 that according to "a very reliable private source—one which can be traced back to the highest echelons of the SS leadership", there was "an intention to carry out a genuine and dramatic pogrom in Germany on a large scale in the near future".[286]

## Expulsion of Polish Jews in Germany

In August 1938 the German authorities announced that residence permits for foreigners were being canceled and would have to be renewed. This included German-born Jews of foreign origin. Poland stated that it would not accept

Jews of Polish origin after the end of October. In the so-called "Polenaktion", more than 12,000 Polish-born Jews, among them the philosopher and theologian Rabbi Abraham Joshua Heschel, and future literary critic Marcel Reich-Ranicki were expelled from Germany on 28 October 1938, on Hitler's orders. They were ordered to leave their homes in a single night and were allowed only one suitcase per person to carry their belongings. As the Jews were taken away, their remaining possessions were seized as loot both by the Nazi authorities and by their neighbors.

The deportees were taken from their homes to railway stations and were put on trains to the Polish border, where Polish border guards sent them back over the river into Germany. This stalemate continued for days in the pouring rain, with the Jews marching without food or shelter between the borders. Four thousand were granted entry into Poland, but the remaining 8,000 were forced to stay at the border. They waited there in harsh conditions to be allowed to enter Poland. A British newspaper told its readers that hundreds "are reported to be lying about, penniless and deserted, in little villages along the frontier near where they had been driven out by the Gestapo and left." Conditions in the refugee camps "were so bad that some actually tried to escape back into Germany and were shot", recalled a British woman who was sent to help those who had been expelled.[287]

## Shooting of vom Rath

Among those expelled was the family of Sendel and Riva Grynszpan, Polish Jews who had emigrated to Germany in 1911 and settled in Hanover, Germany. At the trial of Adolf Eichmann in 1961, Sendel Grynszpan recounted the events of their deportation from Hanover on the night of 27 October 1938: "Then they took us in police trucks, in prisoners' lorries, about 20 men in each truck, and they took us to the railway station. The streets were full of people shouting: *'Juden Raus! Auf Nach Palästina!'*" ("Jews out, out to Palestine!").[288] Their seventeen-year-old son Herschel was living in Paris with an uncle. Herschel received a postcard from his family from the Polish border, describing the family's expulsion: "No one told us what was up, but we realized this was going to be the end ... We haven't a penny. Could you send us something?"[289] He received the postcard on 3 November 1938.

On the morning of Monday, 7 November 1938, he purchased a revolver and a box of bullets, then went to the German embassy and asked to see an embassy official. After he was taken to the office of Ernst vom Rath, Grynszpan fired five bullets at Vom Rath, two of which hit him in the abdomen. Vom Rath was a professional diplomat with the Foreign Office who expressed anti-Nazi sympathies, largely based on the Nazis' treatment of the Jews, and was under Gestapo investigation for being politically unreliable.[290] Grynszpan made no

**Figure 20:** *Herschel Grynszpan, 7 November 1938*

**Figure 21:** *Ernst vom Rath*

attempt to escape the French police and freely confessed to the shooting. In his pocket, he carried a postcard to his parents with the message, "May God forgive me ... I must protest so that the whole world hears my protest, and that I will do." It is widely assumed that the assassination was politically motivated, but historian Hans-Jürgen Döscher says the shooting may have been the result of a homosexual love affair gone wrong. Grynszpan and vom Rath had become intimate after they met in Le Boeuf sur le Toit, which was a popular meeting place for gay men at the time.[291]

The next day, the German government retaliated, barring Jewish children from German state elementary schools, indefinitely suspending Jewish cultural activities, and putting a halt to the publication of Jewish newspapers and magazines, including the three national German Jewish newspapers. A newspaper in Britain described the last move, which cut off the Jewish populace from their leaders, as "intended to disrupt the Jewish community and rob it of the last frail ties which hold it together." Their rights as citizens had been stripped.[292] One of the first legal measures issued was an order by Heinrich Himmler, commander of all German police, forbidding Jews to possess any weapons whatever and imposing a penalty of twenty years confinement in a concentration camp upon every Jew found in possession of a weapon hereafter.[293] In Berlin, the entire Jewish population was "'disarmed' with the confiscation of 2,569 hand weapons, 1,702 firearms and 20,000 rounds of ammunition."[294]

# Pogrom

## Death of vom Rath

Ernst Vom Rath died of his wounds on 9 November. Word of his death reached Hitler that evening while he was with several key members of the Nazi party at a dinner commemorating the 1923 Beer Hall Putsch. After intense discussions, Hitler left the assembly abruptly without giving his usual address. Propaganda Minister Joseph Goebbels delivered the speech, in his place, and said that "the Führer has decided that... demonstrations should not be prepared or organized by the party, but insofar as they erupt spontaneously, they are not to be hampered."[295] The chief party judge Walter Buch later stated that the message was clear; with these words, Goebbels had commanded the party leaders to organize a pogrom.[296]

Some leading party officials disagreed with Goebbels' actions, fearing the diplomatic crisis it would provoke. Heinrich Himmler wrote, "I suppose that it is Goebbels's megalomania...and stupidity which is responsible for starting this operation now, in a particularly difficult diplomatic situation."[297] The Israeli historian Saul Friedländer believes that Goebbels had personal reasons

**Figure 22:** *Telegram sent by Reinhard Heydrich, 10 November 1938*

for wanting to bring about *Kristallnacht*. Goebbels had recently suffered humiliation for the ineffectiveness of his propaganda campaign during the Sudeten crisis, and was in some disgrace over an affair with a Czech actress, Lída Baarová. Goebbels needed a chance to improve his standing in the eyes of Hitler. At 01:20 am on 10 November 1938, Reinhard Heydrich sent an urgent secret telegram to the *Sicherheitspolizei* (Security Police; SiPo) and the *Sturmabteilung* (SA), containing instructions regarding the riots. This included guidelines for the protection of foreigners and non-Jewish businesses and property. Police were instructed not to interfere with the riots unless the guidelines were violated. Police were also instructed to seize Jewish archives from synagogues and community offices, and to arrest and detain "healthy male Jews, who are not too old", for eventual transfer to (labor) concentration camps.[298]

## Riots

The storefronts of about 7,500 Jewish stores and businesses were shattered, hence the appellation *Kristallnacht* (Crystal Night).[299] Jewish homes were ransacked all throughout Germany. Although violence against Jews had not been condoned by the authorities, there were cases of Jews being beaten or assaulted.

Over 1400 synagogues and prayer rooms,[300] many Jewish cemeteries, more than 7,000 Jewish shops, and 29 department stores were damaged, and in many

**Figure 23:** *Kristallnacht, shop damage in Magdeburg*

cases destroyed. More than 30,000 Jewish men were arrested and taken to concentration camps; primarily Dachau, Buchenwald, and Sachsenhausen.[301]

The synagogues, some centuries old, were also victims of considerable violence and vandalism, with the tactics the Stormtroops practiced on these and other sacred sites described as "approaching the ghoulish" by the United States Consul in Leipzig. Tombstones were uprooted and graves violated. Fires were lit, and prayer books, scrolls, artwork and philosophy texts were thrown upon them, and precious buildings were either burned or smashed until unrecognizable. Eric Lucas recalls the destruction of the synagogue that a tiny Jewish community had constructed in a small village only twelve years earlier:

<templatestyles src="Template:Quote/styles.css"/>

> It did not take long before the first heavy grey stones came tumbling down, and the children of the village amused themselves as they flung stones into the many colored windows. When the first rays of a cold and pale November sun penetrated the heavy dark clouds, the little synagogue was but a heap of stone, broken glass and smashed-up woodwork.[302]

After this, the Jewish community was fined 10 billion Reichsmarks. In addition, it cost 40 million marks to repair the windows.[303] The *Daily Telegraph* correspondent, Hugh Greene, wrote of events in Berlin:

<templatestyles src="Template:Quote/styles.css"/>

**Figure 24:** *A ruined synagogue in Munich after Kristallnacht*

*Mob law ruled in Berlin throughout the afternoon and evening and hordes of hooligans indulged in an orgy of destruction. I have seen several anti-Jewish outbreaks in Germany during the last five years, but never anything as nauseating as this. Racial hatred and hysteria seemed to have taken complete hold of otherwise decent people. I saw fashionably dressed women clapping their hands and screaming with glee, while respectable middle-class mothers held up their babies to see the "fun".*[304]

Many Berliners were however deeply ashamed of the pogrom, and some took great personal risks to offer help. The son of a US consular official heard the janitor of his block cry: "They must have emptied the insane asylums and penitentiaries to find people who'd do things like that!"[305]

Tucson News TV channel briefly reported on a 2008 remembrance meeting at a local Jewish congregation. According to eyewitness Esther Harris: "They ripped up the belongings, the books, knocked over furniture, shouted obscenities". Historian Gerhard Weinberg is quoted as saying:

*Houses of worship burned down, vandalized, in every community in the country where people either participate or watch.*

**Figure 25:** *A ruined synagogue in Eisenach after Kristallnacht*

**Figure 26:** *Home movie from Vienna taken likely just after Kristallnacht in 1938.*

# Aftermath

Göring, who was in favor of expropriating the Jews rather than destroying Jewish property as had happened in the pogrom, complained directly to *Sicherheitspolizei* Chief Heydrich immediately after the events: "I'd rather you had done in two-hundred Jews than destroy so many valuable assets!" (*"Mir wäre lieber gewesen, ihr hättet 200 Juden erschlagen und hättet nicht solche Werte vernichtet!"*).[306] Göring met with other members of the Nazi leadership on 12 November to plan the next steps after the riot, setting the stage for formal government action. In the transcript of the meeting, Göring said,

> *I have received a letter written on the Führer's orders requesting that the Jewish question be now, once and for all, coordinated and solved one way or another... I should not want to leave any doubt, gentlemen, as to the aim of today's meeting. We have not come together merely to talk again, but to make decisions, and I implore competent agencies to take all measures for the elimination of the Jew from the German economy, and to submit them to me.*[307]

The persecution and economic damage inflicted upon German Jews continued after the pogrom, even as their places of business were ransacked. They were forced to pay *Judenvermögensabgabe*, a collective fine of one billion marks for the murder of vom Rath (equal to roughly $US 5.5 billion in today's currency), which was levied by the compulsory acquisition of 20% of all Jewish property by the state. Six million Reichsmarks of insurance payments for property damage due to the Jewish community were to be paid to the government instead as "damages to the German Nation".[308]

The number of emigrating Jews surged, as those who were able left the country. In the ten months following *Kristallnacht*, more than 115,000 Jews emigrated from the Reich.[309] The majority went to other European countries, the US and Palestine, and at least 14,000 made it to Shanghai, China. As part of government policy, the Nazis seized houses, shops, and other property the émigrés left behind. Many of the destroyed remains of Jewish property plundered during Kristallnacht were dumped near Brandenburg. In October 2008, this dumpsite was discovered by Yaron Svoray, an investigative journalist. The site, the size of four Association football fields, contained an extensive array of personal and ceremonial items looted during the riots against Jewish property and places of worship on the night of 9 November 1938. It is believed the goods were brought by rail to the outskirts of the village and dumped on designated land. Among the items found were glass bottles engraved with the Star of David, mezuzot, painted window sills, and the armrests of chairs found in synagogues, in addition to an ornamental swastika.

**Figure 27:** *Portrait of Paul Ehrlich, damaged on Kristallnacht, then restored by a German neighbor*

## Responses to *Kristallnacht*

### From the Germans

The reaction of non-Jewish Germans to *Kristallnacht* was varied. Many spectators gathered on the scenes, most of them in silence. The local fire departments confined themselves to prevent the flames from spreading to neighboring buildings. In Berlin, police Lieutenant Otto Bellgardt barred SA troopers from setting the New Synagogue on fire, earning his superior officer a verbal reprimand from the commissioner.[310]

The British historian Martin Gilbert believes that "many non-Jews resented the round-up",[311] his opinion being supported by German witness Dr. Arthur Flehinger who recalls seeing "people crying while watching from behind their curtains".[312] Rolf Dessauers recalls how a neighbor came forward and restored a portrait of Paul Ehrlich that had been "slashed to ribbons" by the *Sturmabteilung*. "He wanted it to be known that not all Germans supported Kristallnacht." The extent of the damage done on Kristallnacht was so great that many Germans are said to have expressed their disapproval of it, and to have described it as senseless.[313]

In an article released for publication on the evening of 11 November, Goebbels ascribed the events of *Kristallnacht* to the "healthy instincts" of the German people. He went on to explain: "The German people are anti-Semitic. It has no desire to have its rights restricted or to be provoked in the future by parasites of the Jewish race."[314] Less than 24 hours after the Kristallnacht Adolf Hitler made a one-hour long speech in front of a group of journalists where he managed to completely ignore the recent events on everyone's mind. According to Eugene Davidson the reason for this was that Hitler wished to avoid being directly connected to an event that he was aware that many of those present condemned, regardless of Goebbels's unconvincing explanation that Kristallnacht was caused by popular wrath.[315] Goebbels met the foreign press in the afternoon of 11 November and said that the burning of synagogues and damage to Jewish owned property had been "spontaneous manifestations of indignation against the murder of Herr Vom Rath by the young Jew Grynsban [sic]"[316]

In 1938, just after Kristallnacht, the psychologist Michael Müller-Claudius interviewed 41 randomly selected Nazi Party members on their attitudes towards racial persecution. Of the interviewed party-members 63% expressed extreme indignation against it, while only 5% expressed approval of racial persecution, the rest being noncommittal. A study conducted in 1933 had then shown that 33% of Nazi Party members held no racial prejudice while 13% supported persecution. Sarah Ann Gordon sees two possible reasons for this difference. First, by 1938 large numbers of Germans had joined the Nazi Party for pragmatic reasons rather than ideology thus diluting the percentage of rabid antisemites; second, the Kristallnacht could have caused party members to reject Antisemitism that had been acceptable to them in abstract terms but which they could not support when they saw it concretely enacted. During the Kristallnacht, several Gauleiter and deputy Gauleiters had refused orders to enact the Kristallnacht, and many leaders of the SA and of the Hitler Youth also openly refused party orders, while expressing disgust. Some Nazis helped Jews during the Kristallnacht.

As it was aware that the German public did not support the Kristallnacht, the propaganda ministry directed the German press to portray opponents of racial persecution as disloyal. The press was also under orders to downplay the Kristallnacht, describing general events at the local level only, with the prohibition against depictions of individual events. In 1939 this was extended to a prohibition on reporting any anti-Jewish measures.

The vast majority of the German public disapproved of the Kristallnacht as for example evidenced by the torrent of reports attesting to this by diplomats in Germany.

The US ambassador to Germany reported:

<templatestyles src="Template:Quote/styles.css"/>
> *In view of this being a totalitarian state a surprising characteristic of the situation here is the intensity and scope among German citizens of condemnation of the recent happenings against Jews.*

To the consternation of the Nazis, the Kristallnacht affected public opinion counter to their desires, the peak of opposition against the Nazi racial policies was reached just then, when according to almost all accounts the vast majority of Germans rejected the violence perpetrated against the Jews. Verbal complaints grew rapidly in numbers, and for example, the Duesseldorf branch of the Gestapo reported a sharp decline in anti-Semitic attitudes among the population.

There are many indications of Protestant and Catholic disapproval of racial persecution; for example the Catholic church had already distributed Pastoral letters critical of Nazi racial ideology, and the Nazi regime expected to encounter organised resistance from it following Kristallnacht. The Catholic leadership however, just as the various Protestant churches, refrained from responding with organised action. While individual Catholics and Protestants took action, the churches as a whole chose silence publicly. Nevertheless, individuals continued to show courage, for example, a Parson paid the medical bills of a Jewish cancer patient and was sentenced to a large fine and several months in prison in 1941, and a Catholic nun was sentenced to death in 1945 for helping Jews. A Protestant parson spoke out in 1943 and was sent to Dachau concentration camp where he died after a few days.

Martin Sasse, Nazi Party member and bishop of the Evangelical Lutheran Church in Thuringia, leading member of the Nazi German Christians, one of the schismatic factions of German Protestantism, published a compendium of Martin Luther's writings shortly after the *Kristallnacht*; Sasse "applauded the burning of the synagogues" and the coincidence of the day, writing in the introduction, "On 10 November 1938, on Luther's birthday, the synagogues are burning in Germany." The German people, he urged, ought to heed these words "of the greatest anti-Semite of his time, the warner of his people against the Jews."[317] Diarmaid MacCulloch argued that Luther's 1543 pamphlet, *On the Jews and Their Lies* was a "blueprint" for the *Kristallnacht*.[318]

**Figure 28:** *After 1945 some synagogues were restored. This one in Berlin features a plaque, reading "Never forget", a common expression around Berlin*

## From the global community

*Kristallnacht* sparked international outrage. It discredited pro-Nazi movements in Europe and North America, leading to an eventual decline in their support. Many newspapers condemned *Kristallnacht*, with some of them comparing it to the murderous pogroms incited by Imperial Russia during the 1880s. The United States recalled its ambassador (but it did not break off diplomatic relations) while other governments severed diplomatic relations with Germany in protest. The British government approved the Kindertransport program for refugee children. As such, *Kristallnacht* also marked a turning point in relations between Nazi Germany and the rest of the world. The brutality of the pogrom, and the Nazi government's deliberate policy of encouraging the violence once it had begun, laid bare the repressive nature and widespread anti-Semitism entrenched in Germany. World opinion thus turned sharply against the Nazi regime, with some politicians calling for war. The private protest against the Germans following *Kristallnacht* was held on 6 December 1938. William Cooper, an Aboriginal Australian, led a delegation of the Australian Aboriginal League on a march through Melbourne to the German Consulate to deliver a petition which condemned the "cruel persecution of the Jewish people by the Nazi government of Germany". German officials refused to accept the tendered document.

After the Kristallnacht, Salvador Allende, Gabriel González Videla, Marmaduke Grove, Florencio Durán and other members of the Congress of Chile sent a telegram to Adolf Hitler denouncing the persecution of Jews. A more personal response, in 1939, was the oratorio *A Child of Our Time* by the English composer Michael Tippett.

## *Kristallnacht* as a turning point

*Kristallnacht* changed the nature of the Nazi persecution of Jews from economic, political, and social to physical with beatings, incarceration, and murder; the event is often referred to as the beginning of the Holocaust. In the words of historian Max Rein in 1988, "Kristallnacht came...and everything was changed."

While November 1938 predated the overt articulation of "the Final Solution", it foreshadowed the genocide to come. Around the time of *Kristallnacht*, the SS newspaper *Das Schwarze Korps* called for a "destruction by swords and flames." At a conference on the day after the pogrom, Hermann Göring said: "The Jewish problem will reach its solution if, in anytime soon, we will be drawn into war beyond our border—then it is obvious that we will have to manage a final account with the Jews."

## Modern references

Many decades later, association with the *Kristallnacht* anniversary was cited as the main reason against choosing 9 November *(Schicksalstag)*, the day the Berlin Wall came down in 1989, as the new German national holiday; a different day was chosen (3 October 1990, German reunification). The avant-garde guitarist Gary Lucas's 1988 composition "Verklärte Kristallnacht", which juxtaposes what would become the Israeli national anthem ten years after *Kristallnacht*, "Hatikvah", with phrases from the German national anthem "Deutschland Über Alles" amid wild electronic shrieks and noise, is intended to be a sonic representation of the horrors of *Kristallnacht*. It was premiered at the 1988 Berlin Jazz Festival and received rave reviews. (The title is a reference to Arnold Schoenberg's 1899 work "Verklärte Nacht" that presaged his pioneering work on atonal music; Schoenberg was an Austrian Jew who would move to the United States to escape the Nazis).

*Kristallnacht* was the inspiration for the 1993 album *Kristallnacht* by the composer John Zorn. The German power metal band Masterplan's debut album, *Masterplan* (2003), features an anti-Nazi song entitled "Crystal Night" as the fourth track. The German band BAP published a song titled "Kristallnaach" in their Cologne dialect, dealing with the emotions engendered by the *Kristallnacht*.

*Kristallnacht* was the inspiration for the 1988 composition *Mayn Yngele* by the composer Frederic Rzewski, of which he says: "I began writing this piece in November 1988, on the 50th anniversary of the Kristallnacht ... My piece is a reflection on that vanished part of Jewish tradition which so strongly colors, by its absence, the culture of our time".

*Kristallnacht* was invoked as a reference point on July 16, 2018 by a former Watergate Prosecutor, Jill Wine-Banks, during an MSNBC segment. Her argument was that President Trump's joint press conference with Russian President Vladimir Putin was a performance that would live in infamy much like the attack on Pearl Harbor and *Kristallnacht*.

*Kristallnacht* has been referenced both explicitly and implicitly in countless cases of vandalism of Jewish property including the toppling of gravestones in a Jewish cemetery in suburban St. Louis, Missouri,[319] and the two 2017 vandalisms of the New England Holocaust Memorial, as the memorial's founder Steve Ross discusses in his book, *From Broken Glass: My Story of Finding Hope in Hitler's Death Camps to Inspire a New Generation.*[320]

## Women in the Pogrom

Kristallnacht was an appalling and traumatic time for both men and women and although women were also beaten and publicly humiliated by side men,[321] one of the greatest damages to women was that they were forced to view their homes being destroyed and their husbands and fathers are taken from them. Since such a large number of the men were captured and imprisoned, many of the women came together for support and guidance. Since the men were imprisoned, women were still forced to hide from additional mistreatment, yet many of their homes were demolished. Many women had nowhere to go and found refuge in hospitals and other public spaces.

The women were in charge of restoring their homes and recovering their family's belongings. The women consulted one another and arranged plans to free their men and rescue them from captivity.[322] Following Kristallnacht in 1938 the wives of the prisoners were informed that they could free their husbands if they obtained emigration papers and many women did what they had to do in order to have the men set free. Women had to travel to a multitude of different locations in order to free their men, including Nazi headquarters and begging their Christian colleagues and people they were familiar with for help. One Erna Zydower took her husband's Iron Cross to a Gestapo office to plead for his release from Sachsenhausen. Some women even went to concentration camps and one woman claimed to have traveled to Dachau concentration camp on a bus filled with SS officers. Women worked to release the men, as well as discover ways to escape and keep their families safe. Testimonies during this time claim that women maintained tranquility and command, even in the course of upheaval.

The issue of sexual assault of women at this time has become clearer. Instances of rape occurred and indeed were punished, but as "racial mixing" rather than as rape *per se*. Sexual assaults of young women were detailed at the Nuremberg Trials.

# References

<templatestyles src="Template:Refbegin/styles.css" />

**Books in English**

- Browning, Christopher R. (2003). *Collected Memories: Holocaust History and Postwar Testimony*. George L. Mosse Series in Modern European Cultural and Intellectual History. Madison: University of Wisconsin Press. ISBN 0-299-18984-8.<templatestyles src="Module:Citation/CS1/styles.css"></templatestyles>
- Mayer, Kurt (2009). *My Personal Brush with History*. Tacoma: Kurt Mayer, Confluence Books. ISBN 978-0-578-03911-4.<templatestyles src="Module:Citation/CS1/styles.css"></templatestyles>
- Friedlander, Saul (1998). *Nazi Germany and the Jews: Volume 1: The Years of Persecution 1933–1939*. New York, NY: Perennial. ISBN 0-06-092878-6.<templatestyles src="Module:Citation/CS1/styles.css"></templatestyles>
- Gilbert, Martin (1986). *The Holocaust: The Jewish Tragedy*. London: Collins. ISBN 0-00-216305-5.<templatestyles src="Module:Citation/CS1/styles.css"></templatestyles>
- Gordon, Sarah Ann (1984). *Hitler, Germans, and the Jewish Question*. Princeton University Press. ISBN 0-691-10162-0.<templatestyles src="Module:Citation/CS1/styles.css"></templatestyles>
- Johnson, Eric J. (1999). *Nazi Terror: The Gestapo, Jews, and Ordinary Germans*. New York: Basic Books. ISBN 0-465-04906-0.<templatestyles src="Module:Citation/CS1/styles.css"></templatestyles>
- Mosse, George L. (1978). *Toward the Final Solution: A History of European Racism*. New York: Howard Fertig. ISBN 0-86527-941-1.<templatestyles src="Module:Citation/CS1/styles.css"></templatestyles>

- Mosse, George L. (2000). *Confronting History: A Memoir*. Madison: University of Wisconsin Press. ISBN 0-299-16580-9.
- Mosse, George L. (2003). *Nazi Culture: Intellectual, Cultural and Social Life in the Third Reich*. Madison: University of Wisconsin Press. ISBN 0-299-19304-7.
- Mosse, George L. (1999). *The Crisis of German Ideology: Intellectual Origins of the Third Reich*. New York: Howard Fertig. ISBN 0-86527-426-6.
- Schwab, Gerald (1990). *The day the Holocaust began: the odyssey of Herschel Grynszpan*. New York: Praeger. ISBN 0-275-93576-0.
- Shirer, William L. (1990). *The Rise and Fall of the Third Reich*. New York: Simon & Schuster. ISBN 0-671-72868-7.
- Yahil, Leni (1990). *The Holocaust: the fate of European Jewry, 1932–1945*. Oxford [Oxfordshire]: Oxford University Press. ISBN 0-19-504523-8.
- Dawidowicz, Lucy (1986). *The War Against the Jews: 1933–1945*. UK: Bantam. ISBN 978-0-553-34532-2.
- Steinweis, Alan E. (2009). *Kristallnacht 1938*. Harvard University Press. ISBN 978-0-674-03623-9.

**Books in German**

- Christian Faludi: Die "Juni-Aktion" 1938. Eine Dokumentation zur Radikalisierung der Judenverfolgung. Campus, Frankfurt a. M./New York 2013, ISBN 978-3-593-39823-5
- Hans-Dieter Arntz. "Reichskristallnacht". Der Novemberpogrom 1938 auf dem Lande – Gerichtsakten und Zeugenaussagen am Beispiel der Eifel und Voreifel, Helios-Verlag, Aachen 2008, ISBN 978-3-938208-69-4
- Döscher, Hans-Jürgen (1988). *Reichskristallnacht: Die Novemberpogrome 1938* (in German). Ullstein. ISBN 978-3-550-07495-0.

- Richter, Hans Peter: "Friedrich" Puffin Books 1970
- Kaul, Friedrich Karl; Herschel Feibel Grynszpan (1965). *Der Fall des Herschel Grynszpan* (in German). Berlin: Akademie-Verl.<templatestyles src="Module:Citation/CS1/styles.css"></templatestyles> ISBN Unknown. ASIN B0014NJ88M. Available at *Oxford Journals*[323] (PDF)
- Korb, Alexander (2007). *Reaktionen der deutschen Bevölkerung auf die Novemberpogrome im Spiegel amtlicher Berichte* (in German). Saarbrücken: VDM Verlag. ISBN 978-3-8364-4823-9.<templatestyles src="Module:Citation/CS1/styles.css"></templatestyles>
- Lauber, Heinz (1981). *Judenpogrom: "Reichskristallnacht" November 1938 in Grossdeutschland : Daten, Fakten, Dokumente, Quellentexte, Thesen und Bewertungen (Aktuelles Taschenbuch)* (in German). Bleicher. ISBN 3-88350-005-4.<templatestyles src="Module:Citation/CS1/styles.css"></templatestyles>
- Pätzold, Kurt; Runge, Irene (1988). *Kristallnacht: Zum Pogrom 1938 (Geschichte)* (in German). Köln: Pahl-Rugenstein. ISBN 3-7609-1233-8.<templatestyles src="Module:Citation/CS1/styles.css"></templatestyles>
- Pehle, Walter H. (1988). *Der Judenpogrom 1938: Von der "Reichskristallnacht" zum Völkermord* (in German). Frankfurt am Main: Fischer Taschenbuch Verlag. ISBN 3-596-24386-6.<templatestyles src="Module:Citation/CS1/styles.css"></templatestyles>
- Schultheis, Herbert (1985). *Die Reichskristallnacht in Deutschland nach Augenzeugenberichten (Bad Neustadter Beiträge zur Geschichte und Heimatkunde Frankens)* (in German). Bad Neustadt a. d. Saale: Rotter Druck und Verlag. ISBN 3-9800482-3-3.<templatestyles src="Module:Citation/CS1/styles.css"></templatestyles>

**Online resources**

- Wroe, David (21 October 2008). "Hitler 'led henchmen' in Kristallnacht riots"[324]. *Daily Telegraph*.<templatestyles src="Module:Citation/CS1/styles.css"></templatestyles>
- Segev, Tom (31 October 2008). "Hitler gave the order"[325]. *Haaretz*. Archived from the original[326] on 8 December 2008.<templatestyles src="Module:Citation/CS1/styles.css"></templatestyles>
- Rabbi Eliahu Ellis; Rabbi Shmuel Silinsky. "Kristallnacht"[327]. *Holocaust studies*. Aish.com. Retrieved 2008-05-20.<templatestyles src="Module:Citation/CS1/styles.css"></templatestyles>
- "Germany commemorates Nazi era 'Kristallnacht'"[328]. CNN.com. 1998-11-09. Archived from the original[329] on 25 February 2008. Retrieved 2008-05-20.<templatestyles src="Module:Citation/CS1/styles.css"></templatestyles>

- "What Was Kristallnacht?"[330]. *THHP Short Essays*. The Holocaust History Project. 28 November 2003. Archived from the original[331] on 11 May 2008. Retrieved 20 May 2008.<templatestyles src="Module:Citation/CS1/styles.css"></templatestyles>
- "Kristallnacht "Night of Crystal" – "Night of Broken Glass""[332]. *Holocaust Prelude*. Holocaust Education & Archive Research Team. 2006–2007. Retrieved 2008-05-20.<templatestyles src="Module:Citation/CS1/styles.css"></templatestyles>
- Frieda S. Miller; Vancouver Holocaust Education Center (2008-02-25). "Kristallnacht"[333]. *From Aryanization to Cultural Loss: The Destruction of the Jewish Fashion Industry in Germany and Austria*. Center for Holocaust & Genocide Studies, University of Minnesota. Archived from the original[334] on 10 December 2008. Retrieved 2008-05-20.<templatestyles src="Module:Citation/CS1/styles.css"></templatestyles>
- "Sitting at Nuremberg, Germany 29th July to 8th August 1946"[335]. *The Trial of German Major War Criminals Volume 20*. The Nizkor Project. 2006. Retrieved 2008-05-20.<templatestyles src="Module:Citation/CS1/styles.css"></templatestyles>
- Allida Black; June Hopkins; et al. (2003). "The Eleanor Roosevelt Papers – Kristallnacht"[336]. *Teaching Eleanor Roosevelt; Eleanor Roosevelt National Historic Site, Hyde Park, New York*. US National Park Service archive (nps.gov). Retrieved 2008-05-20.<templatestyles src="Module:Citation/CS1/styles.css"></templatestyles>
- "Kristallnacht: A Nationwide Pogrom, November 9–10, 1938"[337]. *Holocaust Encyclopedia*. US Holocaust Memorial Museum. Retrieved 2008-05-20.<templatestyles src="Module:Citation/CS1/styles.css"></templatestyles>
- "Kristallnacht: The November 1938 Pogroms"[338]. *Online exhibitions, special topics*. US Holocaust Memorial Museum. Archived from the original[339] on 17 May 2008. Retrieved 20 May 2008.<templatestyles src="Module:Citation/CS1/styles.css"></templatestyles>
- Yad Vashem (2004). "Kristallnacht"[340]. *Yad Vashem's Photo Archives*. The Holocaust Martyrs' and Heroes' Remembrance Authority. Archived from the original[341] on 9 March 2005. Retrieved 2008-05-21.<templatestyles src="Module:Citation/CS1/styles.css"></templatestyles>

## External links

 Wikimedia Commons has media related to *Kristallnacht*.

- Events Leading Up to Kristallnacht – What led to the Night of Broken Glass?[342], by The Center for Holocaust and Humanity Education
- *Voices on Antisemitism* Interview with Susan Warsinger[343] from the United States Holocaust Memorial Museum[344]
- *Synagogues Memorial institute* in Jerusalem[345]
- It Came From Within... 71 Years Since Kristallnacht[346] – Online exhibition from Yad Vashem, including survivor testimonies, archival footage, photos, and stories
- "At 7:00 in the morning I was a student, and at 5:00, I was a criminal"[347] – Interview with Miriam Ron, Witness to the Events of Kristallnacht
- Witness Speech, *Kristallnacht*[348], by George Spooner, Holocaust survivor, at Grace United Methodist Church, St. Louis, Missouri, 29 October 2017.

# The holocaust

## The Holocaust in Poland

<indicator name="pp-default"> 🔒 </indicator>

The Holocaust
in German-occupied Poland

Top, clockwise: Warsaw Ghetto burning, May 1943 • *Einsatzgruppe* shooting of women from the Mizocz Ghetto, 1942 • Selection of people to be sent directly to the gas chamber right after their arrival at Auschwitz-II Birkenau • Jews captured in the Warsaw Ghetto Uprising led to the *Umschlagplatz* by Waffen SS • Łódź Ghetto children deported to Chełmno death camp, 1942

Map of the Holocaust in occupied Poland during World War II with six extermination camps marked with white skulls in black squares: Auschwitz-Birkenau, Bełżec, Chełmno, Majdanek, Sobibór and Treblinka; as well as remote mass killing sites at Bronna Góra, Ponary, Połonka and others. Marked with the Star of David are selected large Polish cities with the extermination ghettos. Solid red line denotes the Nazi–Soviet frontier – starting point for Operation Barbarossa of 1941.

**Overview**

| Period | September 1939 – April 1945 |
|---|---|
| Territory | Occupied Poland, also present day western Ukraine and western Belarus among others |
| **Major perpetrators** | |
| Units | *SS-Totenkopfverbände*, *Einsatzgruppen*, Orpo battalions, Trawnikis, BKA, OUN-UPA, TDA, Ypatingasis būrys |
| Killed | three million Polish Jews, scholars disagree on the classification of three million ethnic Polish victims |
| Survivors | 50,000–120,000; or 210,000–230,000; or a total of 350,000. |
| **Armed resistance** | |
| Jewish uprisings | Będzin, Białystok, Birkenau, Częstochowa, Łachwa, Łuck, Mińsk Mazowiecki, Mizocz, Pińsk, Poniatowa, Sobibór, Sosnowiec, Treblinka, Warsaw, Wilno |

**The Holocaust in German-occupied Poland** was the last and most lethal phase of Nazi Germany's "Final Solution of the Jewish Question" (*Endlösung der Judenfrage*), marked by the construction of death camps on German-occupied Polish soil. The Third Reich's World War II genocide, known as the Holocaust, took the lives of three million Polish Jews, half of all Jews killed during the Holocaust. Scholars disagree on whether to also classify up to three million ethnic-Polish victims of German genocide as Holocaust victims. The extermination camps played a central role in Germany's systematic destruction of over 90% of Poland's Jewish population.

Every branch of the sophisticated German bureaucracy was involved in the killing process, from the Interior and Finance Ministries to German firms and state-run railroads. German companies bid for contracts to build crematoria in concentration camps run by Germany in the General Government and in other areas of occupied Poland and beyond.

During the German occupation, many ethnic Poles, at the greatest risk to themselves and their families, succeeded in saving Jews from the Germans. Polish rescuers represent the greatest number of persons, of any nationality, who saved Jews during the Holocaust.. The State of Israel has recognized 6,863 individuals as Polish Righteous among the Nations.

A small percentage of Polish Jews survived World War II within German-occupied Poland or escaped east, beyond reach of the Germans, into the territories of Poland that had been annexed by the Soviet Union in 1939, only to be deported to forced labor in Siberia along with up to 1 million of Poland's non-Jewish citizens.

# Background

Following the 1939 invasion of Poland in accordance with the secret protocol of the Molotov–Ribbentrop Pact, Nazi Germany and the Soviet Union partitioned Poland into occupation zones. Large areas of western Poland were annexed by Germany. The Soviets had attempted to deceive the Poles into believing that they had invaded eastern Poland to help Poland fight Germany and took over some 52% of Poland's territory. The entire *Kresy* (eastern Poland's borderlands) macroregion – inhabited by between 13.2 and 13.7 million people, including majority-Ukrainian and -Belarusin populations and 1,300,000 Jews – was annexed by the Soviet Union in an atmosphere of terror surrounding a mock referendum staged by the NKVD and the Red Army. Within months, Polish Jews in the Soviet zone who refused to swear allegiance were deported deep into the Soviet interior along with ethnic Poles. The number of deported Polish Jews is estimated at 200,000–230,000 men, women, and children.

Both occupying powers were hostile to the existence of a sovereign Polish state and endorsed policies of genocide. However, Soviet possession was short-lived because the terms of the Nazi–Soviet Pact, signed earlier in Moscow, were broken when the German army invaded the Soviet occupation zone on 22 June 1941 *(see map)*. From 1941 to 1943 all of Poland was under Germany's control. The semi-colonial General Government, set up in central and southeastern Poland, comprised 39 percent of occupied Polish territory.

# Nazi ghettoization policy

Prior to World War II, there were 3,500,000 Jews in Poland, living predominantly in the cities; about 10% of the general population. Database of the POLIN Museum of the History of Polish Jews provides information on 1,926 Jewish communities across the country. Following the conquest of Poland, and the 1939 murder of intelligentsia, the first German anti-Jewish measures involved the policy of expulsion of Jews from the territories annexed by the Third Reich. The westernmost provinces of Greater Poland and Pomerelia were turned into brand new German *Reichsgaue* named Danzig-West Prussia and the Wartheland, with the intention of their complete Germanization through settler colonialism (*Lebensraum*). Annexed directly to the new *Warthegau* district, the city of Łódź absorbed the influx of some 40,000 Polish Jews forced out from the surrounding areas. A total of 204,000 Jewish people passed through the ghetto in Łódź. Initially, they were to be expelled to the *Generalgouvernement*. However, the ultimate destination of the massive removal of Jews was left open until the Final Solution was set in motion two years later.

Persecution of Polish Jews by the German occupation authority began immediately after the invasion particularly in major urban areas. In the first year and a half, the Nazis confined themselves to stripping the Jews of their valuables and property for profit, herding them into makeshift ghettos, and forcing them into slave labor for public works and the war economy. During this period, the Germans ordered Jewish communities to appoint Jewish Councils (*Judenräte*) to administer the ghettos and to be "responsible in the strictest sense" for carrying out orders. Most ghettos were set up in cities and towns where Jewish life was well organized. For logistical reasons, the Jewish communities in settlements without railway connections in occupied Poland were dissolved. In a massive deportation action involving the use of freight trains, all Polish Jews had been segregated from the rest of society in dilapidated neighborhoods (*Jüdischer Wohnbezirk*) adjacent to the existing rail corridors. The food aid was completely dependent on the *SS*. Initially, the Jews were legally banned from baking bread; they were sealed off from the general public in an unsustainable manner.

<templatestyles src="Template:Quote/styles.css"/>

> *The Warsaw ghetto contained more Jews than all of France; the Łódź ghetto more Jews than all of the Netherlands. More Jews lived in the city of Kraków than in all of Italy, and virtually any medium-sized town in Poland had a larger Jewish population than all of Scandinavia. All of southeast Europe – Hungary, Romania, Bulgaria, Yugoslavia, and Greece – had fewer Jews than the original four districts of the General Government.*

The plight of Jews in war-torn Poland could be divided into stages defined by the existence of the ghettos. Before their formation, the escape from persecution did not involve extrajudicial punishment by death. Once the ghettos were sealed off from the outside, death by starvation and disease became rampant, alleviated only by the smuggling of food and medicine, described by Ringelblum as "one of the finest pages in the history between the two peoples". In Warsaw, up to 80 percent of food consumed in the Ghetto was brought in illegally. The food stamps introduced by the Germans, provided 9 percent of the calories necessary for survival. In two and a half years, between November 1940 and May 1943, some 100,000 Jews died in the Warsaw Ghetto of starvation and disease; and around 40,000 in the Łódź Ghetto in the four-and-a-quarter years between May 1940 and August 1944. By the end of 1941, most ghettoized Jews had no savings left to pay the *SS* for further bulk food deliveries. The 'productionists' among the German authorities – who attempted to make the ghettos self-sustaining by turning them into enterprises – prevailed over the 'attritionists' only after the German attack on the Soviet positions in eastern Poland, codenamed Operation Barbarossa. The most prominent ghettos were stabilized through the production of goods needed at the front, and

**Figure 29:** *Jews from Tarnopol Voivodeship shot face-down in an open pit near Złoczów*

death rates among the Jewish population began to decline (at least temporarily).

## Holocaust by bullets

Following the German attack on the USSR in June 1941, Himmler assembled a force of some 11,000 men to pursue, for the first time, a program of physical annihilation of Jews. Also during Operation Barbarossa, the *SS* had recruited collaborationist auxiliary police from among Soviet nationals. The local *Schuma* provided Germany with manpower and critical knowledge of local regions and languages. In what became known as the "Holocaust by bullets", the German police battalions (*Orpo*), *SiPo*, Waffen-SS, and special-task *Einsatzgruppen*, along with Ukrainian and Lithuanian auxiliaries, operated behind front lines, systematically shooting tens of thousands of men, women, and children, independently of the army.

Massacres were committed in over 30 locations across the formerly Soviet-occupied parts of Poland, including in Brześć, Tarnopol, and Białystok, as well as in prewar provincial capitals of Łuck, Lwów, Stanisławów, and Wilno (see Ponary).[349] The survivors of mass killing operations were incarcerated in the new ghettos of economic exploitation, and starved slowly to death by artificial famine at the whim of German authorities. Because of sanitation concerns, the corpses of people who had died as a result of starvation and

**Figure 30:** *Photos from The Black Book of Poland, published in London in 1942 by Polish government-in-exile.*

mistreatment were buried in mass graves in the tens of thousands. Gas vans were made available in November 1941. By December, over 439,800 Jewish people had been murdered, both in the eastern half of Poland and in the Soviet westernmost republics. The 'war of destruction' policy in the east against 'the Jewish race' became common knowledge among the Germans at all levels. Within two years, the total number of shooting victims in the east had risen to between 618,000 and 800,000 Jews. Entire regions behind the German–Soviet Frontier were reported to Berlin by the Nazi death squads to be *"Judenfrei"*.

# Final Solution and liquidation of Ghettos

On January 20, 1942, during the Wannsee conference near Berlin, State Secretary of the Government General, Josef Bühler, urged Reinhard Heydrich to begin the proposed "final solution to the Jewish question" as soon as possible. The industrial killing by exhaust fumes was already tried and tested over several weeks at the Chełmno extermination camp in the then-Wartheland, under the guise of resettlement. All condemned Ghetto prisoners, without exception, were told they were going to labour camps, and asked to pack a carry-on luggage. Many Jews believed in the transfer ruse, since deportations were also part of the ghettoization process. Meanwhile, the idea of mass murder by means

**Figure 31:** *Top: entrance to Auschwitz camp I, with gate sign, Arbeit macht frei. Bottom: the real death factory at nearby Auschwitz II–Birkenau*

of stationary gas chambers was discussed in Lublin already since September 1941. It was a precondition for the newly drafted Operation Reinhard led by Odilo Globocnik who ordered the construction of death camps at Belzec, Sobibór, and Treblinka. At Majdanek and Auschwitz, the work of the stationary gas chambers began in March and May respectively, preceded by experiments with Zyklon B. Between 1942 and 1944, the most extreme measure of the Holocaust, the extermination of millions of Jews from Poland and all over Europe was carried out in six extermination camps. There were no Polish guards at any of the Reinhard camps, despite the sometimes used misnomer Polish death camps. All killing centres were designed and operated by the Nazis in strict secrecy, aided by the Ukrainian Trawnikis. Civilians were forbidden to approach them and often shot if caught near the train tracks.[350]

Systematic liquidation of the ghettos began across General Government in the early spring of 1942. At that point the only chance for survival was escape to the "Aryan side". The German round-ups for the so-called resettlement trains were connected directly with the use of top secret extermination facilities built for the SS at about the same time by various German engineering companies including HAHB, I.A. Topf and Sons of Erfurt, and C.H. Kori GmbH.

Unlike other Nazi concentration camps where prisoners from all across Europe were exploited for the war effort, German death camps – part of secretive

**Figure 32:** *Liquidation of Kraków Ghetto, March 1943. Families walk to Prokocim railway station for "resettlement". Destination: Auschwitz.*

Operation Reinhardt – were designed exclusively for the rapid elimination of Polish and foreign Jews, subsisting in isolation. The camp's German overseers reported to Heinrich Himmler in Berlin, who kept control of the extermination program, but who delegated the work in Poland to SS and police chief Odilo Globocnik of the Lublin Reservation. The selection of sites, construction of facilities and training of personnel was based on a similar (Action T4) "racial hygiene" program of mass murder through involuntary euthanasia, developed in Germany.

## The "resettlement" program

The scale of the Final Solution would not have been possible without the *Reichsbahn*. The extermination of Polish and foreign Jews depended on the railways as much as on the secluded killing centres. The Holocaust trains sped up the scale and duration over which the extermination took place; and, the enclosed nature of freight cars also reduced the number of troops required to guard them. Rail shipments allowed the Nazi Germans to build and operate bigger and more efficient death camps and, at the same time, openly lie to the world – and to their victims – about a "resettlement" program. In one telephone conversation Heinrich Himmler informed Martin Bormann about the Jews already exterminated in Poland, to which Bormann screamed in response: "They were not exterminated, only evacuated, evacuated, evacuated!"

Unspecified number of deportees died in transit during Operation Reinhard from suffocation and thirst. No food or water was supplied. The *Güterwagen* boxcars were only fitted with a bucket latrine. A small barred window provided little ventilation, which oftentimes resulted in multiple deaths. A survivor of the Treblinka uprising testified about one such train, from Biała Podlaska. When the sealed doors flew open, 90 percent of about 6,000 Jewish prisoners were found to have suffocated to death. Their bodies were thrown into smouldering mass grave at the "Lazaret".[351] Millions of people were transported in similar trainsets to the extermination camps under the direction of the German Ministry of Transport, and tracked by an IBM subsidiary, until the official date of closing of the Auschwitz-Birkenau complex in December 1944.

Death factories were just one of a number of ways of mass extermination. There were secluded killing sites set up further east. At Bronna Góra (the Bronna Mount, now Belarus) 50,000 Jews died in execution pits; delivered by the Holocaust trains from the ghettos in Brześć, Bereza, Janów Poleski, Kobryń, Horodec (pl), Antopol and other locations along the western border of *Reichskommissariat Ostland*. Explosives were used to speed up the digging process. At the Sosenki Forest on the outskirts of Równe in prewar Wołyń Voivodeship, over 23,000 Jews were shot, men, women, and children. At the Górka Połonka forest *(see map)* 25,000 Jews forced to disrobe and lay over the bodies of others were shot in waves; most of them were deported there via the Łuck Ghetto.[352] The execution site for the Lwów Ghetto inmates was arranged near Janowska, with 35,000–40,000 Jewish victims killed and buried at the Piaski ravine.[353]

While the Order Police performed liquidations of the Jewish ghettos in occupied Poland, loading prisoners into railcars and shooting those unable to move or attempting to flee, the collaborationist auxiliary police were used as a means of inflicting terror upon the Jewish people by conducting large-scale massacres in the same locations. They were deployed in all major killing sites of Operation Reinhard (terror was a primary aim of their SS training). The Ukrainian Trawniki men formed into units took an active role in the extermination of Jews at Belzec, Sobibór, Treblinka II; during the Warsaw Ghetto Uprising (on three occasions, see Stroop Report), Częstochowa, Lublin, Lwów, Radom, Kraków, Białystok (twice), Majdanek, Auschwitz, the Trawniki concentration camp itself, and the remaining subcamps of KL Lublin/Majdanek camp complex including Poniatowa, Budzyń, Kraśnik, Puławy, Lipowa, and also during massacres in Łomazy, Międzyrzec, Łuków, Radzyń, Parczew, Końskowola, Komarówka and all other locations, augmented by members of the SS, SD, Kripo, as well as the reserve police battalions from Orpo (each, responsible for annihilation of thousands of Jews). Mass executions of Jews (as in Szebnie) was part of regular training of the Ukrainian *Waffen-SS* Division soldiers from

**Figure 33:** *Jews being sent to Chełmno death camp, forced to abandon their bundles along the way. Here: loading of victims being sent from Łódź Ghetto, 1942*

the *SS-Heidelager* troop-training base in Pustków in south-eastern Poland. In the north-east, the "Poachers' Brigade" of Oskar Dirlewanger trained Belarusian Home Guard in murder expeditions with the help of Belarusian Auxiliary Police. By the end of World War II in Europe in May 1945, over 90% of Polish Jewry perished.

## Death camp at Chełmno

The Chełmno extermination camp (German: *Kulmhof*) was built as the first-ever, following Hitler's launch of Operation Barbarossa. It was a pilot project for the development of other extermination sites. The experiments with exhaust gases were finalized by murdering 1,500 Poles at Soldau.[354] The killing method at Chełmno grew out of the 'euthanasia' program in which busloads of unsuspecting hospital patients were gassed in air-tight shower rooms at Bernburg, Hadamar and Sonnenstein. The killing grounds at Chełmno, 50 kilometres (31 mi) from Łódź, consisted of a vacated manorial estate similar to Sonnenstein, used for undressing (with a truck-loading ramp in the back), as well as a large forest clearing 4 kilometres (2.5 mi) northwest of Chełmno, used for the mass burial as well as open-pit cremation of corpses introduced some time later.

All Jews from the *Judenfrei* district of *Wartheland* were deported to Chełmno under the guise of 'resettlement'. At least 145,000 prisoners from the Łódź

**Figure 34:** *Auschwitz II–Birkenau prisoners*

Ghetto perished at Chełmno in several waves of deportations lasting from 1942 to 1944. Additionally, 20,000 foreign Jews and 5,000 Roma were brought in from Germany, Austria and Czechoslovakia. All victims were killed with the use of mobile gas vans (*Sonderwagen*), which had exhaust pipes reconfigured and poisons added to gasoline (see Chełmno Trials for supplementary data). In the last phase of the camp's existence, the exhumed bodies were cremated in open-air for several weeks during Sonderaktion 1005. The ashes, mixed with crushed bones, were trucked every night to the nearby river in sacks made from blankets, to remove the evidence of mass murder.

## Auschwitz-Birkenau

The Auschwitz concentration camp was the largest of the German Nazi extermination centers. Located 64 kilometres (40 mi) west of Kraków, Auschwitz processed an average of 1.5 Holocaust trains per day. The overwhelming majority of prisoners deported there were murdered within hours of their arrival. The camp was fitted with the first permanent gas chambers in March 1942. The extermination of Jews with Zyklon B as the killing agent began in July. At Birkenau, the four killing installations (each consisting of coatrooms, multiple gas chambers and industrial-scale crematoria) were built in the following year. By late 1943, Birkenau was a killing factory with four so-called 'Bunkers' (totaling over a dozen gas chambers) working around the clock.[355]

Up to 6,000 people were gassed and cremated there each day, after the ruthless 'selection process' at the *Judenrampe*. Only about 10 percent of the deportees from transports organized by the Reich Main Security Office (RSHA) were registered and assigned to the Birkenau barracks.

Auschwitz II extermination program resulted in the death of 1.3 to 1.5 million people. Over 1.1 million of them were Jews from across Europe including 200,000 children. Among the registered 400,000 victims (less than one-third of the total Auschwitz arrivals) were 140,000–150,000 non-Jewish Poles, 23,000 Gypsies, 15,000 Soviet POWs and 25,000 others. Auschwitz received a total of about 300,000 Jews from occupied Poland, shipped aboard freight trains from liquidated ghettos and transit camps, beginning with Bytom (February 15, 1942), Olkusz (three days of June), Otwock (in August), Łomża and Ciechanów (November), then Kraków (March 13, 1943), Sosnowiec, Będzin, Dąbrowa (June–August 1943), and several dozen other metropolitan cities and towns,[356] including the last ghetto left standing in occupied Poland, liquidated in August 1944 at Łódź. Auschwitz-Birkenau gas chambers and crematoria were blown up on November 25, 1944, in an attempt to destroy the evidence of mass killings, by the orders of SS chief Heinrich Himmler.

## Treblinka

Designed and built for the sole purpose of killing people, Treblinka was one of only three such facilities in existence; the other two were Bełżec and Sobibór. All of them were situated in wooded areas away from population centres and linked to the Polish rail system by a branch line. They had transferable *SS* staff. There was a railway platform constructed alongside the tracks, surrounded by 2.5 m (8 ft) high barbed-wire fencing. Large barracks were built for storing belongings of disembarking victims. One was disguised as a railway station complete with a fake wooden clock and signage to prevent new arrivals from realizing their fate. Passports and money were collected for "safekeeping" at a cashier's booth set up by the "Road to Heaven", a fenced-off path leading into the gas chambers disguised as communal showers. Directly behind were the burial pits, dug with a crawler excavator.

Located 80 kilometres (50 mi) northeast of Warsaw, Treblinka became operational on July 24, 1942, after three months of forced labour construction by expellees from Germany.[357] The shipping of Jews from the Polish capital – plan known as the *Großaktion Warschau* – began immediately. During two months of the summer of 1942, about 254,000 Warsaw Ghetto inmates were exterminated at Treblinka (by some other accounts, at least 300,000). On arrival, the transportees were made to disrobe, then the men – followed by women and children – were forced into double-walled chambers and gassed to death in batches of 200, with the use of exhaust fumes generated by a tank engine. The

**Figure 35:** *Treblinka II burning during prisoner uprising, 2 August 1943: barracks and petrol tank set ablaze. Clandestine photo by Franciszek Ząbecki*

gas chambers, rebuilt of brick and expanded during August–September 1942, were capable of killing 12,000 to 15,000 victims every day, with a maximum capacity of 22,000 executions in twenty-four hours. The dead were initially buried in large mass graves, but the stench from the decomposing bodies could be smelled up to ten kilometers away. As a result, the Nazis began burning the bodies on open-air grids made of concrete pillars and railway tracks. The number of people killed at Treblinka in about a year ranges from 800,000 to 1,200,000, with no exact figures available. The camp was closed by Globocnik on October 19, 1943 soon after the Treblinka prisoner uprising, with the murderous Operation Reinhard nearly completed.[358]

## Bełżec

The Bełżec extermination camp, set up near the railroad station of Bełżec in the Lublin District, began operating officially on March 17, 1942, with three temporary gas chambers later replaced with six made of brick and mortar, enabling the facility to handle over 1,000 victims at one time. At least 434,500 Jews were exterminated there. The lack of verified survivors however, makes this camp much less known. The bodies of the dead, buried in mass graves, swelled in the heat as a result of putrefaction making the earth split, which was resolved with the introduction of crematoria pits in October 1942.

**Figure 36:** *SS Death's-Head unit, Bełżec extermination camp, 1942*

Kurt Gerstein from *Waffen-SS*, supplying Zyklon B from Degesch during the Holocaust, wrote after the war in his Gerstein Report for the Allies that on August 17, 1942 at Belzec, he had witnessed the arrival of 45 wagons with 6,700 prisoners of whom 1,450 were already dead inside. That train came with the Jewish people of the Lwów Ghetto, less than a hundred kilometers away. The last shipment of Jews (including those who had already died in transit) arrived in Bełżec in December 1942. The burning of exhumed corpses continued until March. The remaining 500 *Sonderkommando* prisoners who dismantled the camp, and who bore witness to the extermination process, were murdered at the nearby Sobibór extermination camp in the following months.

## Sobibór

The Sobibór extermination camp, disguised as a railway transit camp not far from Lublin, began mass gassing operations in May 1942. As in other extermination centers, the Jews, taken off the Holocaust trains arriving from liquidated ghettos and transit camps (Izbica, Końskowola) were met by an SS-man dressed in a medical coat. *Oberscharführer* Hermann Michel gave the command for prisoners' "disinfection".

New arrivals were forced to split into groups, hand over their valuables, and disrobe inside a walled-off courtyard for a bath. Women had their hair cut off by the *Sonderkommando* barbers. Once undressed, the Jews were led down

```
                                            GPDD 355a    2.

12. OMX de OMQ              1000           89 ? ?
    Geheime Reichssache! An das Reichssicherheitshauptamt, zu
    Händen SS Obersturmbannführer EICHMANN, BERLIN ...rest missed..
13/15. OLQ de OMQ           1005           83 234 250
    Geheime Reichssache! An den Befehlshaber der Sicherheitspol.,
    zu Händen SS Obersturmbannführer HEIM, KRAKAU.
    Betr: 14-tägige Meldung Einsatz REINHART. Bezug: dort.
    Fs. Zugang bis 31.12.42, L 12761,B 0, S 515, T 10335 zusammen
    23611. Stand... 31.12.42, L 24733, B 434508, S 101370,
    T 71355, zusammen 1274166.
    SS und Pol.führer LUBLIN, HOEFLE, Sturmbannführer.
```

**Figure 37:** *Top-secret "Höfle Telegram" confirms at least 101,370 train deportations of Jews to Sobibór extermination camp in 1942*

a narrow path to the gas chambers which were disguised as showers. Carbon monoxide gas was released from the exhaust pipes of a gasoline engine removed from a Red Army tank. Their bodies were taken out and burned in open pits over iron grids partly fueled by human body-fat. Their remains were dumped onto seven "ash mountains". The total number of Polish Jews murdered at Sobibór is estimated at a minimum of 170,000. Heinrich Himmler ordered the camp dismantled following a prisoner revolt on October 14, 1943; one of only two successful uprisings by Jewish *Sonderkommando* inmates in any extermination camp, with 300 escapees (most of them were recaptured by the SS and killed).

## Lublin-Majdanek

The Majdanek forced labor camp located on the outskirts of Lublin (like Sobibór) and closed temporarily during an epidemic of typhus, was reopened in March 1942 for Operation Reinhard; first, as a storage depot for valuables stolen from the victims of gassing at the killing centers of Belzec, Sobibór, and Treblinka, It became a place of extermination of large Jewish populations from south-eastern Poland (Kraków, Lwów, Zamość, Warsaw) after the gas chambers were constructed in late 1942.

The gassing of Polish Jews was performed in plain view of other inmates, without as much as a fence around the killing facilities. According to witness's testimony, "to drown the cries of the dying, tractor engines were run near the gas chambers" before they took the dead away to the crematorium. Majdanek was the site of death of 59,000 Polish Jews (from among its 79,000 victims). By the end of Operation *Aktion Erntefest* (Harvest Festival) conducted at Majdanek in early November 1943 (the single largest German massacre of Jews during the entire war), the camp had only 71 Jews left.

**Figure 38:** *Crematorium ovens, Majdanek*

# Armed resistance and ghetto uprisings

There is a popular misconception among the general public that most Jews went to their deaths passively. Nothing could be further from the truth. Jewish resistance to the Nazis comprised not only their armed struggle but also spiritual and cultural opposition which gave the Jews dignity despite the inhumane conditions of life in the ghettos. Many forms of resistance were present, even though the elders were terrified by the prospect of mass retaliation against the women and children in the case of anti-Nazi revolt.[359] As the German authorities undertook to liquidate the ghettos, armed resistance was offered in over 100 locations on either side of Polish-Soviet border of 1939, overwhelmingly in eastern Poland.[360] The uprisings erupted in 5 major cities, 45 provincial towns, 5 major concentration and extermination camps, as well as in at least 18 forced labor camps. Notably, the only rebellions in Nazi camps were Jewish.

The Nieśwież Ghetto insurgents in eastern Poland fought back on July 22, 1942. The Łachwa Ghetto revolt erupted on September 3. On October 14, 1942, the Mizocz Ghetto followed suit. The Warsaw Ghetto firefight of January 18, 1943, led to the largest Jewish uprising of World War II launched on April 19, 1943. On June 25, the Jews of the Częstochowa Ghetto rose up. At Treblinka, the *Sonderkommando* prisoners armed with stolen weapons attacked the guards on August 2, 1943. A day later, the Będzin and Sosnowiec ghetto revolts broke out. On August 16, the Białystok Ghetto uprising erupted.

**Figure 39:** *Photograph of Jewish women insurgents captured by the SS during the Warsaw Ghetto Uprising, from the Stroop Report.*

The revolt in Sobibór extermination camp occurred on October 14, 1943. At Auschwitz-Birkenau, the insurgents blew up one of Birkenau's crematoria on October 7, 1944. Similar resistance was offered in Łuck, Mińsk Mazowiecki, Pińsk, Poniatowa, and in Wilno.

## Poles and the Jews

Only 10 percent of Poland's Jews survived the genocide which is less than in any other occupied country save for Lithuania. However, Polish nationals account for the majority of rescuers with the title of 'Righteous Among the Nations, *honored by Yad Vashem. According to Paulsson it is probable that these 5,000 recognized Poles only "represent only the tip of the iceberg" of Polish rescuers. Some Jews received organized help from Żegota )The Council to Aid Jews) an underground organization of Polish resistance in German-occupied Poland.*[361]

On November 10, 1941, capital punishment was extended by Hans Frank to Poles who helped Jews "in any way: by taking them in for a night, giving them a lift in a vehicle of any sort", or "feeding runaway Jews or selling them foodstuffs." The law was publicized with posters distributed in all major cities. Similar regulations were issues by the Germans in other territories they controlled

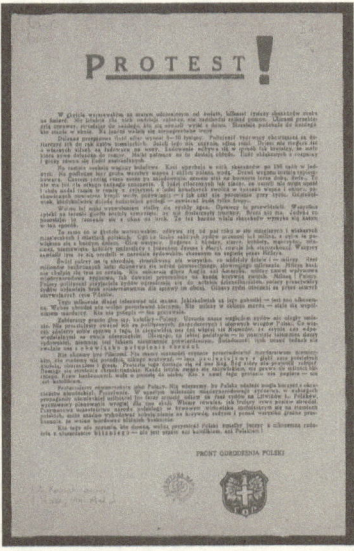

**Figure 40:** *Zofia Kossak-Szczucka's Protest! against killing of Jews, distributed in German-occupied Poland, 28 August 1942*

in the Eastern Front.[362] Capital punishment meted out to entire families was the most draconian penalty ever imposed.Wikipedia:Citation needed Over 700 Polish Righteous among the Nations received that recognition posthumously, having been murdered by the Germans for aiding or sheltering their Jewish neighbors. Many of the Polish Righteous awarded by Yad Vashem came from the capital. In his work on Warsaw's Jews, Gunnar S. Paulsson demonstrated that despite the much harsher conditions, Warsaw's Polish citizens managed to support and hide the same percentage of Jews as did the citizens of cities in reportedly *safer* German-occupied countries of Western Europe.

## Antisemitism

Polish antisemitism was deeply rooted, with two formative motifs: claims of defilement of the Catholic faith; and Żydokomuna (Jew-communism). During the 1930s, Catholic journals in Poland paralleled western European social-Darwinist antisemitism and the Nazi press. However, church doctrine ruled out violence, which only became more common in the mid-1930s. Unlike German antisemitism, Polish antisemities rejected the idea of genocide or pogroms of the Jews, advocating mass emigration instead[363] The German and Soviet occupations brought a sudden upsurge of Polish antisemitism. The Polish narrative was based on a notion of "Jewish collaboration" with the communists

**Figure 41:** *Children, Warsaw Ghetto*

and hatred of the Polish nation. The *szmalcownik* practice of extorting and denouncing Jews to the German authorities was also carried out by ordinary Poles who were acting the traditional "other" who were outside the national consensus. Poles attacked and killed Jews in the 1941 Jedwabne pogrom and other locations in Eastern Poland in the wake of Operation Barbarossa. The question of Jewish property, taken over by Poles, was a driving factor behind the beating and murdering of Jews by Poles between summer 1944 and 1946, including the Kielce pogrom.[364]

## Rescue and aid

The vast majority of Polish Jews were a "visible minority" by modern standards, distinguishable by language, behavior, and appearance. In the 1931 Polish national census, only 12 percent of Jews declared Polish as their first language, while 79 percent listed Yiddish and the remaining 9 percent Hebrew as their mother tongue. In the labour market of many cities and towns, including Poland's provincial capitals, the presence of such large, mostly non acculturated minority, was a source of competitive tension.[365] Here is where the temptation to jump to conclusions with regard to Polish-Jewish relations in wartime should be resisted, wrote Gunnar Paulsson: "leaving aside acts of war and Nazi perfidy, a Jew's chances of survival in hiding were no worse in Warsaw, at any rate, than in the Netherlands" once the Holocaust began.

**Figure 42:** *Public hanging of ethnic Poles, Przemyśl, 1943, for helping Jews*

Toward the end of the ghetto-liquidation period, the largest number of Jews managed to escape to the "Aryan" side, and to survive with the aid of their Polish helpers. During the Nazi occupation, most ethnic Poles were themselves engaged in a desperate struggle to survive. They were in no position to impede the German extermination of Jews. Between 1939 and 1945, nearly 2.8 million gentile Poles died at the hands of the Nazis, and 150,000 due to Soviet repressions. About one fifth of the prewar population of Poland perished. Their deaths were the result of deliberate acts of war, mass murder, incarceration in concentration camps, forced labor, malnutrition, disease, kidnappings, and expulsions. There were, however, many Poles who risked death to hide entire Jewish families or otherwise help Jews on compassionate grounds. Polish rescuers of Jews were sometimes exposed by those very Jews if the Jews were found by the Germans, resulting in the murder of entire helper networks in the General Government. The number of Jews hiding with gentile Poles, quoted by Żarski-Zajdler, was about 450,000. Possibly a million gentile Poles aided their Jewish neighbors. Historian Richard C. Lukas gives an estimate as high as three million Polish helpers; an estimate similar to those cited by other authors.[366]

The Polish Government in Exile was the first (in November 1942), to reveal the existence of German-run concentration camps and the systematic extermination of the Jews. The genocide was reported to the Allies by Lieutenant Jan

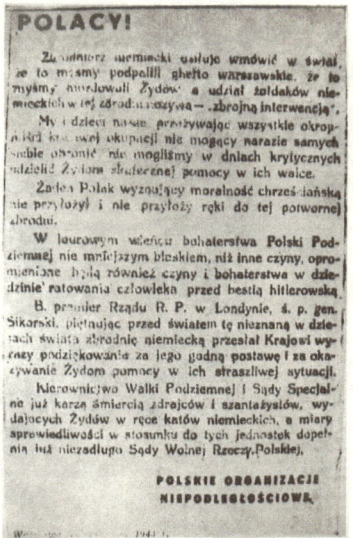

**Figure 43:** *September 1943 Żegota warning about death sentence for denunciations of Jews to the Nazis.*

Karski, as well as Captain Witold Pilecki who volunteered to be imprisoned at Auschwitz in order to gather intelligence and subsequently wrote an official Report of over 100 pages for the West.

In September 1942, with financial assistance from the Underground State, the Provisional Committee to Aid Jews was founded (*Tymczasowy Komitet Pomocy Żydom*) on the initiative of Zofia Kossak-Szczucka, for the purpose of rescuing Jews. It was superseded by the Council for Aid to Jews known by the code-name Żegota (*Rada Pomocy Żydom*) chaired by Julian Grobelny. It is not known how many Jews were helped by Żegota, but at one point in 1943 it had 2,500 Jewish children under its care in Warsaw alone under Irena Sendler. Żegota was granted nearly 29 million zlotys (over $5 million) from 1942 onwards for relief payments to thousands of extended Jewish families in Poland. The government in exile also provided special assistance – funds, arms and other supplies – to Jewish resistance organizations like ŻOB and ŻZW.

## Opportunism and collaboration

No Polish collaborative government was ever formed during World War II. As noted by Piotrowski, the "Poles never produced either a Quisling or any specifically Polish SS divisions. In contrast, almost all other European countries provided Nazi Germany with both." The Polish Underground State strongly opposed collaboration in anti-Jewish persecutions and threatened death to all informers against them, on behalf of the Polish military tribunals of the Home Army. However, the continued brutality of war led to the breakdown of traditional social norms and values. There were people who betrayed Jews in hiding along with the Poles who protected them. The number of notorious blackmailers is estimated at around several thousand, based on the number of death sentences for treason by Poland's Special Courts.[367] Gunnar S. Paulsson in his comment stated that he would probably tag 20,000 Poles with "monstrous deeds". The Holocaust testimonies confirm that, trapped in the ghettos, some Jews took advantage of inside information about the socio-economic standing of other Jews as well (see Group 13).

The phenomenon of Polish collaboration was described by John Connelly and Leszek Gondek as marginal, when seen against the backdrop of European and world history. The crossing of moral boundaries had first occurred under the Soviets with the participation of the Jewish militia (so-called *opaskowcy*) armed by the NKVD, in the mass deportations of Polish families from the east to Siberia in 1940 and 1941 after the Soviet takeover, and again, at the onset of the German-Soviet war, when over 300 Jews perished in Jedwabne on July 10, 1941, locked in a barn set on fire by a group of Polish men in the presence of German *Ordnungspolizei* (IPN Final Findings). The circumstances surrounding the incident in Jedwabne are still debated, and include the ominous presence of the *Einsatzgruppe Zichenau-Schroettersburg* under *SS-Obersturmführer* Hermann Schaper deployed in *Bezirk Bialystok*, as well as German Nazi pressure, but also widespread resentment over the Jewish warm welcome given to the Red Army in 1939.

According to politician Stefan Korboński, some members of the National Armed Forces (NSZ), participated in executions of Jews who belonged to the pro-Soviet underground. Historians Richard Lukas and Tadeusz Piotrowski wrote that NSZ units rendered assistance to the Jews and included them in their ranks along with Polish Righteous Among the Nations. The NSZ Holy Cross Brigade rescued 280 Jewish women among some 1,000 persons from the concentration camp in Holýšov. A Jewish partisan from NSZ, Feliks Parry, suggested that most of them "didn't have the slightest notion of the ideological underpinnings of their organization" and didn't care, focused only on resisting the Nazis. In postwar Poland, the communist secret police routinely tortured the NSZ insurgents in order to force them to confess to killing Jews among other alleged crimes. This was most notably the case with the 1946 trial of 23 officers of the NSZ in Lublin. The torture of political prisoners by the Ministry of Public Security did not stop when the interrogations were concluded. Physical torture was also ordered if they retracted in court their forced confessions of "killing Jews".

# Ethnic Poles as victims of the Holocaust

The Nazis' long-term plans for eastern Europe included the ethnic cleansing of Poland, which would have resulted by their estimates in the death of some 85% of the Poles. By war's end these plans were mostly unfulfilled.

According to Donald Niewyk and Francis Nicosia, whether to include the Poles and other Slavic groups depends on the question of whether the Holocaust should be defined based on the Nazis' motives, or the degree to which they managed to realize their racial agenda. Those who take the first position argue that the Nazi atrocities in Poland, the Ukraine, Byelorussia and the USSR were "a direct result of Nazi contempt for the 'subhuman'":[49]; those who take the second position note that these deaths "were far more selective than was the case with Jews, Gypsies, and the handicapped", and that it is difficult to distinguish between "racially motivated killings of Poles and Soviet citizens, [and] those that resulted directly or indirectly from German military actions.":[49] Niewyk and Niocosia take the second approach.:[52]

# National minorities' role in the Holocaust

| Part of a series of articles on the |
|---|
| ## History of Jews and Judaism in Poland |
| |
| **History of the Jews in Poland** |
| **20th century** |
| • The Holocaust in occupied Poland<br>• Jewish ghettos in German-occupied Poland<br>• Nazi camps<br>• Jewish resistance under Nazi rule<br>• Ghetto uprisings<br>• Rescue of Jews by Poles during the Holocaust |
| Polish Righteous Among the Nations |
| **1989–present** |
| **Timeline of Jewish-Polish history** |
| **List of Polish Jews** |
| • v<br>• t<br>• e[368] |

The Republic of Poland was a multicultural country before the Second World War broke out, with almost a third of its population originating from the minority groups: 13.9 percent Ukrainians; 10 percent Jews; 3.1 percent Belarusians; 2.3 percent Germans and 3.4 percent Czechs, Lithuanians and Russians. Soon after the 1918 reconstitution of an independent Polish state, about 500,000 refugees from the Soviet republics came to Poland in the first spontaneous flight from persecution especially in Ukraine (see, Pale of Settlement) where up to 2,000 pogroms took place during the Civil War. In the second wave of immigration, between November 1919 and June 1924 some 1,200,000 people left the territory of the USSR for new Poland. It is estimated that some 460,000 refugees spoke Polish as the first language. Between 1933 and 1938, around 25,000 German Jews fled Nazi Germany to sanctuary in Poland.

About one million Polish citizens were members of the German minority. Following the invasion of 1939, additional 1,180,000 German speakers came to occupied Poland either from the Reich or from the east with little to lose (the *Volksdeutsche*). Many hundreds of ethnically German men in Poland joined the Nazi *Volksdeutscher Selbstschutz* as well as *Sonderdienst* formations launched in May 1940 by *Gauleiter* Hans Frank stationed in occupied Kraków. Likewise, among some 30,000 Ukrainian nationalists who fled to *polnischen Gebiete*, thousands joined the *pokhidny hrupy* (pl) as saboteurs, interpreters, and civilian militiamen, trained at the German bases across *Distrikt Krakau*.[369]

The existence of *Sonderdienst* formations constituted a grave danger to the Catholic Poles who attempted to help ghettoised Jews in the cities which had a sizable German and pro-German minorities, as in the case of the Izbica Ghetto or the Łuck and the Mińsk Mazowiecki Ghettos among numerous others. Anti-Semitic attitudes were particularly visible in the eastern provinces which had been occupied by the Russians following the Soviet invasion of Kresy. Local people had witnessed the repressions against their own compatriots, and mass deportations to Siberia, conducted by the Soviet security apparatus with some of the local Jews forming militias, taking over key administrative positions, and collaborating with the NKVD. Others assumed that, driven by vengeance, Jewish Communists had been prominent in betraying the ethnically Polish and other non-Jewish victims.

## German-inspired massacres

Many German-inspired massacres were carried out across occupied eastern Poland with the active participation of indigenous people. The guidelines for such massacres were formulated by Reinhard Heydrich, who ordered his officers to induce anti-Jewish pogroms on territories newly occupied by the German forces. In the lead-up to the establishment of the Wilno Ghetto in the

**Figure 44:** *Jewish woman chased along Medova Street during 1941 Lviv pogroms*

fifth largest city of prewar Poland and a provincial capital Wilno (now Vilnius, Lithuania), German commandos and the Lithuanian Auxiliary Police Battalions killed more than 21,000 Jews during the Ponary massacre in late 1941. At that time, Wilno had only a small Lithuanian-speaking minority of about 6 percent of the city's population. In the infamous series of Lviv pogroms committed by the Ukrainian militants in the eastern city of Lwów (now Lviv, Ukraine), some 6,000 Polish Jews were murdered in the streets between June 30 and July 29, 1941, on top of 3,000 arrests and mass shootings by *Einsatzgruppe C*. The Ukrainian militias formed by OUN with the blessings of the SS spread terror across dozens of locations throughout south-eastern Poland.[370]

Long before the Tarnopol Ghetto was set up, and only two days after the arrival of the Wehrmacht, up to 2,000 Jews were killed in the provincial capital of Tarnopol (now Ternopil, Ukraine), one-third of them by the Ukrainian militias. Some of the victims were decapitated.[371] The SS shot the remaining two-thirds, in the same week. In Stanisławów – another provincial capital in the Kresy macroregion (now Ivano-Frankivsk, Ukraine) – the single largest massacre of Polish Jews prior to *Aktion Reinhardt* was perpetrated on 12 October 1941, hand in glove by Orpo, SiPo and the Ukrainian Auxiliary Police (brought in from Lwów); tables with sandwiches and bottles of vodka had been set up about the cemetery for shooters who needed to rest from the deafening noise of gunfire; 12,000 Jews were murdered before nightfall.

A total of 31 deadly pogroms were carried out throughout the region in conjunction with the Belarusian, Lithuanian and Ukrainian Schuma.[372] The genocidal techniques learned from the Germans, such as the advanced planning of the pacification actions, site selection, and sudden encirclement, became the hallmark of the OUN-UPA massacres of Poles and Jews in Volhynia and Eastern Galicia beginning in March 1943, parallel with the liquidation of the ghettos in *Reichskommissariat Ostland* ordered by Himmler. Thousands of Jews who escaped deportations and hid in the forests were murdered by the Banderites.

## Rate of survival

The question regarding the Jews' real chances of survival once the Holocaust began continues to draw the attention of historians. For one, the Germans made it extremely difficult to escape the ghettos just before deportations to death camps deceptively disguised as "resettlement in the East". All passes were cancelled, walls rebuilt containing fewer gates, with policemen replaced by SS-men. Some victims already deported to Treblinka were forced to write form letters back home, stating that they were safe. Around 3,000 others fell into the German Hotel Polski trap. Many ghettoized Jews did not believe what was going on until the very end, because the actual outcome seemed unthinkable at the time. David J. Landau suggested also that the weak Jewish leadership might have played a role. Likewise, Israel Gutman proposed that the Polish Underground might have attacked the camps and blown up the railway tracks leading to them, but as noted by Paulsson, such ideas are a product of hindsight.

The exact number of Holocaust survivors is unknown. Possibly as many as 300,000 Polish Jews escaped to the Soviet-occupied zone soon after the war started. Some estimates go even higher than that. Notably, a very high percentage of the Jews fleeing east were men and women without families. Thousands of them perished at the hands of OUN-UPA, TDA and Ypatingasis būrys during Massacres of Poles in Volhynia, the Holocaust in Lithuania (see Ponary massacre), and in Belarus. The majority of Polish Jews in the *Generalgouvernement* stayed put. Prior to the mass deportations, there was no proven necessity to leave familiar places. When the ghettos were closed from the outside, smuggling of food kept most of the inhabitants alive. Escape into clandestine existence on the "Aryan" side was attempted by some 100,000 Jews, and, contrary to popular misconceptions, the risk of them being turned in by the Poles was very small.

It is estimated that about 350,000 Polish Jews survived the Holocaust. Some 230,000 of them survived in the USSR and the Soviet-controlled territories

**Figure 45:** *The burning Słonim Ghetto during the Jewish revolt which erupted in the course of the final Ghetto extermination action. Before the joint German-Soviet invasion of Poland in 1939 Słonim was a county seat in the Nowogródek Voivodeship. The invading Soviets annexed the city to the Byelorussian SSR in an atmosphere of terror.*

of Poland, including men and women who escaped from areas occupied by Germany. Right after World War II, over 150,000 Polish Jews (Berendt) or 180,000 (Engel) were repatriated or expelled back to new Poland along with the younger men conscripted to the Red Army from Kresy in 1940–1941. Their families died in the Holocaust. Gunnar S. Paulsson estimated that 30,000 Polish Jews survived in the labor camps; but according to Engel as many as 70,000–80,000 of them were liberated from camps in Germany and Austria alone, except that declaring their own nationality was of no use to those who did not intend to return. Madajczyk estimated that as many as 110,000 Polish Jews were in the Displaced Person camps. According to Longerich, up to 50,000 Jews survived in the forests (not counting Galicia) and also among the soldiers who reentered Poland with the pro-Soviet Polish "Berling army" formed by Stalin. The number of Jews who successfully hid on the "Aryan" side of the ghettos could be as high as 100,000 wrote Peter Longerich, although many were killed by the German *Jagdkommandos*. Not all survivors registered with CKŻP after the war ended. Thousands of so-called Convent children hidden by the non-Jewish Poles and the Catholic Church remained in orphanages run by the Sisters of the Family of Mary in more than 20 locations, similar as in other Catholic convents. Given the severity of the German measures designed

**Figure 46:** *1946 meeting of Żegota members on the anniversary of the Warsaw Ghetto Uprising at the Polish Theatre*

to prevent this occurrence, the survival rate among the Jewish fugitives was relatively high and by far, the individuals who circumvented deportation were the most successful.

## Border changes and repatriations

The Western powers remained unaware of the top secret Nazi-Soviet Pact in 1939, which paved the way for World War II. The German surrender in May 1945 was followed by a massive change in the political geography of Europe. Poland's borders were redrawn by the Allies according to the demands made by Josef Stalin during the Tehran Conference, confirmed as not negotiable at the Yalta Conference of 1945. The Polish government-in-exile was excluded from the negotiations. The territory of Poland was reduced by approximately 20 percent. Before the end of 1946 some 1.8 million Polish citizens were expelled and forcibly resettled within the new borders. For the first time in its history Poland became a homogeneous one nation-state by force, with the national wealth reduced by 38 percent. Poland's financial system had been destroyed. Intelligentsia was largely obliterated along with the Jews, and the population reduced by about 33 percent.

Due to the territorial shift imposed from the outside, the number of Holocaust survivors from Poland remains the subject of deliberation. According to official statistics, the number of Jews in the country changed dramatically in a very short time. In January 1946, the Central Committee of Polish Jews (CKŻP) registered the first wave of some 86,000 survivors from the vicinity. By the end of that summer, the number had risen to about 205,000–210,000 (with 240,000 registrations and over 30,000 duplicates). The survivors included 180,000 Jews who arrived from the Soviet-controlled territories as a result repatriation agreements. Another 30,000 Jews returned to Poland from the USSR after the Stalinist repressions ended a decade later.

## *Aliyah Bet* from Europe

In July 1946, right after the rigged referendum held in Poland with the intention of solidifying the communist takeover of power, forty Jews and two ethnic Poles were killed in the Kielce pogrom. Eleven of the victims died from bayonet wounds and eleven more were fatally shot with military assault rifles (official IPN findings), indicating direct involvement of the regular troops.[373] The pogrom prompted General Spychalski of PWP from wartime Warsaw, to sign a legislative decree allowing the remaining survivors to leave Poland without Western visas or Polish exit permits. Poland was the only Eastern Bloc country to allow free Jewish *aliyah* to Mandate Palestine, with Stalin's vexed approval seeking to undermine British influence in the Middle East. Most refugees crossing the new borders left Poland without a valid passport. By contrast, the Soviet Union brought Soviet Jews from DP camps back to USSR by force, along with all other Soviet citizens irrespective of their wishes, as agreed to by the Yalta Conference.

Uninterrupted traffic across the Polish borders increased dramatically. By the spring of 1947 only 90,000 Jews remained in Poland.[374,375] Britain demanded that Poland (among others) halt the Jewish exodus, but their pressure was largely unsuccessful. The massacre in Kielce was condemned by a public announcement sent by the diocese in Kielce to all churches. The letter denounced the pogrom and "stressed – wrote Natalia Aleksiun – that the most important Catholic values were the love of fellow human beings and respect for human life. It also alluded to the demoralizing effect of anti-Jewish violence, since the crime was committed in the presence of youth and children." Priests read it without comments during Mass, hinting that "the pogrom might have in fact been a political provocation."

Approximately 7,000 Jewish men and women of military age left Poland for Mandatory Palestine between 1947 and 1948 as members of Haganah organization, trained in Poland. The boot camp was set up in Bolków, Lower Silesia, with Polish-Jewish instructors. It was financed by JDC in agreement with the

**Figure 47:** *Museum of the History of the Polish Jews, Warsaw, April 2013*

Polish administration. The program which trained mostly men 22–25 years of age for service in the Israel Defense Forces lasted until early 1949. Joining the training was a convenient way to leave the country, since the course graduates were not controlled at the border, and could carry undeclared valuables and even restricted firearms.

## Holocaust memorials and commemoration

There are a large number of memorials in Poland dedicated to Holocaust remembrance. The Monument to the Ghetto Heroes in Warsaw was unveiled in April 1948. Major museums include the Auschwitz-Birkenau State Museum on the outskirts of Oświęcim with 1.4 million visitors per year, and the POLIN Museum of the History of Polish Jews in Warsaw on the site of the former Ghetto, presenting the thousand-year history of the Jews in Poland.[376] Since 1988, an annual international event called March of the Living takes place in April at the former Auschwitz-Birkenau camp complex on Holocaust Remembrance Day, with total attendance exceeding 150,000 young people from all over the world.

There are State museums on the grounds of each of the Operation Reinhard death camps, including the Majdanek State Museum in Lublin, declared a national monument as early as 1946, with intact gas chambers and crematoria from World War II. Branches of the Majdanek Museum include the

Bełżec, and the Sobibór Museums where advanced geophysical studies are being conducted by Israeli and Polish archaeologists. The new Treblinka Museum opened in 2006. It was later expanded and made into a branch of the Siedlce Regional Museum located in a historic Ratusz (see also the Siedlce Ghetto). There is also a small museum in Chełmno nad Nerem.

The Radegast train station is a Holocaust memorial in Łódź. The Oskar Schindler's Enamel Factory covers the Holocaust in Kraków.

There is a Holocaust memorial at the former Umschlagplatz in Warsaw.

# References

- Arad, Yitzhak (1999) [1987]. *Belzec, Sobibor, Treblinka: The Operation Reinhard Death Camps*[377]. Bloomington and Indianapolis: Indiana University Press. ISBN 0-253-34293-7 – via Google Book phrase search.<templatestyles src="Module:Citation/CS1/styles.css"></templatestyles>
- Baumel, Judith Tydor; Laqueur, Walter (2001). *The Holocaust Encyclopedia*[378]. New Haven and London: Yale University Press. ISBN 0-300-13811-3 – via Google Books preview.<templatestyles src="Module:Citation/CS1/styles.css"></templatestyles>
- Bogner, Nahum (2012). "The Convent Children. The Rescue of Jewish Children in Polish Convents During the Holocaust"[379] (PDF). Shoah Resource Center: 41–44. Archived from the original on February 17, 2012 – via direct download, 45.2 KB.<templatestyles src="Module:Citation/CS1/styles.css"></templatestyles>
- Browning, Christopher (2004). *The Origins of the Final Solution : The Evolution of Nazi Jewish Policy, September 1939 – March 1942*[380]. Comprehensive History of the Holocaust. With contributions by Jürgen Matthäus. London: Random House / William Heinemann; University of Nebraska Press 2007 [2004]. ISBN 0-8032-0392-6 – via Google Books preview.<templatestyles src="Module:Citation/CS1/styles.css"></templatestyles>
- Cherry, Robert D.; Orla-Bukowska, Annamaria (2007). *Rethinking Poles and Jews: Troubled Past, Brighter Future*[381]. Rowman & Littlefield. ISBN 0-7425-4666-7.<templatestyles src="Module:Citation/CS1/styles.css"></templatestyles>
- Dobroszycki, Lucjan (1994). *Survivors of the Holocaust in Poland: A Portrait Based on Jewish Community Records, 1944–1947*[382]. Yivo Institute for Jewish Research, M.E. Sharpe. p. 164. ISBN 1-56324-463-2.<templatestyles src="Module:Citation/CS1/styles.css"></templatestyles>

- Engel, David (1993). *Facing a Holocaust: The Polish Government-in-exile and the Jews, 1943–1945*[383]. UNC Press Books. p. 317. ISBN 0-8078-2069-5 – via Google Book preview.
- Hakohen, Devorah (2003). *Immigration from Poland*[384]. *Immigrants in turmoil: mass immigration to Israel and its repercussions in the 1950s and After*. Syracuse University Press, 325 pages. ISBN 0-8156-2969-9.
- Kopówka, Edward; Rytel-Andrianik, Paweł (2011). *Treblinka II Death Camp. Monograph, chapt. 3*[385] [*Treblinka II – Obóz zagłady*] (PDF). *Dam im imię na wieki* [*I will give them an everlasting name. Isaiah 56:5*] (in Polish). Drohiczyńskie Towarzystwo Naukowe [The Drohiczyn Scientific Society]. ISBN 978-83-7257-496-1. With list of Catholic rescuers of Jews imprisoned at Treblinka I, selected testimonies, bibliography, alphabetical indexes, photographs, English language summaries, and forewords by Holocaust scholars – via PDF direct download 20.2 MB.
- Lukas, Richard C. (1989). *Out of the Inferno: Poles Remember the Holocaust*[386]. University Press of Kentucky. ISBN 978-0-8131-1692-1.
- Lukas, Richard C. (2001). *The forgotten Holocaust: the Poles under German occupation, 1939–1944*[387]. Hippocrene Books. ISBN 978-0-7818-0901-6.
- Materski, Wojciech; Szarota, Tomasz; IPN (2009). *Poland 1939–1945. Casualties and the victims of repressions under the Nazi and the Soviet occupations*[388] [*Polska 1939–1945. Straty osobowe i ofiary represji pod dwiema okupacjami*]. *(excerpts online)*. Institute of National Remembrance (IPN). Hardcover, 353 pages. ISBN 978-83-7629-067-6. With a Foreword by Janusz Kurtyka (IPN); and expert contributions by Waldemar Grabowski, Franciszek Piper, and Andrzej Krzysztof Kunert. Archived from the original[389] on March 31, 2012.
- Musiał, Bogdan (ed.), "Treblinka — ein Todeslager der Aktion Reinhard", in: *Aktion Reinhard — Die Vernichtung der Juden im Generalgouvernement*, Osnabrück 2004, pp. 257–281.
- Phayer, Michael (2000). *The Catholic Church and the Holocaust, 1930–1965*[390]. Indiana University Press. pp. 113, 117–120, 250. ISBN 0253214718.

src="Module:Citation/CS1/styles.css"></templatestyles>
- Piotrowski, Tadeusz (1998). *Poland's Holocaust: Ethnic Strife, Collaboration with Occupying Forces and Genocide in the Second Republic, 1918–1947*[391]. Jefferson, NC: McFarland & Company. ISBN 0-7864-0371-3. OCLC 37195289[392].<templatestyles src="Module:Citation/CS1/styles.css"></templatestyles>
- Paulsson, Gunnar S. (March 29, 2003), 'Polish Complicity In The Shoah Is A Myth'[393] (online, *Special Reports*: Commentary).
- Paulsson, Gunnar S. (May 5, 2008), On the Marginal Role of Poles In Abetting the Nazi Perpetrators[394] Isurvived.org
- Paulsson, Gunnar S. *Secret City: The Hidden Jews of Warsaw, 1940–1945*. New Haven: Yale University Press, 2002, <templatestyles src="Module:Citation/CS1/styles.css" />ISBN 978-0-300-09546-3, Review.[395]
- Samson, Naomi (2000), Hide: A Child's View of the Holocaust.[396] U of Nebraska Press, 194 pages.
- Sterling, Eric; Roth, John K. (2005), Life in the Ghettos During the Holocaust.[397] Syracuse University Press, 356 pages.
- Schelvis, Jules (2014) [2007]. *Sobibor: A History of a Nazi Death Camp*[398]. Bloomsbury Publishing. p. 110. ISBN 1-4725-8906-8.<templatestyles src="Module:Citation/CS1/styles.css"></templatestyles>

# Jewish ghettos in German-occupied Poland

| Part of a series on |
|:-:|
| **The Holocaust** |
| Jews on selection ramp at Auschwitz, May 1944 |
| |
| |
| |
| |
| |

**Jewish ghettos in German-occupied Poland** were established during World War II in hundreds of locations across occupied Poland.[400,401] Most Jewish ghettos had been created by Nazi Germany between October 1939 and July 1942 in order to confine and segregate Poland's Jewish population of about 3.5 million for the purpose of persecution, terror, and exploitation. In smaller towns, ghettos often served as staging points for Jewish slave-labor and mass deportation actions, while in the urban centers they resembled walled-off prison-islands described by some historians as little more than instruments of "slow, passive murder," with dead bodies littering the streets.[402]

In most cases, the larger ghettos did not correspond to traditional Jewish neighborhoods, and non-Jewish Poles and members of other ethnic groups were ordered to take up residence elsewhere. Smaller Jewish communities with populations under 500 were terminated through expulsion soon after the invasion.[403,404]

# The Holocaust

The liquidation of the Jewish ghettos across occupied Poland was closely connected with the construction of secretive death camps—industrial-scale mass-extermination facilities—built in early 1942 for the sole purpose of murder.[405] The Nazi extermination program depended on rail transport, which enabled the SS to run and, at the same time, openly lie to their victims about the "resettlement" program. Jews were transported to their deaths in Holocaust trains from liquidated ghettos of all occupied cities, including Łódź, the last ghetto in Poland to be emptied in August 1944.[406,407,408] In some larger ghettos there were armed resistance attempts, such as the Warsaw Ghetto Uprising, the Białystok Ghetto Uprising, the Będzin and the Łachwa Ghetto uprisings, but in every case they failed against the overwhelming German military force, and the resisting Jews were either executed locally or deported with the rest of prisoners to the extermination camps.[409,410,411,412] By the time Nazi-occupied Eastern Europe was liberated by the Red Army, not a single Jewish ghetto in Poland was left standing.[413] Only about 50,000–120,000 Polish Jews survived

**Figure 48:** *A child lies on the street in the Warsaw Ghetto, May 1941. Photo by Nazi officer P.K. Zermin, now in German Federal Archive*

the war on native soil with the assistance of their Polish neighbors, a fraction of their prewar population of 3,500,000.[414,415]

In total, according to USHMM archives, "The Germans established at least 1000 ghettos in German-occupied and annexed Poland and the Soviet Union alone."[416] The list of locations of the Jewish ghettos within the borders of pre-war and post-war Poland is compiled with the understanding that their inhabitants were either of Polish nationality from before the invasion, or had strong historical ties with Poland. Also, not all ghettos are listed here due to their transient nature. Permanent ghettos were created only in settlements with rail connections, because the food aid (paid by the Jews themselves) was completely dependent on the Germans, making even the potato-peels a hot commodity.[417] Throughout 1940 and 1941, most ghettos were sealed off from the outside, walled off or enclosed with barbed wire, and any Jews found outside them could be shot on sight. The Warsaw Ghetto was the largest ghetto in all of Nazi occupied Europe, with over 400,000 Jews crammed into an area of 1.3 square miles (3.4 km$^2$), or 7.2 persons per room.[418] The Łódź Ghetto was the second largest, holding about 160,000 inmates.[419] In documents and signage, the Nazis usually referred to the ghettos they created as *Jüdischer Wohnbezirk* or *Wohngebiet der Juden*, meaning "Jewish Quarter". By the end of 1941, most Polish Jews were already ghettoized, even though the Germans knew that the system was unsustainable; most inmates had no chance of earning their own keep, and no savings left to pay the SS for further deliveries.

**Figure 49:** *Partial liquidation of the Białystok Ghetto, 15–20 August 1943. Jewish men with their hands up, surrounded by military unit*

The quagmire was resolved at the Wannsee conference of 20 January 1942 near Berlin, where the "Final Solution" (die Endlösung der Judenfrage) was set in place.[420]

## List of Jewish ghettos in occupied Poland

The settlements listed in the Polish language,[421] including major cities, had all been renamed after the 1939 joint invasion of Poland by Germany and the Soviet Union. Renaming everything in their own image had been one way in which the invaders sought to redraw Europe's political map. All Polish territories were confiscated as either Nazi zones of occupation (i.e. Bezirk Bialystok, Provinz Ostpreußen, Reichskommissariat Ostland, etc.), or Soviet brand-new extensions to the two fledging western republics (i.e. West Belarus), soon overrun again in Operation Barbarossa. The Soviet Ukraine and Byelorussia witnessed the genocide of Poles just prior to invasion, resulting in the virtual absence of ethnic Poles in the USSR along the pre-war border with Poland since the Great Terror.

| # | Ghetto location in prewar and postwar Poland[422] | Population | Date of creation | Date of liquidation | Final destination |
|---|---|---|---|---|---|
| | (in alphabetical order) | | (year, month) | (year, month) | |

**1939–1940**

Only 38 days after the **1939** Nazi German Invasion of Poland, the first large ghetto of World War II was set up at Piotrków Trybunalski on October 8, 1939. Within months, the most populous Jewish ghettos in World War II included the Łódź Ghetto, and the Warsaw Ghetto.

| # | Ghetto | Population | Date of creation | Date of liquidation | Final destination |
|---|---|---|---|---|---|
| 1 | Aleksandrów Łódzki | 3,500 | 1939 | Dec 1939 | to Głowno ghetto |
| 2 | Bełżyce | 4,500 | Jun 1940 | May 1943 | to Budzyń ghetto → Sobibor and Majdanek |
| 3 | Będzin Ghetto | 7,000–28,000[423] | Jul 1940 | Aug 1943 | to Auschwitz (7,000).[424] |
| 4 | Błonie | 2,100 | Dec 1940 | Feb 1941 | to Warsaw Ghetto (all 2,100) |
| 5 | Bodzentyn | 700 | 1940 | Sep 1942 | to Suchedniów ghetto → Treblinka.[425] |
| 6 | Brześć Kujawski | 630 | 1940 | Apr 1942 | to Łódź Ghetto → Chełmno death camp |
| 7 | Brzeziny | 6,000–6,800 | Feb 1940 | May 1942 | to Łódź Ghetto → Chełmno |
| 8 | Brzozów | 1,000 | 1940 | Aug 1942 | to Bełżec extermination camp |
| 9 | Bychawa | 2,700 | 1940 | Apr 1941 | to Belzyce |
| 10 | Chęciny | 4,000 | 1940 – Jun 1941 | Sep 1942 | to Treblinka |
| 11 | Ciechanów | 5,000 | 1940 | Nov 1942 | to labour camps (1,500), Mława Ghetto → Auschwitz, many killed locally. |
| 12 | Dąbrowa Górnicza | 4,000–10,000 | 1940 | Jun 1943 | to Auschwitz |
| 13 | Dęblin | 3,300–5,800 | Apr 1940 | Oct 1942 | to Sobibor and Treblinka |
| 14 | Działoszyce | 15,000? | Apr 1940 | Oct 1942 | to Płaszów and Bełżec extermination camp |
| 15 | Gąbin | 2,000–2,300 | 1940 | Apr 1942 | to Chełmno extermination camp |
| 16 | Głowno | 5,600 | May 1940 | Mar 1941 | to Łowicz ghetto and Warsaw Ghetto (5,600) |
| 17 | Gorlice (labor camp 1st) | ? | 1940 | 1942 | to Buchenwald, Muszyna, Mielec, see Gorlice Ghetto (1941) |

| | | | | | |
|---|---|---|---|---|---|
| 18 | Góra Kalwaria | 3,300 | Jan 1940 | Feb 1941 | to Warsaw Ghetto (3,000), 300 killed locally |
| 19 | Grodzisk Mazowiecki | 6,000 | 1940 – Jan 1941 | Oct 1942 | to Warsaw Ghetto (all 6,000) |
| 20 | Grójec | 5,200–6,000 | Jul 1940 | Sep 1942 | to Warsaw Ghetto (all 6,000) → Treblinka |
| 21 | Izbica Kujawska | 1,000 | 1940 | Jan 1942 | to Chełmno extermination camp |
| 22 | Jeżów | 1,600 | 1940 | Feb 1941 | to Warsaw Ghetto (all 1,600) |
| 23 | Jędrzejów | 6,000 | Mar 1940 | Sep 1942 | to Treblinka |
| 24 | Kazimierz Dolny | 2,000–3,500 | 1940 – Apr 1941 | Mar 1942 | to Sobibor, and Treblinka |
| 25 | Kobyłka | 1,500 | Sep 1940 | Oct 1942 | to Treblinka |
| 26 | Koło | 2,000–5,000 | Dec 1940 | Dec 1941 | to Treblinka (2,000) and Chełmno |
| 27 | Koniecpol | 1,100–1,600 | 1940 | Oct 1942 | to Treblinka |
| 28 | Konin | 1,500? | Dec 1939 | 1940 – Mar 1941 | to Zagórów & other ghettos → killed locally |
| 29 | Kozienice | 13,000 | Jan 1940 | Sep 1942 | to Treblinka |
| 30 | Koźminek | 2,500 | 1940 | Jul 1942 | to Chełmno |
| 31 | Krasnystaw | 2,000 | Aug 1940 | Oct 1942 | to Bełżec extermination camp |
| 32 | Krośniewice | 1,500 | May 1940 | Mar 1942 | to Chełmno extermination camp |
| 33 | Kutno | 7,000 | Jun 1940 | Mar 1942 | to Chełmno |
| 34 | Legionowo | 3,000 | 1940 | 1942 | to Treblinka |
| 35 | Łańcut | 2,700 | Dec 1939 | Aug 1942 | to Bełżec extermination camp |
| 36 | Łask | 4,000 | Dec 1940 | Aug 1942 | to Chełmno extermination camp |
| 37 | Łowicz | 8,000–8,200 | 1940 | Mar 1941 | to Warsaw Ghetto (all; with labor camp)[426] |
| 38 | Łódź Ghetto | 200,000 | 8 Feb 1940 | Aug 1944 | to Auschwitz and Chełmno extermination camp, labour camps (1,000) |
| 39 | Marki | ? | 1940 – Mar 1941 | 1942 | to Warsaw Ghetto |
| 40 | Mielec | 4,000–4,500 | 1940 | Mar 1942 | to Bełżec extermination camp |

| | | | | | |
|---|---|---|---|---|---|
| 41 | Mińsk Mazowiecki Ghetto | 5,000–7,000 | Oct 1940 | Aug 1942 | to Treblinka, 1,300 killed locally |
| 42 | Mława | 6,000–6,500 | Dec 1940 | Nov 1942 | to Treblinka and Auschwitz |
| 43 | Mogielnica | 1,500 | 1940 | 28 Feb 1942 | to Warsaw Ghetto (all) → Treblinka.[427] |
| 44 | Mordy | 4,500 | Nov 1940 | Aug 1942 | to Treblinka |
| 45 | Myślenice | 1,200 | 1940 | Aug 1942 | to Skawina Ghetto (all) → Bełżec |
| 46 | Nowy Dwór Mazowiecki | 2,000–4,000 | 1940 – Jan 1941 | Dec 1942 | to Pomiechówek ghetto → Auschwitz |
| 47 | Nowy Korczyn | 4,000 | 1940 | Oct 1942 | to Treblinka |
| 48 | Opoczno | 3,000–4,000 | Nov 1940 | Oct 1942 | to Treblinka |
| 49 | Otwock | 12,000–15,000 | Dec 1939 | Aug 1942 | to Treblinka, and Auschwitz |
| 50 | Pabianice | 8,500–9,000 | Feb 1940 | May 1942 | to Łódź Ghetto → Chełmno death camp |
| 51 | Piaseczno | 2,500 | 1940 | Jan 1941 | to Warsaw Ghetto (all 2,500) |
| 52 | Piaski (transit) | 10,000 | 1940 | Nov 1943 | to Bełżec extermination camp, Sobibor, Trawniki concentration camp |
| 53 | Piotrków Trybunalski Ghetto | 25,000[428] | 8 Oct 1939 | 14 / 21 Oct 1944 | to Majdanek and Treblinka (22,000), killed locally also |
| 54 | Płock | 7,000–10,000 | 1939–1940 | Feb 1941 | to Działdowo ghetto |
| 55 | Płońsk | 12,000 | Sep 1940 | Nov 1942 | to Treblinka, Auschwitz |
| 56 | Poddębice | 1,500 | Nov 1940 | Apr 1942 | to Treblinka(?) |
| 57 | Pruszków | 1,400 | 1940 | 1941 | to Warsaw Ghetto (all 1,400) |
| 58 | Przedbórz | 4,000–5,000 | Mar 1940 | Oct 1942 | to Bełżec extermination camp and Treblinka |
| 59 | Puławy | 5,000 | Nov – Dec 1939 | 1940 | to Opole Lubelskie → Sobibor |
| 60 | Radomsko | 18,000–20,000 | 1939 – Jan 1940 | 21 Jul 1943 | to Treblinka extermination camp (18,000) |
| 61 | Radzymin | 2,500 | Sep 1940 | Oct 1942 | to Treblinka |
| 62 | Serock | 2,000 | Feb 1940 | Dec 1940 | to other ghettos |
| 63 | Sieradz | 2,500–5,000 | Mar 1940 | Aug 1942 | to Chełmno extermination camp |

| | | | | | |
|---|---|---|---|---|---|
| 64 | Sierpc | 500–3,000 | 1940 | Feb 1942 | *to* Warsaw Ghetto → Treblinka |
| 65 | Skaryszew | 1,800 | 1940 | Apr 1942 | *to* Szydlowiec |
| 66 | Skierniewice | 4,300–7,000 | Dec 1940 | Apr 1941 | *to* Warsaw Ghetto (all 7,000) |
| 67 | Sochaczew | 3,000–4,000 | Jan 1940 | Feb 1941 | *to* Warsaw Ghetto (all 3,000) |
| 68 | Stalowa Wola | 2,500 | 1940 | Jul 1942 | *to* Bełżec extermination camp |
| 69 | Stryj | 12,000 | 1940–1941 | Jun 1943 | *to* Bełżec extermination camp |
| 70 | Szadek | 500 | 1940 | 1940 | *to* other ghettos |
| 71 | Szczebrzeszyn | 4,000 | 1940 – Apr 1941 | Oct 1942 | *to* Bełżec death camp, killed locally also |
| 72 | Tomaszów Mazowiecki | 16,000–20,000 | Dec 1940 | Nov 1942 | *to* Treblinka (16,000), with 4,000 killed locally |
| 73 | Tuliszków | 230 | Dec 1939 | Jan 1940 | *to* Kowale Pańskie → Chełmno |
| 74 | Turek | 5,000 | 1940 | Oct 1941 | *to* Kowale Pańskie ghetto (all 5,000) |
| 75 | Tyszowce | 1,500–2,000 | 1940 | Sep 1942 | *to* Bełżec extermination camp |
| 76 | Uchanie | 2,000 | 1940 | Nov 1942 | *to* Sobibor |
| 77 | Ulanów | 500 | 1940 | Oct 1942 | *to* other ghettos |
| 78 | Uniejów | 500 | 1940 | Oct 1941 | *to* Kowale Pańskie ghetto (all 500) |
| 79 | Warka | 2,800 | 1940 | Feb 1941 | *to* Warsaw Ghetto (all 2,800) |
| 80 | Warta | 1,000–2,400 | Feb 1940 | Aug 1942 | *to* Chełmno extermination camp |
| 81 | Warsaw Ghetto, see Muranów neighbourhood of Warsaw *(whole)*[429] | 445,000 | Oct – 15 Nov 1940 | Sep 1942 | *to* Treblinka extermination camp (300,000), and Majdanek, Trawniki, Poniatowa |
| 82 | Włocławek | 4,000–13,500 | Oct 1940 | Apr 1942 | *to* Chełmno extermination camp |
| 83 | Włodawa | 10,500 [430] | (sealed) 1941 | Apr – May 1943 | *to* Sobibor, also shot locally |
| 84 | Włoszczowa | 4,000–6,000 | Jul 1940 | Sep 1942 | *to* Treblinka |
| 85 | Wodzisław | 4,000 | Jun 1940 | Nov 1942 | *to* Treblinka |
| 86 | Wołomin | 3,000–5,500 | 1940–1942 | Apr 1943 | *to* Treblinka |
| 87 | Wyszogród | 2,700–3,000 | Dec 1940 | Nov 1942 | *to* Treblinka |

| # | Name | Population | Ghetto established | Liquidated | Fate |
|---|---|---|---|---|---|
| 88 | Zagórów | 2,000–2,500 | Jul 1940 | Oct 1941 | all killed locally |
| 89 | Zamość | 12,000–14,000 | 1940 | May 1943 | to Izbica Ghetto → Bełżec, Majdanek |
| 90 | Zduńska Wola | 8,300–10,000 | 1940 | Aug 1942 | to Chełmno extermination camp |
| 91 | Żychlin | 2,800–4,000 | Jul 1940 | Mar 1942 | to Chełmno extermination camp |
| 92 | Żyrardów | 3,000–5,000 | Dec 1940 | Feb 1941 | to Warsaw Ghetto (all 5,000) |

**1941**
Under the codename Operation Barbarossa Germany entered the Soviet occupation zone of Poland on 22 June 1941. The creation of new Jewish ghettos behind Nazi-Soviet demarcation line and mass executions on-site by mobile killing squads intensified.

| # | Name | Population | Ghetto established | Liquidated | Fate |
|---|---|---|---|---|---|
| 93 | Augustów | 4,000 | Oct 1941 | Jun 1942 | to Treblinka and Auschwitz, shot locally |
| 94 | Bełchatów | 5,500–6,000 | Mar 1941 | Aug 1942 | to Chełmno extermination camp |
| 95 | Biała Podlaska | 7,000–8,400 | Jul 1941 | Sep 1942 | to Majdanek, Sobibor, Treblinka |
| 96 | Biała Rawska | 4,000 | Sep 1941 | Oct 1942 | to Treblinka |
| 97 | Białystok Ghetto | 40,000–50,000 | 26 Jul 1941 | Nov 1943 | to Majdanek, Treblinka |
| 98 | Biłgoraj | 2,500–3,000 | 1941–1942 | Nov 1942 | to Bełżec extermination camp |
| 99 | Bobowa | 658? | Oct 1941 | Aug 1942 | to Gorlice and Biecz ghettos |
| 100 | Bochnia | 14,000–15,000 | Mar 1941 | Sep 1943 | to Szebnie → Bełżec and Auschwitz |
| 101 | Brześć Litewski Ghetto | 18,000 | 16 Dec 1941 | Oct 1942 | 5,000 shot locally before the ghetto was set up → Bronna Góra ravine |
| 102 | Busko Zdrój | 2,000 | 1941 | Oct 1942 | to Treblinka |
| 103 | Chełm | 8,000–12,000 | Jun 1941 | Nov 1942 | to Sobibor |
| 104 | Chmielnik | 10,000–14,000 | Apr 1941 | Nov 1942 | to Treblinka |
| 105 | Chodel | 1,400 | Jun 1941 | 1942 | to other ghettos |
| 106 | Chrzanów | 8,000 | Nov 1941 | Feb 1943 | to Auschwitz |
| 107 | Ciechanowiec | 4,000 | 1941 | Nov 1941 | to Treblinka |
| 108 | Ciepielów | 600 | Dec 1941 | 15 / 29 Oct 1942[431] | to Treblinka → Polish rescuers killed locally 6 Dec 1942.[432] |
| 109 | Czeladź | 800 | | Nov 1941 | Feb 1943 | to Auschwitz |

| | | | | | |
|---|---|---|---|---|---|
| 110 | Częstochowa Ghetto | 48,000 | 9 Apr 1941 | 22 Sep – 9 Oct 1942 | to Treblinka extermination camp |
| 111 | Ćmielów | 1,500–2,000?[433] | 1941 | Oct (end) 1942 | to Treblinka (900), rest murdered locally |
| 112 | Dąbie | 900 | 1941 | Dec 1941 | to Chełmno extermination camp |
| 113 | Dobre | 500–1,000 | 1941 | Sep 1942 | to Treblinka |
| 114 | Drohiczyn | 700 | Jun 1941 | Nov 1942 | to Bransk and Bielsk ghettos |
| 115 | Drzewica | 2,000 | 1941 | Oct 1942 | to Treblinka |
| 116 | Dubienka | 2,500–3,000 | Jun 1941 | Oct 1942 | to other ghettos |
| 117 | Głogów Małopolski | (120)? | 1941 | 1942 | to Rzeszów ghetto → 5,000 shot locally |
| 118 | Gniewoszów (open type) | 6,580 | Dec 1941 | Nov 1942 | to Zwoleń (5,000); 1,000 → Treblinka |
| 119 | Goniądz | 1,000–1,300 | Jun 1941 | Nov 1942 | to Bogusze ghetto |
| 120 | Gorlice | 4,500 | Oct 1941 | Aug 1942 | to Bełżec extermination camp |
| 121 | Gostynin | 3,500 | 1941 | Aug 1942 | to Chełmno extermination camp |
| 122 | Grajewo | 3,000 | Jun 1941 | Nov 1942 | to Bogusze ghetto |
| 123 | Hrubieszów (open type) | 6,800–10,000 | Jun 1941 – May 1942 | May – Nov 1943 | to Sobibor and Budzyn labour camp, many shot locally, 2,000 fled. |
| 124 | Iłża | 1,900–2,000 | 1941 | Oct 1942 | to Treblinka |
| 125 | Inowłódz | 500–600 | 1941 | Aug 1942 | to Tomaszow Mazowiecki ghetto |
| 126 | Iwacewicze | 600 | 1941 | 14 Mar 1942 | to Słonim Ghetto, all killed locally |
| 127 | Izbica Ghetto (transit) | 12,000–22,700[434] | 1941 | 2 Nov 1942 | to Bełżec extermination camp and Sobibor, 4,500 killed locally |
| 128 | Jasło | 2,000–3,000 | 1941 | Aug 1942 | to other ghettos |
| 129 | Jedwabne | 100–130 | Jul 1941 | Nov 1941 | to Łomża Ghetto → Treblinka, 340 killed locally.[435] |
| 130 | Kalisz | 400 | 1941 | 1942 | to other ghettos |
| 131 | Kałusz | 6,000 | Jun 1941 | Nov 1942 | to Bełżec extermination camp, several hundreds executed locally |
| 132 | Karczew | 700 | Mar 1941 | Oct 1941 | to Warsaw Ghetto |

| | | | | | |
|---|---|---|---|---|---|
| 133 | Kielce Ghetto | 27,000 | Mar 1941 | Aug 1942 | to Treblinka, with 6,000 killed locally |
| 134 | Kłobuck | 2,000 | 1941 | Jun 1942 | to Auschwitz |
| 135 | Knyszyn | 2,000 | Jun 1941 | Nov 1942 | to Bialystok Ghetto |
| 136 | Kobryn | 8,000 | Jun 1941 | Oct 1942 | all killed locally |
| 137 | Kock | 2,500–3,000 | Jun 1941 | Dec 1942 | to Treblinka |
| 138 | Kodeń | ? | Jun 1941 | Sep 1942 | to Miedzyrzec Podlaski Ghetto |
| 139 | Kolbuszowa | 2,500 | 1941 | Sep 1942 | to Bełżec extermination camp |
| 140 | Koluszki | 2,000 | 1941 | Oct 1942 | to Treblinka |
| 141 | Końskie | 10,000 | 1941 | Jan 1943 | to Treblinka |
| 142 | Korczyn | 2,000 | 1941 | Aug 1942 | to Bełżec extermination camp |
| 143 | Kraków Ghetto | 20,000 (pop. 68,500) | Mar 1941 | Mar 1943 | to Bełżec extermination camp and Płaszów; 48,000 expelled in 1940.[436] |
| 144 | Kraśnik | 5,000–6,000 | 1940–1941 | Nov 1942 | to Bełżec extermination camp |
| 145 | Krynki | 5,000–6,000 | Jun – Nov 1941 | Nov 1942 | to Kiełbasin transit camp → Treblinka[437] |
| 146 | Książ Wielki | 200?[438] | 1941 | Nov 1942 | to Miechow ghetto |
| 147 | Kunów | 500 | 1941 | Oct 1942 | to Treblinka |
| 148 | Limanowa | 2,000 | 1941 | Aug 1942 | to Bełżec extermination camp |
| 149 | Lipsk | 3,000 | Dec 1941 | Oct 1942 | to Treblinka |
| 150 | Lubartów Ghetto | 3,269–4,500 | Jun 1941 | Oct 1942 | to Bełżec extermination camp |
| 151 | Lublin Ghetto | 30,000–40,000 | 24 Mar 1941 | Nov 1942 | to Bełżec extermination camp (30,000)[439] and Majdanek (4,000) |
| 152 | Lwów Ghetto | 115,000–160,000 | Jun – Nov 1941 | Jun 1943 | to Bełżec extermination camp and Janowska concentration camp |
| 153 | Łapy | 600 | Jun – Jul 1941 | Nov 1942 | to Białystok Ghetto |
| 154 | Łaskarzew | 1,300 | 1941 | Sep 1942 | to Treblinka |
| 155 | Łęczyca | 3,000–4,300 | 1941 | Jun 1942 | to Chełmno, many killed locally |
| 156 | Łomża Ghetto | 9,000–11,000 | Jun 1941 | Nov 1942 | to Auschwitz, many killed locally |

| | | | | | |
|---|---|---|---|---|---|
| 157 | Łosice | 5,500–6,000 | 1941 | Aug 1942 | to Treblinka |
| 158 | Łuków | 10,000 | 1941 | Oct – Nov 1942 | to Treblinka (Oct: 7,000; Nov: 3,000)[440] |
| 159 | Łuck Ghetto | 25,000 | Dec 1941 | 19 / 24 Aug 1942 | all killed locally (most at Polanka)[441] |
| 160 | Maków Mazowiecki | 3,500–5,000 | 1941 | Dec 1942 | to Treblinka |
| 161 | Michałowo | 1,500 | 1941 | Nov 1942 | to Bialystok Ghetto |
| 162 | Miechów | 4,000 | 1941 | 1942 | to Bełżec (1,000 killed locally) |
| 163 | Nowe Miasto | 3,700 | 1941 | 22 Oct 1942 | to Treblinka (3,000), rest killed locally |
| 164 | Nowogródek | 6,000? | Jun 1941 | Oct 1942 | all killed locally |
| 165 | Nowy Sącz Ghetto | 20,000 | Aug 1941 | Aug 1942 | to Bełżec extermination camp |
| 166 | Nowy Targ | 2,500 | 1941 | Aug 1942 | to Bełżec extermination camp |
| 167 | Nowy Żmigród | 1,300 | 1941 | Jul 1942 | all killed locally |
| 168 | Olkusz | 3,000–4,000 | 1941 | Jun 1942 | to Auschwitz |
| 169 | Opatów Ghetto | 10,000 | 1941 | Oct 1942 | to Treblinka |
| 170 | Opole Lubelskie | 8,000–10,000 | 1941 | Oct 1942 | to Sobibor and Poniatowa ghetto |
| 171 | Osiek | 500 | 1941 | Jun 1942 | to Ożarów ghetto → Treblinka |
| 172 | Ostrowiec Świętokrzyski | 16,000 | Apr 1941 | 10 Jan 1943 | to Treblinka |
| 173 | Ozorków | 3,000–5,000 | 1941 | Aug 1942 | to Łódź Ghetto → Chełmno |
| 174 | Pajęczno | 3,000 | 1941 | 1942 | to Łódź Ghetto |
| 175 | Parczew | 7,000 | 1941 | Oct 1942 | to Treblinka |
| 176 | Piątek | ? | 1941 | Jul 1942 | to Chełmno extermination camp |
| 177 | Pilzno | 788? | 1941 | Jun 1942 | to Bełżec extermination camp |
| 178 | Pińczów | 3,000–3,500 | 1941 | Oct 1942 | to Treblinka |
| 179 | Pionki (labor camp) | 682 | 1941 | Aug 1942 | to Zwoleń ghetto → Treblinka |
| 180 | Połaniec | 2,000 | 1941 | 1942 | to Chełmno extermination camp |
| 181 | Praszka | ? | 1941 | Aug 1942 | to Chełmno extermination camp |
| 182 | Rabka | 300 | 1941 | Aug 1942 | to Bełżec extermination camp |

| | | | | | |
|---|---|---|---|---|---|
| 183 | Radom Ghetto | 30,000–32,000 | Mar 1941 | Aug 1942 | to Treblinka extermination camp |
| 184 | Radomyśl Wielki | 1,300? | 1941 | 1942 | to Bełżec extermination camp |
| 185 | Radoszyce | 3,200?[442] | 1941 | Nov 1942 | to Treblinka |
| 186 | Radzyn Podlaski | 2,000–3,000 | 1941 | Dec 1942 | to Treblinka |
| 187 | Rajgród | 1,200 | 1941 | Nov 1942 | to Bogusze |
| 188 | Rawa Mazowiecka | 4,000 | 1941 | Oct 1942 | to Treblinka |
| 189 | Rejowiec | 3,000 | 1941 | 1943 | to Auschwitz, Sobibor and Majdanek |
| 190 | Ropczyce | 800 | 1941 | Jul 1942 | to Bełżec extermination camp |
| 191 | Ryki | 1,800–3,500 | 1941 | Oct 1942 | to Treblinka and Sobibor |
| 192 | Rymanów | 1,600? | 1941 | Aug 1942 | to Kraków Ghetto, Bełżec extermination camp, killed locally |
| 193 | Sędziszów Małopolski | 2,000 | 1941 | Jan 1942 | to Bełżec |
| 194 | Siedlce Ghetto | 12,000–18,000 | Jun – Aug 1941 | Nov 1942 | to Treblinka |
| 195 | Siemiatycze | 7,000 | 1941 | Nov 1942 | to Sobibor |
| 196 | Sieniawa | 3,000 | 1941 | 1942 | all killed locally |
| 197 | Siennica | 700? | 1941 | 15 Sep 1942 | to Treblinka (700) |
| 198 | Skarżysko-Kamienna | 3,000 | 1941 | 1942 | to Treblinka (2,500), the rest killed locally |
| 199 | Skrzynno | ? | 1941 | Oct 1942 | to Opoczno ghetto |
| 200 | Słonim Ghetto | 22,000 | Jul 1941 | 15 Jul 1942[443] | all killed locally (Jul-41: 1,200; Nov: 9,000; Jul-42: 10,000) |
| 201 | Słuck | 3,000–8,500 | Jun 1941 | Nov 1942 | all killed locally |
| 202 | Sokołów Małopolski | 3,000 | 1941 | Jul 1942 | to Bełżec |
| 203 | Sokołów Podlaski | 4,000–7,000 | Jun 1941 | Sep 1942 | to Treblinka |
| 204 | Sokółka | 8,000–9,000 | Jun 1941 | Nov 1942 | to Kiełbasin → Treblinka |
| 205 | Solec | 800 | 1941 | Dec 1942 | to Tarlow ghetto |
| 206 | Stanisławów Ghetto | 20,000 | Dec 1941 | Feb 1943 | killed locally → to Bełżec |
| 207 | Starachowice | 6,000 | Apr 1941 | Oct 1942 | to Treblinka |
| 208 | Stary Sącz | 1,000 | 1941 | Aug 1942 | to Bełżec |
| 209 | Staszów | 7,000 | 1941 | Dec 1942 | to Treblinka |

| | | | | | |
|---|---|---|---|---|---|
| 210 | Stopnica | 5,000 | 1941 | Nov 1942 | to Treblinka, many killed locally |
| 211 | Strzemieszyce Wielkie | 1,800 | 1940–1941 | May – 15 Jun 1942 | to Będzin Ghetto (500), Auschwitz (1,400) |
| 212 | Strzyżów | 1,300 | 1941 | 26 / 28 Jun 1942 | to Rzeszów ghetto, killed locally → Bełżec |
| 213 | Suchedniów | 5,000 | 1941 | Aug 1942 | to Treblinka |
| 214 | Sulejów | 1,500 | 1941 | Oct 1942 | to Treblinka |
| 215 | Szczuczyn | 2,000 | 1941 | Jul – Nov 1942 | to Bogusze transit camp, killed locally |
| 216 | Śniadowo | 650 | 1941 | Nov 1942 | to Zambrow ghetto |
| 217 | Tarczyn | 1,600 | 1941 | Feb 1942 | to Treblinka |
| 218 | Tarnobrzeg (ghetto & camp) | 500[444] | Jun 1941 | Jul 1942 | to Dębica ghetto → Bełżec |
| 219 | Tarnogród | 2,600–5,000 | 1941 | Nov 1942 | to Bełżec from ghetto & camp, many killed locally |
| 220 | Tarnopol Ghetto | 20,000 | Jul – Aug 1941 | Jun 1943 | to Bełżec, many killed locally |
| 221 | Tarnów | 40,000 | Mar 1941 | Sep 1943 | 10,000 killed locally, Bełżec (10,000), Auschwitz |
| 222 | Tomaszów Lubelski | 1,400–1,500 | 1941 | Oct 1942 | to Bełżec |
| 223 | Tyczyn | ? | 1941 | Jul 1942 | to Bełżec extermination camp |
| 224 | Wadowice | 1,400[445] | 1941 | Aug 1943 | to Auschwitz |
| 225 | Wąwolnica | 2,500 | 1941 | May 1942 | to Bełżec extermination camp |
| 226 | Węgrów | 6,000–8,300 | 1941 | Sep 1942 | to Treblinka |
| 227 | Wieliczka | 7,000 | 1941 | Aug 1942 | to Bełżec extermination camp |
| 228 | Wielun | 4,200–7,000 | 1941 | Aug 1942 | to Chełmno extermination camp, killed locally |
| 229 | Wieruszów | 1,400 | 1941 | Aug 1942 | to Chełmno extermination camp |
| 230 | Wilno Ghetto | 30,000–80,000 | Sep 1941 | Sep 1943 | killed locally (21,000 before ghetto was set up)[446] |
| 231 | Wiślica | 2,000 | 1941 | Oct 1942 | to Jędrzejów ghetto |
| 232 | Wolbrom | 3,000–5,000 | 1941 | Sep 1942 | to Bełżec, many killed locally |

| | | | | | |
|---|---|---|---|---|---|
| 233 | Wysokie Mazowieckie | 5,000 | 1941 | Nov 1942 | *to* Zambrow ghetto |
| 234 | Zabłudów | 1,800[447] | Jul 1941 | 2 Nov 1942 | 10th Calvary camp near Białystok → Treblinka (1,400) |
| 235 | Zambrów | 3,200–4,000 | 1941 | Jan 1943 | *to* Auschwitz, mass killings locally |
| 236 | Zawiercie | 5,000–7,000 | 1941 | Oct 1943 | *to* Auschwitz (5,000) |
| 237 | Zelów | ? | 1941 | Sep 1942 | *to* Chełmno extermination camp |
| 238 | Zwoleń (open type) | 6,500–10,000 | 1941 | 29 Sep 1942 | *to* Treblinka extermination camp (8,000) |
| 239 | Żarki | 3,200 | 1941 | Oct 1942 | *to* Treblinka |
| 240 | Żelechów | 5,500–13,000 | 1941 | Sep 1942 | *to* Treblinka |

**1942**

On January 20 at the Wannsee conference near Berlin, Reinhard Heydrich informed senior Nazi officials that "the final solution of the Jewish question" was deportation from the ghettos and subsequent mass extermination of the Jews. Implementation plan developed. Six death factories were built by German firms in occupied Poland within two-to-six months.

| | | | | | |
|---|---|---|---|---|---|
| 241 | Andrychów | 700 | Sep 1942 | Nov 1943 | *to* Auschwitz concentration camp |
| 242 | Annopol | ? | Jun 1942 | Oct 1942 | *to* Kraśnik ghetto |
| 243 | Baranów Sandomierski | 2,000 | Jun 1942 | Jul 1942 | *to* Dębica ghetto, (all) |
| 244 | Biecz | 700–800 | Apr 1942 | Aug 1942 | *to* Bełżec extermination camp |
| 245 | Czortków | 4,000 | Apr 1942 | Sep 1943 | *to* Bełżec extermination camp |
| 246 | Dąbrowa Tarnowska | 2,400–3,000 | Oct 1942 | Sep 1943 | *to* Bełżec extermination camp and Auschwitz |
| 247 | Dębica | 1,500–4,000 | 1942 | Mar 1943 | *to* Bełżec extermination camp |
| 248 | Drohobycz Ghetto | 10,000 | Mar 1942 | Jun 1943 | *to* Bełżec extermination camp |
| 249 | Dubno | 9,000? | Apr 1942 | Oct 1942 | all killed locally |
| 250 | Frysztak | 1,600[448] | 1942 | 18 Aug 1942 | *to* Jasło ghetto → killed in Warzyce forest |
| 251 | Hrubieszów (labor camp) | 200[449] | May 1942 | May 1943 | *to* Budzyn, killed locally, *see* Hrubieszów # 122 above (6,800) |
| 252 | Jasienica Rosielna | 1,500 | 1942 | Aug 1942 | *to* Bełżec extermination camp |

| | | | | | |
|---|---|---|---|---|---|
| 253 | Kołomyja (ghetto & camp) | 18,000 | 1942 | Feb 1943 | to Bełżec extermination camp, many killed locally |
| 254 | Koprzywnica | 1,800 | 1940 | Oct 1942 | to Treblinka |
| 255 | Kowale Pańskie | 3,000–5,000 | 1939–1942 | 1942 | to Chełmno extermination camp |
| 256 | Kowel | 17,000 | May 1942 | Oct 1942 | all killed locally |
| 257 | Kraśnik (ghetto & camp) | 5,000 | 1940–1942 | Nov 1942 | to Bełżec extermination camp |
| 258 | Krosno | 600–2,500 | Aug 1942 | Dec 1942 | to Bełżec extermination camp |
| 259 | Lesko | 2,000 | 1942 | Sep 1942 | to Bełżec extermination camp |
| 260 | Lubaczów | 4,200–7,000 | Oct 1942 | Jan 1943 | to Sobibor, many killed locally |
| 261 | Łachwa Ghetto | 2,350 | 4 Apr 1942 | Sep 1942 | killed locally, 1,500 in an uprising.[450] |
| 262 | Łęczna | 3,000 | Jun 1942 | Nov 1942 | to Sobibor, many killed locally |
| 263 | Międzyrzec Podlaski Ghetto | 20,000 | 28 Aug 1942 | 18 Jul 1943[451] | to Treblinka (17,000), hundreds killed locally.[452] |
| 264 | Ożarów | 4,500 | Jan 1942 | Oct 1942 | to Treblinka |
| 265 | Pińsk Ghetto | 26,200 | Apr 1942 | Oct 1942 | to Bronna Góra (3,500), the rest killed locally |
| 266 | Przemyśl | 22,000–24,000 | Jul 1942 | Sep 1943 | to Bełżec extermination camp, Auschwitz, Janowska |
| 267 | Przeworsk | 1,400? | Jul 1942 | Oct 1942 | to Bełżec extermination camp |
| 268 | Przysucha | 2,500–5,000 | Jul – 15 Aug 1942 | 27 / 31 Oct 1942[453] | to Treblinka (5,000)[454] |
| 269 | Sambor Ghetto | 8,000–9,000 | Mar 1942 | Jul 1943 | to Bełżec extermination camp, many killed locally |
| 270 | Sosnowiec Ghetto | 12,000 | Oct 1942 | Aug 1943 | to Auschwitz |
| 271 | Starachowice (labor camp) | 13,000 | 1942 | 1942 | to Treblinka, see also Starachowice ghetto |
| 272 | Stryj | 4,000–12,000 | 1942 | Jun 1943 | all killed locally |
| 273 | Sucha Beskidzka | 400[455] | 1942 | 1943 | to Auschwitz |
| 274 | Szydłów | 1,000 | Jan 1942 | Oct 1942 | to Chmielnik ghetto |
| 275 | Tarnogród (labor camp) | 1,000 | 1942 | 1942 | see Tarnogród ghetto → Bełżec extermination camp |

| 276 | Tomaszów M. (labor camp) | 1,000 | 1942 | May 1943 | *to* Starachowice,[456] *see also* Tomaszów Mazowiecki Ghetto (1940) |
| 277 | Tuchów | 3,000 | Jun 1942 | Sep 1942 | *to* Bełżec extermination camp |
| 278 | Zdzięcioł Ghetto | 4,500 | 22 Feb 1942 | 30 Apr – 6 Aug 1942 | killed locally during Zdzięcioł massacres |

## Aftermath

The ghetto inhabitants – most of whom were killed during Operation Reinhard – possessed Polish citizenship before the Nazi–Soviet invasion of Poland, which in turn enabled over 150,000 Holocaust survivors registered at CKŻP to take advantage of the later repatriation agreements between the governments of Poland and the Soviet Union, and legally emigrate to the West to help form the nascent State of Israel. Poland was the only Eastern Bloc country to allow free Jewish aliyah without visas or exit permits upon the conclusion of World War II.[457] By contrast, Stalin forcibly brought Soviet Jews back to USSR along with all Soviet citizens, as agreed to in the Yalta Conference.[458]

**Figure 50:** *Jewish women and children rounded up for deportation to a death camp during the Warsaw Ghetto Uprising*

# The Holocaust in Norway

Part of a series on
**The Holocaust**

Jews on selection ramp at Auschwitz, May 1944

- v
- t
- e[459]

In 1941–1942 during the occupation of Norway by Nazi Germany, there were at least 2,173 Jews in Norway. At least 775 of them were arrested, detained and/or deported. More than half of the Norwegians who died in camps in Germany were Jews.[460] 742 Jews were murdered in the camps and 23 Jews died as a result of extrajudicial execution, murder and suicide during the war, bringing the total of Jewish Norwegian dead to at least 765 Jews, comprising 230 complete households.[461] "Nearly two-thirds of the Jews in Norway fled from Norway".[462] Of these, around 900 Jews were smuggled out of the country by the Norwegian resistance movement, mostly to Sweden but some also to the United Kingdom).[463] Between 28 and 34 of those deported survived their continued imprisonment in camps (following their deportation)—and around 25 (of these) returned to Norway after the war.

## Background

The Jewish community in Norway was established in the late 19th century, after a clause in the Norwegian constitution of 1814 that banned Jews from entering Norway was repealed in 1851. The population grew slowly until the early 20th century, when pogroms in Russia and the Baltic states increased the number of immigrants. Another immigration increase came in the 1930s, as Jews fled Nazi persecution in Germany and areas under German control. *See also Nansenhjelpen.*

By 1942, there were 2,173 Jews in Norway. Of these, it is estimated that 1,643 were Norwegian citizens, 240 were foreign citizens, and 290 were stateless.

Much of the prejudice against Jews commonly found in Europe was also evident in Norway in the late 19th and early 20th century, and Nasjonal Samling (NS), the Nazi party in Norway, made antisemitism part of its political platform in the 1930s. Halldis Neegaard Østbye became the de facto spokeswoman for increasingly virulent propaganda against Jews, summarized in her 1938 book *Jødeproblemet og dets løsning* (The Jewish Problem and its Solution). NS had also started gathering information about Jewish Norwegians before the war started, and antisemitic op-ed articles were occasionally published in the mainstream press.

# The Holocaust in Norway

**Figure 51:** *Who's Who in the Jewish World, an attache to an antisemitic periodical listing Jews and presumed Jews in Norway. First edition printed in 1925.*

Following the German invasion and occupation, of Norway, and after the legitimate Norwegian government had left the country, German occupying authorities under the leadership of Reichskommissar Josef Terboven, put Norwegian civilian authorities under his control. This included various branches of Norwegian police, including the district sheriffs (Lensmannsetaten), criminal police, and order police. Nazi police branches, including the SD and Gestapo, also became part of a network that served as tools for increasingly oppressive policies toward the Norwegian populace.

## Preparations

As a deliberate strategy, Terboven's regime sought to use Norwegian, rather than German, officials to subjugate the Norwegian population. Although German police and paramilitary forces reported through the RSHA chain of command, and Norwegian police formally into the newly formed Department of Police, the actual practice was that Norwegian police officials took direction from the German RSHA.

Although several Jewish Norwegians had already been arrested and deported as political prisoners in the early months of the occupation, the first measure targeting all Jews was an order from the German foreign ministry made

| Land | Zahl |
|---|---|
| A. Altreich | 131.800 |
| Ostmark | 43.700 |
| Ostgebiete | 420.000 |
| Generalgouvernement | 2.284.000 |
| Bialystok | 400.000 |
| Protektorat Böhmen und Mähren | 74.200 |
| Estland – judenfrei – | |
| Lettland | 3.500 |
| Litauen | 34.000 |
| Belgien | 43.000 |
| Dänemark | 5.600 |
| Frankreich / Besetztes Gebiet | 165.000 |
| Unbesetztes Gebiet | 700.000 |
| Griechenland | 69.600 |
| Niederlande | 160.800 |
| Norwegen | 1.300 |
| B. Bulgarien | 48.000 |
| England | 330.000 |
| Finnland | 2.300 |
| Irland | 4.000 |
| Italien einschl. Sardinien | 58.000 |
| Albanien | 200 |
| Kroatien | 40.000 |
| Portugal | 3.000 |
| Rumänien einschl. Bessarabien | 342.000 |
| Schweden | 8.000 |
| Schweiz | 18.000 |
| Serbien | 10.000 |
| Slowakei | 88.000 |
| Spanien | 6.000 |
| Türkei (europ. Teil) | 55.500 |
| Ungarn | 742.800 |
| UdSSR | 5.000.000 |
| Ukraine | 2.994.684 |
| Weißrußland aus- schl. Bialystok | 446.484 |
| Zusammen: über | 11.000.000 |

**Figure 52:** *(Incorrect) estimate of the number of Jews presented at the Wannsee Conference*

through Terboven that on 10 May 1941 the police of Oslo were to confiscate radios from all Jews in the city. Within days local sheriffs throughout the entire country received the same orders.

To identify Jewish Norwegians, the authorities relied on information from the police and telegraph service, whilst the synagogues in Oslo and Trondheim were ordered to produce full rosters of their members, including their names, date of birth, profession, and address. Jewish burial societies and youth groups were likewise ordered to produce their lists.

In August, the synagogues were also ordered to produce lists of Jewish individuals who were not members. The resulting lists were cross-referenced with information Nasjonal Samling had compiled previously and information from the Norwegian Central Bureau of statistics. In the end, occupying authorities in Norway had a more complete list of Jewish residents in Norway than most other countries under Nazi rule.[464]

On the basis of the lists compiled in the spring, the Justice Department and county governors started in the fall to register all Jewish property, including commercial holdings. A complete inventory was transmitted to the police department in December 1941, and this also included individuals who were suspected of having a Jewish background.

**Figure 53:** *Anti-Semite graffiti on shop windows in Oslo in 1941. (The location is at the junction of present-day Henrik Ibsen's Street and Crown Prince Street.)*

On 20 December, the Norwegian Department of Police ordered 700 stamps with a 2 cm tall "J" for use by authorities to stamp the identification cards of Jewish individuals in Norway. These were put into use on 10 January 1942, when advertisements in the mainstream press ordered all Norwegian Jews to immediately present themselves at the local police stations to have their identification papers stamped. They were also ordered to complete an extensive form. For purposes of this registration, a Jew was identified as anyone who had at least three "full-Jewish" grandparents; anyone who had two "full-Jewish" grandparents and was married to a Jew; or was a member of a Jewish congregation. This registration showed that about 1,400 Jewish adults lived in Norway.

The Norwegian State Railways "aided without protest in the deportation", according to author Halvor Hegtun.

## Confiscation and arrests

Both the German and Norwegian police officials intensified efforts to target the Jewish population during the course of 1941 and the Falstad concentration camp was established near Levanger, north of Trondheim. Jewish individuals, particularly those who were stateless, were briefly detained in connection with Operation Barbarossa.Wikipedia:Citation needed The first Jewish Norwegian to be deported was Benjamin Bild, a labor union activist and mechanic,

**Figure 54:** *Memorial plaque at Stabekk elementary school over three children who were taken out of their classrooms and sent to Auschwitz*

who died in Gross Rosen.Wikipedia:Citation needed Moritz Rabinowitz, was probably the first to be arrested in March, 1941 for agitating against Nazi antisemitism in the Haugesund press. He was sent to Sachsenhausen concentration camp where he was beaten to death on 27 December 1942.

German troops occupied and vandalized the Trondheim Synagogue on 21 April 1941. The Torah scrolls had been secured in the early days of the war, and before long the Methodist church in Trondheim had provided temporary facilities for Jewish religious services. Several Jewish residents of Trondheim were arrested and detained at Falstad. The first such prisoner was Efraim Koritzinsky, a medical doctor and head of Trondheim hospital. Several others followed; altogether eight of these were shot in the woods outside of the camp that became the infamous site of extrajudicial executions in Norway On 24 February, all remaining Jewish property in Trondheim was seized by Nazi authorities.[465]

By the fall of 1942, about 150 Jews from Norway had fled the country. The Jewish population in Norway had experienced someWikipedia:Please clarify mistreatment specifically targeted at them, but the prevailing senseWikipedia:Citation needed was that their lot was the same as all other Norwegians.

As the brutality of the Terboven regime came to light through the atrocities at Telavåg, Martial law in Trondheim in 1942, etc., persecution against Jews in particular became more pronounced.

After numerous cases of harassment and violence against individuals, orders were issued to Norwegian police authorities on 24 and 25 October 1942, to arrest all Jewish men over the age of 15 and confiscate all their property. On 26 October, several Norwegian police branches and 20 soldiers of Germanic-SS rounded up and arrested Jewish men, oftenWikipedia:Citation needed leaving their wives and children on the street. These prisoners were held primarily at Berg concentration camp in Southern Norway and Falstad concentration camp in central parts of the country; some were held in local jails, while Jewish women were ordered to report in person to their local sheriffs on a daily basis.

On the morning of 26 November, German soldiers and more than 300 Norwegian officials (belonging to *Statspolitiet*, *Kriminalpolitiet*, *Hirden* and *Germanske SS-Norge*)[466] were deployed to arrest and detain Jewish women and children. These were sent by cars and train to the pier in Oslo where a cargo ship, the SS *Donau* was waiting to transport them to Stettin, and from there to Auschwitz.

By 27 November, all Jews in Norway (except one[467]) were either deported and murdered, imprisoned, had fled to Sweden, or were in hiding in Norway.

Around 70[468] Jews remained imprisoned at Berg concentration camp until the end of the war, because they were married to "Aryans".[469]

# Deportation and mass murder

- The first group deportation of Jews from Norway was on 19 November 1942 when the ship *Monte Rosa* left Oslo with 223 prisoners, of which 21Wikipedia:Citation needed were Jewish.
- The original plan was to ship all remaining Jews in Norway in one cargo ship, the SS *Donau*, on 26 November 1942, but only 532 prisoners boarded the SS *Donau* that day. Coincidentally with the departure of the SS *Donau* the same day, the MS *Monte Rosa* carried 26Wikipedia:Citation needed Jews from Oslo. The *Donau* landed in Stettin on 30 November. The prisoners boarded cargo trains at Breslauer Bahnhof, 60 to a car and departed Stettin at 5:12 pm. The train journey to Auschwitz took 28 hours. All the prisoners arrived alive at the camp, and there they were sorted into two lines. 186 were sent to slave labor in the Birkenau subcamp, the rest - 345 - were killed (within hours) in Auschwitz's gas chambers.
- The remaining Jewish prisoners that had been en route to Oslo on 26 November for the departure of the *Donau* were delayed, possibly as a result of delaying tactics by the Red Cross and sympathetic railroad workers. These were imprisoned under harsh conditions at Bredtveit concentration camp in Oslo to await a later transport.
- On 24 February 1943, the Bredtveit prisoners, along with 25 from Grini, boarded the *Gotenland* in Oslo, altogether 158. The ship departed the following day, also landing in Stettin, where they arrived on 27 February. They traveled to Auschwitz via Berlin, where they stayed overnight at

the Levetzowstrasse Synagogue. They arrived at Auschwitz on the night between 2 March and 3 March. Of the 158 who arrived from Norway, only 26 or 28 survived the first day, being sent to the Monowitz subcamp of Auschwitz.

There were smaller and individual deportations after the *Gotenland*'s voyage. A smaller number of Jewish prisoners remained in camps in Norway during the war, primarily those who were married to non-Jewish Norwegians. These were subject to mistreatment and neglect. In the camp in Grini, for example, the group that was harshest treated consisted of violent criminals and Jews.

Altogether, about 767 Jews from Norway were deported and sent to concentration camps under German control, primarily Auschwitz. 26 of these survived the ordeal.[470] In addition to the 741 murdered in the camps, 23 died as a result of extrajudicial execution, murder, and suicide during the war; bringing the total of Jewish Norwegian dead to at least 764, comprising 230 complete households.

The death toll among Jews from Norway constituted about 0.013% of the total death toll of European Jews in the Holocaust.Wikipedia:Citation needed

## Escape to Sweden

Early during the occupation, there was traffic between neutral countries, primarily Sweden over land; and the United Kingdom, by sea. Even as the occupying authorities triedWikipedia:Please clarify to limit such traffic, the underground railroad became more organized. Swedish authorities were at first only willing to accept political refugees and did not count Jews among them. Several Jewish refugees were turned away at the border, and a few were subsequently deported.

The North Sea route would become increasingly challenging as German forces increased their naval presence along the Norwegian coast, limiting the sea route to special operations missions against German military targets. The land routes to Sweden became the main conduit for people and materials that either needed to get out of Norway for their safety, or into Norway for clandestine missions.

There were a few private routes across the border, but most were organized through three resistance groups: Milorg ("military organization"), Sivorg ("civilian organization") and Komorg, the communist resistance group. These routes were carefully guarded, in large part through a network of secret cells. Some efforts to infiltrate them, especially through the Rinnan gang (Sonderabteilung Lola) succeeded, but such holes were quickly plugged.

**Figure 55:** *Backpack used by Jewish refugees, placed at remnants of gate at a border crossing to Sweden*

### Recommendations for (or warnings to) escape

Examples of Jews being recommended to escape include outgoing communication by anti-Nazi Germans in Norway: Theodor Steltzer warned Wolfgang Geldmacher—married to Randi Eckhoff, sister of member of the Resistance "Rolf Eckhoff. From them, warnings were passed on to Lise Børsum, Amalie Christie, Robert Riefling, Ole Jacob Malm and others".

### Report of disappearance—filed in Norway—regarding two Jews on the first transport from Prague to Poland

On 16 December 1941, "secretary of Nansen International Office for Refugees received a letter from the stateless Jews Nora Lustig, Fritz Lusting and Leo Eitinger. They were in Norway, and wrote that Czech Jews that they knew, had been deported to an unknown place in Poland. They asked Filseth, to report missing (through Red Cross), two Jews, shipped with the first transport from Prague to Poland".

## After the arrest of Jewish men (on 26 October 1942)

The arrest and detention of Jewish men on 26 October 1942 changed that premise, but at that point many were afraid of reprisals against the imprisoned men if they left. Some Norwegian Nazis and German officials advised Jews to leave the country as quickly as possible.

On the evening of 25 November, resistance people got a few hours' notice before the scheduled arrests and deportation of all Jews in Norway. Many did their best to notify the remaining Jews who were not already detained, usually by making brief phone calls or short appearances on people's doorsteps. This was more successful in Oslo than other areas. Those who were warned only had a few hours to go into hiding and days to find their way out of the country.

The Norwegian resistance movement had not planned for the contingency that hundreds of individuals had to go underground in one night, and it was left to individuals to improvise shelter out of sight of the arresting authorities. Many were moved several times in just as many days.

Most of the refugees were moved in small groups across the border, typically with the help of taxis or trucks, railroads to areas near the border, and then by foot, car, bicycle, or on skis across the border. It was a particularly cold winter, and the crossing involved considerable hardship and uncertainty. Those who had the means, paid their non-Jewish helpers for their trouble.

The passage was complicated by the vigilance of police who were committed to capturing such refugees, and Terboven imposed the death penalty for anyone caught aiding Jewish refugees. Only individuals who by application were granted "border zone permits" were allowed within easy traveling distance to the border with Sweden. Trains were subject to regular search and inspection, and there were continuous patrols of the area. A failed crossing would have dire consequences for anyone caught, as indeed it turned out for a few.

Still, at least 900 Jewish refugees made their way across the border to Sweden. They usually went through a transit center in Kjesäter in Vingåker, and then found temporary homes throughout Sweden, but mostly in certain towns where Norwegians gathered, such as Uppsala.

## Criticism of the Norwegian government in exile, and of Milorg

Some have said that the Norwegian government in exile should have warned the Jews (and told them to flee), since Trygve Lie already in June 1942 knew about what was happening to Jews in continental Europe, while others say that "What could one expect from Lie while the British and the Americans did not

**Figure 56:** *Terboven, Rediess, and other SS officers on an excursion to Skeikampen in April, 1942*

believe the messages from Poland? Also in Norway there had been difficulty in believing that gruesomness had taken place".

Some have said that Milorg did too little for the Jews, while others[471] say that "The great rescue operation Carl Fredriksens Transport was a result of orders from a *tilbaketrukket* leader of Milorg, Ole Berg, and later financed by Sivorg".

# Criminal culpability and moral responsibility

## Criminal prosecution

Although both the Norwegian Nazi party Nasjonal Samling and the German Nazi establishment had a political platform that called for persecution and ultimately the genocide of European Jewry, the arrest and deportation of Jews in Norway into the hands of the camp officials turned on the actions of several specific individuals and groups.

The ongoing rivalry between Reichskommissar Josef Terboven and Ministerpresident Vidkun Quisling may have played a role, as both were likely presented with the directives from the Wannsee Conference in January 1942. The German policy was to use Norwegian police as a front for the Norwegian implementation of the conference plans, orders for which were issued along two chains of command: from Adolf Eichmann through the RSHA and Heinrich

Fehlis to Hellmuth Reinhard, the Gestapo chief in Norway; and from Quisling through the "minister of justice" Sverre Riisnæs and "minister of police" Jonas Lie through to Karl Marthinsen, the head of the Norwegian state police.

Documentation from the period suggests that the Nazi authorities, and especially the Quisling administration, were loath to initiate actions that might cause widespread opposition among the Norwegian population. Quisling had tried and failed to take over the teachers' unions, the clergy of the State of Norway, athletics, and the arts. Eichmann had de-prioritized the extermination of Jews in Norway, as the number was low and even Nasjonal Samling had claimed that the "Jewish problem" in Norway was minor. Confiscation of Jewish property, the arrest of Jewish men, constant harassment and individual murder was – until late November, 1942 – part of Terboven's approach of terrorizing the Norwegian population into submission.

The evidence suggests that Hellmuth Reinhard took the initiative to put an end to all Jews in Norway. This may have been motivated by his own ambition, and it's possible he was encouraged by the lack of outrage over the initial measures targeting Jews.

According to the trial against him in Baden-Baden in 1964, Reinhard arranged for the SS *Donau* to set aside capacity for prisoner transport on 26 November and ordered Karl Marthinsen to mobilize the necessary Norwegian forces to effect the transit from Norway. In a curious sidenote to all this, he also sent along a typewriter on the *Donau* to properly register all prisoners, and was insistent that it be returned to him on *Donau*'s return voyage – which it was.

A local, Norwegian, police chief in Oslo named Knut Rød provided on-the-ground command of Norwegian police officers for arresting women and children and transporting them as well as the men who had already been detained to the Oslo harbor and putting them in the hands of the German SS troops.

Eichmann was not notified of the transport until the *Donau* had left the harbor, bound for Stettin. Nevertheless, he was able to arrange for box cars to be present for transport to Auschwitz.

Of those involved:

- **Terboven** committed suicide before being captured when the war ended; **Quisling** was convicted for treason and executed. **Jonas Lie** died, apparently of a heart attack before his capture. **Sverre Riisnæs** either feigned insanity or went insane and was put in protective custody. **Marthinsen** was assassinated by the Norwegian resistance in February 1945. Heinrich Fehlis committed suicide by first taking poison and then shooting himself in May 1945.

In the end, only two of the principals were put on trial:

- **Hellmuth Reinhard** left Norway in January 1945 without any clues to his whereabouts. He was presumed dead and his wife was issued a death certificate so she could remarry. But it turned out he had changed his name to his birth name of Hellmuth Patzschke and had actually remarried his "widow," settling down as a publisher in Baden-Baden. His real identity was discovered in 1964, and he was put on trial. In spite of overwhelming evidence about his culpability for the deportation of Jews from Norway and his complicity in their deaths, he was acquitted because statute of limitations had expired. He was convicted and sentenced to five years for his participation in Operation Blumenpflücken.
- **Knut Rød** was put on trial in 1948, acquitted of all charges, and managed to get reinstated as a police officer and retired in 1965. Rød's acquittal remains controversial this day and has been characterized as "the strangest criminal trial [in the legal proceedings after World War II]".
- Another controversial trial was that held against members of the resistance **Peder Pedersen** and **Håkon Løvestad**, who confessed to killing an elderly Jewish couple and stealing their money. The jury found that the killing was justified, but convicted the two of embezzlement. This also became a controversial issue known as the Feldmann case.

The moral culpability among Norwegian police officers and Norwegian informants is a matter of continuing research and debate.

Although the persecution and murder of Jews was raised as a factor in several trials, including that against Quisling, legal scholars agree that in no case was it a decisive or even weighty factor in the conviction or sentencing of these people.

## Moral responsibility

Beyond the criminal actions of individuals in Norway that led to the deportation and murder of Jews from Norway, and indeed also of non-Jews who were persecuted on political, religious or other pretexts, there has been considerable public debate in Norway about the public morals that allowed these crimes to take place and did not prevent them from happening.

### Comparison between Denmark and Norway

The situation of the Jews in Denmark was very different from Norway. Far fewer Danish Jews were arrested and deported, and those who were deported were sent to Theresienstadt, rather than Auschwitz, where a relatively large percentage survived.

Several factors have been cited for these differences[472]

**Figure 57:** *Holocaust memorial at the Jewish cemetery at Lademoen in Trondheim, Norway*

- In Denmark, the German diplomat Georg Ferdinand Duckwitz leaked the plans for arrest and deportation to Hans Hedtoft several days before the plan was to be put in motion. There was no such humanitarian among German officials in Norway.
- The terms of occupation in Denmark gave Danish politicians greater influence over internal affairs in Denmark, and in particular command authority over Danish police forces. Consequently, German occupying authorities had to rely on German police and military to perform arrests. Where Danish police participated, it was to rescue Jews from Germans. Since the Norwegians resisted the Germans more actively, the country never enjoyed the same civil autonomy as did the Danes during the occupation.
- Danish popular opinion was more actively opposed to the Nazi occupation and was more emboldened to take care of its Jewish citizens. Non-Jewish Danes were known to take to the streets to find Jews who needed shelter, and to search the forests for Jews who had hidden there to help them.
- The arrest of Norwegian Jews happened about one year before the arrests in Denmark, and also before the Soviet victory at Stalingrad, which changed nearby Sweden's stand from being supportive of the Germans to lean towards the Allies. As there was considerable contact between the resistance in Denmark and Norway through neutral Sweden it means that the Danes knew what fate the Danish Jews were destined for. That Swe-

den had changed to lean towards the Allies also meant that it was open for Jewish refugees, which had not been the case before and early in the war.

## Issues of moral responsibility

The exiled Norwegian government became part of the Allies upon the invasion on 9 April 1940. Though the most significant contribution of the Allied war effort was through the merchant marine fleet known as Nortraship, a number of Norwegian military forces were established and became part of the Norwegian Armed Forces in exile. Consequently, the Norwegian government was regularly briefed on Allied intelligence relating to atrocities committed by German forces in Eastern Europe and in occupied Netherlands, France, etc.

In addition, the Norwegian government also received regular intelligence from the Norwegian home front, including accounts from returning Norwegian Germanic-SS soldiers, who had firsthand accounts of massacres of Jews in Poland, the Ukraine, etc.[473]

Indeed, both underground resistance newspapers in Norway and the Norwegian press abroad published news about "wholesale murders" of Jews in the late summer and fall of 1942.[474] There is, however, little evidence that either the Norwegian home front or Norwegian government expected that the Jews in Norway would be a target for the genocide that was unfolding on the European continent. On 1 December 1942, the Norwegian foreign minister, Trygve Lie sent a letter to the British section of the World Jewish Congress where he asserted that:

<templatestyles src="Template:Quote/styles.css"/>

> ...it has never been found necessary for the Norwegian Government to appeal to the people of Norway to assist and to protect other individuals of classes in Norway, who have been selected for persecution by the German aggressors, and I feel convinced that such an appeal is not needed in order to urge the population to fulfill their human duty towards the Jews of Norway.
>
> —Abrahamsen 1991, p. 10.

Although the Norwegian resistance by the fall of 1942 had a sophisticated network for transmitting and propagating urgent news among the population that led to very effective passive resistance efforts, e.g., in keeping the teachers' union, athletics, physicians, etc., out of Nazi control, no such notifications were issued to save Jews.[475]

The Protestant religious establishment in Norway did, however, make their opposition known: in a letter to Vidkun Quisling dated 10 November 1942, read out in Norwegian churches on two consecutive Sundays, bishops of the

Church of Norway, the administration of the theological seminaries, the leaders of several leading religious organizations, and the leaders of non-Lutheran Protestant organizations protesting actions against the Jews, calling on Quisling "in the name of Jesus Christ" to "stop the persecution of Jews and stop the bigotry that through the press is disseminated throughout our land."[476]

The discrimination, persecution, and ultimately deportation of Jews was enabled by the cooperation of Norwegian agencies that were not entirely co-opted by Nasjonal Samling or the German occupying powers. In addition to the police and local sheriffs who implemented the directives of Statspolitiet, the taxis aided in transporting Jewish prisoners to their point of deportation and even sued the Norwegian government after the war for wages owed to them for such services.

Jews in Norway had been singled out for persecution also before 26 October 1942. They were the first to have radios confiscated, were forced to register and have identification papers imprinted, and were banned from certain professions. However, it was not widely considered that this would extend to deportation and murder. It wasn't until the night of 26 November that the resistance movement was mobilized to rescue Jews from deportation. It took time for the network to be fully engaged, and until then Jewish refugees had to improvise on their own, and rely on acquaintances to avoid capture. Within a few weeks, however, the Norwegian home front organizations (including Milorg and Sivorg) had developed the means to move relatively large numbers of refugees out of Norway and also financed these escapes when needed.

## The State Railways' role

Bjørn Westlie says that the "Norwegian State Railways transported Jews to the outward shipping from the Oslo harbor (...) the NSB employees did not know what fate awaited the Jews. Naturally they understood that the Jews would be shipped out of the country by force, because the train went to Oslo harbor". Furthermore, Westlie points to "dilemmas [that] NSB's employees found themselves in when the NSB leadership cooperated with the Germans".

Later Westlie said about the extermination of Norwegian Jews: "what else than co-responsible was NSB ? For me, NSB's use of POWs and this deportation of Jews must be viewed as one: namely, that NSB thereby became an agency that participated in Hitler's violence against these two groups, who were the nazism's main enemies. The fact that the pertinent NSB leaders received awards after the war, confirms NSB's and others' desire to conceal this".

There was no investigation of the agencies [or NSB] after the war. However, the former chief Vik was not to be prosecuted if he "did not again work for NSB".

# Post-war reactions

## The post-war Norwegian government's refusal to finance the return of deported Jewish Norwegians

"When the White Buses travelled down [southward from Scandinavia] to fetch prisoners who had survived, Jews were not permitted on board because they were no longer considered Norwegian citizens, and the government after 8 May [1945] refused to finance their transportation home.", according to historian Kjersti Dybvig.[477]

## Skarpnes commission

On 27 May 1995, Bjørn Westlie published an article in the daily, *Dagens Næringsliv*, that highlighted the uncompensated financial loss incurred by the Norwegian Jewish community as a result of Nazi persecution during the war. This brought to public attention the fact that much if not most of the assets confiscated from Jewish owners during the war had been inadequately restored to them and their descendants, even in cases where the Norwegian government or private individuals had benefited from the confiscation after the war.

In response to this debate, the Norwegian Ministry of Justice on 29 March 1996, named a commission to investigate what was done with Jewish assets during the war. The commission consisted of County governor of Vest Agder, Oluf Skarpnes as its chair, professor of law Thor Falkanger, professor of history Ole Kristian Grimnes, district court judge Guri Sunde, director at National Archival Services of Norway, psychologist Berit Reisel, and cand.philol. Bjarte Bruland, Bergen. Consultant Torfinn Vollan from the Skarpnes's office acted as the commission's secretary. Of the commission's members, Dr. Reisel and Mr. Bruland had been nominated by the Jewish community in Norway. Anne Hals resigned from the commission early in the process, and Eli Fure from the same institution was named in her place.

The commission worked together for a year, but it became apparent that were diverging views on premises for the group's analysis.

- The majority focused its effort on arriving at an accurate accounting of the assets lost during the war using conventional assumptions and information in available records.
- The minority, consisting of Reisel and Bruland, sought a more in-depth understanding of the historical sequence of events around the loss of individual assets, as well as both the intended and actual effect of the confiscation and subsequent events, whether the owners were deported, killed, or escaped.

By all accounts, the commission had difficulty unifying these views, and on 23 June 1997, twoWikipedia:Citation needed separate reports were submitted to the Ministry of Justice. After considerable debate in the media, the government accepted the findings of the minority report and initiated financial compensation and issuing a public apology.

**Assessment of financial loss**

The Nazi authorities confiscated allWikipedia:Citation needed Jewish property with an administrative penstroke. This included commercial property such as retail stores, factories, workshops, etc.; and also personal property such as residences, bank accounts, automobiles, securities, furniture, and other fixtures they could find. Jewelry and other personal valuables were usually taken by German officials as "voluntary contributions to the German war effort." In addition, Jewish professionals were typically deprived of any legal right to practice their profession: attorneys were disbarred, physicians and dentists lost their licenses, and craftsmen were locked out of their trade associations. Employers were pressured to fire all Jewish employees. In many cases, Jewish proprietors were forced to continue to work at their confiscated businesses for the benefit of the "new owners."[478]

Assets were often sold at fire sale prices or assigned at a token price to Nazis, Germans, or their sympathizers.

The administration of these assets was performed by a "Liquidation board for confiscated Jewish assets" that accounted for the assets as they were seized and their disposition. For these purposes, the board continued to treat each estate as a bankrupt legal entity, charging expenses even after the assets had been disposed. As a result, there was a significant discrepancy between the value of the assets for the rightful owners, and the value assessed by the confiscating authorities.

This was further complicated by the methodology employed by the legitimate Norwegian government after the war. In order to restore confiscated assets to their owners, the government was guided by public policy to alleviate the economic impact on the economy by reducing compensation to approximate a sense of fairness and finance the reconstruction of the country's economy. The assessed value was thereby reduced by the Nazis' liquidation practices and was further reduced by the discounting applied as a result of governmental policy after the war.[479]

Norwegian estate law imposes estate tax on inheritance passed from the deceased to his/her heirs depending on the relationship between the two. This tax was compounded at each step of inheritance. As no death certificates had been issued for Jews murdered in German concentration camps, the deceased were listed as missing. Their estates were held in probate pending a declaration of death and charged for administrative expenses.

By the time all these factors had had their effect on the valuation of the confiscated assets, very little was left. In total, NOK 7.8 million was awarded to principals and heirs of Jewish property confiscated by the Nazis. This was less than the administrative fees charged by governmental agencies for probate. It did not include assets seized by the government that belonged to non-Norwegian citizens, and that of citizens that left no legal heirs. This last category was formidable, as 230 entire Jewish households were killed during the course of the Shoah.

## Legacy

### Education, remembrance and research

Since 2002, Norway has commemorated International Holocaust Memorial Day on 27 January. In 2003 Norway became a member of IHRA (International Holocaust Remembrance Alliance) and served as Chair in 2009.[480]

### Monuments

The first Holocaust-related monument in Norway was inaugurated in Trondheim in 1947.; in later years, monuments in Haugesund (to commemorate Moritz Rabinowitz), at the pier in Oslo from which the *Donau* sailed, at Falstad, in Kristiansund in Trondheim (over Cissi Klein), and at schools have also raised the awareness. Snublesteiner ("stumbling stones") have been placed in many Norwegian streets outside the apartments where the holocaust victims lived before deportation.

### Notable remorse

- On Holocaust Remembrance Day in 2012,[481] prime minister Jens Stoltenberg expressed regret "that Norwegian citizens aided in the arrests and deportations of Norwegian Jews". [Around] the same time, National Police Commissioner Odd Reidar Humlegård said to *Dagsavisen* that "I wish to-, on behalf of Norwegian police—and those who participated in the deportation of Norwegian Jews to the concentration camps—express regret".
- In 2015 the chief of public relations of the Norwegian State Railways, Åge-Christoffer Lundeby, said that "The transportation of Jews that were to be deported and the use of POWs on the Nordland Line is a dark chapter of NSB's history".

**Figure 58:** *Quisling's former residence, now housing the Norwegian Center for Studies of Holocaust and Religious Minorities*

## Emergence of literature about the Holocaust in Norway

Herman Sachnowitz's *Det angår også deg*,[482] was published in 1978.[483]

The literature since then can be categorized as follows:

- Comprehensive historical accounts of the Holocaust in Norway, which include Abrahamsen 1991 and the first 336 pages of Mendelsohn 1986, but also monographs such as Jan Otto Johansen (1984) and Per Ole Johansen (1984)
- Books that cover specific aspects of the Holocaust, such as Ulstein 2006 about the escapes to Sweden and Ottosen (1994) about the deportation, or Cohen (2000)
- Case studies of individuals and families. Some of these are biographical, such as Komissar (1995), Søbye (2003),
- In-depth studies on specific issues, such as Skarpnesutvalget (1997) and Johansen (2006)

One issue that has been highlighted is the hypothesis that many Norwegians viewed Jews as outsiders, whose fate was of no direct concern to Norwegians.

The Norwegian Center for Studies of Holocaust and Religious Minorities has facilitated research about the holocaust, and the institute has published the findings. The Falstad Center at the former site of the Falstad concentration camp provides another forum on humanitarian aspects of the German occupation. Jewish museums have recently been established in Oslo and Trondheim, and there have been notable papers written within criminology about the legal purge in Norway after World War II.

The author of a 2014 book (*Den største forbrytelsen*) received the Brage Prize. The book received great reviews, but also criticism from historians at Jødisk Museum in Oslo—Mats Tangestuen and Torill Torp-Holte—for losing sight of important nuances in the portrayal of who were helpers and who were violators.

## Research

In 2010 the doctoral dissertation of Synne Corell was published as a book. In it she criticizes major works about the war, and how they deal with the fate of Norwegian Jews during World War Two.

In 2011, historian Odd-Bjørn Fure said that most of the Norwegian research on the Holocaust and World War II is being conducted by the Norwegian Center for Studies of Holocaust and Religious Minorities (HL-Senteret).[484]

In 2014 Jahn Otto Johansen said that "the Norwegian Cabinet [in exile] in London, and Milorg's leadership, as well as large parts of Norwegian society, did not particularly care about the Jews. There is agreement about this among *seriøse* historians. - I can refer to [the book by] Samuel Abrahamsen *Norway's response to the Holocaust*. I cooperated closely with" him "and discovered how many worked against his project because the [Norwegian] Cabinet [in] London's-, Milorg's- and Norwegian society's alleged positive attitude towards the Jews, was not to be doubted".

In 2014 author Marte Michelet said that more research is needed about "What role did the Jewish networks have in organizing the flight[s of individuals]? Who was responsible for the warning[s], and who did the warning reach? - We know little about the money involved in the trafficking of refugees. To what degree did helpers receive payment, what sums were to be paid, and how did that play a role in who was able to flee, and who was not able to flee?"[485]

## Notes

## Bibliography

### Works about the Holocaust in Norway

- "Historikk jøder fra Agder"[486] (in Norwegian). Stiftelsen Arkivet. Archived from the original[487] on 22 July 2011. Retrieved 17 January 2008.<templatestyles src="Module:Citation/CS1/styles.css"></templatestyles> The article depicts the fate of Jews in the Agder counties.

- Abrahamsen, Samuel (1991). *Norway's Response to the Holocaust: A Historical Perspective*. Holocaust Library. ISBN 0-89604-117-4.<templatestyles src="Module:Citation/CS1/styles.css"></templatestyles> One of two comprehensive treatises on the Holocaust in Norway.
- Berman, Irene Levin (2008). *Flukten fra Holocaust*[488] (in Norwegian). Oslo: Orion. ISBN 978-82-458-0865-0;<templatestyles src="Module:Citation/CS1/styles.css"></templatestyles> the history of the Holocaust against the background of the author's memories of her own escape into Sweden. Published in English as: "'We Are Going to Pick Potatoes': Norway and the Holocaust, The Untold Story" (Hamilton Books, 2010, <templatestyles src="Module:Citation/CS1/styles.css" />ISBN 978-0-7618-5011-3).
- Bruland, Bjarte (1995). "Forsøket på å tilintetgjøre de norske jødene" [The attempt to exterminate the Norwegian Jews]. University of Bergen<templatestyles src="Module:Citation/CS1/styles.css"></templatestyles> (academic thesis).
- Feinberg, Kai; Stefansen, Arnt. *Fange 79018 vender tilbake* (in Norwegian). Oslo: Cappelen. ISBN 82-02-15705-6.<templatestyles src="Module:Citation/CS1/styles.css"></templatestyles> Personal account of survivor Kai Feinberg, with historical notes by Arnt Stefansen.
- Gerstenfeld, Manfred. "Norway: The Courage of a Small Jewish Community; Holocaust Restitution and antisemitism: An interview with Bjarte Bruland and Irene Levin"[489]. Jerusalem Center for Public Affairs. Retrieved January 2008. Check date values in: | accessdate= (help)<templatestyles src="Module:Citation/CS1/styles.css"></templatestyles>
- Hegtun, Halvor (2004-10-31). "Auschwitz er en del av livet"[490] (in Norwegian). Aftenposten. Retrieved 2008-01-21.<templatestyles src="Module:Citation/CS1/styles.css"></templatestyles> A newspaper article about a return to Auschwitz by Norwegian survivors.
- Johansen, Jahn Otto (1984). *Det hendte også her* (in Norwegian). Oslo: Cappelen. ISBN 82-02-09894-7.<templatestyles src="Module:Citation/CS1/styles.css"></templatestyles>
- Johansen, Per Ole (1984). *Oss selv nærmest: Norge og jødene 1914-1943* (in Norwegian). Oslo: Gyyldendal. ISBN 82-05-15062-1.<templatestyles src="Module:Citation/CS1/styles.css"></templatestyles>
- Komissar, Vera; Sundvor, Bjørg (1992). *Nådetid: norske jøder på flukt 1942* (in Norwegian). Oslo: Aschehoug. ISBN 82-03-17170-2.<templatestyles src="Module:Citation/CS1/styles.css"></templatestyles> It is about

twelve case examples of Norwegian Jews who escaped and survived.
- Komissar, Vera; Nyrønning, Sverre; Paltiel, Julius (1995). *På tross av alt: Julius Paltiel - norsk jøde i Auschwitz* (in Norwegian). Oslo: Aschehoug. ISBN 82-03-26086-1.<templatestyles src="Module:Citation/CS1/styles.css"></templatestyles> It is about the story of Julius Paltiel, who survived deportation and imprisonment in Auschwitz.
- Lyngvi, Arne (2005). *Fordi de var jøder... Da Holocaust rammet noen medmennesker i Bergen og Hordaland* (in Norwegian). Bergen: Sigma forlag. ISBN 82-7916-035-3.<templatestyles src="Module:Citation/CS1/styles.css"></templatestyles> It covers specifically the Jewish population of Bergen and Hordaland affected by the Holocaust.
- Michelet, Marte (2014). "Den største forbrytelsen" [The greatest crime].<templatestyles src="Module:Citation/CS1/styles.css"></templatestyles>
- Norwegian Government (1997). *Inndragning av jødisk eiendom i Norge under den 2. verdenskrig*[491]. Norges offentlige utredninger (in Norwegian). Oslo: Statens forvaltningstjeneste. ISBN 82-583-0437-2. NOU 1997:22 ("Skarpnesutvalget"). Retrieved 2008-01-16;<templatestyles src="Module:Citation/CS1/styles.css"></templatestyles> report from the governmental commission on the confiscation and disposition of Jewish assets. An English translation of the full minority report and a summary of the majority report was published by the Norwegian Ministry of Foreign Affairs in June 1997, but without the ministry's insignia or an ISBN registration. It was titled "The Reisel/Bruland Report on the Confiscation of Jewish Property in Norway during World War II," and is commonly known as the "blue book" and is on file at the Norwegian Center for Studies of Holocaust and Religious Minorities.
- Ottosen, Kristian (1994). *I slik en natt - historien om deportasjonen av jøder fra Norge*. Oslo: Aschehoug. ISBN 82-03-26049-7;<templatestyles src="Module:Citation/CS1/styles.css"></templatestyles> on the deportation of Jews from Norway to concentration camps, including case studies.
- Sachnowitz, Herman; Arnold Jacoby (1978). *Det angår også deg* (in Norwegian). Stabekk: Den norske bokklubben. ISBN 82-525-0544-9.<templatestyles src="Module:Citation/CS1/styles.css"></templatestyles> - an early personal account of a survivor's experiences.
- Savosnick, Robert; Hans Melien (1986). *Jeg ville ikke dø* (in Norwegian) (2nd ed.). Oslo/Risør: Cappelen (1st), Aktive Fredsforlag (2nd). ISBN 82-92627-00-6.<templatestyles src="Module:Citation/CS1/styles.css"></templatestyles>

- Søbye, Espen (2003). *Kathe, alltid vært i Norge* (in Norwegian). Oslo: Oktober. ISBN 82-7094-926-4.
- Ulstein, Ragnar (2006) [1995]. *Jødar på flukt* (in Norwegian) (2nd ed.). Samlaget. ISBN 82-521-6988-0; on the escape and underground railroad to Sweden, including case studies.

## Works about the Jewish minority in Norway

- Mendelsohn, Oskar (1969). *Jødenes historie i Norge gjennom 300 år: Bind 1 1660-1940* (in Norwegian). Universitetsforlaget. ISBN 82-00-02523-3.
- Mendelsohn, Oskar (1986). *Jødenes historie i Norge gjennom 300 år: Bind 2 1940-1985* (in Norwegian) (2nd ed.). Universitetsforlaget. pp. pps 13–262. ISBN 82-00-02524-1. A comprehensive treatment of the Holocaust in Norway.
- Mendelsohn, Oskar (1992). *Jødene i Norge: Historien om en minoritet* (in Norwegian). Universitetsforlaget. ISBN 82-00-21669-1.
- Reisel (editor), Micha (1992). *Du skal fortelle det til dine barn: Det mosaiske trossamfund i Oslo 1892-1992* (in Norwegian). Oslo: Det mosaiske trossamfund i Oslo. ISBN 82-992611-0-4.
- Reitan, Jon (2005). *Jødene fra Trondheim* (in Norwegian). Trondheim: Tapir akademisk forlag. ISBN 82-519-2044-2.

## Works about Norwegian World War II history

- Cohen, Maynar (2000). *A Stand Against Tyranny: Norway's Physicians and the Nazis*. Wayne State University Press. ISBN 0-8143-2934-9. It is about the resistance network organized by Norwegian physicians.
- Grimnes, Ole Kristian, ed. (1984). *Norge i krig* (in Norwegian). Oslo: Aschehoug. ISBN 82-03-11144-0. A comprehensive, 8-volume survey of the war in Norway, organized by topic.

- Johansen, Per Ole (2006). *På siden av rettsoppgjøret*. Unipub. ISBN 978-82-7477-233-5. - A series of interdisciplinary works at the University of Oslo on bias in the Legal purge in Norway after World War II.
- Books by Kristian Ottosen:
  - O., K. (1989). *Natt og tåke : historien om Natzweiler-fangene* (in Norwegian). Oslo: Aschehoug. ISBN 82-03-16108-1. It is about the Nacht und Nebel prisoners in the Natzweiler concentration camp, with an emphasis on the Norwegians held there.
  - O., K. (1990). *Liv og død : historien om Sachsenhausen-fangene* (in Norwegian). Oslo: Aschehoug. ISBN 82-03-16484-6. It is about the Sachsenhausen concentration camp.
  - O., K. (1991). *Kvinneleiren : historien om Ravensbrück-fangene* (in Norwegian). Oslo: Aschehoug. ISBN 82-03-16791-8. It is about the Ravensbrück concentration camp, primarily for women.
  - O., K. (1993). *Bak lås og slå : historien om norske kvinner og menn i Hitlers fengsler og tukthus* (in Norwegian). Oslo: Aschehoug. ISBN 82-03-26000-4. It is about the deportation and imprisonment of Norwegian men and women in prisons throughout Germany.
  - O., K. (1995). *Nordmenn i fangenskap 1940-1945* (in Norwegian). Oslo: Universitetsforlaget. ISBN 82-00-22372-8. It is an authoritative list of Norwegian individuals who had been held in German captivity during World War II.
- Ringdal, Nils Johan (1987). *Mellom barken og veden: politiet under okkupasjonen*. Oslo: Aschehoug. ISBN 82-03-15616-9. It is about the role of Norwegian police during the occupation.

# External links

- «Holocaust i Norge»[492], from *Store norske leksikon* (Norwegian)
- «Deportasjonen av de norske jødene»[493], from the website norgeshistorie.no (University of Oslo) (Norwegian)
- Norway[494] at European Holocaust Research Infrastructure (EHRI)

# The Holocaust in Belgium

The Holocaust in German-occupied Belgium refers to the persecution and attempted extermination of Jews and Roma between 1940 and 1944 during World War II.

At the start of the war, the population of Belgium was overwhelmingly Catholic. Jews made up the largest non-Christian population in the country, numbering between 70–75,000 out of a population of 8 million. Most lived in the cities of Antwerp, Brussels, Charleroi and Liège. The vast majority were recent immigrants to Belgium who had fled persecution in Germany and Eastern Europe, and, as a result, only a small minority actually possessed Belgian citizenship.

Shortly after the invasion of Belgium, the Military Government passed a series of anti-Jewish laws in October 1940. The Belgian Committee of Secretary-Generals refused from the start to co-operate on passing any anti-Jewish measures and the Military Government seemed unwilling to pass further legislation. The German government began to seize Jewish-owned businesses and forced Jews out of positions in the civil service. In April 1941, without orders from the German authorities, Flemish collaborators pillaged two synagogues in Antwerp and burned the house of the chief rabbi of the town in the Antwerp Pogrom. The Germans created a *Judenrat* in the country, the *Association des Juifs en Belgique* (AJB; "Association of Jews in Belgium"), which all Jews were required to join. As part of the Final Solution from 1942, the persecution of Belgian Jews escalated. From May 1942, Jews were forced to wear yellow Star of David badges to mark them out in public. Using the registers compiled by the AJB, the Germans began deporting Jews to concentration camps in the General Government (the occupied portion of Poland). Jews chosen from the registration lists were required to turn up at the newly established Mechelen transit camp; they were then deported by train to concentration camps, mostly to Auschwitz. Between August 1942 and July 1944, around 25,000 Jews and 350 Roma were deported from Belgium; more than 24,000 were killed before the camps were liberated by the Allies.

From 1942, opposition among the general population to the treatment of the Jews in Belgium grew. By the end of the occupation, more than 40 per cent of all Jews in Belgium were in hiding; many of them were hidden by Gentiles, particularly by Catholic priests and nuns. Some were helped by the organized resistance, such as the *Comité de Défense des Juifs* (CDJ; "Committee of Jewish Defense"), which provided food and refuge to hiding Jews. Many of the Jews in hiding joined the armed resistance. In April 1943, members of the CDJ attacked the twentieth rail convoy to Auschwitz and succeeded in rescuing some of those being deported.

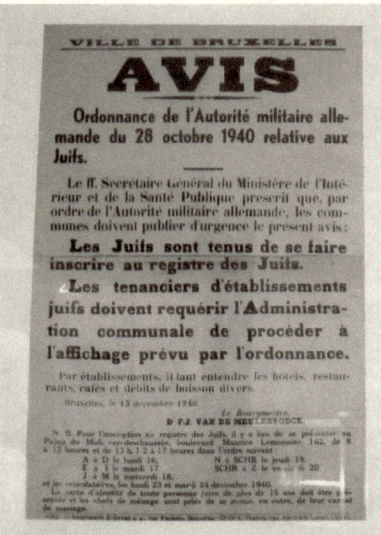

**Figure 59:** *French language poster detailing the Anti-Jewish laws enacted in Belgium on 28 October 1940.*

# Background

### Religion and Anti-Semitism

Before the war, the population of Belgium was overwhelmingly Catholic. Around 98 per cent of the population was baptized and around 80 per cent of marriage ceremonies were held with traditional Catholic services, while politically the country was dominated by the Catholic Party.

The Jewish population of Belgium was comparatively small. Out of a population of around 8 million, there were only 10,000 Jews in the country before World War I. The interwar period saw substantial Jewish immigration to Belgium. By 1930, the population rose to 50,000, and by 1940 it was between 70,000–75,000. Most of the new Jewish immigrants came from Eastern Europe and Nazi Germany, escaping anti-Semitism and poverty in their native countries. The Roma population of Belgium at the same time was approximately 530. Few of the Jewish migrants claimed Belgian citizenship, and many did not speak French or Dutch. Jewish communities developed in Charleroi, Liège, Brussels and, above all, Antwerp, where more than half of the Jews in Belgium lived.

**Figure 60:** *The Great Synagogue of Brussels, built in 1875.*

The Interwar period also saw the rise in popularity of Fascist New Order parties in Belgium. These were chiefly represented by the *Vlaams Nationaal Verbond* (VNV; "Flemish National Union") and *Verdinaso* in Flanders, and *Rex* in Wallonia. Both Flemish parties supported the creation of an ethnically Germanic *"Dietse Natie"* ("Greater Dutch State") from which Jews would be excluded. *Rex*, whose ideology was based on Christian Fascism, was particularly anti-Semitic, but both VNV and *Rex* campaigned under anti-Semitic slogans for the 1938 elections. Their stance was officially condemned by the Belgian authorities, but prominent figures, including King Leopold III, were suspected of holding anti-Semitic attitudes. From June 1938, Jewish illegal immigrants arrested by the Belgian police were deported to Germany, until public condemnation halted the practice after *Kristallnacht* in November 1938. Between 1938 and the start of the war, with the influence of Fascist parties declining in Belgium, the country began accepting more Jewish refugees, including 215 from the MS *St. Louis* who had been refused visas elsewhere.

## German invasion and occupation

In the interwar period, Belgium followed a strict policy of political neutrality. Though the Belgian Army was mobilized in 1939, the country only became involved in the war on 10 May 1940, when it was invaded by Nazi Germany. After a campaign lasting 18 days, the Belgian military, along with its

**Figure 61:** *Trilingual (German-Dutch-French) signs used to mark Jewish-owned shops and businesses in Belgium from October 1940*

commander-in-chief Leopold III, surrendered on 28 May. Belgium, together with the French province of Nord-Pas-de-Calais, were grouped together under the German Military Administration in Belgium and Northern France (*Militärverwaltung in Belgien und Nordfrankreich*). Because the country was under military occupation, it initially fell under the control of the *Wehrmacht* rather than Nazi Party or Schutzstaffel (SS) authorities. In July 1944, the *Militärverwaltung* was replaced with a civilian administration (*Zivilverwaltung*), greatly increasing the power of the more radical Nazi Party and SS organisations until the Allied liberation in September 1944.

## The Holocaust

### Early discrimination and persecution, 1940–41

On 23 October 1940, the German Military Administration adopted anti-Jewish legislation for the first time. The new laws, similar to the Nuremberg Laws adopted in Germany in 1935, coincided with the adoption of similar legislation in the Netherlands and in France. The laws of 28 October forbade Jews to practice certain professions (including the civil service) and forced Jews to register with their local municipality. On the same date, the German administration announced a definition of who was regarded as Jewish. Jewish-owned shops or businesses had to be marked by a sign in the window, and Jewish-owned economic assets had to be registered. From June 1940, a list of Jewish businesses had already been drawn up in Liège.

In 1940, the German government began to liquidate Jewish businesses. Some were transferred to German ownership in a process termed Aryanization. Some 6,300 Jewish-owned businesses were liquidated before 1942, and 600 were Aryanized. Around 600 million Belgian francs was raised from the seizures, much less than anticipated.

In total, between 28 October 1940 and 21 September 1942, 17 anti-Jewish ordinances were proclaimed by the Military Administration.

## *Association des Juifs en Belgique*

The "Association of Jews in Belgium" (AJB) was a *Judenrat* created by the Germans to administer the Jewish population of Belgium from November 1941. Though directed by the Germans, the AJB was run by Jews and acted as an "organizational ghetto", allowing the Nazis to deal with Belgian Jews as a unit. The AJB played a major role in registering Jews in the country. In total, 43,000 Jews were registered with the AJB. This number represents only half of the total Jewish population, reflecting the community's mistrust of the organization, but it was the figure that *SS-Obersturmbannführer* Adolf Eichmann presented as the total number of Jews in Belgium at the Wannsee Conference in January 1942.

During the deportations, around 10,000 Jews were arrested based on their affiliation to the AJB. The AJB, closely supervised by the *SiPo-SD* (*Sicherheitspolizei und Sicherheitsdienst*; "Security Police and Intelligence Service"), was also responsible for the administration of the transit camp at Mechelen. The AJB played a major role in persuading Jews to turn up voluntarily for deportation, though whether they knew the fate awaiting the deportees is disputed. From 1942, following the assassination by the Resistance of Robert Holzinger, an AJB leader, confidence in the association declined and it was regarded with increasing suspicion.

After the war, the leaders of the AJB were tried and acquitted of complicity in the Holocaust.

**Figure 62:** *The Belgian version of the Yellow Badge, compulsory from 1942*

## Radicalisation, 1941–42

### Antwerp Pogrom and Yellow Badge

On 14 April 1941, after watching the German propaganda film *Der Ewige Jude*, Flemish paramilitaries from the *Volksverwering*, VNV and *Algemeene-SS Vlaanderen* began a pogrom in the city of Antwerp. The mob, armed with iron bars, attacked and burned two synagogues in the city and threw the Torah scrolls onto the street. They then attacked the home of Marcus Rottenburg, the town's chief rabbi. The police and fire brigade were summoned, but they were forbidden to intervene by the German authorities.

As in the rest of occupied Europe, compulsory wearing of the yellow badge was enforced from 27 May 1942. The Belgian version of the badge depicted a black letter "J" (standing for "*Juif*" in French and "*Jood*" in Dutch) in the centre of a yellow star of David. The star had to be displayed prominently on all outer clothing when in public and there were harsh penalties for non-compliance. The decree sparked public outrage in Belgium. At great personal risk, the Belgian civil authorities in Brussels and Liège refused to distribute the badge, buying time for many Jews to go into hiding.

The German authorities in Antwerp attempted to enforce the wearing of badges in 1940, but the policy was dropped when non-Jewish citizens protested and wore the armbands themselves.

**Figure 63:** *A modern view of Dossin Barracks in Mechelen which housed Mechelen transit camp during the occupation*

## Deportation and extermination, 1942–44

From August 1942, the Germans began deporting Jews, using *Arbeitseinsatz* ("recruitment for work") in German factories as a pretext. Around half of the Jews turned up voluntarily (though coerced by the German authorities) for transportation although round-ups were begun in late July. Later in the war, the Germans increasingly relied on the police to arrest or round up Jews by force.

The first convoy from Belgium, carrying stateless Jews, left Mechelen transit camp for Auschwitz on 4 August 1942 and was soon followed by others. These trains left for extermination camps in Eastern Europe. Between October 1942 and January 1943, deportations were temporarily halted; by this time 16,600 people have been deported on 17 rail convoys. As the result of Queen Elisabeth's intervention with the German authorities, all of those deported in this first wave were not Belgian citizens. In 1943, the deportations resumed. By the time that deportations to extermination camps had begun, however, nearly 2,250 Belgian Jews had already been deported as forced laborers for *Organisation Todt*, a civil and military engineering group, which was working on the construction of the Atlantic Wall in Northern France.

In September, armed *Devisenschutzkommando* (DSK; "Currency protection command") units raided homes to seize valuables and personal belongings as the occupants were preparing to report to the transit camp, and in the same month, Jews with Belgian citizenship were deported for the first time. DSK units relied on networks of informants, who were paid between 100 and 200 Belgian francs for each person they betrayed. After the war, the collaborator Felix Lauterborn stated in his trial that 80 per cent of arrests in Antwerp used information from paid informants. In total, 6,000 Jews were deported in 1943, with another 2,700 in 1944. Transports were halted by the deteriorating situation in occupied Belgium before the liberation.

The percentages of Jews which were deported varied by location. It was highest in Antwerp, with 67 per cent deported, but lower in Brussels (37 per cent), Liège (35 per cent) and Charleroi (42 per cent). The main destination for the convoys was Auschwitz in German-occupied Poland. Smaller numbers were sent to Buchenwald and Ravensbrück concentration camps, as well as Vittel concentration camp in France.

In total, 25,437 Jews were deported from Belgium. Only 1,207 of these survived the war. Amongst those deported and killed was the surrealist artist Felix Nussbaum in 1944.

## Belgian collaboration in the Holocaust

Members of Belgian fascist political parties actively attempted to assist in the deportation of Jews. The VNV and *Algemeene-SS Vlaanderen* encouraged the deportations, while an association known as *La Défense du Peuple/Volksverwering* ("The People's Defence") was specially formed to bring together Belgian anti-Semites and to assist in the deportations. During the early stages of the occupation, they campaigned for harsher anti-Jewish laws. Both *Rex* and the VNV routinely published anti-Semitic articles in their party newspapers.

Although the Belgian civil authorities (especially the police and security service) were officially forbidden to assist the German authorities in anything other than routine maintenance of order, several incidents occurred where individual policemen or police sections assisted in the German arrest of Jews, against orders. In Antwerp, the Belgian authorities facilitated the conscription of Jews for forced labour in France in 1941 and aided in the rounding up of Jews in August 1942 after the *SiPo-SD* threatened to imprison local officials in Fort Breendonk. Outside Antwerp, the Germans used coercion to force the Belgian police to intervene, and in Brussels at least three police officers disobeyed orders and helped arrest Jews. The historian Insa Meinen argued that around a fifth of the Jews arrested in Belgium were rounded up by the Belgian police.

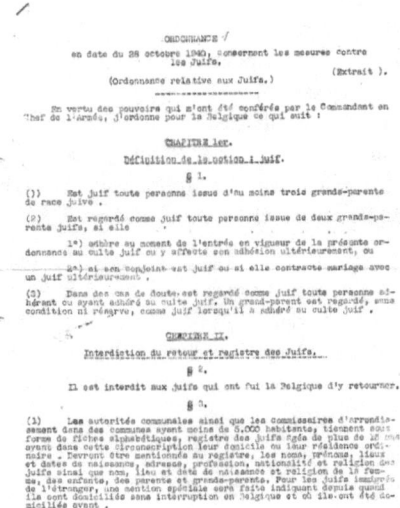

**Figure 64:** *Internal civil service circular outlining the anti-Jewish laws of October 1940*

Nevertheless, the general refusal of the Belgian police to assist in the Holocaust has been cited as a reason for the comparatively high survival rate of Belgian Jews during the Holocaust.

## Belgian opposition to Jewish persecution

Belgian resistance to the treatment of Jews crystallised between August–September 1942, following the passing of legislation regarding wearing yellow badges and the start of the deportations. When deportations began, Jewish partisans destroyed records of Jews compiled by the AJB. The first organization specifically devoted to hiding Jews, the *Comité de Défense des Juifs* (CDJ-JVD), was formed in the summer of 1942. The CDJ, a left-wing organization, may have saved up to 4,000 children and 10,000 adults by finding them safe hiding places. It produced two Yiddish language underground newspapers, *Unzer Wort* (אונזער־ווארט, "Our Word", with a Labour-Zionist stance) and *Unzer Kamf* (אונזער קאמף, "Our Fight", with a Communist one). The CDJ was only one of dozens of organised resistance groups that provided support to hidden Jews. Other groups and individual resistance members were responsible for finding hiding places and providing food and forged papers. Many Jews in hiding went on to join organised resistance groups. Groups from left wing backgrounds, like the *Front de l'Indépendance* (FI-OF), were particularly popular with Belgian Jews. The Communist-inspired *Partisans Armés* (PA) had a particularly large Jewish section in Brussels.

The resistance was responsible for the assassination of Robert Holzinger, the head of the deportation program, in 1942. Holzinger, an active collaborator, was an Austrian Jew selected by the Germans for the role. The assassination led to a change in leadership of the AJB. Five Jewish leaders, including the head of the AJB, were arrested and interned in Breendonk, but were released after public outcry. A sixth was deported directly to Auschwitz.

The Belgian resistance was unusually well informed on the fate of the deported Jews. In August 1942 (two months after the start of the Belgian deportations), the underground newspaper *De Vrijschutter* reported that "They [the deported Jews] are being killed in groups by gas, and others are killed by salvos of machinegun fire."

In early 1943, the *Front de l'Indépendance* sent Victor Martin, an academic economist at the Catholic University of Louvain, to gather information on the fate of deported Belgian Jews using the cover of his research post at the University of Cologne. Martin visited Auschwitz and witnessed the crematoria. Arrested by the Germans, he escaped, and was able to report his findings to the CDJ in May 1943.

## Attack on the 20th transport

The best-known Belgian resistance action during the Holocaust was the attack on the 20th rail convoy to Auschwitz. In the evening of 19 April 1943, three poorly armed members of the resistance attacked the railway convoy as it passed near Haacht in Flemish Brabant. The train, containing over 1,600 Jews, was guarded by 16 Germans from the *SiPo-SD*. Resistance members used a lantern covered with red paper (a danger signal) to stop the train, and freed 17 prisoners from one wagon before they were discovered by the Germans. A further 200 managed to jump from the train later in the journey, as the train's Belgian driver deliberately kept his speed low to allow others to escape. All three resistance members responsible for the attack were arrested before the end of the occupation. Youra Livchitz was executed and Jean Franklemon and Robert Maistriau were deported to concentration camps but survived the war.

The attack on the 20th train was the only attack on a Holocaust train from Belgium during the war, as well as the only transport from Belgium to experience a mass breakout.

**Figure 65:** *A cattle truck used for the transport of Belgian Jews to camps in Eastern Europe. The openings were covered in barbed wire. This example is preserved at Fort Breendonk.*

## Passive resistance

The treatment of Jews by the Germans led to public resistance in Belgium. In June 1942, the representative of the German Foreign Ministry in Brussels, Werner von Bargen, complained the Belgians did not exhibit "sufficient understanding" of Nazi racial policy.

The Belgian underground newspaper *La Libre Belgique* called for Belgian citizens to make small gestures to show their disgust at the Nazi racial policy. In August 1942, the paper called for Belgians to "Greet them [the Jews] in passing! Offer them your seat on the tram! Protest against the barbaric measures that are being applied to them. That'll make the *Boches* furious!"

Discrimination against Jews was condemned by many high-profile figures in the occupied country. As early as October 1940, the senior Catholic clergyman in Belgium, Cardinal Jozef-Ernest van Roey, condemned the German policy and particularly the legislation from 1942.

Van Roey made many of the church's resources available for hiding Jews, but was prevented from publicly condemning the treatment of the Jews by his peers, who feared a Nazi repression of the Church. German attempts to involve the Belgian authorities and local government in its implementation began to arouse protest from 1942. The Committee of Secretary-Generals, a panel of Belgian senior civil servants tasked with implementing German demands, refused from the outset to enforce anti-Jewish legislation. In June 1942, a conference of the 19 mayors of the Greater Brussels region refused to allow its officials to distribute yellow badges to Jews in their districts. At great personal risk, the mayors, led by Joseph Van De Meulebroeck, sent a letter protesting the decree to the German authorities on 5 June. The refusal of Brussels' council, and later that of the city of Liège, to distribute badges allowed many Jews to go into hiding before the deportations began.

In the same year, members of the AJB met with Queen Elisabeth to appeal for her support against the deportations. She appealed to the Military Governor of Belgium, General Alexander von Falkenhausen, who sent Eggert Reeder, his deputy and head of the non-military aspects of the administration, to Berlin to clarify the policy with *Reichsführer-SS* Heinrich Himmler. The *SS-Reichssicherheitshauptamt* (RSHA; "Reich Main Security Office") made concessions to Elisabeth, allowing Jews with Belgian citizenship to be exempt from deportation, and Jewish families would not be broken up. The RSHA also agreed not to deport Jewish men over the age of 65 and women over 60, after Belgian protests that they would be too old to be used as forced labor.

## Legacy and remembrance

In the aftermath of the war, emigration to Israel further decreased the Jewish population of Belgium, which as of 2011 was estimated at between 30,000 and 40,000. The population is still concentrated in Brussels and Antwerp, but new smaller communities (such as those in Ghent, Knokke, Waterloo and Arlon) have developed since 1945. Notable Belgian Holocaust survivors include François Englert, a joint recipient of the Nobel Prize in Physics in 2013, and Paul Lévy, a well-known journalist (who converted to Christianity) who was also responsible for the design of the European flag.

Since the passing of the Holocaust denial law in 1995, it is illegal to deny or attempt to justify the Holocaust. The act follows the Belgian Anti-Racism Law, passed in 1981, which led to the establishment of the Centre for Equal Opportunities and Opposition to Racism, which researches racism and anti-Semitism in Belgium as well as aiding victims of discrimination. Breendonk and Dossin Barracks (at the site of the former Mechelen transit camp) are preserved as museums to the Holocaust and to German repression in Belgium during the occupation.

In 2004, the Belgian Senate commissioned the Centre for Historical Research and Documentation on War and Contemporary Society (Cegesoma) to produce a definitive historical report on Belgian collaboration in the Holocaust.

**Figure 66:** *Stolperstein memorial to a victim of the Holocaust in Schaerbeek, Brussels*

The report, entitled "Docile Belgium" (*La Belgique Docile/Gewillig België*), was published in 2007. It generated significant public interest in Belgium and abroad. The report's findings were controversial, as they emphasised the extent to which the Belgian police and authorities had collaborated in the deportation of Jews.

As of 2013, a total of 1,612 Belgians have been awarded the distinction of Righteous Among the Nations by the State of Israel for risking their lives to save Jews from persecution during the occupation.

# Further reading

<templatestyles src="Template:Refbegin/styles.css" />

- Michman, Dan, ed. (1998). *Belgium and the Holocaust: Jews, Belgians, Germans* (2nd ed.). Jerusalem: Yad Vashem. ISBN 965-308-068-7.<templatestyles src="Module:Citation/CS1/styles.css"></templatestyles>
- Steinburg, Maxime (1983). *L'Étoile et le Fusil* (in French). I: La Question Juive 1940–1942. Brussels: Éd. Vie Ouvrière. ISBN 2870031777.<templatestyles src="Module:Citation/CS1/styles.css"></templatestyles>

- Steinburg, Maxime (1984). *L'Étoile et le Fusil* (in French). II: 1942. Les Cent Jours de la Déportation des Juifs de Belgique. Brussels: Éd. Vie Ouvrière. ISBN 2870031807.<templatestyles src="Module:Citation/CS1/styles.css"></templatestyles>
- Steinburg, Maxime (1987). *L'Étoile et le Fusil* (in French). III: La Traque des Juifs 1942–1944. Brussels: Éd. Vie Ouvrière. ISBN 2870032102.<templatestyles src="Module:Citation/CS1/styles.css"></templatestyles>
- Fraser, David (2009). *The Fragility of Law: Constitutional Patriotism and the Jews of Belgium, 1940–1945*. Abingdon: Routledge-Cavendish. ISBN 978-0-415-47761-1.<templatestyles src="Module:Citation/CS1/styles.css"></templatestyles>
- Schreiber, Marion (2003). *The Twentieth Train: the True Story of the Ambush of the Death Train to Auschwitz* (1st US ed.). New York: Grove Press. ISBN 978-0-8021-1766-3.<templatestyles src="Module:Citation/CS1/styles.css"></templatestyles>
- Vromen, Suzanne (2008). *Hidden Children of the Holocaust: Belgian Nuns and their Daring Rescue of Young Jews from the Nazis*. Oxford: Oxford University Press. ISBN 9780195181289.<templatestyles src="Module:Citation/CS1/styles.css"></templatestyles>

# External links

 Wikimedia Commons has media related to *The Holocaust in Belgium*.

- Belgium[495] at the European Holocaust Research Infrastructure (EHRI)
- Belgium[496] at the United States Holocaust Memorial Museum (USHMM)

<indicator name="good-star"> ⊕ </indicator>

# The Holocaust in Luxembourg

The Holocaust in Luxembourg refers to the persecution and near-annihilation of the 3,500-strong Jewish population of Luxembourg begun shortly after the start of the German occupation during World War II, when the country was officially incorporated into Nazi Germany. The persecution lasted until October 1941, when the Germans declared the territory to be free of Jews who had been deported to extermination camps and ghettos in Eastern Europe.

## History

Before the war, Luxembourg had a population of about 3,500 Jews, many of them newly arrived in the country to escape persecution in Germany. The Nuremberg Laws, which had applied in Germany since 1935, were enforced in Luxembourg from September 1940 and Jews were encouraged to leave the country for Vichy France. Emigration was forbidden in October 1941, but not before nearly 2,500 had fled. In practice they were little better off in Vichy France, and many of those who left were later deported and killed. From September 1941, all Jews in Luxembourg were forced to wear the yellow Star of David badge to identify them.

From October 1941, Nazi authorities began to deport the around 800 remaining Jews from Luxembourg to Łódź Ghetto and the concentration camps at Theresienstadt and Auschwitz. Around 700 were deported from the Transit Camp at Fuenfbrunnen in Ulflingen in the north of Luxembourg.

Luxembourg was declared "*Judenfrei*" ("cleansed of Jews") except for those in hiding on 19 October 1941. Of the original Jewish population of Luxembourg, only 36 are known to have survived the war.

## Further reading

- Artuso, Vincent (October 2012). "Des excuses, mais au nom de qui? L'administration luxembourgeoise et la Shoah". *Forum* (322): 9–11.<templatestyles src="Module:Citation/CS1/styles.css"></templatestyles>
- Cerf, Paul. *L'étoile juive au Luxembourg*. Luxembourg: Editions RTL, 1986.
- Clesse, René (1991). "Die Natur is gnädiger als die Menschen". *Ons Stad*. **36**: 22–25.<templatestyles src="Module:Citation/CS1/styles.css"></templatestyles>
- Clesse, René (2002). "Shoah in Luxemburg". *Ons Stad*. **71**: 18–19.<templatestyles src="Module:Citation/CS1/styles.css"></templatestyles>

**Figure 67:** *A Nazi parade by the Synagogue in Luxembourg in 1941. It was destroyed in 1943.*

- Hoffmann, Serge (1996). "Luxemburg - Asyl und Gastfreundschaft in einem kleinen Land". In Benz, Wolfgang; Wetzel, Juliane. *Solidarität und Hilfe für Juden während der NS-Zeit*. Regionalstudien I: Polen, Rumänien, Griechenland, Luxemburg, Norwegen, Schweiz. Berlin: Metropol-Verl. pp. 187–204. ISBN 9783926893437.<templatestyles src="Module:Citation/CS1/styles.css"></templatestyles>

# External links

 Wikimedia Commons has media related to *The Holocaust in Luxembourg*.

- Luxembourg[497] at United States Holocaust Memorial Museum (USHMM)
- Luxembourg[498] at European Holocaust Research Infrastructure (EHRI)
- Memoshoah.lu[499] at MemoShoah association

# The Holocaust in France

The Holocaust in France refers to the persecution, deportation, and annihilation of Jews and Roma between 1940 and 1944 in occupied France, metropolitan Vichy, and in Vichy-North Africa, during World War II. The persecution began in 1940, and culminated in deportations of Jews from France to concentration camps in Germany and Nazi-occupied Poland from 1942 which lasted until July 1944. Of the 340,000 Jews living in metropolitan/continental France in 1940, more than 75,000 were deported to death camps, where about 72,500 were killed. French Vichy government[500] and the French police participated in the roundup of Jews. Although most deported Jews died, the survival rate of the Jewish population in France was up to 75% which is one of the highest survival rates in Europe.[501]

## Background

In the summer of 1940, there were around 700,000 Jews living in French-ruled territory, of which 400,000 lived in French Algeria, then an integral part of France, and in the two French protectorates of Tunisia and Morocco. Metropolitan France had a population of about 150,000 Jewish nationals during the Interwar period. In addition, France hosted a large population of foreign Jews who had fled persecutions in Germany. By 1939, the Jewish population had increased to 330,000 due to the refusal of the United States and the United Kingdom to accept any more Jewish refugees following the Évian Conference. After the occupation of Belgium and the Netherlands in 1940, France hosted a new wave of Jewish immigrants and Jewish population peaked at 340,000 individuals.

At the declaration of World War II, French Jews were mobilized into the French military like their compatriots, and, like in 1914, a significant number of foreign Jews enlisted in regiments of foreign volunteers.[502] Jewish refugees from Germany were interned as enemy aliens. In general, the Jewish population of France was confident in the ability of France to defend them against the occupiers, but some, particularly from Alsace and the Moselle regions fled westwards into the unoccupied zone from July 1940.[503]

The armistice of 22 June 1940, signed between the Third Reich and the government of Marshal Philippe Pétain, did not contain any overtly anti-Jewish

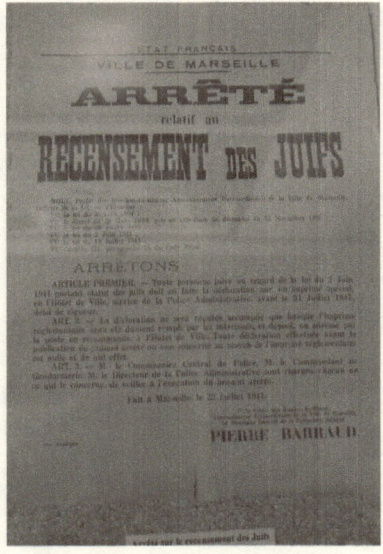

**Figure 68:** *1941 poster from Marseilles announcing the order for Jews to register*

clauses, but did indicate that the Germans intended the racial order existent in Germany since 1933 to spread to Metropolitan France and its overseas territories:

- Article 3 warned that in the regions of France occupied directly by the Germans, the French administration must "by all means facilitate the regulations" relating to the exercise of the rights of the Reich;
- Articles 16 and 19 warned that the French government had to proceed to repatriate refugees from the occupied territory and that "The French government is required to deliver on demand all German nationals designated by the Reich and who are in France, in French possessions, colonies, protectorates and territories under mandate"

Under the terms of the armistice, only part of Metropolitan France was occupied by Germany. From the city of Vichy, the government of Marshal Pétain governed a new French State (*l'État français*) in southern France and the departments of French Algeria, together with France's overseas territories such as Morocco, Tunisia, Indochina, the Levant, etc. The Vichy regime saw its empire as an integral part of non-occupied France, and its anti-Jewish decrees were immediately implemented there, because of the Vichy vision of the empire as a territorial continuation of metropolitan France

**Figure 69:** *An anti-Semitic exhibition, entitled "The Jew and France", in Paris, 1941*

# History

### From the Armistice to the invasion of the *Zone libre*

From the summer of 1940, Otto Abetz, the German ambassador in Paris, organized the expropriation of rich Jewish families.[504] The Vichy regime took the first anti-Jewish measures slightly after the German authorities in the autumn of 1940. On 3 October 1940, Vichy passed a set of anti-Jewish laws called the *Statut des Juifs* ("statute on Jews") to solve the Jewish question in areas under its control. Article 9.of the Statut stated that the law are applicable to France's possessions of French Algeria, the colonies, the Protectorates of Tunisia and Morocco, and mandates territories. The October 1940 Statut was prepared by Raphaël Alibert. According to a document made public in 2010, Pétain himself made slight moderations to the term of the law. The Jewish Statute, "embraced the definition of a Jew established in the Nuremberg Laws",[505] deprived the Jews of their civil rights, and fired them from many jobs. The *statut* also forbade Jews from working in certain professions (teachers, journalists, lawyers, etc.) while a Law of 4 October 1940 envisaged the incarceration of foreign Jews in internment camps in southern France such as the one at Gurs. These internees were joined by convoys of Jews deported

**Figure 70:** *Two Jewish women in occupied Paris wearing Yellow badges in June 1942, a few weeks before the mass arrest*

**Figure 71:** *Yellow badge made mandatory by the Nazis in France*

from regions of France, including 6,500 Jews who had been deported from Alsace-Lorraine during Operation *Bürckel*.

During Operation *Bürckel*, *Gauleiters* Josef Bürckel and Robert Heinrich Wagner oversaw the expulsion of Jews into unoccupied France from their *Gaues* and the parts of Alsace-Lorraine that had been annexed in the summer of 1941 to the *Reich*. Only those Jews in mixed marriages were not expelled. The 6,500 Jews affected by Operation *Bürckel* were given at most two hours warning on the night of 22–23 October 1940, before being rounded up. The nine trains carrying the deported Jews crossed over into France "without any warning to the French authorities", who were not happy with receiving them. The deportees had not been allowed to take any of their possessions with them, these being confiscated by the German authorities. The German Foreign Minister Joachim von Ribbentrop treated the ensuing complaints by the Vichy government over the expulsions in a "most dilatory fashion". As a result, the Jews expelled in Operation *Bürckel* were interned in harsh conditions by the Vichy authorities at the camps in Gurs, Rivesaltes and Les Milles while awaiting a chance to return them to Germany.

The *Commissariat Général aux Questions juives* ("Commissariat-General for Jewish Affairs"), created by the Vichy State in March 1941, managed the seizure of Jewish assets and organized anti-Jewish propaganda.[506] At the same time, the Germans began compiling registers of Jews in the occupied zone. The Second *Statut des Juifs* of 2 June 1941 systematized this registrations across the country and in Vichy-North Africa. Because the yellow star-of-David badge was not made compulsory in the unoccupied zone, these records would provide the basis for the future round-ups and deportations. In the occupied zone, a German order enforced the wearing of the yellow star for all Jews aged over 6 on 29 May 1942.[507]

In order to more closely control the Jewish community, on 29 November 1941, the Germans created the *Union Générale des Israélites de France* (UGIF) in which all Jewish charitable works were subsumed. The Germans were thus able to learn where the local Jews lived. Many of the leaders of the UGIF were also deported, such as René-Raoul Lambert and André Baur.[508]

# Drancy camp

The arrests of Jews in France began from 1940 for individuals, and general round ups began in 1941. The first raid (*rafle*) took place on 14 May 1941. The Jews arrested, all men and foreigners, were interned in the first transit campas at Pithiviers and Beaune-la-Rolande in the Loiret (3,747 men). The second round-up, between 20–1 August 1941, led to the arrest of 4,232 French and foreign Jews who were taken to Drancy internment camp.

**Figure 72:** *French Jews being deported from Marseilles, 1943*

Deportations began on 27 March 1942, when the first convoy left Paris for Auschwitz.[509] Women and children were also targeted, for instance during the Vel' d'Hiv Roundup on 16–17 July 1942, in which 13,000 Jews were arrested by the French police. In the occupied zone, the French police was effectively controlled by the German authorities. They carried out the measures ordered by the Germans against Jews, and in 1942, delivered non-French Jews from internment camps to the Germans.[510] They also contributed to the sending of tens of thousands from those camps to extermination camps in German occupied Poland, via Drancy.[511]

In the unoccupied zone, from August 1942, foreign Jews who had been deported to refugee camps in south-west France, in Gurs and elsewhere, were again arrested and deported to the occupied zone, from where they were sent to extermination camps in Germany and occupied Poland.

## From the invasion of the *Zone libre* to 1945

In November 1942, the whole of France came under direct German control, apart from a small sector occupied by Italy. In the Italian zone, Jews were generally spared persecution, until the fall of the Fascist regime in Italy led to the establishment of the German-controlled Italian Social Republic in northern Italy in September 1943.Wikipedia:Citation needed

The German authorities took increasing charge of the persecution of Jews, while the Vichy authorities were forced towards a more sensitive approach by public opinion. However, the Milice, a French paramilitary force inspired by Nazi ideology, was heavily involved in rounding up Jews for deportation during this period. The frequency of German convoys increased. The last, from the camp at Drancy, left the Gare de Bobigny on 31 July 1944.

In French Algeria, General Henri Giraud and later Charles de Gaulle, the French exile government restored (*de jure*) French citizenship to Jews on 20 October 1943.[512]

# Results

Of the approximately 330,000 Jews in metropolitan France in 1939, 75% survived the Holocaust, which is one of the highest survival rates in Europe. France has the third highest number of citizens who were awarded the Righteous Among the Nations, an award given to "non-Jews who acted according to the most noble principles of humanity by risking their lives to save Jews during the Holocaust".[513] About 75,000 Jews were deported to Nazi concentration camps and death camps and 72,500 of them died.

# Government admission

For decades the French government declined to apologize for the role of French policemen in the roundup or for any other state complicity. It was argued that the French Republic had been dismantled when Philippe Pétain instituted a new French State during the war and that the Republic had been re-established when the war was over. It was not for the Republic, therefore, to apologise for events that happened while it had not existed and which had been carried out by a state which it did not recognise. For example, former President François Mitterrand had maintained this position. The claim was more recently reiterated by Marine Le Pen, leader of the National Front Party, during the 2017 election campaign.[514,515]

On 16 July 1995, the President, Jacques Chirac, stated that it was time that France faced up to its past and he acknowledged the role that the state had played in the persecution of Jews and other victims of the German occupation. Those responsible for the roundup, according to Chirac, were "4500 policemen and gendarmes, French, under the authority of their leaders [who] obeyed the demands of the Nazis."

To mark the 70th anniversary of the roundup, President François Hollande gave a speech at a monument of the Vél d'Hiv roundup on 22 July 2012. The president recognized that this event was a crime committed "in France, by

France," and emphasized that the deportations in which French police participated were offenses committed against French values, principles, and ideals. He continued his speech by remarking on French tolerance towards others.[516]

In July 2017, also in commemoration of the victims of the roundup at the Vélodrome d'Hiver, President Emmanuel Macron denounced his country's role in the Holocaust and the historical revisionism that denied France's responsibility for 1942 roundup and subsequent deportation of 13,000 Jews. "It was indeed France that organised this [roundup]", he said, French police collaborating with the Nazis. "Not a single German took part," he added. Neither Chirac nor Hollande had specifically stated that the Vichy government, in power during WW II, actually represented the French State.[517] Macron on the other hand, made it clear that the Government during the War was indeed the French State. "It is convenient to see the Vichy regime as born of nothingness, returned to nothingness. Yes, it's convenient, but it is false. We cannot build pride upon a lie."[518,519]

Macron did make a subtle reference to Chirac's 1995 apology when he added, "I say it again here. It was indeed France that organized the roundup, the deportation, and thus, for almost all, death."[520,521]

# References

## Bibliography

- Berg, Roger (1947). *Crimes ennemis en France*[522] (in French). vol. V - La Persécution raciale. Paris: Service d'information des crimes de guerre - Office français d'édition.<templatestyles src="Module:Citation/CS1/styles.css"></templatestyles>
- Blumenkranz, Bernhard (1972). *Histoire des Juifs en France* (in French). Toulouse: Éditeur. OCLC 417454239[523].<templatestyles src="Module:Citation/CS1/styles.css"></templatestyles>
- Cohen, Asher (1996). *The Shoah in France*. Jerusalem: Yad Vashem.<templatestyles src="Module:Citation/CS1/styles.css"></templatestyles>
- Kaspi, André (1991). *Les Juifs pendant l'Occupation* (in French). Paris: Seuil. ISBN 978-202013509-2.<templatestyles src="Module:Citation/CS1/styles.css"></templatestyles>
- Marrus, Michael; Paxton, Robert (1995). *Vichy France and the Jews*. Stanford University Press. ISBN 0-8047-2499-7.<templatestyles src="Module:Citation/CS1/styles.css"></templatestyles>
- Philippe, Beatrice (1979). *Être juif dans la société française* (in French). Montalba. ISBN 2-8587-0017-6.<templatestyles src="Module:Citation/CS1/styles.css"></templatestyles>

- Poliakov, Léon (1966). "France. The Fate of the French Jews". *Algemeyne Entsiklopedye* (in Yiddish). New York: Shulsinger Pubs. and Dubnov Fund & Entsiklopedye Komitet.<templatestyles src="Module:Citation/CS1/styles.css"></templatestyles>.
- Poznanski, Renée (1997). *Les Juifs en France pendant la Seconde Guerre mondiale* (in French). Hachette. ISBN 978-2012352704.<templatestyles src="Module:Citation/CS1/styles.css"></templatestyles>
- Yahil, Leni (1990). *The Holocaust: The Fate of European Jewry, 1932–1945*. New York: Oxford University Press. ISBN 0195045238.<templatestyles src="Module:Citation/CS1/styles.css"></templatestyles>

## Further reading

- Carroll, David (1998). "What It Meant to Be "A Jew" in Vichy France: Xavier Vallat, State Anti-Semitism, and the Question of Assimilation". *SubStance*. **27** (3): 36–54. JSTOR 3685578[524].<templatestyles src="Module:Citation/CS1/styles.css"></templatestyles>
- Weisberg, Richard H. (1996). *Vichy law and the Holocaust in France*. Studies in Antisemitism. Amsterdam: Harwood Academic. ISBN 3718658925.<templatestyles src="Module:Citation/CS1/styles.css"></templatestyles>
- Zuccotti, Susan (1999). *The Holocaust, the French, and the Jews* (Repr. ed.). Lincoln: University of Nebraska Press. ISBN 0803299141.<templatestyles src="Module:Citation/CS1/styles.css"></templatestyles>
- Poznanski, Renée (2001). *Jews in France during World War II*. Hanover: Brandeis University Press. ISBN 978-1-58465-144-4.<templatestyles src="Module:Citation/CS1/styles.css"></templatestyles>

## External links

 Wikimedia Commons has media related to ***The Holocaust in France***.

- France[525] at the European Holocaust Research Infrastructure (EHRI)
- France[526] at the United States Holocaust Memorial Museum (USHMM)
- The Holocaust in France[527] - at Yad Vashem website
- Children's homes in France during the Holocaust[528] - an online exhibition at Yad Vashem website

# The Holocaust in Serbia

**The Holocaust in Serbia** was the Nazi genocide against Jews and Romani during World War II in the Territory of the Military Commander in Serbia[529,530]</ref> supported by the puppet government led by Milan Nedić. Serbia today includes areas outside the Military Commander of Serbia's Territory in 1941 to 1945: especially the Vojvodina then made up of the Hungarian Delvidek with its major city of Novi Sad or Ujvidek and Serbian Banat, and today it also includes an area then part of Croatia, called Srem or Syrmia. The main perpetrator of the crimes was the Nazi German *Wehrmacht* stationed in Serbia, which carried out the operations with the assistance of Dimitrije Ljotić's Serbian fascist movement Zbor and the quisling regime of Milan Nedić.[531]

## Background

Yugoslav Foreign Secretary Anton Korošec, who was Roman Catholic priest and leader of Slovenian conservatives, stated in September 1938, that "Jewish issue did not exist in Yugoslavia.... Jewish refugees from the Nazi Germany are not welcome here." In December 1938 Rabbi Isaac Alkalai, the only Jewish member of government was dismissed from the government.

On 25 March 1941, Prince Paul of Yugoslavia signed the Tripartite Pact, allying the Kingdom of Yugoslavia with the Axis powers. The Pact was extremely unpopular, particularly in Serbia and Montenegro, and demonstrations broke out. On March 27, Serb military officers overthrew Prince Paul. The new government withdrew its support for the Axis, but did not repudiate the Tripartite Pact. Nevertheless, Axis forces, led by Nazi Germany invaded Yugoslavia in April 1941.

In central Serbia the Germans occupiers established the Territory of the Military Commander in Serbia (*Gebiet des Militärbefehlshabers in Serbien*), the only area of partitioned Yugoslavia under direct German military government, with the day-to-day administration of the territory controlled by the German Chief of the Military Administration. The German Military Commander in Serbia appointed a Serbian civil puppet government to carry out administrative tasks in accordance with German direction and supervision. The police and army of the puppet government were placed under German commanders.

In July 1941, a major uprising began in Serbia against the German occupiers, which included the establishment of the Republic of Užice, the first liberated territory in World War II Europe. To assist in quelling the rebellion the Nazi occupiers in August 1941 put in place the puppet government of Milan Nedic,

**Figure 73:** *Concentration camps in Yugoslavia in World War II.*

**Figure 74:** *Jews in Belgrade in 1941.*

**Figure 75:** *A Jewish prisoner in Belgrade*

which was also given responsibility for many Holocaust-related activities, including the registration and arrest of Jews and joint control over the Banjica concentration camp in Belgrade.

## The Holocaust

On April 13, 1941, before the Yugoslav Army formally capitulated, Wilhelm Fuchs – Chief of the Einsatzgruppen based in Belgrade – ordered the registration of the city's Jews. His order stated that all those who did not register, will be shot. Shortly after, Field Commander Colonel von Keisenberg, issued a decree which limited their freedom of movement. On 29 April 1941, the Chief of the German Military Administration in Serbia, Harald Turner issued the order to register all Jews and Gypsies throughout Serbia. The order prescribed the wearing of yellow armbands, introduced forced labor and curfew, limited access to food and other provisions and banned the use of public transport.

On May 30, the German Military Commander in Serbia, Helmuth Förster, issued the main race laws - The Regulation Concerning Jews and Gypsies (*Verordnung Betreffend Die Juden Und Zigeuner*), which defined who is considered Jewish and Gypsy. The law excluded Jews and Roma from public and economic life, their property was seized, they were obliged to register in special lists (*Judenregister and Zigeunerlisten*) and for forced labor. In addition, the order prescribed the obligatory wearing of yellow tape for Jews and Roma, prohibited them from work in public institutions and professions as lawyers, doctors, dentists, veterinarians and pharmacists, as well as visits to cinemas, theaters, entertainment venues, public baths, sports fields and markets.

The destruction of Serbian Jews by the Nazis was carried out in 2 distinct phases. The first, which lasted between July and November 1941 involved the murder of Jewish men, who were shot as part of retaliatory executions carried out by German forces in response to the rising anti-Nazi, partisan insurgency in Serbia. In October 1941. the German general, Franz Böhme, ordered the execution of 100 civilians for every German soldier killed and 50 for every wounded. Böhme's order stated that hostages are to be drawn from "all Communists, people suspected of being Communists, all Jews, and a given number of nationalist and democratically minded inhabitants". Altogether some 30.000 people were executed by the Nazi's during the first 2 months of this policy, including nearly all Serbian Jewish males, as well as tens of thousands of Serbs. After executing tens of thousands of Jewish males, the Wehrmacht in Belgrade refused to kill women and children because that would be "dishonourable".[532]

The second genocidal attempt between December 1941 and May 1942 involved the incarceration of the women and children at the Semlin concentration camp and former fairgrounds in Belgrade and their gassing in a mobile gas van called a Sauerwagen. The Nazi concentration camp, the old fairgrounds or Stare Sajmište, near Zemun/Semlin was established across the Sava river from Belgrade, on the territory of the Independent State of Croatia, to process and eliminate the captured Jews, Serbs, Roma, and others. Some 7,000 to 10,000 Jews are estimated to have been exterminated by the Nazis in the Semlin concentration camp alone, along with more than 10,600 Serbs and uncounted Romani (see Sajmište concentration camp)

The SS-commander Harald Turner, Chief of the German military administration in Serbia described how the Nazis carried out the genocide of Serbian Jews:

<templatestyles src="Template:Quote/styles.css"/>

> *Already some months ago, I shot dead all the Jews I could get my hands on in this area, concentrated all the Jewish women and children in a camp and with the help of the SD (i.e. Sicherheitsdienst – Nazi Security Services) got my hands on a "delousing van," that in about 14 days to 4 weeks will have brought about the definitive clearing out of the camp...*
>
> *—Dr. Harold Turner's letter to Karl Wolff, dated April 11, 1942.*[533]

While the Nazis were exclusively responsible for attempted extermination the Jews of Serbia proper, they were assisted by local quislings in the Nedic government and others, who helped round up the Jews, Romani and Serbs who opposed the Nazi occupation. Dimitrije Ljotić, who was a leading Serbian Nazi ideologist founded a pan-Serbian, pro-Nazi and Fascist party Zbor. It was very active organization that published a large number extreme anti-Semitic literature. The military part of Zbor renowned as the Serbian Voluntary Guard acted as a reliable ally of Gestapo in elimination of Jews.

Emanuel Schäfer, commander of the Security Police and Gestapo in Serbia, convicted in Germany in 1953 for the death van killings of 6.000 Serbian Jews at Sajmiste, famously cabled Berlin after last Jews were killed in May 1942:

> *Serbien ist judenfrei.*

Similarly Harald Turner of the SS, later executed in Belgrade for his war crimes, stated in 1942 that:

> *Serbia is the only country in which the Jewish question and the Gypsy question has been solved.*

By the time Serbia and Yugoslavia were liberated in 1944, most of the Serbian Jewry had been murdered. Of the 82,500 Jews of Yugoslavia alive in 1941, only 14,000 (17%) survived the Holocaust.[534] Of the Serbian Jewish population of 16,000, the Nazis murdered approximately 14,500.[535]

Historian Christopher Browning who attended the conference on the subject of Holocaust and Serbian involvement stated:

<templatestyles src="Template:Quote/styles.css"/>

> *Serbia was the only country outside Poland and the Soviet Union where all Jewish victims were killed on the spot without deportation, and was the first country after Estonia to be declared 'Judenfrei,'" a term used by the Nazis during the Holocaust to denote an area free of all Jews.*
>
> —*Christopher Browning*

## The Holocaust in Vojvodina

Unlike Serbia proper, which was under Nazi control, control of the Serbian province of Vojvodina was divided between Hungary (Bačka/Batschka), local ethnic German Danube Swabian or Shwovish authorities ( in Banat), and the Independent State of Croatia authorities in Srem/Syrmia, all of whom helped carry out the Jewish genocide in those areas.

In January 1942 Hungarian military units under Shwovish leadership conducted a Razzia/police raid nominally against a communist insurgency. This occurred in several villages of the Vojvodina and the literature is replete with varying estimates of the number of victims. In Novi Sad alone one estimate offers a total of 600 Jews and 2,500 Serbs, ostensibly in retaliation for an act of sabotage. One expert of the Holocaust in Hungary, Ralph L. Braham estimates 3,309 victims ( 2,550 Serbs and 700 Jews). After the Germans occupied Hungary in March 1944, and then the Hungarian Arrow Cross fascists overthrew the Horthy government in October, Hungarian gendarmerie units rounded up some 16,000 Jews from the Bačka area of Vojvodina and nearby Baranja (then a part of Hungary), deported them into the custody of German police, who transported them to Auschwitz, where the majority died in the gas chambers. and to the Austrian concentration and work camp of Strasshof where 70% or so survived.[536]

Approximately 4,000 to 10,000 Jews from the Serbian Banat were deported to the German military authorities in Serbia by the local ethnic German authorities under Sepp Janko to be killed in Nazi concentration camps (Semlin and others – see Axis occupation of Vojvodina). Jews in Ustasha-controlled Syrmia, were sent to concentration camps in the Independent State of Croatia, such as Jasenovac where approximately 17,000 of a total population of 20,000 in Croatia were likewise killed.

## Role of the *Wehrmacht*

Although the *Wehrmacht*, after the war, stated that it took no part in the genocidal programmes, General Böhme and his men planned and executed the slaughter of over 20,000 Jews and Gypsies without any signal from Berlin.

## Number of victims

Of the Jewish population of 16,000 in Serbia Proper, the Nazis murdered approximately 14,500.

In the Hungarian, ethnic German (Danube Swabian and Shwovish) and Ustasha-controlled province of Vojvodina, an additional 17,000 Jews were murdered (see Axis occupation of Vojvodina)

## Help given by Serbian civilians

Serbian civilians were involved in saving thousands of Yugoslavian Jews during this period. Miriam Steiner-Aviezer, a researcher into Yugoslavian Jewry and a member of Yad Vashem's Righteous Gentiles committee states: "The Serbs saved many Jews. Contrary to their present image in the world, the Serbs are a friendly, loyal people who will not abandon their neighbors."[537] CurrentlyWikipedia:Manual of Style/Dates and numbers#Chronological items, Yad Vashem recognizes 135 Serbians as Righteous Among Nations, the highest of any Balkan country.[538]

## Restitution of properties

Serbia is the first country in Europe which adopted a law for restitution of properties of Jewish heirless victims of Holocaust. According to this law, besides this restitution, Serbia will make 950,000 EUR annual payment from its budget to the Union of Jewish Municipalities starting from 2017. The World Jewish Restitution Organization (WJRO) praised adoption of this law while its chair of operations invited other countries to follow Serbias example. The Embassy of Israel in Serbia issued a release welcoming the adoption of this law and emphasizing that Serbia should be an example for other countries in Europe. The release of Embassy of Israel concluded: "The new law is a noble act of a great country that will breathe new life into the small Jewish community that it is today."

## Serbian historiography

During the 1990s, the role Nedić and Ljotić played in the extermination of Serbia's Jews was downplayed by a number of Serbian historians. In 1993, the Serbian Academy of Sciences and Arts listed Nedić among *The 100 most prominent Serbs*.

Following the breakup of Yugoslavia, local councillors in Smederevo campaigned to have the town's largest square named after Ljotić. The councillors defended Ljotić's wartime record and justified the initiative by stating that "[collaboration] ... is what the biological survival of the Serbian people demanded" during World War II.[539] Later, the Serbian magazine *Pogledi* published a series of articles attempting to exonerate Ljotić.[540] In 1996, future Yugoslav President Vojislav Koštunica praised Ljotić in a public statement.[541] Koštunica and his Democratic Party of Serbia (*Demokratska stranka Srbije*, DSS) actively campaigned to rehabilitate figures such as Ljotić and Nedić following the overthrow of Slobodan Milošević and his socialist government in October 2000.[541]

# References

## Bibliography

- Hehn, Paul N. (1971). "Serbia, Croatia and Germany 1941–1945: Civil War and Revolution in the Balkans"[542]. *Canadian Slavonic Papers*. University of Alberta. **13** (4): 344–373. Retrieved 8 April 2012.<templatestyles src="Module:Citation/CS1/styles.css"></templatestyles>
- Pavlowitch, Stevan K. (2002). *Serbia: the History behind the Name*[543]. London: C. Hurst & Co. Publishers. ISBN 978-1-85065-476-6.<templatestyles src="Module:Citation/CS1/styles.css"></templatestyles>

## External links

 Wikimedia Commons has media related to *The Holocaust in Serbia*.

- Holokaust u Srbiji[544]
- Against serbian chetnik revisionism[545]
- Browning, Christopher R. (1983). «The Final Solution in Serbia; The Semlin Judenlager — A Case study». Yad Vashem Studies 15: pp. 55–90.[546]

# The Holocaust in the Independent State of Croatia

**The Holocaust in the Independent State of Croatia** refers primarily to the genocide of Jews, but sometimes also include that of Serbs (the "Serbian Genocide") and Romani (*Porajmos*), during World War II within the Independent State of Croatia, a fascist puppet state ruled by the Ustashe regime, that included most of the territory of modern-day Croatia, the whole of modern-day Bosnia and Herzegovina and the eastern part of Syrmia (Serbia). 90% of Croatian Jews were exterminated in Ustashe-run concentration camps like Jasenovac and others, while a considerable number of Jews were rounded up and turned over by the Ustashe for extermination in Nazi Germany.

**Figure 76:** *Concentration camps in the Independent State of Croatia on a map of all camps in Yugoslavia in World War II.*

# Background

On 25 March 1941, Prince Paul of Yugoslavia signed the Tripartite Pact, allying the Kingdom of Yugoslavia with the Axis powers. Prince Paul was overthrown, and a new anti-German government under Peter II and Dušan Simović took power. The new government withdrew its support for the Axis, but did not repudiate the Tripartite Pact. Nevertheless, Axis forces, led by Nazi Germany invaded Yugoslavia in April 1941.

The Independent State of Croatia was proclaimed by the Ustaše - a Croatian fascist, racist, ultra-nationalist and terrorist organization - on 10 April 1941. Within the new state lived approximately 40,000 Jews, only 9,000 of whom would ultimately survive the war.[547]

Already prior to the war the Ustaše forged close ties to fascist Italy and Nazi Germany. In 1933 the Ustaše presented "The Seventeen Principles", which proclaimed the uniqueness of the Croatian nation, promoted collective rights over individual rights, and declared that people who were not Croat by race and blood, would be excluded from political life. In 1936, the Ustaše leader, Ante Pavelić, wrote in "The Croat Question":

*'Today, practically all finance and nearly all commerce in Croatia is in Jewish hands. This became possible only through the support of the state, which*

**Figure 77:** *A Jewish prisoner is forced to remove his ring upon arrival in the Jasenovac concentration camp.*

*thereby seeks, on one hand, to strengthen the pro-Serbian Jews, and on the other, to weaken Croat national strength. The Jews celebrated the establishment of the so-called Yugoslav state with great joy, because a national Croatia could never be as useful to them as a multi-national Yugoslavia; for in national chaos lies the power of the Jews... In fact, as the Jews had foreseen, Yugoslavia became, in consequence of the corruption of official life in Serbia, a true Eldorado of Jewry...The entire press in Croatia is also in Jewish-masonic hands..."*[548]

# The Holocaust

## Anti-Semitic legislation and start of persecution

The main race laws in the Independent State of Croatia were adopted and signed by the Ustaše leader Ante Pavelić on 30 April 1941: the "Legal Decree on Racial Origins" (*Zakonska odredba o rasnoj pripadnosti*) and the "Legal Decree on the Protection of Aryan Blood and the Honour of the Croatian People" (*Zakonska odredba o zaštiti arijske krvi i časti hrvatskog naroda*).[549] The "Legal Decree on the Nationalization of the Property of Jews and Jewish Companies" was declared on 10 October 1941.

**Figure 78:** *Ustaše executing people over a mass grave near Jasenovac.*

Actions against Jews began immediately after the Independent State of Croatia was founded. On 10–11 April 1941 a group of prominent Jews in Zagreb was arrested by the Ustaše and held for ransom. On 13 April the same was done in Osijek, where Ustaše and Volksdeutscher mobs destroyed the synagogue and Jewish graveyard. This procedure was repeated in 1941 and 1942 several times with groups of Jews.

## Anti-Semitic propaganda

The Ustaše immediately initiated intensive anti-Semitic propaganda. A day after the signing of the main race laws on 30 April 1941, the newspaper of the Ustaše movement, *Hrvatski narod (Croatian Nation)*, published across its entire front page: "The Blood and Honor of the Croatian people protected by special provisions".[550]

Two days later, the newspaper *Novi list* concluded that Croatians must "be more alert than any other ethnic group to protect their racial purity, ... We need to keep our blood clean of the Jews". The newspaper also wrote that Jews are synonymous with "treachery, cheating, greed, immorality and foreigness", and therefore "wide swaths of the Croatian people always despised the Jews and felt towards them natural revulsion". *Nova Hrvatska* (New Croatia) added that according to the Talmud, "this toxic. hot well-spring of Jewish wickedness and malice, the Jew is even free to kill Gentiles".

One of the main claims of Ustaše propaganda was that the Jews have always been against an independent Croatian state and against the Croatian people. In April 1941 the newspaper *Hrvatski narod* (The Croatian People) accused Jews of being responsible for the "many failures and misfortunes of so many

Croatian people", which led the Poglavnik [the Ustaše leader Ante Pavelic] to "eradicate these evils". A *Spremnost* article stated that the Ustaša movement defines "Judaism as one of the greatest enemies of the people".

Some in the Catholic Church joined the anti-Semitic propaganda. Thus the Catholic Bishop of Sarajevo, Ivan Šarić, published in his diocesan newspaper that "the movement to free the world of Jews, represents the movement for the restoration of human dignity. Omniscient and omnipotent God is behind this movement ".[551] And in July 1941, the Franciscan priest, Dionysius Juričev, in *Novi list* wrote that "it is no longer a sin to kill a seven year-old child".[552]

## Ustaše concentration camps

Already in April 1941 the Ustaše established the concentration camps Danica (near Koprivnica), Kruščica concentration camp near Travnik and Kerestinec, where along with communists and other political opponents, the Ustaše imprisoned Jews.

In May 1941, the Ustaše rounded up 165 Jewish youth in Zagreb, ages 17–25, most of them members of the Jewish sports club Makabi, and sent them to the Danica concentration camp (all but 3 were killed by the Ustaše).

In May and June the Ustaše established new camps, primarily for Jews who came to Croatia as refugees from Germany and countries which Germany had previously occupied, and some of these were quickly killed. Also arrested and sent to the Ustaše camps were larger groups of Jews from Zagreb (June 22), Bihac (June 24), Karlovac (June 27), Sarajevo, Varaždin, Bjelovar, etc.Wikipedia:Citation needed

On 8 July 1941 the Ustaše ordered that all arrested Jews be sent to Gospić, from where they took the victims to death camps Jadovno on Velebit, and Slano on the island of Pag, where they carried out mass executions. The historian Paul Mojzes lists 1,998 Jews, 38,010 Serbs, and 88 Croats killed at Jadovno and related execution grounds,[553] among them 1,000 children.

Other sources generally offer a range of 10,000–68,000 deaths at the Jadovno system of camps, with estimates of the number of Jewish deaths ranging from several hundred[553] to 2,500–2,800.[554]

In August 1941 the Ustaše established the Jasenovac concentration camp, one of the largest in Europe.[555] This included the Stara Gradiška concentration camp for women and children. The United States Holocaust Memorial Museum (USHMM) in Washington, D.C. presently estimates that the Ustaša regime murdered between 77,000 and 99,000 people in Jasenovac system of camps between 1941 and 1945. The Jasenovac Memorial Site quotes a similar figure of between 80,000 and 100,000 victims.[556] Of these, the United States Holocaust Museum says that at least 20.000 were Jews.

The Jasenovac Memorial site lists the individual names of 83,145 victims, including 13,116 Jews, 16,173 Roma, 47,627 Serbs, 4,255 Croats, 1,128 Bosnian Muslims, etc. Of the total 83,145 named Jasenovac victims, 20,101 were children under the age of 12, and 23,474 were women.

## Other events

The destruction of the Sephardi Il Kal Grande synagogue in Sarajevo was carried out by Nazi German soldiers and their local Ustaše allies soon after their arrival in the city on 15 April.[557] The Sarajevo Haggadah was the most important artifact which survived this period, smuggled out of Sarajevo and saved from the Nazis and Ustaše by the chief librarian of the National Museum, Derviš Korkut. The demolition of the Zagreb Synagogue was ordered by the Ustaše mayor Ivan Werner and was carried out from 10 October 1941 to April 1942. The two Jewish football clubs in the state, ŽGiŠK Makabi Zagreb and ŽŠK Makabi Osijek, were banned in 1941.[558]

In April 1942, the Jews of Osijek were forced to build a "Jewish settlement" at Tenja, into which they were herded along with Jews from the surrounding region. Approximately 3,000 Jews were moved to Tenja in June and July 1942. From Tenja, 200 Jews were transported to the Jasenovac concentration camp and 2,800 Jews were transported to the Auschwitz concentration camp.

In February 1942 the Ustaše Interior Minister, Andrija Artuković, in a speech to the Croatian Parliament declared that:

> "The Independent State of Croatia through its decisive action has solved the so-called Jewish question ... This necessary cleansing procedure finds its justification not only from a moral, religious and social point of view, but also from the national-political point of view: it is international Jewry associated with international communism and Freemasonry, that sought and still seeks to destroy the Croatian people". The speech was accompanied by shouts of approval -" yes! - from the parliamentary benches.

On 5 May 1943, Nazi SS leader Heinrich Himmler paid a short visit to Zagreb in which he held talks with Ante Pavelić.[559] Starting on 7 May, a roundup of the remaining Jews in Zagreb was carried out by the Gestapo under the command of Franz Abromeit.[560] During this period, Archbishop Stepinac offered the head rabbi in Zagreb Miroslav Šalom Freiberger help to escape the roundup, which he ultimately declined.[561] The operation lasted for the following week, and resulted in the capture of 1,700 Jews from Zagreb and 300 from the surrounding area. All of these people were taken to the Auschwitz concentration camp.[562]

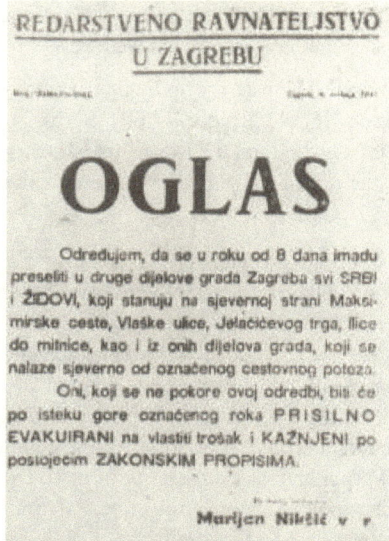

**Figure 79:** *Order for Serbs and Jews to move out of their homes in specified parts of Zagreb to other parts of the city, Croatia and a warning of forcible expulsion and punishment of those that failed to comply.*

After the capitulation of Italy on 8 September 1943, Nazi Germany annexed the Croat-populated Italian provinces of Pula and Rijeka into its Operational Zone Adriatic Coast. On 25 January 1944, the Germans demolished the Jewish synagogue in Rijeka. The region of Međimurje had been annexed by the Kingdom of Hungary in 1941. In April 1944, the Jews of Međimurje were taken to a camp in Nagykanizsa where they were held until their transport to Auschwitz. An estimated 540 Međimurje Jews were murdered at Auschwitz, while 29 were murdered at Jasenovac.[563]

# Other ethnicities

## Serbs

Many historians describe the Ustasha regime's mass killings of Serbs as meeting the definition of genocide.[564] Some racist laws, brought from Germany, in addition to Jews and Roma, were applied to the Serbs. Vladimir Žerjavić estimates that 322,000 Serbs were killed in the Independent State of Croatia, out of a total population of 1.8 million Serbs. Thus one in six Serbs were killed, which represents the highest percentage killed in Europe, after the Jews and Roma. Of these Žerjavić estimates that about 78,000 Serbs were killed at Jasenovac and other Ustasha camps. According to the United States Holocaust Memorial Museum[565] in Washington, D.C., between 320,000 and 340,000 Serbs were killed in the NDH.

### Roma

The Ustasha regime launched the persecution of the Roma in May 1942. Whole families were arrested and transported to the Jasenovac concentration camp, where they were immediately, or within a few months, killed. Estimates of the number of victims vary from 16,000 (this figure is given Vladimir Žerjavić) to 40,000. The Jasenovac Memorial[566] at Jasenovac, Croatia lists the names of 16,173 Roma killed at that concentration camp. Due to their way of life, many more victims are probably unrecorded. The German historian Alexander Korb[567] and the United States Holocaust Memorial Museum[565] in Washington, D.C., both estimate at least 25,000 casualties among the Roma, which represents nearly the total Roma population in the Independent State of Croatia.

## Abolition of racial laws

On 5 May 1945, the *Legal Decree on the Equalization of Members of the NDH Based on Racial Origin* (Zakonska odredba o izjednačavanju pripadnika NDH s obzirom na rasnu pripadnost) was declared which repealed the racial laws enacted over the course of the war.Wikipedia:Citation needed

## Number of victims

| Part of a series on |
|---|
| **Genocide** |
| Issues |
| • Cultural genocide |
| • Democide |
| • Ethnic cleansing |
| • Ethnic relations |
| • Ethnocide |
| • Genocide |
| • Genocidal rape |
| • Utilitarian genocide |
| • Double genocide <br>    • Holocaust uniqueness debate <br>    • Rwandan genocide |

| |
|---|
| **Genocide of indigenous peoples** |
| European colonization of the Americas |

- Dzungar genocide, 1750s
- Manifest Destiny
  - Indian Removal, 1830s
  - California Genocide, 1848–1873
- Circassian genocide, 1860s
- Selk'nam genocide, 1890s–1900s
- Herero and Namaqua genocide, 1904–1907
- Greek genocide, 1914–1923
- Assyrian genocide, 1914–1925
- Armenian Genocide, 1915–1923
- Libyan Genocide, 1923–1932

| |
|---|
| **Soviet genocide** |
| Ethnic cleansing in the Soviet Union |

- Soviet famine of 1932–33
  - Holodomor, 1931–1933
  - Kazakhstan, 1930–1933
- Mass Deportations during World War II
  - Kalmyks, 1943
  - Chechens and Ingush, 1944
  - Crimean Tatars, 1944

| |
|---|
| **Nazi Holocaust and genocide (1941–1945)** |

- Final Solution
- Porajmos
- Nazi crimes against ethnic Poles
- Nazi crimes against Soviet POWs
- Serbian genocide

| |
|---|
| **Cold War** |

- Indonesian genocide (1965–1966)
- 1971 Bangladesh genocide (1971)
- Burundian genocides (1972 & 1993)
- East Timorese genocide (1974–1999)
- Cambodian genocide (1975–1979)
- Guatemalan genocide (1981–1983)
- Kurdish genocide (1986–1989)
- Isaaq genocide (1988–1989)

| |
|---|
| **Contemporary genocide** |

- Rwandan genocide (1994)
- Bosnian genocide (1992–1995)
  - Srebrenica massacre (1995)
- Darfur genocide (2003–)
- Genocides by ISIS (2014–)
  - Yazidi genocide
  - Shia genocide
  - Christian genocide
- Central African genocide
- Rohingya genocide (2017–)

| |
|---|
| **Related topics** |

# The Holocaust in the Independent State of Croatia 203

- Genocides in history
- Khmer Rouge Killing Fields
- Hutu Power
- Holodomor genocide question
- Extermination camp
- Effects of genocide on youth
- List by death toll
- Mass killings under Communist regimes
- Rohingya people
- Anti-communist mass killings
- Mass killings compilation

**Category**

- v
- t
- e[568]

**The United States Holocaust Memorial Museum** lists the following number of victims in the Independent State of Croatia:

- 32,000 Jews, with 12,000 to 20,000 Jews killed at the Jasenovac system of camps
- At least 25,000 Roma, or virtually the entire Roma population in the Independent State of Croatia
- Between 320,000 and 340,000 Serbs, most killed by the Ustasha authorities

Slavko Goldstein estimates that approximately 30,000 Jews were killed from the Independent State of Croatia, with approximately 12,790 of those killed in Croatia. Vladimir Žerjavić's demographics research produced an estimate of 25,800 to 26,700 Jewish victims, of which he estimates that 19,000 were killed by the Ustasha in Croatia and Bosnia, and the rest abroad.

## By site

The Jasenovac Memorial Site maintains the names of 13,116 Jews killed at the Jasenovac concentration camp.

# Concentration camps

- Jadovno concentration camp
- Jasenovac concentration camp
- Sisak children's concentration camp
- Stara Gradiška concentration camp
- Lobor concentration camp

- Sajmište concentration camp (run by German forces in Serbia)
- Tenja concentration camp

## Notable people

### Victims

- Lea Deutsch, Croatian Jewish child actress
- Kalmi Baruh, Bosnian Jewish scholar
- Laura Papo Bohoreta, Bosnian Jewish feminist writer and Ladino scholar
- Sava Šumanović, Serb painter

### Survivors

- Amiel Shomrony
- Branko Lustig
- Esther Gitman
- Isak Samokovlija

### Other

- Diana Budisavljević

## Righteous among the Nations

Over one hundred Croatians have been recognized as Righteous among the Nations. They include Žarko Dolinar and Mate Ujević.

## Sources

<templatestyles src="Template:Refbegin/styles.css" />

- Bartulin, Nevenko (2008). "The Ideology of Nation and Race: The Croatian Ustasha Regime and its Policies toward the Serbs in the Independent State of Croatia 1941-1945"[569]. *Croatian Studies Review*. **5**: 75–102.<templatestyles src="Module:Citation/CS1/styles.css"></templatestyles>
- Bulajić, Milan (1992). *Tudjman's "Jasenovac Myth": Ustasha Crimes of Genocide*[570]. Belgrade: The Ministry of information of the Republic of Serbia.<templatestyles src="Module:Citation/CS1/styles.css"></templatestyles>
- Bulajić, Milan (1994). *Tudjman's "Jasenovac Myth": Genocide against Serbs, Jews and Gypsies*[571]. Belgrade: Stručna knjiga.<templatestyles src="Module:Citation/CS1/styles.css"></templatestyles>

- Bulajić, Milan (1994). *The Role of the Vatican in the break-up of the Yugoslav State: The Mission of the Vatican in the Independent State of Croatia*[572]. Ustashi Crimes of Genocide. Belgrade: Stručna knjiga.
- Bulajić, Milan (2002). *Jasenovac: The Jewish-Serbian Holocaust (the role of the Vatican) in Nazi-Ustasha Croatia (1941-1945)*[573]. Belgrade: Fund for Genocide Research, Stručna knjiga.
- Cvetković, Dragan (2011). "Holokaust u Nezavisnoj Državi Hrvatskoj - numeričko određenje"[574] (PDF). *Istorija 20. veka: Časopis Instituta za savremenu istoriju.* **29** (1): 163–182.
- Dedijer, Vladimir (1992). *The Yugoslav Auschwitz and the Vatican: The Croatian Massacre of the Serbs During World War II*[575]. Amherst: Prometheus Books. ISBN 9780879757526.
- Hory, Ladislaus; Broszat, Martin (1964). *Der kroatische Ustascha-Staat1941-1945*[576]. Stuttgart: Deutsche Verlags-Anstalt.
- Kolstø, Pål (2011). "The Serbian-Croatian Controversy over Jasenovac". *Serbia and the Serbs in World War Two*[577]. Palgrave Macmillan UK. pp. 225–246. ISBN 9780230347816.
- Korb, Alexander (2010). "A Multipronged Attack: Ustaša Persecution of Serbs, Jews, and Roma in Wartime Croatia". *Eradicating Differences: The Treatment of Minorities in Nazi-Dominated Europe*[578]. Newcastle upon Tyne: Cambridge Scholars Publishing. pp. 145–163. ISBN 9781443824491.
- Levy, Michele Frucht (2011). "'The Last Bullet for the Last Serb': The Ustaša Genocide against Serbs: 1941–1945". *Crimes of State Past and Present: Government-Sponsored Atrocities and International Legal Responses*[579]. Routledge. pp. 54–84. ISBN 9781317986829.
- Lituchy, Barry M., ed. (2006). *Jasenovac and the Holocaust in Yugoslavia: Analyses and Survivor Testimonies*[580]. New York: Jasenovac Research Institute. ISBN 9780975343203.
- McCormick, Robert B. (2014). *Croatia Under Ante Pavelić: America, the Ustaše and Croatian Genocide*[581]. London-New York: I.B. Tauris.

- Mojzes, Paul (2008). "The Genocidal Twentieth Century in the Balkans". *Confronting Genocide: Judaism, Christianity, Islam*[582]. Lanham: Lexington Books. pp. 151–182.
- Mojzes, Paul (2011). *Balkan Genocides: Holocaust and Ethnic Cleansing in the 20th Century*[583]. Lanham: Rowman & Littlefield.
- Novak, Viktor (2011). *Magnum Crimen: Half a Century of Clericalism in Croatia*[584]. **1**. Jagodina: Gambit.
- Novak, Viktor (2011). *Magnum Crimen: Half a Century of Clericalism in Croatia*[585]. **2**. Jagodina: Gambit.
- Paris, Edmond (1961). *Genocide in Satellite Croatia, 1941-1945: A Record of Racial and Religious Persecutions and Massacres*[586]. Chicago: American Institute for Balkan Affairs.
- Pavlowitch, Stevan K. (2008). *Hitler's New Disorder: The Second World War in Yugoslavia*[587]. New York: Columbia University Press.
- Phayer, Michael (2000). *The Catholic Church and the Holocaust, 1930–1965*[588]. Bloomington and Indianapolis: Indiana University Press.
- Phayer, Michael (2008). *Pius XII, the Holocaust, and the Cold War*[589]. Bloomington and Indianapolis: Indiana University Press.
- Rivelli, Marco Aurelio (1998). *Le génocide occulté: État Indépendant de Croatie 1941–1945*[590] [*Hidden Genocide: The Independent State of Croatia 1941–1945*] (in French). Lausanne: L'age d'Homme.
- Rivelli, Marco Aurelio (1999). *L'arcivescovo del genocidio: Monsignor Stepinac, il Vaticano e la dittatura ustascia in Croazia, 1941-1945*[591] [*The Archbishop of Genocide: Monsignor Stepinac, the Vatican and the Ustaše dictatorship in Croatia, 1941-1945*] (in Italian). Milano: Kaos.
- Rivelli, Marco Aurelio (2002). *"Dio è con noi!": La Chiesa di Pio XII complice del nazifascismo*[592] [*"God is with us!": The Church of Pius XII

*accomplice to Nazi Fascism*] (in Italian). Milano: Kaos.<templatestyles src="Module:Citation/CS1/styles.css"></templatestyles>
- Tomasevich, Jozo (2001). *War and Revolution in Yugoslavia, 1941–1945: Occupation and Collaboration*[593]. Stanford: Stanford University Press.<templatestyles src="Module:Citation/CS1/styles.css"></templatestyles>
- Yeomans, Rory (2013). *Visions of Annihilation: The Ustasha Regime and the Cultural Politics of Fascism, 1941-1945*[594]. Pittsburgh: University of Pittsburgh Press.<templatestyles src="Module:Citation/CS1/styles.css"></templatestyles>

## External links

 Wikimedia Commons has media related to *The Holocaust in Croatia*.

- Holocaust Era in Croatia[595] at the United States Holocaust Memorial Museum

# Jews of Libya during the Holocaust

Conditions worsened for the Jews of Libya after the passage of Italy's Manifesto of Race in 1938. Following the German intervention in 1941, some of the Jews of Libya were sent to camps in continental Europe, where those who survived stayed until the end of World War II.

Italian Libya had two large Jewish communities, one in the western district of Tripolitania, and mainly in its capital Tripoli, and the other in the eastern district of Barka (Cyrenaica) and its capital Benghazi. During the Holocaust hundreds of Jews died of starvation. With approximately 40,000 Jews living in Libya before the war, as a result of the later Jewish exodus from Arab and Muslim countries, there are no Jews left in the country today.

**Figure 80:** *A 1940 "imperial Italia" map of Libya under Italian control*

## Background: the beginning of the Italian occupation

In July 1911 the Italian government demanded control of Libya from the Ottoman Empire. When the demand was not met, Italy declared war and quickly conquered the main cities along the coast of Libya. Some of the Jews of Libya supported Italy, and some actively contributed to the war effort. One of the reasons behind the support of Italy and a regime change began with the Italian influence on Libya through commercial and cultural ties. Other causes were the recurring pogroms the Jews suffered from at the hands of their Muslim neighbors; the wave of anti-Semitism that spread through the Ottoman Empire during the mid-19th century did not pass over the Jews of Libya. The autonomy that they received from the empire didn't prevent the recurring pogroms.

After the Italian conquest, the Jews received official status and were an important religious-ethnic group due to their key role in the Libyan economy. The studying of the Italian language and European country,Wikipedia:Please clarify which began before the conquest, became more common. The Italian government, which at first saw the Jews as Italians—just like the Italian Jews—began to consider them as indigenous Muslims.Wikipedia:Please clarify In 1934, after the fascists' rise to power, Italo Balbo was appointed as the governor-general of Italian Libya. He developed the "Italian colony" and, like many fascists, saw it as symbol of Italy's returning to the greatness of the Roman Empire—the last time that Italy controlled Libya. During his term in office, the process of modernizing Jewish communities accelerated, and Jews took part in government establishments. Balbo respected the Jewish tradition so long as it did not prevent the progress he brought to Libya. One instance of conflict occurred when Jews closed their shops on the Sabbath, even outside the Jewish community. Balbo sentenced the Jews to be punished by flogging, but later, in October 1937, he admitted at a gathering of the Fascist Party that he had been mistaken and that he did not distinguish between Catholics and Jews - they were all Italian. Earlier that year, Benito Mussolini came to the Jewish community during a visit to Italian Libya and received a warm reception. He promised that the Jews of Libya would be safe and that Italy would respect the Jewish community and their traditions, religion and leadership.

# During the Holocaust

Part of a series on
## The Holocaust

Jews on selection ramp at Auschwitz, May 1944

- v
- t
- e[596]

## Worsening status of the Jews

Italy's aggressive policies led to its isolation within Europe, and to a pact with Nazi Germany in 1936. The Rome-Berlin axis forced the countries to operate based on common principles, so the German race laws applied to Italy and its colonies. In the racial manifesto, which was published in Italy in 1938, racist and anti-semitic laws appeared as representing the Italian Fascist Party's position. The main laws were:

- Jews with foreign citizenship were banned from leaving the country- Wikipedia:Please clarify
- Jewish students were banned from high schools and higher education establishments
- Any Jew with a government position was to be fired
- All Jewish soldiers in the Italian army were to be demoted.
- Jews were forbidden from participating in government bids.

Italian Libya's governor, Balbo, tried to convince Mussolini to postpone the application of the laws in Libya, claiming that they would destroy the Libyan economy. Mussolini allowed Balbo to apply the laws as he saw fit. Despite the relative protection that the Jews enjoyed under Balbo, Jewish government workers were fired, Jewish children were expelled from schools, and Jews wishing to move between cities required a license. Balbo was killed in July 1940, when an Italian ship shot down his airplane. Italian officials explained the incident as an accident.

In the second half of 1940, after Italy joined World War II on the side of Germany, the Jews' situation worsened. Tripoli was in chaos, and the Jewish quarter in Italy Wikipedia:Please clarify was heavily damaged by Allied bombings, leaving many Jews dead. Some Jews, like the Muslim population, escaped inland. The Jewish community in Tripoli rented homes for the needy, constructed underground bomb shelters and supplied education for the children who were expelled.

As time went by, the race laws became worse - the Jews of Cyrenaica were sent to a concentration camp in Tripolitania, and most of the community's workforce was sent to labor camps. Jews who were citizens of enemy countries were expelled from the country, and the rest suffered from racist and oppressive laws that hurt them socially and economically. In mid-1942, the governor decreed that Jews were forbidden to enter into real estate deals or commerce outside the community, to publish any material that did not relate to religion, and subject to other oppressive laws.

## The Jews of Cyrenaica under regime changes

The accelerated application of the Race Laws caused the Jews to lose trust in the Italian government and led them to support the British instead. When Britain first conquered Cyrenaica in December 1940, the Jews were freed from the race laws. They did not hide their support of the conquering army, especially due to the meetings between the community and the Jewish soldiers who joined the war as part of the unit of Jewish soldiers.Wikipedia:Please clarify The soldiers met with the Benghazi community many times, renewed Zionist activities, and supported educational activity. On April 3, 1941, the Italian-German forces managed to push the British forces out of Benghazi, and 250 Jews left with them. The Italian citizens who lived in the city during the British control held a grudge towards the Jews, and conducted pogroms during which two Jews were killed, and a great deal of property was pillaged and damaged. When order was restored and anti-Semitism began to increase , the Italian government arrested many Jews on charge of assisting enemy forces.

In November of that year, Britain reconquered Cyrenaica. The unit of JewishWikipedia:Please clarify soldiers tried to support the community, but in February 1942 the Italian-German army returned, and only a small number of Jews managed to escape with the retreating British army. Italy decided to expel all the Jews to Tripolitania and imposed harsh punishments on the remaining Jews, including the death penalty for three of them. During the last British conquest of Cyrenaica in November 1942, the remaining 360 Jews were deterred from contacting the British army for fear of another regime change. The Jewish Wikipedia:Please clarify soldiers were an important part of the rehabilitation of the community's remains. The blow to the Jewish community was the worst of any Libyan community. Over 500 Jews were killed, out of a community of 4,000. The lives of the survivors were in danger. Close to 2,600 Jews were sent to the Giado concentration camp; some families were sent to other camps. About 200 British citizens were transferred to Italy and some 250 French citizens to Tunisia.

## Giado concentration camp

The majority of the Jewish community in Cyrenaica was sent to the Giado concentration camp, approximately 240 km (150 mi) south of Tripoli. The prosperous urban community of 2,600 people was crammed into booths in an old military camp that had been converted into a concentration camp. The health and sanitation conditions were terrible, and many of the Jews suffered from malnutrition. The camp was run by Italian officers, headed by the anti-Semitic Ettore Bastico, who supplied the detainees with just 100-150 grams of bread a day, in addition to a small weekly allocation of food. The Jews were in charge of distributing this insufficient food supply. After many rejections of the requests by Jewish leaders to increase the food allowance, the camp officers permitted Arab merchants to sell basic food supplies to the Jews, which they did for a high price - one that few could afford. After further requests, they were allowed to receive aid from Tripoli.

Rabbi Frigia Zuaretz requested permission to set up a synagogue in the camp, and was allocated one of the booths. With the first death in the community, the community leaders needed to make burial arrangements. They found a Jewish cemetery from the 18th century where they were able to bury their dead - in numbers that grew daily, mainly due to malnutrition and the spread of typhus.

In January 1943, a few days before the Allies liberated the camp, all the prisoners were called to the plaza and brought before armed soldiers, and it was believed that the order to shoot would come at any moment.Wikipedia:Citation needed The order wasn't carried out. After a few days, the camp's officers retreated and some of the prisoners escaped. When the British arrived, they found the Jews in an unstable and disorganized state. In March of that year, the British military Rabbi Orbach visited, and received permission to send 60 Jews to Palestine. The camp survivors were sent at first to Tripoli, where they became a burden on the local community, until October 1943 when most of the survivors moved to Benghazi. The community never returned to its previous prosperity, and few managed to return to economic stability. Close to 600 out of the 2600 Jewish residents of the Benghazi camp perished.

## Forced labor

In June 1942, Italian Libya's governor decreed that the legal status of Libyan and Italian men was the same, which meant that men aged 18-45 were drafted into military service. Men from Tripolitania county were sent to work in Sidi Azaz and Bukbuk. In August, 3,000 Jews were sent to the Sidi Azaz labor camp but, due to the lack of infrastructure, most were sent back to their homes, to serve the country and to work camps in Cyrenaica. The Jews were a substantial work force that the community was lacking.

The camp was isolated and desert-like, with few Italian guards and tents. It was an open camp, which allowed the rich to purchase food which they sometimes shared with others. After a while, residents of Tripoli traveled out to meet their family members. The camp residents started their day at 6:00 am with roll call and it ended at 5:00 pm. They received 500 grams of bread, rice, or pasta as food. Unprecedented consideration was shown when the Italian guards allowed the prisoners to rest on the Sabbath. There was one violent incident, when a prisoner argued with an Italian guard as was shot dead as a result. The guard was transferred and the Jews learned to stay out of arguments with the guards.

**Figure 81:** *Jewish Holocaust survivors return to Libya from Concentration Camp Bergen-Belsen*

The Bukbuk camp was set up in East Cyrenaica, on the Egyptian border. The prisoners were tasked with paving roads from Libya to Egypt for the army's purposes. The camp was so remote that there were no guards or fences. There was a lack of water, for a supply arrived only every few days. The work day was officially from 7:00 am to 5:00 pm, but the lack of supervision allowed the prisoners to work at a leisurely pace and, despite the complaints of the Italian supervisor who came every few days, the camp was short of guards. The camp did have an Italian doctor who ignored the mostly invented diseases and injuries of the prisoners, which allowed them to claim they were not suited for work and be released. In October 1942, Bukbuk was the target of multiple bombings, and only in November, with the retreat of Italian forces, were the prisoners released and allowed to find their own way back to Tripoli, most of them with the aid of passing vehicles.

## Expulsion of Jews with foreign citizenship

German soldiers entered Italian Libya in 1941 after the Italian army was defeated in Cyrenaica, but German influence was felt starting in 1938. Due to the involvement and importance that the foreign Jews had in economy and commerce, they were treated normally, and the Italian government wasn't quick to apply the racial laws and expel the foreign Jews. Yet, there were incidents of German soldiers harassing Jews. After Italy joined the war in June 1940 the Jews' conditions worsened, and in September all the citizens of enemy countries were put in detention camps, in decent conditions. They were all expelled during the second half of 1941, mainly due to the fact that the detention camps became an economic burden. Many of those expelled had lived in Libya their whole lives, holding a second citizenship for convenience only. Approximately 1,600 Jews with French citizenship were expelled to Tunisia. Over 400 with British citizenship were sent to Italy. Those expelled from Benghazi were allowed to take valuables and were sent to a detention camp in Bologna, while those leaving Tripoli were allowed only personal items, and sent mainly to camps in Siena and Firenze. Living conditions were tight but they were treated well by the guards. In September 1943, Italy fell under German control, and in October Jewish men were sent from Arzo camp, east of Siena, to forced labor. Between February and May 1944, the expellees from Tripoli and some from Benghazi were sent to Bergen-Belsen camp, while most of the Benghazi expellees were sent to Innsbruck-Reichenau camp.

The food supply in Bergen Belsen was terrible, working conditions were very hard and prisoners were abused and harassed by SS soldiers.

The Innsbruck-Reichenau camp was located in western Austria and was an offshoot of the Dachau camp. It was surrounded by an electric fence, there was separation between men and women and the inmates were all forced to work. Unlike the other prisoners, the Jews of Libya were allowed to stay in their civilian clothes. The SS guards were cruel to the Jews- they were banned from any religious expression or worship, and punishment such as flogging, imprisonment and death by shooting were common.

Beyond the known horrors of the Holocaust, the Jews of Libya were a foreign element in frigid Europe, which made survival much harder. Beyond the different climate, the cultural difference was a major obstacle. In both camps the Jews of Libya made an effort to observe Jewish dietary restrictions despite the hardships, and traded their cooked meals for bread. Many of the Jews of Libya perished in the camp, mainly elderly people who couldn't withstand the hunger, torture and disease.

## Aftermath

According to Maurice Roumani, a Libyan emigrant who was previously the Executive Director of WOJAC,[597] the most important factors which influenced the Libyan Jewish community to emigrate were "the scars left from the last years of the Italian occupation and the entry of the British Military in 1943 accompanied by the Jewish Palestinian soldiers".[598]

Following the allied victory at the Battle of El Agheila in December 1942, German and Italian troops were driven out of Libya. The British installed the

Palestine Regiment in Cyrenaica, which later became the core of the Jewish Brigade which was later also stationed in Tripolitania. The pro-Zionist soldiers encouraged the spread of Zionism throughout the local Jewish population[599,600,601]

In 1943, Mossad LeAliyah Bet began to send emissaries to prepare the infrastructure for the emigration of the Libyan Jewish community.[602]

The most severe post-World War II anti-Jewish violence in Arab countries was in Tripolitania (North-West Libya), then a British-military-controlled state, in November 1945. Over a period of several days more than 130 Jews (including 36 children) were killed, hundreds were injured, 4,000 were left homeless (displaced) and 2,400 were reduced to poverty. Five synagogues in Tripoli and four in provincial towns were destroyed, and over 1,000 Jewish residences and commercial buildings were plundered in Tripoli alone.[603] Further riots took place in Tripolitania in June 1948, when 15 Jews were killed and 280 Jewish homes destroyed.[604] In November 1948, a few months after the events in Tripolitania, the American consul in Tripoli Orray Taft Jr. reported that: "There is reason to believe that the Jewish Community has become more aggressive as the result of the Jewish victories in Palestine. There is also reason to believe that the community here is receiving instructions and guidance from the State of Israel. Whether or not the change in attitude is the result of instructions or a progressive aggressiveness is hard to determine. Even with the aggressiveness or perhaps because of it, both Jewish and Arab leaders inform me that the inter-racial relations are better now than they have been for several years and that understanding, tolerance and cooperation are present at any top level meeting between the leaders of the two communities."[605,606]

Emigration to Israel began in 1949, following the establishment of a Jewish Agency office in Tripoli. According to Harvey E. Goldberg, "a number of Libyan Jews" believe that the Jewish Agency was behind the riots, given that the riots helped them achieve their goal.[607] Between the establishment of the State of Israel in 1948 and Libyan independence in December 1951 over 30,000 Libyan Jews emigrated to Israel.

Soon, the Jewish community of Libya ceased to exist, with most of its members emigrating to Israel and other countries, mainly Italy.

# Further reading

- Renzo De Felice (1985). *Jews in an Arab land: Libya, 1835-1970*[608]. University of Texas Press.<templatestyles src="Module:Citation/CS1/styles.css"></templatestyles>

- *The Jews of Arab Lands: A History and Source Book*[609]. Jewish Publication Society. 1979. ISBN 978-0-8276-0370-7.<templatestyles src="Module:Citation/CS1/styles.css"></templatestyles>
- Ariel, Ari (2013), *Jewish-Muslim Relations and Migration from Yemen to Palestine in the Late Nineteenth and Twentieth Centuries*[610], BRILL, ISBN 9789004265370<templatestyles src="Module:Citation/CS1/styles.css"></templatestyles>
- Fischbach, Michael R. (2008), *Claiming Jewish Communal Property in Iraq*[611], Middle East Report, retrieved 2010-04-05<templatestyles src="Module:Citation/CS1/styles.css"></templatestyles>
- Stillman, Norman (2003). *Jews of Arab Lands in Modern Times*. Jewish Publication Society, Philadelphia. <templatestyles src="Module:Citation/CS1/styles.css" />ISBN 0-8276-0370-3
- Goldberg, Harvey E. (1990), *Jewish Life in Muslim Libya: Rivals and Relatives*[612], University of Chicago Press, ISBN 9780226300924<templatestyles src="Module:Citation/CS1/styles.css"></templatestyles>
- Roumani, Maurice (2009), *The Jews of Libya: Coexistence, Persecution, Resettlement*, Sussex Academic Press, ISBN 9781845193676<templatestyles src="Module:Citation/CS1/styles.css"></templatestyles>

# External links

- Blog on Jewish refugees[613]
- Libyan Jews to get Holocaust benefits[614] on Jpost
- Holocaust Survivor Testimonies: Libya[615] on YouTube
- Jewish History In Libya - Brief Biography[616]
- Personal experiences of survivor Benjamin Doron from Benghazi, Libya[617] on Yad Vashem

# Concentration and labor camps

## Nazi concentration camps

<indicator name="pp-default"> 🔒 </indicator>

**Nazi concentration camps**

U.S. Army soldiers show the German civilians of Weimar the corpses found in Buchenwald Concentration Camp

| | Main concentration camps across Europe |
|---|---|
| Excluding listing of SS sub-camps and transit camps | • Auschwitz-Birkenau<br>• Belzec<br>• Bergen-Belsen<br>• Buchenwald<br>• Chelmno<br>• Dachau<br>• Ebensee<br>• Flossenbürg<br>• Gross-Rosen<br>• Janowska<br>• Kaiserwald<br>• Majdanek<br>• Mauthausen-Gusen<br>• Natzweiler-Struthof<br>• Neuengamme<br>• Nordhausen (Dora-Mittelbau)<br>• Sachsenhausen (Oranienburg)<br>• Plaszow<br>• Ravensbrück<br>• Sobibor<br>• Stutthof<br>• Terezin (Theresienstadt)<br>• Treblinka<br>• Westerbork |

Nazi Germany maintained concentration camps (German: *Konzentrationslager*, KZ or KL) throughout the territories it controlled before and during the Second World War. The first Nazi camps were erected in Germany in March 1933 immediately after Hitler became Chancellor and his Nazi Party was given control of the police by Reich Interior Minister Wilhelm Frick and Prussian Acting Interior Minister Hermann Göring.[618] Used to hold and torture political opponents and union organizers, the camps initially held around 45,000 prisoners.[619]

Heinrich Himmler's *Schutzstaffel* (SS) took full control of the police and the concentration camps throughout Germany in 1934–35.[620] Himmler expanded the role of the camps to hold so-called "racially undesirable elements", such as Jews, Romanis, Serbs, Poles, disabled people, and criminals.[621,622,623] The number of people in the camps, which had fallen to 7,500, grew again to 21,000 by the start of World War II[624] and peaked at 715,000 in January 1945.[625]

The concentration camps were administered since 1934 by the Concentration Camps Inspectorate (CCI) which in 1942 was merged into *SS-Wirtschafts-Verwaltungshauptamt* and they were guarded by *SS-Totenkopfverbände* (SS-TV).

Holocaust scholars draw a distinction between *concentration* camps (described in this article) and extermination camps, which were established by Nazi Germany for the industrial-scale mass murder of Jews in the ghettos by way of gas chambers.

**Figure 82:** *The Dachau concentration camp was created for the purpose of holding political opponents. In time for Christmas of 1933, roughly 600 of the inmates were released as part of a pardoning action. The picture above depicts a speech by camp commander Theodor Eicke to prisoners who were about to be released.*

## Pre-war camps

Use of the word "concentration" came from the idea of confining people in one place because they belong to a group that is considered undesirable in some way. The term itself originated in 1897 when the "reconcentration camps" were set up in Cuba by General Valeriano Weyler. In the past, the U.S. government had used concentration camps against Native Americans and the British had also used them during the Second Boer War. Between 1904 and 1908, the *Schutztruppe* of the Imperial German Army operated concentration camps in German South-West Africa (now Namibia) as part of its genocide of the Herero and Namaqua peoples. The Shark Island Concentration Camp in Lüderitz was the largest camp and the one with the harshest conditions.

When the Nazis came to power in Germany, they quickly moved to suppress all real and potential opposition. The general public was intimidated by the arbitrary psychological terror that was used by the special courts (*Sondergerichte*). Especially during the first years of their existence when these courts "had a strong deterrent effect" against any form of political protest.

The first camp in Germany, Dachau, was founded in March 1933. The press announcement said that "the first concentration camp is to be opened

**Figure 83:** *Reichsführer-SS Heinrich Himmler inspecting Dachau concentration camp on 8 May 1936.*

in Dachau with an accommodation for 5,000 people. All Communists and – where necessary – Reichsbanner and Social Democratic functionaries who endanger state security are to be concentrated there, as in the long run it is not possible to keep individual functionaries in the state prisons without overburdening these prisons." Dachau was the first regular concentration camp established by the German coalition government of National Socialist Workers' Party (Nazi Party) and the Nationalist People's Party (dissolved on 6 July 1933). Heinrich Himmler, then Chief of Police of Munich, officially described the camp as "the first concentration camp for political prisoners."

On 26 June 1933, Himmler appointed Theodor Eicke commandant of Dachau, who in 1934 was also appointed the first Inspector of Concentration Camps (CCI). In addition, the remaining SA-run camps were taken over by the SS.[626,627,628] Dachau served as both a prototype and a model for the other Nazi concentration camps. Almost every community in Germany had members who were taken there. The newspapers continuously reported on "the removal of the enemies of the Reich to concentration camps" making the general population more aware of their presence. There were jingles warning as early as 1935: "Dear God, make me dumb, that I may not come to Dachau."

Between 1933 and the fall of Nazi Germany in 1945, more than 3.5 million Germans were forced to spend time in concentration camps and prisons for political reasons, and approximately 77,000 Germans were executed for one

**Figure 84:** *Jewish prisoners are issued food on a building site at Salaspils concentration camp, Latvia, in 1941.*

or another form of resistance by Special Courts, courts-martial, and the civil justice system. Many of these Germans had served in government, the military, or in civil positions, which enabled them to engage in subversion and conspiracy against the Nazis.

As a result of the Holocaust, the term "concentration camp" carries many of the connotations of "extermination camp" and is sometimes used synonymously. Because of these ominous connotations, the term "concentration camp", originally itself a euphemism, has been replaced by newer terms such as internment camp, resettlement camp, detention facility, etc., regardless of the actual circumstances of the camp, which can vary a great deal.

# World War II

After September 1939, with the beginning of the Second World War, concentration camps became places where millions of ordinary people were enslaved as part of the war effort, often starved, tortured and killed. During the war, new Nazi concentration camps for "undesirables" spread throughout the continent. According to statistics by the German Ministry of Justice, about 1,200 camps and subcamps were run in countries occupied by Nazi Germany, while the Jewish Virtual Library estimates that the number of Nazi camps was closer to 15,000 in all of occupied Europe and that many of these camps were run for a limited amount of time before they were closed. Camps were being created near the centers of dense populations, often focusing on areas with large communities of Jews, Polish intelligentsia, Communists or Romani. Since millions of Jews lived in pre-war Poland, most camps were located in the area of the General Government in occupied Poland, for logistical reasons. The location also allowed the Nazis to quickly remove the German Jews from within Germany proper.

By 1940, the CCI came under the control of the *Verwaltung und Wirtschaftshauptamt Hauptamt* (VuWHA; Administration and Business office) which was set up under Oswald Pohl.[629] Then in 1942, the CCI became *Amt D* (Office D) of the consolidated main office known as the *SS-Wirtschafts-Verwaltungshauptamt* (SS Economic and Administrative Department; WVHA) under Pohl.[629] In 1942, the SS built a network of extermination camps to systematically kill millions of prisoners by gassing. The extermination camps (*Vernichtungslager*) and death camps (*Todeslager*) were camps whose primary function was genocide. The Nazis themselves distinguished the concentration camps from the extermination camps. The British intelligence service had information about the concentration camps, and in 1942 Jan Karski delivered a thorough eyewitness account to the government.

## Internees

The two largest groups of prisoners in the camps, both numbering in the millions, were the Polish Jews and the Soviet prisoners of war (POWs) held without trial or judicial process. There were also large numbers of Romani people, ethnic Poles, Serbs, political prisoners, homosexuals, people with disabilities, Jehovah's Witnesses, Catholic clergy, Eastern European intellectuals and others (including common criminals, as the Nazis declared). In addition, a small number of Western Allied aviators were sent to concentration camps as punishment for spying. Western Allied POWs who were Jews, or who were suspected of being Jews by the Nazis, were usually sent to ordinary POW camps; however, a small number of them were sent to concentration camps because of antisemitic policies.

Sometimes the concentration camps were used to hold important prisoners, such as the generals involved in the attempted assassination of Hitler; U-boat Captain-turned-Lutheran pastor Martin Niemöller; and Admiral Wilhelm Canaris, who was interned at Flossenbürg on February 7, 1945, until he was hanged on April 9, shortly before the war's end.

In most camps, prisoners were forced to wear identifying overalls with colored badges according to their categorization: red triangles for Communists and other political prisoners, green triangles for common criminals, pink triangles

**Figure 85:** *American soldiers view a pile of corpses found in the newly liberated Buchenwald concentration camp in April 1945*

for homosexual men, purple triangles for Jehovah's Witnesses, black triangles for asocials and the "work shy", yellow triangle for Jews, and later the brown triangle for Romanis.

## Treatment

Many of the prisoners died in the concentration camps due to deliberate maltreatment, disease, starvation, and overwork, or they were executed as unfit for labor. Prisoners were transported in inhumane conditions by rail freight cars, in which many died before reaching their final destination. The prisoners were confined in the boxcars for days or even weeks, with little or no food or water. Many died of dehydration in the intense heat of summer or froze to death in winter. Concentration camps also existed in Germany itself, and while they were not specifically designed for systematic extermination, many of their inmates perished because of harsh conditions or they were executed.

In the spring of 1941, the SS—along with doctors and officials of the T-4 Euthanasia Program—introduced the Action 14f13 programme meant for extermination of selected concentration camp prisoners. The Inspectorate of the Concentration Camps categorized all files dealing with the death of prisoners as 14f, and those of prisoners sent to the T-4 gas chambers as 14f13.

**Figure 86:** *A mass grave inside Bergen-Belsen concentration camp*

Under the language regulations of the SS, selected prisoners were designated for "special treatment (German: *Sonderbehandlung*) 14f13". Prisoners were officially selected based on their medical condition; namely, those permanently unfit for labor due to illness. Unofficially, racial and eugenic criteria were used: Jews, the handicapped, and those with criminal or antisocial records were selected.:p.144 For Jewish prisoners there was not even the pretense of a medical examination: the arrest record was listed as a physician's "diagnosis".:pp. 147–148 In early 1943, as the need for labor increased and the gas chambers at Auschwitz became operational, Heinrich Himmler ordered the end of Action 14f13.:p.150

After 1942, many small subcamps were set up near factories to provide forced labor. IG Farben established a synthetic rubber plant in 1942 at Monowitz concentration camp (Auschwitz III); other camps were set up next to airplane factories, coal mines and rocket propellant plants. Conditions were brutal and prisoners were often sent to the gas chambers or killed on site if they did not work quickly enough.

On 31 July 1941 Hermann Göring gave written authorization to SS-*Obergruppenführer* Reinhard Heydrich, Chief of the Reich Main Security Office (RSHA), to prepare and submit a plan for a "total solution of the Jewish question" in territories under German control and to coordinate the participation of all involved government organisations.[630] The resulting *Generalplan Ost* (General Plan for the East) called for deporting the population of occupied

**Figure 87:** *Commander-in-Chief of all Allied Forces, General Dwight D. Eisenhower, witnesses the corpses found at Ohrdruf concentration camp in May 1945.*

Eastern Europe and the Soviet Union to Siberia, for use as slave labour or to be murdered.[631]

Towards the end of the war, the camps became sites for medical experiments. Eugenics experiments, freezing prisoners to determine how downed pilots were affected by exposure, and experimental and lethal medicines were all tried at various camps. A cold water immersion experiments at Dachau concentration camp were performed by Sigmund Rascher.

## Total number of camps and casualties

The lead editors of the *Encyclopedia of Camps and Ghettos, 1933–1945* of the United States Holocaust Memorial Museum, Geoffrey Megargee and Martin Dean, cataloged some 42,500 Nazi ghettos and camps throughout Europe, spanning German-controlled areas from France to Russia and Germany itself, operating from 1933 to 1945. They estimate that 15 million to 20 million people died or were imprisoned in the sites.[632]

Some of the most notorious slave labour camps included a network of subcamps. Gross-Rosen had 100 subcamps, Auschwitz had 44 subcamps,[633] Stutthof had 40 sub-camps set up contingently. Prisoners in these subcamps were

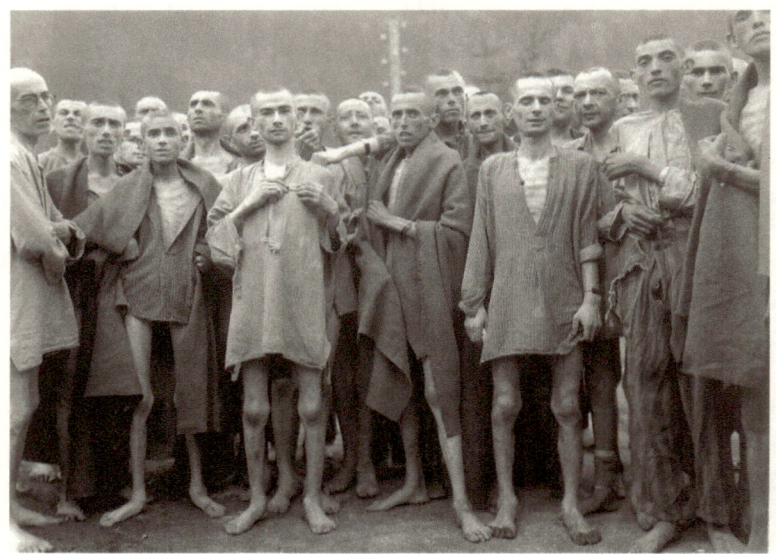

**Figure 88:** *Starving prisoners in Ebensee concentration camp, part of the Mauthausen concentration camp liberated on May 5, 1945*

dying from starvation, untreated disease and summary executions by the tens of thousands already since the beginning of war.[634]

## Liberation

The camps were liberated by the Allied forces between 1944 and 1945. The first major camp, Majdanek, was discovered by the advancing Soviets on July 23, 1944. Auschwitz was liberated, also by the Soviets, on January 27, 1945; Buchenwald by the Americans on April 11; Bergen-Belsen by the British on April 15; Dachau by the Americans on April 29; Ravensbrück by the Soviets on the same day; Mauthausen by the Americans on May 5; and Theresienstadt by the Soviets on May 8. Treblinka, Sobibór, and Bełżec were never liberated, but were destroyed by the Nazis in 1943. Colonel William W. Quinn of the U.S. 7th Army said of Dachau: "There our troops found sights, sounds, and stenches horrible beyond belief, cruelties so enormous as to be incomprehensible to the normal mind."

In most of the camps discovered by the Soviets, almost all the prisoners had already been removed, leaving only a few thousand alive—7,000 inmates were found in Auschwitz, including 180 children who had been experimented on by doctors. Some 60,000 prisoners were discovered at Bergen-Belsen by the

**Figure 89:** *The main German camps and extermination centers, 1943–44*

British 11th Armoured Division, 13,000 corpses lay unburied, and another 10,000 died from typhus or malnutrition over the following weeks. The British forced the remaining SS guards to gather up the corpses and place them in mass graves.

## Types of camps

The Nazi concentration camps have been divided by historians into several major categories based on purpose, administrative structure, and inmate population profile. The system of camps preceded the onset of World War II by several years and was developed gradually.

1. Early camps, usually without proper infrastructure, sprang up everywhere in Germany when the Nazi reached power in 1933: rising "like mushrooms after the rain", Himmler recollected.[635] These early camps, called also "Wild camps" because some were set up with little supervision from higher authorities, were overseen by Nazi paramilitaries, political police forces, and sometimes local police authority utilizing any lockable larger space, e.g. engine rooms, brewery floors, storage facilities, cellars, etc.[636]
2. State camps (e.g. Dachau, Oranienburg, Esterwegen) guarded by the SA; prototypes for future SS concentration camps, with a total of 107,000 prisoners already in 1935.[637]

3. Hostage camps (*Geisellager*), known also as police prison camps (e.g. Sint-Michielsgestel, Haaren) where hostages were held and later killed in reprisal actions.
4. Labor camps (*Arbeitslager*): concentration camps where interned captives had to perform hard physical labor under inhumane conditions and cruel treatment. Some of these were sub-camps, called "Outer Camps" (*Aussenlager*), built around a larger central camp (*Stammlager*), or served as "operational camps" established for a temporary need.
5. POW camps (*Kriegsgefangenen-Mannschafts-Stammlager / Stalag*) a.k.a. Main Camps for Enlisted Prisoners of War: concentration camps where enlisted prisoners-of-war were held after capture. They were usually assigned soon to nearby labor camps (*Arbeitskommandos*), i.e. the Work Details. POW officers had their own camps (*Offizierslager / Oflag*). Stalags were for Army prisoners, but specialized camps (*Marinelager / Marlag* ("Navy camps") and *Marineinterniertenlager / Milag* ("Merchant Marine Internment Camps")) existed for the other services. *Kriegsgefangenen-Mannschafts-Stammlager Luftwaffe / Stalag Luft* ("Air Forces Camps") were the only camps that detained both officers and non-commissioned personnel together.
6. Camps for the so-called "rehabilitation and re-education of Poles" (*Arbeitserziehungslager* - "Work Instruction Camps"): camps where the intelligentsia of the ethnic Poles were held, and "re-educated" according to Nazi values as slaves.
7. Collection and Transit camps: camps where inmates were collected (*Sammellager*) or temporarily held (*Durchgangslager / Dulag*) and then routed to main camps.
8. Extermination camps (*Vernichtungslager*): These camps differed from the rest, since not all of them were also concentration camps. Although none of the categories are independent, many camps could be classified as a mixture of several of the above. All camps had some of the elements of an extermination camp, but systematic extermination of new arrivals by gas chambers only occurred in specialized camps. These were extermination camps, where all new-arrivals were simply killed—the "Aktion Reinhard" camps (Treblinka, Sobibór and Belzec), together with Chelmno. Two others (Auschwitz and Majdanek) were combined concentration and extermination camps. Others like Maly Trostenets were at times classified as "minor extermination camps".

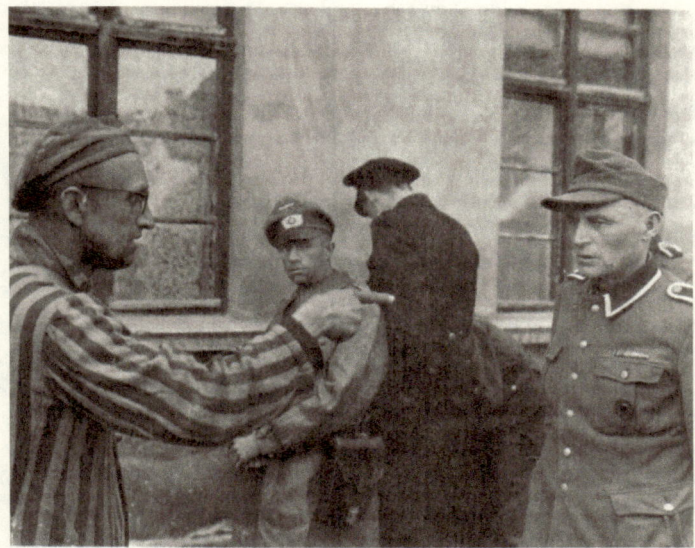

**Figure 90:** *A concentration camp victim identifies an SS guard in June 1945*

## Post-war use

Though most Nazi concentration and extermination camps were destroyed after the war, some of them were turned into permanent memorials. In Communist Poland, some camps such as Majdanek, Jaworzno, Potulice and Zgoda were used by the Soviet NKVD to hold German prisoners of war, suspected or confirmed Nazis and Nazi collaborators, anti-Communists and other political prisoners, as well as civilian members of the German-speaking, Silesian and Ukrainian ethnic minorities. Currently, there are memorials to the victims of both Nazi and communist camps at Potulice; they have helped to enable a German-Polish discussion on historical perceptions of World War II. In East Germany, the concentration camps at Buchenwald and Sachsenhausen were used for similar purposes. Dachau concentration camp was used as a detention centre for the arrested Nazis.

## Bibliography

- Browning, Christopher R. (2004). *The Origins of the Final Solution : The Evolution of Nazi Jewish Policy, September 1939 – March 1942*. Comprehensive History of the Holocaust. Lincoln: University of Nebraska Press. ISBN 0-8032-1327-1.<templatestyles src="Module:Citation/CS1/styles.css"></templatestyles>

- Evans, Richard J. (2003). *The Coming of the Third Reich*. Penguin Group. ISBN 978-0-14-303469-8.<templatestyles src="Module:Citation/CS1/styles.css"></templatestyles>
- Evans, Richard J. (2005). *The Third Reich in Power*. New York: Penguin Group. ISBN 978-0-14-303790-3.<templatestyles src="Module:Citation/CS1/styles.css"></templatestyles>
- Evans, Richard J. (2008). *The Third Reich at War*. New York: Penguin Group. ISBN 978-0-14-311671-4.<templatestyles src="Module:Citation/CS1/styles.css"></templatestyles>
- Kershaw, Ian (2008). *Hitler: A Biography*. W. W. Norton & Company. ISBN 978-0-393-06757-6.<templatestyles src="Module:Citation/CS1/styles.css"></templatestyles>
- McNab, Chris (2009). *The SS: 1923–1945*. London: Amber Books. ISBN 978-1-906626-49-5.<templatestyles src="Module:Citation/CS1/styles.css"></templatestyles>
- Snyder, Timothy (2010). *Bloodlands: Europe between Hitler and Stalin*. New York: Basic Books. ISBN 978-0-465-00239-9.<templatestyles src="Module:Citation/CS1/styles.css"></templatestyles>
- Wachsmann, Nikolaus (2015). *KL: A History of the Nazi Concentration Camps*[638]. Macmillan. ISBN 978-142994372-7.<templatestyles src="Module:Citation/CS1/styles.css"></templatestyles>
- Weale, Adrian (2012). *Army of Evil: A History of the SS*. New York: Caliber Printing. ISBN 978-0-451-23791-0.<templatestyles src="Module:Citation/CS1/styles.css"></templatestyles>

# Further reading

- Megargee, Geoffrey P., ed. (2012). *Encyclopedia of Camps and Ghettos, 1933–1945*. in association with United States Holocaust Memorial Museum. Bloomington: Indiana University Press. ISBN 978-0-253-35599-7.<templatestyles src="Module:Citation/CS1/styles.css"></templatestyles>

## External links

 Wikimedia Commons has media related to *Nazi concentration camps*.

- Nazi Concentration Camps newsreel[639] on YouTube
- The World of the Camps: Labor and Concentration Camps[640] on the Yad Vashem website
- Pages show pictures and videos of the day taken at places connected with World War II (Second World War)[641]
- Yad VaShem—The Holocaust Martyrs' and Heroes' Remembrance Authority[642]
- United States Holocaust Memorial Museum Personal Histories – Camps[643] at United States Holocaust Memorial Museum
- The Holocaust History Project[644]
- Official U.S. National Archive Footage of Nazi camps[645]
- Concentration Camps[646] at Jewish Virtual Library
- *Memory of the Camps*[647], as shown by PBS Frontline
- Podcast with one of 2,000 Danish policemen in Buchenwald[648]
- Nazi Concentration Camp Page with links to original documents[649]

# List of Nazi concentration camps

This article presents a partial list of the most prominent **Nazi German concentration camps and extermination camps set up across Europe** before and during the course of World War II and the Holocaust. A more complete list drawn up in 1967 by the German Ministry of Justice names about 1,200 camps and subcamps in countries occupied by Germany,[650] while the Jewish Virtual Library writes: "It is estimated that the Germans established 15,000 camps in the occupied countries."[651] Some of the data presented in this table originates from the monograph titled *The War Against the Jews* by Lucy Dawidowicz among similar others.[652]

In 1933–1939, before the onset of war, most prisoners consisted of German Communists, Socialists, Social Democrats, Roma, Jehovah's Witnesses, homosexuals, and persons accused of 'asocial' or socially 'deviant' behavior by the Germans.[653] They were not utilized to sustain the German war effort.

Although the term 'concentration camp' is often used as a general term for all German camps during World War II, there were in fact several types of concentration camps in the German camp system. Holocaust scholars make a clear distinction between death camps and concentration camps which served

**Figure 91:** *The main gate into Auschwitz II (Birkenau) concentration camp, where an estimated 1.1 million people were killed.*

a number of war related purposes including prison facilities, labor camps, prisoner of war camps, and transit camps among others.[654]

Concentration camps served primarily as detention and slave labor exploitation centers. An estimated 15 to 20 million people were imprisoned in 42,500 camps and ghettos, and often pressed into slavery during the subsequent years, according to research by the United States Holocaust Memorial Museum conducted more recently. The system of about 20,000 concentration camps in Germany and German-occupied Europe played a pivotal role in economically sustaining the German reign of terror. Most of them were destroyed by the Germans in an attempt to hide the evidence of war crimes and crimes against humanity; nevertheless tens of thousands of prisoners sent on death marches were liberated by the Allies afterward.

Extermination camps were designed and built exclusively to kill prisoners on a massive scale, often immediately upon arrival. The extermination camps of Operation Reinhard such as Bełżec, Sobibór and Treblinka served as "death factories" in which German SS and police murdered nearly 2,700,000 Jews by asphyxiation with poison gas, shooting, and extreme work under starvation conditions.[655,656]

List of Nazi concentration camps

The concentration camps held large groups of prisoners without trial or judicial process. In modern historiography, the term refers to a place of systemic mistreatment, starvation, forced labour and murder.

## Selected examples

Statistical and numerical data presented in the table below originates from a wide variety of publications and therefore does not constitute a representative sample of the total.

The Ghettos in German-occupied Europe are generally not included in this list. Relevant information can be found at the separate List of Nazi-era ghettos.

Extermination camps

Concentration camps

Labor camps

Main camps, including collection points

| # | Camp name | Country (today) | Camp type | Dates of use | Est. prisoners | Est. deaths | Sub-camps | Web-page |
|---|---|---|---|---|---|---|---|---|
| 1 | Alderney | United Kingdom | Labour camps | Jan 1942 – Jun 1944 | 6,000 | 700 | Lager Borkum, Lager Helgoland, Lager Norderney, Lager Sylt | 657 |
| 2 | Amersfoort | Netherlands | Transit camp and prison | Aug 1941 – Apr 1945 | 35,000 | 1,000 | | 658 |
| 3 | Arbeitsdorf | Germany | Labour camp | 8 Apr 1942 – 11 Oct 1942 | | 600 min. | none | |
| 4 | Auschwitz-Birkenau | Poland | Extermination and labour camp | Apr 1940 – Jan 1945 | 135,000 min.[659] in August 1944 | 1,100,000 min.[659] with 400,000 recorded arrivals | list of **48** sub-camps with description at the Auschwitz-Birkenau State Museum [659] | |
| 5 | Banjica | Serbia | Concentration camp | Jun 1941 – Sep 1944 | 23,637 | 3,849[660] | | |
| 6 | Bardufoss | Norway | Concentration camp | Mar 1944 – ???? | 800 | 250 | | |

| # | Name | Country | Type | Dates | | | | |
|---|---|---|---|---|---|---|---|---|
| 7 | Bełżec | Poland | Extermination camp | Oct 1941 – Jun 1943 | | 434,508 min. | | 661 |
| 8 | Bergen-Belsen | Germany | Concentration camp | Apr 1943 – Apr 1945 | 120,000 | 52,000 | 2 | 662 |
| 9 | Berlin-Marzahn | Germany | Early a "rest place" then labour camp for Roma | July 1936 – ???? | | | none | 663 |
| 10 | Bernburg | Germany | Collection point | Apr 1942 – Apr 1945 | | 14,385 | 2 | |
| 11 | Bogdanovka | Ukraine | Concentration camp | 1941 | 54,000 | 40,000 | | |
| 12 | Bolzano | Italy | Transit camp | Jul 1944 – Apr 1945 | 11,116 | | | |
| 13 | Bor | Serbia | Labour camp | July 1943 – September 1944 | 6,000 | 1,800–2,800 | | 664 |
| 14 | Bredtvet | Norway | Concentration camp | Fall, 1941 – May, 1944 | 1,000 min. | | none | |
| 15 | Breendonk | Belgium | Prison and labour camp | 20 Sep 1940 – Sep 1944 | 3532 min. | 391 min. | none | 665 |
| 16 | Breitenau | Germany | "Early wild camp", then labour camp | Jun 1933 – Mar 1934, 1940–1945 | 470 – 8500 | | | 666 |
| 17 | Buchenwald | Germany | Concentration camp | Jul 1937 – Apr 1945 | 266,000 | 56,545 | list | 667 |
| 18 | Chełmno (Kulmhof) | Poland | Extermination camp | Dec 1941 – Apr 1943, Apr 1944 – Jan 1945 | | 152,000 min. | | 668 |
| 19 | Crveni Krst | Serbia | Concentration camp | 1941–1944 | 30,000 | 10,000 | | |
| 20 | Dachau | Germany | Concentration camp | Mar 1933 – Apr 1945 | 200,000 | 31,591 | list | 669 |
| 21 | Drancy | France | Internment camp, transit | 20 Aug 1941 – 17 Aug 1944 | 70,000 | | Three of five Paris annexes: Austerlitz, Lévitan and Bassano camps | 670 |
| 22 | Falstad | Norway | Prison camp | Dec 1941 – May 1945 | | 200 min. | none | 671 |
| 23 | Flossenbürg | Germany | Concentration camp | May 1938 – Apr 1945 | 96,000 | 30,000 | list of subcamps | 672 |

# List of Nazi concentration camps

| | | | | | | | | |
|---|---|---|---|---|---|---|---|---|
| 24 | Fort de Romainville | France | Prison and transit camp | 1940 – Aug 1944 | 8,100 min. | 200 min. | none | 673 |
| 25 | Fort VII (Posen) | Poland | Concentration, detention, transit | Oct 1939 – Apr 1944 | 18,000 min. | 4,500 min. | | 674 |
| 26 | Fossoli | Italy | Prison and transit camp | 5 Dec 1943 – Nov 1944 | 2,800 | | | |
| 27 | Grini | Norway | Prison camp | 2 May 1941 – May 1945 | 19,788 | 8 | Fannrem Bardufoss Kvænangen | |
| 28 | Gross-Rosen | Poland | Labour camp; Nacht und Nebel camp | Aug 1940 – Feb 1945 | 125,000 | 40,000 | list | 675 |
| 29 | Herzogenbusch (Vught) | Netherlands | Concentration camp | 1943 – Summer 1944 | 31,000 | 750 | list | 676 |
| 30 | Hinzert | Germany | Collection point and subcamp | Jul 1940 – Mar 1945 | 14,000 | 302 min. | | 677 |
| 31 | Jägala | Estonia | Labour camp | Aug 1942 – Aug 1943 | 200 | 3,000 | none | 678 |
| 32 | Janowska (Lwów) | Ukraine | Ghetto; transit, labour, & extermination camp | Sep 1941 – Nov 1943 | | 40,000 min. | none | 679 (see "A-Z") |
| 33 | Kaiserwald (Mežaparks) | Latvia | Concentration camp | 1942 – 6 Aug 1944 | 20,000? | | 16, incl. Eleja-Meitenes | 680 |
| 34 | Kaufering/Landsberg | Germany | Concentration camp | Jun 1943 – Apr 1945 | 30,000 | 14,500 min. | | 681 682 |
| 35 | Kauen (Kaunas) | Lithuania | Ghetto and internment camp | June 22, 1941 - August 1, 1944 | | | Prawienischken | 683 |
| 36 | Kemna | Germany | Early concentration camp | Jun 1933 – Jan 1934 | 4,500 | | none | 684 |
| 37 | Kistarcsa | Hungary | Concentration camp | 1944 – 1945 | | 1,800 | | 685 |
| 38 | Klooga | Estonia | Labour camp | Summer 1943 – 28 Sep 1944 | | 1,800 | | |
| 39 | Koldichevo | Belarus | Labour camp | Summer 1942 – Jun 1944 | | 22,000 | | |

| # | Name | Country | Type | Dates | Prisoners | Deaths | Subcamps | Ref |
|---|---|---|---|---|---|---|---|---|
| 40 | Le Vernete | France | Internment camp | 1939–1944 | | | | |
| 41 | Majdanek (KZ Lublin) | Poland | Extermination and concentration camp | Oct 1941 – Jul 1944 | | 78,000 | | 686 |
| 42 | Malchow | Germany | Concentration and transit camp | Winter 1943 – 8 May 1945 | 5,000 | | | |
| 43 | Maly Trostenets | Belarus | Extermination camp | Jul 1941 – Jun 1944 | | 60,000-65,000 | | |
| 44 | Mauthausen-Gusen | Austria | Concentration camp | Aug 1938 – May 1945 | 195,000 | 55,000–60,000 | list | 687 |
| 45 | Mechelen | Belgium | Transit camp | July 1942 – Sep 1944 | 25267 min. | 300 min. | none | 665 |
| 46 | Mittelbau-Dora | Germany | Concentration camp | Sep 1943 – Apr 1945 | 60,000 | 20,000 min. | list | 688 |
| 47 | Natzweiler-Struthof (Struthof) | France | Concentration camp; Nacht und Nebel camp; extermination camp | May 1941 – Sep 1944 | 52,000 | 22,000 | list | 689 |
| 48 | Neuengamme | Germany | Concentration camp | 13 Dec 1938 – 4 May 1945 | 106,000 | 42,900+ | list | 690 |
| 49 | Niederhagen | Germany | Concentration and labour camp | Sep 1941 – early 1943 | 3,900 | 1,285 | none | 691 |
| 50 | Oberer Kuhberg concentration camp | Germany | Concentration camp | Nov 1933 – 1935 | 600 | 0 | Former infantry base Gleißelstetten (Fortress of Ulm) | 692 |
| 51 | Oranienburg | Germany | Early concentration camp | Mar 1933 – Jul 1934 | 3,000 | 16 min. | | |
| 52 | Osthofen | Germany | Collective point | Mar 1933 – Jul 1934 | | | | |
| 53 | Płaszów | Poland | Labour camp | Dec 1942 – Jan 1945 | 150,000 min. | 9,000 min. | list | |
| 54 | Ravensbrück | Germany | Concentration camp for women | May 1939 – Apr 1945 | 132,000 | 28,000 | list | 693 694 |
| 55 | Risiera di San Sabba (Trieste) | Italy | Police detainment camp, transit camp | Sep 1943 – 29 Apr 1945 | 25,000 | 5,000 | | 695 |
| 56 | Sachsenhausen | Germany | Concentration camp | Jul 1936 – Apr 1945 | 200,000 min. | 30,000 | list | 696 |

| | | | | | | | | |
|---|---|---|---|---|---|---|---|---|
| 57 | Sajmište | Serbia | Extermination camp | Oct 1941 – Jul 1944 | 50,000 | 20,000–23,000 | | |
| 58 | Salaspils (Kirchholm) | Latvia | Concentration camp | Oct 1941 – Summer 1944 | | 2,000 | | 697 |
| 59 | Skrochowitz (Skrochovice) | Czech Republic | Transit (1939) and labour camp | Sept 1939 - Dec 1939, 1940–1943 | 700 | 13 | | 698 |
| 60 | Sobibór | Poland | Extermination camp | May 1942 – Oct 1943 | | 170,165 | | 699 |
| 61 | Soldau | Poland | Labour and transit camp | Winter 1939/40 – Jan 1945 | 30,000 | 13,000 | 3 | |
| 62 | Stutthof | Poland | Concentration camp | Sep 1939 – May 1945 | 110,000 | 65,000 | list | 700 |
| 63 | Syrets (Kiev) | Ukraine | Labor and extermination camp | July 1942 – spring 1943 | 2,000 | | | 701 |
| 64 | Theresienstadt (Terezín) | Czech Republic | Transit camp and Ghetto | Nov 1941 – May 1945 | 140,000 | 33,000 min. | | 702 |
| 65 | Treblinka | Poland | Extermination camp | Jul 1942 – Nov 1943 | | aprox 1,000,000 | | 703 |
| 66 | Vaivara | Estonia | Concentration and transit camp | 15 Sep 1943 – 29 Feb 1944 | 20,000 | 950 | 22 | 704 705 |
| 67 | Warsaw | Poland | Concentration and extermination camp | 1942–1944 | 400,000 max. | 20,000–35,000 | | |
| 68 | Westerbork | Netherlands | Transit camp | May 1940 – Apr 1945 | 102,000 | | | |

# Bibliography

- Megargee, Geoffrey P., ed. (2012). *Encyclopedia of Camps and Ghettos, 1933–1945*. in association with United States Holocaust Memorial Museum. Bloomington: Indiana University Press. ISBN 978-0-253-35599-7.<templatestyles src="Module:Citation/CS1/styles.css"></templatestyles>

## External links

- Media related to Germany concentration camps at Wikimedia Commons
- The World of the Camps: Labor and Concentration Camps[706] on the Yad Vashem website
- List of German Concentration Camps During the Holocaust[707], Holocaust Center of Northern California

# Extermination through labour

**Extermination through labour** is a term sometimes used to describe the operation of labour camps in Nazi Germany, the Soviet Union, North Korea, and elsewhere, defined as the deliberate strategy of (often random and indiscriminate) killing prisoners by means of forced labour.

## Use as a term

The term "extermination through labour" (*Vernichtung durch Arbeit*) was not generally used by the Nazi SS, but the phrase was notably used in late 1942 in negotiations between Albert Bormann, Joseph Goebbels, Otto Georg Thierack and Heinrich Himmler, relating to the transfer of prisoners to concentration camps. Thierack and Goebbels specifically used the term. The phrase was used again during the post-war Nuremberg trials.

In the 1980s and 1990s, however, historians have debated the appropriate use of the term. Falk Pingel believed the phrase should not be applied to all Nazi prisoners, while Hermann Kaienburg and Miroslav Kárný believed "extermination through labour" was a consistent goal of the SS. More recently, Jens-Christian Wagner has also argued that not all Nazi prisoners were targeted with annihilation.

## In Nazi Germany

The Nazis persecuted many individuals because of their race, political affiliation, disability, religion, or sexual orientation.[708] Groups marginalized by the majority population in Germany included welfare-dependent families with many children, alleged vagrants and transients, as well as members of perceived problem groups, such as alcoholics and prostitutes. While these people were considered "German-blooded", they were also categorized as "social misfits" (*Asoziale*) as well as superfluous "ballast-lives" (*Ballastexistenzen*). They were recorded in lists (as were homosexuals) by civil and police

**Figure 92:** *The Todesstiege ("Stairs of Death") at the Mauthausen concentration camp quarry in Upper Austria. Inmates were forced to carry heavy rocks up the stairs. In their severely weakened state, few prisoners could cope with this back-breaking labour for long.*

authorities and subjected to myriad state restrictions and repressive actions, which included forced sterilization and ultimately imprisonment in concentration camps. Anyone who openly opposed the Nazi regime (such as communists, social democrats, democrats, and conscientious objectors) was detained in prison camps. Many of them did not survive the ordeal.

While others could possibly redeem themselves in the eyes of the Nazis, there was no room in Hitler's world-view for Jews, although Germany encouraged and supported emigration of Jews to Palestine and elsewhere from 1933 until 1941 with arrangements such as the Haavara Agreement, or the Madagascar Plan. During the war in 1942, the Nazi leadership gathered to discuss what had come to be called "the final solution to the Jewish question" at a conference in Wannsee, Germany. The transcript of this gathering gives historians insight into the thinking of the Nazi leadership as they devised the details of the Jews' future destruction, including using extermination through labour as one component of their so-called "Final Solution".

<templatestyles src="Template:Quote/styles.css"/>

**Figure 93:** *Commemorative plaque in Hamburg-Neugraben*

> *Under proper leadership, the Jews shall now in the course of the Final Solution be suitably brought to their work assignments in the East. Able-bodied Jews are to be led to these areas to build roads in large work columns separated by sex, during which a large part will undoubtedly drop out through a process of natural reduction. As it will undoubtedly represent the most robust portion, the possible final remainder will have to be handled appropriately, as it would constitute a group of naturally-selected individuals, and would form the seed of a new Jewish resistance.*
> — *Wannsee Protocol, 1942.*[709]

In Nazi camps, "extermination through labour" was principally carried out through a slave-based labour organization, which is why, in contrast with the forced labour of foreign work forces, a term from the Nuremberg Trials is used for "slave work" and "slave workers".

Working conditions were characterized by: no remuneration of any kind; constant surveillance of workers; physically demanding labour (for example, road construction, farm work, and factory work, particularly in the arms industry); excessive working hours (often 10 to 12 hours per day); minimal nutrition, food rationing; lack of hygiene; poor medical care and ensuing disease; insufficient clothing (for example, summer clothes even in the winter).

# Extermination through labour

**Figure 94:** *Jewish forced labourers, marching with shovels, Mogilev, 1941*

Torture and physical abuse were also used. *Torstehen* ("Gate Hanging") forced victims to stand outside naked with arms raised, like a gate hanging on its hinges. When they collapsed or passed out, they would be beaten until they re-assumed the position. *Pfahlhängen* ("Post Attachment") involved tying the inmate's hands behind their back and then hanging them by their hands from a tall stake. This would dislocate and disjoint the arms, and the pressure would be fatal within hours. (Cf. strappado.)

## Concentration camps

Imprisonment in concentration camps was intended not merely to break, but to destroy inmates. The admission and registration of the new prisoners, the forced labour, the prisoner housing, the roll calls—all aspects of camp life were accompanied by humiliation and harassment.

Admission, registration and interrogation of the detainees was accompanied by scornful remarks from SS officials. The prisoners were stepped on and beaten during roll call. Forced labour partly consisted of pointless tasks and heavy labour, which was intended to wear down the prisoners.

At many of the concentration camps, forced labour was channeled for the advancement of the German war machine. In these cases, excessive working hours were also seen as a means to maximizing output. Oswald Pohl, the leader

**Figure 95:** *Gate in the Dachau concentration camp memorial.*

of the *SS-Wirtschafts-Verwaltungshauptamt* ("SS Economy and Administration Main Bureau", or SS-WVHA), who oversaw the employment of forced labour at the concentration camps, ordered on April 30, 1942.

> *The camp commander alone is responsible for the use of man power. This work must be exhausting in the true sense of the word in order to achieve maximum performance. [...] There are no limits to working hours. [...] Time consuming walks and mid-day breaks only for the purpose of eating are prohibited. [...] He [the camp commander] must connect clear technical knowledge in military and economic matters with sound and wise leadership of groups of people, which he should bring together to achieve a high performance potential.*[710]

Up to 25,000 of the 35,000 prisoners appointed to work for IG Farben in Auschwitz died. The average life expectancy of a slave laborer on a work assignment amounted to less than four months.[711] The emaciated forced labourers died from exhaustion or disease or they were deemed to be incapable of work and killed. About 30 percent of the forced labourers who were assigned to dig tunnels, which were created for weapon factories in the last months of the war, died.[712] In the satellite camps, which were established in the vicinity of mines and industrial firms, death rates were even higher, since accommodations and supplies were often even less adequate there than in the main camps.

The phrase "Arbeit macht frei" ("work shall set you free"), which could be found in various places in some Nazi concentration camps, e.g. on the entrance gates, seems particularly cynical in this context. The Buchenwald concentration camp was the only concentration camp with the motto "Jedem das Seine" ("To each what he deserves") on the entrance gate.

# Deadly labour outside Nazi Germany

## In the African slave trade

Some scholars refer to the slave trade as a Holocaust. though many prefer the neologism Maafa which means 'great disaster'.[713,714,715]

The Arab slave trade is estimated to have killed between 4.4 and 19 million Africans, mostly in slave raids.

Likewise, the Atlantic slave trade resulted in a vast and as yet still unknown loss of life for African captives both inside and outside America. Approximately 1.2 – 2.4 million Africans died during their transport to the New World.[716] More died soon after their arrival. The number of lives lost in the procurement of slaves remains a mystery, but it may equal or exceed the number of Africans who survived only to be enslaved.[717]

Estimates by Patrick Manning are that about 12 million slaves entered the Atlantic trade between the 16th and 19th century, but about 1.5 million died on board ship. About 10.5 million slaves arrived in the Americas. Besides the slaves who died on the Middle Passage, more Africans likely died during the slave raids in Africa and forced marches to ports. Manning estimates that 4 million died inside Africa after capture, and many more died young. Manning's estimate covers the 12 million who were originally destined for the Atlantic, as well as the 6 million destined for Asian slave markets and the 8 million destined for African markets.[718]

## In Leopold II's Congo Free State

In the period from 1885 to 1908, a number of well-documented atrocities were perpetrated in the Congo Free State (today the Democratic Republic of the Congo) which, at the time, was a colony under the personal rule of King Leopold II of Belgium. These atrocities were sometimes collectively referred to by European contemporaries as the "Congo Horrors", and were particularly associated with the labour policies used to collect natural rubber for export. With the majority of the Free State's revenues derived from the export of rubber, a labour policy (known by critics as the "Red Rubber system") was created to maximise its extraction. Labour was demanded by the administration as taxation.[719] </ref>

This created a "slave society", as companies became increasingly dependent on forcibly mobilising Congolese labour for their collection of rubber.[720] Workers who refused to supply their labour were coerced with "constraint and repression". Dissenters were beaten or whipped with the *chicotte*, hostages were taken to ensure prompt collection and punitive expeditions were sent to destroy villages which refused.[721] The policy led to a collapse of Congolese economic and cultural life, as well as farming in some areas.[722] Together with epidemic disease, famine, and a falling birth rate caused by these disruptions, the atrocities contributed to a sharp decline in the Congolese population. The magnitude of the population fall over the period is disputed, but it is thought by multiple historians that 10 or more million[723,724] Vansina has since revised down his own estimate.[725]</ref>[726] Congolese perished during the period, mostly due to disease.[727]

One of the enduring images of the Free State was the severed hands which became "the most potent symbol of colonial brutality".[728] The practice of hacking the hands off corpses in the aftermath of punitive expeditions became common as evidence (*pièces justificatives*) that government supplies had not been misused.[729] When soldiers did misuse their equipment, they cut hands from living people to cover their activities.[730]

## In the Soviet Union

The Soviet Gulag is sometimes presented as a system of death camps,[731,732,733,734] particularly in post-Communist Eastern European politics. This controversial position has been criticized as Holocaust trivialization, considering that with the obvious exception of the war years, a very large majority of people who entered the Gulag left alive. Alexander Solzhenitsyn introduced the expression *camps of extermination by labour* in his non-fiction work *The Gulag Archipelago*.[735] According to him, the system eradicated opponents by forcing them to work as prisoners on big state-run projects (for example the White Sea-Baltic Canal, quarries, remote railroads and urban development projects) under inhumane conditions. Roy Medvedev comments: "The penal system in the Kolyma and in the camps in the north was deliberately designed for the extermination of people." Alexander Nikolaevich Yakovlev expands upon this, claiming that Stalin was the "architect of the gulag system for totally destroying human life".[736] Writer Stephen Wheatcroft argues that the scale and nature of the Soviet Gulag repressions need to be looked at through the perspective of the greater populations of the USSR.[737]

Hannah Arendt argued that although the Soviet government deemed them all "forced labor" camps, this in fact highlighted that the work in the camps was deliberately pointless, since "forced labor is the normal condition of all Russian workers, who have no freedom of movement and can be arbitrarily drafted for work at any place and at any time."[738] The only real economic purpose they typically served was financing the cost of supervision. Otherwise the work performed was generally useless, either by design or made that way through extremely poor planning and execution; some workers even preferred more difficult work if it was actually productive. She differentiated between "authentic" forced-labor camps, concentration camps, and "annihilation camps". In authentic labor camps, inmates worked in "relative freedom and are sentenced for limited periods." Concentration camps had extremely high mortality rates and but were still "essentially organized for labor purposes." Annihilation camps were those where the inmates were "systematically wiped out through starvation and neglect." She criticizes other commentators' conclusion that the purpose of the camps was a supply of cheap labor. According to her, the Soviets were able to liquidate the camp system without serious economic consequences, showing that the camps were not an important source of labor and were overall economically irrelevant.[739]

According to formerly secret internal Gulag documents, some 1.6 million people must have died in the period between 1930 and 1956 in Soviet forced labour camps and colonies (excluding prisoner-of-war camps), though these figures only include the deaths in the colonies beginning in 1935. The majority (about 900,000) of these deaths therefore fall between 1941 and 1945,[740] coinciding with the period of the German-Soviet War when food supply levels were low in the entire country.

These figures are consistent with the archived documents that Russian historian Oleg Khlevniuk presents and analyzes in his study *The History of the Gulag: From Collectivization to the Great Terror*, according to which some 500,000 people died in the camps and colonies from 1930 to 1941.[741] Khlevniuk points out that these figures don't take into account any deaths that occurred during transport.[742] Also excluded are those who died shortly after their release owing to the harsh treatment in the camps,[743] who, according to both archives and memoirs, were numerous.[744] The historian J. Otto Pohl estimates that some 2,749,163 prisoners perished in the labour camps, colonies and special settlements, although stresses that this is an incomplete figure.[745] Though the death toll is still widely debated, no state or national institution has recognized the Gulag system as a genocide.Wikipedia:Citation needed

## In Maoist China

Like the Soviet system, Mao Zedong's rule of China also installed an extremely deadly forced labor and prison system known as the Laogai or "reform through labour". According to Jean-Louis Margolin during the Campaign to Suppress

Counterrevolutionaries, the harshness of the official prison system reached unprecedented levels, and the mortality rate until 1952 was "certainly in excess" of 5 percent per year, and reached 50 percent during six months in Guangxi.[746] In Shanxi, more than 300 people died per day in one mine. Torture was commonplace and the suppression of revolts, which were quite numerous, resulted in "veritable massacres". One Chinese priest died after being interrogated for over 100 hours. Of the 20,000 inmates who worked in the oilfields of Yanchang, several thousand were executed.

In *Mao: The Unknown Story*, the Mao biographer Jung Chang and historian Jon Halliday estimate that perhaps 27 million people died in prisons and labor camps during Mao Zedong's rule.[747] They claim that inmates were subjected to back-breaking labor in the most hostile wastelands, and that executions and suicides by any means (like diving into a wheat chopper) were commonplace. Frank Dikötter estimates that 1 to 3 million Chinese citizens committed suicide[748] during the Great Leap Forward, likely referring in part to suicides in the labor camps.

Writing in *The Black Book of Communism*, which describes the history of repressions by Communist states, Jean-Louis Margolin claims that perhaps 20 million died in the prison system.[749] Professor R.J. Rummel puts the number of forced labor "democides" at 15,720,000, excluding "all those collectivized, ill-fed and clothed peasants who would be worked to death in the fields."[750] Harry Wu puts the death toll at 15 million.[751]

## Other deadly labour systems

### In Africa

- Like Leopold's Free State, Portugal also used brutal forced labour in their African colonies, resulting in 325,000 deaths over the first quarter of the 20th century.

752

- France's colonies have meet similar scrutiny, with estimates of forced labour deaths ranging from under 200,000 by Rudolph Rummel to almost 800,000 by other scholars. Adam Hoschild estimated half the human population in rainforests within French African colonies perished. Tom Conner goes as far as to posit a population decline in the millions, or essentially that most of French Equatorial Africa's populace perished during the Colonial period of 1900 to the early 1920s partially as a result of forced labour. 14 to 20 thousand are estimated to have perished in the building of the Congo Ocean railroad under French administration.[753]

- Putting an end to most foreign trade relationships, Ranavalona I pursued a policy of self-reliance in Madagascar, made possible through frequent use of the long-standing tradition of *fanompoana*—forced labor in lieu of tax payments in money or goods. Ranavalona continued the wars of expansion conducted by her predecessor, Radama I, in an effort to extend her realm over the entire island, and imposed strict punishments on those who were judged as having acted in opposition to her will. Due in large part to loss of life throughout the years of military campaigns, high death rates among *fanompoana* workers, and harsh traditions of justice under her rule, the population of Madagascar is estimated to have declined from around 5 million to 2.5 million between 1833 and 1839, and from 750,000 to 130,000 between 1829 and 1842 in Imerina. These statistics have contributed to a strongly unfavorable view of Ranavalona's rule in historical accounts.[754]

## In Asia

- Forced labour was used in Japan's construction of the Burma Railway. More than 180,000—possibly many more—Southeast Asian civilian labourers (Romusha) and 60,000 Allied prisoners of war (POWs) worked on the railway. Javanese, Malayan Tamils of Indian origin, Burmese, Chinese, Thai and other Southeast Asians, forcibly drafted by the Imperial Japanese Army to work on the railway, died in its construction — including 100,000 Tamils alone.WP:NOTRS 12,621 Allied POWs died during the construction. The dead POWs included 6,904 British personnel, 2,802 Australians, 2,782 Dutch, and 133 Americans.
- The U.S. Library of Congress estimates that during the Japanese occupation of the Dutch East Indies, between 4 and 10 million *romusha* (Japanese: "manual laborer"), were forced to work by the Japanese military.[755] About 270,000 of these Javanese laborers were sent to other Japanese-held areas in southeast Asia. Only 52,000 were repatriated to Java, meaning that there was a death rate as high as 80%. (For further details, see Japanese war crimes.)[756] A later UN report stated that four million people died in Indonesia as a result of the Japanese occupation.[757] About 2.4 million people died in Java from famine during 1944–45.[758]
- Hundreds of thousands to millions of Cambodians were worked to death during the Cambodian genocide which killed around 1,700,000 or more than a fifth of citizens in Cambodia.[759]
- 400,000[760] to 1,500,000[761] have perished in camps similar to the Soviet Gulag and Chinese Laogai that are operating in North Korea. They resulted in the death of at least 20,000 political prisoners in 2013 alone, with at least 130,000 held therein.

- Foreign observers of the Chinese government's ongoing persecution of Falun Gong, starting from 1999, have estimated that hundreds of thousands—and perhaps millions—of Falun Gong practitioners have been held extra-legally in reeducation-through-labor camps, prisons, and other detention facilities.[762] 3,700 named Falun Gong practitioners have died as a result of torture and abuse in custody, typically after they refused to recant their beliefs.[763] In 2006, allegations emerged that a large number of Falun Gong practitioners had been killed to supply China's organ transplant industry.[764] These allegations prompted an investigation by former Canadian Secretary of State David Kilgour and human rights lawyer David Matas. In July 2006, the Kilgour-Matas report[765] found that "the source of 41,500 transplants for the six year period 2000 to 2005 is unexplained" and concluded that "the government of China and its agencies in numerous parts of the country, in particular hospitals but also detention centres and 'people's courts', since 1999 have put to death a large but unknown number of Falun Gong prisoners of conscience". In 2016, the researchers published a joint update to their findings showing that the number of organ transplants conducted in China is much higher than previously believed, and that 60,000 to 100,000 could be harvested from political prisoners per year. The 789-page report is based on an analysis of records from hundreds of Chinese transplant hospitals. In 2009, courts in Spain and Argentina indicted senior Chinese officials for genocide and crimes against humanity for their role in orchestrating the suppression of Falun Gong.[766,767,768]

## In Europe

- Over 10,000,000 Slavs across Southern Europe, the Polish–Lithuanian Commonwealth, and the Grand Duchy of Moscow are estimated to have perished from the Arab Slave Trade and Ottoman Slave Trade.[769,770]
- Separate from the GULAG, estimates of German POW in the Soviet Union casualties (in both east and west and cumulative for both the war and peace-time period) range from 600,000 to 1,000,000.[771] According to the section of the German Red Cross dealing with tracing the captives, the ultimate fate of 1,300,000 German POWs in Allied custody is still unknown; they are still officially listed as missing.[772] The capture and transfer of civilian ethnic Germans to the Soviet Union began as soon as countries with a German minority began to be overrun in 1944. Large numbers of civilians were taken from countries such as Romania, Yugoslavia, and from the eastern parts of Germany itself. For example, between 27,000 and 30,000 ethnic Germans (aged 18–40) were sent to the USSR from Yugoslavia after Christmas 1944. Women made up 90% of the group. Most were sent to labor camps in the Donbass (Donez

# Extermination through labour

**Figure 96:** *A photo of enslaved Amazon Indians from the 1912 book The Putumayo, the Devil's Paradise*

basin) where 16% of them died.[773] After the war, many Germans in what would become East Germany were forced by the Communist authorities to work in German uranium mines producing the majority of the raw material of the Soviet atomic bomb project. Beginning in the summer of 1946, the Soviets began explorations in the Erzgebirge, sealing off the old radium hot springs by September of the same year. The work was dangerous and stressful, and the Soviets made no effort to improve it; as a result the mines became filled with forced labor conscripts and has been compared to a death march and the Gulags of Kolyma. An additional 200,000 ethnic Germans died in the Soviet-run slave labour camps in Poland.[774]

- 200,000 perished in the Forced labor of Hungarians in the Soviet Union
- Over 10 to up to 40 thousand perished in the construction of the Danube-Black Sea Canal.

## In the Americas

- The conditions of haciendas and chattel slavery in Mexico has been compared to those of a Soviet Gulag by R.J. Rummel, an analyst of what he calls democides, estimating 69,000 Mexicans or 0.5 percent of Mexico's population perished annually from the system or 825,000 deaths overall.
- During the Yaqui genocide the Mexican government established large concentration camps at San Marcos, where the remaining Yaqui families

were broken up and segregated. Individuals were then sold into slavery inside the station and packed into train cars which took them to Veracruz, where they were embarked yet again for the port town of Progreso in the Yucatán. There they were transported to their final destination, the nearby henequen plantations. By 1908, at least 5,000 Yaqui had been sold into slavery.[775,776] At Valle Nacional, the enslaved Yaquis were worked until they died. While there were occasional escapes, the escapees were far from home and, without support or assistance, most died of hunger while begging for food on the road out of the valley toward Córdoba. At Guaymas, thousands more Yaquis were put on boats and shipped to San Blas, where they were forced to walk more than 200 miles to San Marcos and its train station. Many women and children could not withstand the three-week journey over the mountains, and their bodies were left by the side of the road. Yaquis (particularly children) were rattled off in Train cars to be sold as slaves in this process having 1/3 die simply in the process of deportation. The deaths were mostly caused by unfettered smallpox epidemics.[777] On the plantations, the Yaquis were forced to work in the tropical climate of the area from dawn to dusk. Yaqui women were allowed to marry only non-native Chinese workers. Given little food, the workers were beaten if they failed to cut and trim at least 2,000 henequen leaves per day, after which they were then locked up every night. Most of the Yaqui men, women and children sent for slave labor on the plantations died there, with two-thirds of the arrivals dying within a year. The Haciendas have been compared to those of the Stalinist Gulags.

- Like the rubber boom in the Congo, the Amazon rubber boom also utilized extremely inhumane forced labour. The rubber boom and the associated need for a large workforce had a significant negative effect on the indigenous population across Brazil, Peru, Ecuador and Colombia. As rubber plantations grew, labor shortages increased. The owners of the plantations or rubber barons were rich, but those who collected the rubber made very little as a large amount of rubber was needed to be profitable. The rubber barons rounded up all the Indians and forced them to tap rubber out of the trees. One plantation started with 50,000 Indians and when discovered of the killings, only 8,000 were still alive. Slavery and systematic brutality were widespread, and in some areas, 90% of the Indian population was wiped out. These rubber plantations were part of the Brazilian rubber market, which declined as rubber plantations in southeast Asia became more effective.[778]

# Further reading

- (in German) Stéphane Courtois: *Das Schwarzbuch des Kommunismus, Unterdrückung, Verbrechen und Terror.* Piper, 1998. 987 pages. <templatestyles src="Module:Citation/CS1/styles.css" />ISBN 3-492-04053-5
- (in German) Jörg Echternkamp: *Die deutsche Kriegsgesellschaft: 1939 bis 1945: Halbband 1. Politisierung, Vernichtung, Überleben.* Deutsche Verlags-Anstalt, Stuttgart 2004. 993 pages, graphic representation. <templatestyles src="Module:Citation/CS1/styles.css" />ISBN 3-421-06236-6
- Oleg V. Khlevniuk: *The History of the Gulag: From Collectivization to the Great Terror* New Haven: Yale University Press 2004, <templatestyles src="Module:Citation/CS1/styles.css" />ISBN 0-300-09284-9
- (in Russian) A. I. Kokurin/N. V. Petrov (Ed.): *GULAG (Glavnoe Upravlenie Lagerej): 1918–1960* (Rossija. XX vek. Dokumenty), Moskva: Materik 2000, <templatestyles src="Module:Citation/CS1/styles.css" />ISBN 5-85646-046-4
- (in German) Joel Kotek/Pierre Rigoulot: *Das Jahrhundert der Lager.Gefangenschaft, Zwangsarbeit, Vernichtung,* Propyläen 2001, <templatestyles src="Module:Citation/CS1/styles.css" />ISBN 3-549-07143-4
- (in German) Rudolf A. Mark (Ed.): *Vernichtung durch Hunger: der Holodomor in der Ukraine und der UdSSR.* Wissenschaftlicher Verlag Berlin, Berlin 2004. 207 pages <templatestyles src="Module:Citation/CS1/styles.css" />ISBN 3-8305-0883-2
- Hermann Kaienburg (1990). *Vernichtung durch Arbeit. Der Fall Neuengamme (Extermination through labour: Case of Neuengamme)* (in German). Bonn: Dietz Verlag J.H.W. Nachf. p. 503. ISBN 3-8012-5009-1.<templatestyles src="Module:Citation/CS1/styles.css"></templatestyles>
- Gerd Wysocki (1992). *Arbeit für den Krieg (Work for the War)* (in German). Braunschweig.<templatestyles src="Module:Citation/CS1/styles.css"></templatestyles>
- Donald Bloxham (2001). *Genocide on Trial: War Crimes Trials and the Formation of History and Memory*[779]. Oxford: Oxford University Press. p. 296. ISBN 0-19-820872-3.<templatestyles src="Module:Citation/CS1/styles.css"></templatestyles>
- Nikolaus Wachsmann (1999). "Annihilation through labor: The Killing of State Prisoners in the Third Reich". *Journal of Modern History.* **71** (3): 624–659. doi: 10.1086/235291[780]. JSTOR 2990503[781].<templatestyles src="Module:Citation/CS1/styles.css"></templatestyles>
- various authors (2002). Michael Berenbaum, Abraham J Peck, ed. *The Holocaust and History: The Known, the Un-*

known, the Disputed, and the Reexamined[782]. Indiana University Press. pp. 370–407. ISBN 0-253-21529-3.<templatestyles src="Module:Citation/CS1/styles.css"></templatestyles>
- Eugen Kogon; Heinz Norden; Nikolaus Wachsmann (2006). *The Theory and Practice of Hell: The German Concentration Camps and the System Behind Them*. Farrar, Straus and Giroux. p. 368. ISBN 0-374-52992-2.<templatestyles src="Module:Citation/CS1/styles.css"></templatestyles>

# External links

- (in German) Lemo *Die nationalsozialistischen Konzentrationslager*[783]
- (in German) *Frauen im Gulag*, Deutschlandradio, May 11, 2003[784]

# Nazi ghettos

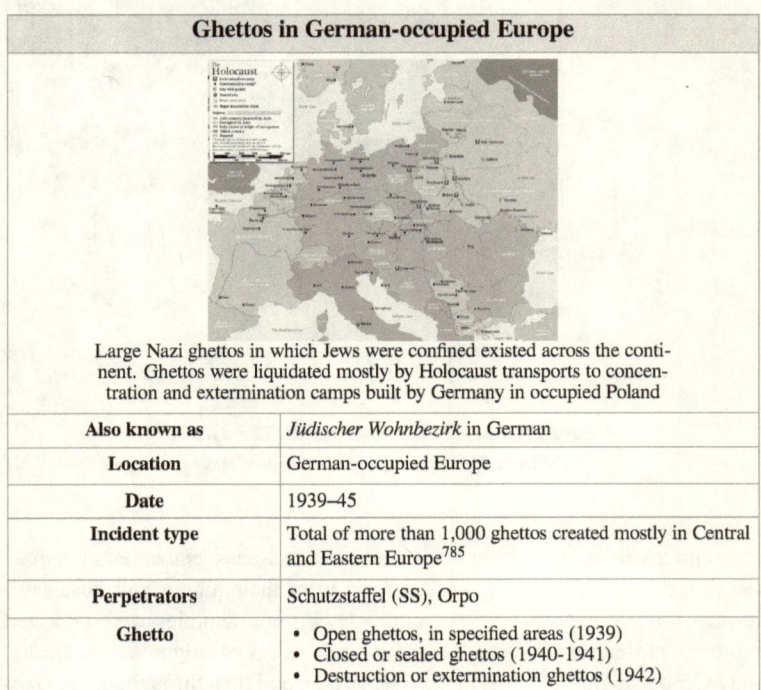

**Ghettos in German-occupied Europe**

Large Nazi ghettos in which Jews were confined existed across the continent. Ghettos were liquidated mostly by Holocaust transports to concentration and extermination camps built by Germany in occupied Poland

| Also known as | *Jüdischer Wohnbezirk* in German |
|---|---|
| Location | German-occupied Europe |
| Date | 1939–45 |
| Incident type | Total of more than 1,000 ghettos created mostly in Central and Eastern Europe[785] |
| Perpetrators | Schutzstaffel (SS), Orpo |
| Ghetto | • Open ghettos, in specified areas (1939)<br>• Closed or sealed ghettos (1940-1941)<br>• Destruction or extermination ghettos (1942) |

Beginning with the invasion of Poland during World War II, the regime of Nazi Germany set up ghettos across occupied Europe in order to segregate and confine Jews, and sometimes Romani people, into small sections of towns and cities furthering their exploitation. In German documents, and signage at ghetto entrances, the Nazis usually referred to them as *Jüdischer Wohnbezirk* or *Wohngebiet der Juden*, both of which translate as the Jewish Quarter. There were several distinct types including *open ghettos*, *closed ghettos*, *work*, *transit*, and *destruction ghettos*, as defined by the Holocaust historians. In a number of cases, they were the place of Jewish underground resistance against the German occupation, known collectively as the ghetto uprisings.

## History

The first anti-Jewish measures were enacted in Germany with the onset of Nazism, without the actual ghettoization planning for the German Jews which was rejected in the post-Kristallnacht period.[786] However, soon after the 1939 German invasion of Poland, the Nazis began to designate areas of larger Polish

**Figure 97:** *Jews being forced into the new Grodno Ghetto in Bezirk Białystok, November 1941*

cities and towns as exclusively Jewish, and within weeks, embarked on a massive programme of uprooting Polish Jews from their homes and businesses through forcible expulsions. The entire Jewish communities were deported into these closed off zones by train from their places of origin systematically, using Orpo battalions,[787] first in the *Reichsgaue*, and then throughout the *Generalgouvernement* territory.

The first ghetto of World War II was established on 8 October 1939 at Piotrków Trybunalski (38 days after the invasion),[788] with the Tuliszków ghetto established in December 1939. The first large metropolitan ghetto known as the Łódź Ghetto (*Litzmannstadt*) followed them in April 1940, and the Warsaw Ghetto in October. Most Jewish ghettos were established in 1940 and 1941. Subsequently, many ghettos were sealed from the outside, walled off with brickwork, or enclosed with barbed wire. In the case of sealed ghettos, any Jew found leaving there could be shot. The Warsaw Ghetto, located in the heart of the city, was the largest ghetto in Nazi occupied Europe, with over 400,000 Jews crammed into an area of 1.3 square miles (3.4 km$^2$).[789] The Łódź Ghetto was the second largest, holding about 160,000 people.[790] According to the United States Holocaust Memorial Museum archives, there were at least 1,000 such ghettos in German-occupied and annexed Poland and the Soviet Union alone.

**Figure 98:** *Warsaw Ghetto; walling-off Świętokrzyska Street (seen from "Aryan side" of Marszałkowska)*

## Living conditions

Ghettos across Eastern Europe varied in their size, scope and living conditions.[791] The conditions in the ghettos were generally brutal. In Warsaw, the Jews, comprising 30% of the city overall population, were forced to live in 2.4% of the city's area, a density of 7.2 people per room. In the ghetto of Odrzywół, 700 people lived in an area previously occupied by five families, between 12 and 30 to each room. The Jews were not allowed out of the ghetto, so they had to rely on smuggling and the starvation rations supplied by the Nazis: in Warsaw this was 253 calories (1,060 kJ) per Jew, compared to 669 calories (2,800 kJ) per Pole and 2,613 calories (10,940 kJ) per German. With the crowded living conditions, starvation diets, and insufficient sanitation (coupled with lack of medical supplies), epidemics of infectious disease became a major feature of ghetto life.[792] In the Łódź Ghetto some 43,800 people died of 'natural' causes, 76,000 in the Warsaw Ghetto before July 1942.

## Types of ghettos

To prevent unauthorised contact between the Jewish and non-Jewish populations, German Order Police formations were assigned to patrol the perimeter. Within each ghetto, a Jewish Police force was created to ensure that no prisoners tried to escape. In general terms, there were three types of ghettos maintained by the Nazi administration.

- *Open ghettos* did not have walls or fences, and existed mostly in initial stages of World War II in German-occupied Poland and the occupied Soviet Union, but also in Transnistria province of Ukraine occupied and administered by Romanian authorities. There were severe restrictions on entering and leaving them.
- *Closed or sealed ghettos* were situated mostly in German-occupied Poland. They were surrounded by brick walls, fences or barbed wire stretched between posts. Jews were not allowed to live in any other areas under the threat of capital punishment. In the closed ghettos the living conditions were the worst. The quarters were extremely crowded and unsanitary. Starvation, chronic shortages of food, lack of heat in winter and inadequate municipal services led to frequent outbreaks of epidemics such as dysentery and typhus and to a high mortality rate.[793] Most Nazi ghettos were of this particular type.
- The *destruction or extermination ghettos* existed in the final stages of the Holocaust, for between two and six weeks only, in German-occupied Soviet Union - especially in Lithuania and the Soviet Ukraine - in Hungary, and in occupied Poland. They were tightly sealed off. The Jewish population was imprisoned in them only to be deported or taken out of town and shot by the German killing squads, often with the aid of local collaborationist Auxiliary Police battalions.

## Aryan side

The parts of a city outside the walls of the Jewish Quarter were called "Aryan." For example, in Warsaw, the city was divided into Jewish, Polish, and German Quarters. Those living outside the ghetto had to have identification papers proving they were not Jewish (none of their grandparents was a member of the Jewish community), such as a baptism certificate. Such documents were sometimes called "Christian" or "Aryan papers." Poland's Catholic clergy massively forged baptism certificates,[794] which were given to Jews by the dominant Polish resistance movement, the Home Army (*Armia Krajowa*, or AK). Any Pole found by the Germans to be giving any help to a Jew was subject to the death penalty.

# Liquidation

In 1942, the Nazis began Operation Reinhard, the systematic deportation of Jews to extermination camps. Nazi authorities throughout Europe deported Jews to ghettos in Eastern Europe or most often directly to extermination

**Figure 99:** *Deportation to a death camp during liquidation of the Biała Podlaska Ghetto conducted by the Reserve Police Battalion 101 in 1942*

camps built by Nazi Germany in occupied Poland. Almost 300,000 people were deported from the Warsaw Ghetto alone to Treblinka over the course of 52 days. In some ghettos, local resistance organizations staged ghetto uprisings. None were successful, and the Jewish populations of the ghettos were almost entirely killed. On June 21, 1943, Heinrich Himmler issued an order to liquidate all ghettos and transfer remaining Jewish inhabitants to concentration camps. A few ghettos were re-designated as concentration camps and existed until 1944.

## References

- Megargee, Geoffrey P., ed. (2012). *Encyclopedia of Camps and Ghettos, 1933-1945*. in association with United States Holocaust Memorial Museum. Bloomington: Indiana University Press. ISBN 978-0253355997.<templatestyles src="Module:Citation/CS1/styles.css"></templatestyles>
- Browning, Christopher R. (2007) [2004]. *The Origins of the Final Solution: The Evolution of Nazi Jewish Policy 1939-1942*[795]. Lincoln: University of Nebraska Press. ISBN 0803203926.<templatestyles src="Module:Citation/CS1/styles.css"></templatestyles>

# The Holocaust in Ukraine

| The Holocaust in Ukraine ||
|---|---|
| 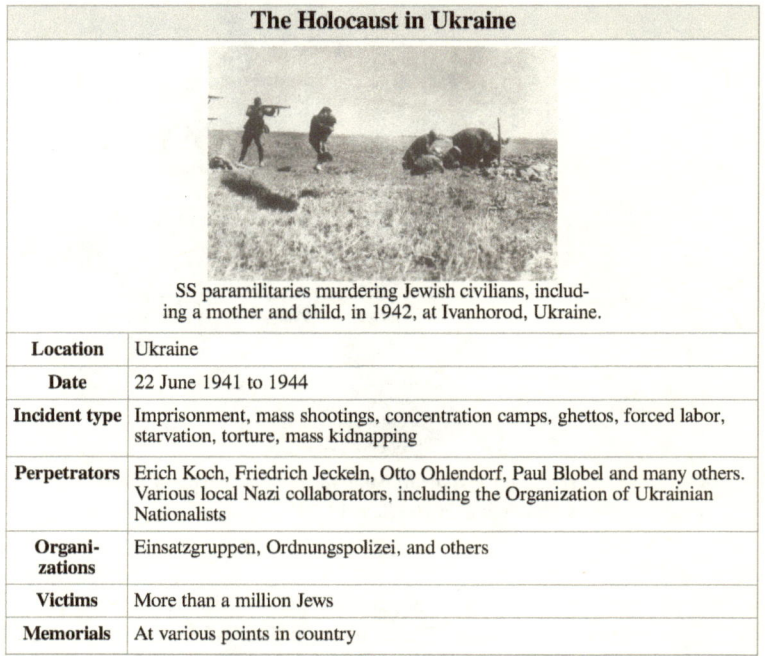<br>SS paramilitaries murdering Jewish civilians, including a mother and child, in 1942, at Ivanhorod, Ukraine. ||
| Location | Ukraine |
| Date | 22 June 1941 to 1944 |
| Incident type | Imprisonment, mass shootings, concentration camps, ghettos, forced labor, starvation, torture, mass kidnapping |
| Perpetrators | Erich Koch, Friedrich Jeckeln, Otto Ohlendorf, Paul Blobel and many others. Various local Nazi collaborators, including the Organization of Ukrainian Nationalists |
| Organizations | Einsatzgruppen, Ordnungspolizei, and others |
| Victims | More than a million Jews |
| Memorials | At various points in country |

The **Holocaust in Ukraine** took place in *Reichskommissariat Ukraine* during the occupation of the Soviet Ukraine by Nazi Germany in World War II. Between 1941 and 1944 more than a million Jews living in Ukrainian SSR were murdered as part of *Generalplan Ost* and the Final Solution extermination policies.

According to Yale historian Timothy D. Snyder, "the Holocaust is integrally and organically connected to the *Vernichtungskrieg*, to the war in 1941, and is organically and integrally connected to the attempt to conquer Ukraine."

## Generalplan Ost

One of Hitler's ambitions at the start of the war was to exterminate, expel, or enslave most or all Slavs from their native lands so as to make living space for German settlers. This plan of genocide[796] was to be carried into effect gradually over a period of 25–30 years.[797]

According to historian William W. Hagen, "*Generalplan Ost* . . . forecast the diminution of the targeted east European peoples' populations by the following measures: Poles – 85 percent; Belarusians – 75 percent; Ukrainians – 65

**Figure 100:** *A map of the Holocaust in Ukraine*

percent; Czechs – 50 percent. ... The Russian people, once subjugated in war, would join the four Slavic-speaking nations whose fate *Generalplan Ost* foreshadowed."

## Death squads (1941–1943)

Total civilian losses during the war and German occupation in Ukraine are estimated at four million, including up to a million Jews who were murdered by the Einsatzgruppen and local Nazi collaborators. Einsatzgruppe C (SS-*Gruppenführer* Dr. Otto Rasch) was assigned to north and central Ukraine, and Einsatzgruppe D (SS-*Gruppenführer* Dr. Otto Ohlendorf) to Moldavia, south Ukraine, the Crimea, and, during 1942, the north Caucasus. According to Ohlendorf at his trial, "the *Einsatzgruppen* had the mission to protect the rear of the troops by killing the Jews, Romani, Communist functionaries, active Communists, uncooperative slavs, and all persons who would endanger the security." In practice, their victims were nearly all Jewish civilians (not a single *Einsatzgruppe* member was killed in action during these operationsWikipedia:Citation needed). The United States Holocaust Memorial Museum tells the story of one survivor of the Einsatzgruppen in Piryatin, Ukraine, when they killed 1,600 Jews on April 6, 1942, the second day of Passover:

<templatestyles src="Template:Quote/styles.css"/>

> *I saw them do the killing. At 5:00 p.m. they gave the command, "Fill in the pits." Screams and groans were coming from the pits. Suddenly I saw my neighbor Ruderman rise from under the soil ... His eyes were bloody and he was screaming: "Finish me off!" ... A murdered woman lay at my feet. A boy of five years crawled out from under her body and*

**Figure 101:** *A member of Einsatzgruppe D is about to shoot a man sitting by a mass grave in Vinnytsia, Ukraine in 1942. Present in the background are members of the German Army, the German Labor Service, and the Hitler Youth.*[798] *The back of the photograph is inscribed "The last Jew in Vinnitsa"*

*began to scream desperately. "Mommy!" That was all I saw, since I fell unconscious.*

From September 16–30, 1941 the Nikolaev massacre in and around the city of Mykolaiv resulted in the deaths of 35,782 Soviet citizens, most of whom were Jews, as was reported to Hitler.

<templatestyles src="Template:Quote_box/styles.css" />

Jews of the city of Kiev and vicinity! On Monday, September 29, you are to appear by 08:00 a.m. with your possessions, money, documents, valuables, and warm clothing at Dorogozhitskaya Street, next to the Jewish cemetery. Failure to appear is punishable by death.

*– Order posted in Kiev in Russian and Ukrainian on or around September 26, 1941.*[799]

The most notorious massacre of Jews in Ukraine was at the Babi Yar ravine outside Kiev, where 33,771 Jews were killed in a single operation on September 29–30, 1941. (An amalgamation of 100,000 to 150,000 Ukrainian and other Soviet citizens were also killed in the following weeks). The mass killing of Jews in Kiev was decided on by the military governor Major-General

**Figure 102:** *Jews digging their own graves. Storow, July 4, 1941*

Friedrich Eberhardt, the Police Commander for Army Group South (SS-*Obergruppenführer* Friedrich Jeckeln) and the *Einsatzgruppe* C Commander Otto Rasch. It was carried out by a mixture of SS, SD and Security Police, assisted by the Ukrainian Auxiliary Police. On the Monday, the Jews of Kiev gathered by the cemetery, expecting to be loaded onto trains. The crowd was large enough that most of the men, women, and children could not have known what was happening until it was too late: by the time they heard the machine-gun fire, there was no chance to escape. All were driven down a corridor of soldiers, in groups of ten, and then shot. A truck driver described the scene:

<templatestyles src="Template:Quote/styles.css"/>

> [O]ne after the other, they had to remove their luggage, then their coats, shoes, and overgarments and also underwear ... Once undressed, they were led into the ravine which was about 150 meters long and 30 meters wide and a good 15 meters deep ... When they reached the bottom of the ravine they were seized by members of the Schutzmannschaft and made to lie down on top of Jews who had already been shot ... The corpses were literally in layers. A police marksman came along and shot each Jew in the neck with a submachine gun ... I saw these marksmen stand on layers of corpses and shoot one after the other ... The marksman would walk across the bodies of the executed Jews to the next Jew, who had meanwhile lain down, and shoot him.[799]

## Collaboration in Ukraine

The *National Geographic* reported:

> A number of Ukrainians had collaborated: According to German historian Dieter Pohl, around 100,000 joined police units that provided key assistance to the Nazis. Many others staffed the local bureaucracies or lent a helping hand during mass shootings of Jews. Ukrainians, such as the infamous Ivan the Terrible of Treblinka, were also among the guards who manned the German Nazi death camps.[800]

According to The Simon Wiesenthal Center (in January 2011) "Ukraine has, to the best of our knowledge, never conducted a single investigation of a local Nazi war criminal, let alone prosecuted a Holocaust perpetrator."[801]

According to the Israeli Holocaust historian Yitzhak Arad, "In January 1942 a company of Tatar volunteers was established in Simferopol under the command of *Einsatzgruppe 11*. This company participated in anti-Jewish manhunts and murder actions in the rural regions."

According to Timothy Snyder, "something that is never said, because it's inconvenient for precisely everyone, is that more Ukrainian Communists collaborated with the Germans, than did Ukrainian nationalists." As well, very many of those who collaborated with the German occupation, also collaborated Soviet policies of the 1930s.[802]

## Death toll

Until the fall of the Soviet Union, it was believed that about 900,000 Jews were murdered as part of the Holocaust in Ukraine. This is the estimate found in such respected works as *The Destruction of the European Jews* by Raul Hillberg. In the late 1990s, access to Soviet archives increased the estimates of the prewar population of Jews and as a result, the estimates of the death toll have been increasing. In the 1990s, Dieter Pohl estimated 1.2 million Jews murdered, and more recent estimates have been up to 1.6 million. Some of those Jews added to the death toll attempted to find refuge in the forest, but were killed later on by Home Army, the Ukrainian Insurgent Army, or other partisan groups during the German retreat. According to American historian Wendy Lower, "there were many perpetrators, albeit with different political agendas, who killed Jews and suppressed this history".

**Figure 103:** *Lvov Ghetto, 1942*

# Executor units

- Einsatzgruppen C & D (Einsatzkommando)
- Abwehr/Brandemburg special saboteur unit Nachtigall Battalion
- Freiwilligen-Stamm-Regiment 3 & 4 (Russians & Ukrainians)
- Ukrainian auxiliary units:[803] *Schutzmannschaft* as well as *Ukrainische Hilfspolizei*

# Survivors

- Mina Rosner
- Roald Hoffmann
- Shevah Weiss
- Simon Wiesenthal
- Adam Daniel Rotfeld
- Mordechai Rokeach
- Stefan Petelycky

# Rescuers

Ukraine rates the 4th in the number of people recognized as "Righteous Among the Nations" for saving Jews during the Holocaust, with the total of 2,515 individuals recognized as of 1 January 2015.

The Shtundists, an evangelical Protestant denomination which emerged in late 19th century Ukraine, helped hide Jews.

## Massacres

- Babi Yar
- Bila Tserkva
- Dnipropetrovsk
- Feodosiya
- Ivano-Frankivsk
- Klevan
- Lviv pogroms
- Massacre of Lviv professors
- Mezhirichi
- Mizoch
- Nikolaev massacre
- Olyka
- Plyskiv
- Terebovl
- Zhytomyr

## External links

- The Holocaust in Ukraine: New Sources and Perspectives[804], Center for Advanced Holocaust Studies of the United States Holocaust Memorial Museum, Conference Papers, 2013
- Holocaust, Fascism, and Ukrainian History: Does It Make Sense to Rethink the History of Ukrainian Perpetrators in the European Context, published by the American Association for Polish-Jewish Studies, April 2016.[805]

# The Holocaust in Lithuania

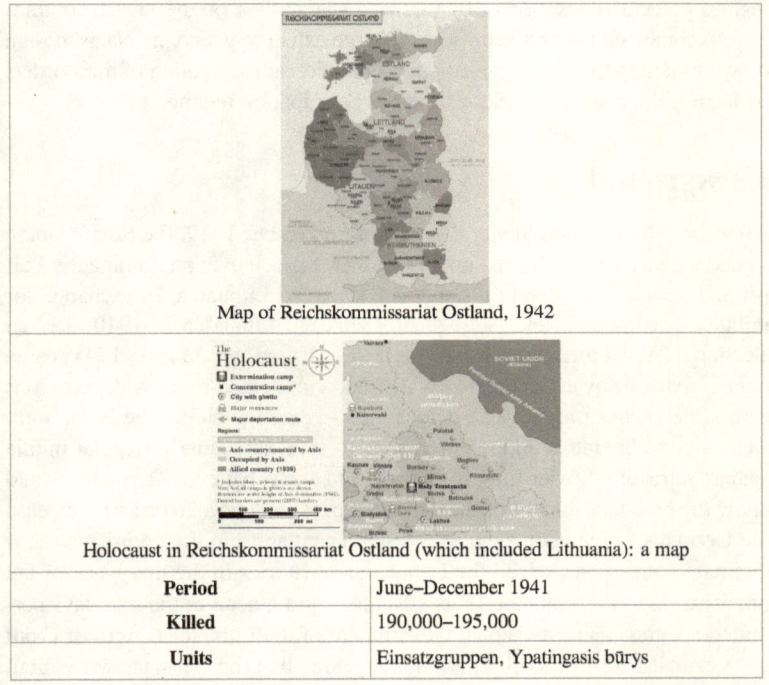

Map of Reichskommissariat Ostland, 1942

Holocaust in Reichskommissariat Ostland (which included Lithuania): a map

| Period | June–December 1941 |
|---|---|
| Killed | 190,000–195,000 |
| Units | Einsatzgruppen, Ypatingasis būrys |

**The Holocaust in German occupied Lithuania** resulted in the near total destruction of Lithuanian (Litvaks) and Polish Jews,[a] living in *Generalbezirk Litauen* of Reichskommissariat Ostland within the Nazi-controlled Lithuanian SSR. Out of approximately 208,000-210,000 Jews, an estimated 190,000–195,000 were murdered before the end of World War II (wider estimates are sometimes published), most between June and December 1941. More than 95% of Lithuania's Jewish population was massacred over the three-year German occupation — a more complete destruction than befell any other country affected by the Holocaust. Historians attribute this to the massive collaboration in the genocide by the non-Jewish local paramilitaries, though the reasons for this collaboration are still debated.[806] The Holocaust resulted in the largest-ever loss of life in so short a period of time in the history of Lithuania.

The events that took place in the western regions of the USSR occupied by Nazi Germany in the first weeks after the German invasion, including Lithuania, marked the sharp intensification of the Holocaust.[b]

An important component to the Holocaust in Lithuania was that the occupying Nazi German administration fanned antisemitism by blaming the Soviet regime's recent annexation of Lithuania, a year earlier, on the Jewish community. Another significant factor was the large extent to which the Nazis' design drew upon the physical organization, preparation and execution of their orders by local Lithuanian auxiliaries of the Nazi occupation regime.

## Background

After the joint German-Soviet invasion of September 1939, the Soviet Union signed a treaty with Lithuania on 10 October, handed over predominantly Polish and Jewish city of Wilno (renamed Vilna) to Lithuania, in exchange for military concessions, and subsequently annexed Lithuania in 1940 after an election. The German invasion of the Soviet Union, on 22 June 1941, came after a year of Soviet occupation which had culminated in mass deportations across the Baltics only a week before the German invasion. The Nazis were welcomed as liberators and received support from Lithuania's irregular militia against retreating Soviet forces. Many Lithuanians believed Germany would allow the re-establishment of the country's independence. In order to appease the Germans, some people expressed significant antisemitic sentiments. Nazi Germany, which had seized the Lithuanian territories in the first week of the offensive, used this situation to its advantage and indeed in the first days permitted a Lithuanian Provisional Government of the Lithuanian Activist Front to be established. For a brief period it appeared that the Germans were about to grant Lithuania significant autonomy, comparable with that given to Slovak Republic. However, after about a month, the more independently minded Lithuanian organizations were disbanded around August and September 1941, as the Germans seized more control.

## Destruction of Jewry

### Estimated number of victims

Prior to the German invasion, the population of Jews was estimated to be about 210,000, although according to data from the Lithuanian statistics department, as of 1 January 1941 there were 208,000 Jews. This estimate, based on the officially accounted for prewar emigration within the USSR (approx. 8,500), the number of escapees from the Kaunas and Vilnius Ghettos, (1,500-2,000), as well as the number of survivors in the concentration camps when they were liberated by the Red Army, (2,000-3,000), puts the number of Lithuanian Jews murdered in the Holocaust at 195,000 to 196,000. It is difficult to estimate the exact number of casualties of the Holocaust and the

The Holocaust in Lithuania

**Figure 104:** *Map titled "Jewish Executions Carried Out by Einsatzgruppe A" from the Stahlecker's report. Marked "Secret Reich Matter", the map shows the number of Jews shot in Reichskommissariat Ostland. According to this map the estimated numbers of Jews killed in Lithuania is 136,421 by the date that his map was created.*

latter number cannot be final or indisputable. The numbers given by historians differ significantly ranging from 165,000 to 254,000, the higher number probably including non-Lithuanian Jews among other Reich (empirical) dissenters labeled as Jewish killed in Lithuania.

## The Holocaust events

Chronologically, the genocide in Lithuania can be divided into three phases: phase 1. summer to the end of 1941; phase 2. December 1941 – March 1943; phase 3. April 1943 – mid-July 1944. The Lithuanian port city of Klaipėda (Memel in German) had historically been a member of the German Hanseatic League, and had belonged to Germany and East Prussia prior to 1918. The city was semi-autonomous during the period of Lithuanian independence, and under League of Nations supervision. Approximately 8,000 Jews lived in Memel when it was absorbed into the Reich on March 15, 1939. Its Jewish residents were expelled, and most fled into Lithuania proper. In 1941, German killing squads, the Einsatzgruppen, followed the advance of the German army units and immediately began organizing the murder of Jews.

**Figure 105:** *Kaunas Ninth Fort*

Most Lithuanian Jews perished in the first phase during the first months of the occupation and before the end of 1941. The first recorded action of the Einsatzgruppen (Einsatzgruppe A) took place on June 22, 1941, in the border town of Gargzdai (called Gorzdt in Yiddish and Garsden in German), which was one of the oldest Jewish settlements in the country and only 18 kilometres (11 mi) from Germany's recovered Memel. Approximately 800 Jews were shot that day in what is known as the Garsden Massacre. Approximately 100 non-Jewish Lithuanians were also executed, many for trying to aid the Jews. About 80,000 Jews were killed by October and about 175,000 by the end of the year. The majority of Jews in Lithuania were not required to live in ghettos[c] nor sent to the Nazi concentration camps which at that time were just in the preliminary stages of operation. Instead they were shot in pits near their places of residence with the most infamous mass murders taking place in the Ninth Fort near Kaunas and the Ponary Forest near Vilnius. By 1942 about 45,000 Jews survived, largely those who had been sent to ghettos and camps.[c] In the second phase, the Holocaust slowed, as Germans decided to use the Jews as forced labor to fuel the German war economy. In the third phase, the destruction of Jews was again given a high priority; it was in that phase that the remaining ghettos and camps were liquidated.

Two factors contributed to the rapid destruction of Lithuanian Jewry. The first was the significant support for the "de-Jewification" of Lithuania coming

# The Holocaust in Lithuania

**Figure 106:** *German soldiers and locals watch a Lithuanian synagogue burn, 9 July 1941*

from the Lithuanian populace. The second was the German plan for early colonization of Lithuania – which shared a border with German East Prussia – in accordance with their Generalplan Ost; hence the high priority given to the extermination of the relatively small Lithuanian Jewish community.

## Participation of local collaborators

The Nazi German administration directed and supported the organized killing of Lithuanian Jews. Local Lithuanian auxiliaries of the Nazi occupation regime carried out logistics for the preparation and execution of the murders under Nazi direction. Nazi SS Brigadeführer Franz Walter Stahlecker arrived in Kaunas on 25 June 1941 and gave agitation speeches in the city to instigate the murder of Jews. Initially this was in the former State Security Department building, but officials there refused to take any action. Later, he gave speeches in the city. In a report of October 15, Stahlecker wrote that they had succeeded in covering up their vanguard unit (Vorkommando) actions, and it was made to look like it was the initiative of the local population. Groups of partisans, civil units of nationalist-rightist anti-Soviet affiliation, initiated contact with the Germans as soon as they entered the Lithuanian territories. A rogue unit of insurgents headed by Algirdas Klimaitis and encouraged by Germans from the Sicherheitspolizei and Sicherheitsdienst, started anti-Jewish pogroms

**Figure 107:** *Holocaust mass graves near city of Jonava.*

in Kaunas (Kovno) on the night of 25–26 June 1941. Over a thousand Jews perished over the next few days in what was the first pogrom in Nazi-occupied Lithuania. Different sources give different figures, one being 1,500 and another 3,800, with additional victims in other towns of the region.

On 24 June 1941, the Lithuanian Security Police (*Lietuvos saugumo policija*), subordinate to Nazi Germany's Security Police and Nazi Germany's Criminal Police, was created. It would be involved in various actions against the Jews and other enemies of the Nazi regime. Nazi commanders filed reports purporting the "zeal" of the Lithuanian police battalions surpassed their own. The most notorious Lithuanian unit participating in the Holocaust was the Ypatingasis būrys (a subdivision of German SD) from the Vilnius (Vilna, Wilno) area whichWikipedia:Citation needed killed tens of thousands of Jews, Poles and others in the Ponary massacre. Another Lithuanian organization involved in the Holocaust was the Lithuanian Labor Guard. Many Lithuanian supporters of the Nazi policies came from the fascist Iron Wolf organization. Overall, the nationalistic Lithuanian administration was interested in the liquidation of the Jews as a perceived enemy and potential rivals of ethnic Lithuanians and thus not only did not oppose Nazi Holocaust policy but in effect adopted it as their own.

A combination of factors serves as an explanation for participation of some Lithuanians in genocide against Jews. Those factors include national traditions and values, including antisemitism, common throughout contemporary Central Europe, and a more Lithuanian-specific desire for a "pure" Lithuanian nation-state with which the Jewish population was believed to be incompatible. There were a number of additional factors, such as severe economic problems which led to the killing of Jews over personal property. Finally the Jews were seen as having supported the Soviet regime in Lithuania during 1940–1941.[d] During the period leading up to the German invasion, the Jews were blamed by some for virtually every misfortune that had befallen Lithuania.

The involvement of the local population and institutions, in relatively high numbers, in the destruction of Lithuanian Jewry became a defining factor of the Holocaust in Lithuania.

Not all of the Lithuanian populace supported the killings, and many hundreds risked their lives sheltering the Jews. Israel has recognized 891 Lithuanians (as of January 1, 2017) as Righteous Among the Nations for risking their lives to save Jews during the Holocaust. In addition, many members of the Polish minority in Lithuania also helped to shelter the Jews. Lithuanians and Poles who risked their lives saving Jews were persecuted and often executed by the Nazis.

## Comprehension and remembrance

The genocide in Lithuania is seen by some historians as one of the earliest large-scale implementations of the Final Solution, leading some scholars to express an opinion that the Holocaust began in Lithuania in the summer of 1941.* Other scholars say the Holocaust started in September 1939 with the onset of the Second World War, or even earlier, on Kristallnacht in 1938, or, according to the Jewish Virtual Library, when Hitler became Chancellor of Germany in 1933.

The Soviet government, for political reasonsWikipedia:Vagueness, tried to minimize the unique suffering of the Jews. In Lithuania and throughout the Soviet Union, memorials did not mention Jews in particular; instead they were built to commemorate the suffering of "local inhabitants". People guilty of Nazi collaboration and crimes against Jews were not punished severely.

Since Lithuania regained independence from the Soviet Union in 1991, the debate over Lithuanian participation in the Holocaust has been fraught with difficulty. Modern Lithuanian nationalists stress anti-Soviet resistance, but some Lithuanian partisans, seen in Lithuania as heroes in the struggle against Soviet occupation, were also Nazi collaborators who had cooperated in the murder of Lithuanian Jewry. The post-Soviet Lithuanian government has on a number of occasions stated a commitment to commemorating the Holocaust, combating antisemitism, and bringing Nazi-era war criminals to justice. The National

**Figure 108:** *Kaunas pogrom in June 1940, Vilna Gaon Jewish State Museum in Vilnius, Lithuania*

Coalition Supporting Soviet Jewry have said "Lithuania has made slow but significant progress in the prosecution of suspected Lithuanian collaborators in the Nazi genocide". Lithuania was the first of the newly independent post-Soviet states to legislate for the protection and marking of Holocaust-related sites. In 1995, president of Lithuania Algirdas Brazauskas speaking before the Israeli Knesset, offered a public apology to the Jewish people for the Lithuanian participation in the Holocaust. On 20 September 2001, to mark the 60th anniversary of the Holocaust in Lithuania, the Seimas (Lithuanian parliament) held a session during which Alfonsas Eidintas, the historian nominated as the Republic's next ambassador to Israel, delivered an address accounting for the annihilation of Lithuania's Jews.

There has been criticism that Lithuania is dragging its feet on the issue; in 2001 Dr. Efraim Zuroff, Director of the Simon Wiesenthal Center, criticized the Lithuanian government for its unwillingness to prosecute Lithuanians involved in the Holocaust. In 2002 the Simon Wiesenthal Center declared its dissatisfaction with the Lithuanian government's efforts and launched a controversial "Operation Last Chance" offering monetary rewards for evidence that leads to the prosecution of war criminals; this campaign has encountered much resistance in Lithuania and the other former Soviet bloc countries. More recently, in 2008, the Simon Weisenthal Center which had initially ranked

Lithuania high during on-going trials to bring Lithuanian war criminals to justice, noted, in its annual report, no progress and the lack of any real punishment by Lithuanian justice organs for Holocaust perpetrators.

There has been limited debate on the place of the Holocaust in Lithuanian national memory; historically Lithuanians have denied national participation in the Holocaust or labeled the Lithuanian participants in genocide as fringe extreme elements. The memories of that time and the discussion of those events in Jewish and Lithuanian historiographies are quite different, although Lithuanian historiography in the past two decades has improved, compared to the Soviet historiography, with the works of scholars such as Alfonsas Eidintas, Valentinas Brandišauskas and Arūnas Bubnys, among others, being positively reviewed by the Western and Jewish historians. The issue remains controversial to this day. According to Lithuanian historians, the contentious issues involve the role of the Lithuanian Activist Front, the Lithuanian Provisional Government and participation of Lithuanian civilians and volunteers in the Holocaust.

# Notes

<templatestyles src="Template:Refbegin/styles.css" />

**a** ^ While this article discusses the Holocaust on the Lithuanian territories, which primarily affected and resulted in the destruction of Lithuanian Jewry, tens of thousands of non-Lithuanian Jews also died on Lithuanian territories. This included primarily: 1) Polish Jews from Vilnius and others who sought refuge in Lithuania escaping the invasion of Poland in 1939 and 2) Jews from various Western countries shipped to extermination sites in Lithuania.

**b** ^ Some scholars have noted that the German Final Solution and the Holocaust actually began in Lithuania.
Dina Porat: "The Final Solution – the systematic overall physical extermination of Jewish communities one after the other – began in Lithuania."
Konrad Kwiet: "Lithuanian Jews were among the first victims of the Holocaust [...] The Germans carried out the mass executions [...] signalling the beginning of the "Final Solution." See also, Konrad Kwiet, "The Onset of the Holocaust: The Massacres of Jews in Lithuania in June 1941." Annual lecture delivered as J. B. and Maurice Shapiro Senior Scholar-in-Residence at the United States Holocaust Memorial Museum on 4 December 1995. Published under the same title but expanded in Power, Conscience and Opposition: Essays in German History in Honour of John A Moses, ed. Andrew Bonnell et al. (New York: Peter Lang, 1996), pp. 107–21

c ˆ Three major ghettos in Lithuania were established: Vilnius ghetto (with a population of about 20,000), Kaunas Ghetto (17,500) and the Shavli Ghetto (5,000); there were also a number of smaller ghettos and labor camps.

d ˆ The propaganda line of Jewish Bolshevism was used intensively by Nazis in instigating antisemitic feelings among Lithuanians. It built upon the pre-invasion antisemitic propaganda of the anti-Soviet Lithuanian Activist Front which had seized upon the fact that more Jews than Lithuanians supported the Soviet regime. This had helped to create an entire mythos of Jewish culpability for the sufferings of Lithuania under the Soviet regime (and beyond). A LAF pamphlet read: "For the ideological maturation of the Lithuanian nation it is essential that anticommunist and anti-Jewish action be strengthened [...] It is very important that this opportunity be used to get rid of the Jews as well. We must create an atmosphere that is so stifling for the Jews that not a single Jew will think that he will have even the most minimal rights or possibility of life in the new Lithuania. Our goal is to drive out the Jews along with the Red Russians. [...] The hospitality extended to the Jews by Vytautas the Great is hereby revoked for all time because of their repeated betrayals of the Lithuanian nation to its oppressors." An extreme faction of the supporters of Augustinas Voldemaras, a group which also worked within the LAF, actually envisioned a racially exclusive "Aryan" Lithuanian state. With the start of German occupation, one of Kaunas' newspapers – *Į Laisvę* (Towards Freedom), commenced a spirited antisemitic crusade, reinforcing the identity of the Jew with communism in popular consciousness: "Jewry and Bolshevism are one, parts of an indivisible entity."

## Further reading

- Arūnas Bubnys, *The Holocaust in Lithuania between 1941 and 1944*, Genocide and Resistance Research Centre of Lithuania, 2005, <templatestyles src="Module:Citation/CS1/styles.css" />ISBN 9986-757-66-5 abstract[807]
- Alfonsas Eidintas, *Jews, Lithuanians and the Holocaust*, Versus Aureus, 2003, <templatestyles src="Module:Citation/CS1/styles.css" />ISBN 978-9955-9613-8-3
- Alfonsas Eidintas, *A "Jew-Communist" Stereotype in Lithuania, 1940–1941*, Lithuanian Political Science Yearbook (01/2000), pp. 1–36,[808]
- Harry Gordon, *The Shadow of Death: The Holocaust in Lithuania*, University Press of Kentucky, 2000, <templatestyles src="Module:Citation/CS1/styles.css" />ISBN 0-8131-9008-8

- Rose Lerer-Cohen, Saul Issroff, *The Holocaust in Lithuania 1941–1945: A Book of Remembrance*, Gefen Booksm, 2002, <templatestyles src="Module:Citation/CS1/styles.css" />ISBN 965-229-280-X
- Dov Levin, *Lithuanian Attitudes toward the Jewish Minority in the Aftermath of the Holocaust: The Lithuanian Press, 1991–1992*, # Holocaust and Genocide Studies, Volume 7, Number 2, pp. 247–262, 1993,[809]
- Dov Levin, *On the Relations between the Baltic Peoples and their Jewish Neighbors before, during and after World War II*, Holocaust and Genocide Studies, Volume 5, Number 1, pp. 53–6, 1990,[810]
- Josifas Levinsonas, Joseph Levinson, *The Shoah (Holocaust) in Lithuania*, The Vilna Gaon Jewish State Museum, 2006, <templatestyles src="Module:Citation/CS1/styles.css" />ISBN 5-415-01902-2
- Alfred Erich Senn, *Lithuania 1940: Revolution from Above*, Rodopi, 2007, <templatestyles src="Module:Citation/CS1/styles.css" />ISBN 90-420-2225-6
- Vytautas Tininis, *"Kolaboravimo" sąvoka Lietuvos istorijos kontekste* (Definition of Lithuanian collaborationists),[811], Lietuvos gyventojų genocido ir rezistencijos tyrimo centras, 2004-01-30

Sepetys, Ruta. *Between shades of gray*. New York, N.Y.: Speak, 2012. Print.

# External links

- Lithuanian Holocaust Atlas[812] – Vilna Gaon State Jewish Museum, Lithuania
- United States Holocaust Memorial Museum, Holocaust Encyclopedia: Lithuania[813]
- The Genocide and Resistance Research Centre of Lithuania[814]
- Memorial to Murdered Jews of Lithuania[815] (w/ photos of the memorial)
- Atamukas, Solomonas. (2001), *The hard long road toward the truth: on the sixtieth anniversary of the holocaust in Lithuania*.[816] in Lithuanus/Lithuanian Quarterly Journal of Arts and Sciences, vol. 47, 4.
- Kulikauskas, Andrius. (2015), *How did Lithuanians wrong Litvaks?*[817]
- Holocaust In The Baltics[818] Information and updates on the ongoing debate, edited by Dovid Katz
- The Holocaust in Lithuania[819]
- German soldiers and Lithuanians watch a "partisan" murder Jewish men at the Lietukis garage, Kovno, June 27, 1941.[820]
- Chronicles of the Vilna Ghetto[821]
- Lietukis Garage Massacre in Kaunas (27 June 1941)[822]
- Lithuanian militiamen in Kovno round up Jews during an early pogrom. Kovno, Lithuania, June 25-July 8, 1941.[823]

- Kovno, Lithuania, Jews who were murdered by Lithuanian nationalists...[824]
- District of Kaunas / Kovno[825]
- Lithuanian Testimonies' Project[826]
- Jewish children on the streets of the Kovno ghetto. Lithuania, 1941–1943[827]
- Association of Lithuanian Jews in Israel[828]
- Как литовцы евреев убивали[829]
- Центр исследования геноцида и резистенции жителей Литвы[830]
- Double Genocide: Lithuania wants to erase its ugly history of Nazi collaboration[831]
- The Holocaust in Lithuania, and Its Obfuscation, in Lithuanian Sources[832]
- Kulikauskas, Andrius. Documents Which Argue for Ethnic Cleansing (by Kazys Škirpa, Stasys Raštikis, Stasys Lozoraitis and Petras Klimas in 1940-1941 and by Birutė Teresė Burauskaitė in 2015)[833]

<indicator name="good-star"> ⊕ </indicator>

# The Holocaust in Latvia

| | The Holocaust in Latvia |
|---|---|
| | Exhibit presented at the Wannsee (Holocaust planning) Conference on January 20, 1942, showing only 3,500 Jews left alive in Latvia of about 60,000 in the country at the time of the Nazi takeover. |
| Also known as | *Churbns Lettlands* |
| Location | Latvia |
| Date | 22 June 1941 to late 1944 |
| Incident type | Imprisonment, mass shootings, concentration camps, ghettos, forced labor, starvation, mass kidnapping, |
| Perpetrators | Rudolf Lange, Friedrich Jeckeln, Franz Walter Stahlecker, Viktors Arājs and others |
| Organizations | Einsatzgruppen, Ordnungspolizei, Wehrmacht, Arajs Kommando, Latvian Auxiliary Police, Kriegsmarine, and others. |
| Victims | About 66,000 Latvian Jews, 19,000 German, Austrian and Czech Jews, unknown numbers of Lithuanian and Hungarian Jews; unknown but substantial number of Gypsies, Communists, and mentally disabled persons; unknown number of non-Jewish Latvians shot or imprisoned in reprisals and so-called "anti-partisan" activities |
| Memorials | At various points in country, including multiple locations in the Riga area |

**The Holocaust in Latvia** refers to the war crimes of Nazis and Nazi collaborators victimizing Jews during the occupation of Latvia by Nazi Germany.

## German occupation

The German army crossed the Soviet frontier early in the morning on Sunday, 22 June 1941, on a broad front from the Baltic Sea to Hungary. The German

**Figure 109:** *Holocaust in Reichskommissariat Ostland (which included Latvia): a map*

**Figure 110:** *Fire damage in Daugavpils, July 1941*

army advanced quickly through Lithuania towards Daugavpils and other strategic points in Latvia. The Nazi police state included an organisation called the Security Service (German: *Sicherheitsdienst*), generally referred to as the SD, and its headquarters in Berlin was known as the National (or Reich) Security Main Office (*Reichssicherheitshauptamt*), known by its initials RSHA.[834]

## The SD in Latvia

In advance of the invasion, the SD had organised four "Special Assignment Units", which have become known in history by their German name of Einsatzgruppen. The name of these units was a euphemism, as their real purpose was to kill large numbers of people whom the Nazis regarded as "undesirable". These included Communists, Gypsies, the mentally ill, and especially, Jews. The Einsatzgruppen followed closely behind the German invasion forces, and established a presence in Latvia within days, and sometimes hours, of the occupation of a given area of the country by the German Wehrmacht.

The SD in Latvia can be distinguished in photographs and descriptions by their uniforms. The full black of the Nazi SS was seldom worn, instead the usual attire was the grey Wehrmacht uniform with black accents. They wore the SD patch on the left sleeve, a yellowish shirt, and the Death's Head (*Totenkopf*) symbol on their caps. The SD ranks were identical to the SS. The SD did not wear the SS lightning rune symbol on their right collar tabs, but replaced it with either the Totenkopf or the letters "SD".

The SD first established its power in Latvia through Einsatzgruppe A, which was subdivided into units called Einsatzkommandos 1a, 1b, 2 and 3. As the front line moved further east, Einsatzgruppe A moved out of Latvia, remaining in the country only a few weeks, after which its functions were taken over by the "resident" SD, under the authority of the *Kommandant der Sicherheitspolizei un SD*, generally referred to by the German initials of KdS. The KdS took orders both from RSHA in Berlin and from another official called the *Befehlshaber* (commander) *der Sicherheitspolizei und des SD*, or BdS. Both the KdS and the BdS were subordinate to another official called the Ranking (or Higher) SS and Police Commander (*Höherer SS-und Polizeiführer*), or HPSSF. The lines of authority were overlapping and ambiguous.[835] The eastern part of Latvia, including Daugavpils and the Latgale region, was assigned to Einsatzkommandos 1b (EK 1b) and 3 (EK 3). EK 1b had about 50 to 60 men and was commanded by Erich Ehrlinger.

**Figure 111:** *Members of a Latvian self-defence unit assemble a group of Jewish women for execution on a beach near Liepāja, 15 December 1941.*

## Murders commence with Nazi invasion

In Latvia, the Holocaust started on the night of 23 to 24 June 1941, when in the Grobiņa cemetery an SD detachment killed six local Jews, including the town chemist.[836] On the following days 35 Jews were exterminated in Durbe, Priekule and Asīte. On June 29 the Nazi invaders started forming the first Latvian SD auxiliary unit in Jelgava. Mārtiņš Vagulāns, member of the Pērkonkrusts organisation, was chosen to head it. In the summer of 1941, 300 men in the unit took part in the extermination of about 2000 Jews in Jelgava and other places in Zemgale. The killing was supervised by the officers of the German SD Rudolf Batz and Alfred Becu, who involved the SS people of the Einsatzgruppe in the action. The main Jelgava Synagogue was burnt down through their joint effort. After the invasion of Riga, Walter Stahlecker, assisted by the members of Pērkonkrusts and other local collaborationists, organised the pogrom of Jews in the capital of Latvia. Viktors Arājs, aged 31 at the time, possible former member of Pērkonkrusts and a member of a student fraternity, was appointed direct executor of the action. He was an idle eternal student who was supported by his wife, a rich shop owner, who was ten years older than he was. Arājs had worked in the Latvian Police for a certain period of time. He stood out with his power-hungry and extreme thinking. The man was well fed, well dressed, and "with his student's hat proudly cocked on one ear".

**Figure 112:** *'Two Worlds": An anti-communist and anti-semitic propaganda board, Latvia, Summer, 1941.*

## Arājs commando formed

On 2 July Viktors Arājs started to form his armed unit of men who were responding to the appeal of Pērkonkrusts to take arms and to clear Latvia of Jews and communists. In the beginning the unit mainly included members of different student fraternities. In 1941 altogether about 300 men had applied. The closest assistants of Viktors Arājs included Konstantīns Kaķis, Alfrēds Dikmanis, Boris Kinsler and Herberts Cukurs. On the night of July 3, Arājs Kommando started arresting, beating and robbing the Riga Jews. On 4 July, the choral synagogue at Gogoļa Street was burnt, and thereafter, the synagogues at Maskavas and Stabu Streets. Many Jews were killed during those days, including the refugees from Lithuania. In carts and blue buses the men of Arājs Commando went to different places in Courland, Zemgale and Vidzeme, killing thousands of Jews there.

These killings were supposed to serve as an example to other anti-Semitic supporters of the Nazi invaders. Individual Latvian Selbstschutz units were also involved in the extermination of Jews. In the district of Ilūkste, for instance, Jews were killed by the Selbstschutz death unit of commander Oskars Baltmanis, which consisted of 20 cold-blooded murderers. All killings were supervised by the officers of the German SS and SD. In July 1941 the mass killing of Riga Jews took place in the Biķernieku Forest. About 4,000 people died there. The executions were headed by Sturmbannführers (majors) H. Barth, R. Batz, and the newly appointed chief of the Riga SD Rudolf Lange.

**Figure 113:** *Members of Latvian Auxiliary Police assemble a group of Jews, Liepāja, July, 1941.*

# Massacres

As stated by the Latvian historian Andrievs Ezergailis, this was the beginning of "the greatest criminal act in the history of Latvia". From July 1941 the Jews of Latvia were also humiliated in different ways and deprived of the rights that were enjoyed by the other citizens of Latvia. Jews were strictly forbidden to leave their homes in the evening, at night and in the morning. They were allotted lower food rations, they could only shop in some special stores, and they had to wear the mark of recognition – the yellow Star of David on their clothes. It was forbidden for them to attend places where public events took place, including cinemas, athletic fields and parks. They were not allowed to use trains and trams, to go to bath-houses, use pavements, attend libraries and museums or to go to schools, and they had to hand over bicycles and radios. Jewish doctors were only allowed to advise and treat Jews, and they were forbidden to run pharmacies. Maximum norms for furniture, clothes and linen were also soon introduced for Jews. All articles above the norm were subject to confiscation for the needs of the Reich. All jewelry, securities, gold and silver coins had to be surrendered on demand. Anti-Semitism thus became the source of enrichment of Nazi officials and their local collaborators who confiscated Jewish property. The extermination of Jews suited the purposes of these Nazis, since nobody would remain alive to demand the return of stolen items.

## Liepāja

In Liepāja the first mass killing of Jews took place on July 3 and 4, when about 400 people were shot dead, and on July 8 when 300 Jews were killed. The German group of SD and policemen did the shooting, while the members of Latvian Selbstschutz convoyed victims to the killing site.[837] On July 13 the destroying of the large choral synagogue of Liepāja began. The rolls of the Scripture were spread on the Ugunsdzēsēju Square, and the Jews were forced to march across their sacred things, with watchers merrily laughing at the amusing scene. The above operations took place under the direct leadership of Erhard Grauel, commander of the Einsatzgruppe's Sonderkommando.

## Ventspils

Thereafter Grauel went to Ventspils. The killings were jointly carried out by German Ordnungspolizei and the men of the local Selbstschutz. On July 16-July 18, 300 people were shot dead in the Kaziņu Forest. In July–August the remaining 700 Jews of the town were shot dead, while the Jews of the region were killed in the autumn. The shooting was carried out by German, Latvian and Estonian SD men who had arrived by ship. Soon a poster appeared on the Kuldīga-Ventspils highway, which said that Ventspils was Judenfrei (free of Jews).

## Daugavpils

In Daugavpils the extermination of Jews was initially commanded by Erich Ehrlinger, chief of Einsatzkommando 1b. By July 11 they had killed about 1150 people. Ehrlinger's work was continued by Joachim Hamann, who was liable for the killing of 9012 Jews in the city and in southern Latgale. The chief of the local auxiliary police Roberts Blūzmanis had rendered active assistance by ensuring the moving of the Jews to the Grīva ghetto and transporting them to the killing places.

## Rēzekne

In Rēzekne killings were carried out by a German SD group, which was helped by Selbstschutz men and Arājs murderers. About 2,500 people were exterminated. By October 1941, altogether about 35,000 Latvian Jews were killed.

**Figure 114:** *Hinrich Lohse in the Riga Central Railway Station.*

## Varaklani

Varaklani, a relatively small town, had about 540 remaining Jews when the Germans gained control. They were shot into graves they were forced to dig on August 4, 1941. The fate of this small town is similar to many other towns, documented by JewishGen and others.

## Confinement

### Riga Ghetto

 Wikisourcehas original text related to this article:
**Comprehensive report of Einsatzgruppe A up to 15 October 1941**

# The Holocaust in Latvia

**Figure 115:** *The Jews with Yellow badges, Riga, 1942.*

**Figure 116:** *Riga ghetto, 1942*

**Figure 117:** *Jewish prisoners in Salaspils concentration camp*

**Figure 118:** *An Anti-partisan operation, March 1943.*

On July 27, 1941, State Commissar (Reichskommissar) Hinrich Lohse (earlier Gauleiter of Schleswig-Holstein), ruler of the Baltic lands and Belarus or Ostland as the territory was called by the invaders – made his guidelines on Jewish question public. Jews, in his opinion, had to be used as a cheap labour force by paying them minimum wages or by providing them with a minimum food ration – with whatever may be left over after supplying the indigenous Aryan population. In order to govern the Jews they had to be moved to special areas where ghettos would be arranged and they would be forbidden to leave the area. Walter Stahlecker protested against the idea of Hinrich Lohse and demanded that the extermination of the Jews be continued. Berlin, however, passed the power to the civil administration of occupation force and it did things its own way. The area of the Latgale suburbs in Riga was chosen for the Riga Ghetto. It was mainly inhabited by poor people: Jews, Russians and Belarusians. The ghetto bordered on Maskavas, Vitebskas, Ebreju (Jewish), Līksnas, Lauvas, Lazdonas, Lielā Kalnu, Katoļu, Jēkabpils and Lāčplēša Streets. About 7000 non-Jews were moved from there to other flats in Riga. More than 23,000 Riga Jews were ordered to move to the territory of the ghetto. There now were more than 29,000 inmates in the ghetto, including those who had already previously resided there. The Jewish Council was formed within the ghetto, which was assigned the task of regulating social life. The Jewish police force for the maintenance of order formed there. It consisted of 80 men armed with sticks and rubber truncheons. The ghetto was enclosed by a barbed-wire fence. Wooden barriers (logs) were placed on the main streets at the entrance, and the Latvian police were stationed as guards there. Jews were allowed to leave the ghetto only in work columns and in the accompaniment of guards. Individual Jewish specialists could come and go by displaying a special yellow ID. Leaving independently was severely punished.

In the ghetto the Jews were very crowded: 3-4 square metres were allotted per person. There was also great poverty, as food rations were given only to those who worked, i.e. to about a half of the ghetto inmates. They had to maintain their 5,652 children and 8,300 elderly and disabled people. The ghetto only had 16 groceries, a pharmacy and a laundry, and a hospital was arranged, which was headed by Professor Vladimir Mintz, a surgeon. The Council of the ghetto was situated in the former Jewish school building at 141 Lāčplēša Street. The historian Marģers Vestermanis writes: "The members of the Jewish Council, including the lawyers D. Elyashev, M. Mintz and Iliya Yevelson, and their volunteer assistants did all they could to somehow relieve general suffering."[838] Jewish policemen, too, tried to somehow protect their fellowmen. The inmates strived to preserve themselves, and there was even an illusion of survival. A resistance group was formed that bought weapons.[839]

## Daugavpils ghetto

The Daugavpils Ghetto was set up in Grīva at the end of July, 1941, when all surviving Jews in the city were moved there. Jews from other towns and villages of Latgale and even Vidzeme were also brought there. Altogether the ghetto had about 15,000 prisoners. The engineer Misha Movshenson ran the Council of the ghetto. His father had headed the city of Daugavpils in 1918 during the previous period of German occupation.

## Gypsy Holocaust in Latvia

Less is known about the Holocaust of the Romani people (called "Gypsy" in English and *Ziguener* in German) than for other groups.[840] Most of the available information about the persecution of the Gypsies in Nazi-occupied eastern Europe comes from Latvia.[841] According to Latvia's 1935 census, 3,839 Gypsies lived in the country, the largest population of any of the Baltic States. Many of them did not travel about the country, but lived settled, or "sedentary" lives.

On December 4, 1941, Hinrich Lohse issued a decree which stated:

<templatestyles src="Template:Quote/styles.css"/>

> *Gypsies who wander about in the countryside represent a two-fold danger. 1. As carriers of contagious diseases, especially typhus; 2. As unreliable elements who neither obey the regulations issued by German authorities, nor are willing to do useful work.*
>
> *There exists well-founded suspicion that they provide intelligence to the enemy and thus damage the German cause. I therefore order that they are to be treated as Jews.*

Although Lohse's name was on the order, it was actually issued at the behest of Bruno Jedicke,[842] the Ordnungspolizei chief in the Baltic States. Jedicke in turn was subordinate to Friedrich Jeckeln, the senior SS man in the Baltic States and Belarus.[843]

Gypsies were also forbidden to live along the coast. Historian Lewy believes this restriction may have occasioned the first large killing of Gypsies in Latvia. On December 5, 1941, the Latvian police in Liepāja arrested 103 Gypsies (24 men, 31 women, and 48 children). Of these people, the Latvian police turned over 100 to the custody of the German police chief Fritz Dietrich "for follow up" (*zu weiteren Veranlassung*), a Nazi euphemism for murder. On December 5, 1941, all 100 were all killed near Frauenburg.

On January 12, 1942, Jedicke distributed Lohse's order of December 4, 1941, ordering his subordinates that in all cases, they were to make sure to implement the necessary "follow up." By May 18, 1942 the German police and SS commander in Liepāja indicated in a log that over a previous unspecified period, 174 Gypsies had been killed by shooting. The German policy on Gypsies varied. In general, it seemed that wandering or "itinerate" Gypsies (*vagabundierende Zigeuner*) were targeted, as opposed to the non-wandering, or "sedentary" population. Thus, on May 21, 1942, the SS commander in Liepāja police and SS commander recorded the execution of 16 itinerate Gypsies from the Hasenputh district. The documentation however does not always distinguish between different Gypsy groups, thus on April 24, 1942, EK A reported having killed 1,272 people, including 71 Gypsies, with no further description. In addition, the Nazi policy shifted back and forth as to how the Gypsies were to be treated, and the treatment of any particular group of Gypsies did not necessarily reflect what might appear to have been the official policy of the moment.[844]

Like the Jews, the killing of the Gypsies proceeded through Latvia's smaller towns, and with the aid of Latvians. The Arājs Commando was reported to have killed many Gypsies between July and September 1941. In April, 1942, 50 Gypsies, mostly women and small children, were assembled at the jail in Valmiera, then taken out and shot. Other massacres were reported at Bauska and Tukums.

It is not known how many of Latvia's Gypsies were killed by the Nazis and their Latvian collaborators. Professor Ezergailis estimated that one-half of the Gypsy population was killed, but there will probably never be a more definite number.[845]

## Justice

Some of the Rumbula murderers were captured after the fact.

- Hinrich Lohse was a member of a Nazi class that "was to receive surprisingly light treatment" at the Nuremberg trials.[846] In Lohse's case, apparently because the British authorities believed him to have been innocent of the Nazi crimes in the Baltic states, he was handed over to a West German "denazification" court. Sentenced to the maximum of 10 years, Lohse was released early in 1951 "on the familiar grounds of ill health."
- Victors Arajs was charged in a British court with war crimes, but was released in 1948, and afterwards hid out in West Germany for many years; although he was still a wanted war criminal, he found work as a driver for a British military unit in the western occupation zone.[847] Eventually Arajs was caught, and, in 1979, tried and convicted of murder in a West German court.[848,849]

**Figure 119:** *SS-Obergruppenführer Hans-Adolf Prützmann.*

- Friedrich Jahnke, a Nazi policeman who had been instrumental in setting up the Riga Ghetto and organizing the march out to the pits, was likewise apprehended and tried in West Germany in the 1970s.[850]
- Herberts Cukurs escaped to South America, where he was later murdered. It is said that he was assassinated by Mossad agents, who attracted him from Brazil to Uruguay under a fake intention of starting an aviation business,[851] after it was found out that he would not stand trial for his alleged participation in the Holocaust.
- Eduard Strauch, SS Lieutenant Colonel, commanded a subunit of the Rumbula killers called "Einsatzkommando 2.".[852] Despite an effort to sham mental illness, he was convicted by the Nuremberg Military Tribunal in the Einsatzgruppen trial for having a key role in the Rumbula and a number of other mass murders in Eastern Europe. On April 9, 1948, Presiding judge Michael Musmanno pronounced the tribunal's sentence on Strauch: "Defendant EDUARD STRAUCH, on the counts of the indictment on which you have been convicted, the Tribunal sentences you to death by hanging."[853] Unlike his co-defendants Otto Ohlendorf and Paul Blobel, Strauch did not hang. Instead, he was handed over to authorities in Belgium, where he had committed other crimes, for trial. He died in Belgian custody on September 11, 1955.[854,855]

- Friedrich Jeckeln came into Soviet custody after the war. He was interrogated, tried, convicted and hanged in Riga on February 3, 1946. Against popular misconception, the execution did not happen in the territory of the former Riga ghetto, but in Victory Square (Uzvaras laukums).[856]

# Historiography and memorials

## Soviet period

After the Second World War, the Soviet Union again occupied Latvia, this time from 1944 to 1990. It did not suit Soviet purposes to memorialize the Rumbula site or to acknowledge that the victims were Jewish. Until 1960 nothing was done to preserve or memorialize the killing grounds. In 1961 young Jews from Riga searched for the site and found charred bones and other evidence of the murders. In 1962 the Soviets staged an officially sanctioned memorial service at Bikernieki (another murder site) which made no mention of the Jews but spoke only of "Nazi victims". In 1963 groups of young Jews from Riga came out to Rumbula weekly and cleaned up and restored the site using shovels, wheelbarrows and other hand tools.[857] The site has been marked by a series of makeshift memorials over the years. Throughout the Soviet domination of Latvia the Soviets refused to allow any memorial which would specifically identify the victims as Jews.

The Soviet Union suppressed research into and memorials of the Holocaust in Latvia until 1991, when Soviet rule over Latvia ended.[858] In one case a memorial at Rumbula of which the authorities did not approve was simply hauled away in the middle of the night, with no explanation given. Occasional references were made to the Holocaust in literature during the Soviet era. A folkloric figure called "žīdu šāvējs" (Jew shooter) turned up in stories on occasion. The poet Ojārs Vācietis often referred to the Holocaust in his work, including in particular his well-regarded poem "Rumbula", written in the early 1960s.[859] One notable survivor of the Latvian Holocaust was Michael Genchik, who escaped from Latvia and joined the Red Army, where he served for 30 years. His family was killed at Rumbula. Many years later he recalled:

> In later years the officials held memorial services every year in November or December. There were speeches reminding of the atrocities of the Nazis. But saying kaddish was forbidden. Once after the official part of the meeting, Jews tried to say Kaddish and tell a little about the ghetto, but the police didn't permit to do so. Until 1972, when I retired from the army, I did my best to keep the place neat.

## Independent Latvia

In Latvia, Holocaust scholarship could only be resumed once Soviet rule had ended.[860] Much of the post-1991 work was devoted to identification of the victims. This was complicated by the passage of time and the loss of some records and the concealment of others by the NKVD and its successor agencies of the Soviet secret police.[861]

On November 29, 2002, sixty-one years after the murders, the highest officials of the Republic of Latvia, together with representatives of the Latvian Jewish community, foreign ambassdors, and others attended a memorial dedication at the Rumbula site. The President and the Prime Minister of the Republic walked to the forest from where the Riga ghetto had been. Once they arrived, President Vaira Vīķe-Freiberga addressed the gathering:

<templatestyles src="Template:Quote/styles.css"/>

> *The Holocaust, in its many forms, has painfully struck Latvia. Here in Rumbula where the earthly remains of Latvia's Jews rest, we have come to honour and remember them. I wish therefore to extend a special greeting to the representatives of Latvia's Jewish community for whom this is special day of mourning, all the more so since here lie their loved ones, relatives, and members of their faith.* \* \* \*
>
> *This is an atrocious act of violence, an atrocious massacre. And it is our duty, the duty of those of us who have survived, to pass on the commemoration of these innocent victims to future generations, to remember with compassion, sorrow and reverence. Our duty is to teach our children and children's children about it, our duty is to seek out the survivors and record their recollections, but, above all, our duty is to see that this will never happen again.*[862]

# References

## Historiographical

- Anders, Edward, and Dubrovskis, Juris, "Who Died in the Holocaust? Recovering Names from Official Records", Holocaust and Genocide Studies 17.1 (2003) 114-138[863]
- (in German) Angrick, Andrej, and Klein, Peter, *Die "Endlösung" in Riga.*, (English: *The Final Solution in Riga*), Darmstadt 2006, <templatestyles src="Module:Citation/CS1/styles.css" />ISBN 3-534-19149-8

- Bloxham, Donald, Genocide on Trial; war crimes trials and the formation of Holocaust History and Memory, *Oxford University Press, New York NY 2001* <templatestyles src="Module:Citation/CS1/styles.css" />ISBN 0-19-820872-3
- Browning, Christopher, and Matthäus, Jürgen, *The Origins of the Final Solution: The Evolution of Nazi Jewish Policy, September 1939 – March 1942*, University of Nebraska Press, Lincoln, NE 2004 <templatestyles src="Module:Citation/CS1/styles.css" />ISBN 978-0-8032-5979-9
- Dribins, Leo, Gūtmanis, Armands, and Vestermanis, Marģers, "Latvia's Jewish Community: History, Trajedy, Revival", Ministry of Foreign Affairs, Republic of Latvia[864]
- Edelheit, Abraham J. and Edelheit, Hershel, *History of the Holocaust : A Handbook and Dictionary*, Westview Press, Boulder, CO 1994 <templatestyles src="Module:Citation/CS1/styles.css" />ISBN 0-8133-1411-9
- Eksteins, Modris, *Walking Since Daybreak: A story of Eastern Europe, World War II, and the Heart of our Century*, Houghton Mifflin, Boston 1999 <templatestyles src="Module:Citation/CS1/styles.css" />ISBN 0-395-93747-7
- Ezergailis, Andrew, *The Holocaust in Latvia 1941-1944—The Missing Center*, Historical Institute of Latvia (in association with the United States Holocaust Memorial Museum) Riga 1996 <templatestyles src="Module:Citation/CS1/styles.css" />ISBN 9984-9054-3-8
- Ezergailis, Andrew, "Latvia", in *The World Reacts to the Holocaust*, Wyman, David S., and Rosenzveig, Charles H., Eds., at pages 354-388, Johns Hopkins University Press, Baltimore 1996 <templatestyles src="Module:Citation/CS1/styles.css" />ISBN 0-8018-4969-1
- Fleming, Gerald, *Hitler and the Final Solution*, Berkeley : University of California Press, Berkeley,1994 <templatestyles src="Module:Citation/CS1/styles.css" />ISBN 0-520-06022-9
- Friedländer, Saul, *The years of extermination : Nazi Germany and the Jews, 1939-1945*, New York, NY 2007 <templatestyles src="Module:Citation/CS1/styles.css" />ISBN 978-0-06-019043-9
- Hancock, Ian, "Genocide of the Roma in the Holocaust", Excerpted from Charny, Israel, W., *Encyclopedia of Genocide* (1997) available on-line at the Patrin Web Journal[865] at the Wayback Machine (archived October 26, 2009)
- Hilberg, Raul, *The Destruction of the European Jews* (3d Ed.) Yale University Press, New Haven, CT 2003. <templatestyles src="Module:Citation/CS1/styles.css" />ISBN 0-300-09557-0
- Kaufmann, Max, *Die Vernichtung des Judens Lettlands* (*The Destruction of the Jews of Latvia*), Munich, 1947, English translation by Laimdota Mazzarins available on-line as Churbn Lettland – The Destruction of the

Jews of Latvia[866] (all references in this article are to page numbers in the on-line edition) <templatestyles src="Module:Citation/CS1/styles.css" />ISBN 978-3866283152
- Klee, Ernst, Dressen, Willi, and Riess, Volker, eds., *The Good Old Days: The Holocaust as seen by its Perpetrators and Bystanders*, (English translation) MacMillan Free Press, NY 1991 <templatestyles src="Module:Citation/CS1/styles.css" />ISBN 0-02-917425-2
- Latvia Institute, The Holocaust in German-Occupied Latvia[867]
- Lewy, Guenter, *The Nazi Persecution of the Gypsies*, Oxford University Press 2000 <templatestyles src="Module:Citation/CS1/styles.css" />ISBN 0-19-512556-8
- Lumans, Valdis O., *Latvia in World War II*, New York : Fordham University Press, 2006 <templatestyles src="Module:Citation/CS1/styles.css" />ISBN 0-8232-2627-1
- Michelson, Frida, *I Survived Rumbuli*, Holocaust Library, New York, NY 1979 <templatestyles src="Module:Citation/CS1/styles.css" />ISBN 0-89604-029-1
- Ministry of Foreign Affairs of the Republic of Latvia, Holocaust Remembrance - Rumbula Memorial Site Unveiled, December 2002[868]
- Niewyk, Donald L., and Nicosia, Francis R., *The Columbia Guide to the Holocaust*, New York : Columbia University Press, 2003
- Press, Bernhard (2000). *The Murder of the Jews in Latvia: 1941-1945*[869]. Northwestern University Press. ISBN 978-081011729-7.<templatestyles src="Module:Citation/CS1/styles.css"></templatestyles>
- Reitlinger, Gerald, *The SS—Alibi of a Nation*, at 186, 282, Viking Press, New York, 1957 (Da Capo reprint 1989) <templatestyles src="Module:Citation/CS1/styles.css" />ISBN 0-306-80351-8
- Roseman, Mark, *The Wannsee Conference and the Final Solution—A Reassessment*, Holt, New York, 2002 <templatestyles src="Module:Citation/CS1/styles.css" />ISBN 0-8050-6810-4
- Rubenstein, Richard L., and Roth, John K., *Approaches to Auschwitz*, page 179, Louisville, Ky. : Westminster John Knox Press, 2003. <templatestyles src="Module:Citation/CS1/styles.css" />ISBN 0-664-22353-2
- (in German) Scheffler, Wolfgang, "Zur Geschichte der Deportation jüdischer Bürger nach Riga 1941/1942", Volksbund Deutsche Kriegsgräberfürsorge e.V. – 23.05.2000[870]
- Schneider, Gertrude, ed., *The Unfinished Road: Jewish Survivors of Latvia Look Back*, Praeger Publishers (1991) <templatestyles src="Module:Citation/CS1/styles.css" />ISBN 978-0-275-94093-5
- Smith, Lyn, *Remembering: Voices of the Holocaust*, Carroll & Graf, New York 2005 <templatestyles src="Module:Citation/CS1/styles.css"

/>ISBN 0-7867-1640-1
- Winter, Alfred, "Rumbula Viewed From The Riga Ghetto" from *The Ghetto of Riga and Continuance - A Survivor's Memoir* 1998[871]

## War crimes trials and evidence

- Bräutigam, Otto, Memorandum dated 18 Dec. 1941, "Jewish Question re correspondence of 15 Nov. 1941" translated and reprinted in Office of the United States Chief of Counsel For Prosecution of Axis Criminality, OCCPAC: *Nazi Conspiracy and Aggression*, Exhibit 3666-PS, Volume VII, pages 978-995, USGPO, Washington DC 1946 ("Red Series")
- Jeckeln, Friedrich, excerpts from minutes of interrogation, 14 December 1945 (Maj. Zwetajew, interrogator, Sgt. Suur, interpreter), pages 8–13, from the Historical State Archives, as reprinted in Fleming, *Hitler and the Final Solution*, at pages 95–100 (Portions of the Jeckeln interrogation are also available online at the Nizkor website[872]).
- Stahlecker, Franz W., "Comprehensive Report of Einsatzgruppe A Operations up to 15 October 1941", Exhibit L-180, translated in part and reprinted in Office of the United States Chief of Counsel For Prosecution of Axis Criminality, OCCPAC: *Nazi Conspiracy and Aggression*, Volume VII, pages 978-995, USGPO, Washington DC 1946 ("Red Series")
- *Trials of War Criminals before the Nuernberg Military Tribunals under Control Council Law No. 10, Nuernberg, October 1946 - April 1949*, Volume IV, ("Green Series) (the "Einsatzgruppen case")[873] also available at Mazel library[874] (well indexed HTML version)

# Further reading

- Hancock, Ian "Downplaying the Porrajmos: The Trend to Minimize the Romani Holocaust—A review of Guenther Lewy, *The Nazi Persecution of the Gypsies* on-line edition[875] (criticizing Guenter Lewy's treatment of the Gypsy holocaust)
- Margalit, Gilad, *Germany and its gypsies—A Post-Auschwitz Ordeal* Madison, Wisc.: University of Wisconsin Press2002 <templatestyles src="Module:Citation/CS1/styles.css" />ISBN 0-299-17670-3
- Fings, Karola; Kenrick, Donald; Heuss, Herbert; and Sparing, Frank, *The Gypsies during the Second World War*, Hatfield, Hertfordshire : Gypsy Research Centre, University of Hertfordshire Press, 1997 <templatestyles src="Module:Citation/CS1/styles.css" />ISBN 0-900458-78-X

## External links

 Wikimedia Commons has media related to *The Holocaust in Latvia*.

- The Death of the Jewish Community of Kraslava[876]
- Holocaust in the Baltics[877], a site by Professor Dovid Katz of the Vilnius Yiddish Institute at Vilnius University
- Propagandistic German video[878] showing the entrance of the Wehrmacht in Riga.

# The Holocaust in Estonia

**The Holocaust in Estonia** refers to the Nazi crimes during the occupation of Estonia by Nazi Germany. Prior to the war, there were approximately 4,300 Estonian Jews. After the Soviet 1940 occupation about 10% of the Jewish population was deported to Siberia, along with other Estonians. About 75% of Estonian Jews, aware of the fate that awaited them from Nazi Germany, escaped to the Soviet Union; virtually all of those who remained (between 950 and 1,000 people) were killed by Einsatzgruppe A and local collaborators before the end of 1941. Roma people of Estonia were also murdered and enslaved by the Nazi occupiers and their collaborators. The Nazis and their allies also killed around 6,000 ethnic Estonians and 1,000 ethnic Russians who were accused of being communist sympathizers or the relatives of communist sympathizers. In addition around 25,000 Soviet prisoners-of-war and Jews from other parts of Europe were killed in Estonia during the German occupation.

## Jewish life pre-Holocaust

Prior to World War II, Jewish life flourished with the level of cultural autonomy accorded being the most extensive in all of Europe, giving full control of education and other aspects of cultural life to the local Jewish population. In 1936, the British-based Jewish newspaper The Jewish Chronicle reported that *"Estonia is the only country in Eastern Europe where neither the Government nor the people practice any discrimination against Jews and where Jews are left in peace and are allowed to lead a free and unmolested life and fashion it in accord with their national and cultural principles."*

**Figure 120:** *Map titled "Jewish Executions Carried Out by Einsatzgruppe A" from the Stahlecker's report. Marked "Secret Reich Matter," the map shows the number of Jews shot in Ostland, and reads at the bottom: "the estimated number of Jews still on hand is 128,000". Estonia is marked as judenfrei.*

## Murder of Jewish population

Round-ups and killings of the remaining Jews began immediately as the first stage of Generalplan Ost which would require the "removal" of 50% of Estonians.:[54] Undertaken by the extermination squad Einsatzkommando (Sonderkommando) 1A under Martin Sandberger, part of Einsatzgruppe A led by Walter Stahlecker, who followed the arrival of the first German troops on July 7, 1941. Arrests and executions continued as the Germans, with the assistance of local collaborators, advanced through Estonia. Estonia became a part of the Reichskommissariat Ostland. A Sicherheitspolizei (Security Police) was established for internal security under the leadership of Ain-Ervin Mere in 1942. Estonia was declared *Judenfrei* quite early by the German occupation regime at the Wannsee Conference.[879] The Jews who had remained in Estonia (929 according to the most recent calculation) were killed. Fewer than a dozen Estonian Jews are known to have survived the war in Estonia.

## German policy toward the Jews in Estonia

The Estonian state archives contain death certificates and lists of Jews shot dated July, August, and early September 1941. For example, the official death certificate of Rubin Teitelbaum, born in Tapa on January 17, 1907, states laconically in a form with item 7 already printed with only the date left blank: "7. By a decision of the Sicherheitspolizei on September 4, 1941, condemned to death, with the decision being carried out the same day in Tallinn." Teitelbaum's crime was "being a Jew" and thus constituting a "threat to the public order".

On September 11, 1941 an article entitled "Juuditäht seljal" – "A Jewish Star on the Back" appeared in the Estonian mass-circulation newspaper *Postimees*. It stated that Dr. Otto-Heinrich Drechsler, the High Commissioner of Ostland, had proclaimed ordinances in accordance with which all Jewish residents of Ostland from that day onward had to wear visible yellow six-pointed Star of David at least 10 cm (4 in). in diameter on the left side of their chest and back.

On the same day regulations[880] issued by the Sicherheitspolizei were delivered to all local police departments proclaiming that the Nuremberg Laws were in force in Ostland, defining who is a Jew, and what Jews could and could not do. Jews were prohibited from changing their place of residence, walking along the sidewalk, using any means of transportation, going to theatres, museums, cinema, or school. The professions of lawyer, physician, notary, banker, or real estate agent were declared closed to Jews, as was the occupation of street hawker. The regulations also declared that the property and homes of Jewish residents were to be confiscated. The regulations emphasized that work to this ends was to be begun as soon as possible, and that lists of Jews, their addresses, and their property were to be completed by the police by September 20, 1941.

These regulations also provided for the establishment of a concentration camp near the south-eastern Estonian city of Tartu. A later decision provided for the construction of a Jewish ghetto near the town of Harku, but this was never built, a small concentration camp being built there instead. The Estonian State Archives contain material pertinent to the cases of about 450 Estonian Jews. They were typically arrested either at home or in the street, taken to the local police station, and charged with the 'crime' of being Jews. They were either shot outright or sent to concentration camp and shot later. An Estonian woman, E. S. describes the arrest of her Jewish husband as follows:[881]

<templatestyles src="Template:Quote/styles.css"/>

> As my husband did not go out of the house, I was the one to go to town every day to see what was going on. I was very frightened when I saw a poster at the corner of Vabaduse Square and Harju Street calling for people to show where the apartments of Jews were located. On that fatal

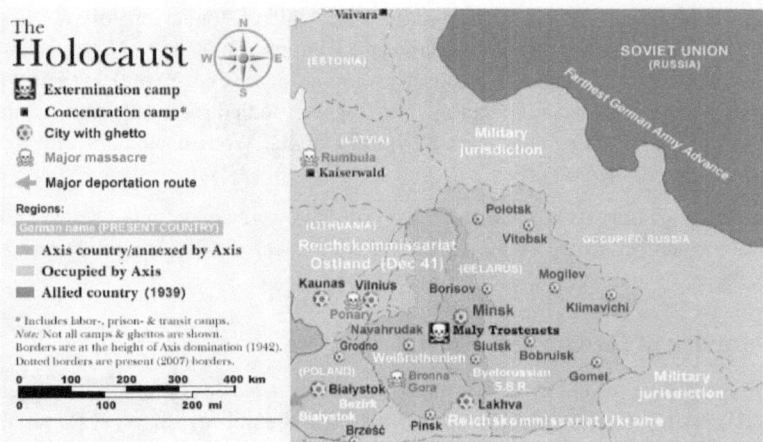

**Figure 121:** *Holocaust in Reichskommissariat Ostland (which included Estonia): a map*

day of September 13, I went out again because the weather was fine but I remember being very worried. I rushed home and when I got there and heard some voices in our apartment I had a foreboding that something bad had happened. There were two men in our apartment from the Selbstschutz who said they were taking my husband to the police station. I ran after them and went to the chief officer and asked for permission to see my husband. The chief officer said that he could not give me permission but added, in a low voice, that I should come the next morning when the prisoners would be taken to prison and perhaps I could see my husband in the corridor. I returned the next morning as I had been advised, and it was the last time I saw my husband. On September 15 I went to the German Sicherheitspolizei on Tõnismägi in an attempt to get information about my husband. I was told he had been shot. I asked the reason since he had not been a communist but a businessman, The answer was: "Aber er war doch ein Jude." [But he was a Jew.].

## Concentration camps established for foreign Jews

After the invasion of the Baltic States, it was the intention of the Nazi government to use the Baltic countries as their main area of mass genocide. Consequently, Jews from countries outside the Baltics were deported there to be killed.[882] An estimated 10,000 Jews were killed in Estonia after having been deported to camps there from elsewhere in Eastern Europe. The Nazi regime also established 22 concentration camps in occupied Estonian territory for foreign Jews, where they would used as slave laborers. The largest, Vaivara concentration camp, served as a transit camp and processed 20,000 Jews from Latvia and the Lithuanian ghettos. Usually able-bodied men were selected to work in the oil shale mines in northeastern Estonia. Women, children, and old people were killed on arrival.

At least two trainloads of Central European Jews were deported to Estonia and were killed on arrival at the Kalevi-Liiva site near the Jägala concentration camp.

## Murder of foreign Jews at Kalevi-Liiva

According to testimony of the survivors, at least two transports with about 2,100–2,150 Central European Jews, arrived at the railway station at Raasiku, one from Theresienstadt (Terezin) with Czechoslovakian Jews and one from Berlin with German citizens. Around 1,700–1,750 people were immediately taken to an execution site at the Kalevi-Liiva sand dunes and shot. About 450 people were selected for work at the Jägala camp

Transport *Be 1.9.1942* from Theresienstadt arrived at the Raasiku station on September 5, 1942, after a five-day trip.[883] According to testimony by Ralf Gerrets, one of the accused at the war crimes trials in 1961, eight busloads of Estonian auxiliary police had arrived from Tallinn. The selection process was supervised by Ain-Ervin Mere, chief of Security Police in Estonia; those transportees not selected for slave labor were sent by bus to a killing site near the camp. Later the police, in teams of 6 to 8 men, killed the Jews by machine gun fire,. During later investigations, however, some guards of camp denied the participation of police and said that executions were done by camp personnel. On the first day, a total of 900 people were murdered in this way. Gerrets testifies that he had fired a pistol at a victim who was still making noises in the pile of bodies. The whole operation was directed by SS commanders Heinrich Bergmann and Julius Geese.[884] Few witnesses pointed out Heinrich Bergmann as the key figure behind the extermination of Estonian gypsies. In the case of *Be 1.9.1942*, the only ones chosen for labor and to survive the war were a small group of young women who were taken through a series of concentration camps in Estonia, Poland and Germany to Bergen-Belsen, where they were liberated. Camp commandant Laak used the women as sex slaves, killing many after they had outlived their usefulness.[885]

A number of foreign witnesses were heard at the post-war trials in Soviet Estonia, including five women who had been transported on *Be 1.9.1942* from Theresienstadt.

*The accused Mere, Gerrets and Viik actively participated in crimes and mass killings that were perpetrated by the Nazi invaders on the territory of the Estonian SSR. In accordance with the Nazi racial theory, the Sicherheitspolizei and Sicherheitsdienst were instructed to exterminate the Jews and Gypsies. To that end, during August and September of 1941, Mere and his collaborators set up a death camp at Jägala, 30 km (19 mi) from Tallinn. Mere put Aleksander Laak in charge of the camp; Ralf Gerrets was appointed his deputy. On September 5, 1942, a train with approximately 1,500 Czechoslovak citizens arrived at the Raasiku railway station. Mere, Laak and Gerrets personally selected who of them should be executed and who should be moved to the Jägala death camp. More than 1,000 people, mostly children, the old, and the infirm, were transported to a wasteland at Kalevi-Liiva, where they were monstrously executed in a special pit. In mid-September, the second troop train with 1,500 prisoners arrived at the railway station from Germany. Mere, Laak, and Gerrets selected another thousand victims, who were then condemned by them to extermination. This group of prisoners, which included nursing women and their new-born babies, were transported to Kalevi-Liiva where they were killed.*
*In March 1943, the personnel of the Kalevi-Liiva camp executed about fifty Gypsies, half of whom were under 5 years of age. Also were executed 60 Gypsy children of school age...*

### Roma people murdered

A few witnesses pointed out Heinrich Bergmann as the key figure behind the extermination of Estonian Roma people.

## Estonian collaboration

The Germans recruited tens of thousands of native Estonians into the Waffen SS and the Wehrmacht. Formations of note in such forces were the Estonian Legion, the 3rd Estonian SS Volunteer Brigade, and the 20th Waffen Grenadier Division of the SS (1st Estonian) among others.

Units of the *Eesti Omakaitse* (Estonian Home Guard; approximately 1000 to 1200 men) were directly involved in criminal acts, taking part in the roundup of 200 Roma people and 950 Jews. Units of Estonian Auxiliary Police participated in the extermination of Jews in the Pskov region of Russia Wikipedia:Verifiability and provided guards for concentration camps for Jews and Soviet POWs in Jägala, Vaivara, Klooga, and Lagedi.

The final acts of liquidating the camps, such as Klooga, which involved the mass-shooting of roughly 2,000 prisoners, were carried out by German units belonging to the Schutzmannschaftsbataillon of the KdS. Survivors report that, during these last days before liberation, when Jewish slave labourers were visible, the Estonian population in part attempted to help the Jews by providing food and other types of assistance."[886]

## War crimes trials

Four Estonians deemed most responsible for the murders at Kalevi-Liiva were accused at the war crimes trials in 1961. Two were later executed, while the Soviet occupation authorities were unable to press charges against the other two due to the fact that they lived in exile.[887] There have been 7 known ethnic Estonians (Ralf Gerrets, Ain-Ervin Mere, Jaan Viik, Juhan Jüriste, Karl Linnas, Aleksander Laak and Ervin Viks) who have faced trials for crimes against humanity committed during the Nazi occupation in Estonia. The accused were charged with murdering up to 5,000 German and Czechoslovakian Jews and Romani people near the Kalevi-Liiva concentration camp in 1942–1943. Ain-Ervin Mere, commander of the Estonian Security Police (Group B of the Sicherheitspolizei) under the Estonian Self-Administration, was tried *in absentia*. Before the trial, Mere had been an active member of the Estonian community in England, contributing to Estonian language publications.[888] At the time of the trial, however, he was being held in custody in England, having been accused of murder. He was never deported and died a free man in England in 1969. Ralf Gerrets, the deputy commandant at the Jägala camp. Jaan Viik, *(Jan Wijk, Ian Viik)*, a guard at the Jägala labor camp, out of the hundreds of Estonian camp guards and police, was singled out for prosecution due to his particular brutality.[889] Witnesses testified that he would throw small children into the air and shoot them. He did not deny the charge. A fourth accused, camp commandant Aleksander Laak (*Alexander Laak*), was discovered living in Canada, but committed suicide before he could be brought to trial.

In January 1962, another trial was held in Tartu. Juhan Jüriste, Karl Linnas and Ervin Viks were accused of murdering 12,000 civilians in the Tartu concentration camp.

## Number of victims

Soviet-era Estonian era sources estimate the total number of Soviet citizens and foreigners to be murdered in Nazi-occupied Estonian Soviet Socialist Republic to be 125,000. The bulk of this number consists Jews from Central and Western Europe and Soviet prisoners-of-war killed or starved to death in prisoner-of-war camps on Estonian territory. The Estonian History Commission estimates the total number of victims to be roughly 35,000, consisting of the following groups:

**Figure 122:** *Holocaust memorial at the site of the former Klooga concentration camp, opened on July 24, 2005*

- 1000 Estonian Jews,
- about 10,000 foreign Jews,
- 1000 Estonian Roma,
- 7000 other Estonians,
- 15,000 Soviet POWs.

The number of Estonian Jews killed is less than 1,000; the German Holocaust perpetrators Martin Sandberger and Walter Stahlecker cite the numbers 921 and 963 respectively. In 1994 Evgenia Goorin-Loov calculated the exact number to be 929.

## Modern memorials

Since the reestablishment of the Estonian independence, markers were put in place for the 60th anniversary of the mass executions that were carried out at the Lagedi, Vaivara and Klooga (Kalevi-Liiva) camps in September 1944. On February 5, 1945 in Berlin, Ain Mere founded the *Eesti Vabadusliit* together with SS-Obersturmbannführer Harald Riipalu.[890] He was sentenced to the capital punishment during the Holocaust trials in Soviet Estonia but was not extradited by Great Britain and died there in peace. In 2002 the Government of the Republic of Estonia decided to officially commemorate the Holocaust.

**Figure 123:** *Kiviõli Concentration Camp Holocaust Memorial, northeastern Estonia.*

In the same year, the Simon Wiesenthal Center had provided the Estonian government with information on alleged Estonian war criminals, all former members of the 36th Estonian Police Battalion. In August 2018 it was reported that the memorial at Kalevi-Liiva was defaced[891].

## Collaborators

- Ralf Gerrets
- Juhan Jüriste
- Friedrich Kurg[892]
- Aleksander Laak
- Karl Linnas
- Ain-Ervin Mere
- Hjalmar Mäe
- Jaan Viik
- Ervin Viks

## Organizations

- Einsatzgruppe A
- Estonian Auxiliary Police
- Omakaitse
- Ordnungspolizei
- Sonderkommando 1a
- Sicherheitspolizei

## Concentration camps

### KZ-Stammlager

- KZ Vaivara
  - Klooga

### KZ-Außenlager

- KZ Aseri
- KZ Auvere
- KZ Erides
- KZ Goldfields (Kohtla)
- KZ Ilinurme
- KZ Jewe
- KZ Kerestowo (Karstala in Viru Ingria, now in Gatchinsky District)
- KZ Kiviöli
- KZ Kukruse
- KZ Kunda
- KZ Kuremaa
- KZ Lagedi
- KZ Klooga, Lodensee. Commandant SS-Untersturmführer Wilhelm Werle. (b. 1907, d. 1966),; September 1943 – September 1944. There were held 2 000 – 3 000 prisoners, most of them the Lithuanian Jews. When the Red Army approached, SS-men shot the 2 500 prisoners on September 19, 1944 and burned most of the bodies. The fewer than 100 prisoners succeeded in surviving by hiding. There is a monument on the location of the concentration camp.
- KZ Narwa
- KZ Pankjavitsa, Pankjewitza. It was situated app. 15 km south of the village of Pankjavitsa near the hamlet of Roodva in the former Estonian province of Petserimaa. Since 1945 Russia occupies a large part of this province including Roodva/Rootova. The camp was established in November 1943. On 11 November that year 250 prisoners from Klooga arrived. Their accommodations were barracks. Already in January 1944

the camp was shut down and the inmates were relocated to Kūdupe (in Latvia near the Estonian border), Petseri and Ülenurme. Likely the camp was closed after some kind of work was finished. It was affiliated to the Vaivara camp.[893]
- KZ Narwa-Hungerburg
- KZ Putki (in Piiri Parish, near Slantsy)
- KZ Reval (Ülemiste?)
- KZ Saka
- KZ Sonda
- KZ Soski (in Vasknarva Parish)
- KZ Wiwikond
- KZ Ülenurme

## Arbeits- und Erziehungslager

- AEL Jägala (August 1942 – September 1943)
- AEL Murru
- AEL Reval
  - Harku (243 Estonian Romani people were executed in the Harku concentration camp on 27 October 1942)
  - Lasnamäe
- AEL Tartu (commandant Karl Linnas)
- AEL Turba (in Ellamaa)[894]

## Prisons

- Haapsalu
- Kuressaare
- Narva (in Vestervalli Street, 1941–1944)
- Petseri
- Pärnu
- Tartu
- Valga
- Võru

## Other concentration camps

- Dvigatel[895]
- Essu
- Järvakandi
- Laitse
- Lavassaare[896]
- Lehtse
- Lelle[897] (1942 – May 1943)

- Roela
- Sitsi (In Tallinn, at the end of Tööstuse Street where was 10 barracks; until 17 September 1944)[898]
- Vasalemma
- Vaste

# Bibliography

- 12000: Tartus 16.-20.jaanuaril 1962 massimõrvarite Juhan Jüriste, Karl Linnase ja Ervin Viksi üle peetud kohtuprotsessi materjale. Karl Lemmik and Ervin Martinson. Eesti Riiklik Kirjastus. 1962
- Ants Saar, *Vaikne suvi vaikses linnas*. Eesti Raamat. 1971
- "Eesti vaimuhaigete saatus Saksa okupatsiooni aastail (1941–1944)", *Eesti Arst*, nr. March 3, 2007
- Ervin Martinson. *Elukutse – reetmine*. Eesti Raamat. 1970
- Ervin Martinson. *Haakristi teenrid*. Eesti Riiklik Kirjastus. 1962
- *Inimesed olge valvsad*. Vladimir Raudsepp. Eesti Riiklik Kirjastus. 1961
- *Pruun katk: Dokumentide kogumik fašistide kuritegude kohta okupeeritud Eesti NSV territooriumil*. Ervin Martinson and A. Matsulevitš. Eesti Raamat. 1969
- *SS tegutseb: Dokumentide kogumik SS-kuritegude kohta*. Eesti Riiklik Kirjastus. 1963

# External links

- Birn, Ruth Bettina (2001), Collaboration with Nazi Germany in Eastern Europe: the Case of the Estonian Security Police[899]. *Contemporary European History* 10.2, 181–198.
- Extermination of the Gypsies in Estonia during World War II[900]
- Operation 1005 in Riga by Jens Hoffmann[901]

# The Holocaust in Belarus

> Part of a series on
> **The Holocaust**
>
> Jews on selection ramp at Auschwitz, May 1944
>
> - v
> - t
> - e[902]

**The Holocaust in Belarus** in general terms refers to the Nazi crimes committed during World War II on the territory of Belarus against Jews. The borders of Belarus however, changed dramatically following the Soviet invasion of Poland in 1939, which has been the source of confusion especially in the Soviet era as far as the scope of the Holocaust in Belarus is concerned.

When World War II began, with the September 1, 1939 attack on Poland by Nazi Germany, the sovereign Belarus of today did not exist. The Nazi-Soviet Pact signed in secrecy led to the parallel Soviet invasion of Poland from the east on September 17, 1939. The eastern half of prewar Poland was annexed by the USSR to the two republics of Soviet Belarus and Soviet Ukraine.

The entire territory of modern-day Belarus was occupied by Nazi Germany by the end of August 1941. American historian Lucy Dawidowicz, author of *The War Against the Jews* estimated that 66% of the Jewish people residing in Belarusian SSR died in the Holocaust, out of 375,000 Jews in Belarus prior

**Figure 124:** *Masza Bruskina and two other resistance members before hanging, Minsk, October 26, 1941.*

to World War II according to Soviet data. By comparison, in the Baltics about 90% of Jews were killed in the same period.

## Background

Resulting from the Soviet invasion of Poland in 1939, the territory of Belarusian SSR was almost doubled in size through the annexation of Kresy. The act of aggression against the Second Polish Republic was followed by the mock elections conducted in the atmosphere of terror. Polish cities were renamed in Russian, and the new Oblasts created.[903] Millions of Polish citizens were turned by force into the new Soviet subjects. Within two years, the Jewish population of Minsk, the capital of the Byelorussian Soviet Socialist Republic, had swelled to 90,000 due to an influx of Polish Jews escaping German occupation.

The Holocaust perpetrated by the Third Reich in the territory of Soviet Belarus began in the summer of 1941, during the German attack on the Soviet positions in Operation Barbarossa. Minsk was bombed and taken over by the Wehrmacht on 28 June 1941. In Hitler's view, Operation Barbarossa was Germany's war against "Jewish Bolshevism". On 3 July 1941 during the first "selection" in Minsk 2,000 Jewish members of the intelligentsia were marched off to a forest and massacred. The atrocities committed beyond the German–Soviet frontier were summarized by *Einsatzgruppen* for both sides of the prewar border

**Figure 125:** *Jewish prisoners of the Minsk Ghetto clearing snow at the station, February 1942*

between BSSR and Poland. The Nazis made Minsk the administrative centre of *Reichskomissariat Ostland*. As of 15 July 1941 all Jews were ordered to wear a yellow badge on their outer garments under penalty of death, and on 20 July 1941 the creation of the Minsk Ghetto was pronounced. Within two years, it became the largest ghetto in German-occupied Soviet Union, with over 100,000 Jews.

A fair percentage of ethnic Belarusians supported Nazi Germany, especially in the early years. Some nationalists out of Minsk including sworn Germanophile Ivan Yermachenka hoped for the formation of a Belarusian national state under protectorate of the Reich. By the end of 1942 the Yermachenka's group known as BNS had 30,000 members in a dozen different Soviet cities. The Belarusian Auxiliary Police was established by the Nazi authorities in the summer of 1941.[904] High-ranking positions in the police were also kept by BNS. "Known to the Germans as the *Schutzmannschaft* – wrote Martin Dean – the local police were recruited from volunteers at the start of the occupation. These men played an indispensable role in the killing process." Eventually, the number of local auxiliary police in German-occupied Soviet Union reached 300,000 men.

The southern part of the modern-day Belarus was annexed to the newly formed *Reichskommissariat Ukraine* on 17 July 1941 including the eastern-

**Figure 126:** *Holocaust in Reichskommissariat Ostland, which included Soviet Belarus*

most Gomel Region of the Russian SFSR, and several others. They became part of the *Shitomir Generalbezirk* centred around Zhytomyr. The Germans determined the identities of the Jews either through registration, or by issuing decrees. The Jews were separated from the general population and confined to makeshift ghettos. Because the Soviet leadership fled from Minsk without ordering evacuation, most Jewish inhabitants have been captured. There were 100,000 prisoners held in the Minsk Ghetto, in Bobruisk 25,000, in Vitebsk 20,000, in Mogilev 12,000, in Gomel over 10,000, in Slutsk 10,000, in Borisov 8,000, and in Polotsk 8,000. In the Gomel Region alone, twenty ghettos were established in which no less than 21,000 people were imprisoned.

In November 1941 the Nazis rounded up 12,000 Jews in the Minsk Ghetto to make room for the 25,000 foreign Jews slated for expulsion from Germany, Austria and the Protectorate of Bohemia and Moravia. On the morning of 7 November 1941 the first group of prisoners were formed into columns and ordered to march singing revolutionary songs. People were forced to smile for the cameras. Once beyond Minsk, 6,624 Jews were taken by lorries to the nearby village of Tuchinka (Tuchinki) and shot by members of *Einsatzgruppe* A. The next group of over 5,000 Jews followed them to Tuchinka on 20 November 1941.

## Holocaust by bullet

Resulting from the Soviet 1939 annexation of Polish territory comprising the Soviet Western Belorussia, the Jewish population of BSSR nearly tripled. In June 1941, at the beginning of Operation Barbarossa, there were 670,000 Jews on the Polish side and 405,000 Jews on the Soviet side of present-day Belarus. On 8 July 1941 the SS-*Obergruppenführer* Reinhard Heydrich gave the order for all male Jews in the occupied territory – between the ages of 15 and 45 – to be shot on sight as Soviet partisans. By August, the victims targeted in the shootings included women, children, and the elderly. The German police battalions as well as the *Einsatzgruppen* carried out the first wave of killings.

<templatestyles src="Multiple_image/styles.css" />

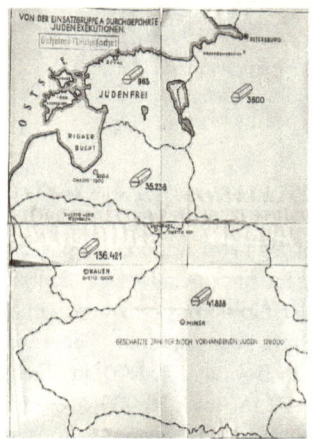

Original map from Franz Walter Stahlecker's Report, summarizing murders committed by *Einsatzgruppen* in *Reichskommissariat Ostland* until January 1942

Notably, the Stahlecker's map *(top)* had shown the Soviet Byelorussia – not from before, but after the Soviet annexation of Polish Kresy in 1939 following the Nazi-Soviet invasion of Poland. The Byelorussian SSR in 1939 is marked in pink. Territory of prewar Poland inhabited by Polish Jews is marked in yellow.

The role of the Belarusian Auxiliary Police, established on 7 July 1941, was crucial in the totality of procedures, as only they – wrote Martin Dean – knew the identity of the Jews. The pacification actions were conducted using local *Schutzmannschaft* during roundups (as in Homel, Mozyrz, Kalinkowicze, Korma). The local police took on a secondary role. The ghettoised Jews were controlled by them and brutalized before mass executions (as in Dobrusz, Czeczersk, Żytkowicze). After a while the already-trained auxiliary police not only led the Jews out of the ghettos to places of massacres but also took active part in the shootings. Such tactic was successful (without much exertion of force) in places where the killings of Jews were carried out in early September, and throughout October and November 1941. In winter 1942, a different tactic was introduced - the pacification raids, conducted in Żłobin, Petryków, Streszyn, Czeczersk. The role of the Belarusian police in the killings became particularly noticeable during the second wave of the ghetto liquidations, starting in February–March 1942.[904]

In the Holocaust by bullet, no less than 800,000 Jews perished in the territory of modern-day Belarus. Most of them were shot by *Einsatzgruppen*, *Sicherheitsdienst* and Orpo battalions aided by *Schutzmannschaften*. Notably, when the bulk of the Jewish communities were annihilated in first major killing spree, the number of Belarusian collaborators was still considerably small, therefore the Eastern European destruction battalions consisted in most part of Lithuanian, Ukrainian, and Latvian volunteers. Historian Martin Gilbert wrote that the General-Commissar for *Generalbezirk Weißruthenien*, Wilhelm Kube, personally participated in the March 2, 1942 killings in the Minsk Ghetto. During the search of the ghetto area by the Nazi police, a group of children were seized and thrown into deep pit of sand covered with snow. "At that moment, several SS officers, among them Wilhelm Kube, arrived, whereupon Kube, immaculate in his uniform, threw handfuls of sweets to the shrieking children. All the children perished in the sand."

## Mass murders in Nawahrudak

On 22 June 1941 Nazi Germany launched Operation Barbarossa against the Soviet Union. The city of Navahrudak (Nowogródek in Polish), capital of the Nowogródek Voivodship in interwar Poland), was occupied on 4 July during the Battle of Białystok–Minsk when two armies of the Red Army were surrounded in the Navahrudak pocket. The city became part of the Reichskommissariat Ostland and Immediately Nazi occupiers staged their racial persecution and segregation policies, in particular against Poles of Jewish ethnicity, who were forced into a newly established ghetto.

According to the Polish census of 1931 the Nowogródek Voivodeship was home to about 616,000 ethnic Belorussians, or ~39% of the total population of the province, exceeding the number of ethnic Poles by eight percentage points. Prior to the war, the town had a population of 20,000, about half of which were Polish Jews.

During winter 1941-42 the German occupiers killed all but 550 of the approximately 10,000 Jews in a series of actions by bullet,. Those not killed were forced into slave labour and worked to death. Thus partisan resistance immediately began; local Jews volunteers, who later were known as the Bielski partisans, fled into nearby forests engaging in combat activity and in the same time providing shelter to Jewish families, many of whom were able to survive the war.

Ethnic Poles and Belorussians were not spared by Nazi terrorism either, in particular during 1943 when more civilians were imprisoned and subject to harsh retaliatory actions and forced labour. On 31 July 1943 11 Sisters of the Holy Family of Nazareth were imprisoned, and on the next day loaded into a van, driven out of town, in the woods 5 km (3.1 mi) beyond Navahrudak, killed by bullet, and buried in a mass grave.

The Red Army liberated the city almost exactly three years after its occupation, on July 8, 1944. During the war more than 45,000 people were killed in town and in surrounding areas. Over 60% of buildings was destroyed.

## Saving Jews

As of 1 January 2017, the Yad Vashem in Israel recognized 641 Belarusians as Righteous Among the Nations, including citizens of modern-day Belarus with distinctly Polish names who used to live in the territories of the Second Polish Republic annexed after the Soviet invasion of Poland, and incorporated into the USSR in 1945 at the insistence of Joseph Stalin.[905] All of the awards were granted after the dissolution of the Soviet Union. Many of the distinguished individuals came from Minsk, and are already deceased.[906]

# Anti-partisan operations

On 22 September 1943, Wilhelm Kube was assassinated in Minsk by his Belarusian mistress. His death was caused by a bomb hidden in a hot water bottle, which was placed in his bed by Jelena Mazanik, coerced by the Soviet agents who knew where her son was. The SS executed more than 1,000 male citizens of Minsk in retaliation, though SS leader Heinrich Himmler reportedly said the assassination was a "blessing" since Kube did not support some of the harsh measures mandated by the SS.[907] Mazanik escaped and joined the partisans.

**Figure 127:** *Kampfgruppe Schimana of the 14th Waffen Grenadier Division of the SS Galicia (1st Ukrainian), summer 1943.*

SS and Police Leader Curt von Gottberg was appointed *Generalkommissar* for Belarus on October 27, 1943 after Kube was killed by a bomb in Minsk on October 23.Wikipedia:Please clarify Gottberg developed a new "strategy" in the fight against partisans on the occupied territory of the Soviet Union, mounting aggressive operations against suspected "partisan bases" (generally ordinary villages; Gottberg's strategy seems to have largely involved terrorising the civilian population). Whole regions were classified as "bandit territory" (German: *Bandengebiet*): residents were expelled or murdered and dwellings destroyed. Gottberg said in an order "In the evacuated areas all people are in future fair game". Another order of Gottberg's of December 7, 1942, stated: "Each bandit, Jew, gypsy, is to be regarded as an enemy". After his first operation, *Nürnberg*, Gottberg reported on December 5, 1942: "Enemy dead: 799 bandits, over 300 suspected gangsters and over 1800 Jews [...] Our losses: 2 dead and 10 wounded. One must have luck".Wikipedia:Citation needed

The cruelty during anti-partisan operations, especially in Belarus, has been pointed out in the past, indicating a high degree of identification with their deeds rather than an unwilling execution. The meanness of their actions is evidenced by the means of mass killings employed by the Germans in their fight against partisans. Most of the victims were women and children, as the male population of the villages had been evacuated or drafted into the Red

**Figure 128:** *Bronislav Kaminski and 29th Waffen Grenadier Division of the SS RONA (1st Russian), spring 1944.*

Army, or joined the partisans. They were also used as a labor force. Similar aspects also apply to the murder of Jews, prisoners of war, political opponents, and the ill.

The 36th Waffen Grenadier Division of the SS on July 21, 1943, during "Operation Hermann", chased the inhabitants of the village of Dory together with the priest into a church and burned them alive there. Only men able to work were let out of the church, women only if they left their children behind. At another place hundreds of selected children, two to ten years old, were locked in freight cars and left to their fate until half of them had died. While Max von Schenckendorff in 1942 called for measures against the soldiers, the generally organized sequence of the destruction of villages shows how little was left to chance.

Photo albums were prepared for higher SS commanders after anti-partisan actions. Thus, Erich von dem Bach-Zelewski readily admitted to have possessed thousands of color photographs of the fight against partisans, photos which were confiscated after the war. After "Operation Hermann" in the summer of 1943, Curt von Gottberg requested appropriate pictures for an album on partisan fighting, to be handed to Himmler. Some months later, he was sent an album featuring photos from Operation Heinrich, which Bach-Zelewski had dedicated to Himmler by naming it after him. The rank and file behaved in a similar manner. Many German participants had a camera in their backpack during the operations. The respective pictures mostly show rather uncompromising scenes, but often also the burning of villages.

Another aspect was the fact that inhabitants of the countryside were forced to remove mines from the roads and other pathways to partisan camps, a dangerous task that killed several thousand Belarusians. Such cases already occurred in Wehrmacht-controlled areas 1942, at the remote village of Uchwała, Krupki, where a total of 360 people perished. In the area of the 286th Security Division, the civilian population had to walk, plough and harrow the roads on the orders of Major General Richert from the autumn of 1942. At Artiszewo near Orsza, 28 people, 18 of which were children, perished during this operation. The LIX Army Corps had issued a corresponding order already on March 2, 1942.

Later, they also used herds of sheep. But in most cases people were used, on an ever-larger scale. During Operation Cottbus, between 2,000 and 3,000 Belarusians whom the Germans drove before them into the swamps were torn apart by mines, according to Bach-Zelewski. After preparation by artillery and flak, entering the swamp area was only possible by chasing inhabitants of the region across the heavily mined paths through the swamp. Oskar Dirlewanger's corresponding order of May 25, 1943 had read:

> *Roadblocks and artificial obstacles are almost always mined. So far we have suffered 1 dead and 4 wounded during removal. Thus the order is: Never remove obstacles yourselves, but always let natives do it. The blood thus saved justifies the loss of time.*

For "Operation Hermann" conducted in July–August 1943 partly by *Einsatzgruppe Dirlewanger* the same directive applied right from the beginning. The commanders carried out the instructions. The same occurred during Operation Frühlingsfest (April 16 till May 10, 1944), which was carried out in equal parts by Wehrmacht and SS units. A corresponding suggestion is said to have come from the already mentioned Richert. But in the meantime, this method had become routine also outside the scope of major actions. It was also applied by Wehrmacht frontline troops in their direct rear area. All Belarusians had become hostages of the Germans. The 78th Infantry division ordered the whole civilian population in its area to de-mine the roads area every morning for six hours:

> *I thus order that all roads that must be driven on by German troops are to be walked first by all inhabitants of the location (including women and children) with cows, horses and vehicles up to the next command post, or that marching columns must be preceded at a distance of at least 150*

**Figure 129:** *Minsk Memorial "Yama"*

*meters by such inhabitants. The civilians must close up tightly and walk the whole width of the road.*

Rear area command 532 proceeded in a similar manner, and an officer in the high command of Army Group Center wanted to recommend this procedure as exemplary to other units. As of February 18, 1944, General Commissar v. Gottberg issued a Directive for the *Securing of Traffic Roads in White Ruthenia against Bandits and Mines*. Therein the whole population of villages in White Ruthenia was obliged to de-mine streets and roads every day at the regional police commanders instructions. Whoever refused the de-mining and road supervision service was to be punished by death.

## Massacres

The pacifications, and the ghetto liquidation actions in the territories occupied by the Germans since June 1941, were conducted in a number of notable locations in present-day Belarus. The victims, including Polish Jews from the territories annexed into the Soviet Belarus from the Polish Kresy, were also transported by rail to the Bronna Góra extermination site whenever deemed necessary by the executioners. The towns (in alphabetical order) included Antopol, Berazino, Novogrudok (see Martyrs of Nowogródek), Bobruisk, Chavusy, Davyd-Haradok, Dzyatlava (see Dzyatlava massacre), Grodno (see

Grodno Ghetto), Iwye, Khatyn (see Khatyn massacre), Lakhva (see Łachwa Ghetto), Lida, Luniniec, Lyubavichi, Trostenets (see Maly Trostenets extermination camp), Minsk (see Minsk Ghetto), Motal, Obech, Pinsk (see Pińsk Ghetto), Polotsk, Ponary (see Ponary massacre), Shkloŭ, Slonim (see Słonim Ghetto), Slutsk (see Slutsk Affair), Vitebsk (see Vitebsk Ghetto), and Zhetel (see Zdzięcioł Ghetto).

According to State Memorial Complex "Khatyn" created by the Central Committee of the Communist Party of Belarus, the Nazi regime deported some 380,000 Belarusians to Germany for slave labour and killed hundreds of thousands of civilians. At least 5,295 Belarusian settlements were destroyed and their inhabitants murdered (out of 9,200 settlements that were burned or otherwise destroyed in Belarus during World War II). According to SMC "Khatyn", 243 Belarusian villages were burned twice, 83 villages three times, and 22 villages were burned four or more times in the Vitebsk region. In the Mińsk region 92 villages were burned twice, 40 villages three times, nine villages four times, and six villages five or more times. More than 600 villages like Khatyn (see: the Khatyn massacre) were annihilated with their entire population. More than 209 cities and towns (out of 270 total) were destroyed.

## Postwar research

The communist Soviet-era sources estimated that Belarus lost a quarter of its prewar population in World War II, including most of its intellectual elite. It is a myth believed to have been concocted by the local 1st Secretary Pyotr Masherov in a speech of 8 May 1965 according to western historians who point out to evidence of manipulation by the Extraordinary State Commission inflating the figure considerably by including victims who were not citizens of the republic. The official memorial narrative of Belarus allows only a "pro-Soviet version of the resistance to the German invaders." The Constitution of the Republic under Article 28 denies access to information about Belarusians who served with the Nazis.

In the 1970s and 1980s historian and Soviet refusenik Daniel Romanovsky who later emigrated to Israel, interviewed over 100 witnesses, including Jews, Russians, and Belarusians from the vicinity, recording their accounts of the Holocaust by bullet.[908] Research on the topic was difficult in the Soviet Union because of government restrictions. Nevertheless, based on his interviews Romanovsky concluded that the open-type ghettos in Belarusian towns were the result of prior concentration of the entire Jewish communities in prescribed areas. No walls were required. The collaboration with the Germans by most non-Jewish people was in part a result of attitudes developed under the Soviet rule; namely, the practice of conforming to a totalitarian state. Sometimes called Homo Sovieticus.[909]

# The Holocaust in Russia

The **Holocaust in Russia** refers to the Nazi crimes during the occupation of Russia (Russian Soviet Federative Socialist Republic) by Nazi Germany.

## On the eve of the Holocaust

Beyond longstanding controversies, ranging from the Molotov–Ribbentrop Pact to anti-Zionism, the Soviet Union did grant official "equality of all citizens regardless of status, sex, race, religion, and nationality." The years before the Holocaust were an era of rapid change for Soviet Jews, leaving behind the dreadful poverty of the Pale of Settlement. 40% of the population in the former Pale left for large cities within the USSR. Emphasis on education and movement from countryside *shtetls* to newly industrialized cities allowed many Soviet Jews to enjoy overall advances under Joseph Stalin and to become one of the most educated population groups in the world. Due to Stalinist emphasis on its urban population, interwar migration inadvertently rescued countless Soviet Jews—Nazi Germany penetrated the entire former Jewish Pale, but were kilometers short of Leningrad and Moscow. The great wave of deportations from the areas annexed by Soviet Union according to the Nazi-Soviet pact, often seen by victims as genocide, paradoxically also saved lives of a few hundred thousand Jewish deportees. However horrible their conditions, the fate of Jews in Nazi Germany was much worse. The migration of many Jews deeper East from the part of the Jewish Pale that would become occupied by Germany saved at least forty percent of this area's Jewish population.

## World War II

On 22 June 1941, Adolf Hitler abruptly broke the non–aggression pact and invaded the Soviet Union. The Soviet territories occupied by early 1942, including all of Belarus, Estonia, Latvia, Lithuania, Ukraine, and Moldova and most Russian territory west of the line Leningrad-Moscow-Rostov, contained about four million Jews, including hundreds of thousands who had fled Poland in 1939. Despite the chaos of the Soviet retreat, some effort was made to evacuate Jews, who were either employed in the military industries or were family members of servicemen. Of 4 million about a million succeeded in escaping further east. The remaining three million were left at the mercy of the Nazis. Despite the subservience of the Oberkommando des Heeres to Adolf Hitler, Heinrich Himmler did not trust the Army to approve of, let alone carry out, the large-scale killings of Jews in the occupied Soviet territories. This task was assigned to SS formations called *Einsatzgruppen* ("task groups"), under

**Figure 130:** *A map of the Holocaust in Reichskommissariat Ostland, which included Russia*

**Figure 131:** *Russia. Jewish women and children being forced out of their homes. A Romanian soldier is marching along as a guard, 17 July 1941*

the overall command of Reinhard Heydrich. These had been used on a limited scale in Poland in 1939, but were now organized on a much larger scale. According to Otto Ohlendorf at his trial, "the *Einsatzgruppen* had the mission to protect the rear of the troops by killing the Jews, gypsies, Communist functionaries, active Communists, and all persons who would endanger the security." In practice, their victims were nearly all defenseless Jewish civilians (not a single *Einsatzgruppe* member was killed in action during these operations). Raul Hilberg writes that the *Einsatzgruppe* member were ordinary citizens; the great majority were university-educated professionals.[910] They used their

**Figure 132:** *Map titled "Jewish Executions Carried Out by Einsatzgruppe A" from Stahlecker's report. Marked "Secret Reich Matter," the map shows the number of Jews shot, and reads at the bottom: "the estimated number of Jews still on hand is 128,000"*

skills to become efficient killers, according to Michael Berenbaum.[911] By the end of 1941, however, the *Einsatzgruppen* had killed only 15 percent of the Jews in the occupied Soviet territories, and it was apparent that these methods could not be used to kill all the Jews of Europe. Even before the invasion of the Soviet Union, experiments with killing Jews in the back of vans using gas from the van's exhaust had been carried out, and when this proved too slow, more lethal gasses were tried. For large-scale killing by gas, however, fixed sites would be needed, and it was decided—probably by Heydrich and Eichmann—that the Jews should be brought to camps specifically built for the purpose.

Although the Soviet Union was victorious in World War II, the war resulted in around 26–27 million Soviet deaths (estimates vary)[912] and had devastated the Soviet economy in the struggle. Some 1,710 towns and 70 thousand settlements were destroyed.[913] The occupied territories suffered from the ravages of German occupation and deportations of slave labor in Germany.[914] Thirteen million Soviet citizens became victims of a repressive policy of Germans and their allies in occupied territory, where they died because of mass murders, famine, absence of elementary medical aid and slave labor.[915,916] The Nazi

Genocide of the Jews carried by German *Einsatzgruppen*, along the local collaborators resulted in almost complete annihilation of the Jewish population over the entire territory temporary occupied by Germany and its allies. During occupation, Russia's Leningrad, now Saint Petersburg, region lost around a quarter of its population. 3.6 million Soviet prisoners of war (of 5.5 million) died in German camps.[917,918] British historian Martin Gilbert used a similar approach in his *Atlas of the Holocaust,* but arrived at a number of 5.75 million Jewish victims, since he estimated higher numbers of Jews killed in Russia and other locations.[919] Lucy S. Dawidowicz used pre-war census figures to estimate that 5.934 million Jews died. In October 1943, 600 Jewish and Russian prisoners attempted an escape at the Sobibór extermination camp. About 60 survived and joined the Belarusian partisans. In Eastern Europe, many Jews joined the ranks of the Soviet partisans: throughout the war, they faced anti-semitism and discrimination from the Soviets and some Jewish partisans were killed, but over time, many of the Jewish partisan groups were absorbed into the command structure of the much larger Soviet partisan movement. Soviet partisans were not in a position to ensure protection to the Jews in the Holocaust. The fit Jews were usually welcomed by the partisans (sometimes only if they brought their own weapons); however women, children, and the elderly were mostly unwelcome. Eventually, however, separate Jewish groups, both guerrilla units and mixed family groups of refugees (like the Bielski partisans), were subordinated to the communist partisan leadership and considered as Soviet assets. Even as some assisted the Germans, a significant number of individuals in the territories under German control also helped Jews escape death (*see Righteous Among the Nations*). During World War II, Léon Poliakov established the Center of Contemporary Jewish Documentation (1943) and after the war, he assisted Edgar Faure at the Nuremberg Trial. By 1944, the Germans had been pushed out of the Soviet Union onto the banks of the Vistula River, just east of Prussia. With Soviet Marshal Georgy Zhukov attacking from Prussia, and Marshal Konev slicing Germany in half from the south the fate of Nazi Germany was sealed. It is estimated that up to 1.4 million Jews fought in Allied armies; 40% of them in the Red Army.[920] In total, at least 142 500 Soviet soldiers of Jewish nationality lost their lives fighting against the German invaders and their allies Salomon Smolianoff was selected for Operation Bernhard, transferred to the Sachsenhausen concentration camp in 1944, and eventually to the Ebensee site of the Mauthausen camp network,[921] where he was liberated by the US Army on 6 May 1945.[922] Without changing its official anti-Zionist stance, from late 1944 until 1948 Joseph Stalin had adopted a *de facto* pro-Zionist foreign policy, apparently believing that the new country would be socialist and would speed the decline of British influence in the Middle East.[923]

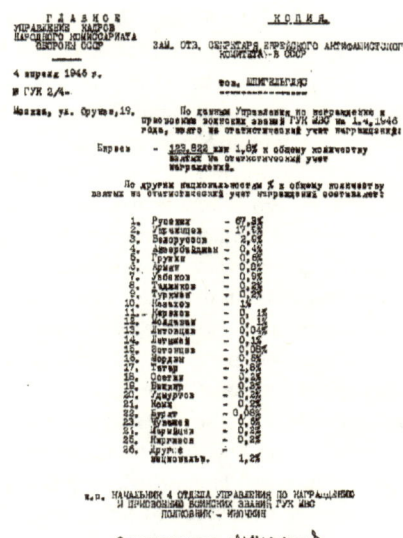

**Figure 133:** *1946. The official response to an inquiry by the Jewish Anti-Fascist Committee about the military decorations of Jews during the war (1.8% of the total number). Some antisemites accused Jews of lack of patriotism and of hiding from military service*

## After World War II

Following the war, the Soviet Union suppressed or downplayed the impact of the Nazi crimes on its Jewish citizens. An anti-semitic campaign against "rootless cosmopolitans" (i.e. "Zionists") followed. On 12 August 1952, in the event known as the Night of the Murdered Poets, thirteen most prominent Yiddish writers, poets, actors and other intellectuals were executed on the orders of Joseph Stalin, among them Peretz Markish, Leib Kvitko, David Hofstein, Itzik Feffer and David Bergelson.[924]

In 2012, Yad Vashem began releasing more than a million new testimonial pages about Jews in the Soviet Union that are expected to help researchers measure the scope of persecution and extermination of Jews in the former Soviet Union.

**Figure 134:** *The Grand Mufti of Jerusalem, Haj Amin al-Husseini, talking to Azerbaijani Legion volunteers*

## Perpetrators and commanders

- Gruppenführer Otto Ohlendorf
- SS-Gruppenführer Walter Schimana
- SS-Brigadeführer Christoph Diehm
- SS-Obersturmbannführer Hans Siegling
- SS-Hauptsturmführer Albert Löffler
- SS-Sturmbannführer Franz Henningfeld
- SS-Brigadeführer Peter Hansen
- SS-Standartenführer Gustav Lombard
- SS-Oberführer Constantin Heldmann
- Waffen-Brigadefuhrer der SS Bronislaw Kaminski
- Sonderführer (K) (later Major-General of Wehrmacht) Boris Smyslovsky, a.k.a. Artur Holmston
- Otto Brautigam

## Executor units

### German security and police units

- Schutzmannschaft-Brigade Siegling
- Einsatzgruppen (Einsatzkommando)

## Volunteers in German armed forces

- According to Yitzhak Arad, "In January 1942 a company of Tatar volunteers was established in Simferopol under the command of *Einsatzgruppe 11*. This company participated in anti-Jewish manhunts and murder actions in the rural regions."[925]
- Hilfswillige or Hiwi Russians
- Ostlegionen (Russian sections)
- 29th Waffen Grenadier Division of the SS RONA (1st Russian)
- 29th Waffen Grenadier Division of the SS (1st Italian) (Russian volunteers unit)
- 30th Waffen Grenadier Division of the SS (2nd Russian)
- Guard Corps Brigade of ROA
- "Schutzmannschaft-Brigade Siegling" or "SS-Polizei-Bataillon-Siegling"
- 2nd KNOR Division (600. (Russische) Infanterie-Division)
- 1st KNOR Division (650. (Russische) Infanterie-Division)
- 3rd KNOR Division (in development still at the end of the war)
- Freiwilligen-Stamm-Regiment 3 (Russians & Ukrainians)
- Freiwilligen-Stamm-Regiment 4 (Russians & Ukrainians)
- Freiwillige SS reg. Warager (Wrangel SS Regiment)
- 1st Russian National Army (1st RNA, also known as Boyarski Brigade)
- Sonderheadquarters R (special headquarters Russia)
- Special division R (12 training reconnaissance battalions)
- 1064th Russian Grenadier Regiment of 599th Russian Brigade
- 1st Russian National SS brigade Drushina
- Russkiy Okhranniy Korpus
- Otdel'niy Russkiy Korpus
- Russisches Schutzkorps or Russisches Schutzkorps Serbien (Russian Units in Balkans area)
- Russian fighter volunteers on Fehrbelliner Platz (Berlin U-Bahn)

## Collaborationist parties

### European front

- *Narodnaya Socialisticheskaya Partiya* (Russian National Socialist Party), later renamed *Nacional-Socialisticheskaya Rabochaya Partiya Rossiya* (National-Socialist Labour Party of Russia) with first led by Ivan K. Voskoboinikov, later for Bronislav Kaminski in the Lokot Republic

**Pacific front**

- Russian Fascist Party, led by Konstantin Rodzaevsky in exile from Manchukuo (Japanese satellite Chinese 'empire' in Manchuria).
- Monarchist Party, led by General Kislitsin, in Manchukuo.

# Death squads

## Einsatzgruppen

<indicator name="pp-default"> 🔒 </indicator> <indicator name="pp-default"> 🔒 </indicator>

<indicator name="good-star"> ⊕ </indicator>

*Einsatzgruppen*

The *Einsatzgruppen* operated under the administration of the *Schutzstaffel* (SS)

Killing of Jews in Ivanhorod, Ukraine, 1942. A woman is attempting to protect a child with her own body just before they are fired upon with rifles at close range.

| Agency overview | |
|---|---|
| Formed | c. 1939 |
| Preceding agency | • *Einsatzkommando* |
| Jurisdiction | 🇩🇪 Nazi Germany<br>Occupied Europe |
| Head-quarters | RSHA, Prinz-Albrecht-Straße, Berlin<br>52°30′26″N 13°22′57″E[926] |
| Employees | c. 3,000 (1941) |

| Minister responsible | • Heinrich Himmler, Reichsführer-SS |
|---|---|
| Agency executives | • SS-*Obergruppenführer* Reinhard Heydrich, Director, RSHA (1939–1942)<br>• SS-*Obergruppenführer* Ernst Kaltenbrunner, Director, RSHA (1943–1945) |
| Parent agency | ᛋᛋ Allgemeine SS and RSHA |

*Einsatzgruppen*[927] (German: [ˈʔaɪnzats̩ˌɡʁʊpn̩], "task forces"[928] or "deployment groups")[929] were *Schutzstaffel* (SS) paramilitary death squads of Nazi Germany that were responsible for mass killings, primarily by shooting, during World War II (1939–45). The *Einsatzgruppen* were involved in the murder of much of the intelligentsia, including members of the priesthood,[930] and cultural elite of Poland, and had an integral role in the implementation of the so-called "Final Solution to the Jewish Question" (*Die Endlösung der Judenfrage*) in territories conquered by Nazi Germany. Almost all of the people they killed were civilians, beginning with the intelligentsia and swiftly progressing to Soviet political commissars, Jews, and Romani people as well as actual or alleged partisans throughout Eastern Europe.

Under the direction of *Reichsführer-SS* Heinrich Himmler and the supervision of SS-*Obergruppenführer* Reinhard Heydrich, the *Einsatzgruppen* operated in territories occupied by the Wehrmacht (German armed forces) following the invasion of Poland in September 1939 and the invasion of the Soviet Union in June 1941. The *Einsatzgruppen* worked hand-in-hand with the Orpo Police Battalions on the Eastern Front to carry out operations ranging from the murder of a few people to operations which lasted over two or more days, such as the massacre at Babi Yar with 33,771 Jews killed in two days, and the Rumbula massacre (with about 25,000 killed in two days of shooting). As ordered by Nazi leader Adolf Hitler, the Wehrmacht cooperated with the *Einsatzgruppen* and provided logistical support for their operations. Historian Raul Hilberg estimates that between 1941 and 1945 the *Einsatzgruppen* and related auxiliary troops killed more than two million people, including 1.3 million Jews. The total number of Jews murdered during the Holocaust is estimated at 5.5 to 6 million people.

After the close of World War II, 24 senior leaders of the *Einsatzgruppen* were prosecuted in the Einsatzgruppen Trial in 1947–48, charged with crimes against humanity and war crimes. Fourteen death sentences and two life sentences were handed out. Four additional *Einsatzgruppe* leaders were later tried and executed by other nations.

## Formation and Action T4

The *Einsatzgruppen* were formed under the direction of SS-*Obergruppenführer* Reinhard Heydrich and operated by the *Schutzstaffel* (SS) before and during World War II.[931] The *Einsatzgruppen* had its origins in the ad hoc *Einsatzkommando* formed by Heydrich to secure government buildings and documents following the *Anschluss* in Austria in March 1938.[932] Originally part of the *Sicherheitspolizei* (Security Police; SiPo), two units of *Einsatzgruppen* were stationed in the Sudetenland in October 1938. When military action turned out not to be necessary due to the Munich Agreement, the *Einsatzgruppen* were assigned to confiscate government papers and police documents. They also secured government buildings, questioned senior civil servants, and arrested as many as 10,000 Czech communists and German citizens.[932,933] From September 1939, the *Reichssicherheitshauptamt* (Reich Main Security Office; RSHA) had overall command of the *Einsatzgruppen*.[934]

As part of the drive to remove so-called "undesirable" elements from the German population, from September to December 1939 the *Einsatzgruppen* and others took part in Action T4, a programme of systematic murder undertaken by the Nazi regime of persons with physical and mental disabilities and patients of psychiatric hospitals. Action T4 mainly took place from 1939 to 1941, but the killings continued until the end of the war. Initially the victims were shot by the *Einsatzgruppen* and others, but gas chambers were put into use by spring 1940.[935]

## Invasion of Poland

In response to Adolf Hitler's plan to invade Poland on 1 September 1939, Heydrich re-formed the *Einsatzgruppen* to travel in the wake of the German armies.[936] Membership at this point was drawn from the SS, the *Sicherheitsdienst* (Security Service; SD), the police, and the Gestapo.[937,938] Heydrich placed SS-*Obergruppenführer* Werner Best in command, who assigned Hans-Joachim Tesmer to choose personnel for the task forces and their subgroups, called *Einsatzkommandos*, from among educated people with military experience and a strong ideological commitment to Nazism.[939] Some had previously been members of paramilitary groups such as the *Freikorps*.[940] Heydrich instructed Wagner in meetings in late July that the *Einsatzgruppen* should undertake their operations in cooperation with the *Ordnungspolizei* (Order Police; Orpo) and military commanders in the area.[941] Army intelligence was in constant contact with *Einsatzgruppen* to coordinate their activities with other units.[942]

Initially numbering 2,700 men (and ultimately 4,250 in Poland),[940,943] the *Einsatzgruppen*'s mission was to kill members of the Polish leadership most

**Figure 135:** *Execution of Poles in Kórnik, 20 October 1939*

clearly identified with Polish national identity: the intelligentsia, members of the clergy, teachers, and members of the nobility.[937,944] As stated by Hitler: "... there must be no Polish leaders; where Polish leaders exist they must be killed, however harsh that sounds".[945] SS-*Brigadeführer* Lothar Beutel, commander of *Einsatzgruppe* IV, later testified that Heydrich gave the order for these killings at a series of meetings in mid-August.[946] The *Sonderfahndungsbuch Polen* — lists of people to be killed — had been drawn up by the SS as early as May 1939, using dossiers collected by the SD from 1936 forward.[937,947] The *Einsatzgruppen* performed these murders with the support of the *Volksdeutscher Selbstschutz*, a paramilitary group consisting of ethnic Germans living in Poland.[948] Members of the SS, the Wehrmacht, and the *Ordnungspolizei* also shot civilians during the Polish campaign.[949] Approximately 65,000 civilians were killed by the end of 1939. In addition to leaders of Polish society, they killed Jews, prostitutes, Romani people, and the mentally ill. Psychiatric patients in Poland were initially killed by shooting, but by spring 1941 gas vans were widely used.[950,951]

Seven *Einsatzgruppen* of battalion strength (around 500 men) operated in Poland. Each was subdivided into five *Einsatzkommandos* of company strength (around 100 men).[938]

- *Einsatzgruppe* I, commanded by SS-*Standartenführer* Bruno Streckenbach, acted with 14th Army
- *Einsatzgruppe* II, SS-*Obersturmbannführer* Emanuel Schäfer, acted with 10th Army

- *Einsatzgruppe* III, SS-*Obersturmbannführer und Regierungsrat* Herbert Fischer, acted with 8th Army
- *Einsatzgruppe* IV, SS-*Brigadeführer* Lothar Beutel, acted with 4th Army
- *Einsatzgruppe* V, SS-*Standartenfürer* Ernst Damzog, acted with 3rd Army
- *Einsatzgruppe* VI, SS-*Oberführer* Erich Naumann, acted in Wielkopolska
- *Einsatzgruppe* VII, SS-*Obergruppenführer* Udo von Woyrsch and SS-*Gruppenführer* Otto Rasch, acted in Upper Silesia and Cieszyn Silesia[952]

Though they were formally under the command of the army, the *Einsatzgruppen* received their orders from Heydrich and for the most part acted independently of the army.[953,954] Many senior army officers were only too glad to leave these genocidal actions to the task forces, as the killings violated the rules of warfare as set down in the Geneva Conventions. However, Hitler had decreed that the army would have to tolerate and even offer logistical support to the *Einsatzgruppen* when it was tactically possible to do so. Some army commanders complained about unauthorised shootings, looting, and rapes committed by members of the *Einsatzgruppen* and the *Volksdeutscher Selbstschutz*, to little effect.[955] For example, when *Generaloberst* Johannes Blaskowitz sent a memorandum of complaint to Hitler about the atrocities, Hitler dismissed his concerns as "childish", and Blaskowitz was relieved of his post in May 1940. He continued to serve in the army but never received promotion to field marshal.[956]

The final task of the *Einsatzgruppen* in Poland was to round up the remaining Jews and concentrate them in ghettos within major cities with good railway connections. The intention was to eventually remove all the Jews from Poland, but at this point their final destination had not yet been determined.[957,958] Together, the Wehrmacht and the *Einsatzgruppen* also drove tens of thousands of Jews eastward into Soviet-controlled territory.[949]

## Preparations for Operation Barbarossa

On 13 March 1941, in the lead-up to Operation Barbarossa, the planned invasion of the Soviet Union, Hitler dictated his "Guidelines in Special Spheres re: Directive No. 21 (Operation Barbarossa)". Sub-paragraph B specified that *Reichsführer-SS* Heinrich Himmler would be given "special tasks" on direct orders from the Führer, which he would carry out independently.[959,960] This directive was intended to prevent friction between the Wehrmacht and the SS in the upcoming offensive.[959] Hitler also specified that criminal acts against civilians perpetrated by members of the Wehrmacht during the upcoming campaign would not be prosecuted in the military courts, and thus would go unpunished.[961]

In a speech to his leading generals on 30 March 1941, Hitler described his envisioned war against the Soviet Union. General Franz Halder, the Army's Chief of Staff, described the speech:<templatestyles src="Template:Quote/styles.css"/>

> *Struggle between two ideologies. Scathing evaluation of Bolshevism, equals antisocial criminality. Communism immense future danger ... This a fight to the finish. If we do not accept this, we shall beat the enemy, but in thirty years we shall again confront the Communist foe. We don't make war to preserve the enemy ... Struggle against Russia: Extermination of Bolshevik Commissars and of the Communist intelligentsia ... Commissars and GPU personnel are criminals and must be treated as such. The struggle will differ from that in the west. In the east harshness now means mildness for the future.*[962]

Though General Halder did not record any mention of Jews, German historian Andreas Hillgruber argued that because of Hitler's frequent contemporary statements about the coming war of annihilation against "Judeo-Bolshevism", his generals would have understood Hitler's call for the destruction of the Soviet Union as also comprising a call for the destruction of its Jewish population.[962] The genocide was often described using euphemisms such as "special tasks" and "executive measures"; *Einsatzgruppe* victims were often described as having been shot while trying to escape.[963] In May 1941, Heydrich verbally passed on the order to kill the Soviet Jews to the SiPo NCO School in Pretzsch, where the commanders of the reorganised *Einsatzgruppen* were being trained for Operation Barbarossa.[964] In spring 1941, Heydrich and the First Quartermaster of the *Wehrmacht Heer*, General Eduard Wagner, successfully completed negotiations for co-operation between the *Einsatzgruppen* and the German Army to allow the implementation of the "special tasks".[965] Following the Heydrich-Wagner agreement on 28 April 1941, Field Marshal Walther von Brauchitsch ordered that when Operation Barbarossa began, all German Army commanders were to immediately identify and register all Jews in occupied areas in the Soviet Union, and fully co-operate with the *Einsatzgruppen*.[966]

In further meetings held in June 1941 Himmler outlined to top SS leaders the regime's intention to reduce the population of the Soviet Union by 30 million people, not only through direct killing of those considered racially inferior, but by depriving the remainder of food and other necessities of life.[967]

## Organisation starting in 1941

For Operation Barbarossa, initially four *Einsatzgruppen* were created, each numbering 500–990 men to comprise a total force of 3,000.[968] *Einsatzgruppen* A, B, and C were to be attached to Army Groups North, Centre, and South; *Einsatzgruppe* D was assigned to the 11th Army. The *Einsatzgruppe* for Special Purposes operated in eastern Poland starting in July 1941.[968] The *Einsatzgruppen* were under the control of the RSHA, headed by Heydrich and later by his successor, SS-*Obergruppenführer* Ernst Kaltenbrunner. Heydrich gave them a mandate to secure the offices and papers of the Soviet state and Communist Party;[969] to liquidate all the higher cadres of the Soviet state; and to instigate and encourage pogroms against Jewish populations.[970] The men of the *Einsatzgruppen* were recruited from the SD, Gestapo, *Kriminalpolizei* (Kripo), Orpo, and Waffen-SS.[968] Each *Einsatzgruppe* was under the operational control of the Higher SS Police Chiefs in its area of operations.[966] In May 1941, General Wagner and SS-*Brigadeführer* Walter Schellenberg agreed that the *Einsatzgruppen* in front-line areas were to operate under army command, while the army provided the *Einsatzgruppen* with all necessary logistical support.[971] Given their main task was defeating the enemy, the army left the pacification of the civilian population to the *Einsatzgruppen*, who offered support as well as prevented subversion.[972] This did not preclude their participation in acts of violence against civilians, as many members of the Wehrmacht assisted the *Einsatzgruppen* in rounding up and killing Jews of their own accord.[973]

Heydrich acted under orders from *Reichsführer-SS* Himmler, who supplied security forces on an "as needed" basis to the local SS and Police Leaders.[931] Led by SD, Gestapo, and Kripo officers, *Einsatzgruppen* included recruits from the Orpo, Security Service and Waffen-SS, augmented by uniformed volunteers from the local auxiliary police force.[974] Each *Einsatzgruppe* was supplemented with a reserve battalion of Orpos and Waffen-SS as well as support personnel such as drivers and radio operators.[968] On average, the Orpo formations were larger and better armed, with heavy machine-gun detachments, which enabled them to carry out operations beyond the capability of the SS.[974] Each death squad followed an assigned army group as they advanced into the Soviet Union.[975] During the course of their operations, the *Einsatzgruppen* commanders received assistance from the Wehrmacht.[975] Activities ranged from the murder of targeted groups of individuals named on carefully prepared lists, to joint citywide operations with *SS Einsatzgruppen* which lasted for two or more days, such as the massacres at Babi Yar, perpetrated by the Orpo Reserve Battalion 45, and at Rumbula, by Battalion 22, reinforced by local *Schutzmannschaften* (auxiliary police).[976,977] The SS brigades, wrote historian Christopher Browning, were "only the thin cutting edge of German units that became involved in political and racial mass murder."[978]

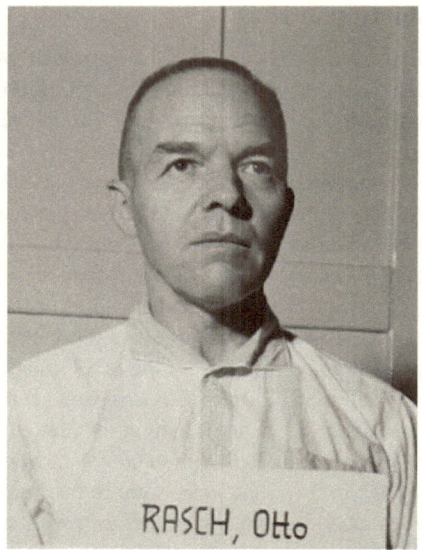

**Figure 136:** *Otto Rasch photographed by Allied forces at the Nuremberg Trials, circa 1948*

Many *Einsatzgruppe* leaders were highly educated; for example, nine of seventeen leaders of *Einsatzgruppe* A held doctorate degrees.[979] Three *Einsatzgruppen* were commanded by holders of doctorates, one of whom (SS-*Gruppenführer* Otto Rasch) held a double doctorate.[980]

Additional *Einsatzgruppen* were created as additional territories were occupied. *Einsatzgruppe* E operated in Independent State of Croatia under three commanders, SS-*Obersturmbannführer* Ludwig Teichmann, SS-*Standartenführer* Günther Herrmann, and lastly SS-*Standartenführer* Wilhelm Fuchs. The unit was subdivided into five *Einsatzkommandos* located in Vinkovci, Sarajevo, Banja Luka, Knin, and Zagreb.[981,982] *Einsatzgruppe* F worked with Army Group South.[982] *Einsatzgruppe* G operated in Romania, Hungary, and Ukraine, commanded by SS-*Standartenführer* Josef Kreuzer.[981] *Einsatzgruppe* H was assigned to Slovakia.[983] *Einsatzgruppen* K and L, under SS-*Oberführer* Emanuel Schäfer and SS-*Standartenführer* Ludwig Hahn, worked alongside 5th and 6th Panzer Armies during the Ardennes offensive.[984] Hahn had previously been in command of *Einsatzgruppe Griechenland* in Greece.[985]

Other *Einsatzgruppen* and *Einsatzkommandos* included *Einsatzgruppe Iltis* (operated in Carinthia, on the border between Slovenia and Austria) under SS-*Standartenführer* Paul Blobel,[986] *Einsatzgruppe Jugoslawien* (Yugoslavia)[987]

*Einsatzkommando Luxemburg* (Luxembourg),[982] *Einsatzgruppe Norwegen* (Norway) commanded by SS-*Oberführer* Franz Walter Stahlecker,[988] *Einsatzgruppe Serbien* (Yugoslavia) under SS-*Standartenführer* Wilhelm Fuchs and SS-*Gruppenführer* August Meysner,[989] *Einsatzkommando Tilsit* (Lithuania, Poland),[990] and *Einsatzgruppe Tunis* (Tunis), commanded by SS-*Obersturmbannführer* Walter Rauff.[991]

## Killings in the Soviet Union

Map of the *Einsatzgruppen* operations behind the German-Soviet frontier with the location of the first shooting of Jewish men, women and children, 30 July 1941

After the invasion of the Soviet Union on 22 June 1941, the *Einsatzgruppen*'s main assignment was to kill civilians, as in Poland, but this time its targets specifically included Soviet Communist Party commissars and Jews.[970] In a letter dated 2 July 1941 Heydrich communicated to his SS and Police Leaders that the *Einsatzgruppen* were to execute all senior and middle ranking Comintern officials; all senior and middle ranking members of the central, provincial, and district committees of the Communist Party; extremist and radical Communist Party members; people's commissars; and Jews in party and government posts. Open-ended instructions were given to execute "other radical elements (saboteurs, propagandists, snipers, assassins, agitators, etc.)." He instructed that any pogroms spontaneously initiated by the population of the occupied territories were to be quietly encouraged.[992]

On 8 July, Heydrich announced that all Jews were to be regarded as partisans, and gave the order for all male Jews between the ages of 15 and 45 to be shot.[993] On 17 July Heydrich ordered that the *Einsatzgruppen* were to kill all Jewish Red Army prisoners of war, plus all Red Army prisoners of war from Georgia and Central Asia, as they too might be Jews.[994] Unlike in Germany, where the Nuremberg Laws of 1935 defined as Jewish anyone with at least three Jewish grandparents, the *Einsatzgruppen* defined as Jewish anyone with at least one Jewish grandparent; in either case, whether or not the person practised the

**Figure 137:** *A teenage boy stands beside his murdered family shortly before his own death by the SS. Zboriv, Ukraine, 5 July 1941*

religion was irrelevant.[995] The unit was also assigned to exterminate Romani people and the mentally ill. It was common practice for the *Einsatzgruppen* to shoot hostages.[996]

As the invasion began, the Germans pursued the fleeing Red Army, leaving a security vacuum. Reports surfaced of Soviet guerrilla activity in the area, with local Jews immediately suspected of collaboration. Heydrich ordered his officers to incite anti-Jewish pogroms in the newly occupied territories.[997] Pogroms, some of which were orchestrated by the *Einsatzgruppen*, broke out in Latvia, Lithuania, and Ukraine.[998] Within the first few weeks of Operation Barbarossa, 40 pogroms led to the deaths of 10,000 Jews, and by the end of 1941 some 60 pogroms had taken place, claiming as many as 24,000 victims.[998,999] However, SS-*Brigadeführer* Franz Walter Stahlecker, commander of *Einsatzgruppe* A, reported to his superiors in mid-October that the residents of Kaunas were not spontaneously starting pogroms, and secret assistance by the Germans was required.[1000] A similar reticence was noted by *Einsatzgruppe* B in Russia and Belarus and *Einsatzgruppe* C in Ukraine; the further east the *Einsatzgruppen* travelled, the less likely the residents were to be prompted into killing their Jewish neighbours.[1001]

All four main *Einsatzgruppen* took part in mass shootings from the early days of the war.[1002] Initially the targets were adult Jewish men, but by August the net had been widened to include women, children, and the elderly—the entire Jewish population. Initially there was a semblance of legality given to the shootings, with trumped-up charges being read out (arson, sabotage, black marketeering, or refusal to work, for example) and victims being killed by a firing squad. As this method proved too slow, the *Einsatzkommandos* began to take their victims out in larger groups and shot them next to, or even inside, mass graves that had been prepared. Some *Einsatzkommandos* started to use automatic weapons, with survivors being killed with a pistol shot.[1003]

As word of the massacres got out, many Jews fled; in Ukraine, 70 to 90 per cent of the Jews ran away. This was seen by the leader of *Einsatzkommando* VI as beneficial, as it would save the regime the costs of deporting the victims further east over the Urals.[1004] In other areas the invasion was so successful that the *Einsatzgruppen* had insufficient forces to immediately kill all the Jews in the conquered territories.[1005] A situation report from *Einsatzgruppe* C in September 1941 noted that not all Jews were members of the Bolshevist apparatus, and suggested that the total elimination of Jewry would have a negative impact on the economy and the food supply. The Nazis began to round their victims up into concentration camps and ghettos and rural districts were for the most part rendered *Judenfrei* (free of Jews).[1006] Jewish councils were set up in major cities and forced labour gangs were established to make use of the Jews as slave labour until they were totally eliminated, a goal that was postponed until 1942.[1007]

The *Einsatzgruppen* used public hangings as a terror tactic against the local population. An *Einsatzgruppe B* report, dated 9 October 1941, described one such hanging. Due to suspected partisan activity near Demidov, all male residents aged 15 to 55 were put in a camp to be screened. The screening produced seventeen people who were identified as "partisans" and "Communists". Five members of the group were hanged while 400 local residents were assembled to watch; the rest were shot.[1008]

## Babi Yar

The largest mass shooting perpetrated by the *Einsatzgruppen* took place on 29 and 30 September 1941 at Babi Yar, a ravine northwest of Kiev, a city in Ukraine that had fallen to the Germans on 19 September.[1009,1010] The perpetrators included a company of Waffen-SS attached to *Einsatzgruppe* C under Rasch, members of *Sonderkommando* 4a under SS-*Obergruppenführer* Friedrich Jeckeln, and some Ukrainian auxiliary police.[1011] The Jews of Kiev were told to report to a certain street corner on 29 September; anyone who disobeyed would be shot. Since word of massacres in other areas had not yet reached Kiev and the assembly point was near the train station, they assumed they were being deported. People showed up at the rendezvous point in large numbers, laden with possessions and food for the journey.[1012]

After being marched two miles north-west of the city centre, the victims encountered a barbed wire barrier and numerous Ukrainian police and German troops. Thirty or forty people at a time were told to leave their possessions and were escorted through a narrow passageway lined with soldiers brandishing clubs. Anyone who tried to escape was beaten. Soon the victims reached an open area, where they were forced to strip, and then were herded down into the ravine. People were forced to lie down in rows on top of the bodies of other victims, and they were shot in the back of the head or the neck by members of the execution squads.[1013]

The murders continued for two days, claiming a total of 33,771 victims.[1010] Sand was shovelled and bulldozed over the bodies and the sides of the ravine were dynamited to bring down more material.[1014] Anton Heidborn, a member of *Sonderkommando* 4a, later testified that three days later that there were still people alive among the corpses. Heidborn spent the next few days helping smooth out the "millions" of banknotes taken from the victims' possessions.[1015] The clothing was taken away, destined to be re-used by German citizens.[1014] Jeckeln's troops shot more than 100,000 Jews by the end of October.[1010]

## Killings in the Baltic states

*Einsatzgruppe* A operated in the formerly Soviet-occupied Baltic states of Estonia, Latvia, and Lithuania. According to its own reports to Himmler, *Einsatzgruppe* A killed almost 140,000 people in the five months following the invasion: 136,421 Jews, 1,064 Communists, 653 people with mental illnesses, 56 partisans, 44 Poles, five Romani, and one Armenian were reported killed between 22 June and 25 November 1941.[1016]

Upon entering Kaunas, Lithuania, on 25 June 1941, the *Einsatzgruppe* released the criminals from the local jail and encouraged them to join the pogrom which was underway.[1017] Between 23–27 June 1941, 4,000 Jews were killed on the streets of Kaunas and in nearby open pits and ditches.[1018] Particularly active in the Kaunas pogrom was the so-called "Death Dealer of Kaunas", a young man who murdered Jews with a crowbar at the Lietukis Garage before a large crowd that cheered each killing with much applause; he occasionally paused to play the Lithuanian national anthem "Tautiška giesmė" on his accordion before resuming the killings.[1018,1019]

As *Einsatzgruppe* A advanced into Lithuania, it actively recruited local nationalists and antisemitic groups. In July 1941, members of the *Baltaraisciai* movement joined the massacres.[999] A pogrom in Riga in early July killed 400

Jews. Latvian nationalist Viktors Arājs and his supporters undertook a campaign of arson against synagogues.[1020] On 2 July, *Einsatzgruppe* A commander Stahlecker appointed Arājs to head the *Arajs Kommando*,[999] a *Sonderkommando* of about 300 men, mostly university students. Together, *Einsatzgruppe* A and the *Arājs Kommando* killed 2,300 Jews in Riga on 6–7 July.[1020] Within six months, Arājs and his men would kill about half of Latvia's Jewish population.[1021]

Local officials, the *Selbstschutz*, and the *Hilfspolizei* (Auxiliary Police) played a key role in rounding up and massacring Jewish Lithuanians, Latvians, and Estonians.[1022] These groups helped the *Einsatzgruppen* and other killing units to quickly identify Jews.[1022] The *Hilfspolizei*, consisting of auxiliary police organised by the Germans and recruited from former Latvian Army and police officers, ex-*Aizsargi*, members of the Pērkonkrusts, and university students, assisted in the murder of Latvia's Jewish citizens.[1021] Similar units were created elsewhere, and provided much of the manpower for the Holocaust in Eastern Europe.[1023]

With the creation of units such as the *Arājs Kommando* and the *Rollkommando Hamann* in Lithuania,[1024] the attacks changed from the spontaneous mob violence of the pogroms to more systematic massacres.[1021] With extensive local help, *Einsatzgruppe* A was the first *Einsatzgruppe* to attempt to systematically exterminate all the Jews in its area.[1025,1022] Latvian historian Modris Eksteins wrote: <templatestyles src="Template:Quote/styles.css"/>

> *Of the roughly 83,000 Jews who fell into German hands in Latvia, not more than 900 survived; and of the more than 20,000 Western Jews sent into Latvia, only some 800 lived through the deportation until liberation. This was the highest percentage of eradication in all of Europe.*[1026]

In late 1941, the *Einsatzkommandos* settled into headquarters in Kovno, Riga, and Tallinn. *Einsatzgruppe* A grew less mobile and faced problems because of its small size. The Germans relied increasingly on the *Arājs Kommando* and similar groups to perform massacres of Jews.[1024]

Such extensive and enthusiastic collaboration with the *Einsatzgruppen* has been attributed to several factors. Since the Russian Revolution of 1905, the *Kresy Wschodnie* and other borderlands had experienced a political culture of violence.[1027] The period of Soviet rule had been profoundly traumatic for residents of the Baltic states and areas that had been part of Poland until 1939; the population was brutalised and terrorised by the imposed Soviet rule, and the existing familiar structures of society were destroyed.[1028]

Historian Erich Haberer notes that many survived and made sense of the "totalitarian atomization" of society by seeking conformity with communism.[1029] As a result, by the time of the German invasion in 1941, many had come

**Figure 138:** *Dog tag issued by Einsatzgruppen SD*

to see conformity with a totalitarian regime as socially acceptable behaviour; thus, people simply transferred their allegiance to the German regime when it arrived.[1029] Some who had collaborated with the Soviet regime sought to divert attention from themselves by naming Jews as collaborators and killing them.[1030]

## Rumbula

In November 1941 Himmler was dissatisfied with the pace of the exterminations in Latvia, as he intended to move Jews from Germany into the area. He assigned SS-*Obergruppenführer* Jeckeln, one of the perpetrators of the Babi Yar massacre, to liquidate the Riga ghetto. Jeckeln selected a site about 10 kilometres (6.2 mi) southeast of Riga near the Rumbula railway station, and had 300 Russian prisoners of war prepare the site by digging pits in which to bury the victims. Jeckeln organised around 1,700 men, including 300 members of the *Arajs Kommando*, 50 German SD men, and 50 Latvian guards, most of whom had already participated in mass killings of civilians. These troops were supplemented by Latvians, including members of the Riga city police, battalion police, and ghetto guards. Around 1,500 able-bodied Jews would be spared execution so their slave labour could be exploited; a thousand men were relocated to a fenced-off area within the ghetto and 500 women were temporarily housed in a prison and later moved to a separate nearby ghetto, where they were put to work mending uniforms.[1031]

Although Rumbula was on the rail line, Jeckeln decided that the victims should travel on foot from Riga to the execution ground. Trucks and buses were arranged to carry children and the elderly. The victims were told that they were being relocated, and were advised to bring up to 20 kilograms (44 lb) of possessions. The first day of executions, 30 November 1941, began with the perpetrators rousing and assembling the victims at 4:00 am. The victims were moved in columns of a thousand people toward the execution ground. As they walked, some SS men went up and down the line, shooting people who could not keep up the pace or who tried to run away or rest.[1032]

When the columns neared the prepared execution site, the victims were driven some 270 metres (300 yd) from the road into the forest, where any possessions that had not yet been abandoned were seized. Here the victims were split into groups of fifty and taken deeper into the forest, near the pits, where they were ordered to strip. The victims were driven into the prepared trenches, made to lie down, and shot in the head or the back of the neck by members of Jeckeln's bodyguard. Around 13,000 Jews from Riga were killed at the pits that day, along with a thousand Jews from Berlin who had just arrived by train. On the second day of the operation, 8 December 1941, the remaining 10,000 Jews of Riga were killed in the same way. About a thousand were killed on the streets of the city or on the way to the site, bringing the total deaths for the two-day extermination to 25,000 people. For his part in organising the massacre, Jeckeln was promoted to Leader of the SS Upper Section, Ostland.[1033]

## Second sweep

*Einsatzgruppe B, C*, and *D* did not immediately follow *Einsatzgruppe* A's example in systematically killing all Jews in their areas. The *Einsatzgruppe* commanders, with the exception of *Einsatzgruppe* A's Stahlecker, were of the opinion by the fall of 1941 that it was impossible to kill the entire Jewish population of the Soviet Union in one sweep, and thought the killings should stop.[1034] An *Einsatzgruppe* report dated 17 September advised that the Germans would be better off using any skilled Jews as labourers rather than shooting them.[1034] Also, in some areas poor weather and a lack of transportation led to a slowdown in deportations of Jews from points further west.[1035] Thus, an interval passed between the first round of *Einsatzgruppen* massacres in summer and fall, and what American historian Raul Hilberg called the second sweep, which started in December 1941 and lasted into the summer of 1942.[1036] During the interval, the surviving Jews were forced into ghettos.[1037]

*Einsatzgruppe* A had already murdered almost all Jews in its area, so it shifted its operations into Belarus to assist *Einsatzgruppe* B. In Dnepropetrovsk in February 1942, *Einsatzgruppe* D reduced the city's Jewish population from

**Figure 139:** *Magirus-Deutz van found near Chełmno extermination camp is the same type as those used as gas vans.*

30,000 to 702 over the course of four days.[1038] The German Order Police and local collaborators provided the extra manpower needed to perform all the shootings. Haberer wrote that, as in the Baltic states, the Germans could not have killed so many Jews so quickly without local help. He points out that the ratio of Order Police to auxiliaries was 1 to 10 in both Ukraine and Belarus. In rural areas the proportion was 1 to 20. This meant that most Ukrainian and Belarusian Jews were killed by fellow Ukrainians and Belarusians commanded by German officers rather than by Germans.[1039]

The second wave of exterminations in the Soviet Union met with armed resistance in some areas, though the chance of success was poor. Weapons were typically primitive or home-made. Communications were impossible between ghettos in various cities, so there was no way to create a unified strategy. Few in the ghetto leadership supported resistance for fear of reprisals on the ghetto residents. Mass break-outs were sometimes attempted, though survival in the forest was nearly impossible due to the lack of food and the fact that escapees were often tracked down and killed.[1040]

# Transition to gassing

After a time, Himmler found that the killing methods used by the *Einsatzgruppen* were inefficient: they were costly, demoralising for the troops, and sometimes did not kill the victims quickly enough.[1041] Many of the troops found the massacres to be difficult if not impossible to perform. Some of the perpetrators suffered physical and mental health problems, and many turned to drink.[1042] As much as possible, the *Einsatzgruppen* leaders militarized the genocide. The historian Christian Ingrao notes an attempt was made to make the shootings a collective act without individual responsibility. Framing the shootings in this way was not psychologically sufficient for every perpetrator to feel absolved of guilt.[1043] Browning notes three categories of potential perpetrators: those who were eager to participate right from the start, those who participated in spite of moral qualms because they were ordered to do so, and a significant minority who refused to take part.[1044] A few men spontaneously became excessively brutal in their killing methods and their zeal for the task. Commander of *Einsatzgruppe* D, SS-*Gruppenführer* Otto Ohlendorf, particularly noted this propensity towards excess, and ordered that any man who was too eager to participate or too brutal should not perform any further executions.[1045]

During a visit to Minsk in August 1941, Himmler witnessed an *Einsatzgruppen* mass execution first-hand and concluded that shooting Jews was too stressful for his men.[1046] By November he made arrangements for any SS men suffering ill health from having participated in executions to be provided with rest and mental health care.[1047] He also decided a transition should be made to gassing the victims, especially the women and children, and ordered the recruitment of expendable native auxiliaries who could assist with the murders.[1047,1048] Gas vans, which had been used previously to kill mental patients, began to see service by all four main *Einsatzgruppen* from 1942.[1049] However, the gas vans were not popular with the *Einsatzkommandos*, because removing the dead bodies from the van and burying them was a horrible ordeal. Prisoners or auxiliaries were often assigned to do this task so as to spare the SS men the trauma.[1050] Some of the early mass killings at extermination camps used carbon monoxide fumes produced by diesel engines, similar to the method used in gas vans, but by as early as September 1941 experiments were begun at Auschwitz using Zyklon B, a cyanide-based pesticide gas.[1051]

Plans for the total eradication of the Jewish population of Europe—eleven million people—were formalised at the Wannsee Conference, held on 20 January 1942. Some would be worked to death, and the rest would be killed in the implementation of the Final Solution of the Jewish question (German: *Die Endlösung der Judenfrage*).[1052] Permanent killing centres at Auschwitz, Belzec, Sobibor, Treblinka, and other Nazi extermination camps replaced mobile death squads as the primary method of mass killing.[1053] The *Einsatzgruppen* remained active, however, and were put to work fighting partisans, particularly in Belarus.[1054]

After the fall of Stalingrad in February 1943, Himmler realised that Germany would likely lose the war, and ordered the formation of a special task force, *Sonderkommando* 1005, under SS-*Standartenführer* Paul Blobel. The unit's assignment was to visit mass graves all along the Eastern Front to exhume bodies and burn them in an attempt to cover up the genocide. The task remained unfinished at the end of the war, and many mass graves remain unmarked and unexcavated.[1055]

By 1944 the Red Army had begun to push the German forces out of Eastern Europe, and the *Einsatzgruppen* retreated alongside the Wehrmacht. By late 1944, most *Einsatzgruppen* personnel had been folded into Waffen-SS combat units or transferred to permanent death camps. Hilberg estimates that between 1941 and 1945 the *Einsatzgruppen* and related agencies killed more than two million people, including 1.3 million Jews.[1056] The total number of Jews murdered during the war is estimated at 5.5 to six million people.[1057]

## Plans for the Middle East and Britain

According to research by German historians Klaus-Michael Mallmann and Martin Cüppers, an *Einsatzgruppe* was created in 1942 to kill the half-million Jews living in the British Mandate of Palestine and the 50,000 Jews of Egypt. *Einsatzgruppe* Egypt, standing by in Athens, was prepared to go to Palestine once German forces arrived there.[991] SS-*Obersturmbannführer* Walter Rauff was to lead the unit.[1058] Given its small staff of only 24 men, *Einsatzgruppe* Egypt would have needed help from local residents and from the *Afrika Korps* to complete their assignment. Its members planned to enlist collaborators from the local population to perform the killings under German leadership.[1059] Former Iraqi prime minister Rashid Ali al-Gaylani and the Grand Mufti of Jerusalem Haj Amin al-Husseini played roles, engaging in antisemitic radio propaganda, preparing to recruit volunteers, and in raising an Arab-German Battalion that would also follow *Einsatzgruppe* Egypt to the Middle East.[1060] On 20 July 1942, Walther Rauff, who was responsible for the unit, was sent to Tobruk to report to Field Marshal Erwin Rommel, Commander of the *Afrika Korps*. However, since Rommel was 500 km away at the First Battle of El Alamein, it is unlikely that the two were able to meet.[1061] The plans for *Einsatzgruppe* Egypt were set aside after the Allied victory at the Second Battle of El Alamein.[1062] Historian Jean-Christophe Caron opines that there is no evidence that Rommel knew of or would have supported Rauff's mission.[1063]

Had Operation Sea Lion, the German plan for an invasion of the United Kingdom been launched, six *Einsatzgruppen* were scheduled to follow the invasion force into Britain. They were provided with a list called *die Sonderfahndungsliste, G.B.* ("Special Search List, G.B"), known as The Black Book after

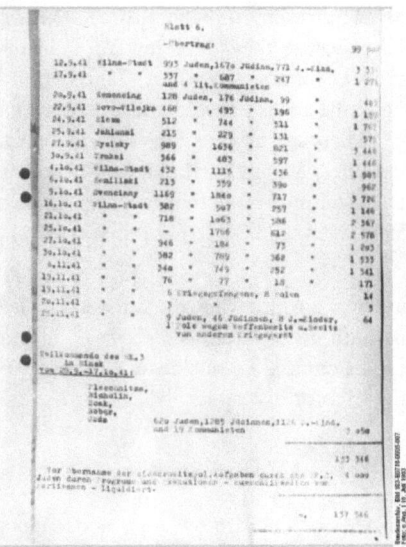

**Figure 140:** *Page 6 of the Jäger Report shows the number of people killed by Einsatzkommando III alone in the five-month period covered by the report as 137,346.*

the war, of 2,300 people to be immediately imprisoned by the Gestapo. The list included Churchill, members of the cabinet, prominent journalists and authors, and members of the Czechoslovak government-in-exile.[1064]

## Jäger Report

The *Einsatzgruppen* kept official records of many of their massacres and provided detailed reports to their superiors. The Jäger Report, filed by Commander *SS-Standartenführer* Karl Jäger on 1 December 1941 to his superior, Stahlecker (head of *Einsatzgruppe* A), covers the activities of *Einsatzkommando* III in Lithuania over the five-month period from 2 July 1941 to 25 November 1941.[1065]

Jäger's report provides an almost daily running total of the liquidations of 137,346 people, the vast majority of them Jews.[1065] The report documents the exact date and place of massacres, the number of victims, and their breakdown into categories (Jews, Communists, criminals, and so on).[1066] Women were shot from the very beginning, but initially in fewer numbers than men.[1067] Children were first included in the tally starting in mid-August, when 3,207 people were murdered in Rokiškis on 15–16 August 1941.[1066] For the most part the report does not give any military justification for the killings; people were killed solely because they were Jews.[1066] In total, the report lists over 100 executions in 71 different locations. Jäger wrote: "I can state today that the goal of solving the Jewish problem in Lithuania has been reached by *Einsatzkommando* 3. There are no more Jews in Lithuania, apart from working Jews and their families."[1065] In a February 1942 addendum to the report, Jäger increased the total number of victims to 138,272, giving a breakdown of 48,252 men, 55,556 women, and 34,464 children. Only 1,851 of the victims were non-Jewish.[1068]

Jäger escaped capture by the Allies when the war ended. He lived in Heidelberg under his own name until his report was discovered in March 1959.[1069] Arrested and charged, Jäger committed suicide on 22 June 1959 in a Hohenasperg prison while awaiting trial for his crimes.[1070]

## Involvement of the Wehrmacht

The killings took place with the knowledge and support of the German Army in the east.[1071] On 10 October 1941 Field Marshal Walther von Reichenau drafted an order to be read to the German Sixth Army on the Eastern Front. Now known as the Severity Order, it read in part: <templatestyles src="Template:Quote/styles.css"/>

> *The most important objective of this campaign against the Jewish-Bolshevik system is the complete destruction of its sources of power and the extermination of the Asiatic influence in European civilization ... In this eastern theatre, the soldier is not only a man fighting in accordance with the rules of the art of war, but also the ruthless standard bearer of a national conception ... For this reason the soldier must learn fully to appreciate the necessity for the severe but just retribution that must be meted out to the subhuman species of Jewry.*[1072]

Field Marshal Gerd von Rundstedt of Army Group South expressed his "complete agreement" with the order. He sent out a circular to the generals under his command urging them to release their own versions and to impress upon their troops the need to exterminate the Jews.[1073] General Erich von Manstein, in an order to his troops on 20 November, stated that "the Jewish-Bolshevist system must be exterminated once and for all."[1071] Manstein sent a letter to *Einsatzgruppe* D commanding officer Ohlendorf complaining that it was unfair that the SS was keeping all of the murdered Jews' wristwatches for themselves instead of sharing with the army.[1074]

Beyond this trivial complaint, the Army and the *Einsatzgruppen* worked closely and effectively. On 6 July 1941 *Einsatzkommando* 4b of *Einsatzgruppe* C reported that "Armed forces surprisingly welcome hostility against the Jews".[1075] Few complaints about the killings were ever raised by Wehrmacht officers.[1076] On 8 September, *Einsatzgruppe* D reported that relations with the German Army were "excellent".[1075] In the same month, Stahlecker of *Einsatzgruppe* A wrote that Army Group North had been exemplary in co-operating with the exterminations and that relations with the 4th Panzer Army, commanded by General Erich Hoepner, were "very close, almost cordial".[1077] In the south, the Romanian Army worked closely with *Einsatzgruppe* D to massacre Ukrainian Jews,[1037] killing around 26,000 Jews in the Odessa massacre.[1078] The German historian Peter Longerich thinks it probable that the Wehrmacht, along with the Organization of Ukrainian Nationalists (OUN), incited the Lviv pogroms, during which 8,500 to 9,000 Jews were killed by the native population and *Einsatzgruppe* C in July 1941.[1079] Moreover, most people on the home front in Germany had some idea of the massacres being committed by the *Einsatzgruppen*.[1080] British historian Hugh Trevor-Roper noted that although Himmler had forbidden photographs of the killings, it was common for both the men of the *Einsatzgruppen* and for bystanders to take pictures to send to their loved ones, which he felt suggested widespread approval of the massacres.[1081]

Officers in the field were well aware of the killing operations being conducted by the *Einsatzgruppen*.[1082] The Wehrmacht tried to justify their considerable involvement in the *Einsatzgruppen* massacres as being anti-partisan operations rather than racist attacks, but Hillgruber wrote that this was just an excuse. He states that those German generals who claimed that the *Einsatzgruppen* were a necessary anti-partisan response were lying, and maintained that the slaughter of about 2.2 million defenceless civilians for reasons of racist ideology cannot be justified.[1083]

## Einsatzgruppen Trial

After the close of World War II, 24 senior leaders of the *Einsatzgruppen* were prosecuted in the Einsatzgruppen Trial in 1947–48, part of the Subsequent Nuremberg Trials held under United States military authority. The men were charged with crimes against humanity, war crimes, and membership in the SS (which had been declared a criminal organization). Fourteen death sentences and two life sentences were among the judgments; only four executions were carried out, on 7 June 1951; the rest were reduced to lesser sentences. Four additional *Einsatzgruppe* leaders were later tried and executed by other nations.[1084]

Several *Einsatzgruppen* leaders, including Ohlendorf, claimed at the trial to have received an order before Operation Barbarossa requiring them to murder all Soviet Jews.[1085] To date no evidence has been found that such an order was

**Figure 141:** *Otto Ohlendorf, 1943*

ever issued.[1086] German prosecutor Alfred Streim noted that if such an order had been given, post-war courts would only have been able to convict the *Einsatzgruppen* leaders as *accomplices* to mass murder. However, if it could be established that the *Einsatzgruppen* had committed mass murder without orders, then they could have been convicted as *perpetrators* of mass murder, and hence could have received stiffer sentences, including capital punishment.[1087]

Streim postulated that the existence of an early comprehensive order was a fabrication created for use in Ohlendorf's defence. This theory is now widely accepted by historians.[1088] Longerich notes that most orders received by the *Einsatzgruppen* leaders—especially when they were being ordered to carry out criminal activities—were vague, and couched in terminology that had a specific meaning for members of the regime. Leaders were given briefings about the need to be "severe" and "firm"; all Jews were to be viewed as potential enemies that had to be dealt with ruthlessly.[1089] British historian Sir Ian Kershaw argues that Hitler's apocalyptic remarks before Barbarossa about the necessity for a war without mercy to "annihilate" the forces of "Judeo-Bolshevism" were interpreted by *Einsatzgruppen* commanders as permission and encouragement to engage in extreme antisemitic violence, with each *Einsatzgruppen* commander to use his own discretion about how far he was prepared to go.[1090]

Most of the perpetrators of Nazi war crimes were never charged, and returned unremarked to civilian life. The West German Central Prosecution Office of Nazi War Criminals only charged about a hundred former *Einsatzgruppe* members with war crimes.[1091] And as time went on, it became more difficult to obtain prosecutions; witnesses grew older and were less likely to be able to offer valuable testimony. Funding for trials was inadequate, and the governments of Austria and Germany became less interested in obtaining convictions for wartime events, preferring to forget the Nazi past.[1092]

# References

## Sources

<templatestyles src="Template:Refbegin/styles.css" />
- Browning, Christopher R. (1998) [1992]. *Ordinary Men: Reserve Police Battalion 101 and the Final Solution in Poland*. London; New York: Penguin.<templatestyles src="Module:Citation/CS1/styles.css"></templatestyles>
- Browning, Christopher; Matthäus, Jürgen (2004). *The Origins of the Final Solution: The Evolution of Nazi Jewish Policy, September 1939 – March 1942*. Comprehensive History of the Holocaust. Lincoln: University of Nebraska Press. ISBN 978-0-8032-1327-2.<templatestyles src="Module:Citation/CS1/styles.css"></templatestyles>
- Caron, Jean-Christophe (22 December 2007). "Erwin Rommel: Auf der Jagd nach dem Schatz des "Wüstenfuchses""[1093]. *Spiegel Online* (in German): 2. Retrieved 9 September 2016.<templatestyles src="Module:Citation/CS1/styles.css"></templatestyles>
- Conze, Eckart; Frei, Norbert; Hayes, Peter; Zimmermann, Moshe (2010). *Das Amt und die Vergangenheit : deutsche Diplomaten im Dritten Reich und in der Bundesrepublik* (in German). Munich: Karl Blessing. ISBN 978-3-89667-430-2.<templatestyles src="Module:Citation/CS1/styles.css"></templatestyles>
- Craig, William (1973). *Enemy at the Gates: The Battle for Stalingrad*. Old Saybrook, CT: Konecky & Konecky. ISBN 1-56852-368-8.<templatestyles src="Module:Citation/CS1/styles.css"></templatestyles>
- Crowe, David (2007) [2004]. *Oskar Schindler: The Untold Account of his Life, Wartime Activities and the True Story Behind the List*. New York: Basic Books. ISBN 978-0-465-00253-5.<templatestyles src="Module:Citation/CS1/styles.css"></templatestyles>

- Dams, Carsten; Stolle, Michael (2012) [2008]. *Die Gestapo: Herrschaft und Terror im Dritten Reich*. Becksche Reihe (in German). Munich: Beck. ISBN 978-3-406-62898-6.
- Edeiken, Yale F. (22 August 2000). "Introduction to the Einsatzgruppen"[1094]. Holocaust History Project. Archived from the original[1095] on 7 October 2015. Retrieved 10 June 2018.
- "Einsatzgruppen case"[1096] (PDF). *Trials of War Criminals before the Nuernberg Military Tribunals under Control Council Law No. 10*[1097] (PDF). Green Series. Volume 4. Nürnberg. October 1946 – April 1949. Retrieved 10 June 2018.
- Evans, Richard J. (2008). *The Third Reich at War*. New York: Penguin Group. ISBN 978-0-14-311671-4.
- Gerwarth, Robert (2011). *Hitler's Hangman: The Life of Heydrich*. New Haven, CT: Yale University Press. ISBN 978-0-300-11575-8.
- Haberer, Erich (2001). "Intention and Feasibility: Reflections on Collaboration and the Final Solution"[1098]. *East European Jewish Affairs*. **31** (2): 64–81. doi: 10.1080/13501670108577951[1099]. OCLC 210897979[1100].
- Headland, Ronald (1992). *Messages of Murder: A Study of the Reports of the Security Police and the Security Service*[1101]. London: Associated University Presses. ISBN 0-8386-3418-4.
- Hilberg, Raul (1985). *The Destruction of the European Jews*. New York: Holmes & Meier. ISBN 978-0-8419-0832-1.
- Hillgruber, Andreas (1989). "War in the East and the Extermination of the Jews". In Marrus, Michael. *Part 3, The "Final Solution": The Implementation of Mass Murder, Volume 1*. The Nazi Holocaust. Westpoint, CT: Meckler. pp. 85–114. ISBN 0-88736-266-4.
- Ingrao, Christian (2013). *Believe and Destroy: Intellectuals in the SS War Machine*. Malden, MA: Polity. ISBN 978-0-7456-6026-4.
- Kershaw, Ian (2008). *Hitler, the Germans, and the Final Solution*. New Haven, Conn.: Yale Univer-

- sity Press. ISBN 978-0-300-12427-9.
- Klee, Ernst; Dressen, Willi; Riess, Volker (1991). *'The Good Old Days" – The Holocaust as Seen by its Perpetrators and Bystanders*. Trans. Burnstone, Deborah. New York: MacMillan. ISBN 0-02-917425-2. (originally published as Klee, Ernst; Dreßen, Willi; Rieß, Volker (Hrsg.) (1988). *Schöne Zeiten. Judenmord aus der Sicht der Täter und Gaffer* (in German). Frankfurt / Main: S. Fischer. ISBN 978-3-10-039304-3.
- Krumenacker, Thomas (7 April 2006). "Nazis Planned Holocaust for Palestine: historians"[1102]. Red Orbit. Archived from the original[1103] on 22 December 2017. Retrieved 10 June 2018.
- Langerbein, Helmut (2003). *Hitler's Death Squads: The Logic of Mass Murder*. College Station, TX: Texas A&M University Press. ISBN 978-1-58544-285-0.
- Larsen, Stein Ugelvik (2008). *Meldungen aus Norwegen 1940–1945: Die geheimen Lagesberichte des Befehlshabers der Sicherheitspolizei und des SD in Norwegen, 1* (in German). Munich: Oldenburg. ISBN 978-3-486-55891-3.
- LEO Dictionary Team. "LEO Deutsch-Englisches Wörterbuch "einsatzgruppe""[1104] (in German). Dict.leo.org. Retrieved 10 January 2013.
- Longerich, Peter (2010). *Holocaust: The Nazi Persecution and Murder of the Jews*. Oxford; New York: Oxford University Press. ISBN 978-0-19-280436-5.
- Longerich, Peter (2012). *Heinrich Himmler: A Life*. Oxford; New York: Oxford University Press. ISBN 978-0-19-959232-6.
- MacLean, French L. (1999). *The Field Men: The SS Officers Who Led the Einsatzkommandos—The Nazi Mobile Killing Units*. Schiffer Military History. Madison, WI: Schiffer. ISBN 978-0-7643-0754-6.
- Mallmann, Klaus-Michael; Cüppers, Martin (2006). *Crescent and Swastika: The Third Reich, the Arabs and Palestine*. Ann Arbor: University of Michigan Press. ISBN 978-3-534-19729-3.

- src="Module:Citation/CS1/styles.css"></templatestyles>
- Mallmann, Klaus-Michael; Cüppers, Martin; Smith, Krista (2010). *Nazi Palestine: The Plans for the Extermination of the Jews in Palestine.* New York: Enigma. ISBN 1-929631-93-6.<templatestyles src="Module:Citation/CS1/styles.css"></templatestyles>
- Marrus, Michael (2000). *The Holocaust in History.* Toronto: Key Porter. ISBN 978-1-55263-120-1.<templatestyles src="Module:Citation/CS1/styles.css"></templatestyles>
- Mayer, Arno J (1988). *Why Did The Heavens Not Darken?.* New York: Pantheon. ISBN 0-394-57154-1.<templatestyles src="Module:Citation/CS1/styles.css"></templatestyles>
- "Nuremberg Trial Proceedings, Volume 20, Day 194"[1105]. *The Avalon Project.* Yale Law School Lillian Goldman Law Library. Retrieved 10 January 2013.<templatestyles src="Module:Citation/CS1/styles.css"></templatestyles>
- Rabitz, Cornelia (21 June 2011). "Biography of Nazi criminal meets resistance from small German town"[1106]. *dw.de.* Deutsche Welle. Retrieved 9 September 2016.<templatestyles src="Module:Citation/CS1/styles.css"></templatestyles>
- Rees, Laurence (1997). *The Nazis: A Warning From History.* Foreword by Sir Ian Kershaw. New York: New Press. ISBN 1-56584-551-X.<templatestyles src="Module:Citation/CS1/styles.css"></templatestyles>
- "Reflections on the Holocaust: "The Einsatzgruppen""[1107]. Encyclopædia Britannica. Archived from the original[1108] on 11 October 2016. Retrieved 10 June 2018.<templatestyles src="Module:Citation/CS1/styles.css"></templatestyles>
- Rhodes, Richard (2002). *Masters of Death: The SS-Einsatzgruppen and the Invention of the Holocaust.* New York: Vintage Books. ISBN 0-375-70822-7.<templatestyles src="Module:Citation/CS1/styles.css"></templatestyles>
- Robertson, Struan. "The genocidal missions of Reserve Police Battalion 101 in the General Government (Poland) 1942–1943"[1109]. *Hamburg Police Battalions during the Second World War.* Regionalen Rechenzentrum der Universität Hamburg. Archived from the original[1110] on 22 February 2008. Retrieved 2 January 2015.<templatestyles src="Module:Citation/CS1/styles.css"></templatestyles>
- Rossino, Alexander B. (2003). *Hitler Strikes Poland: Blitzkrieg, Ideology, and Atrocity.* Lawrence, Kansas: University Press of Kansas. ISBN 0-7006-1234-3.<templatestyles src="Module:Citation/CS1/styles.css"></templatestyles>

- Segev, Tom (2010). *Simon Wiesenthal: The Life and Legends*. New York: Doubleday. ISBN 978-0-385-51946-5.
- Shelach, Menachem (1989). "Sajmište: An Extermination Camp in Serbia". In Marrus, Michael Robert. *The Victims of the Holocaust: Historical Articles on the Destruction of European Jews*. **2**. Westport, CT: Meckler.
- Shirer, William L. (1960). *The Rise and Fall of the Third Reich*. New York: Simon & Schuster. ISBN 978-0-671-62420-0.
- Smelser, Ronald; Davies, Edward (2008). *The Myth of the Eastern Front: The Nazi-Soviet War in American Popular Culture*. Cambridge: Cambridge University Press. ISBN 978-0-521-83365-3.
- Staff. "Book review: *Tasks of the Einsatsgruppen* by Alfred Streim"[1111]. *Museum of Tolerance Online Multimedia Learning Center, Annual 4, Chapter 9*. Los Angeles: Simon Wiesenthal Center. Retrieved 10 June 2018.
- Streim, Alfred (1989). "The Tasks of the SS Einsatzgruppen". In Marrus, Michael. *The Nazi Holocaust, Part 3, The "Final Solution": The Implementation of Mass Murder, Volume 2*. Westpoint, CT: Meckler. pp. 436–454. ISBN 0-88736-266-4.
- Thomas, David (April 1987). "Foreign Armies East and German Military Intelligence in Russia 1941–45". *Journal of Contemporary History*. **22** (2): 261–301. JSTOR 260933[1112].
- Urban, Thomas (1 September 2001). "Poszukiwany Hermann Schaper"[1113]. *Rzeczpospolita* (in Polish) (204). Archived from the original[1114] on 24 November 2007. Retrieved 5 January 2015.
- Weale, Adrian (2012). *Army of Evil: A History of the SS*. New York; Toronto: Penguin Group. ISBN 978-0-451-23791-0.
- Wette, Wolfram (2007). *The Wehrmacht: History, Myth, Reality*. Cambridge, MA: Harvard University Press. ISBN 978-0-67402-577-6.

## Further reading

- Earl, Hilary (2009). *The Nuremberg SS-Einsatzgruppen Trial, 1945–1958: Atrocity, Law, and History*. Cambridge; New York: Cambridge University Press. ISBN 978-0-521-45608-1.<templatestyles src="Module:Citation/CS1/styles.css"></templatestyles>
- Förster, Jürgen (1998). "Complicity or Entanglement? The Wehrmacht, the War and the Holocaust". In Berenbaum, Michael; Peck, Abraham. *The Holocaust and History: The Known, the Unknown, the Disputed and the Reexamined*. Bloomington: Indian University Press. pp. 266–283. ISBN 978-0-253-33374-2.<templatestyles src="Module:Citation/CS1/styles.css"></templatestyles>
- Krausnick, Helmut; Wilhelm, Hans-Heinrich (1981). *Die Truppe des Weltanschauungskrieges. Die Einsatzgruppen der Sicherheitspolizei und des SD 1938–1942* (in German). Stuttgart: Deutsche Verlags-Anstalt. ISBN 3-421-01987-8.<templatestyles src="Module:Citation/CS1/styles.css"></templatestyles>
- Snyder, Timothy (2010). *Bloodlands: Europe Between Hitler and Stalin*. New York: Basic Books. ISBN 978-0-465-00239-9.<templatestyles src="Module:Citation/CS1/styles.css"></templatestyles>
- Stang, Knut (1996). *Kollaboration und Massenmord. Die litauische Hilfspolizei, das Rollkommando Hamann und die Ermordung der litauischen Juden* (in German). Frankfurt am Main: Peter Lang. ISBN 3-631-30895-7.<templatestyles src="Module:Citation/CS1/styles.css"></templatestyles>

## External links

Wikimedia Commons has media related to *Einsatzgruppen*.

Wikisourcehas original text related to this article:
**Comprehensive report of Einsatzgruppe A up to 15 October 1941**

- United States Holocaust Memorial Museum article on *Einsatzgruppen*[1115]
- "Einsatzgruppen"[1116] The Holocaust Education & Archive Research Team

# Final Solution

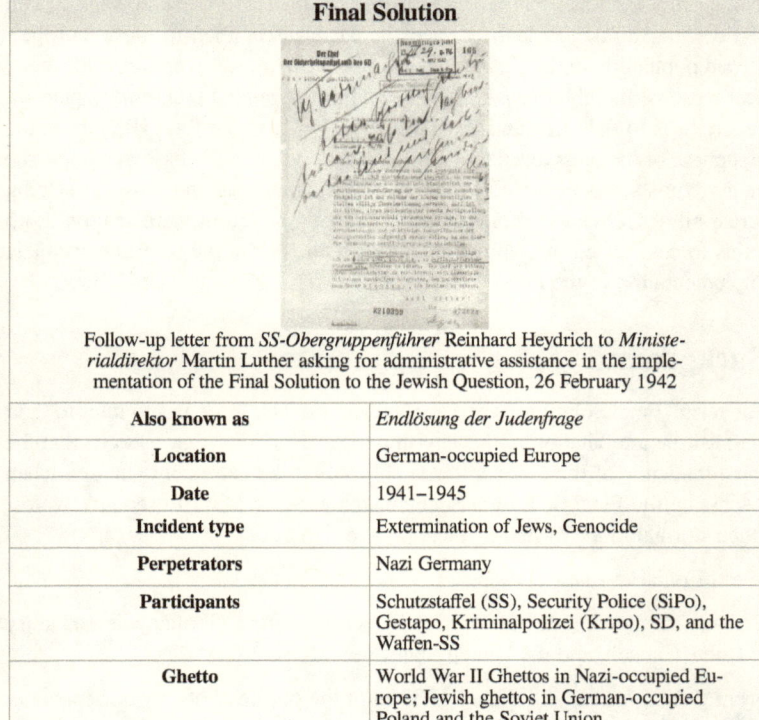

| | Final Solution |
|---|---|
| | Follow-up letter from *SS-Obergruppenführer* Reinhard Heydrich to *Ministerialdirektor* Martin Luther asking for administrative assistance in the implementation of the Final Solution to the Jewish Question, 26 February 1942 |
| Also known as | *Endlösung der Judenfrage* |
| Location | German-occupied Europe |
| Date | 1941–1945 |
| Incident type | Extermination of Jews, Genocide |
| Perpetrators | Nazi Germany |
| Participants | Schutzstaffel (SS), Security Police (SiPo), Gestapo, Kriminalpolizei (Kripo), SD, and the Waffen-SS |
| Ghetto | World War II Ghettos in Nazi-occupied Europe; Jewish ghettos in German-occupied Poland and the Soviet Union |

The **Final Solution** (German: *Endlösung*) or the **Final Solution to the Jewish Question** (German: *die Endlösung der Judenfrage*, pronounced [diː ˈɛntˌløːzʊŋ deːɐ̯ ˈjuːdn̩ˌfʁaːɡə]) was a Nazi plan for the Genocide or extermination of the Jews during World War II. The "Final Solution of the Jewish Question" was the official code name for the murder of all Jews within reach, which was not restricted to the European continent. This policy of deliberate and systematic genocide starting across German-occupied Europe was formulated in procedural and geo-political terms by Nazi leadership in January 1942 at the Wannsee Conference held near Berlin, and culminated in the Holocaust, which saw the killing of 90% of Polish Jews, and two thirds of the Jewish population of Europe.

The nature and timing of the decisions that led to the Final Solution is an intensely researched and debated aspect of the Holocaust. The program evolved during the first 25 months of war leading to the attempt at "murdering every last Jew in the German grasp". Most historians agree, wrote Christopher

Browning, that the Final Solution cannot be attributed to a single decision made at one particular point in time. "It is generally accepted the decision-making process was prolonged and incremental." In 1940, following the Fall of France, Adolf Eichmann devised the Madagascar Plan to move Europe's Jewish population to the French colony, but the plan was abandoned for logistical reasons, mainly a naval blockade. There were also preliminary plans to deport Jews to Palestine and Siberia.[1117] In 1941, wrote Raul Hilberg, in the first phase of the mass murder of Jews, the mobile killing units began to pursue their victims across occupied eastern territories; in the second phase, stretching across all of German-occupied Europe, the Jewish victims were sent on death trains to centralized extermination camps built for the purpose of systematic implementation of the Final Solution.

## Background

The term "Final Solution" was a euphemism used by the Nazis to refer to their plan for the annihilation of the Jewish people. Historians have shown that the usual tendency of the German leadership was to be extremely guarded when discussing the Final Solution. Euphemisms were, in Mark Roseman's words, "their normal mode of communicating about murder".[1118]

File:StLouisHavana.jpg

German ship MS St. Louis with Jewish refugees from Germany denied entry to Cuba, Canada, and the United States in mid-1939

From gaining power in January 1933 until the outbreak of war in September 1939, the Nazi persecution of the Jews in Germany was focused on intimidation, expropriating their money and property, and encouraging them to emigrate. According to the Nazi Party policy statement, the Jews, and Roma (although numerically fewer), were the only "alien people in Europe".[1119] In 1936 the Bureau of Romani Affairs in Munich was taken over by the Interpol and renamed as the Center for Combating the Gypsy Menace. Introduced at the end of 1937,[1120] the "final solution of the Gypsy Question" entailed round-ups, expulsions, and incarceration of Romani in concentration camps built at Dachau, Buchenwald, Flossenbürg, Mauthausen, Natzweiler, Ravensbruck, Taucha, and Westerbork until this point in time. After the Anschluss with Austria in 1938, special offices were established in Vienna and Berlin to "facilitate" Jewish emigration, without covert plans for their forthcoming annihilation.

The outbreak of war and the invasion of Poland brought a population of 3.5 million Polish Jews under the control of the Nazi and Soviet security forces,[1121] and marked the start of a far more savage persecution, including mass killings. In the German-occupied zone of Poland, Jews were forced into hundreds of makeshift ghettos pending other arrangements. Two years later, with the launch of Operation Barbarossa against the USSR, in late June 1941, the German top echelon began to pursue Hitler's new anti-Semitic plan to eradicate, rather than expel, Jews. Hitler's earlier ideas about forcible removal of Jews from the German-controlled territories in order to achieve *Lebensraum* were abandoned after the failure of the air campaign against Britain, initiating a naval blockade of Germany. *Reichsführer-SS* Heinrich Himmler became the chief architect of a new plan, which came to be called "the Final Solution to the Jewish Question".[1122] On 31 July 1941, *Reichsmarschall* Hermann Göring wrote to Reinhard Heydrich (Himmler's deputy and chief of the RSHA),[1123,1124] instructing Heydrich to submit concrete proposals for the implementation of the projected new goal.

Broadly speaking, the extermination of Jews was carried out in two major operations. With the onset of Operation Barbarossa launched from occupied Poland in June 1941, mobile killing units of the SS and Orpo were dispatched to Soviet controlled territories of eastern Poland and further into the Soviet republics for the express purpose of killing all Jews, both Polish and Soviet. During the massive chase after the fleeing Red Army, Himmler himself visited Białystok in the beginning of July 1941, and requested that, "as a matter of principle, any Jew" behind the German-Soviet frontier "was to be regarded as a partisan". His new orders gave the SS and police leaders full authority for the mass murder behind the front-lines. By August 1941, all Jewish men, women, and children were shot.[1125] In the second phase of annihilation, the Jewish inhabitants of central, western, and south-eastern Europe were transported by Holocaust trains to camps with newly-built gassing facilities. Raul Hilberg wrote: "In essence, the killers of the occupied USSR moved to the victims, whereas outside this arena, the victims were brought to the killers. The two operations constitute an evolution not only chronologically, but also in complexity." Massacres of about one million Jews occurred before plans for the Final Solution were fully implemented in 1942, but it was only with the decision to annihilate the entire Jewish population that extermination camps such as Auschwitz II Birkenau and Treblinka were fitted with permanent gas chambers to kill large numbers of Jews in a relatively short period of time.[1126]

The plans to exterminate all the Jews of Europe was formalized at the SS's guesthouse on the Wannsee[1127] near Berlin on 20 January 1942. The conference was chaired by Heydrich and attended by 15 senior officials of the Nazi Party and the German government. Most of those attending were representatives of the Interior Ministry, the Foreign Ministry, and the Justice Ministry, including Ministers for the Eastern Territories.[1128] At the conference, Heydrich indicated that approximately 11,000,000 Jews in Europe would fall under

**Figure 142:** *The villa at 56–58 Am Großen Wannsee, where the Wannsee Conference was held, is now a memorial and museum.*

the provisions of the "Final Solution". This figure included not only Jews residing in Axis-controlled Europe, but also the Jewish populations of the United Kingdom, and of neutral nations (Switzerland, Ireland, Sweden, Spain, Portugal, and European Turkey). Eichmann's biographer David Cesarani wrote that Heydrich's main purpose in convening the conference was to assert his authority over the various agencies dealing with Jewish issues. "The simplest, most decisive way that Heydrich could ensure the smooth flow of deportations" to death camps, according to Cesarani, "was by asserting his total control over the fate of the Jews in the Reich and the east" under the single authority of the RSHA.[1129] A copy of the minutes of this meeting was found by the Allies in March 1947; it was too late to serve as evidence during the first Nuremberg Trial, but was used by prosecutor General Telford Taylor in the subsequent Nuremberg Trials.[1130]

After the end of World War II, surviving archival documents provided a clear record of the Final Solution policies and actions of Nazi Germany. They included the Wannsee Conference Protocol, which documented the co-operation of various German state agencies in the SS-led Holocaust, as well as some 3,000 tons of original German records captured by Allied armies, including the Einsatzgruppen reports, which documented the progress of the mobile killing units assigned, among other tasks, to kill Jewish civilians during the attack on the Soviet Union in 1941. The evidential proof which documented the mechanism of the Holocaust were submitted at Nuremberg.

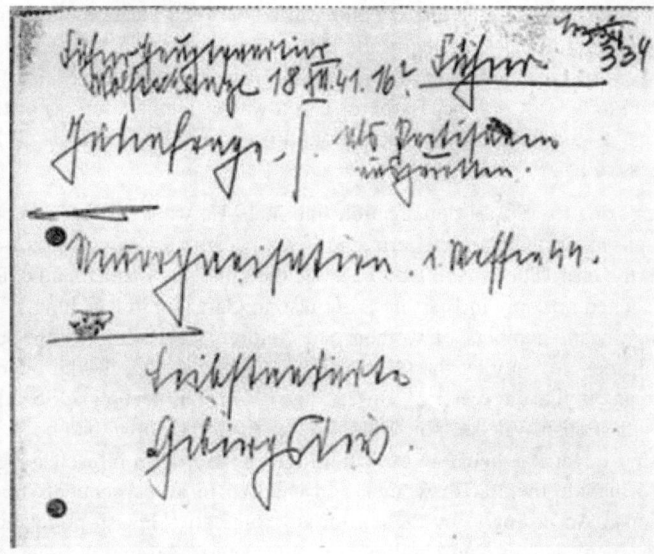

**Figure 143:** *Himmler note 18 December 1941: 'als Partisanen auszurotten'*

## Phase one: killing squads of Operation Barbarossa

The Nazi invasion of the Soviet Union codenamed Operation Barbarossa, which commenced on 22 June 1941, set in motion a "war of destruction" which quickly opened the door to systematic mass murder of European Jews.[1131] For Hitler, Bolshevism was merely "the most recent and most nefarious manifestation of the eternal Jewish threat".[1132] On 3 March 1941, Wehrmacht Joint Operations Staff Chief Alfred Jodl repeated Hitler's declaration that the "Jewish-Bolshevik intelligentsia would have to be eliminated" and that the forthcoming war would be a confrontation between two completely opposing cultures.[1133] In May 1941, Gestapo leader Heinrich Müller wrote a preamble to the new law limiting the jurisdiction of military courts in prosecuting troops for criminal actions because: "This time, the troops will encounter an especially dangerous element from the civilian population, and therefore, have the right and obligation to secure themselves."[1134]

Himmler assembled a force of about 3,000 men from Security Police, Gestapo, Kripo, SD, and the Waffen-SS, as the so-called "special commandos of the security forces" known as the *Einsatzgruppen*, to eliminate both communists and Jews in occupied territories.[1135] These forces were supported by 21 battalions of Orpo Reserve Police under Kurt Daluege, adding up to 11,000 men.[1136] The explicit orders given to the Order Police varied between locations, but for Police Battalion 309 participating in the first mass murder of 5,500 Polish Jews in the Soviet-controlled Białystok (a Polish provincial capital), Major Weiss explained to his officers that Barbarossa is a war of annihilation against Bolshevism,[1137] and that his battalions would proceed ruthlessly against all Jews, regardless of age or sex.[1138]

After crossing the Soviet demarcation line in 1941, what had been regarded as exceptional in the Greater Germanic Reich became a normal way of operating in the east. The crucial taboo against the killing of women and children was breached not only in Białystok, but also in Gargždai in late June.[1139] By July, significant numbers of women and children were being killed behind all front-lines not only by the Germans, but also by the local Ukrainian and Lithuanian auxiliary forces.[1140] On 29 July 1941, at a meeting of SS officers in Vileyka (Polish Wilejka, now Belarus), the *Einsatzgruppen* had been given a dressing-down for their low execution figures. Heydrich himself issued an order to include the Jewish women and children in all subsequent shooting operations. Accordingly, by the end of July the entire Jewish population of Vileyka, men, women and children were murdered. Around 12 August, no less than two-thirds of the Jews shot in Surazh were women and children of all ages. In late August 1941 the *Einsatzgruppen* murdered 23,600 Jews in the Kamianets-Podilskyi massacre. A month later, the largest mass shooting of Soviet Jews took place on 29–30 September in the ravine of Babi Yar, near Kiev, where more than 33,000 Jewish people of all ages were systematically machine-gunned.[1141] In mid-October 1941, HSSPF South, under the command of Friedrich Jeckeln, had reported the indiscriminate killing of more than 100,000 people.[1142]

By the end of December 1941, before the Wannsee Conference, over 439,800 Jewish people had been murdered, and the Final Solution policy in the east became common knowledge within the SS. Entire regions were reported "free of Jews" by the *Einsatzgruppen*. Addressing his district governors in the General Government on 16 December 1941, Governor-General Hans Frank said: "But what will happen to the Jews? Do you believe they will be lodged in settlements in Ostland? In Berlin, we were told: why all this trouble; we cannot use them in the Ostland or the Reichskommissariat either; liquidate them yourselves!"[1143] Two days later, Himmler recorded the outcome of his discussion with Hitler. The result was: *"als Partisanen auszurotten"* ("exterminate them as partisans"). Israeli historian Yehuda Bauer wrote that the remark is probably as close as historians will ever get to a definitive order from Hitler for the genocide carried out during the Holocaust. Within two years, the total number of shooting victims in the east had risen to between 618,000 and 800,000 Jews.[1144]

Original annotated map from Stahlecker's Report, summarizing murders committed by *Einsatzgruppen* in Estonia, Latvia, Lithuania, Belarus and Russia until January 1942

Notably, the Stahlecker's map *(top)* had shown the Soviet Byelorussia according to bilateral terms of the Nazi-Soviet invasion of Poland, not the Byelorussian SSR (marked in pink), from before the Soviet annexation of Kresy. In this map, territory of prewar Poland inhabited by Polish Jews is marked in yellow.

## *Bezirk Białystok* and *Reichskommissariat Ostland*

Several scholars have suggested that the Final Solution began in the newly formed district of *Bezirk Białystok*.[1145] The German army took over Białystok within days. On Friday, 27 June 1941, the Reserve Police Battalion 309 arrived in the city and set the Great Synagogue on fire with hundreds of Jewish men locked inside.[1146] The burning of the synagogue was followed by a frenzy of killings both inside the homes around the Jewish neighbourhood of Chanajki, and in the city park, lasting until night time. The next day, some 30 wagons of dead bodies were taken to mass graves. As noted by Browning, the killings were led by a commander "who correctly intuited and anticipated the wishes of his Führer" without direct orders.[1146] For reasons unknown, the number of victims in the official report by Major Weis was cut in half. The next mass shooting of Polish Jews within the newly formed *Reichskommissariat Ostland* took place in two days of 5–7 August in occupied Pińsk, where over 12,000 Jews died at the hands of Waffen SS, not the *Einsatzgruppen*. An additional 17,000 Jews perished there in a ghetto uprising crushed a year later with the aid of Belarusian Auxiliary Police.

An Israeli historian Dina Porat claimed that the Final Solution, i.e.: "the systematic overall physical extermination of Jewish communities one after the other – began in Lithuania" during the massive German chase after the Red Army across the Baltic states in *Reichskommissariat Ostland*. The subject of the Holocaust in Lithuania has been analysed by Konrad Kweit from USHMM who wrote: "Lithuanian Jews were among the first victims of the Holocaust [beyond the eastern borders of occupied Poland]. The Germans carried out the mass executions [...] signaling the beginning of the 'Final Solution'."[1147] About 80,000 Jews were killed in Lithuania by October (including in formerly Polish Wilno) and about 175,000 by the end of 1941 according to official reports.

## *Reichskommissariat Ukraine*

Within one week from the start of Operation Barbarossa, Heydrich issued an order to his *Einsatzkommandos* for the on-the-spot execution of all Bolsheviks, interpreted by the SS to mean all Jews. One of the first indiscriminate massacres of men, women, and children in *Reichskommissariat Ukraine* took the lives of over 4,000 Polish Jews in occupied Łuck on 2–4 July 1941, murdered by *Einsatzkommando* 4a assisted by the Ukrainian People's Militia. Formed officially on 20 August 1941, the *Reichskommissariat Ukraine* – stretching from prewar east-central Poland to Crimea – had become operational theatre of the *Einsatzgruppe* C. Within the Soviet Union proper, between 9 July 1941 and 19 September 1941 the city of Zhytomyr was made *Judenfrei* in three murder operations conducted by German and Ukrainian police in which 10,000 Jews perished. In the Kamianets-Podilskyi massacre of 26–28 August 1941 some 23,600 Jews were shot in front of open pits (including 14,000–18,000 people expelled from Hungary). After an incident in Bila Tserkva in which 90 small children left behind had to be shot separately, Blobel requested that Jewish mothers hold them in their arms during mass shootings. Long before the conference at Wannsee, 28,000 Jews were shot by SS and Ukrainian military in Vinnytsia on 22 September 1941, followed by the 29 September massacre of 33,771 Jews at Babi Yar. In Dnipropetrovsk, on 13 October 1941 some 10,000–15,000 Jews were shot. In Chernihiv, 10,000

Jews were put to death and only 260 Jews were spared. In mid-October, during the Krivoy-Rog massacre of 4,000–5,000 Soviet Jews the entire Ukrainian auxiliary police force actively participated.[1148] In the first days of January 1942 in Kharkiv, 12,000 Jews were murdered, but smaller massacres continued in this period on daily basis in countless other locations.[1149] In August 1942 in the presence of only a few German SS men over 5,000 Jews were massacred in Polish Zofjówka by the Ukrainian Auxiliary Police leading to the town's complete sweep from existence.[1150]

## *Distrikt Galizien*

Historians find it difficult to determine precisely when the first concerted effort at annihilation of all Jews began in the last weeks of June 1941 during Operation Barbarossa. Dr. Samuel Drix (*Witness to Annihilation*), Jochaim Schoenfeld (*Holocaust Memoirs*), and several survivors of the Janowska concentration camp, who were interviewed in the film *Janovska Camp at Lvov*, among other witnesses, have argued that the Final Solution began in Lwów (Lemberg) in *Distrikt Galizien* of the General Government during the German advance across Soviet-occupied Poland. Statements and memoirs of survivors emphasize that, when Ukrainian nationalists and *ad hoc* Ukrainian People's Militia (soon reorganized as the Ukrainian Auxiliary Police) began to murder women and children, rather than only male Jews, the "Final Solution" had begun. Witnesses have said that such murders happened both prior to and during the pogroms reportedly triggered by the NKVD prisoner massacre. The question of whether there was some coordination between the Lithuanian and Ukrainian militias remains open (i.e. collaborating for a joint assault in Kovno, Wilno, and Lwów).

The killings continued uninterrupted. On 12 October 1941, in Stanisławów, some 10,000–12,000 Jewish men, women, and children were shot at the Jewish cemetery by the German uniformed SS-men and Ukrainian Auxiliary Police during the so-called "Bloody Sunday" *(de)*. The shooters began firing at 12 noon and continued without stopping by taking turns. There were picnic tables set up on the side with bottles of vodka and sandwiches for those who needed to rest from the deafening noise of gunfire. It was the single largest massacre of Polish Jews in *Generalgouvernement* prior to mass gassings of *Aktion Reinhard*, which commenced at Bełżec in March 1942. Notably, the extermination operations in Chełmno had begun on 8 December 1941, one-and-a-half month before Wannsee, but Chełmno – located in *Reichsgau Wartheland* – was not a part of Reinhard, and neither was Auschwitz-Birkenau functioning as an extermination center until November 1944 in Polish lands annexed by Hitler and added to Germany proper.

**Figure 144:** *Nazi extermination camps marked with black and white skulls. General Government territory: centre, Distrikt Galizien: lower–right. Death camp at Auschwitz: lower–left (in Provinz Oberschlesien), Nazi-Soviet line in red*

The conference at Wannsee gave impetus to the so-called *second sweep* of the Holocaust by the bullet in the east. Between April and July 1942 in Volhynia, 30,000 Jews were murdered in death pits with the help of dozens of newly formed Ukrainian *Schutzmannschaft*. Owing to good relations with the Ukrainian *Hilfsverwaltung*, these auxiliary battalions were deployed by the SS also in Russia Center, Russia South, and in Byelorussia; each with about 500 soldiers divided into three companies. They participated in the extermination of 150,000 Volhynian Jews alone, or 98 percent of the Jewish inhabitants of the entire region. In July 1942 the Completion of the Final Solution in the General Government territory which included *Distrikt Galizien*, was ordered personally by Himmler. He set the initial deadline for 31 December 1942.

# Phase two: deportations to killing centres

When in 1941 the Wehrmacht forces attacked the Soviet positions in eastern Poland during the initially successful Operation Barbarossa, the area of the General Government was enlarged by the inclusion of regions that had been occupied by the Red Army since 1939. The killings of Jews from the Łódź Ghetto in the *Warthegau* district began in early December 1941 with the use of gas vans [approved by Heydrich] at the Kulmhof extermination camp. The deceptive guise of "Resettlement in the East" organised by SS Commissioners, was also tried and tested at Chełmno. By the time the European-wide Final Solution was formulated two months later, Heydrich's RSHA had already confirmed the effectiveness of industrial killing by exhaust fumes, and the strength of deception.

Construction work on the first killing centre at Bełżec in occupied Poland began in October 1941, three months before the Wannsee Conference. The new facility was operational by March the following year. By mid-1942, two more death camps had been built on Polish lands: Sobibór operational by May 1942, and Treblinka operational in July. From July 1942, the mass murder of Polish and foreign Jews took place at Treblinka as part of Operation Reinhard, the deadliest phase of the Final Solution. More Jews were killed at Treblinka than at any other Nazi extermination camp apart from Auschwitz. By the time the mass killings of Operation Reinhard ended in 1943, roughly two million Jews in German-occupied Poland had been murdered. The total number of people killed in 1942 in Lublin/Majdanek, Bełżec, Sobibór, and Treblinka was 1,274,166 by Germany's own estimation, not counting Auschwitz II Birkenau nor *Kulmhof*. Their bodies were buried in mass graves initially.[1151] Both Treblinka and Bełżec were equipped with powerful crawler excavators from Polish construction sites in the vicinity, capable of most digging tasks without disrupting surfaces. Although other methods of extermination, such as the cyanic poison Zyklon B, were already being used at other Nazi killing centres such as Auschwitz, the *Aktion Reinhard* camps used lethal exhaust gases from captured tank engines.

The *Holocaust by bullets* (as opposed to the *Holocaust by gas*) went on in the territory of occupied Poland in conjunction with the ghetto uprisings, irrespective of death camps' quota. In two weeks of July 1942, the Słonim Ghetto revolt, crushed with the help of Latvian, Lithuanian, and Ukrainian *Schutzmannschaft*, cost the lives of 8,000–13,000 Jews.[1152] The second largest mass shooting (to that particular date) took place in late October 1942 when the insurgency was suppressed in the Pińsk Ghetto; over 26,000 men, women and children were shot with the aid of Belarusian Auxiliary Police before the ghetto's closure.[1153] During the suppression of the Warsaw Ghetto Uprising (the largest single revolt by Jews during World War II), 13,000 Jews were killed in action before May 1943. Numerous other uprisings were quelled without impacting the pre-planned Nazi deportations actions.

About two-thirds of the overall number of victims of the Final Solution were killed before February 1943, which included the main phase of the extermination programme in the West launched by Eichmann on 11 June 1942 from Berlin. The Holocaust trains run by the *Deutsche Reichsbahn* and several other national railway systems delivered condemned Jewish captives from as far as Belgium, Bulgaria, France, Greece, Hungary, Italy, Moravia, Netherlands, Romania, Slovakia, and even Scandinavia. The cremation of exhumed corpses to destroy any evidence left behind began in early spring and continued throughout summer.[1154] The nearly completed clandestine programme of murdering all deportees was explicitly addressed by Heinrich Himmler in his Posen speeches made to the leadership of the Nazi Party on 4 October and during the Posen Conference of 6 October 1943 in occupied Poland. Himmler explained why the Nazi leadership found it necessary to kill Jewish women and children along with the Jewish men. The assembled functionaries were told that the Nazi state policy was "the extermination of the Jewish people" as such.[1155]

<templatestyles src="Template:Quote/styles.css"/>

> *We were faced with the question: what about the women and children? — I have decided on a solution to this problem. I did not consider myself justified to exterminate the men only — in other words, to kill them or have them killed while allowing the avengers, in the form of their children, to grow up in the midst of our sons and grandsons. The difficult decision had to be made to have this people disappear from the earth.*
>
> —*Heinrich Himmler, 6 October 1943*[1156]

On 19 October 1943, five days after the prisoner revolt in Sobibór, Operation Reinhard was terminated by Odilo Globocnik on behalf of Himmler. The camps responsible for the killing of nearly 2,700,000 Jews were soon closed. Bełżec, Sobibór, and Treblinka were dismantled and ploughed over before spring.[1157] The operation was followed by the single largest German massacre of Jews in the entire war carried out on 3 November 1943; with approximately 43,000 prisoners shot one-by-one simultaneously in three nearby locations by the Reserve Police Battalion 101 hand-in-hand with the Trawniki men from Ukraine.[1158] Auschwitz alone had enough capacity to fulfill the Nazis' remaining extermination needs.[1151]

## Auschwitz II Birkenau

Unlike Belzec, Sobibor, Treblinka, and Lublin-Majdanek,[1159] which were built in the occupied General Government territory inhabited by the largest concentrations of Jews, the killing centre at Auschwitz subcamp of Birkenau operated in Polish areas annexed by Nazi Germany directly. The new gas chambers at Bunker I were finished around March 1942 when the Final Solution was officially launched at Belzec. Until mid-June 20,000 Silesian Jews were killed there using Zyklon B. In July 1942, Bunker II became operational. In August, another 10,000-13,000 Polish Jews from Silesia perished, along with 16,000 French Jews declared 'stateless', and 7,700 Jews from Slovakia.[1160]

The infamous 'Gate of Death' at Auschwitz II for the incoming freight trains was built of brick and cement mortar in 1943, and the three-track rail spur was added. Until mid-August, 45,000 Thessaloniki Jews were murdered in a mere six months, including over 30,000 Jews from Sosnowiec (Sosnowitz) and Bendzin Ghettos.[1161] The spring of 1944 marked the beginning of the last phase of the Final Solution at Birkenau. The new big ramps and sidings were constructed, and two freight elevators were installed inside Crematoria II and III for moving the bodies faster. The size of the *Sonderkommando* was nearly quadrupled in preparation for the Special Operation Hungary (*Sonderaktion Ungarn*). In May 1944, Auschwitz-Birkenau became the site of one of the two largest mass murder operations in modern history, after the *Großaktion Warschau* deportations of the Warsaw Ghetto inmates to Treblinka in 1942. It is estimated that until July 1944 approximately 320,000 Hungarian Jews were gassed at Birkenau in less than eight weeks.[1162] The entire operation was photographed by the SS. In total, between April and November 1944, Auschwitz II received over 585,000 Jews from over a dozen regions as far as Greece, Italy, and France, including 426,000 Jews from Hungary, 67,000 from Łódź, 25,000 from Theresienstadt, and the last 23,000 Jews from the General Government. Auschwitz was liberated by the Red Army on 27 January 1945, when the gassing had already stopped.[1163]

# Historiographic debate about the decision

Part of a series on
## The Holocaust

Jews on selection ramp at Auschwitz, May 1944

Historians disagree as to when and how the Nazi leadership decided that the European Jews should be exterminated. The controversy is commonly described as the functionalism versus intentionalism debate which began in the 1960s, and subsided thirty years later. In the 1990s, the attention of mainstream historians moved away from the question of top executive orders triggering the Holocaust, and focused on factors which were overlooked earlier, such as personal initiative and ingenuity of countless functionaries in charge of the killing fields. No written evidence of Hitler ordering the Final Solution has ever been found to serve as a "smoking gun", and therefore, this one particular question remains unanswered.

Hitler made numerous predictions regarding the Holocaust of the Jews of Europe prior to the beginning of World War II. During a speech given on 30 January 1939, on the sixth anniversary of his accession to power, Hitler said:

<templatestyles src="Template:Quote/styles.css"/>

> *Today I will once more be a prophet: If the international Jewish financiers in and outside Europe should succeed in plunging the nations once more into a world war, then the result will not be the Bolshevization of the earth, and thus the victory of Jewry, but the annihilation of the Jewish race in Europe!*
>
> —*Adolf Hitler, 1939*[1165]

Raul Hilberg, in his book *The Destruction of the European Jews*, was the first historian to systematically document and analyse the Nazi project to kill every Jew in Europe. The book was initially published in 1961, and issued in an enlarged version in 1985.

Hilberg's analysis of the steps that led to the destruction of European Jews revealed that it was "an administrative process carried out by bureaucrats in a network of offices spanning a continent".[1166] Hilberg divides this bureaucracy into four components or hierarchies: the Nazi Party, the civil service, industry, and the Wehrmacht armed forces – but their cooperation is viewed as "so complete that we may truly speak of their fusion into a machinery of destruction".[1167] For Hilberg, the key stages in the destruction process were: definition and registration of the Jews; expropriation of property; concentration into ghettoes and camps; and, finally, annihilation.[1168] Hilberg gives an estimate of 5.1 million as the total number of Jews killed. He breaks this figure down into three categories: Ghettoization and general privation: over 800,000; open-air shootings: over 1,300,000; extermination camps: up to 3,000,000.[1169]

With respect to the "functionalism versus intentionalism" debate about a master plan for the Final Solution, or the lack thereof, Hilberg posits what has been described as "a kind of structural determinism". Hilberg argues that "a destruction process has an inherent pattern" and the "sequence of steps in a destruction process is thus determined". If a bureaucracy is motivated "to inflict maximum damage upon a group of people", it is "inevitable that a bureaucracy—no matter how decentralized its apparatus or how unplanned its activities—should push its victims through these stages", culminating in their annihilation.[1170]

In his monograph, *The Origins Of The Final Solution: The Evolution of Nazi Jewish Policy, September 1939 – March 1942*, Christopher Browning argues that Nazi policy toward the Jews was radicalized twice: in September 1939, when the invasion of Poland implied policies of mass expulsion and massive loss of Jewish lives; and in spring 1941, when preparation for Operation Barbarossa involved the planning of mass execution, mass expulsion, and starvation – to dwarf what had happened in Jewish Poland.[1171]

Browning believes that the "Final Solution as it is now understood—the systematic attempt to murder every last Jew within the German grasp" took shape during a five-week period, from 18 September to 25 October 1941. During this time: the sites of the first extermination camps were selected, different methods of killing were tested, Jewish emigration from the Third Reich was forbidden, and 11 transports departed for Łódź as a temporary holding station. During this period, Browning writes, "The vision of the Final Solution had crystallised in the minds of the Nazi leadership, and was being turned into reality." This period was the peak of Nazi victories against the Soviet Army on the Eastern Front, and, according to Browning, the stunning series of German victories led to both an expectation that the war would soon be won, and the planning of the final destruction of the "Jewish-Bolshevik enemy".[1172]

Browning describes the creation of the extermination camps, which were responsible for the largest number of deaths in the Final Solution, as bringing together three separate developments within the Third Reich: the concentration camps which had been established in Germany since 1933; an expansion of the gassing technology of the Nazi euthanasia programme to provide killing mechanism of greater efficiency and psychological detachment; and the creation of "factories of death" to be fed endless streams of victims by mass uprooting and deportation that utilized the experience and personnel from earlier population resettlement programmes—especially the HSSPF and Adolf Eichmann's RSHA for "Jewish affairs and evacuations".[1173]

Peter Longerich argues that the search for a finite date on which the Nazis embarked upon the extermination of the Jews is futile, in his book *Holocaust: The Nazi Persecution and Murder of the Jews* (2011). Longerich writes: "We should abandon the notion that it is historically meaningful to try to filter the wealth of available historical material and pick out a single decision" that led to the Holocaust.[1174]

Timothy Snyder writes that Longerich "grants the significance of Greiser's murder of Jews by gas at Chełmno in December 1941", but also detects a significant moment of escalation in spring 1942, which includes "the construction of the large death factory at Treblinka for the destruction of the Warsaw Jews, and the addition of a gas chamber to the concentration camp at Auschwitz for the murder of the Jews of Silesia". Longerich suggests that it "was only in the summer of 1942, that mass killing was finally understood as the realization of the Final Solution, rather than as an extensively violent preliminary to some later program of slave labor and deportation to the lands of a conquered USSR". For Longerich, to see mass killing as the Final Solution was an acknowledgement by the Nazi leadership that there would not be a German military victory over the USSR in the near future.

David Cesarani emphasises the improvised, haphazard nature of Nazi policies in response to changing war time conditions in his overview, *Final Solution: The Fate Of The European Jews 1933-49* (2016). "Cesarani provides telling examples", wrote Mark Roseman, "of a lack of coherence and planning for the future in Jewish policy, even when we would most expect it. The classic instance is the invasion of Poland in 1939, when not even the most elementary consideration had been given to what should happen to Poland's Jews either in the shorter or longer term. Given that Poland was home to the largest Jewish population in the world, and that, in a couple of years, it would house the extermination camps, this is remarkable."

Whereas Christopher Browning places the Nazi plan to exterminate the Jews in the context of the Wehrmacht victories on the Eastern front, Cesarani argues that the German subsequent realisation that there would be no swift victory over the Soviet Union "scuppered the last territorial 'solution' still on the table: expulsion to Siberia". Germany's declaration of war on the United States on December 11, 1941, "meant that holding European Jews hostage to deter the US from entering the conflict was now pointless. As Joseph Goebbels put it when he summarised a secret speech Hitler made on 12 December 1941: 'The world war is here, the destruction of the Jews must be the inevitable consequence'."[1175] Cesarani concludes, the Holocaust "was rooted in anti-Semitism,

**Figure 145:** *Berlin, Reichstag session of 11 December 1941: Adolf Hitler declares war on the United States of America*

but it was shaped by war". The fact that the Nazis were, ultimately, so successful in killing between five and six million Jews was not due to the efficiency of the Third Reich or the clarity of their policies. "Rather, the catastrophic rate of killing was due to German persistence ... and the duration of the murderous campaigns. This last factor was largely a consequence of allied military failure."[1176]

The entry of the U.S. into the War is also crucial to the time-frame proposed by Christian Gerlach, who argued in his 1997 thesis,[1177] that the Final Solution decision was announced on 12 December 1941, when Hitler addressed a meeting of the Nazi Party (the *Reichsleiter*) and of regional party leaders (the *Gauleiter*).[1178] </ref> The day after Hitler's speech, on 13 December 1941 Joseph Goebbels wrote in his diary:

<templatestyles src="Template:Quote/styles.css"/>

> *With respect of the Jewish Question, the Führer has decided to make a clean sweep. He prophesied to the Jews that if they again brought about a world war, they would see their annihilation in it. That wasn't just a catch-word. The world war is here and the annihilation of the Jews must be the necessary consequence.*

Cesarani notes that by 1943, as the military position of the German forces deteriorated, the Nazi leadership became more openly explicit about the Final Solution. In March, Goebbels confided to his diary: "On the Jewish question especially, we are in it so deeply that there is no getting out any longer. And that is a good thing. Experience teaches that a movement and a people who have burned their bridges fight with much greater determination and fewer constraints than those that have a chance of retreat."

When Himmler addressed senior SS personnel and leading members of the regime in the Posen speeches on October 4, 1943, he used "the fate of the Jews as a sort of blood bond to tie the civil and military leadership to the Nazi cause".

<templatestyles src="Template:Quote/styles.css"/>

> *Today, I am going to refer quite frankly to a very grave chapter. We can mention it now among ourselves quite openly and yet we shall never talk about it in public. I'm referring to the evacuation of the Jews, the extermination of the Jewish people. Most of you will know what it's like to see 100 corpses side by side or 500 corpses or 1,000 of them. To have coped with this and—except for cases of human weakness—to have remained decent, that has made us tough. This is an unwritten—never to be written—and yet glorious page in our history.*

In May 1944, Himmler told senior army officers that, "The Jewish question has been solved in Germany and in the countries occupied by Germany. It has been solved uncompromisingly, as was appropriate in view of the struggle in which we were engaged for the life of our nation." Himmler explained that it was important that even women and children had to die, so that no "hate-filled avengers" would be able to confront our children and grandchildren.[1179]

# References

<templatestyles src="Template:Refbegin/styles.css" />

- Arad, Yitzhak (1987). *Belzec, Sobibor, Treblinka. The Operation Reinhard Death Camps*[1180]. Bloomington: Indiana University Press. ISBN 0-253-21305-3.<templatestyles src="Module:Citation/CS1/styles.css"></templatestyles>
- Baumslag, Naomi (2005). *Murderous Medicine: Nazi Doctors, Human Experimentation, and Typhus*. Praeger Publishers. ISBN 0-275-98312-9.<templatestyles src="Module:Citation/CS1/styles.css"></templatestyles>

- Breitman, Richard (1991). *The Architect of Genocide: Himmler and The Final Solution*. New York: Alfred A. Knopf. ISBN 0-394-56841-9.<templatestyles src="Module:Citation/CS1/styles.css"></templatestyles>
- Browning, Christopher R. (1998) [1992]. *Ordinary Men: Reserve Police Battalion 101 and the Final Solution in Poland*[1181] (PDF). Penguin Books. Archived[1182] (PDF) from the original on 19 October 2013. Retrieved 7 May 2013.<templatestyles src="Module:Citation/CS1/styles.css"></templatestyles>
- ────── (2004). *The Origins of the Final Solution : The Evolution of Nazi Jewish Policy, September 1939 – March 1942*. Comprehensive History of the Holocaust. With contributions by Jürgen Matthäus. London: Random House / William Heinemann;. ISBN 0803203926.<templatestyles src="Module:Citation/CS1/styles.css"></templatestyles> Newer edition by Univ. of Nebraska Press / Yad Vashem 2007[1183].
- Cesarani, David (2005) [2004]. *Eichmann: His Life and Crimes*. London: Vintage. ISBN 978-0-099-44844-0.<templatestyles src="Module:Citation/CS1/styles.css"></templatestyles>
- ────── (2016). *Final Solution: The Fate of the Jews 1933-1949*[1184]. London: Macmillan. ISBN 978-0-330-53537-3.<templatestyles src="Module:Citation/CS1/styles.css"></templatestyles>
- Dawidowicz, Lucy (1975). *The War Against the Jews*. Holt, Rinehart and Winston. ISBN 003013661X.<templatestyles src="Module:Citation/CS1/styles.css"></templatestyles>
- Fleming, Gerald (1984). *Hitler and the Final Solution*. Berkeley: University of California Press.<templatestyles src="Module:Citation/CS1/styles.css"></templatestyles>
- Gerlach, Christian (December 1998). "The Wannsee Conference, the Fate of German Jews, and Hitler's decision in principle to exterminate all European Jews"[1185] (PDF). *The Journal of Modern History*. Chicago. **70** (4): 759–812. doi: 10.1086/235167[1186].<templatestyles src="Module:Citation/CS1/styles.css"></templatestyles>
- Głowacka-Penczyńska, Anetta; Kawski, Tomasz; Mędykowski, Witold; Horev, Tuvia, eds. (2015). *The First to be Destroyed: The Jewish Community of Kleczew and the Beginning of the Final Solution*. Boston: Academic Studies Press. ISBN 9781618112842.<templatestyles src="Module:Citation/CS1/styles.css"></templatestyles>
- Hilberg, Raul (1985). *The Destruction of the European Jews: The Revised and Definitive Edition*[1187]. New York: Holmes and Meier. ISBN 0-8419-0832-X – via Archive.org search inside. <q>The deportations ... were the work of a much larger apparatus that had to deal with a host of constraints and requirements. The ef-

fort, as we shall see, was deemed necessary to accomplish the Final Solution on a European-wide scale.[p.273] </q><templatestyles src="Module:Citation/CS1/styles.css"></templatestyles>
- Laqueur, Walter; Baumel, Judith Tydor (2001). *The Holocaust Encyclopedia*. New Haven and London: Yale University Press. ISBN 978-0-30008-432-0.<templatestyles src="Module:Citation/CS1/styles.css"></templatestyles>
- Longerich, Peter (2003). *The Unwritten Order: Hitler's Role in The Final Solution*. Stroud: Tempus Publishing. ISBN 978-075242564-1.<templatestyles src="Module:Citation/CS1/styles.css"></templatestyles>
- ——— (2010). *Holocaust: The Nazi Persecution and Murder of the Jews*[1188]. Oxford University Press. ISBN 0192804367.<templatestyles src="Module:Citation/CS1/styles.css"></templatestyles>
- ——— (2012). *Heinrich Himmler*[1189]. Translation by Jeremy Noakes and Lesley Sharpe. Oxford University Press. ISBN 978-019959232-6.<templatestyles src="Module:Citation/CS1/styles.css"></templatestyles>
- Niewyk, Donald; Nicosia, Francis (2000). *The Columbia Guide to the Holocaust*. New York: Columbia University Press. ISBN 978-0-23111-201-7.<templatestyles src="Module:Citation/CS1/styles.css"></templatestyles>
- Roseman, Mark (2002). *The Villa, The Lake, The Meeting: Wannsee and the Final Solution*. Allen Lane. ISBN 0-713-99570-X.<templatestyles src="Module:Citation/CS1/styles.css"></templatestyles>
- Schultheis, Herbert; Wahler, Isaac E. (1988). *Bilder und Akten der Gestapo Wuerzburg ueber die Judendeportationen 1941–1943* (German-English ed.). Bad Neustadt a. d. Saale. ISBN 978-3-9800482-7-9.<templatestyles src="Module:Citation/CS1/styles.css"></templatestyles>

# External links

- Website of the House of the Wannsee Conference[1190]
- The Development of the Final Solution[1191]—lecture from Dr. Havi Dreifuss, Yad Vashem
- Elimination of the Jewish National Home in Palestine: The Einsatzkommando of the Panzer army Africa, 1942[1192] by Klaus-Michael Mallmann and Martin Cüppers
- Death Decree: Göring directive officially launches the Final Solution[1193]

# Flow of information about the mass murder

## The Black Book of Polish Jewry

The Black Book of Polish Jewry

Plates inserted between pages 128 and 129 illustrating *Part One. Chapter 8. Extermination*

| | |
|---|---|
| Author | Jacob Apenszlak, Jacob Kenner, Isaac Lewin, Moses Polakiewicz |
| Published | Roy Publishers, New York |
| Publisher | American Federation for Polish Jews in cooperation with the Association of Jewish Refugees and Immigrants from Poland |
| Publication date | 1943 |
| Pages | 400 |
| OCLC | 1265138[1194] |

**The Black Book of Polish Jewry** is a 400-page report about the progress of the Holocaust in Poland published in 1943 during World War II by the American Federation for Polish Jews in cooperation with the Association of Jewish Refugees and Immigrants from Poland. It was compiled by Jacob Apenszlak with Jacob Kenner, Isaac Lewin and Moses Polakiewicz, and released by Roy

Publishers of New York with Introduction by Ignacy Schwarzbart from the National Council of the Polish Republic. The book was Sponsored by Eleanor Roosevelt, Albert Einstein, US Senator Robert Wagner, and other high-ranking community leaders. Historian Michael Fleming suggests it downplayed the true scale and manner of the Holocaust in an effort to elicit the empathy of its readership.[1195]</ref>

# Contents

*The Black Book of Polish Jewry* is a compendium of information collected and summarized from the plethora of already available sources including *The Polish Fortnightly Review* series published by the Polish Ministry of Information, the heavily-censored *Gazeta Żydowska* published in occupied Poland, as well as depositions of refugees who managed to escape from occupied Poland to Palestine via Wilno; articles by Swiss and Swedish correspondents, daily bulletins of the Polish Telegraphic Agency, the Jewish news agencies in Geneva, Hungary, Slovakia and Constantinople, and many others. The 400-page volume is divided into Part One, consisting of 17 chapters devoted to all stages of the mass extermination of Jews during the Final Solution; and Part Two, presenting an overview of the thousand-year-old Jewish community in Poland, in 12 chapters.

The 1943 estimates of how many Jews have died in General Government, are based on data collected while the Holocaust was still in progress, mostly from the preceding year.[pp. 200-201] Notably, the Birkenau killing installations are missing from the book entirely, and only the concentration camps quota from 1942 are partially summarized. Nevertheless, it estimates the loss of over 700,000 Jewish lives directly due to Nazi persecution.

The Report correctly identified Treblinka, Bełżec, and Sobibór, as extermination camps where prisoners were killed by means of poison gas, but the fate of the Nazi ghetto deportees was not as clearly defined: <templatestyles src="Template:Quote/styles.css"/>

> About 25,000 Jews were deported from Lublin in sealed railway cars to an unknown destination and all trace of them was lost" [and] "of the 250,000 Jews deported from the Warsaw Ghetto up to September 1, 1942, only two small transports, numbering about 4,000 people, are known to have been sent eastwards in the direction of Brzesc and Malachowicze, allegedly to be employed on work behind the front lines. It was not possible to ascertain whether any of the other Jews deported from the Warsaw Ghetto still survive and it must be feared that they have been all put to death.

The report documented with high accuracy the progress of the Holocaust by bullets in the east as far as localities, but the number of victims was underestimated, with significant percentage of deaths unaccounted for by year's end:
<templatestyles src="Template:Quote/styles.css"/>

> In many places the Jews were deported to an unknown destination and killed in neighboring woods. In Lwow 30,000 Jews were killed in that way, at Stanislawow 15,000, at Tarnopol 5,000, at Zloczow 2,000, at Brzezany 4,000. The same things happened at Zborow, Kolomyja, Sambor, Stryj, Drohobycz, Zbaraz, Przemyslany, Kuty, Sniatyn, Zaleszczyki, Brody, Przemysl, Rawa-Ruska, etc. In Wilno 50,000 Jews were murdered ... all Jews in Zurawicze, Mir, Lachowice, Kosow ... in Slonim ... nearly 9,000 Jews were slaughtered. In Rowno ... nearly 15,000 Jews were shot, men, women and children ... This mass-slaughter of Jew has taken place in all the Polish territories east of the rivers San and Bug.

According to Michael Fleming, neither the editor, Jacob Apenszlak, nor his collaborators, stated the true scale and manner of the Holocaust in Poland, seeking to elicit empathy from an American public which at that time "was marked by a high level of antisemitism". Fleming further wrote that "the fate of Polish Jewry was narrated without, in the most part, reference to the death camps". He attributed those issues to self-censorship and compromises made to satisfy the "US censorship and propaganda organs". The book was sponsored by Eleanor Roosevelt (wife of President Franklin D. Roosevelt), Albert Einstein, Senator Robert Wagner and several prominent Americans, Jews, and Poles including high-ranking officials and community leaders.

# External links

- Archive.org, *Black Book of Polish Jewry*.[1196] Digitized; link to Collection.
- Jewish Telegraphic Agency (New York, December 15, 1943), "*Black Book of Polish Jewry* Estimates 1,000,000 Polish Jews Killed by Nazis".[1197] JTA Archive.
- YivoArchives.org, "American Federation for Polish Jews".[1198] Administrative History.

# The Polish White Book

### The Polish White Book

| Author | Authority of the Polish Ministry of Information |
|---|---|
| Series | Volume 1: *Official Documents Concerning Polish-German and Polish-Soviet Relations 1933–1939*<br>Volume 2: *German Invasion of Poland*<br>Volume 3: *German Occupation of Poland. Extract of Note Addressed to The Allied and Neutral Powers* |
| Published | The Greystone Press, New York and wydawnictwo RÓJ in exile, Publishers |
| Publisher | Republic of Poland Ministry of Forein Affairs of the Polish government-in-exile |
| Publication date | 1941 |
| Media type | Hardcover |
| Pages | 243 |
| OCLC | 82971798[1199] |

**The Polish White Book** is a semi-official name of a series of comprehensive reports published during World War II by the Ministry of Information of the Polish government-in-exile in London, England; dealing with the Polish-German relations before-and-after the joint Nazi-Soviet aggression against Poland in 1939. Each publication, released in English, French, German and Polish between 1940 and 1941, consisted of official documents and affidavits, supplemented with an overview by the Ministry. Notably the *Polish White Book* was released parallel with *The Black Book of Poland* series by G.P. Putnam's Sons of New York, published in London by Hutchinson & Co under a differing title in 1942.

## Publishing history

The first volume of the *White Book* publication series, released in spring 1940, was titled *Official Documents Concerning Polish-German and Polish-Soviet Relations 1933–1939 – Polish White Book.* The book described and documented the Polish-German negotiations in the lead-up to World War II. The second volume of the *White Book* – sometimes considered to be the first volume of *The Black Book of Poland* – was titled *German Invasion of Poland* (*L'Invasion Allemande en Pologne*, Paris: Flammarion, 1940).

The third volume of *The Polish White Book* was titled the *German Occupation of Poland. Extract of Note Addressed to The Allied and Neutral Powers.* It is a

240-page report published in 1941 during World War II by the Ministry of Information of the Polish government-in-exile, describing atrocities committed by Germany in occupied Poland. It contains 180 appendixes with lists, names, dates and the circumstances of Nazi brutality toward Polish civilians including men, women and children. Most of the book consists of appendixes, documenting the locations of Nazi ghettos where thousands of Jews perished; and the shift in extermination tactics from shootings to poisoning by gas. The affidavits confirm Heinrich Himmler's personal involvement in the liquidation of the Warsaw Ghetto and the final transports to death camps. The *Polish White Book* was written as a plea for help to the world community. At the time of its compilation, there were two million Polish Jews still alive in occupied Poland and hoping for an international rescue effort.

## Contents

As the reports of Nazi war crimes in occupied Poland increased dramatically, new volumes of *The Polish White Book* series were released. The *German Occupation of Poland* (1941) – also known as the second volume of *The German Invasion of Poland* (1940) – is sometimes considered a preamble to *The Black Book of Poland* (1942) by the Polish government-in-exile. The *White Books* by the Polish Ministry were released over the course of two years. The original *Polish White Book*, along with its subsequent volumes were published in both Paris by *Flammarion* and in London by Hutchinson & Co.[p.13 of 253 in PDF]

The final *White Book* titled *German Occupation of Poland. Extract of Note Addressed to the Allied and Neutral Powers* was released by Greystone Press of New York in 1941. The book contained 55-page overview, signed by Auguste Zaleski in London on May 3, 1941, and 180 Appendixes with evidence of forced expulsions and deportations of Jews to overcrowded ghettos where starvation and disease were commonplace, along with evidence of deliberate destruction of the Polish nationhood; for the total of 243 printed pages.

The *White Book* was followed by *The Black Book of Poland* printed by G.P. Putnam's Sons of New York in 1942. It was a collection of authenticated documents, depositions, eye-witness accounts, and Ministerial summaries, describing and illustrating with photographs, the Nazi crimes against the Polish nation and War crimes in occupied Poland during World War II committed in mere two years: including massacres, tortures, expulsions, forced colonization, persecution, destruction of culture, and humiliation of a nation.

***German Occupation of Poland* (1941). Sections**

1. *Note*
2. *Outrages Against Persons*
3. *Outrages Against Religion*
4. *Outrages Against Polish Culture*
5. *Outrages Against Property*

**Apendices**

1. *The Law and Customs of War on Land-ivth Hague Convention*
2. *German Documents*
3. *Polish Documents*

# External links

- Archive.org, 'German Occupation of Poland Extract of Note Addressed to The Allied and Neutral Powers'.[1200]
- Worldcat.org, 'German Occupation od Poland'[1201]

# The Black Book of Poland

The Black Book of Poland

The German New Order in Poland

Plates 21–24 inserted between pages 74 and 75 of *The Black Book*, illustrating *Part I. Massacres and Tortures*
- 21–22: Hangings of civilians
- 23. Page from Special Prosecution Book-Poland
- 24. Aftermath of a massacre

| | |
|---|---|
| Author | Authority of the Polish Ministry of Information |
| Published | G.P. Putnam's Sons, New York<br>London edition has title: *The German New Order in Poland*. Published by Hutchinson & Co., London, UK |
| Publisher | Ministry of Information of the Polish government-in-exile |
| Publication date | 1942 |
| Media type | Hardcover |
| Pages | 750 |
| OCLC | 489805[1202] |

***The Black Book of Poland*** is a 750-page report published in 1942 by the Ministry of Information of the Polish government-in-exile, describing atrocities committed by Germany in occupied Poland in twenty-two months between the invasion of Poland in September 1939, and the end of June 1941. All estimates, presented in the book section by section, are based on data collected while the war in the East was in progress, and the killing of Jews by means of carbon monoxide gas during Operation Reinhard – launched in 1942 for the implementation of the "Final Solution" – only began. All casualties are partially summarized. The book includes documentation proving more than 400,000 cases of deliberate killings at an average of 1,576 per day. It is also considered a follow-up to *The Polish White Book* of 1941.

## Contents

*The Black Book* is a collection of authenticated documents, depositions, eye-witness accounts, and Ministerial summaries, describing and illustrating with photographs, the Nazi crimes against the Polish nation and War crimes in occupied Poland during World War II committed in mere two years: including massacres, tortures, expulsions, forced colonization, persecution, destruction of culture, and humiliation of a nation.

The book is a sequel to *The German Invasion of Poland* compiled by the Polish government-in-exile and published in 1940, sometimes considered as the first volume of this publication series. The original volume deals with the war crimes of the September 1939 invasion of Poland. *The Black Book* by G.P. Putnam's Sons of New York (or the 'second volume' of *The Black Book of Poland*) was published in London by Hutchinson under a different title: *The German New Order in Poland*, with only 585 pages and 61 plates. *The Black Book* is composed of nine sections, preceded by an Introduction titled 'Hora Tenebrarum'. All sections include long Appendices.

### Book sections

1. *Part I. Massacres and Tortures*
2. *Part II. The Expulsion of the Polish Population from its Land*
3. *Part III. The Persecution of the Jews, and the Ghettos*
4. *Part IV. The Robbery of Public and Private Property*
5. *Part V. The Economic Exploitation of Polish Territories under German Occupation*
6. *Part VI. Religious Persecution*
7. *Part VII. Humiliation and Degradation of the Polish Nation*
8. *Part VIII. The Destruction of Polish Culture*
9. *Part IX. Violations by the Reich of International Law.*

## External links

- Worldcat.org, 'The Black Book of Poland / The German New Order in Poland'.[1203]
- Photograph of the book with dust jacket.[1204] *The German New Order in Poland*. Reprint. Archive.is[1205]
- German Occupation of Poland, ['https://en.wikipedia.org/wiki/White_Book_-_German_Occupation_of_Poland']

# Raczyński's Note

**Raczyński's Note** was the official diplomatic note of the Government of Poland in exile from December 10, 1942, signed by Minister of Foreign Affairs Edward Raczyński regarding the extermination of the Jews in Poland occupied by Germany. It was the first official report on the Holocaust, informing the Western public about these crimes. It was also the first official speech of one of the governments in defense of all Jews persecuted by Nazi Germany – not only citizens of their country.[1206,1207,1208]

## History

The note was written by the Polish diplomat, Minister of Foreign Affairs of the Exile Government in London Edward Raczyński on the basis of documents imported in the form of microfilm (materials prepared by the Jewish Affairs Department of the Home Army Headquarters) to London by courier Jan Karski and confirmed by his certificate, and Karski's reports prepared in 1940-1942 by Jan Karski. Raczyński's note was sent on December 10, 1942 to the governments of the signatory countries of the United Nations Declaration. It was personally addressed to other foreign ministers.[1209,1210]

On behalf of the Polish government, Raczyński informed the governments of all Allied countries about the desperate situation of Jews in the German-occupied Poland and the unfolding genocide being carried by the Germans, calling for help.[1211,1212,1213]

## Contents

<templatestyles src="Template:Quote/styles.css"/>

> The Polish Government — as the representatives of the legitimate authority on territories in which the Germans are carrying out the systematic extermination of Polish citizens and of citizens of Jewish origin of many other European countries — consider it their duty to address themselves to the Governments of the United Nations, in the confident belief that they will share their opinion as to the necessity not only of condemning the crimes committed by the Germans and punishing the criminals, but also of finding means offering the hope that Germany might be effectively restrained from continuing to apply her methods of mass extermination.
>
> —*Edward Bernard Raczyński (1891–1993) Note to United Nations, 10 December 1942.*[1214]

**Figure 146:** *Edward Bernard Raczyński during office work*

The note has been written on 9 pages of the typescript. In 21 points it presented a description of the background of the problem and the current situation of Jews in occupied Poland, a chronological description of the information campaign of the Polish government on this area, and a call for allied governments to stop the crime. The note was sent to foreign ministers of the 26 governments that signed the Declaration by United Nations in 1942.[1215,1216] Below is the note sent to Anthony Eden on 10 December 1942:[1217]

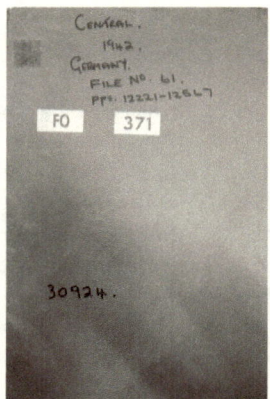

**Figure 147:** *Cover of document*

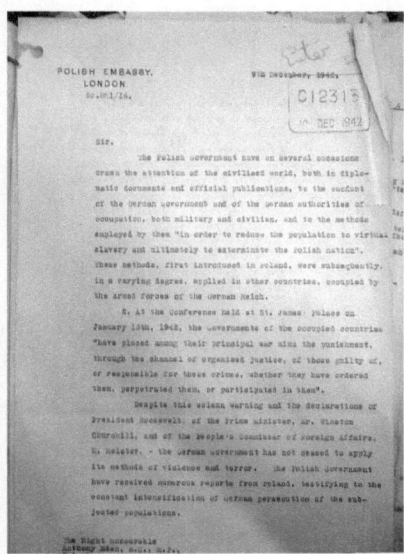

**Figure 148:** *Page I, addressed to Anthony Eden (10 December 1942)*

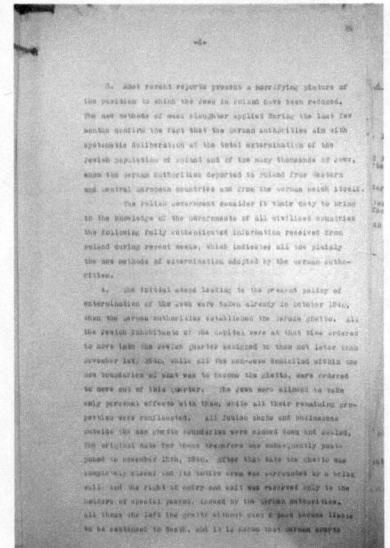

**Figure 149:** *Page II*

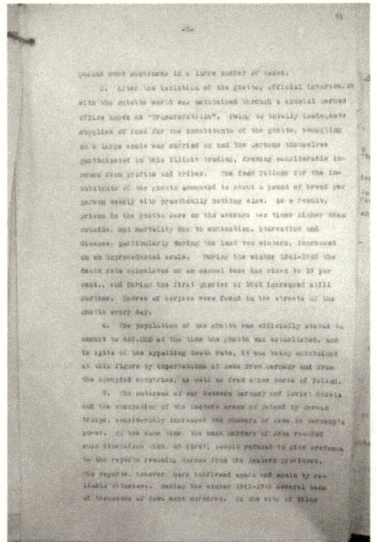

**Figure 150:** *Page III*

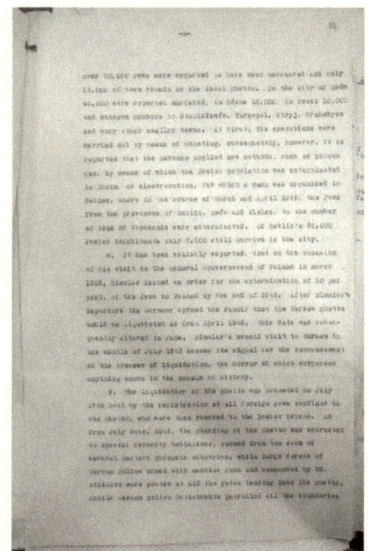

**Figure 151:** *Page IV*

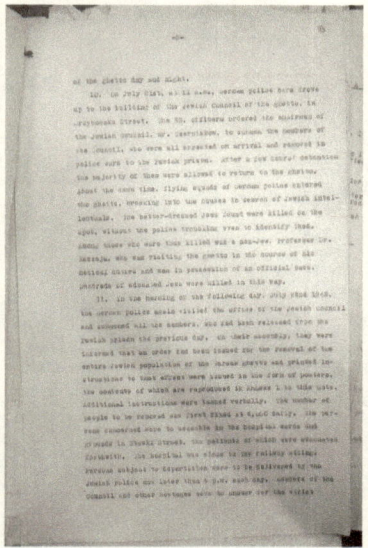

**Figure 152:** *Page V*

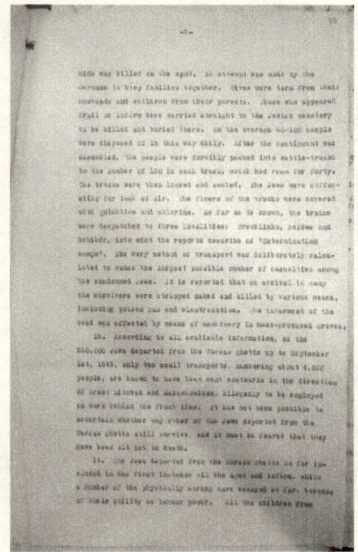

**Figure 153:** *Page VII*

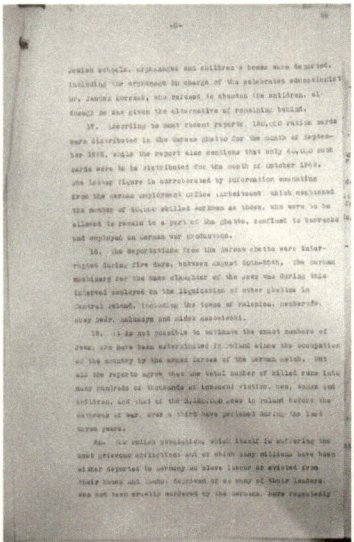

**Figure 154:** *Page VIII*

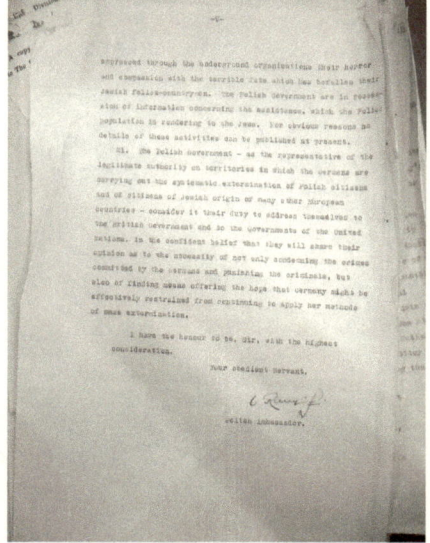

**Figure 155:** *Page IX*

## Bibliography

<templatestyles src="Template:Refbegin/styles.css" />

- Raczyński, Edward (1942). *The Mass Extermination of Jews in German Occupied Poland*[1218]. London, New York, Melbourne: Republic of Poland Ministry of Foreign Affairs.<templatestyles src="Module:Citation/CS1/styles.css"></templatestyles>
- Wroński, Stanisław (1971). *Polacy i Żydzi 1939–1945, (eng. "Poles and Jews" 1939-1945)* (in Polish). Warsaw: Książka i Wiedza.<templatestyles src="Module:Citation/CS1/styles.css"></templatestyles>
- Engel, David (2014). *In the Shadow of Auschwitz: The Polish Government-in-exile and the Jews, 1939-1942*. UNC Press Books. ISBN 9781469619576.<templatestyles src="Module:Citation/CS1/styles.css"></templatestyles>

## External links

- 75th Anniversary of "Raczyński's Note". The full content of the brochure in PDF format: The Mass Extermination of Jews in German Occupied Poland.[1219]
- The Mass Extermination of Jews in German Occupied Poland (PDF), Polish Ministry of Foreign Affairs.[1220]

# Witold's Report

**Witold's Report**, also known as **Pilecki's Report**, is an official report of over 100 pages (in its final version) written in 1943 by Witold Pilecki, a Polish soldier and agent of the Polish resistance, who entered and escaped from the Auschwitz concentration camp. It was the first comprehensive record of a Holocaust death camp to be obtained by the Allies.

The report includes details about the gas chambers, "selektion", and the sterilization experiments. It states that there were three crematoria in Birkenau able to burn 8000 people daily. Raul Hilberg wrote that the Office of Strategic Services in London, which received the report, filed it away with a note that there was no indication as to its reliability.

Pilecki's Report preceded and supplemented the "Polish Major's Report" by Jerzy Tabeau (who escaped with Roman Cieliczko on 19 November 1943 and compiled the report between December 1943 and January 1944), the earliest of the three eyewitness reports known jointly as the Auschwitz Protocols which warned about the mass murder and other atrocities that were taking place inside the camp.

**Figure 156:** *Witold Pilecki*

# Background

On November 9, 1939, after the Polish Army was defeated in the Invasion of Poland, the cavalryman Witold Pilecki together with his commander Major Jan Włodarkiewicz founded the Secret Polish Army (*Tajna Armia Polska*, TAP). In 1940, Pilecki presented to his superiors a plan to enter Germany's Auschwitz concentration camp, gather intelligence on the camp from the inside, and organize inmate resistance. At that time little was known about the Germans' running of the camp, as it was then an internment or large prison camp. His superiors approved the plan and provided him with a false identity card in the name of "Tomasz Serafiński". On September 19, 1940, he deliberately went out during a Warsaw street roundup (łapanka), and was caught by the Germans along with some 2,000 innocent civilians. After two days' detention in the Light Horse Guards Barracks, where prisoners suffered beatings with rubber batons, Pilecki was sent to Auschwitz and was assigned inmate number 4859.

## In Auschwitz

Inside the camp Pilecki organized the underground Union of Military Organizations (Związek Organizacji Wojskowej, ZOW), which was connected with other smaller underground organizations. Pilecki planned a general uprising in Auschwitz and hoped that the Allies would drop arms or troops into the camp (most likely the Polish 1st Independent Parachute Brigade, based in Britain), and that the Home Army would organize an assault on the camp from outside. In 1943, the Gestapo redoubled its efforts to ferret out ZOW members, succeeding in killing many of them. Pilecki decided to break out of the camp, hoping to personally convince Home Army leaders about his idea of uprising in Auschwitz. On the night of April 26/27, 1943, Pilecki made a daring escape from the camp, but the Home Army did not accept his plan, as the Allies considered his reports about the Holocaust exaggerated.Wikipedia:Citation needed

# Report

ZOW's intelligence network inside the camp started to send regular reports to the Home Army from October 1940. Starting in November 1940, the first information about the genocide that was occurring in the camp was sent via ZOW to Home Army Headquarters in Warsaw. From March 1941 Witold Pilecki's reports were forwarded to the Polish government in exile and through it, to the British government in London and other Allied governments. These reports informed the Allies about the Holocaust and were the principal source of intelligence on Auschwitz-Birkenau for the Western Allies.

On June 20, 1942, four Poles, Eugeniusz Bendera,[1221] Kazimierz Piechowski, Stanisław Gustaw Jaster and Józef Lempart made a daring escape from Auschwitz camp.[1222] Dressed as members of the SS-Totenkopfverbände, fully armed and in an SS staff car they drove out the main gate in a stolen automobile, a Steyr 220 belonging to Rudolf Höss. Jaster, a member of ZOW, carried with him a detailed report about conditions in the camp, written by Pilecki. The Germans never recaptured any of them.

After a daring escape from Auschwitz on April 27, 1943, Pilecki wrote "Raport W". The report was signed by other members of the Polish underground who worked with ZOW: Aleksander Wielopolski, Stefan Bielecki, Antoni Woźniak, Aleksander Paliński, Ferdynand Trojnicki, Eleonora Ostrowska and Stefan Miłkowski, and it included a section called "Teren S" that contained a list of ZOW members. Later, after his release from the German prisoner-of-war camp at Murnau in 1945, Pilecki prepared a version of the report that was over 100 pages long.

The first publication of Witold's Report took place in 2000, 55 years after the war.Wikipedia:Citation needed An English translation was published in 2015 under the title *The Auschwitz Volunteer: Beyond Bravery*.

# Further reading

1. Adam Cyra, *Ochotnik do Auschwitz. Witold Pilecki 1901–1948*, <templatestyles src="Module:Citation/CS1/styles.css" />ISBN 83-912000-3-5, Chrześcijańskie Stowarzyszenie Rodzin Oświęcimskich, Oświęcim 2000
2. Cyra, Adam *Spadochroniarz Urban* [Paratrooper Urban], Oświęcim 2005.
3. Cyra, Adam and Wiesław Jan Wysocki, *Rotmistrz Witold Pilecki*, Oficyna Wydawnicza VOLUMEN, 1997. <templatestyles src="Module:Citation/CS1/styles.css" />ISBN 83-86857-27-7
4. Jacek Pawłowicz, *Rotmistrz Witold Pilecki 1901–1948*, 2008, <templatestyles src="Module:Citation/CS1/styles.css" />ISBN 978-83-60464-97-7.
5. Foot, Michael Richard Daniell (2003), Six Faces of Courage. Secret agents against Nazi tyranny. Witold Pilecki, Leo Cooper, <templatestyles src="Module:Citation/CS1/styles.css" />ISBN 0-413-39430-1
6. Lewis, Jon E. (1999), The Mammoth Book of True War Stories, Carroll & Graf Publishers, <templatestyles src="Module:Citation/CS1/styles.css" />ISBN 0-7867-0629-5
7. Piekarski, Konstanty R. (1990), Escaping Hell: The Story of a Polish Underground Officer in Auschwitz and Buchenwald, Dundurn Press Ltd., <templatestyles src="Module:Citation/CS1/styles.css" />ISBN 1-55002-071-4
8. Tchorek, Kamil (March 12, 2009), Double life of Witold Pilecki, the Auschwitz volunteer who uncovered Holocaust secrets, London: The Times, http://www.timesonline.co.uk/tol/news/world/europe/article5891132.ece, retrieved March 16, 2009
9. Wyman, David S.; Garlinski, Jozef (December 1976), "Review: Jozef Garlinski. Fighting Auschwitz: The Resistance Movement in the Concentration Camp", American Historical Review (American Historical Association) 81 (5): 1168–1169, doi: 10.2307/1853043[1223], <templatestyles src="Module:Citation/CS1/styles.css" />ISSN 0002-8762[1224]
10. Ciesielski E., *Wspomnienia Oświęcimskie* [Auschwitz Memoirs], Kraków, 1968
11. Garlinski, Jozef, *Fighting Auschwitz: the Resistance Movement in the Concentration Camp*, Fawcett, 1975, <templatestyles src="Module:Citation/CS1/styles.css" />ISBN 0-449-22599-2, reprinted by Time Life Education, 1993. <templatestyles

src="Module:Citation/CS1/styles.css" />ISBN 0-8094-8925-2 (see also review in The Times[1225])
12. Gawron, W. *Ochotnik do Oświęcimia* [Volunteer for Auschwitz], Calvarianum, Auschwitz Museum, 1992
13. Patricelli, M. "Il volontario" [The Volunteer], Laterza 2010, <templatestyles src="Module:Citation/CS1/styles.css" />ISBN 88-420-9188-X.
14. Wysocki, Wiesław Jan. *Rotmistrz Pilecki*, Pomost, 1994. <templatestyles src="Module:Citation/CS1/styles.css" />ISBN 83-85209-42-5
15. Kon Piekarski "Escaping Hell: The Story of a Polish Underground Officer in Auschwitz and Buchenwald", Dundurn Press Ltd., 1989, <templatestyles src="Module:Citation/CS1/styles.css" />ISBN 1-55002-071-4, <templatestyles src="Module:Citation/CS1/styles.css" />ISBN 978-1-55002-071-7

# External links

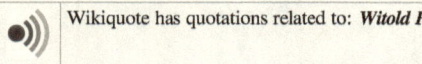

- Staff correspondent (March 5, 1948), Polish Left-Wing Relations: No Fusion as Yet[1226], London: The Times, pp. 3, retrieved March 12, 2009
- (in English) Witold Pilecki Video[1227] on YouTube
- (in English) *The mass extermination of Jews in German occupied Poland : note addressed to the governments of the United Nations on December 10th, 1942, and other documents*[1228] full color scan of the original pamphlet
- (in English) "Witold Pilecki's full report"[1229]. at *Volunteer for Auschwitz* (Online, Translated into English for the Let's Reminisce about Witold Pilecki initiative ed.). May 2008.<templatestyles src="Module:Citation/CS1/styles.css"></templatestyles>
- (in English) The Murder of Cavalry Captain Witold Pilecki[1230]
- (in Polish) Witold Pilecki's report from Auschwitz[1231] (rtf) / mirror[1232] (HTML)
- (in Polish) Additional reports of Pilecki[1233]
- (in Polish) Andrzej M. Kobos, Witold Pilecki w Piekle XX Wieku[1234], Zwoje 5 (9), 1998
- Biography of Witold Pilecki on Diapozytyw[1235]
- Józef Garlinski, The Polish Underground Movement and Auschwitz Concentration Camp[1236], 2003
- Episodes from Auschwitz: Witolds Report.[1237] Witold Pilecki's time at Auschwitz and post-War fate presented as a graphic history.
- Meet The Man Who Sneaked Into Auschwitz.[1238]

# Death marches

## Death marches (Holocaust)

**Death marches** (*Todesmärsche* in German) refer to the forcible movements of prisoners of Nazi Germany between Nazi camps on pain of death during World War II. They occurred at various points during the Holocaust, including in 1939 in the Lublin province of Poland, in 1942 in *Reichskommissariat Ukraine* and across General Government, and between Autumn 1944 and late April 1945 near the Soviet front, from the Nazi concentration camps and prisoner of war camps situated in the new *Reichsgaue*, to camps inside Germany proper, away from reach of the Allied forces. The purpose was to remove evidence of crimes against humanity committed inside the camps and to prevent the liberation of German-held prisoners of war.

### Overview

Towards the end of World War II in 1945, Nazi Germany had evacuated an estimated 10 to 15 million people, mostly from East Prussia and occupied Eastern and Central Europe. While the Allied forces advanced from the West, and the Red Army advanced from the East, trapped in the middle, the German SS divisions abandoned all Nazi concentration camps, moving or destroying evidence of the atrocities they had committed. Thousands of prisoners were killed in the camps before the marches commenced. These executions were deemed crimes against humanity during the Nuremberg trials.

Although most of the prisoners were already very weak or ill after enduring the routine violence, overwork, and starvation of concentration camp or prison camp life, they were marched for kilometres in the snow to railway stations, then transported for days at a time without food, water, or shelter in freight carriages originally designed for cattle. On arrival at their destination, they

**Figure 157:** *May 11, 1945: German civilians are forced to walk past the bodies of 30 Jewish women starved to death by German SS troops in a 500-kilometre (300 mi) march across Czechoslovakia. Buried in shallow graves in Volary, Czechoslovakia, the bodies were exhumed by German civilians working under the direction of Medics of the 5th Infantry Division, US Third Army. The bodies were later placed in coffins and reburied in the cemetery in Volary.*

were then forced to march again to new camps. Prisoners who were unable to keep up due to fatigue or illness were usually executed by gunshot.

The first evacuation of Majdanek inmates started in April 1944. The prisoners of Kaiserwald were transported to Stutthof or killed in August. Mittelbau-Dora was evacuated in April 1945.

The largest death march in World War II was from Auschwitz-Birkenau to Loslau in January 1945.

The SS killed large numbers of prisoners by starvation before the marches, and shot many more dead both during and after for not being able to keep pace. Seven hundred prisoners were killed during one ten-day march of 7,000 Jews, including 6,000 women, who were being moved from camps in the Danzig region. Those still alive when the marchers reached the coast were forced into the Baltic Sea and shot.

Elie Wiesel, Holocaust survivor and winner of the 1986 Nobel Peace Prize, describes in his 1958 book *Night* how he and his father, Shlomo, were forced on a death march from Buna to Buchenwald.

## Chełm to Hrubieszów, Sokal and Belz

In December 1939, male Jews from Chełm, Poland aged between 16 and 60, were forced on a death march to the nearby town of Hrubieszów. There, Jews were rounded up and forced to join the Chełm Jews. They were split into two groups on separate marches to Sokal and Belz, both across the modern border between Poland and Ukraine. In all, an estimated 2,000 Jews were murdered on this death march. There were only a handful of survivors.[1239]

## Lublin to Biała Podlaska and Parczew

In January 1940, the Germans deported a group of prisoners from the Lipowa 7 prisoner of war camp to Biała Podlaska and then to Parczew. They rushed them on foot among snowstorms and temperatures below −20 °C (−4 °F). Those POWs who did not follow orders were killed by the German guards. The inhabitants of the nearby villages were forced to collect and bury the bodies in mass graves. Only a small group of prisoners survived this march of death. A few were able to escape into the woods and join the partisans.[1240]

## Belz to Hrubieszow

In early June 1942, Jews concentrated in Belz were driven in a 60-kilometre (37 mi) death march to Hrubieszow. Those who could not continue on the way were shot by the SS guards. All death march survivors were deported along with about 3,000 Jews from Hrubieszow to Sobibor.[1241]

## Auschwitz to Loslau

The largest and the most notorious of the death marches took place in January 1945, when the Soviet army advanced on occupied Poland. Nine days before the Soviets arrived at the death camp at Auschwitz, the SS marched nearly 60,000 prisoners out of the camp toward Loslau (polish: Wodzisław Śląski), 63 km (39 mi) away, where they were put on freight trains to other camps. Approximately 15,000 prisoners died on the way. In the days when prisoners arrived at Loslau temperatures of a freezing −20 °C (−4 °F) and lower were recorded. Some residents of Upper Silesia tried to help the prisoners, and many prisoners also escaped and regained freedom between Auschwitz and Loslau.

## Stutthof to Lauenburg

The evacuation of the about 50,000 prisoners from the Stutthof camp system in northern Poland began in January 1945. About 5,000 prisoners from Stutthof subcamps were marched to the Baltic Sea coast, forced into the water, and machine gunned. The rest of the prisoners were marched in the direction of Lauenburg in eastern Germany. They were cut off by the advancing Soviet forces. The Germans forced the surviving prisoners back to Stutthof. Marching in severe winter conditions and treated brutally by SS guards, thousands died during the march.

In late April 1945, the remaining prisoners were removed from Stutthof by sea, since it was completely encircled by Soviet forces. Again, hundreds of prisoners were forced into the sea and shot. Over 4,000 were sent by small boat to Germany, some to the Neuengamme concentration camp near Hamburg, and some to camps along the Baltic coast. Many drowned along the way. Shortly before the German surrender, some prisoners were transferred to Malmö, Sweden, and released to the care of that neutral country. It has been estimated that over 25,000 prisoners, around half, died during the evacuation from Stutthof and its subcamps. One hundred prisoners were liberated from Stutthof on May 9, 1945.

## Buchenwald to Dachau, Flossenbürg and Theresienstadt

In early 1945, Buchenwald had received numerous prisoners moved from camps further east in territory lost to the Soviets, and camp authorities began to close the outlying camps of Buchenwald (such as those in Apolda and Altenburg) to concentrate prisoners in the main camp. In April 1945, about 28,000 prisoners were marched from Buchenwald on a journey of over 300 kilometers through Jena, Eisenberg, Bad Köstritz, and Gera[1242] with the intended destination of Dachau, Flossenbürg, and Theresienstadt. The remaining 21,000 prisoners in Buchenwald were liberated by the U.S. Third Army on April 11, 1945.

## Dachau to the Austrian border

On April 24, 1945, the satellite labor camps around Dachau were being cleared out by the Nazis ahead of the advancing Allied troops, and some 15,000 prisoners were first marched to the Dachau camp, only to be sent southwards on a death march towards the Austrian border, the path for which generally headed southwards, partly along the eastern shore of the *Starnberger See*, taking a left turn to the east in the town of Eurasburg and heading towards the *Tegernsee*. By the timeframe of the second of May 1945, only some of the 6,000 prisoners sent on the death march were still alive, as those in failing health were being

**Figure 158:** *Memorial plaque to the victims of the death march in Jena*

shot dead as they fell along the route. On that day, as the eastwards-marching prisoners had passed through Bad Tölz and were nearing Waakirchen, nearly sixty kilometres (37 miles) south of Dachau, several hundred of them were lying on the open ground in ill health, and among them were some who had already died from ill health and exposure to the elements, nearly all covered in freshly-fallen snow. These prisoners were spotted by advance scouts of the U.S. Army's 522nd Field Artillery Battalion, the only segregated Japanese American-manned military unit in Germany at the time — who had, only days before, liberated the *Kaufering IV Hurlach* satellite slave labor camp of the Dachau main camp's "system", and many of whose own relatives were themselves interned during the war on American soil — with the American troops doing what they could in attempts to save those left alive, for at least two days before dedicated medical personnel could take over. A memorial to the rescue by the 522nd exists at 47°46′6.15″N 11°38′55.30″E[1243], just under two kilometres west of the Waakirchen town centre.[1244]

**Figure 159:** *Memorial in Wodzisław Śląski of the death march from Auschwitz Birkenau*

**Figure 160:** *This memorial in Blievenstorf of the death march from Sachsenhausen concentration camp includes a red triangle emblem*

**Figure 161:** *Memorial in Putlitz of the death march from Sachsenhausen concentration camp*

**Figure 162:** *Holocaust cemetery in Nawcz for victims of the death march from Stutthof concentration camp*

## Further reading

- Goldhagen, Daniel (1997). *Hitler's Willing Executioners: Ordinary Germans and the Holocaust*. Vintage. ISBN 978-0-679-77268-2.<templatestyles src="Module:Citation/CS1/styles.css"></templatestyles>
- Death Marches of Prisoners Map (from the U.S. Holocaust Memorial Museum)[1245]
- Iwo Cyprian Pogonowski, A map of the Death March of Brandenburg[1246].
- Todesmarsch Dachau[1247]: Death marches from Dachau, Kaufering, Mühldorf and Allach (in German)
- USHMM Photos page of Waakirchen and 522nd FA BN Nisei soldiers[1248]
- Memorial to the Death March Victims: Chelm and Hrubieszow, Poland[1249]
- The Death March to Volary[1250], at Yad Vashem website

# Victims and death toll

## Holocaust victims

| Victims | Killed | Source |
|---|---|---|
| Jews | 5–6 million | |
| Soviet citizens | 4.5 million | 1251 |
| Soviet POWs | 2.8–3.3 million | 1252 |
| Poles | 1.8–3 million | 1253,1253 |
| Serbs | 300,000–600,000 | |
| Disabled | 270,000 | |
| Romani | 130,000–500,000 | 1254,1255 |
| Freemasons | 80,000–200,000 | 1256 |
| Slovenes | 20,000–25,000 | 1257 |
| Spanish Republicans | 7,000 | 1258 |
| Homosexuals | 5,000–15,000 | |
| Jehovah's Witnesses | 1,250–5,000 | 1259 |

Part of a series on
### The Holocaust

Jews on selection ramp at Auschwitz, May 1944

**Holocaust victims** were people who were targeted by the government of Nazi Germany for various discriminatory practices due to their ethnicity, religion, political beliefs, or sexual orientation. These institutionalized practices came to be called The Holocaust, and they began with legalized social discrimination against specific groups, and involuntary hospitalization, euthanasia, and forced sterilization of those considered physically or mentally unfit for society. These practices escalated during World War II to include non-judicial incarceration, confiscation of property, forced labor, sexual slavery, medical experimentation, and death through overwork, undernourishment, and execution through a variety of methods, with the genocide of different groups as the primary goal.

According to the United States Holocaust Memorial Museum (USHMM), the country's official memorial to the Holocaust, "The Holocaust was the murder of six million Jews and millions of others by the Nazis and their collaborators during World War II." Of those murdered for being Jewish, more than half were Ashkenazi Polish Jews.[1261]Wikipedia:Identifying reliable sources

## Scope of usage

While the term Holocaust generally refers to the systematic mass murder of the Jewish people in German-occupied Europe, the Nazis also murdered a large number of non-Jewish people who were also considered subhuman (*Untermenschen*) or undesirable. Some victims belonged to several categories targeted for extermination, e.g. an assimilated Jew who was a member of a communist party or someone of Jewish ancestry who identified as one of Jehovah's Witnesses.

Non-Jewish victims of Nazism included Slavs (e.g. Russians, Poles, Ukrainians and Serbs), Romanis (gypsies), French, Belgians, Dutch, Greeks, Italians (after 1943), LGBT people (lesbian, gay, bisexual, transgender, pansexual, etc);[1262] the mentally or physically disabled, mentally ill;[1263] Soviet POWs, Roman Catholics, Protestants, Orthodox Christians, Jehovah's Witnesses, Muslims,[1264] Spanish Republicans, Freemasons,[1265] people of color (especially the Afro-German *Mischlinge*, called "Rhineland Bastards" by Hitler and the Nazi regime); leftists, communists, trade unionists, capitalists, social democrats, socialists, anarchists, and every other minority or dissident not considered Aryan (*Herrenvolk*, or part of the "master race") as well as those who disagreed with the Nazi regime.[1266,1267]

Taking into account all of the victims of persecution, the Nazis systematically killed an estimated six million Jews and an additional 11 million people during the war. Donald Niewyk suggests that the broadest definition, including Soviet civilian deaths, would produce a death toll of 17 million.[1268]

Despite widely varying treatment (some groups were actively targeted for genocide, while others were not), some died in concentration camps such as Dachau and others from various forms of Nazi brutality. According to extensive documentation (written and photographic) left by the Nazis, eyewitness testimony by survivors, perpetrators and bystanders and records of the occupied countries, most perished in death camps such as Auschwitz-Birkenau.

# Ethnic criteria

## Jews

The military campaign to remove certain classes of persons (above all, Jews) from Germany and other German-held territories during World War II, often with extreme brutality, is known as the Holocaust. It was carried out primarily by German forces and collaborators, German and non-German. Early in the war, millions of Jews were concentrated in urban ghettos. In 1941 Jews were massacred, and by December Hitler had decided to exterminate all Jews living in Europe at that time. The European Jewish population was reduced from 9,740,000 to 3,642,000; the world's Jewish population was reduced by one-third, from roughly 16.6 million in 1939 to about 11 million in 1946.[1269] The extermination of Jews had been priority to the Nazis regardless of the consequences.[1270]

In January 1942, during the Wannsee Conference, several Nazi leaders discussed the details of the "Final Solution to the Jewish Question" (*Endlösung der Judenfrage*) and German State Secretary Josef Bühler urged conference

**Figure 163:** *Jews delivered to Chełmno death camp were forced to abandon their bundles along the way. In this photo, loading of victims sent from the ghetto in Łódź in 1942*

chairman Reinhard Heydrich to proceed with the Final Solution in the General Government. Jewish populations were systematically deported from the ghettos and the occupied territories to the seven camps designated as *Vernichtungslager* (extermination camps): Auschwitz-Birkenau, Belzec, Chelmno, Majdanek, Maly Trostenets, Sobibór and Treblinka. In 1978 Sebastian Haffner wrote that in December 1941 Hitler began to accept the failure of his primary goal (to dominate Europe) after his declaration of war against the United States, and his withdrawal was compensated for by his secondary goal: the extermination of the Jews.[1271] As the Nazi war machine faltered during the war's final years, military resources such as fuel, transport, munitions, soldiers and industrial resources were still diverted from the fronts to the death camps.

Poland, home of the world's largest Jewish community before the war, lost 3,300,000 (90 percent) of its Jewish population. Although the Germans rigorously imposed the death penalty for hiding Jews, some Poles hid Jews (saving their lives) despite the risk to themselves and their families. Although reports of the Holocaust had reached Western leaders, public awareness in the United States and other democracies of the mass murder of Jews in Poland was low at the time; the first references in *The New York Times*, in 1942, were unconfirmed reports rather than front-page news.

Greece, Yugoslavia, Hungary, Lithuania, Bohemia, the Netherlands, Slovakia and Latvia lost over 70 percent of their Jewish population; in Belgium, Roma-

**Figure 164:** *A photograph depicting Polish Jews captured by Germans during the Warsaw Ghetto Uprising, May 1943*

nia, Luxembourg, Norway, and Estonia the figure was about 50 percent. Over one-third of the Soviet Union's Jews were killed; France lost about 25 percent of its Jewish population, Italy between 15 and 20%. Denmark evacuated nearly all its Jews to nearby, neutral Sweden; the Danish resistance movement, with the assistance of many Danish citizens, evacuated 7,220 of the country's 7,800 Jews by sea to Sweden[1272] in vessels ranging from fishing boats to private yachts. The rescue allowed the vast majority of Denmark's Jewish population to avoid capture by the Nazis. Jews outside Europe under Axis occupation were also affected by the Holocaust in Italian Libya, Algeria, Tunisia, Morocco, Iraq, Japan, and China.

Although Jews are an ethnoreligious group, they were defined by the Nazis on purely racial grounds. The Nazi Party viewed the Jewish religion as irrelevant, persecuting Jews in accordance with antisemitic stereotypes of an alleged biologically determined heritage. Defining Jews as the chief enemy, Nazi racial ideology was also used to persecute other minorities.

**Figure 165:** *Polish priests and civilians in Bydgoszcz's Old Market Square, 9 September 1939. The Polish Church experienced brutal persecution under Nazi occupation.*

## Slavs

The Slavs were one of the most widely persecuted groups during the war, with many Poles, Russians, Ukrainians, Serbs and others killed by the Nazis. According to British historian Ian Kershaw, the Nazis' genocide and brutality was their way of ensuring *Lebensraum* ("living space") for those who met Hitler's narrow racial requirements; this necessitated the elimination of Bolsheviks and Slavs:

<templatestyles src="Template:Quote/styles.css"/>

> *The Nazi revolution was broader than just the Holocaust. Its second goal was to eliminate Slavs from Central and Eastern Europe and to create a Lebensraum for Aryans ... As Bartov (The Eastern Front; Hitler's Army) shows, it barbarised the German armies on the eastern front. Most of their three million men, from generals to ordinary soldiers, helped exterminate captured Slav soldiers and civilians. This was sometimes cold and deliberate murder of individuals (as with Jews), sometimes generalised brutality and neglect ... German soldiers' letters and memoirs reveal their terrible reasoning: Slavs were 'the Asiatic-Bolshevik' horde, an inferior but threatening race. Only a minority of officers and men were Nazi members.*[1273]

## Poles

The Nazi occupation of Poland was among the most brutal of the war, resulting in the death of more than 3 million ethnic Poles and about 3 million

Polish Jews. The six million Jewish, Roman Catholic and Orthodox Poles represented nearly 17 percent of the country's population.[1274] Poles were one of Hitler's first extermination targets, as he outlined in an August 22, 1939 speech to Wehrmacht commanders before the invasion. Intelligentsia, socially prominent and influential people were primarily targeted, although ethnic Poles and other Slavic groups were also killed *en masse*. Hundreds of thousands of Roman Catholic and Orthodox Poles were sent to Auschwitz-Birkenau and other concentration camps, and the intelligentsia were the first targets of the *Einsatzgruppen* death squads. The anti-Polish campaign culminated in the near-complete destruction of Warsaw, ordered by Hitler and Himmler in 1944. The original assumptions of Generalplan Ost were based on plans to exterminate around 85% (over 20 million) of ethnically Polish citizens of Poland, with the remaining 15% to be used as slaves.

## Ukrainians

Between 1941 and 1945, approximately three million Ukrainian and other gentiles were killed as part of Nazi extermination policies in present-day Ukraine.More Ukrainians were killed fighting the Wehrmacht in the Red Army than American, British and French soldiers combined. Original Nazi plans called for the extermination of 65 percent of the nation's 23.2 million Ukrainians,[1275] with the survivors treated as slaves.[1276] Over two million Ukrainians were deported to Germany as slave labor. The ten-year plan would have exterminated, expelled, Germanized or enslaved most (or all) Ukrainians.

## Soviet Slavs and POWs

During Operation Barbarossa (the Axis invasion of the Soviet Union), millions of Red Army prisoners of war were summarily executed in the field by German armies (the Waffen SS in particular), died under inhumane conditions in German prisoner of war camps and death marches or shipped to concentration camps for execution. The Germans killed an estimated 2.8 million Soviet POWs by starvation, exposure and execution over an eight-month period in 1941–42.[1277] According to the U.S. Holocaust Memorial Museum, by the winter of 1941 "starvation and disease resulted in mass death of unimaginable proportions". 140,000-500,000 people were killed in the concentration camps.

Soviet civilian populations in the occupied areas were severely persecuted and endured the treacherous conditions of the Eastern Front, which spawned atrocities such as the siege of Leningrad (when more than 1.2 million civilians died). Thousands of peasant villages across Russia, Belarus and Ukraine were annihilated by German troops. During the occupation the Leningrad, Pskov and Novgorod region lost about a quarter of its population. An estimated one-quarter of Soviet civilian deaths at the hands of the Nazis and their allies (five

**Figure 166:** *Naked Soviet prisoners of war in Mauthausen concentration camp.*

million Russians, three million Ukrainians and 1.5 million Belarusians) were racially motivated.[1278] In 1995 the Russian Academy of Sciences reported that civilian deaths in the occupied USSR, including Jews, at the hands of the Germans totaled 13.7 million dead (20 percent of the population of 68 million). The figure includes 7.4 million victims of Nazi genocide and reprisals; 2.2 million deaths of persons deported to Germany as forced labour, and 4.1 million famine and disease deaths. An estimated three million people also died of starvation in unoccupied territory. The losses occurred within the 1946–1991 borders of the USSR, and include territories annexed in 1939–40.[1279] The deaths of 8.2 million Soviet civilians, including Jews, were documented by the Soviet Extraordinary State Commission.[1280]

## Romani

The Nazi genocide of the Romani people was ignored by scholars until the 1980s, and opinions continue to differ on its details. According to historians Donald Niewyk and Francis Nicosia, the genocide of the Romani began later than that of the Jews and a smaller percentage was killed.[1281] Hitler's genocidal campaign against Europe's Romani population involved the application of Nazi "racial hygiene" (selective breeding applied to humans). Although despite discriminatory measures some Romani (including some of Germany's Sinti and Lalleri) were spared deportation and death, the remaining Romani groups suffered a fate similar to that of the Jews. Romani were deported to the

**Figure 167:** *German troops round up Romani in Asperg, Germany in May 1940*

Jewish ghettos, shot by SS *Einsatzgruppen* in their villages, or deported and gassed in Auschwitz-Birkenau and Treblinka.

Estimates of the Romani death toll in World War II range from 220,000 to 1,500,000. The Romani genocide was formally recognized by West Germany in 1982 and by Poland in 2011.[1282]

## Spanish Republicans

Thousands of Spanish Republican refugees were living in France at the time of its occupation by Nazi Germany in 1940; 15,000 were detained in concentration camps, including 7,000 in Mauthausen-Gusen. About 7,000 died.

# People with disabilities

According to their eugenics policy, the Nazis believed that the disabled were a burden to society because they needed care and were considered an affront to their notion of a society composed of a perfect race. About 375,000 people were sterilized against their will due to their disabilities.

Those with disabilities were among the first to be killed by the Nazis; according to the U.S. Holocaust Memorial Museum, the T-4 Program (established in 1939) was the model for future Nazi exterminations and it set a precedent for the genocide of what they described as the Jewish race. The program attempted to maintain the "purity" of the Aryan race by systematically killing

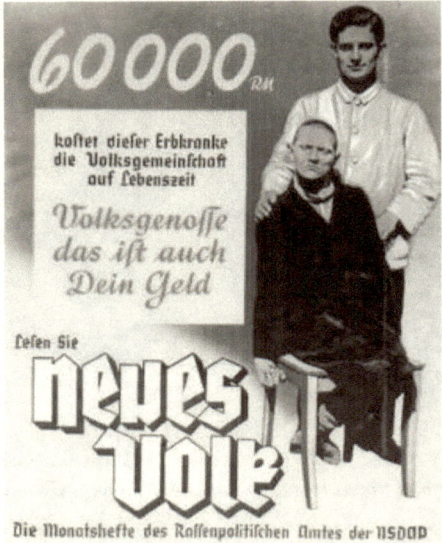

**Figure 168:** *This poster (from around 1938) reads: "60,000 Reichsmark is what this person suffering from a hereditary defect costs the People's community during his lifetime. Fellow citizen, that is your money too. Read '[A] New People', the monthly magazine of the Bureau for Race Politics of the NSDAP."*

children and adults with physical deformities or suffering from mental illness, using gas chambers for the first time. Although Hitler formally halted the program in late August 1941, the killings secretly continued until the end of the war and an estimated 275,000 people with congenital disabilities died.

## Non-Europeans

The Nazis promoted xenophobia and racism against all "non-Aryan" races. African (black sub-Saharan or North African) and Asian residents of Germany and black prisoners of war, such as French colonial troops and African Americans, were also victims of Nazi racial policy. When the Nazis came to power hundreds of African-German children, the offspring of German mothers and African soldiers brought in during the French occupation, lived in the Rhineland. In *Mein Kampf*, Hitler described the children of marriages to African occupation troops as a contamination of the white race "by Negro blood on the Rhine in the heart of Europe"[1283] who were "bastardising the European continent at its core". According to Hitler, "Jews were responsible for bringing Negroes into the Rhineland, with the ultimate idea of bastardising

**Figure 169:** *Nazi propaganda about the differences between German Aryans and blacks.*

the white race which they hate and thus lowering its cultural and political level so that the Jew might dominate".[1284]

Japan signed the Tripartite Pact with Germany and Italy on September 27, 1940, and was part of the Axis. No Japanese people were known to be deliberately imprisoned or killed, since they were considered "honorary Aryans". In his political testament Hitler wrote:

<templatestyles src="Template:Quote/styles.css"/>

> *I have never regarded the Chinese or the Japanese as being inferior to ourselves. [...] and I admit freely that their past history is superior to our own. They have the right to be proud of their past, just as we have the right to be proud of the civilisation to which we belong.*[1285] Wikipedia:Identifying reliable sources

South Africans, white people and Europeans of gentile ancestry from other continents were exempt, as were Latin Americans of "evident" Germanic or White "Aryan" (non-mestizo) ancestry.

## Gay men and lesbians

Non-heterosexual people were also targets of the Holocaust, since male homosexuality was deemed incompatible with Nazism. The Nazis believed that gay men were weak, effeminate and unable to fight for the German nation; homosexuals were unlikely to produce children and increase the German birthrate. According to the Nazis, "inferior races" produced more children than Aryans, so anything which diminished Germany's reproductive potential was considered a racial danger. Homosexuality was also thought to be contagious by the Nazis. By 1936, Heinrich Himmler was leading efforts to persecute gay men under existing and new anti-homosexual laws. More than one million gay Germans were targeted, of whom at least 100,000 were arrested and 50,000 were convicted and imprisoned. An unknown number were institutionalized in state-run mental hospitals. Hundreds of European gay men living under Nazi occupation were chemically castrated by court order. Although an estimated 5,000 to 15,000 gay men were imprisoned in concentration camps, the number who died is uncertain. According to Austrian survivor Heinz Heger, gay men "suffered a higher mortality rate than other relatively small victim groups, such as Jehovah's Witnesses and political prisoners".[1286] Gay men in Nazi concentration camps were identified by a pink triangle on their shirts, along with men convicted of sexually assaulting children and bestiality.[1287] Lesbians were not usually treated as harshly as gay men; although they were labelled "asocial", they were rarely imprisoned on sexual-orientation charges. In the concentration camps, they usually wore a black triangle. U.S. Holocaust Memorial Museum's website, "Nazi Germany did not seek to kill all homosexuals. Nevertheless, the Nazi state, through active persecution, attempted to terrorise German homosexuals into sexual and social conformity, leaving thousands dead and shattering the lives of many more."

Many homosexuals who were liberated from the concentration camps were persecuted in postwar Germany. Survivors were subject to prosecution under Paragraph 175 (which forbade "lewdness between men"), with time served in the concentration camps deducted from their sentences. This contrasted with the treatment of other Holocaust victims, who were compensated for the loss of family members and educational opportunities.

# Political victims

## Political prisoners

Another large group of victims was composed of German and foreign civilian activists across the political spectrum who opposed the Nazi regime, captured resistance fighters (many of whom were executed during—or immediately after—their interrogation, particularly in occupied Poland and France) and, sometimes, their families. German political prisoners were a substantial proportion of the first inmates at Dachau (the prototypical Nazi concentration camp). The political People's Court was notorious for the number of its death sentences.Wikipedia:Citation needed

## Leftists

German Communists were among the first to be imprisoned in concentration camps. Their ties to the USSR concerned Hitler, and the Nazi Party was intractably opposed to communism. Rumors of communist violence were spread by the Nazis to justify the Enabling Act of 1933, which gave Hitler his first dictatorial powers. Hermann Göring testified at Nuremberg that Nazi willingness to repress German Communists prompted Hindenburg and the old elite to cooperate with them. Hitler and the Nazis also despised German leftists because of their resistance to Nazi racism. Many German leftist leaders were Jews who had been prominent in the 1919 Spartacist uprising. Hitler referred to Marxism and "Bolshevism" as means for "the international Jew" to undermine "racial purity", stir up class tension and mobilize trade unions against the government and business. When the Nazis occupied a territory, communists, socialists and anarchists were usually among the first to be repressed; this included summary executions. An example is Hitler's Commissar Order, in which he demanded the summary execution of all Soviet troops who were political commissars who offered resistance or were captured in battle.

## Enemy nationals

Thousands of people, primarily diplomats, of nationalities associated with the Allies (China and Mexico, for example) and Spanish Civil War refugees in occupied France were interned or executed. After Italy's 1943 surrender, many Italian nationals (including partisans and Italian soldiers disarmed by the Germans) were sent to concentration camps.

**Figure 170:** *German nun Edith Stein; ethnically Jewish, she was arrested at a Netherlands convent and killed at Auschwitz after a protest by Dutch bishops against the abduction of Jews.*

## Other religious persecution

The Nazis also targeted religious groups for political and ideological reasons. Thousands of Catholic clergy and nuns were killed, including some with a Jewish background (Edith Stein, for example). The Nazis considered Jews a racial group; secular people and those of other religions who had Jewish ancestry were, therefore, Jews (a belief shared by some Jews).

### Jehovah's Witnesses

Historian Detlef Garbe, director of the Neuengamme Memorial in Hamburg, wrote about Jehovah's Witnesses: "No other religious movement resisted the pressure to conform to National Socialism [Nazism] with comparable unanimity and steadfastness".[1288] Between 2,500 and 5,000 Witnesses died in the concentration camps; unwilling to fight for any cause, they refused to serve in the army.

## Roman Catholics

The Catholic Church was persecuted under the Third Reich,[1289] with the Nazi leadership hoping to gradually de-Christianize Germany. Millions of Catholics were imprisoned and killed. According to the World Holocaust Remembrance Center, "By the latter part of the decade of the Thirties church officials were well aware that the ultimate aim of Hitler and other Nazis was the total elimination of Catholicism and of the Christian religion." Hitler vehemently despised Christianity, calling it the enemy of National Socialism. According to historian William Shirer, "under the leadership of Rosenberg, Bormann and Himmler—backed by Hitler—the Nazi regime intended to destroy Christianity in Germany, if it could, and substitute the old paganism of the early tribal Germanic gods and the new paganism of the Nazi extremists". He also wrote that Hitler "inveighed against political Catholicism in Mein Kampf and attacked both of the Christian Churches for their failure to recognise the racial problem...". As reported in the New York Times, Hitler's forces wished to de-Christianize Germany after "the final victory" and destroy Christianity. According to historian Alan Bullock, "Once the war was over, [Hitler] promised himself, he would root out and destroy the influence of the Christian Churches, but until then he would be circumspect."[1290] Political Catholicism was a target of Hitler's 1934 Night of the Long Knives.[1291,1292,1293] German clergy, nuns and lay leaders were also targeted after the Nazi takeover, leading to thousands of arrests over the following years.[1294] Priests who were part of the Catholic resistance were killed. Hitler's invasion of Catholic Poland in 1939 began World War II, and the Nazis targeted clergy, monks and nuns in their campaign to destroy Polish culture.

In 1940, the Priest Barracks of Dachau Concentration Camp was established.[1295] Of 2,720 clergy imprisoned at Dachau, the overwhelming majority (94.88 percent) were Catholic.[1296] According to Ian Kershaw, about 400 German priests were sent to the camp.[1297] Although the Holy See concluded a 1933 concordat with Germany to protect Catholicism in the Third Reich, the Nazis frequently violated the pact in their *Kirchenkampf* ("struggle with the churches").[1298] They shut down the Catholic press, schools, political parties and youth groups in Germany amid murder and mass arrests.[1299,1300,1301] In March 1937, Pope Pius XI issued his *Mit brennender Sorge* encyclical accusing the Nazi government of violating the 1933 concordat and sowing the "tares of suspicion, discord, hatred, calumny, of secret and open fundamental hostility to Christ and His Church".

The church was especially harshly treated in annexed regions, such as Austria. Viennese *Gauleiter* Odilo Globocnik confiscated property, closed Catholic organizations and sent many priests to Dachau. In the Czech lands, religious orders were suppressed, schools closed, religious instruction forbidden

**Figure 171:** *The Mortal Agony of Christ Chapel at Dachau commemorates the clergy who were imprisoned there.*

and priests sent to concentration camps.[1302] Catholic bishops, clergy, nuns and laypeople protested and attacked Nazi policies in occupied territories; in 1942, the Dutch bishops protested the mistreatment of Jews. When Archbishop Johannes de Jong refused to yield to Nazi threats, the Gestapo rounded up Catholic "Jews" and sent 92 to Auschwitz.[1303] One Dutch Catholic abducted in this manner was nun Edith Stein, who died at Auschwitz along with Poland's Maximilian Kolbe. Other Catholic victims of the Holocaust have been beatified, including Poland's 108 Martyrs of World War II, the Martyrs of Nowogródek, Dutch theologian Titus Brandsma and Germany's Lübeck martyrs and Bernhard Lichtenberg.

**Poland**

According to Norman Davies, the Nazi terror was "much fiercer and more protracted in Poland than anywhere in Europe."[1304] Polish Catholic victims of the Third Reich numbered in the millions. Nazi ideology viewed ethnic Poles—the mainly Catholic ethnic majority of Poland—as subhuman. After their 1939 invasion of Poland, the Nazis instituted a policy of murdering (or suppressing) the ethnic-Polish elite (including Catholic religious leaders). The Nazi plan for Poland was the nation's destruction, which necessitated attacking the Polish Church (particularly in areas annexed by Germany). About the

**Figure 172:** *Polish Franciscan Maximillian Kolbe died at Auschwitz.*

brief period of military control from September 1 to October 25, 1939, Davies wrote: "According to one source, 714 mass executions were carried out, and 6,376 people, mainly Catholics, were shot. Other put the death toll in one town alone at 20,000. It was a taste of things to come."[1305]

In Polish areas annexed by Nazi Germany, severe persecution began. The Nazis systematically dismantled the church, arresting its leaders, exiling its clergy and closing its churches, monasteries and convents. Germanization of the annexed regions began in December 1939 with deportations of men, women and children.[1306] According to Richard J. Evans, in the Reichsgau Wartheland "numerous clergy, monks, diocesan administrators and officials of the Church were arrested, deported to the General Government, taken off to a concentration camp in the Reich, or simply shot. Altogether some 1700 Polish priests ended up at Dachau: half of them did not survive their imprisonment."[1307] Among the clergy who died at Dachau were many of the 108 Polish Martyrs of World War II.

Hans Frank said in 1940, "Poles may have only one master—a German. Two masters cannot exist side by side, and this is why all members of the Polish intelligentsia must be killed." Thomas J. Craughwell wrote that from 1939 to 1945, an estimated 3,000 members of the Polish clergy (18 percent) were murdered; of these, 1,992 died in concentration camps.[1308] According to the *Encyclopædia Britannica*, 1,811 Polish priests died in Nazi concentration camps.[1309] Among the persecuted resisters was Irena Sendlerowa, head of the children's section of Żegota, who placed more than 2,500 Jewish children in convents, orphanages, schools, hospitals and homes. Captured by the Gestapo in 1943, Sendlerowa was crippled by torture.[1310]

## Protestants

The Nazis attempted to deal with Protestant dissent with their ideology by creating the Reich Church, a union of 28 existing Protestant groups espousing Positive Christianity (a doctrine compatible with Nazism). Non-Aryan ministers were suspended and church members called themselves German Christians, with "the swastika on their chest and the cross in their heart." The Protestant opposition to the Nazis established the Confessing Church, a rival umbrella organization of independent German regional churches which was persecuted.[1311]

## Bahá'í Faith

The Bahá'í Faith was formally banned in the Third Reich. Heinrich Himmler signed a 1937 order disbanding Bahá'í institutions in Germany because of their "international and pacifist tendencies". In 1939 and 1942, there were sweeping arrests of former members of the German Spiritual Assembly. May 1944 saw a public trial in Darmstadt; although Hermann Grossmann defended the faith, the Bahá'ís were steeply fined and their institutions continued to be disbanded.

## Freemasons

The Nazis claimed that high-degree Masons were willing members of "the Jewish conspiracy" and Freemasonry was a cause of Germany's defeat in World War I. Reich Main Security Office (*Reichssicherheitshauptamt*, or RSHA) records indicate the persecution of Freemasons during the Holocaust. RSHA Amt VII (written records), overseen by Franz Six, was responsible for "ideological" tasks: the creation of antisemitic and anti-Masonic propaganda. Although the exact number is unknown, an estimated 80,000 to 200,000 Freemasons were killed as a result of Hitler's December 1941 *Nacht und Nebel* directive. Masonic concentration-camp inmates, considered political prisoners, wore an inverted red triangle.

Small blue forget-me-nots were first used by the Zur Sonne Grand Lodge in 1926 as a Masonic emblem at its annual convention in Bremen. In 1938 a forget-me-not badge made by the factory which produced the Masonic badge was chosen for the annual Nazi *Winterhilfswerk*, the charity drive of the National Socialist People's Welfare (the party's welfare branch). The coincidence enabled Freemasons to wear the forget-me-not badge as a secret sign of Masonic membership.[1312]

After the war, the forget-me-not was again used as a Masonic emblem at the first annual United Grand Lodges of Germany convention in 1948. The badge is worn on the lapels of Masons worldwide in remembrance of those who have suffered in the name of Freemasonry, particularly during the Nazi era.

### Esperantists

Speakers of Esperanto, an international auxiliary language, were viewed with suspicion by the Nazis. Hitler considered it a language of the "Jewish conspiracy" because its creator, L. L. Zamenhof, was Jewish. Because of this, people who spoke Esperanto were sent to death camps.

## Others

The SS and police conducted mass actions against civilians with alleged links to resistance movements, their families, and villages or city districts. Notorious killings occurred in Lidice, Khatyn, Sant'Anna and Oradour-sur-Glane, and a district of Warsaw was obliterated. In occupied Poland, Nazi Germany imposed the death penalty on those found sheltering (or aiding) Jews. "Social deviants"—prostitutes, vagrants, alcoholics, drug addicts, open dissidents, pacifists, draft resisters and common criminals—were also imprisoned in concentration camps. The common criminals frequently became Kapos, inmate guards of fellow prisoners.

Some Germans and Austrians who lived abroad for much of their lives were considered to have too much exposure to foreign ideas, and they were sent to concentration camps. These prisoners, known as "emigrants", each wore a blue triangle.WP:NOTRS

On rare occasions, POWs from Western Allied armies were sent to concentration camps, including 350 Americans – some chosen for being Jewish, but mostly for looking Jewish or for being troublemakers or otherwise 'undesirable' – captured in the Battle of the Bulge were forced into slave labor at the Berga concentration camp, a subcamp of Buchenwald; over 70 died. The "KLB Club" was a group of 168 Allied airmen – mainly American, British, and Canadian – considered *Terrorfliegers* ("terror fliers"), denied POW status, and held at Buchenwald for two months until a German officer arranged for their transfer to a standard POW camp, a week before their scheduled execution.

# References

**Informational notes**

**Citations**

**Bibliography**

- Berenbaum, Michael (2005). *The World Must Know: The History of the Holocaust as Told in the United States Holocaust Memorial Museum*[1313]. United States Holocaust Memorial Museum, Johns Hopkins University Press. ISBN 978-0801883583.<templatestyles src="Module:Citation/CS1/styles.css"></templatestyles>
- Hancock, Ian (2004). "Romanies and the Holocaust: A Reevaluation and Overview". In Dan Stone. *The Historiography of the Holocaust*[1314]. New York City: Palgrave-Macmillan.<templatestyles src="Module:Citation/CS1/styles.css"></templatestyles>

# External links

- Non-Jewish Victims of Persecution in Nazi Germany[1315] on the Yad Vashem website
- The Central Database of Shoah Victims' Names[1316]
- Stills from Soviet documentary "The Atrocities committed by German Fascists in the USSR" ( (1)[1317]; (2)[1318]; (3)[1319])
- Slide show "Nazi Crimes in the USSR (Graphic images!)"[1320]
- Yahad in Nunum on Shoah victiums[1321]
- 'Chronicles of Terror' testimony database[1322]

# Responsibility for the Holocaust

> **Part of a series on**
> **The Holocaust**
>
> Jews on selection ramp at Auschwitz, May 1944
>
> - v
> - t
> - e[1323]

**Responsibility for the Holocaust** is the subject of an ongoing historical debate that has spanned several decades. The debate about the origins of the Holocaust is known as functionalism versus intentionalism. Intentionalists such as Lucy Dawidowicz argue that Adolf Hitler planned the extermination of the Jewish people as early as 1918, and that he personally oversaw its execution. However, Functionalists such as Raul Hilberg argue that the extermination plans evolved in stages, as a result of initiatives by bureaucrats who were responding to other policy failures. The debate has settled to a large degree as historians have conceded that both positions have merit.

The primary responsibility for the Holocaust rests on Hitler, and the Nazi Party leadership, but initiatives to persecute Jews, Gypsies, and others were also perpetrated by the *Schutzstaffel* (SS), the German military, ordinary German citizens, as well as by collaborationist members of various European governments, including their military personnel and civilians alike. A host of factors contributed to the environment under which atrocities were committed across the continent, ranging from general racism (including anti-semitism), religious hatred, blind obedience, political opportunism, coercion, profiteering, and xenophobia.

## Historical and philosophical interpretations

The enormity of the Holocaust has prompted much analysis. The Holocaust has been characterized as a project of industrial extermination.[1324] This led authors such as Enzo Traverso to argue in *The Origins of Nazi Violence* that Auschwitz was explicitly a product of Western civilization originating from medieval religious and racial persecution that brought together a "particular kind of stigmatization...rethought in the light of colonial wars and genocides."[1325,1326] Beginning his book with a description of the guillotine, which according to him marks the entry of the Industrial Revolution into capital punishment, he writes: "Through an irony of history, the theories of Frederick Taylor" (taylorism) were applied by a totalitarian system to serve "not production, but extermination."[1327,1328]

Others like Russell Jacoby contend that the Holocaust is a product of German history with deep roots in German society ranging from, "German authoritarianism, feeble liberalism, brash nationalism or virulent anti-Semitism. From A. J. P. Taylor's *The Course of German History* fifty-five years ago to Daniel Goldhagen's controversial work, *Hitler's Willing Executioners*, Nazism is understood as the outcome of a long history of uniquely German traits".[1329] While some claim that the specificity of the Holocaust was also rooted in the constant antisemitism from which Jews had been the target since the foundation of Christianity, intellectual historian George Mosse argued that the extreme form of European racism that led to the Holocaust fully emerged in the eighteenth century.[1330] Others argue that pseudo-scientific racist theories were elaborated upon in order to justify white supremacy, and that they were accompanied by the Darwinian belief in the survival of the fittest and eugenic notions of racial hygiene—particularly within the German scientific community.[1331,1332,1333]

## Authorization

The question of overall responsibility for the atrocities committed under the Nazi regime traverses the oligarchy of those in command, foremost among them Adolf Hitler. In October 1939, he authorized the first Nazi mass killing for those labeled "undesirables" in the T-4 Euthanasia Program.[1334,1335] The Nazis termed such people as being "Lives unworthy of life." or *lebensunwertes Leben* in German.[1336] Before the euthanasia program in Germany-proper was over, the Nazis killed between 65,000–70,000 persons.[1337] Historian Henry Friedlander calls this period during which the 70,000 adults were killed, the "first phase" of the T4 Program since the program and its contributors precipitated the Holocaust.[1338] Sometime between late June 1940 when planning for Operation Barbarossa first started and March 1941, orders were approved by Hitler for the re-establishment of the *Einsatzgruppen* (the surviving historical record does not permit firm conclusions to be drawn about the precise date).[1339] Hitler encouraged the killings of the Jews of Eastern Europe by the *Einsatzgruppen* death squads in a speech of July 1941.[1340] Evidence suggests that in the fall of 1941, *Reichsführer-SS* Heinrich Himmler and Hitler agreed in principle on the complete mass extermination of the Jews of Europe by gassing, with Hitler explicitly ordering the "annihilation of the Jews" in a speech on 12 December 1941, by which time the Jewish populations in the Baltic states had been effectively eliminated.[1341] To make for smoother intra-governmental cooperation in the implementation of this so-called "Final Solution to the Jewish Question", the Wannsee conference was held near Berlin on 20 January 1942, with the participation of fifteen senior officials, led by Reinhard Heydrich and Adolf Eichmann; the records of which provide the best evidence of the central planning of the Holocaust. Just five weeks later on 22 February, Hitler was recorded saying to his closest associates: "We shall regain our health only by eliminating the Jew."[1342]

## Allied knowledge of the atrocities

Upwards of three-hundred Jewish organizations attempted to provide information to U.S. President Franklin Roosevelt about the persecution of Jews in Europe, but the ethnic and cultural diversity of American immigrant Jewish communities and their comparative lack of political power in the U.S. hindered their ability to influence policy.[1343] Various strategies, such as ransoming Jews following the Anschluss of 1938, failed for a host of reasons, not to exclude the unwillingness and inability of Jewish communities in the U.S. to extend financial aid to their suffering brethren.[1344] Clear evidence exists that Winston Churchill was privy to intelligence reports derived from decoded German transmissions in August 1941, during which he stated:

<templatestyles src="Template:Quote/styles.css"/>

> *Whole districts are being exterminated. Scores of thousands – literally scores of thousands – of executions in cold blood are being perpetrated by the German police-troops upon the Russian patriots who defend their native soil. Since the Mongol invasions of Europe in the sixteenth century,*

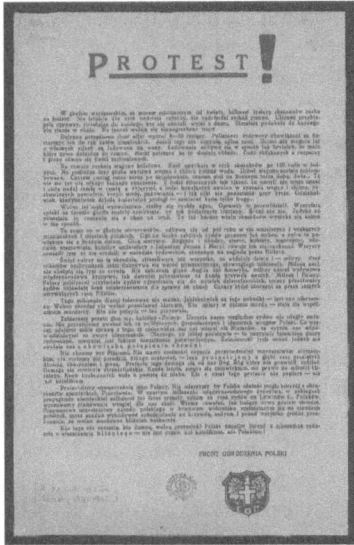

**Figure 173:** *Protest! against killing Jews in Poland of Kossak-Szczucka printed in occupied Poland - 28 August 1942.*

*there has never been methodical, merciless butchery on such a scale, or approaching such a scale.*
—*Winston Churchill, 24 August 1941.*[1345]

During the early years of the war, the Polish government-in-exile published documents and organised meetings to spread word about the fate of the Jews (see Witold Pilecki's Report). In the summer of 1942, a Jewish labor organization (the Bund) leader, Leon Feiner got word to London that 700,000 Polish Jews had already died. The *Daily Telegraph* published it on 25 June 1942,[1346] and the BBC took the story seriously, though the U.S. State Department doubted it.[1347]

On 10 August 1942, the Riegner Telegram to New York described the Nazi plan to murder all the Jews in the occupied states by deporting them to concentration camps in the east, to be exterminated in one blow, possibly by prussic acid, starting at autumn 1942. It was released in the United States by Stephen Wise of the World Jewish Congress in November 1942 after a long wait for permission from the government.[1348] This led to attempts by Jewish organizations to put President Roosevelt under pressure to act on behalf of the European Jews, many of whom had tried in vain to enter either Britain or the U.S.[1349]

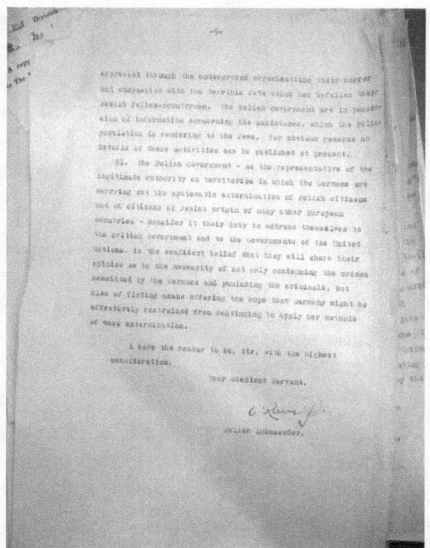

**Figure 174:** *Last page of "Raczyński's Note" - official note of Polish government-in-exile to Anthony Eden 10 December 1942.*

Reports were also coming into Palestine about the German atrocities during the autumn of 1942.[1350] The allies received a detailed eyewitness account from Polish resistance fighter and later Georgetown University professor, Jan Karski. On 10 December 1942, the Polish government-in-exile published a 16-page report addressed to the Allied governments, titled *The Mass Extermination of Jews in German Occupied Poland*.[1351]

On 17 December 1942, as the answer to Raczyński's Note, the Allies issued the *Joint Declaration by Members of the United Nations*, a formal declaration confirming and condemning Nazi extermination policy toward the Jews and describing the ongoing events of the Holocaust in Nazi-occupied Europe.[1352] The statement was read to British House of Commons in a floor speech by Foreign secretary Anthony Eden.[1353]

The death camps were discussed between American and British leaders at the Bermuda Conference in April 1943.[1354] On 12 May 1943, Polish government-in-exile member and Bund leader Szmul Zygielbojm committed suicide in London to protest the inaction of the world with regard to the Holocaust,[1355] stating in part in his suicide letter:

<templatestyles src="Template:Quote/styles.css"/>

*I cannot continue to live and to be silent while the remnants of Polish Jewry, whose representative I am, are being killed. My comrades in the Warsaw ghetto fell with arms in their hands in the last heroic battle. I was not permitted to fall like them, together with them, but I belong with them, to their mass grave. By my death, I wish to give expression to my most profound protest against the inaction in which the world watches and permits the destruction of the Jewish people.*[1356]

The large camps near Auschwitz were finally surveyed by plane in April 1944. While all important German cities and production centers were bombed by Allied forces until the end of the war, no attempt was made to interdict the system of mass annihilation by destroying pertinent structures or train tracks, even though Churchill was a proponent of bombing parts of the Auschwitz complex. The US State Department was aware of the use and the location of the gas chambers of extermination camps, but refused to bomb them.[1357,1358] Throughout the war, Britain pressed European leaders to prevent "illegal" Jewish immigration and sent ships to block the sea-route to Palestine (from which Britain withdrew in 1948), turning back many refugees.[1359]

## The German people

Debate continues on how much average Germans knew about the Holocaust. Robert Gellately, a historian at Oxford University, conducted a widely respected survey of the German media before and during the war and concluded that there was substantial participation and consent from large numbers of ordinary Germans in various aspects of the Holocaust, that German civilians frequently saw columns of slave laborers, and that the basics of the concentration camps, if not the extermination camps, were widely known.[1360] The German scholar, Peter Longerich, in a study looking at what Germans knew about the mass murders concluded that: "General information concerning the mass murder of Jews was widespread in the German population."[1361]

The British Historian Nicholas Stargardt presents evidence of widespread knowledge, agreement and collusion in the destruction of European Jewry, as well of the insane, feeble, disabled, Poles, Roma and other nationals.[1362] His evidence includes speeches by Nazi leaders,[1363] which were broadcast or heard by a wide audience that included mention or inferences concerning the plans to destroy the Jews, along with letters written between soldiers and their families describing the slaughter.[1364] Historian Claudia Koonz relates how reports of the SD described public opinion as favorable where it concerned the killing of Jews;[1365] one must take into consideration the possible extent to which SD reports were evaluated and/or manipulated by the Nazi propaganda machine however.[1366]

The earliest systematic studies relied on reports of the Nazi security services. The historian Lawrence D. Stokes concluded that much, although not all, of the terror inflicted on the Jewish people was generally understood in the German public. Marliss Steinert came to an opposite conclusion through his own studies, contending that only a few were aware of the immense scale of the atrocities.[1367,1368] </ref>

Historians Eric Johnson and Karl-Heinz Reuband conducted interviews with more than 3,000 Germans and 500 German Jews about daily life in the Third Reich. From the Jewish questionnaires, the authors found that German society was not nearly as rife with anti-Semitism as one might otherwise have believed, but this changed dramatically with Hitler's ascension to power.[1369] German Jews claimed that they knew of the Holocaust from a wide range of sources, which included radio broadcasts from Italy and what they heard from friends or acquaintances, but they did not know details until 1943.[1370] Responses from non-Jewish Germans indicate that "the majority of Germans identified with the Nazi regime."[1371] Contrary to many other accounts and/or historical interpretations, which portray rule under the Nazis as terrifying for German citizens, most of the German respondents who participated in the interviews stated that they never really feared arrest from the Gestapo.[1371,1372]</ref> Concerning the mass murder of the Jews, the survey results were contingent to some degree on geography, but roughly 27–29% of Germans had information about the Holocaust at some point before the war's end, and another 10–13% suspected something terrible was happening all along. Based on this information, Johnson and Reuband surmise that one-in-three Germans either heard or knew that the Holocaust was taking place before the end of the war from sources which included family members, friends, neighbors or professional colleagues.[1373] Johnson suggests (in disagreement with his co-author) that it is more likely that about 50% of the German population were aware of the atrocities being committed against the Jewish people and other enemies identified by the Nazi regime.[1374]

During the years 1945 through 1949, polls indicated that a majority of Germans felt that Nazism was a "good idea, badly applied". In a poll conducted in the American German occupation zone, 37% replied that 'the extermination of the Jews and Poles and other non-Aryans was necessary for the security of Germans'.[1375,1376] Sarah Ann Gordon in *Hitler, Germans, and the Jewish Question* notes that the surveys are very difficult to draw conclusions from as respondents were given only three options from which to choose: (1) Hitler was right in his treatment of the Jews, to which 0% agreed; (2) Hitler went too far in his treatment of the Jews, but something had to be done to keep them in bounds - 19% agreed; and (3) The actions against the Jews were in no way justified - 77% agreed. She also noted that another revealing example emerges from the question whether an Aryan who marries a Jew should be condemned, a question to which 91% of the respondents answered "No". To the question: "All those who ordered the murder of civilians or participated in the murders should be made to stand trial", 94% responded "Yes".[1377] Historian Tony Judt highlights how denazification and the subsequent fear of retribution from the Allies likely obscured justice due to some of the perpetrators and camouflaged underlying societal truths.[1378]

Public recollection from Germans about the atrocities was also "marginalized by postwar reconstruction and diplomacy" according to historian Nicholas Wachsmann; a delay, which obscured the complexities of understanding both the Holocaust and the concentration camps that aided in its facilitation.[1379] Wachsmann notes how the German people often claimed that the crimes occurred behind their backs and were perpetrated by Nazi fanatics, or that they frequently dodged responsibility by equating their suffering with that of the prisoners, avowing they too had been victimized by the National Socialist regime.[1380] Initially the memory of the Holocaust was repressed and set aside, but eventually the young Federal Republic of Germany commenced its own investigations and trials.[1381] Political pressure on the prosecutors and judges tempered any extensive probes and very few systematic investigations in the first decade after the war took place.[1382] Later research efforts in Germany revealed that there were a "myriad" of links between the wider population and the SS camps.[1383] In Austria—once part of the Greater German Reich of the Nazis—the situation was much different, as they conveniently evaded accountability through the trope of being the Nazi's first foreign victim.[1384]

## Implementation

During the perpetration of the Holocaust, participants came from all over Europe but the impetus for the pogroms was provided by German and Austrian Nazis. According to Holocaust historian, Raul Hilberg, the "anti-Jewish work" of the regime was "carried out in the civil service, the military, business, and the party" where "every specialization was utilized" and "every stratum of society was represented in the envelopment of the victims."[1385] Sobibor death camp guard Werner Debois stated:

<templatestyles src="Template:Quote/styles.css"/>

> *I am clear about the fact that annihilation camps were used for murder. What I did was aiding in murder. If I should be sentenced, I would consider that correct. Murder is murder. In weighing the guilt, one should not in my opinion consider the specific function in the camp. Wherever we were posted there: we were all equally guilty. The camp functioned in a chain of functions. If only one element in that chain is missing, the entire enterprise comes to a stop.*[1386]

In an entry in the Friedrich Kellner diary, "My Opposition", dated 28 October 1941, the German justice inspector recorded a conversation he had in Laubach with a German soldier who had witnessed a massacre in Poland.[1387,1388]</ref> Nazi bankers at the Paris branch of Barclays Bank volunteered the names of their Jewish employees to Nazi authorities, and many of them ended up in the death camps.[1389] An insightful perspective is provided by Konnilyn G. Feig, who wrote:

<templatestyles src="Template:Quote/styles.css"/>

> *Hitler exterminated the Jews of Europe. But he did not do so alone. The task was so enormous, complex, time-consuming, and mentally and economically demanding that it took the best efforts of millions of Germans... All spheres of life in Germany actively participated: Businessmen, policemen, bankers, doctors, lawyers, soldiers, railroad and factory workers, chemists, pharmacists, foremen, production managers, economists, manufacturers, jewelers, diplomats, civil servants, propagandists, film makers and film stars, professors, teachers, politicians, mayors, party members, construction experts, art dealers, architects, landlords, janitors, truck drivers, clerks, industrialists, scientists, generals, and even shopkeepers—all were essential cogs in the machinery that accomplished the final solution.*[1390]

Additional scholars also point out that a wide range of German soldiers, officials, and civilians were in some way involved in the Holocaust, from clerks and officials in the government to units of the army, police, and the SS.[1391,1392] Many ministries, including those of armaments, interior, justice, railroads, and foreign affairs, had substantial roles in orchestrating the Holocaust; similarly, German physicians participated in medical experiments and the T-4 euthanasia program as did civil servants;[1393] German physicians also made the selections as to who was fit to work and who would die at the concentration camps.[1394] Though there was no single department in charge of the Holocaust, the SS and Waffen-SS under Himmler had a leading role and operated with military efficiency in killing enemies of the Nazi state. From the SS came the *SS-Totenkopfverbände* concentration camp guard units, the *Einsatzgruppen* killing squads, and the main administrative offices behind the Holocaust, including the RSHA and WVHA.[1395,1396] The regular army participated in the atrocities along with the SS on some occasions by taking part in the massacre of Jews in the Soviet Union, Serbia, Poland, and Greece. The German Army also logistically supported the *Einsatzgruppen*, helped form the ghettos, ran prison camps, occasionally provided concentration camp guards, transported prisoners to camps, had medical experiments performed on prisoners, and substantially used slave labor.[1397] Significant numbers of Wehrmacht soldiers accompanied the SS in their macabre tasks or provided other forms of support for killing operations.[1398] The killings by the *Einsatzgruppen* required cooperation between the *Einsatzgruppen* chief and Wehrmacht unit commander so they could coordinate and control access to and from the execution grounds.[1399]

## Obedience

Stanley Milgram was one of a number of post-war psychologists and sociologists who tried to address why people obeyed immoral orders in the Holocaust. Milgram's findings demonstrated that reasonable people, when instructed by a person in a position of authority, obeyed commands entailing what they believed to be the suffering of others. After making his results public, Milgram sparked direct critical response in the scientific community by claiming that "a common psychological process is centrally involved in both" his laboratory experiments and the Holocaust. Professor James Waller, Chair of Holocaust and Genocide Studies at Keene State College, formerly Chair of Whitworth College Psychology Department, expressed the opinion that Milgram experiments "do not correspond well" to the Holocaust events:[1400]

1. The subjects of Milgram's experiments were assured in advance that "no permanent physical damage would result from their actions." However, the Holocaust perpetrators were fully aware of their hands-on killing and maiming of the victims.
2. Milgram's guards did not know their victims and were not motivated by racism. On the other hand, the Holocaust perpetrators displayed an "intense devaluation of the victims" through a lifetime of personal development.
3. The subjects were not selected for sadism or loyalty to Nazi ideology, and often "exhibited great anguish and conflict" in the experiment, unlike the designers and executioners of the Final Solution (see Holocaust trials), who had a clear "goal" on their hands, set beforehand.
4. The experiment lasted for an hour, insufficient time for participants to consider the moral implications of their actions. Meanwhile, the Holocaust lasted for years with ample time for a moral assessment of all individuals and organizations involved.[1401]

In the opinion of Thomas Blass—who is the author of a scholarly monograph on the experiment (*The Man Who Shocked The World*) published in 2004—the historical evidence pertaining to actions of the Holocaust perpetrators speaks louder than words:

<templatestyles src="Template:Quote/styles.css"/>

*My own view is that Milgram's approach does not provide a fully adequate explanation of the Holocaust. While it may well account for the dutiful destructiveness of the dispassionate bureaucrat who may have shipped Jews to Auschwitz with the same degree of routinization as potatoes to Bremerhaven, it falls short when one tries to apply it to the more zealous, inventive, and hate-driven atrocities that also characterized the Holocaust.*[1402]

## Religious hatred and racism

Throughout the Middle Ages in Europe, Jews were subjected to antisemitism based on Christian theology, which blamed them for rejecting and killing Jesus.[1403] Numerous attempts were made by early Christians to convert the Jews to Christianity in the collective, but when they refused, this made them into a "pariah" to many Europeans.[1404] The consequences for this resistance to Christianity were varied. There were an extensive series of attacks against Jews during the religious fervor accompanying the First and Second Crusades (1095–1149).[1404] Jews were slaughtered in the wake of the Italian famine (1315–1317), attacked following the outbreak of the Black Death in the Rhineland in 1347, expelled from both England and Italy in the 1290s, from France in 1306 and 1394, from Spain and Portugal in 1492 and 1497.[1405] By the time of the Reformation in the 16th century, historian Peter Hayes stresses that "hatred of Jews was widespread" throughout Europe.[1406]

Martin Luther (a German leader of the Protestant Reformation) made a specific written call for harsh persecution of the Jewish people in *On the Jews and Their Lies*, published in 1543. In it, he urged that Jewish synagogues and schools be set on fire, prayer books destroyed, rabbis forbidden to preach, homes razed, and property and money confiscated.[1407] Luther argued that Jews should be shown no mercy or kindness, should have no legal protection, and that these "poisonous envenomed worms" should be drafted into forced labor or expelled for all time.[1408] American historian Lucy Dawidowicz asserted in her book *The War Against the Jews* that a clear path of anti-Semitism passes from Luther to Hitler and that "modern German anti-Semitism is the bastard child of Christian anti-Semitism and German nationalism."[1409] Even after the Reformation, Catholics and Lutherans continued to persecute Jews, accusing them of blood libels and subjecting them to pogroms and expulsions.[1410,1411] The second half of the 19th century saw the emergence of the *Völkisch* movement in Germany and Austria-Hungary, which was developed and incentivized by authors like Houston Stewart Chamberlain and Paul de Lagarde. The movement presented a pseudo-scientific, biologically based form of racism that viewed Jews as a race whose members were locked in mortal combat with the Aryan race for world domination.[1412]

**Figure 175:** *Bones of murdered prisoners in the crematoria in the German concentration camp at Weimar, Germany. Photo taken by the 3rd U.S. Army, 14 April 1945*

Some authors, such as liberal philosopher Hannah Arendt in *The Origins of Totalitarianism* (1951),[1413] Swedish writer Sven Lindqvist, historian Hajo Holborn, and Ugandan academic, Mahmood Mandani, have also linked the Holocaust to colonialism, but moreover, place the tragedy into the context of the European tradition of anti-Semitism and the genocide of colonized peoples.[1414] Arendt claimed for instance that nationalism and imperialism were literally bridged together by racism.[1415] Pseudo-scientific theories elaborated upon during the 19th century (e.g. Arthur de Gobineau's 1853 *Essay on the Inequality of the Human Races*) were fundamental in preparing the conditions for the Holocaust according to some scholars.[1416] While other historical incidences of wholesale slaughter exist, there are still scholars who remain adamant about the "uniqueness" of the Holocaust, as compared to other genocides.[1417] Philosopher Michel Foucault also traced the origins of the Holocaust to "racial policies" and "state racism", which are subsumed within the framework of "biopolitics".[1418]

The Nazis considered it their duty to overcome natural compassion and execute orders for what they believed to be higher ideals; members of the SS in particular, perceived that they had a state-legitimized mandate and obligation to eliminate those perceived as racial enemies.[1419] Crowd psychology has been attributed to some of the heinous acts committed by the Nazis and Gustave Le Bon's *The Crowd: A Study of the Popular Mind* (1895) provided influence to Hitler's infamous tome, *Mein Kampf*,[1420] Le Bon claimed that Hitler and the Nazis used propaganda to deliberately shape group-think and related behaviors, especially in cases where people committed otherwise aberrant violent acts due to the anonymity resultant from being a member of the collective.[1421] Sadistic acts of this sort were notable in the case of the genocide committed by members of the Croatian Ustashe, whose enthusiasm and sadism in their killings of Serbs appalled the Italians and Germans to the point that the German Army field police "moved in and disarmed them" at one point.[1422] One might describe the behavior of the Croatians as a sort of quasi-religious eliminationist opportunism, but this same thing might be said of the Germans, whose anti-Semitism was likewise religious and racialist in nomenclature.[1423]

A controversy erupted in 1997 when historian Daniel Goldhagen argued in *Hitler's Willing Executioners* that ordinary Germans were knowing and willing participants in the Holocaust, which he writes, had its roots in a deep racially motivated eliminationist antisemitism that was uniquely manifested in German society.[1424] Historians who disagree with Goldhagen's thesis argue that, while antisemitism undeniably existed in Germany, Goldhagen's idea of a uniquely German "eliminationist" version is untenable.[1425]

## Functionalism versus intentionalism

A major issue in contemporary Holocaust studies is the question of *functionalism* versus *intentionalism*. The terms were coined during the Cumberland Lodge Conference of May 1979 entitled, "The National Socialist Regime and German Society" by British Marxist historian Timothy Mason to describe two schools of thought about the origins of the Holocaust.[1426]

Intentionalists hold that the Holocaust was the result of a long-term masterplan on the part of Hitler, and that he was the driving force behind it.[1427] Functionalists hold that Hitler was antisemitic, but that he did not have a masterplan for genocide. They see the Holocaust as coming from the ranks of the German bureaucracy, with little or no involvement on the part of Hitler.[1428] Within the content of Hitler biographies written by Joachim Fest and Alan Bullock, one encounters a "Hitler-centric explanation of genocide" even though other psycho-historians like Rudolph Binion, Walter Langer, and Robert Waite raised issues about Hitler's ability to make rational decisions; his anti-Semitism remained nonetheless unquestioned, the latter authors merely juxtaposed it against his general mental health.[1429]

Historian and intentionalist Lucy Dawidowicz argues that the Holocaust was planned by Hitler from the very beginning of his political career, traceable

**Figure 176:** *Frontispiece of the Nuremberg's 1940 copy of Mein Kampf*

back to his traumatic experience at the end of the First World War.[1430] Other intentionalists, such as Andreas Hillgruber, Karl Dietrich Bracher, and Klaus Hildebrand, have suggested that Hitler had decided upon the Holocaust sometime in the early 1920s.[1431] Historian Eberhard Jäckel postulates that the extermination order placed upon the Jews may have occurred during the summer of 1940.[1432] Another intentionalist historian, the American Arno J. Mayer, argued that Hitler first ordered the mass murder of the Jews in December 1941, due principally to the failed Blitzkrieg against the Soviet Union.[1433] Saul Friedländer has argued that Hitler was an extreme anti-Semite early on and drove Nazi policy to exterminate the Jews, but he also recognizes the technocratic rationality of the regime that helped bring Hitler's ideological goals to fruition.[1434] While others, like Gerhard Weinberg, remain in the intentionalist camp and see Hitler's part as essential to the unfolding of the Final Solution—he also points out the importance of Nazi ideological imperatives such as the Wannsee Conference, and like many scholars, demonstrates that there is still "much to be discovered and learned."[1435]

Functionalists such as Hans Mommsen, Martin Broszat, Götz Aly, Raul Hilberg, and Christopher Browning hold that the Holocaust was started in 1941–1942 either as a result of the failure of the Nazi deportation policy and/or the impending military losses in Russia.[1436] Functionalists contend that what some see as extermination fantasies outlined in Hitler's *Mein Kampf* and other

Nazi literature were simply propaganda and did not constitute concrete plans. In *Mein Kampf*, Hitler repeatedly states his inexorable hatred of the Jewish people, but nowhere does he proclaim his intention to exterminate them. They also argue that, in the 1930s, Nazi policy aimed at making life so unpleasant for German Jews that they would leave Germany.[1437] Adolf Eichmann was in charge of facilitating Jewish emigration by whatever means possible from 1937[1438] until 23 October 1941, when German Jews were forbidden to leave.[1439] Functionalists see the SS's support in the late 1930s for Zionist groups as the preferred solution to the "Jewish Question" as another sign that there was no master-plan for genocide. Essentially the view of functionalists concerning the Holocaust is that it came about via improvisation as opposed to deliberate planning.[1440]

To that end, functionalists argue that, in German documents from 1939 to 1941, the term "Final Solution to the Jewish Question" was meant to be a "territorial solution"; that is, the entire Jewish population was to be expelled somewhere far from Germany.[1441] At first, the SS planned to create a gigantic Jewish reservation in the Lublin, Poland area, but the so-called "Lublin Plan" was vetoed by Hans Frank, the Governor-General of occupied Poland, who refused to allow the SS to ship any more Jews to the Lublin area after November 1939. The reason Frank vetoed the "Lublin Plan" was not due to any humane motives, but rather because he was opposed to the SS "dumping" Jews into the Government-General.[1442] In 1940, the SS and the German Foreign Office had the so-called "Madagascar Plan" to deport the entire Jewish population of Europe to a "reservation" on Madagascar.[1443] The "Madagascar Plan" was canceled because Germany could not defeat the UK and until the British blockade was broken, the "Madagascar Plan" could not be put into effect.[1444] Finally, functionalist historians have made much of a memorandum written by Himmler in May 1940 explicitly rejecting extermination of the entire peoples as "un-German" and recommending to Hitler instead, the "Madagascar Plan" as the preferred "territorial solution" to the "Jewish Question".[1445,1446] Not until July 1941 did the term "Final Solution to the Jewish Question" come to mean extermination.[1447]

Recently, a synthesis of the two schools has emerged that has been championed by diverse historians such as the Canadian historian Michael Marrus, the Israeli historian Yehuda Bauer, and the British historian Ian Kershaw that contends Hitler was the driving force behind the Holocaust, but that he did not have a long-term plan and that much of the initiative for the Holocaust came from below in an effort to meet Hitler's perceived wishes. As historian Omer Bartov relates, "the "intentionalists" and "functionalists" have gradually come closer, as further research now seems to indicate that the more extreme new interpretations are just as impossible to sustain as the traditional ones."[1448]

# Involved

## Hitler

Most historians take the view that Hitler was the opposite of a pragmatist: his overriding obsession was hatred of the Jews, and he showed on a number of occasions that he was willing to risk losing the war to achieve their destruction. There is no "smoking gun" in the form of a document which shows Hitler ordering the Final Solution. Hitler did not have a bureaucratic mind and many of his most important instructions were given orally.[1449] There is ample documentary evidence however, that Hitler desired to eradicate Jewry and that the order to do so originated from him, including the authorization for mass deportations of the Jews to the east beginning in October 1941.[1450] He cannot have imagined that these hundreds of thousands of Jews would be housed, clothed, and fed by the authorities of the Government-General, and in fact Hans Frank frequently complained that he could not cope with the influx.[1451,1452]

Historian Paul Johnson writes that some writers, such as David Irving, have claimed that because there were no written orders, "the Final Solution was Himmler's work and [...] Hitler not only did not order it but did not even know it was happening." Johnson states, however, that "this argument will not stand up. The administration of the Third Reich was often chaotic but its central principle was clear enough: all key decisions emanated from Hitler."[1449]

According to Kershaw, "Hitler's authority – most probably given as verbal consent to propositions usually put to him by Himmler – stood behind every decision of magnitude and significance."[1453] Hitler continued to be closely involved in the "Final Solution."[1454] Kershaw also points out that, "in the wake of the German military crisis following the catastrophe at Stalingrad" that "Hitler took a direct hand" in convincing his Hungarian and Romanian allies "sharpen the persecution" of the Jews.[1455] Hitler's role in the Final Solution was often indirect rather than overt, frequently granting approval rather than initiating. The unparalleled outpourings of hatred were a constant even amid all the policy shifts of the Nazis. They often had a propaganda or mobilizing motive, and usually remained generalized. Even so, Kershaw remains adamant that Hitler's role was decisive and indispensable in the unfolding of the "Final Solution."[1456]

In a letter dated 1919 Hitler mentions that part of the ultimate aim of a strong national government must "unshakably be the removal of the Jews".[1457,1458]

In 1922 Hitler told Major Josef Hell (a journalist at the time):

<templatestyles src="Template:Quote/styles.css"/>

> *Once I really am in power, my first and foremost task will be the annihilation of the Jews. As soon as I have the power to do so, I will have gallows*

*built in rows—at the Marienplatz in Munich, for example—as many as traffic allows. Then the Jews will be hanged indiscriminately, and they will remain hanging until they stink; they will hang there as long as the principles of hygiene permit. As soon as they have been untied, the next batch will be strung up, and so on down the line, until the last Jew in Munich has been exterminated. Other cities will follow suit, precisely in this fashion, until all Germany has been completely cleansed of Jews.*[1459]

On 21 January 1939 Hitler spoke with František Chvalkovský and said:

<templatestyles src="Template:Quote/styles.css"/>

*We are going to destroy the Jews. They are not going to get away with what they did on 9 November 1918. The day of reckoning has come.*[1460]

On 30 January at the Sports Palace in Berlin, Hitler told the crowd:

<templatestyles src="Template:Quote/styles.css"/>

*And we say that the war will not end as the Jews imagine it will, namely with the uprooting of the Aryans, but the result of this war will be the complete annihilation of the Jews.*[1461]

In Mein Kampf, Hitler argued that a war against Jews would have saved Germany from losing World War I.[1462]

<templatestyles src="Template:Quote/styles.css"/>

*If at the beginning of the war and during the war twelve or fifteen thousand of these Hebrew corrupters of the people had been held under poison gas, as happened to hundreds of thousands of our very best German workers in the field, the sacrifice of millions at the front would not have been in vain.*[1463]

In the following widely cited speech made on 30 January 1939, Hitler says to the Reichstag:

<templatestyles src="Template:Quote/styles.css"/>

*I want to be a prophet again today: if international finance Jewry in Europe and beyond should succeed once more in plunging the peoples into a world war, then the result will be not the Bolshevization of the earth and thus the victory of Jewry, but the annihilation of the Jewish race in Europe.*[1464]

According to historian Klaus Hildebrand, moral responsibility for the Holocaust resides with Hitler and was nothing less than the culmination of his pathological hatred of the Jews, which for all intents and purposes formed the basis of Nazi genocide and drove the regime to pursue its racial-eliminationist goals.[1465] Whether or not Hitler never gave a direct order for the implementation of the Final Solution is immaterial and nothing more than a "red herring", which fails to recognize Hitler's leadership style, particularly since his verbal commands were sufficient to launch initiatives—due largely to the fact that his subordinates were always "working towards the Führer" in an effort to implement "his totalitarian vision" even in cases "without written authority."[1466] Throughout Gerald Fleming's notable work, *Hitler and the Final Solution*, he demonstrates that on numerous occasions, Himmler mentioned a "Führer-Order" concerning the annihilation of the Jews, which indicates that at the very least, Hitler verbally issued a command on the subject.[1467]

Journal entries from Propaganda Minister Joseph Goebbels support the position that Hitler was the driving force behind the destruction of the Jews as well; Goebbels wrote that Hitler followed the subject closely and described the Führer as "uncompromising" about eliminating the Jews.[1468] As historian David Welch asserts, if one takes the scale of the logistical operations that the Holocaust comprised (in the middle of a worldwide war) into consideration alone, it is nearly impossible that the extermination of so many people and the coordination of such an extensive effort could have occurred without Hitler's authorization.[1469]

## Other Nazi leaders

While significant numbers of Germans and other Europeans collectively participated in the Holocaust, it was Hitler and his Nazi paladins who share the greatest responsibility for incentivizing, coercing, and/or overseeing the extermination of millions of people.[1470] Among those most responsible for the Final Solution were Heinrich Himmler, Reinhard Heydrich, Odilo Globocnik, Ernst Kaltenbrunner, Adolf Eichmann, Heinrich Müller, and Oswald Pohl. Key roles were also played by Fritz Sauckel, Hans Frank, Wilhelm Frick and Robert Ley.[1471]

Other top Nazi leaders such as Goebbels, Hermann Göring, and Martin Bormann contributed in various ways, whether administratively supporting killing efforts or providing ideological fodder to encourage the Holocaust.[1472] For example, Goebbels carried on an intensive antisemitic propaganda campaign and also had frequent discussions with Hitler about the fate of the Jews, when they met.[1473] He was aware throughout that the Jews were being exterminated, and completely supported this decision.[1474] In July 1941, Göring issued a memo to Heydrich ordering him to organise the practical details of a solution to the "Jewish Question". This led to the Wannsee Conference held on 20 January 1942, where Heydrich formally announced that genocide of the Jews of Europe was now official Reich policy.[1475] That same year, Bormann signed the decree of 9 October 1942 prescribing that the permanent Final Solution in

Greater Germany could no longer be solved by emigration, but only by the use of "ruthless force in the special camps of the East", that is, extermination in Nazi death camps.[1476]

Although the Nazi regime is often depicted as a super-centralized vertically hierarchical state, individual initiative was an important element in how Nazi Germany functioned.[1477] Millions of people were rounded up, bureaucratically processed and transported across Europe due to the vigorous initiative of those Nazis most committed to carrying out their duties to the state, an operation involving thousands of officials and a great deal of paperwork. This was a coordinated effort among the SS and its sprawling police apparatus with the Reich ministries and the national railways, all under the supervision of the Nazi Party.[1478] Most of the Party's regional leaders (*Gauleiters*) also knew of the Holocaust since many were present for Himmler's October 1943 speech at Posen, during which he explicitly mentioned the extermination of the Jews.[1479]

## The German military

The extent to which the officers of the regular German military knew of the Final Solution has been much debated. Political imperatives in postwar Germany led to the army being generally absolved from responsibility, apart from the handful of "Nazi generals" such as Alfred Jodl and Wilhelm Keitel who were tried and hanged at Nuremberg. There is an abundance of evidence, however, that the top officers of the Wehrmacht certainly knew about the killings and in a number of instances, approved and/or sanctioned them.[1480] The exhibit "War of Extermination: The Crimes of the Wehrmacht"[1481] showed the extent to which the military was involved in the Holocaust.[1482,1483]

It was particularly difficult for commanders on the eastern front to avoid knowing what was happening in the areas behind the front. Many individual soldiers photographed the massacres of Jews by the *Einsatzgruppen*.[1484] Some generals and officers, such as Walther von Reichenau, Erich Hoepner, and Erich von Manstein, actively supported the work of the *Einsatzgruppen*.[1485] A number of Wehrmacht units provided direct or indirect assistance to the *Einsatzgruppen*—all the while mentally normalizing amoral behaviors in the conduct of war through specious justification that they were destroying the Reich's enemies.[1486] Many individual soldiers who ventured to the killing sites behind the lines voluntarily participated in the mass shootings.[1487] Cooperation between the SS police units and Wehrmacht also occurred when they took hostages and carried out reprisals against partisans, particularly in the Eastern theater, where the war took on the complexion of a racial war as opposed to the conventional one being fought in the West.[1488]

Other front-line officers went through the war without coming into direct contact with the machinery of extermination, choosing to focus narrowly on their duties and not noticing the wider context of the war. On 20 July 1942, an extermination unit under the command of Walther Rauff was sent to Tobruk and assigned to the Afrika Korps led by Erwin Rommel. However, since Rommel was 500 km away at the First Battle of El Alamein, it is unlikely that the two were able to meet.[1489] The plans for *Einsatzgruppe* Egypt were set aside after the Allied victory at the Second Battle of El Alamein.[1490] Historian Jean-Christoph Caron opines that there is no evidence that Rommel knew of or would have supported Rauff's mission.[1491] Relations between some Army commanders and the SS were not friendly, as officers occasionally refused to co-operate with Himmler's forces; General Johannes Blaskowitz for instance, was relieved of his command after officially protesting about SS atrocities in Poland.[1492,1493] Such behaviors were uncommon however, as a significant portion of the German military acculturated to the norms of the Nazi regime and the SS in particular, and were likewise censurable for carrying out atrocities during the course of the Second World War.[1494]

## Other states

Although the Holocaust was planned and directed by Germans, the Nazi regime found willing collaborators in other countries, both those allied to Germany and those under German occupation and by 1942, the atrocities across the continent became a "pan-European program."[1495] The civil service and police of the Vichy regime in occupied France actively collaborated in persecuting French Jews.[1496] Germany's allies, Italy, Finland, Hungary, Romania, and Bulgaria, were all pressured to introduce anti-Jewish measures. Bulgaria refused to co-operate, and all 50,000 Bulgarian Jews survived (though most lost their possessions and many were imprisoned), but thousands of Greek and Yugoslavian Jews were deported from the Bulgarian-occupied territories.[1497] Finland officially refused to participate in the Holocaust and only 7 out of 300 Jewish alien refugees were turned over to the Germans.[1498] The Hungarian regime of Miklós Horthy also refused to cooperate until the German invasion of Hungary of 1944, after which its 750,000 Jews were no longer safe.[1499] Between May through July 1944, upwards of 437,000 Jews were deported from Hungary to Auschwitz.[1500] The Romanian regime of Ion Antonescu actively persecuted Jews, and while they were inefficient, 120,000 or more Jews were killed.[1501,1502] The German puppet regime in Croatia actively persecuted Jews on its own initiative.[1503,1504]

The Nazis sought to enlist support for their programs in all the countries they occupied, although their recruitment methods differed in various countries according to Nazi racial theories. In the "Nordic" countries of Denmark, Norway, Netherlands, and Estonia they tried to recruit young men into the Waffen-SS, with sufficient success to create the "Wiking" SS division on the Eastern

Front, many of whose members fought for Germany with great fanaticism until the end of the war.[1505] In Lithuania and Ukraine, on the other hand, they recruited large numbers of auxiliary troops that were used for anti-partisan work and guard duties at extermination and concentration camps.[1506]

In recent years, the extent of local collaboration with the Nazis in Eastern Europe has become more apparent. Historian Alan Bullock writes: "The opening of the archives both in the Soviet Union and in Eastern Europe has produced incontrovertible evidence [of] ... collaboration on a much bigger scale than hitherto realized of Ukrainians and Lithuanians as well as Hungarians, Croats and Slovaks in the deportation and murder of Jews."[1507] Historians have been examining the question whether it is fair to connote the Holocaust as a European Project. Historian Dieter Pohl has estimated that more than 200,000 non-Germans "prepared, carried out and assisted in acts of murder"; that is about the same number as Germans and Austrians.[1508] Such numbers have elicited a similar reaction from other historians; Götz Aly for instance, has come to the conclusion that the Holocaust was in fact a "European project."[1509] While the Holocaust was perpetrated at the urging of the Nazis and constituted part of the SS vision for a "pan-European racial community", the subsequent outbursts of anti-Semitic violence in Croatia, France, Romania, Slovakia, the Baltic states among others, make the catastrophe a "European project" according to historian Dan Stone.[1510]

**Belgium**

In Belgium the state has been accused of having actively collaborated with Nazi Germany. An official 2007 report commissioned by the Belgian senate concluded that the Belgians were indeed complicit for participating in the Holocaust. According to the report, the Belgian authorities "adopted a docile attitude providing collaboration unworthy of a democracy in its treatment of Jews."[1511] The report also identified three crucial moments that showed the attitude of Belgian authorities toward the Jews: (1) During the autumn of 1940 when they complied with the order of the German occupier to register all Jews even though it was contrary to the Belgium constitution; this led to a number of measures including the firing of all Jews from official positions in December 1940 and the expelling of all Jewish children from their schools in December 1941;[1512] (2) In summer 1942, when over one thousand Jews were deported to the death camps, particularly Auschwitz during the month of August. This was only the first of such actions as the deportations to the east continued resulting in the death of some 25,000 people;[1513] and (3) At the end of 1945, the Belgian state officials decided that its authorities bore no legal responsibility for the persecution of the Jews, even though many Belgian police officers participated in the rounding up and deportation of Jews.[1514]

However, collaboration is not the whole story. While there is little doubt that there were strong antisemitic feelings in Belgium, after November 1942, the German roundups became less successful as large-scale rescue operations were carried out by ordinary Belgians. This resulted in the survival of about 25,000 Jews from Belgium.[1515] Unlike other states, which were immediately annexed, Belgium was initially placed under German military administration, which the Belgian authorities exploited by refusing to carry out some of the Nazi directives against the Jews. Roughly 60 percent of Belgium's Jews, who were there at the start of the war, survived the Final Solution.[1516]

## Bulgaria

Bulgaria, mainly through the influence of the Bulgarian Orthodox Church, saved nearly all of its indigenous Jewish population from deportation and certain death. This is not to imply that Bulgaria was entirely blameless, as they passed specials laws to confiscate Jewish property and remove them from public service in early 1941.[1517] Once civil and military administration over parts of Northern Greece and Macedonia were turned over to Bulgaria by Germany, Bulgarian authorities deported Jews from those territories to concentration camps. Originally SS Captain Theodor Dannecker and the head of the Commissariat for Jewish Affairs, Alexander Belev, agreed to deport as many as 20,000 Jews from Macedonia and Thrace.[1518] These deportation were set to be completed by May 1943.[1519] Belev had agreed to these measures without the knowledge or approval from officials in the Bulgarian government, which sparked protests that reached the Bulgarian National Assembly in Sofia.[1520] Before the matter was over however, Bulgaria deported some 11,000 foreign Jews to Nazi-held territory.[1521] Once those Jews were handed over to the Germans, they were sent to the extermination camp at Treblinka where they perished.[1522]

## Channel Islands

Channel Islands police collaborated with the Nazis deporting local Jews, some of whom were sent to Auschwitz in 1942, others were deported in 1943 as retaliation for the British commando raid on the small Channel Island of Sark, when most of the Jews were shipped to internment camps in France and Germany.[1523] On the Channel Island of Alderney a labor camp for Jews was established, one which was notable for the brutality of the German guards; hundreds of Jews died there and 384 were buried within the camp itself, while many others were simply dumped into the sea.[1524] Some 250—mostly French—Jews perished on a ship headed from Germany to the Alderney camp when it was sunk by British warships on 4 July 1944.[1525]

## Croatia

Croatia was a satellite state created by the Germans and ruled by the vehemently racist head of the Ustasha,[1526] Ante Pavelić.[1527] As early as May 1941, the Croatian government forced all Jews to wear the yellow badge and by the summer of that same year, they had enacted laws excluding them from the economy and society.[1528,1529] The Croatian Ustaše regime killed thousands of people, the majority of whom were Serbs, (estimates vary widely, but most modern and qualified sources put the numbers around 45,000 to 52,000), about 12,000 to 20,000 Jews and 15,000 to 20,000 Roma,[1530] primarily in the Ustasha's Jasenovac concentration camp near Zagreb.[1531] Historians Donald Niewyk and Francis Nicosia provide higher estimates for the numbers killed, reporting the following ranges: 500,000 Serbs, 25,000 Gypsies, and 32,000 Jews; most of whom (75%) were murdered, not by the Nazis but the Croatians themselves.[1532,1533] According to the 2001 census in Croatia, only 495 Jews were listed of the 25,000 that had previously lived there before the Second World War, accounting for less than 1/10th of one-percent of Croatia's population.[1534]

## Denmark

Due in part to the fact that the Germans were dependent upon an "uninterrupted supply of Danish agricultural products to the Reich" they tolerated the status quo of 6,500 Jews living unmolested in Denmark.[1535] Disquiet with German policies and wishing for democracy, the Danes began demonstrating against the Germans, which incited a military response from the Nazis that included dismantling the Danish military forces and correspondingly placed Danish Jews at increased risk.[1536]

Most of the Danish Jews were rescued by the unwillingness of the Danish government and people to acquiesce to the demands of the occupying forces and through their concerted efforts to ferry Danish Jews to Sweden during October 1943.[1537] In total, this endeavor saved nearly 8,000 Jews from certain death; another 425 who were sent to Theresienstadt[1538] </ref> were also saved due to the determination of the Danes and returned to their homes following the war.[1539] About 1,500 of the roughly 8,000 Jews rescued by the Danes were recent refugees from Czechoslovakia, Austria, and Germany.[1540]

## Estonia

Prior to the Second World War, there were approximately 5,000 Estonian Jews.[1541] About 50% of Estonia's Jewish community, aware of the fate that otherwise awaited them following the Nazi invasion, managed to escape to the Soviet Union;[1542] virtually all those remaining were forced to wear badges identifying them as Jews, stripped of their property, and eventually killed by

*Einsatzgruppe A* and local collaborators before the end of 1941.[1543] With the invasion of the Baltics, the Nazi government found willing volunteers to assist the *Einsatzgruppen* and auxiliary police from this region, which incidentally enabled them carry-out mass genocide in this region.[1544] Right-wing Estonian units, known as the *Omakaitse* were among those who aided the *Einsatzgruppen* in killing Jews.[1545] At the Wannsee Conference in January 1942, Estonia was reported to be Jew-free.[1545] Jews from countries outside the Baltics were shipped there to be exterminated—as was the case for 7,130 Jews sent to Estonia in September 1943, where just a few months later, they were murdered.[1546] During the winter of 1941–1942, *Einsatzgruppe A* operating in *Ostland* and the Army Group Rear, reported having killed 2,000 Jews in Estonia.[1547] An estimated 20,000 Jews were sent to labor camps in Estonia from elsewhere in Eastern Europe.[1548]

### Finland

Despite being at times a co-belligerent of Nazi Germany, Finland remained independent and its leadership flatly refused to cooperate with Heinrich Himmler's request to relinquish its 2,000 Jews.[1498] Some Jews were even able to flee Nazi occupied Europe and make their way into Finland.[1549] Only seven of the 300 alien Jews living in Finland were turned over to the Germans.[1498] Even the deportation of a handful of Jews did not go unnoticed, as there were protests in Finland from members of its indigenous Social Democratic Party, by a number of Lutheran ministers, the Archbishop, and the Finnish Cabinet.[1550] Like Denmark, Finland was one of only two countries in the orbit of Nazi domination that refused to cooperate fully with Hitler's regime.[1551] These historical observations do not outright excuse the Finns entirely, as some scholars point out—in particular, the *Einsatzkommando Finnland* was formed during the joint invasion of the Soviet Union, which received collaboration from Finnish police units and Finnish military intelligence in capturing partisans, Jews, and Soviet POWs as part of their operations— exactly how many of each group remains unclear and is a subject needing further research according to historian Paul Lubotina.[1552]

### France

Anti-Semitism, as the Dreyfus Affair had shown at the end of the 19th century, was widespread in France, especially among anti-republican sympathizers.[1553] Long before the rise of the Nazis, anti-Semtism was so pronounced in France, that according to intellectual historian George Mosse, France seemed like it would be the country where racism might direct its political future.[1554] Before the onset of World War II, there were roughly 350,000 Jews residing in France with only 150,000 being native-born. Approximately 50,000 were refugees fleeing Germany, Austria, and Czechoslovakia, while another 25,000 came to

France from Belgium and Holland; the remaining Jews were arrivals to France in the 1920s and 30s from Eastern Europe.[1555]

Once the Germans invaded, many Jews fled away from the advancing forces but France's rapid collapse both militarily and politically, the armistice, and the speed at which everything happened trapped many of them in southern France.[1556] Philippe Pétain, who became the French premier after Paris had fallen to the German Army, arranged the surrender to Germany.[1557] He then became the head of the Vichy government, which collaborated with the Nazis, claiming that it would soften the hardships of occupation.[1558] Opposition to the German occupation of northern France and the collaborationist Vichy government was left to the French Resistance within France and the Free French Forces led by Charles de Gaulle outside France.[1559] German occupation was quickly accompanied by harsh treatment; Jews were expelled from Alsace Lorraine and their property was confiscated, whereas foreign Jews—around 32,000—were interned following a Vichy decree on 4 October 1940.[1560] Additional discriminatory measures soon followed and intensified after the Nazis issued an ordinance on 27 September 1940; these were carried out by the French administration and included: identification requirements for Jews, a census to account for all Jewish persons and businesses, expropriation and "Aryanization" of property, along with occupational restrictions and bans.[1560] On 7 October 1940, Pétain's government repealed the Crémieux Law, a move which deprived 117,000 French Jews of the civil rights they were granted in 1870.[1561]

By the end of 1940, more Jews were arrested in Vichy France than in the German occupied region of the country.[1562] Another 1,112 Jews were arrested during French round-ups in May and December 1941; later, when they were deported, they constituted some of the earliest arrivals to Auschwitz at the end of March 1942.[1563] Five-thousand additional Jews were sent from France to Auschwitz at the end of April and during June 1942.[1564] Chief of police for the Vichy government, René Bousquet, agreed to arrest foreign and stateless Jews in the unoccupied region of France starting in July 1942, and he acceded to availing French police to collaborate with arresting Jews in the occupied zone.[1565] Per agreement between the Vichy government and the Nazis, another 10,000 Jews were added to the total departing between 19 July and 7 August 1942.[1566] Some 2,000 Jewish children whose parents had already been shipped to Auschwitz were also sent to the camp during the period 17–26 August 1942, and by the end of the year the total figure of deportees from France reached 42,000 persons.[1567] From the first transport of March 1942 to the last one during July 1944, as many as 77,911 Jews were deported from France to Poland.[1568][1569] </ref> Most of the Jews in France were transported to Auschwitz, but some were sent to Majdanek and Sobibór with a few ending up at Buchenwald.[1570]

**Figure 177:** *Budapest, Hungary – Captured Jewish women in Wesselényi Street, 20–22 October 1944*

## Greece

The Jews of Greece mainly lived in the area around Thessaloniki, where a large and influential Sephardi community had lived since the 15th century, where some 55,000 Jews comprised nearly 20% of the city.[1571] Following the German invasion and occupation of Salonika in 1941, an antisemitic nationalist party called National Union of Greece (*Ethniki Enosis Ellados*, EEE), which had existed between 1927 and 1935, was revived by Nazi authorities.[1572,1573]

The Greek governor, Vasilis Simonides, cooperated with the Nazi authorities and supplied local police forces to aide in deporting 48,500 Jews from Salonika to Auschwitz-Birkenau during March to August 1943.[1574] Both Greeks and Germans looted the businesses and homes vacated by the expelled Jews.[1518] Greek Jews residing in the areas occupied by Bulgaria were also deported following the deportations from Salonika. In March 1944, German forces and Greek police in Athens rounded-up Jews and deported them. Upwards of 2,000 Jews from Corfu and another 2,200 from Rhodes were transported to concentration camps in June 1944.[1575] Before the end of the war, over 60,000 Greek Jews were murdered, the vast majority of whom were sent to Auschwitz.[1576]

## Hungary

In March 1938, several years before the German occupation of Hungary, anti-Jewish measures were already enacted by the Hungarian Parliament in the wake of Prime Minister Kálmán Darányi's announcement about the need to solve the Jewish question.[1577] This legislation and the second set of anti-Jewish laws restricted Jews from certain professions and economic sectors, it also forbade Jews from becoming Hungarian citizens by means of either marriage, naturalization, or legitimization. Approximately 90,000 Jews and their family members who relied on their support (upwards of 220,000 people) lost their means of economic survival and when the third anti-Jewish law went into effect, it nearly mirrored the Nazi Nuremberg Laws.[1578]

Once the legal exclusion of Jews from Hungarian society was complete, the National Central Alien Control Office (*Külföldieket Ellenőrző Országos Központi Hatóság*, KEOKH), turned its attention almost exclusively to expelling "undesirable" Jews.[1579] By the summer of 1941, the Hungarians carried out their first series of mass murders, and again in early January 1942 when they slaughtered 2,500 Serbs and 700 Jews, demonstrating that the political leadership in Hungary authorized the commission of atrocities even before the German occupation.[1580] Sometime in August 1941, the Hungarian authorities deported 16,000 "alien" Jews, most of whom were shot by the SS and Ukrainian collaborators.[1581] In the spring of 1942, the Hungarian Minister of Defense ordered the majority of Jewish forced labor to the theater of military operations. Due to this order as many as 50,000 Jews worked in forced labor companies starting in the spring of 1942 through 1944.[1582] Accompanying Hungarian troops during Operation Barbarossa, Jews in these units were poorly treated, insufficiently housed, ill-fed, routinely used to clear minefields, and placed in constant unnecessary danger; estimates indicate that "at least 33,000 Hungarian Jewish males in the prime of life" died in Russia.[1583]

During parts of May through June 1944, some 10,000 Hungarian Jews were gassed on a daily basis at Auschwitz-Birkenau, a pace with which the crematoria could not maintain, so many of the bodies were burned in open pits.[1584] The 410,000 Jews killed during this period represents the "largest single group of Jews murdered after 1942" according to historian Christian Gerlach.[1585] Much of the efficiency with which the Germans were able to deport and kill Hungarian Jews stemmed from the "frictionless cooperation of Hungary's politicians, bureaucracy, and gendarmerie", and popular Hungarian anti-Semitism served to block any Jews trying to escape.[1586] After the fascist Arrow Cross coup in October 1944, Arrow Cross militias shot as many as 20,000 Jews in Budapest and dumped their bodies into the Danube River between December 1944 and the end of January 1945.[1587] Jews in labor battalions were sent on death marches into Germany and Austria.[1588]

Nearly one-tenth of the Holocaust's Jewish victims were Hungarian Jews, accounting for a total of over 564,000 deaths; some 64,000 Jews were killed prior to the German occupation of Hungary.[1589] Despite the atrocities in Hungary, approximately 200,000 Jews in total survived the war.[1590]

## Italy

Among Germany's allies, Italy was not known for its anti-Semitism and had a relatively well assimilated Jewish population and its policies were essentially about domination as opposed to "destruction."[1591] National pride and the need to express sovereignty had as much to do with Italian behaviors than any general benevolence towards the Jews.[1591] Approximately 57,000 Jews resided in pre-war Italy comprising less than one-tenth of one-percent, about 10,000 of whom were refugees from Austria and Germany.[1592] An Italian law was passed in 1938 as part of Mussolini's effort to align his country more with Germany; the law restricted the civil liberties of Jews. This effectively reduced the country's Jews to second-class status, though the Italians never made it official policy to deport Jews to concentration camps. Edging closer towards Germany, the Italian Ministry of the Interior established 43 camps where enemy "aliens" (to include Jews) were detained—these camps were not pleasant but they were "a far cry from the Nazi concentration camps."[1593]

After the fall of Benito Mussolini and the Italian Social Republic, Jews started being deported to German camps by the Italian puppet regime, which issued a police order to that effect on 30 November 1943.[1594] While Jews understandably fled once the puppet regime came to power, the Italian police nonetheless captured and sent over 7,000 Jews to camps at Fossoli di Carpi and Bolzano, both of which served as assembly points for deportations to Auschwitz-Birkenau.[1595] Italian prisons were used to house Jews as well, the most infamous of them was San Vittorio in Milan where "torture and murder were common."[1596] Nazi Germany's Propaganda Minister, Joseph Goebbels, complained throughout the war about Italy's "lax" policies against the Jews.[1597] Through 1944, no less than 15 transports carrying around 3,800 Jews made their way from Italy to Auschwitz nevertheless.[1598] Estimates from a number of sources place the total death count for Italian Jews between 6,500 and 9,000.[1599] The generally accepted death tolls for Italy are about 8,000 Jews and as many as 1,000 Gypsies.[1600]

## Latvia

Before the war over 93,000 Jews resided in Latvia, comprising less than 5 percent of the country's population.[1601] Immediately in the wake of the German attack on the former Soviet Union in June 1941, Latvia was occupied and incorporated into the *Reichskommissariat Ostland* as *Generalbezirk Lettland* with a Latvian civil administration under the D. Heinrich Drechsler.[1602] Latvian auxiliary forces aided the SS *Einsatzgruppen* by following behind the advancing German forces, shooting Jews who they lined up in anti-tank trenches.[1603] Other instances of Latvian brutality against the Jews manifested before troops even arrived, as the local populations attacked and killed entire communities across hundreds of small villages.[1604] Zealous Latvians assisted the German forces in collecting all males between the ages of 16 and 60 in the city of Dvinsk for support operations; hundreds of Jewish males never returned from these duties as they were often murdered.[1605] In the areas in and around Warsaw, Latvian guards accompanied the SS in securing the ghetto and deporting Jews to Treblinka.[1606]

Former head of the Latvian police, Viktors Arājs, willingly collaborated with the Nazis by forming the Arājs *Kommando*, a Latvian volunteer police unit, which worked in-tandem with the SS *Einsatzgruppe* A to kill Jews.[1607] As early as July 1941, they were already burning synagogues in Riga.[1608] According to historian Timothy Snyder, the Arājs *Kommando* shot 22,000 Latvian Jews at various locations after they had been brutally rounded-up for this purpose by the regular police and auxiliaries, and were responsible for assisting in the killing of some 28,000 more Jews.[1609] Aggregate figures indicate that around 70,000 Latvian Jews died during the Holocaust.[1547]

### Liechtenstein

Only a handful of Jews lived in the small neutral state of Liechtenstein at the outbreak of the Second World War.[1610] </ref> Between 1933 and 1945, approximately 400 Jews were taken in by Liechtenstein, but another 165 were turned away.[1611] According to a 2005 study, the royal family of Liechtenstein purchased once Jewish-owned property and furniture that the Nazis seized after annexing Austria and Czechoslovakia. Liechtenstein's royal family also rented inmates from Strasshoff concentration camp near Vienna, where they employed forced labor on nearby royal estates.[1612]

### Lithuania

Nearly 7 percent of Lithuania's population was Jewish, totaling approximately 160,000 persons.[1613] For the most part, the Nazis considered the majority of non-Jewish people in the Baltics as racially assimilable with the exception of Jews, against whom some discrimination was already present in Lithuania before the occupation, but it was generally confined to edicts against Jews being in certain occupations and/or educational discrimination.[1614] Lithuania's Jewish population quickly swelled in the aftermath of the territorial arrangement between Nazi Germany and the Soviet Union, which proved a tumultuous time for many Jews who fled there to escape persecution; meanwhile, it increased the Jewish population of Lithuania to approximately 250,000.[1615] Angry about the Nazi-Soviet pact, many Lithuanians began taking their anger out on the country's Jews by attacking them and their property.[1616] The situation deteriorated further due to the see-saw of political power that started when the Soviet Army took control of Lithuania in June 1940 and persecuted thousands of its citizens through a program of Sovietization (approximately 17,000 Lithuanians were sent to Siberia right before the Germans arrived).[1617] Many Jews were asked to join the short-lived Soviet government and were allowed integration into Lithuanian society. Just seven-weeks later however, the Nazis invaded and were greeted as liberators. Subsequent blame for the ill-fortune that befell the Lithuanians under the Soviets landed on the Jews, which started even before the Germans had finished conquering the country;[1618] Lithuanians carried out pogroms in at least 40 different places, where Jews were raped, severely injured, and killed.[1619] Blaming the Jews also afforded any Lithuanians who had cooperated with the Soviets the means to exonerate themselves by diverting attention onto a Jewish conspiratorial scapegoat.[1620]

On 25 June 1941 Nazi forces arrived in Kaunas, where they witnessed local Lithuanians drag about 50 male Jews into the center of the city while one Lithuanian man beat them to death with a crowbar (cheered on by spectators) in a public display of brutality that shocked many Germans. Once the Jews were all dead, the man who had beaten them to death, climbed atop their corpses and played the Lithuanian national anthem on an accordion.[1621] These deaths were part of the Kaunas pogrom during which many thousands of Jews were killed by the Nazis with local acquiesance or assistance.[1622] Mere weeks after arrival, the Nazis instituted a systematic campaign to eliminate the Jews of Lithuania by identifying them, rounding them up, guarding them, and transporting them to extermination sites—during which they were aided by Lithuanian soldiers and police.[1623] The pace of murder increased and spread across Lithuania as the Germans consolidated their rule, sometimes by way of Lithuanian initiative, other times triggered at the arrival of Sipo-SD contingents.[1624] Within the last 6 months of 1941 following the June invasion by Germany, the majority of Lithuanian Jews were executed, the biggest crime being the Ponary massacre.[1625] The remnants trapped in ghettos were killed in occupied Lithuania and sent to death German Nazi camps in Poland.[1626] By the end of June 1941, around 80 percent of Lithuania's Jews had been "wiped out."[1627] Scholars believe the overall Holocaust-related death rate in Lithuania was approximately 90 percent, making Nazi-occupied Lithuania the European territory with the lowest number of Jewish survivors from World War II. While estimates vary, the number of Lithuanian Jews murdered in the Holocaust is assessed to be between 195,000 and 196,000.[1628]

Additionally, Lithuanian auxiliary police troops assisted in killing Jews in Poland, Belarus and Ukraine.[1629] One distinguished Lithuanian historian claims that there were five motivational factors eliciting participation in the atrocities by his countrymen. These were: (1) revenge against those who aided the Soviets; (2) expiation for those who wanted to demonstrate loyalty to the Nazis after collaborating previously with the Soviets; (3) anti-Semitism; (4) opportunism; and (5) self-enrichment.[1630]

## Netherlands

Known prior to the war for racial and religious tolerance, the Netherlands had taken in Jews since the 16th century, many of whom had found refuge there after fleeing Spain.[1631] Before the German invasion of May 1940, approximately 140,000 Jews resided in the Netherlands, around 30,000 of them were refugees from Austria and Germany.[1632] Nearly 60 percent of Dutch Jews lived in Amsterdam, constituting some 80,000 people.[1633] Once the Nazis invaded, a host of anti-Semitic measures were enacted to include exclusion from professions like the civil service.[1634] Anti-Jewish legislation that had taken years to institute in Germany was enacted within just months in the Netherlands.[1635] On 22 October 1940, all Jewish banks and businesses had to register and all assets, whether private or those in banks, had to be declared.[1636] Even radio sets in possession of Jewish persons were forbidden and confiscated.[1637] By January 1941, the Jews of the Netherlands were being defined by racist criteria, had to be registered, and merely a month later in February, many were being deported to Westerbork transit camp in the eastern part of the country. From there, most Dutch Jews were first sent to Mauthausen concentration camp.[1637] While there was participation from some Dutch volunteers in various acts against the Jews, there was more of a tacit and begrudging acquiesance in the Netherlands, which required a very visible Nazi presence throughout the entire war to exploit the country's economic wealth and enforce Nazi occupation policies.[1638,1639] </ref>

From the summer of 1942 forward, upwards of 102,000 Dutch Jews were deported and killed—much of which was made possible by the "cooperation and efficiency of the Dutch civil service and police" who willingly served the Germans.[1640] Not only was there relatively smooth cooperation between Dutch authorities and Dutch police, the SS and the Nazi police organizations in the Netherlands also worked well together there; additionally, volunteers from indigenous fascist organizations assisted in persecuting Jews, and the Jewish council in Amsterdam unfortunately spread undue optimism and as a result, very few Dutch Jews went into hiding.[1641] In all fairness to the Jewish council however, they were deceived and provided misinformation by the Nazi commissioner for Amsterdam, Hans Bömcker.[1642] Historians Deborah Dwork and Robert Jan van Pelt report the Jewish death rate in the Netherlands at nearly 80% for the 140,000 originally living there.[1643,1644] </ref>[1645]

## Norway

Amid a prewar population of 3 million, there were only 2,100 Jews living there, the largest contingency residing in Oslo.[1646] After Norway was invaded, the Nazis took control of the government by June 1940 and the true government went into exile.[1647] Power was given to the German Reichskommissar Josef Terboven and the Norwegian Fascist Party leader Vidkun Quisling, who supported the institution of anti-Jewish legislation.[1648] Quisling attempted to establish himself as the ruler of occupied Norway, but the Nazis only used him as leader of a puppet government.[1649] Like in Denmark, radios were confiscated from Jews by Norwegian police in May 1940.[1650] On 20 April 1940, SS *Einsatzkommandos* were established in Oslo, Bergen, Stavanger, Kristiansand, and Trondheim.[1650] The Nazis, assisted by Norwegian police units, managed to round up 763 Jews, who were deported to Auschwitz where they died.[1651] Another 930 Jews escaped to Sweden from Norway.[1652] However, the Nazis and their collaborators were very unpopular in Norway, causing a strong resistance movement, so the German government's aims for Norway were never fulfilled. Many Jews and other people were saved by the actions of Norwegians, including Norwegian police.[1653] Quisling and other Norwegians, who collaborated with the Nazis, were executed as traitors after the war, at least partly due to their involvement in the Holocaust.[1654]

## Palestine

A Palestinian Arab nationalist and a Muslim religious leader, the Grand Mufti of Jerusalem Haj Amin al-Husseini worked for the Nazi Germany as a propagandist and a recruiter of Muslim volunteers for the Waffen-SS and other units.[1655] On 28 November 1941, Hitler officially received al-Husseini in Berlin.[1656] Hitler told al-Husseini of the Germans' "uncompromising fight against the Jews", which included the Jews in Arab territories.[1657] The Mufti spent the remainder of the war assisting with the formation of Muslim Waffen-SS units in the Balkans and the formation of schools and training centers for imams and mullahs who would accompany the Muslim SS and Wehrmacht units.[1658] Beginning in 1943, al-Husseini was involved in the organization and recruitment of Bosnian Muslims into several divisions. The largest of which was the 13th "Handschar" division.[1659]

## Poland

Polish Jews comprised roughly 10 percent of the country's population at upwards of 3.3 million persons before the Second World War began, most of whom were well-integrated into Polish society in various industries.[1660] Most Polish Jews lived in the cities and were self-employed.[1661] Economic depression during the 1920s and 30s changed the situation for Jews in Poland, as a subsequent emergence of anti-Semitism yielded government programs to reduce their economic standing.[1662] German occupation in 1939 only worsened matters for the Jews, as they started isolating them by forcing them into ghettos, eventually transporting them to camps established in Poland itself.[1663]

Poland was the country with the most ghettos, the only camps designed exclusively for extermination, and trains from all across northern, southern, and western Europe carried Jewish deportees into the country.[1664] Far right-wing party members in Poland saw the deportation of the Jews in a favorable light, but for the majority of Poles, their thoughts on the matter were far more complex.[1665] When the Nazis attacked the Red Army in Soviet-occupied Poland during Operation Barbarossa of 1941, a series of massacres of Jews were committed by the SS *Einsatzgruppen* in the new German *Bezirk Bialystok* district, such as in Jedwabne, Radzilow, and Kolno villages. The extent of local collaboration in these massacres is a controversial issue, as is the pivotal role of the *Einsatzgruppe Zichenau-Schroettersburg* under Hermann Schaper.[1666] According to Timothy Snyder, there were about a dozen German-instigated pogroms in Poland resulting in several thousand deaths, but "the scale of the murder was inferior" compared against what happened further north and east of Poland.[1667]

There were also multiple occurrences of individual *Volksdeutsche* turning in, chasing down, or blackmailing Jews; such people were condemned as collaborators and under threat of execution by the Polish resistance. Emmanuel Ringelblum wrote that he saw Polish Blue Police beating Jews and that they participated in street rounds up.[1668] But according to Raul Hilberg, "Of all the native police forces in occupied Eastern Europe, those of Poland were least involved in anti-Jewish actions.... They [the Polish Blue Police] could not join the Germans in major operations against Jews or Polish resistors, lest they be considered traitors by virtually every Polish onlooker."[1669] Poland never surrendered to the Germans so there was no collaboration on a national governmental level as took place elsewhere in occupied Europe. There also were no Polish SS battalions, though there were SS volunteer battalions from almost all of the German-occupied countries. Attempts to organize Polish SS battalions resulted in immediate, large-scale desertions, and so these attempts were abandoned.[1670] Polish Jew, Nechama Tec, an expert on the Holocaust who herself was saved by Polish Catholics, writes that she knew of no Polish concentration camp guards.[1671] In general the machinery of the Holocaust ran with little Polish collaboration, though collaboration did take place on occasion as Yisrael Gutman and Shmuel Krakowski reported in their work *Unequal Victims* that a notable number of Poles turned their backs on the Jews, extorted them (see Szmalcownik ), and in the rural parts of Poland, peasants joined the Germans in hunting down and killing Jews who escaped from ghettos.[1672] They also claim that there were more bystander crimes than those willing to aide the Jews.[1672] Nonetheless, Polish citizens have the world's highest count of individuals recognized as Righteous Among the Nations by Yad Vashem; a list consisting of Gentiles who risked their lives to save Jews from extermination during the Holocaust.[1673,1674] It was also the nation where the infamous killing centers of Belzec, Chelmno, Sobibor, Treblinka, Majdanek, and Auschwitz-Birkenau were located.[1675] Before the killing came to its conclusion, upwards of ninety-percent of all Poland's Jews—amounting to some three-million persons in total—were murdered by the Nazis.[1676] </ref>

## Romania

 Wikimedia Commons has media related to *The Holocaust in Romania*.

Assimilation was common for Jews in Romania, where some 757,000 of them lived but not necessarily in total peace there. Following the First World War, attacks against Jews intensified, as many Jews were stripped of citizenship. According to historian Lucy Dawidowicz, economic discrimination as well as violent anti-Semitism was present in Romania concomitant with Germany.[1677] Similar to Germany, Jews were forbidden full participation in Romanian society and culture, and under Antonescu the Romanianization of Jewish property was carried out, Jews were forbidden gainful employment, made to work as forced laborers, and a process of ghettoization and deportation was begun.[1678] Leading figures in Romania's anti-Semitic movement included the economics professor, Alexander Cuza, who founded the Fascist League of National Christian Defense, an organization that begat the notorious Iron Guard under Corneliu Zelea Codreanu.[1679] Cuza wanted to expel all Jews out of Romania; poet Octavian Coga wished to send them to Madagascar. The fascist Alexandru Razmerita advocated imprisoning the Jews in concentration camps and working them to death, while a Romanian Orthodox priest suggested drowning them all in the Black Sea.[1679] Copying the Nazis, the Romanian government enacted its version of the Nuremberg Laws in 1936.[1680] Iron Guard leader Codreanu once exclaimed that he was in favor of "eliminating the Jews completely, totally and without exception."[1681,1682] </ref>

The Romanian Antonescu regime was responsible for the deaths of approximately 380,000 Jews according to historian Yehuda Bauer.[1683] An official declaration by the Romanian government that denied the existence of Holocaust within the country's borders during World War II led in 2003 to the creation of the International Commission on the Holocaust in Romania.[1684] The official report of the Commission released jointly with the Romanian government concluded:

<templatestyles src="Template:Quote/styles.css"/>

> The Commission concludes, together with the large majority of bona fide researchers in this field, that the Romanian authorities were the main perpetrators of this Holocaust, in both its planning and implementation. This encompasses the systematic deportation and extermination of nearly all the Jews of Bessarabia and Bukovina as well some Jews from other parts of Romania to Transnistria, the mass killings of Romanian and local Jews in Transnistria, the massive execution of Jews during the Iasi pogrom; the systematic discrimination and degradation applied to Romanian Jews during the Antonescu administration — including the expropriation of assets, dismissal from jobs, the forced evacuation from rural areas and concentration in district capitals and camps, and the massive utilization of Jews as forced laborers under the same administration. Jews were degraded solely on account of their Jewish origin, losing the protection of the state and becoming its victims. A portion of the Roma population of Romania was also subjected to deportation and death in Transnistria.[1685]

In cooperation with German *Einsatzgruppen* and Ukrainian auxiliaries, Romanian troops killed hundreds of thousands of Jews in Bessarabia, northern Bukovina, and Transnistria; some of the larger massacres of Jews occurred at Bogdanovka, a Romanian concentration camp along the Bug River in Transnistria, between 21 and 30 December 1941.[1686] Nearly 100,000 Jews were killed in occupied Odessa[1687] and well over 10,000 were killed in the Iași pogrom of June 1941.[1688] Romanian troops also massacred Jews in the Domanevka and Akhmetchetka concentration camps.[1689,1690]

Jean Ancel, who headed the commission along with Elie Wiesel, spent his entire life researching Romania's treatment of Jews. In his book he provides a confirmation using Romania's own archives, made available in 1994–95 after the collapse of the Soviet Union, and with Nazi documents, survivor testimonies, war crimes trial transcripts, that Romania not only participated in but independently implemented its own autonomous genocide of Jews in Bessarabia, Bukovina, and in Ukraine—the only Nazi ally to do so during the war.[1691]

The protests of various public, political and religious figures, including Prince Constantin Karadja, against the deportation of the Jews from the Romanian Kingdom contributed to the change of policy toward the Jews starting with October 1942.[1692] The result of this change of policy and that of the actions of a relatively small number of individuals, was that at least 290,000 Romanian Jews survived.[1693]

## Serbia

Before the First World War, Serbia existed as an independent country before being incorporated into Yugoslavia in 1919. Approximately 16,000 Jews resided there.[1694] During the interwar years, Serbia constituted one of the places where it was comparatively safe to be a Jew, despite the presence of some general xenophobia.[1695] Serbia was occupied by Germany in April 1941.[1398] As part of their effort to occupy the northern regions of Yugoslavia, the Germans established a military government in Serbia.[1696] Serbia's collaborationist government was led by General Milan Nedić.[1697] The internal affairs of the Serbian occupied territory were moderated by German racial laws, that were introduced in all occupied territories with immediate effects on the Jewish and Roma populations.[1698] Indigenous Serbians who harbored democratic beliefs were also targeted.[1699] Partisan activities in Serbia elicited harsh pacification measures from the SD and Wehrmacht.[1700,1701] </ref> The Nazis had a policy of killing 100 Serbs for each German soldier killed and another 50 Serbs for every German soldiers who was wounded.[1694] Resistance activities continued for some time in Serbia nonetheless.[1702]

Sometimes the Serbian authorities cooperated with the Germans as matter of course, whereas others took individual initiative; some Serbian military commanders rounded-up Gypsies so they could be concentrated in one area, where they were shot.[1703] German occupiers declared Serbia *Judenfrei* in August 1942.[1704] The major concentration camps in Serbia were Sajmište and Banjica but many others like Topovske Šupe, Šabac, and Niš concentration camps also interned considerable numbers of Jews.[1705] Before the war was concluded, upwards of 14,500 Serbian Jews were murdered.[1706] Legends about Serbs saving the Jews in World War II are widespread in Serbia, and 132 Serbs have been honored as righteous Gentiles.[1673]

## Slovakia

In 1938 approximately 135,000 Jews resided in Slovakia, around 40,000 of them lived in Ruthenia and Subcarpathia, areas previously ceded to Hungary; most of whom, led good lives despite the presence of anti-Semitism among the peasant population of Slovakia.[1707] As early as April 1939, anti-Jewish legislation was enacted, but this was religious and not racial in nomenclature. Nonetheless, the restrictions against Jews proceeded accordingly, blocking them from various professions, which was accompanied by violence against the Jews from the indigenous Hlinka Guard.[1708] Slovakian Jews were among the first to be handed over en masse to the Nazis following the Wannsee Conference.[1709] Members of the Hlinka Guard went house to house and brutally seized young and fit Jews from their homes in March and April 1942, sending them to Auschwitz as slave laborers.[1710] The Hlinka Guard was assisted by the *Freiwillige Schutzstaffel* (Slovak volunteers in the SS).[1708] Between March through October 1942, Tiso's Slovakian regime deported approximately 58,000 Jews to the German-occupied part of Poland.[1708] The Slovak government even paid the Germans for the Jews that were deported.[1711] The deportation of the remaining 24,000 was stopped due to the intervention of a Papal nuncio, whereby the Slovak president was informed that the German authorities were killing the Jews deported from Slovakia. Despite this action, approximately 12,600 Slovak Jews were still sent to Auschwitz, Theresienstadt, and other camps in Germany before the deportations ceased. Around half of them were killed in concentration camps.[1712] Aggregate numbers of Holocaust victims tabulated by experts indicate that at least 60,000 Jews as well as 400 Slovakian Gypsies were killed; high estimates place the total number of Jewish victims from Slovakia at 71,000 persons.[1713]

**Spain**

During World War II, Francisco Franco remained largely silent in regard to Jewish matters, and Spain became an unlikely escape route and haven for thousands of Jews. Franco was known to harbor virulent anti-Semitic beliefs and agreed with Hitler that Judaism, Communism, and cosmopolitanism were related threats to European society.[1714] Western European Jews still fled to Spain, as they sought to escape deportation to concentration camps from German occupied France, but also Sephardic Jews from Eastern Europe, especially in Hungary. Trudy Alexy refers to the "absurdity" and "paradox of refugees fleeing the Nazis' Final Solution to seek asylum in a country where no Jews had been allowed to live openly as Jews for over four centuries."[1715] In the first years of the war, "Laws regulating their admittance were written and mostly ignored."[1716] Once the tide of war began to turn against the Germans, and Count Francisco Gómez-Jordana succeeded Franco's brother-in-law Serrano Súñer as Spain's foreign minister, Spanish diplomacy became "more sympathetic to Jews", although Franco himself "never said anything" about it.[1716] Around that same time, a contingent of Spanish doctors traveling in Poland were fully informed of the Nazi extermination plans by the *Gauleiter* Frankel of Warsaw, who was under the misimpression that they would share his views about the matter; when they returned home, they passed the information to Admiral Luís Carrero Blanco, who told Franco.[1717]

Diplomats discussed the possibility of Spain as a route to a containment camp for Jewish refugees near Casablanca, but it came to nothing due to lack of Free French and British support.[1718] Nonetheless, control of the Spanish border with France relaxed somewhat[1719] and thousands of Jews managed to cross into Spain (many by smugglers' routes). Almost all of them survived the war.[1720] The American Jewish Joint Distribution Committee operated openly in Barcelona.[1721,1722] </ref> Francoist Spain, despite its aversion to Zionism and "Judeo"-Freemasonry, does not appear to have shared the rabid anti-Semitic ideology promoted by the Nazis.[1723] About 20,000 to 30,000 refugees, mainly Jews, were allowed to transit through Spain to Portugal and beyond.[1724] About 5,000 Jews in occupied Europe benefitted from Spanish legal protection.[1725,1726]

In 2010, a document was found in Spanish archives, which revealed that Franco's government gave a main architect of the Nazi "Final Solution", Heinrich Himmler, a list of six thousand Jews living in Spain, upon his request. Jose Maria Finat y Escriva de Romani, Franco's chief of security issued an official order dated 13 May 1941 to all provincial governors requesting a list of all Jews, both local and foreign, present in their districts. After the list was compiled, Romani was appointed Spain's ambassador to Germany, enabling him to deliver the list to Himmler. Following the defeat of Germany in 1945, the Spanish government attempted to destroy all evidence of cooperation with the Nazis, but this official order survived. Spanish diplomats did save thousands of Jews, but it was done on their personal initiative.[1727]

**The Soviet Union**

As early as 1903, Vladimir Lenin had already formulated a Communist ideology about the Jews, who he avowed, were not a nation since they did not possess any specified territory; this position was shared by Stalin and in the 1920s as many as 830,000 Soviet Jews were considered *lishentsy* (non-citizens).[1728] Some of those Jewish non-citizens eventually applied to work in factories and subsequently gained their citizenship but Jewish culture and literature faded fast under the Stalinist government.[1729] Nearly 90 percent of Russian Jews were urbanized and lived in one of eleven cities, with the largest groups in Moscow, Kiev, and Leningrad.[1730] Anti-Semitic literature like the *Protocols of the Learned Elders of Zion*—which advocates a Jewish conspiracy for world domination—was popular in prewar Russia.[1731] Russian pogroms targeting the Jews were among the first in the modern period to incite its citizens to violence for the sake of political expediency.[1732] Still, around three-million Jews lived across the vast expanse of the Soviet Union in January 1939.[1733] The Jewish population within the Soviet territories was distributed as follows: 300,000 in Bessarabia and northern Bukovina, 5,000 in Estonia, 95,000 in Latvia, 155,000 in Lithuania (excluding Vilna), 1.5 to 1.6 million in Soviet-occupied Poland, and another 3.1 million in the USSR.[1734]

During the invasion of the Soviet Union, the Jews were unaware of the Nazi anti-Jewish policies, partly as a result of Soviet silence about the matter.[1735] In the German-occupied Soviet territories, local Nazi collaborationist units represented over 80% of the available German forces, which provided them with a total of nearly 450,000 personnel organised in so-called *Schutzmannschaften* formations. Practically all of these units participated in the round-ups and mass-shootings. The overwhelming majority were recruited in the western USSR and the Baltic region, areas recently occupied by the Soviets where the Jews were typically scapegoated, which exacerbated pre-Nazi antisemitic attitudes.[1736] Ukrainians in particular, displayed some of the most virulent hatred of the Jews and approved of German measures against them, despite their initial constraint in persecuting them.[1737] Eventually some 12,000 Ukrainian auxiliaries joined the Nazis in perpetrating the Final Solution and while many of them participated as Ukrainian nationalists, anti-Semitism proved a factor, one which they acquired on the job.[1738] Thousands of Ukrainians rushed to occupy businesses and homes vacated by persecuted Jews.[1739]

German *Einsatzgruppen* units, members of the Wehrmacht, Order Police, and auxiliary units mostly from Latvia, Lithuania and the Ukraine were already engaged in killing operations in the summer of 1941 and by July of that year, they had helped kill 39,000 Ukrainian Jews, and another 26,000 Jews in Belarus.[1740] Local citizens aided by militias in Latvia, Bukovina, Romania, Bessarabia, Moldavia, Lithuania, Bialystok, Galicia, and elsewhere killed tens-of-thousands of Jews on their own accord.[1741] Throughout the remainder of 1941 to the autumn of 1942, the concerted murder operations proceeded apace.[1742] Not accounting for the deaths of victims from its territories, at least 700,000 Soviet Jews and 30,000 Gypsies were killed in the Holocaust.[1743] Another three-million Soviet soldiers were killed or starved-to-death by the Germans.[1744]

**Sweden**

Before the onset of the Second World War, approximately 7,000 Jews resided in Sweden, most of whom lived in Stockholm.[1745] Like Switzerland, the Swedish government remained neutral due to its financial ties and the economic advantages it secured from a friendly relationship with Germany.[1746] There was even a small fascist pro-Nazi political group—known as the Swedish National Socialist Party—but they were unable to rally support for their cause.[1747] Swedish authorities were initially resistant to Jewish immigration into the country and several thousands were turned away.[1748] That was not to last, as by 1942 the Swedish government started allowing Norwegian and Finnish immigrants, as well as taking in some 900 Norwegian Jews.[1749] Another 7,000 Danish Jews and some 9,000 Danish Christians were permitted entrance to Sweden in 1943. During 1944, the Swedish diplomat Raoul Wallenberg traveled to Budapest and negotiated for the release of thousands of Hungarian Jews.[1750] Wallenberg's efforts secured passports for 15,000–20,000

Jews; he and those collaborating with him very likely saved the lives of some 70,000 Jewish persons before the Red Army's arrival in Hungary during January 1945.[1751]

## Switzerland

Proximity to Nazi Germany as a bordering nation made the Swiss government very tentative about dealing with the Jews.[1752] Sharing a physical border with Germany was also part of the reason that the Swiss maintained amicable economic relations with Germany.[1753] Correspondingly, both Sweden and especially Switzerland cooperated with the Nazis concerning banking and the exploitation of financial opportunities, as they knowingly accepted expropriation of money and goods, which previously belonged to Jewish companies and/or families for their own gain.[1754] Before 1938, Swiss alien and refugee policy was already restrictive toward certain people and groups, notably foreign Roma and Sinti. However, from that date, restrictions were intensified, particularly towards Jews. As part of that policy, the Swiss government requested that the German government mark the passports of German Jews with a "J" as they were not ready to grant asylum on the grounds of racial persecution.[1755,1756] This policy took effect following the Anschluß with Austria, as the Swiss government was concerned about potential Jewish refugees fleeing and inundating them accordingly.[1757] In 1942 Swiss borders were completely closed to all Jewish refugees, which even included Jewish children.[1758]

By late October 1942, news of the Jewish catastrophe had reached Switzerland.[1758] After German troops seized control of Italy, which had withdrawn its political and military support when non-fascist Italians overthrew Mussolini, hundreds of Jews escaped over the mountain passes into neutral Switzerland.[1759] French resistance fighters and activists were also instrumental in helping smuggle Jews from France into neutral Spain and Switzerland, where they were able to find shelter.[1760] Sometime in 1944, some 1,684 Hungarian Jews arrived in Switzerland from Bergen-Belsen concentration camp, another 1,200 Jews from Theresienstadt concentration camp found safety in Switzerland and by February 1945, over 115,000 refugees of various types had made their way across the Swiss border to safety.[1761]

The International Commission of Experts (ICE) set up in 1996 by the Swiss parliament to examine relations between Nazi Germany and Switzerland reported: "Anti-Semitic views were more or less widespread amongst the political classes, the civil service, the military and the church."[1762] The ICE wrote: "by progressively closing the borders, delivering captured refugees over to their persecutors, and adhering to restrictive principles for far too long, the country stood by as many people were undoubtedly driven to certain death."[1763] Although accurate statistics are hard to put together, the commission concluded that "It must therefore be assumed that Switzerland turned back or deported over 20,000 refugees during the Second World War. Furthermore, between 1938 and November 1944, around 14,500 applications for entry visas submitted by hopeful emigrants to the Swiss diplomatic missions abroad were refused."[1764,1765]

### United States

According to *The Encyclopedia of the Holocaust*, the U.S. failed to live up to its creed about accepting the "tired, poor, huddled masses" of the world during the Holocaust.[1766] The U.S. policy towards Jews fleeing Germany and claiming asylum was restrictive. In 1939, the annual combined German-Austrian immigration quota was 27,370.[1767] A famous incident was the U.S. denial of entry to the *St. Louis*, a ship loaded with 938 passengers. Almost all passengers aboard the vessel were Jews fleeing from Nazi Germany. Most were German citizens, some were from Eastern Europe, and a few were officially "stateless." The ship's original destination was Cuba, but the Cuban government, after admitting 28 refugees, ordered the ship to leave. The ship continued to the U.S., sailing so close to Florida that the passengers could see the lights of Miami. Some passengers on the *St. Louis* cabled President Franklin D. Roosevelt asking for refuge. Roosevelt never responded, though he could have issued an executive order to admit the *St. Louis* refugees. A State Department telegram sent to a passenger stated that the passengers must "await their turns on the waiting list and qualify for and obtain immigration visas before they may be admissible into the United States."[1767] Finally, the ship was forced to return to Europe and the majority of its Jewish passengers died in the Holocaust. On 17 December 1942, the United States finally issued a statement condemning the Nazi extermination program, but this turned out to be a meaningless gesture as did the follow-on Bermuda Conference of April 1943.[1768] The United States did not lift its immigration restriction against Jews until after the Second World War was over.[1769]

# Legal proceedings against Nazis

The juridical notion of crimes against humanity was developed following the Holocaust. The sheer number of people murdered and the transnational nature of the mass killing shattered any notion of national sovereignty taking precedence over international law when prosecuting these crimes. There were a number of legal efforts established to bring Nazis and their collaborators to justice. Some of the higher-ranking Nazi officials were tried as part of the Nuremberg Trials, presided over by an Allied court; the first international tribunal of its kind. Other trials were conducted in the countries in which the defendants were citizens — in West Germany and Austria, many Nazis were let off with light sentences, with the claim of "following orders" ruled a mitigating circumstance, and many returned to society soon afterwards.[1770]

An ongoing effort to pursue Nazis and collaborators resulted, famously, in the 1960 capture of Holocaust organizer Adolf Eichmann in Argentina (an operation led by Rafi Eitan) and to his subsequent trial in Israel in 1961.[1771,1772] Simon Wiesenthal became one of the most famous Nazi hunters.[1773]

## Flight from justice and other obfuscations

Some former Nazis escaped any charges. For example, Reinhard Gehlen, a former intelligence officer of the Wehrmacht, managed to turn around and work for the CIA, and created what informally became known as the Gehlen Organization. He recruited ex–intelligence-officers of the Wehrmacht and Nazis from the SS and SD to work for him.[1774] On 1 April 1956, the *Bundesnachrichtendienst* (BND; the German intelligence agency) was created from the Gehlen Organization, and transferred to the West German government. Reinhard Gehlen became President of the BND and remained its head until 1968.[1775]

Klaus Barbie, known as "the Butcher of Lyon" for his role at the head of the Gestapo, was protected from 1945 to 1955 by MI5 and the CIA, before fleeing to South America where he had a hand in Luis García Meza Tejada's 1980 *Cocaine Coup* in Bolivia.[1776] Barbie was finally arrested in 1983 and sentenced to life imprisonment for crimes against humanity in 1987.[1777]

# References

## Bibliography

<templatestyles src="Template:Refbegin/styles.css" />

- Aderet, Ofer (2010). "WWII Document Reveals: General Franco Handed Nazis List of Spanish Jews"[1778]. *Haaretz*. Retrieved 4 October 2017.<templatestyles src="Module:Citation/CS1/styles.css"></templatestyles>
- Alexy, Trudy (1993). *The Mezuzah in the Madonna's Foot*. New York: Simon and Schuster. ISBN 978-0-671-77816-3.<templatestyles src="Module:Citation/CS1/styles.css"></templatestyles>
- Arendt, Hannah (1994) [1963]. *Eichmann in Jerusalem: A Report on the Banality of Evil*. New York: Penguin. ISBN 0-14-018765-0.<templatestyles src="Module:Citation/CS1/styles.css"></templatestyles>
- Arendt, Hannah (1973). *The Origins of Totalitarianism*. Orlando, FL: Harcourt Inc. ISBN 978-0156701532.<templatestyles src="Module:Citation/CS1/styles.css"></templatestyles>

- Ascher, Abraham (2012). *Was Hitler a Riddle? Western Democracies and National Socialism*. Stanford, CA: Stanford University Press. ISBN 978-0156701532.
- Bartov, Omer (1999). "Soldiers, Nazis and War in the Third Reich". In Christian Leitz, ed. *The Third Reich: The Essential Readings*. Oxford: Blackwell Publishing. ISBN 978-0-63120-700-9.
- Bartov, Omer (2000). "Introduction". In Omar Bartov, ed. *Holocaust: Origins, Implementation, Aftermath*. New York: Routledge. ISBN 0-415-15036-1.
- Bascomb, Neal (2009). *Hunting Eichmann*. Boston; New York: Houghton Mifflin Harcourt. ISBN 978-0-618-85867-5.
- Bauer, Yehuda (1982). *A History of the Holocaust*. New York: Franklin Watts. ISBN 978-9-91163-612-6.
- Bauer, Yehuda (2002). *Rethinking the Holocaust*. New Haven; London: Yale University Press. ISBN 978-0-30009-300-1.
- *BBC News* (2001-11-29). "Croatian Holocaust still stirs controversy"[1779]. Retrieved 2015-06-04.
- *BBC News* (2005-04-14). "Nazi crimes taint Liechtenstein"[1780]. Retrieved 2018-01-01.
- Benz, Wolfgang (2007). *A Concise History of the Third Reich*. Berkeley and Los Angeles: University of California Press. ISBN 978-0-52025-383-4.
- Bergen, Doris (1996). *Twisted Cross: The German Christian Movement in the Third Reich*. Chapel Hill, NC; London: The University of North Carolina Press. ISBN 978-0-80784-560-8.
- Bergen, Doris (2009). *War & Genocide: A Concise History of the Holocaust* (Second, revised ed.). Lanham, MD: Rowman & Littlefield. ISBN 978-0-7425-5715-4.
- Bessel, Richard (2003). "Functionalists vs. Intentionalists: The Debate Twenty Years On *or* Whatever Happened to Functionalism and Intentionalism?"[1781] (PDF). *German Studies Review*. **26** (1): 15–20.

estyles src="Module:Citation/CS1/styles.css"></templatestyles>
- Bessel, Richard (2006). *Nazism and War*. New York: Modern Library. ISBN 978-0-81297-557-4.<templatestyles src="Module:Citation/CS1/styles.css"></templatestyles>
- Bialas, Wolfgang (2013). "The Eternal Voice of the Blood: Racial Science and Nazi Ethics". In Anton Weiss-Wendt; Rory Yeomans, eds. *Racial Science in Hitler's New Europe, 1938–1945*. Lincoln, NE: University of Nebraska Press. ISBN 978-0-80324-605-8.<templatestyles src="Module:Citation/CS1/styles.css"></templatestyles>
- Black, Jeremy (2016). *The Holocaust: History and Memory*. Indianapolis and Bloomington: Indiana University Press. ISBN 978-0-25302-214-1.<templatestyles src="Module:Citation/CS1/styles.css"></templatestyles>
- Blass, Thomas (1998). "The Roots of Milgram's Obedience Experiments and Their Relevance to the Holocaust"[1782] (PDF). *Analyse & Kritik*. **20** (1): 46–53.<templatestyles src="Module:Citation/CS1/styles.css"></templatestyles>
- Bloxham, Donald (2009). *The Final Solution: A Genocide*. New York: Oxford University Press. ISBN 978-0-19955-034-0.<templatestyles src="Module:Citation/CS1/styles.css"></templatestyles>
- Breitman, Richard (2001). "What Chilean Diplomats Learned about the Holocaust"[1783]. *U.S. National Archives*. Retrieved 12 February 2011.<templatestyles src="Module:Citation/CS1/styles.css"></templatestyles>
- Breitman, Richard (1992). "The Final Solution". In Gordon Martel, ed. *Modern Germany Reconsidered: 1870–1945*. London; New York: Routledge. ISBN 978-0-41507-812-2.<templatestyles src="Module:Citation/CS1/styles.css"></templatestyles>
- Browning, Christopher R. (1992). *The Path to Genocide: Essays on Launching the Final Solution*. Cambridge and New York: Cambridge University Press. ISBN 0-521-42695-2.<templatestyles src="Module:Citation/CS1/styles.css"></templatestyles>
- Browning, Christopher R. (2004). *The Origins of the Final Solution: The Evolution of Nazi Jewish Policy, September 1939 – March 1942*. Lincoln: University of Nebraska Press. ISBN 0-8032-1327-1.<templatestyles src="Module:Citation/CS1/styles.css"></templatestyles>
- Bruland, Bjarte (2011). "Norway's Role in the Holocaust: The Destruction of Norway's Jews". In Jonathan C. Friedman, ed. *The Routledge History of the Holocaust*. New York: Routledge. ISBN 978-0-41577-956-2.<templatestyles src="Module:Citation/CS1/styles.css"></templatestyles>

- Bubnys, Arūnas (2004). "Holocaust in Lithuania: An Outline of the Major Stages and Their Results". In Schreiner, Stefan; Donskis, Leonidas; Nikzentaitis, Alvydas; Staliūnas, Darius, eds. *The Vanished World of Lithuanian Jews*. Amsterdam; New York: Rodopi. ISBN 978-9-04200-850-2.<templatestyles src="Module:Citation/CS1/styles.css"></templatestyles>
- Bullock, Alan (1993). *Hitler and Stalin: Parallel Lives*. New York: Vintage Books. ISBN 978-0-679-72994-5.<templatestyles src="Module:Citation/CS1/styles.css"></templatestyles>
- Burleigh, Michael; Wippermann, Wolfgang (1991). *The Racial State: Germany 1933–1945*. Cambridge and New York: Cambridge University Press. ISBN 978-0521398022.<templatestyles src="Module:Citation/CS1/styles.css"></templatestyles>
- Burleigh, Michael (2000). *The Third Reich: A New History*. New York: Hill and Wang. ISBN 978-0-80909-325-0.<templatestyles src="Module:Citation/CS1/styles.css"></templatestyles>
- Caron, Jean-Christoph (2007). "Erwin Rommel: Auf der Jagd nach dem Schatz des "Wüstenfuchses""[1784]. *Spiegel Online* (in German): 2. Retrieved 9 September 2016.<templatestyles src="Module:Citation/CS1/styles.css"></templatestyles>
- Cesarani, David (2016). *Final Solution: The Fate of the Jews, 1933–1945*. New York: St. Martin's Press. ISBN 978-1-25000-083-5.<templatestyles src="Module:Citation/CS1/styles.css"></templatestyles>
- Cockburn, Alexander (1999). *Whiteout: The CIA, Drugs and the Press*. New York: Verso. ISBN 978-1-85984-139-6.<templatestyles src="Module:Citation/CS1/styles.css"></templatestyles>
- Confino, Alon (2011). *Foundational Pasts: The Holocaust as Historical Understanding*. Cambridge and New York: Cambridge University Press. ISBN 978-0-52173-632-9.<templatestyles src="Module:Citation/CS1/styles.css"></templatestyles>
- Confino, Alon (2014). *A World Without Jews: The Nazi Imagination from Persecution to Genocide*. London and New Haven: Yale University Press. ISBN 978-0-30018-854-7.<templatestyles src="Module:Citation/CS1/styles.css"></templatestyles>
- Cooper, Matthew (1979). *The Nazi War Against Soviet Partisans, 1941–1944*. New York: Stein and Day. ISBN 978-0-81282-600-5.<templatestyles src="Module:Citation/CS1/styles.css"></templatestyles>
- Dawidowicz, Lucy S. (1975). *The War Against the Jews: 1933–1945*. New York: Holt, Rinehart and Winston. ISBN 0-03-013661-X.<templatestyles

- Dawidowicz, Lucy S.; Altshuler, David A. (1978). *Hitler's War Against the Jews*. Springfield, NJ: Behrman House. ISBN 0-87441-222-6.
- DW Staff (2005-04-14). "Nazi Camp Labor Used in Liechtenstein"[1785]. *Deutsche Welle*. Retrieved 2018-01-01.
- Dmitrów, Edmund; Szarota, Tomasz; Machcewicz, Paweł (2004). *Der Beginn der Vernichtung—zum Mord an den Juden in Jedwabne und Umgebung im Sommer 1941: neue Forschungsergebnisse polnischer Historiker* (in German). Osnabrück: Fibre Verlag. ISBN 978-3-92975-987-7.
- Dulić, Tomislav (2005). *Utopias of Nation: Local Mass Killings in Bosnia and Herzegovina, 1941–42*. Uppsala, Sweden: Uppsala University Library. ISBN 978-91-554-6302-1.
- Dutton, Donald G. (2007). *The Psychology of Genocide, Massacres, and Extreme Violence*. Westport, CT; London: Praeger. ISBN 978-0275990008.
- Dwork, Deborah; van Pelt, Robert Jan (2002). *Holocaust: A History*. New York: W. W. Norton & Company. ISBN 978-0-39305-188-9.
- Evans, Richard (2010). *The Third Reich at War*. New York: Penguin. ISBN 978-0-14311-671-4.
- Evans, Richard (2015). *The Third Reich in History and Memory*. New York: Oxford University Press. ISBN 978-0-19022-839-2.
- Feig, Konnilyn G. (1981). *Hitler's Death Camps: The Sanity of Madness*. New York: Holmes & Meier. ISBN 0-8419-0675-0.
- Fischer, Conan (2002). *The Rise of the Nazis*. Manchester: Manchester University Press. ISBN 978-0-71906-067-0.
- Fleischhauer, Jan (2011). "Nazi War Crimes as Described by German Soldiers"[1786]. *Spiegel ONLINE*. Retrieved 16 July 2017.

- Fleming, Gerald (1994). *Hitler and the Final Solution*. Berkeley and Los Angeles: University of California Press. ISBN 0-520-06022-9.
- Fleming, Michael (2014). *Auschwitz, the Allies and Censorship of the Holocaust*. Cambridge and New York: Cambridge University Press. ISBN 978-1107062795.
- Friedlander, Henry (1995). *The Origins of Nazi Genocide: From Euthanasia to the Final Solution*. Chapel Hill: University of North Carolina Press. ISBN 978-0-80782-208-1.
- Friedländer, Saul (2007). *Nazi Germany and the Jews 1939–1945: The Years of Extermination*. New York: HarperCollins. ISBN 978-0-06019-043-9.
- Fritzsche, Peter (2008). *Life and Death in the Third Reich*. Cambridge, MA: Harvard University Press. ISBN 978-0-67403-465-5.
- Fromjimovics, Kinga (2011). "The Special Characteristics of the Holocaust in Hungary, 1938–45". In Jonathan C. Friedman, ed. *The Routledge History of the Holocaust*. New York: Routledge. ISBN 978-0-41577-956-2.
- Gaunt, David (2011). "Reichskommissariat *Ostland*". In Jonathan C. Friedman, ed. *The Routledge History of the Holocaust*. New York: Routledge. ISBN 978-0-41577-956-2.
- Gellately, Robert (2001). *Backing Hitler: Consent and Coercion in Nazi Germany*. Oxford and New York: Oxford University Press. ISBN 978-0-19820-560-9.
- Gerlach, Christian (2000). "The Wannsee Conference, the fate of German Jews, and Hitler's decision in principle to exterminate all European Jews". In Omar Bartov, ed. *Holocaust: Origins, Implementation, Aftermath*. New York: Routledge. ISBN 0-415-15036-1.
- Gerlach, Christian (2016). *The Extermination of the European Jews*. Cambridge; New York: Cambridge University Press. ISBN 978-0-52170-689-6.

- Gilbert, Martin (1985). *The Holocaust: A History of the Jews of Europe during the Second World War*. New York: Henry Holt and Company. ISBN 0-8050-0348-7.<templatestyles src="Module:Citation/CS1/styles.css"></templatestyles>
- Gordon, Sarah Ann (1984). *Hitler, Germans, and "the Jewish Question"*. Princeton, NJ: Princeton University Press. ISBN 978-0691101620.<templatestyles src="Module:Citation/CS1/styles.css"></templatestyles>
- Hayes, Peter (2017). *Why? Explaining the Holocaust*. New York: Norton. ISBN 978-0-39325-436-5.<templatestyles src="Module:Citation/CS1/styles.css"></templatestyles>
- Heer, Hannes (2000). "How Amorality Became Normality: Reflections on the Mentality of German Soldiers on the Eastern Front". In Hannes Heer; Klaus Naumann, eds. *War of Extermination: The German Military in World War II*. New York: Berghahn Books. ISBN 978-1-57181-232-2.<templatestyles src="Module:Citation/CS1/styles.css"></templatestyles>
- Hiio, Toomas; Maripuu, Meelis; Paavle, Indrek (2006). Estonia 1940–1945: Reports of the Estonian International Commission for the Investigation of Crimes Against Humanity[1787] (Report). Retrieved 10 August 2017.<templatestyles src="Module:Citation/CS1/styles.css"></templatestyles>
- Hilberg, Raul (1985). *The Destruction of the European Jews*. New York: Holmes & Meier. ISBN 0-8419-0910-5.<templatestyles src="Module:Citation/CS1/styles.css"></templatestyles>
- Hilberg, Raul (1992). *Perpetrators, Victims, Bystanders: The Jewish Catastrophe, 1933–1945*. New York: Harper Collins. ISBN 0-8419-0910-5.<templatestyles src="Module:Citation/CS1/styles.css"></templatestyles>
- Hildebrand, Klaus (1984). *The Third Reich*. London and New York: Routledge. ISBN 0-0494-3033-5.<templatestyles src="Module:Citation/CS1/styles.css"></templatestyles>
- Hillgruber, Andreas (1989). "War in the East and the Extermination of the Jews". In Marrus, Michael. *Part 3, The "Final Solution": The Implementation of Mass Murder*. The Nazi Holocaust. Vol. 1. Westpoint, CT: Meckler. ISBN 0-88736-266-4.<templatestyles src="Module:Citation/CS1/styles.css"></templatestyles>
- Hoffmann, Peter (1977). *The History of the German Resistance, 1933–1945*. Cambridge, MA: MIT Press. ISBN 978-0-26208-088-0.<templatestyles src="Module:Citation/CS1/styles.css"></templatestyles>

- Höhne, Heinz; Zolling, Hermann (1972). *The General was a Spy*. New York: Coward, McCann & Geoghegan, Inc. ISBN 978-0-69810-430-3.
- Ingrao, Christian (2013). *Believe and Destroy: Intellectuals in the SS War Machine*. Malden, MA: Polity. ISBN 978-0-74566-026-4.
- Jacoby, Russell (2003). "Savage Modernism"[1788]. *The Nation*. Retrieved 16 July 2017.
- Jewish Heritage Europe (2016). "Serbia"[1789]. *Jewish Heritage Europe*. Retrieved 1 October 2017.
- JTA—Jewish Telegraph Agency (1999). "Parisian Branch of British Bank Offered to Turn Jews in During War"[1790]. Retrieved 16 July 2017.
- Johnson, Paul (1988). *A History of the Jews*. New York: Harper Perennial. ISBN 978-0060915339.
- Johnson, Eric; Reuband, Karl-Heinz (2005). *What We Knew: Terror, Mass Murder, and Everyday Life in Nazi Germany*. New York: Basic Books. ISBN 978-0-46508-571-2.
- Jones, Adam (2006). *Genocide: A Comprehensive Introduction*. London: Routledge. ISBN 0-415-35384-X.
- Judt, Tony (2005). *Postwar: A History of Europe Since 1945*. New York: Penguin. ISBN 978-1-59420-065-6.
- Kaes, Anton; Jay, Martín; Dimendberg, Edward (1995). *The Weimar Republic Sourcebook*. Berkeley and Los Angeles: University of California Press. pp. 133, 806. ISBN 0-520-06775-4.
- Kellner, Robert Scott (2017). "Selected Diary Entries (October 28, 1941)"[1791]. *The Diary of Friedrich Kellner*. Retrieved 16 July 2017.
- Kershaw, Ian (2005). "OU Lecture 2005: Hitler's Place in History: Transcript"[1792]. *Open Learn*. The Open University—Royal Charter (RC 000391). Retrieved 22 March 2014.

- Kershaw, Ian (2008). *Hitler, the Germans, and the Final Solution*. New Haven; London: Yale University Press. ISBN 978-0-30015-127-5.<templatestyles src="Module:Citation/CS1/styles.css"></templatestyles>
- Koehl, Robert (2004). *The SS: A History 1919–45*. Stroud: Tempus. ISBN 978-0-7524-2559-7.<templatestyles src="Module:Citation/CS1/styles.css"></templatestyles>
- König, Mario; Zeugin, Bettina, eds. (2002). *Switzerland, National Socialism and the Second World War - Final Report of the Independent Commission of Experts Switzerland – Second World War*[1793]. Zürich: Pendo Verlag. p. 496–7. ISBN 3-85842-603-2. Archived from the original[1794] (PDF) on 12 February 2011.<templatestyles src="Module:Citation/CS1/styles.css"></templatestyles>
- Koonz, Claudia (2005). *The Nazi Conscience*. Cambridge, MA: Belknap Press of Harvard University Press. ISBN 978-0-67401-842-6.<templatestyles src="Module:Citation/CS1/styles.css"></templatestyles>
- Krausnick, Helmut (1968). "The Persecution of the Jews". In Krausnick, Helmut; Buchheim, Hans; Broszat, Martin; Jacobsen, Hans-Adolf, eds. *Anatomy of the SS State*. New York: Walker and Company. ISBN 978-0-00211-026-6.<templatestyles src="Module:Citation/CS1/styles.css"></templatestyles>
- Krumenacker, Thomas (7 April 2006). "Nazis Planned Holocaust for Palestine: historians"[1795]. Red Orbit. Retrieved 9 September 2016.<templatestyles src="Module:Citation/CS1/styles.css"></templatestyles>
- Langbehn, Volker; Salama, Mohammad (2011). "Introduction". In Langbehn, Volker; Salama, Mohammad, eds. *German Colonialism: Race, the Holocaust, and Postwar Germany*. New York: Columbia University Press. ISBN 978-0231149730.<templatestyles src="Module:Citation/CS1/styles.css"></templatestyles>
- Laqueur, Walter; Baumel, Judith Tydor (2001). *The Holocaust Encyclopedia*. New Haven and London: Yale University Press. ISBN 978-0-30008-432-0.<templatestyles src="Module:Citation/CS1/styles.css"></templatestyles>
- Lemkin, Raphael (2005). *Axis Rule in Occupied Europe: Laws of Occupation, Analysis of Government, Proposals for Redress*. Clark, NJ: The Lawbook Exchange Ltd. ISBN 978-1584779018.<templatestyles src="Module:Citation/CS1/styles.css"></templatestyles>
- Levy, Alan (2006) [1993]. *Nazi Hunter: The Wiesenthal File* (Revised 2002 ed.). London: Constable & Robinson. ISBN 978-1-84119-607-7.<templatestyles src="Module:Citation/CS1/styles.css"></templatestyles>

- Levy, Robert (2003). "Transnistria, 1941–1942: The Romanian Mass Murder Campaigns (review)"[1796] (PDF). *Project Muse*. Retrieved 24 September 2013.
- Lifton, Robert J. (1986). *The Nazi Doctors: Medical Killing and the Psychology of Genocide*. New York: Basic Books. ISBN 978-0-465-04904-2.
- Longerich, Peter (2006). *Davon haben wir nichts gewusst! Die Deutschen und die Judenverfolgung 1933–1945* (in German). München: Siedler Verlag. ISBN 978-3-88680-843-4.
- Longerich, Peter (2010). *Holocaust: The Nazi Persecution and Murder of the Jews*. Oxford; New York: Oxford University Press. ISBN 978-0-19-280436-5.
- Longerich, Peter (2012). *Heinrich Himmler*. Oxford and New York: Oxford University Press. ISBN 978-0199592326.
- Lubotina, Paul (2015). "Reconciling History: The Holocaust in Scandinavia". In Nancy E. Rupprecht and Wendy Koenig, eds. *Global Perspectives on the Holocaust*. Newcastle upon Tyne, UK: Cambridge Scholars Publishing. ISBN 978-1-44387-606-3.
- Luther, Martin (1971). *Selected Works*. Vol. 47 [The Christian in Society, IV]. Translated by Franklin Sherman. Philadelphia: Fortress Press. ISBN 978-0800603472.
- Mallmann, Klaus-Michael; Cüppers, Martin (2006). *Halbmond und Hakenkreuz: das Dritte Reich, die Araber und Palästina* (in German). Darmstadt: Wissenschaftliche Buchgesellschaft. ISBN 978-3-534-19729-3.
- Manvell, Roger; Fraenkel, Heinrich (2011) [1962]. *Goering: The Rise and Fall of the Notorious Nazi Leader*. London: Skyhorse. ISBN 978-1-61608-109-6.
- Marrus, Michael R. (1987). *The Holocaust in History*. New York: Meridian. ISBN 978-0-45200-953-0.
- Marrus, Michael R. (1989). "The History of the Holocaust: A Survey of Recent Literature". In Michael R. Marrus, ed. *The Nazi Holo-*

*caust. Part 1: Perspectives on the Holocaust.* The Nazi Holocaust: Historical Articles on the Destruction of European Jews. Westport and London: De Gruyter. ISBN 0-88736-266-4.
- Mazower, Mark (2001). *Inside Hitler's Greece: The Experience of Occupation, 1941–44.* New Haven and London: Yale University Press. ISBN 978-0-30008-923-3.
- McDonough, Frank (2008). *The Holocaust.* New York: Palgrave Macmillan. ISBN 978-0-23020-387-7.
- McWhorter, Ladelle (2017). "From Scientific Racism to Neoliberal Biopolitics: Using Foucault's Toolkit". In Zack, Naomi, ed. *The Oxford Handbook of Philosophy and Race.* Oxford; New York: Oxford University Press. ISBN 978-0190236953.
- Miller, Michael (2006). *Leaders of the SS and German Police, Vol. 1.* San Jose, CA: R. James Bender. ISBN 978-93-297-0037-2.
- Millo, Belle (ed.). "Teaching about the Shoah"[1797] (PDF). *Freeman Family Holocaust Education Centre.* Retrieved 16 January 2014.
- Mosse, George (1980). *Toward the Final Solution: A History of European Racism.* New York: Harper & Row. ISBN 978-0-06090-756-3.
- Motadel, David (2014). *Islam and Nazi Germany's War.* Cambridge, MA: The Belknap Press of Harvard University Press. ISBN 978-0-67472-460-0.
- Niewyk, Donald; Nicosia, Francis (2000). *The Columbia Guide to the Holocaust.* New York: Columbia University Press. ISBN 978-0-23111-201-7.
- NS-Archiv (2017). "Hitlers Gutachten über den Antisemitismus: 1919 erstellt im Auftrag seiner militärischen Vorgesetzten"[1798] (in German). NS-Archiv.de. Retrieved 2014-03-22.
- O'Neil, Robin (2005). "Poland and her Jews 1941–1944"[1799]. *JewishGen.* Retrieved 16 July 2017.

- Paldiel, Mordecai (2007). *Diplomat Heroes of the Holocaust*. Jersey City: KTAV Publishing Inc. ISBN 978-0-88125-909-4.<templatestyles src="Module:Citation/CS1/styles.css"></templatestyles>
- Perry, Marvin (2012). *World War II in Europe: A Concise History*. Boston: Wadsworth. ISBN 978-1-11183-652-8.<templatestyles src="Module:Citation/CS1/styles.css"></templatestyles>
- Petropoulos, Jonathan; Roth, John K. (2005). "Part One: Ambiguity and Compromise in Writing and Depicting Holocaust History". In Jonathan Petropoulos; John K. Roth, eds. *Gray Zones: Ambiguity and Compromise in the Holocaust and its Aftermath*. Oxford and New York: Berghahn Books. ISBN 978-1-84545-302-2.<templatestyles src="Module:Citation/CS1/styles.css"></templatestyles>
- Piotrowski, Tadeusz (1998). *Poland's Holocaust*. Jefferson, NC: Mcfarland & Co. ISBN 0-7864-0371-3.<templatestyles src="Module:Citation/CS1/styles.css"></templatestyles>
- Price, Roger (2005). *A Concise History of France*. Cambridge; New York: Cambridge University Press. ISBN 978-0-52160-656-1.<templatestyles src="Module:Citation/CS1/styles.css"></templatestyles>
- Proctor, Robert (1988). *Racial Hygiene: Medicine under the Nazis*. Cambridge, MA: Harvard University Press. ISBN 978-0674745780.<templatestyles src="Module:Citation/CS1/styles.css"></templatestyles>
- Rees, Laurence (2005). *Auschwitz: A New History*. New York: MJF Books. ISBN 978-1-56731-946-0.<templatestyles src="Module:Citation/CS1/styles.css"></templatestyles>
- Rees, Laurence (2017). *The Holocaust: A New History*. New York: PublicAffairs. ISBN 978-1-61039-844-2.<templatestyles src="Module:Citation/CS1/styles.css"></templatestyles>
- Ringelblum, Emmanuel (1992). *Polish–Jewish Relations During the Second World War*. Evanston, IL: Northwestern University Press. ISBN 0-8101-0963-8.<templatestyles src="Module:Citation/CS1/styles.css"></templatestyles>
- Rozett, Robert; Spector, Shmuel (2009). *Encyclopedia of the Holocaust*. Jerusalem: JPH. ISBN 978-0-81604-333-0.<templatestyles src="Module:Citation/CS1/styles.css"></templatestyles>
- Shapiro, Robert Moses (2003). *Why Didn't the Press Shout?: American & International Journalism During the Holocaust*[1800]. KTAV Publishing House. ISBN 978-0-88125-775-5.<templatestyles src="Module:Citation/CS1/styles.css"></templatestyles>
- Shepherd, Ben (2016). *Hitler's Soldiers: The German Army in the Third Reich*. New Haven and London: Yale Uni-

versity Press. ISBN 978-0-300-17903-3.<templatestyles src="Module:Citation/CS1/styles.css"></templatestyles>
- Schuman, Michael (2004). *Croatia*. New York: Facts on File. ISBN 978-0-81605-053-6.<templatestyles src="Module:Citation/CS1/styles.css"></templatestyles>
- Sivathambu, Shamillia (2003). "Romania denies Holocaust (June 14, 2003)"[1801]. *The Daily Telegraph*. London. Retrieved 22 May 2010.<templatestyles src="Module:Citation/CS1/styles.css"></templatestyles>
- Snyder, Timothy (2010). *Bloodlands: Europe between Hitler and Stalin*. New York: Basic Books. ISBN 978-0-46503-147-4.<templatestyles src="Module:Citation/CS1/styles.css"></templatestyles>
- Snyder, Timothy (2015). *Black Earth: The Holocaust as History and Warning*. New York: Tim Duggan Books. ISBN 978-1-10190-345-2.<templatestyles src="Module:Citation/CS1/styles.css"></templatestyles>
- Spiegel Staff. "The Dark Continent: Hitler's European Holocaust Helpers (20 May 2009)"[1802]. *Spiegel Online—International*. Retrieved 11 February 2011.<templatestyles src="Module:Citation/CS1/styles.css"></templatestyles>
- Stackelberg, Roderick (2007). *The Routledge Companion to Nazi Germany*. New York: Routledge. ISBN 978-0-41530-861-8.<templatestyles src="Module:Citation/CS1/styles.css"></templatestyles>
- Stargardt, Nicholas (2015). *The German War: A Nation Under Arms, 1939–1945*. New York: Basic Books. ISBN 978-0-46501-899-4.<templatestyles src="Module:Citation/CS1/styles.css"></templatestyles>
- Stein, George H. (1984). *The Waffen SS: Hitler's Elite Guard at War, 1939–1945*. Ithaca, NY: Cornell University Press. ISBN 0-8014-9275-0.<templatestyles src="Module:Citation/CS1/styles.css"></templatestyles>
- Steinacher, Gerald (2011). *Nazis on the Run: How Hitler's Henchmen Fled Justice*. Oxford; New York: Oxford University Press. ISBN 978-0-19957-686-9.<templatestyles src="Module:Citation/CS1/styles.css"></templatestyles>
- Stone, Dan (2010). *Histories of the Holocaust*. Oxford; New York: Oxford University Press. ISBN 978-0-19956-679-2.<templatestyles src="Module:Citation/CS1/styles.css"></templatestyles>
- Tec, Nechama (1986). *When Light Pierced the Darkness*. New York: Oxford University Press. ISBN 0-19-503643-3.<templatestyles src="Module:Citation/CS1/styles.css"></templatestyles>
- Thacker, Toby (2010) [2009]. *Joseph Goebbels: Life and Death*. New York: Palgrave Macmillan. ISBN 978-0-230-27866-0.<templatestyles

- Traverso, Enzo (2003). *The Origins of Nazi Violence*. New York and London: The New Press. ISBN 978-1-56584-788-0.
- United States Holocaust Memorial Museum (1996). *Historical Atlas of the Holocaust*. New York: Macmillan Publishing. ISBN 978-0-02897-451-4.
- U.S. Department of State (2012). "International Religious Freedom Report for 2012"[1803]. *U.S. Department of State*. Retrieved 1 January 2018.
- USHMM. "Budapest"[1804]. *United States Holocaust Memorial Museum—Holocaust Encyclopedia*. Retrieved 19 August 2017.
- USHMM. "Bulgaria"[1805]. *United States Holocaust Memorial Museum—Holocaust Encyclopedia*. Retrieved 10 August 2017.
- USHMM. "Escape from German-Occupied Europe"[1806]. *United States Holocaust Memorial Museum—Holocaust Encyclopedia*. Retrieved 4 October 2017.
- USHMM. "Lithuania"[1807]. *United States Holocaust Memorial Museum—Holocaust Encyclopedia*. Retrieved 21 August 2017.
- USHMM. "Romania: Facing Its Past"[1808]. *United States Holocaust Memorial Museum—Holocaust Encyclopedia*. Retrieved 2 September 2017.
- USHMM. "The Holocaust in Slovakia"[1809]. *United States Holocaust Memorial Museum—Holocaust Encyclopedia*. Retrieved 4 October 2017.
- USHMM. "Voyage of the St. Louis"[1810]. *United States Holocaust Memorial Museum—Holocaust Encyclopedia*. Retrieved 4 October 2017.
- Van Doorslaer, Rudi (2007). *La Belgique docile: Les autorités belges et la persécution des Juifs en Belgique pendant la Seconde Guerre mondiale* (in French). Brussels: Centre d'Études et de Documentation Guerre et Sociétés contemporaines.

- Vromen, Suzanne (2008). *Hidden Children of the Holocaust: Belgian Nuns and their Daring Rescue of Young Jews from the Nazis*. Oxford; New York: Oxford University Press. ISBN 978-0-19973-905-9.<templatestyles src="Module:Citation/CS1/styles.css"></templatestyles>
- Wachsmann, Nikolaus (2015). *KL: A History of the Nazi Concentration Camps*. New York: Farrar, Straus and Giroux. ISBN 978-0-37411-825-9.<templatestyles src="Module:Citation/CS1/styles.css"></templatestyles>
- Waite, Robert (1993). *The Psychopathic God: Adolf Hitler*. New York: Da Capo Press. ISBN 978-0306805141.<templatestyles src="Module:Citation/CS1/styles.css"></templatestyles>
- Waller, James (2007). *Becoming Evil: How Ordinary People Commit Genocide and Mass Killing*. Oxford; New York: Oxford University Press. ISBN 978-0-19518-093-0.<templatestyles src="Module:Citation/CS1/styles.css"></templatestyles>
- Wallmann, Johannes (1987). "The Reception of Luther's Writings on the Jews from the Reformation to the End of the 19th Century". *Lutheran Quarterly*. **1**: 72–97.<templatestyles src="Module:Citation/CS1/styles.css"></templatestyles>
- Weikart, Richard (2006). *From Darwin to Hitler: Evolutionary Ethics, Eugenics, and Racism in Germany*. New York: Palgrave Macmillan. ISBN 978-1-40396-502-8.<templatestyles src="Module:Citation/CS1/styles.css"></templatestyles>
- Welch, David (2001). *Hitler: Profile of a Dictator*. New York: Routledge. ISBN 978-0415250757.<templatestyles src="Module:Citation/CS1/styles.css"></templatestyles>
- Wette, Wolfram (2007). *The Wehrmacht: History, Myth, Reality*. Cambridge, MA: Harvard University Press. ISBN 978-0-67402-577-6.<templatestyles src="Module:Citation/CS1/styles.css"></templatestyles>
- Wistrich, Robert (2001). *Hitler and the Holocaust*. New York: Modern Library Chronicles. ISBN 0-679-64222-6.<templatestyles src="Module:Citation/CS1/styles.css"></templatestyles>
- Yad Vashem. "Names of Righteous by Country"[1811]. *Yad Vashem—The World Holocaust Remembrance Center*. Retrieved 19 August 2017.<templatestyles src="Module:Citation/CS1/styles.css"></templatestyles>
- Yahil, Leni (1990). *The Holocaust: The Fate of European Jewry, 1932–1945*. Oxford and New York: Oxford University Press. ISBN 0-19-504522-X.<templatestyles src="Module:Citation/CS1/styles.css"></templatestyles>

- Zentner, Christian; Bedürftig, Friedemann (1991). *The Encyclopedia of the Third Reich*. (2 vols.) New York: MacMillan Publishing. ISBN 0-02-897500-6.<templatestyles src="Module:Citation/CS1/styles.css"></templatestyles>

# List of major perpetrators of the Holocaust

This is a **list of major perpetrators of the Holocaust**.

| Name | Photograph | Date of birth | Date of death | Age at death | Role | Fate |
|---|---|---|---|---|---|---|
| Adolf Hitler | | April 20, 1889 | April 30, 1945 | 56 years, 10 days | Leader of the Nazi Party during the Third Reich Chancellor of Germany Führer | Committed suicide by gunshot[1812,1813] |
| Heinrich Luitpold Himmler | | October 7, 1900 | May 23, 1945 | 44 years, 228 days | *Reichsführer-SS* Chief of German Police Reich Minister of the Interior | Arrested; committed suicide by biting down on a cyanide capsule |
| Reinhard Tristan Eugen Heydrich | | March 7, 1904 | June 4, 1942 | 38 years, 89 days | Chief of the Reich Main Security Office Deputy Reich-Protector of Bohemia and Moravia (acting Protector) | Assassinated in Operation Anthropoid |
| Otto Adolf Eichmann | | March 19, 1906 | May 31, 1962 | 56 years, 73 days | Head of the Gestapo Office of Jewish Affairs (*RSHA* Sub-Department IV-B4). Charged by Reinhard Heydrich with facilitating and managing the mass deportations of Jews to ghettos and extermination camps in Eastern Europe. | Evaded arrest after the war and escaped to Argentina in 1950. Discovered and kidnapped by Israeli agents in May 1960; subsequently brought to Israel, tried and executed by hanging in June 1962. |
| Hermann Wilhelm Göring | | January 12, 1893 | October 15, 1946 | 53 years, 276 days | Commander-in-Chief of the Luftwaffe President of the Reichstag Reichsminister of Aviation | Sentenced to death by hanging; committed suicide by cyanide poisoning |
| Heinrich Müller | | April 28, 1900 | | | *SS-Gruppenführer und Generalleutnant der Polizei*, Chief of the Gestapo 1939–1945 | Disappeared; possibly killed in Berlin during May 1945 (unconfirmed) |

## List of major perpetrators of the Holocaust

| Name | | Born | Died | Age | Role | Fate |
|---|---|---|---|---|---|---|
| Odilo Globocnik | | April 21, 1904 | May 31, 1945 | 41 years, 40 days | SS and Police Leader in the General Government Head of Operation Reinhard | Committed suicide by cyanide poisoning |
| Theodor Eicke | | October 17, 1892 | February 26, 1943 | 50 years, 132 days | A major figure in the creation of the Nazi concentration camps First commander of SS Division Totenkopf, which became notorious for its war crimes. | Killed in action |
| Richard Glücks | | April 22, 1889 | May 10, 1945 | 56 years, 18 days | Head of Concentration Camp Operations (*Amt D: Konzentrationslagerwesen*) in the SS Main Economic and Administrative Department (*SS-Wirtschafts-Verwaltungshauptamt*) | Committed suicide by cyanide poisoning |
| Ernst Kaltenbrunner | | October 4, 1903 | October 16, 1946 | 43 years, 12 days | Chief of the Reich Main Security Office after Heydrich was assassinated President of Interpol | Executed by hanging |
| Paul Joseph Goebbels | | October 29, 1897 | May 1, 1945 | 47 years, 184 days | Ministry of Public Enlightenment and Propaganda High-ranking Nazi Party member | Committed suicide by gunshot |
| Hans Michael Frank | | May 23, 1900 | October 16, 1946 | 46 years, 146 days | Governor-General of the General Government | Executed by hanging |
| Arthur Seyss-Inquart | | July 22, 1892 | October 16, 1946 | 54 years, 86 days | Ruler of the Netherlands after its conquest, and effectively deputy to Hans Frank in occupied Poland | Executed by hanging |
| Kurt Daluege | | September 15, 1897 | October 24, 1946 | 49 years, 39 days | Chief of the *Ordnungspolizei* Deputy Reich-Protector of Bohemia and Moravia (acting Protector) Organized the massacres of the Czech villages of Lidice and Ležáky after the assassination of Heydrich | Executed by hanging |

# List of major perpetrators of the Holocaust

| Name | | Born | Died | Age | Role | Fate |
|---|---|---|---|---|---|---|
| Hans Günther | | August 22, 1910 | May 5, 1945 | 34 years, 256 days | Elder brother of Rolf Günther; head of the Central Office for Jewish Emigration in Prague (1939–1945). Directly in charge of the Final Solution in the Protectorate of Bohemia and Moravia | Killed by Czech partisans during the Prague Uprising |
| Rolf Günther | | January 8, 1913 | August 15, 1945 | 32 years, 219 days | First deputy to Adolf Eichmann in the Gestapo Office of Jewish Affairs and head of the "Emigration Section" (*RSHA* Sub-Department IV-B4-a). Direct overseer of the deportations of Jews to concentration camps; personally oversaw the deportations of Greek Jews. Chief of Security Police and SD in Vienna (1943–1944) and in Prague (1944–1945) | Taken into American custody in May 1945; committed suicide by cyanide poisoning in August 1945. |
| Franz Novak | | January 10, 1913 | October 21, 1983 | 70 years, 284 days | Deputy to Adolf Eichmann in the Office of Jewish Affairs; logistics and timetable coordinator for railway deportations of Jews under Rolf Günther (*RSHA* Sub-Department IV-B4-a-"Transport"). | Arrested in 1961; tried and acquitted in 1964 and 1966. Sentenced to 9 years in 1969; verdict reduced to 7 years in 1972; pardoned by the President of Austria with credit for time served. |
| Oswald Ludwig Pohl | | June 30, 1892 | June 8, 1951 | 58 years, 343 days | Chief of the SS-*Wirtschafts-Verwaltungshauptamt* (SS Main Economic and Administrative Department), the central SS financial office responsible for overall administration of the concentration camps. | Executed by hanging |
| Arthur Greiser | | January 22, 1897 | July 21, 1946 | 49 years, 180 days | *Gauleiter* of Wartheland; active participant in organising the Holocaust in Poland | Executed by hanging |
| Alois Brunner | | April 8, 1912 | c. 2010 | c. 98 | Deputy to Adolf Eichmann; organised the deportations of at least 140,000 Jews from France, Greece, Slovakia and Austria. Commandant of the Drancy internment camp | Escaped to Egypt around 1954, then fled to Syria. Served as a consultant to the al-Assad regime on torture techniques; died in Syria of natural causes around 2010. |

| Name | | Born | Died | Age | Role | Fate |
|---|---|---|---|---|---|---|
| Theodor Dannecker | | March 27, 1913 | December 10, 1945 | 32 years, 258 days | Deputy to Adolf Eichmann; Head of the *SD Hauptamt – Judenreferat* (SD Head Office – Jewish Affairs Department) for Paris: September 1940 – July 1942. In charge of the Final Solution in Bulgaria, the Balkans and Hungary (from 1943) | Arrested by the U.S. military; committed suicide |
| Martin Ludwig Bormann | | June 17, 1900 | May 2, 1945 | 44 years, 319 days | Head of the Nazi Party Chancellery Private Secretary to Adolf Hitler | Sentenced to death by hanging *in absentia*; believed to have committed suicide to avoid capture in Berlin; the buried body was not found until 1972; the remains were conclusively identified in 1998.[1814,1815] |
| Alfred Ernst Rosenberg | | January 12, 1893 | October 16, 1946 | 53 years, 277 days | Nazi theoretician and head of the Reich Ministry for the Occupied Eastern Territories | Executed by hanging |
| Rudolf Hermann Brandt | | June 2, 1909 | June 2, 1948 | 39 years, 0 days | Chief of the Ministerial Office of the Reich Ministry of the Interior and personal deputy of administration to Heinrich Himmler | Executed by hanging |
| Roland Freisler | | October 30, 1893 | February 3, 1945 | 51 years, 96 days | Prominent lawyer/judge and State Secretary of the Reich Ministry of Justice and President of the People's Court (*Volksgerichtshof*) in Nazi Germany. Between 1942 and 1945, more than 5,000 death sentences were handed out, and of these, 2,600 through the court's First Senate, which Freisler headed | Killed during an Allied bombing raid |
| Wilhelm Bodewin Johann Gustav Keitel | | September 22, 1882 | October 16, 1946 | 64 years, 24 days | Minister of War and chief of the Supreme Command of the Armed Forces | Executed by hanging |
| Hermann Julius "Hans" Höfle | | June 19, 1911 | August 20, 1962 | 51 years, 62 days | Coordinator of Operation Reinhard | Arrested; committed suicide by hanging |

# List of major perpetrators of the Holocaust

| Name | | Born | Died | Age | Role | Fate |
|---|---|---|---|---|---|---|
| Richard Wolfgang Thomalla | | October 23, 1903 | May 12, 1945 | 41 years, 201 days | Head of extermination camp construction during Operation Reinhard | Executed by the NKVD (presumed) |
| Erwin Hermann Lambert | | December 7, 1909 | October 15, 1976 | 66 years, 313 days | Head of gas chamber construction during Operation Reinhard | Arrested but acquitted |
| Karl Steubl | | October 25, 1910 | September 21, 1945 | 34 years, 331 days | Commander of transportation units during Operation Reinhard | Arrested; committed suicide |
| Karl Bischoff | | August 9, 1897 | October 2, 1950 | 53 years, 54 days | Head of extermination camp construction at Auschwitz II-Birkenau | Died without being suspected of a crime |
| Christian Wirth | | November 24, 1885 | May 26, 1944 | 58 years, 184 days | Inspector of Action T4 and Operation Reinhard; Commandant of Bełżec, March 17, 1942—end of August 1942 (1/2) | Assassinated |
| Rudolf Franz Ferdinand Höss | | November 25, 1900 | April 16, 1947 | 46 years, 142 days | Commandant of Auschwitz, May 4, 1940—December 1, 1943, May 8, 1944—January 18, 1945 (1/2) | Executed by hanging |
| Arthur Liebehenschel | | November 25, 1901 | January 28, 1948 | 46 years, 64 days | Commandant of Auschwitz, December 1, 1943—May 8, 1944 (2/2); Commandant of Majdanek, May 19, 1944—July 22, 1944 (5/5) | Executed by hanging |
| Martin Gottfried Weiss | | June 3, 1905 | May 29, 1946 | 40 years, 360 days | Commandant of Dachau, January 3, 1942—September 30, 1943 (8/12) Commandant of Dachau, April 26, 1945—April 28, 1945 (10/12) Commandant of Neuengamme, April 1940—August 1942 (2/3) Commandant of Majdanek, November 1943—May 1944 (4/5) | Executed by hanging |
| Irmfried Eberl | | September 8, 1910 | February 16, 1948 | 37 years, 161 days | Commandant of Treblinka, July 11, 1942—August 26, 1942 (1/3) | Arrested; committed suicide by hanging |
| Hans Bothmann | | November 11, 1911 | April 4, 1946 | 34 years, 144 days | Commandant of Chelmno, April 1942—July 1944 (2/2) | Arrested by the British Army; committed suicide by hanging |

| Name | | Born | Died | Age | Role | Fate |
|---|---|---|---|---|---|---|
| Herbert Lange | | September 29, 1909 | April 20, 1945 | 35 years, 203 days | Commandant of Chelmno, December 1941—March 1942 (1/2) | Killed in action during the Battle of Berlin |
| Franz Paul Stangl | | March 26, 1908 | June 28, 1971 | 63 years, 94 days | Commandant of Sobibór, April 28, 1942—August 30, 1942 (1/2); Commandant of Treblinka, September 1, 1942—August 1943 (2/3) | Arrested on February 28, 1967; sentenced to life imprisonment on October 22, 1970; died in prison |
| Kurt Hubert Franz | | January 17, 1914 | July 4, 1998 | 84 years, 168 days | Commandant of Treblinka, August 1943—October 19, 1943 (3/3) | Arrested on December 2, 1959; sentenced to life imprisonment in 1965; released on health grounds in 1993 |
| Franz Karl Reichleitner | | December 2, 1906 | January 3, 1944 | 37 years, 32 days | Commandant of Sobibór, September 1, 1942—October 17, 1943 (2/2) | Assassinated |
| Gottlieb Hering | | June 2, 1887 | October 9, 1945 | 58 years, 129 days | Commandant of Bełżec, end of August 1942—June 1943 (2/2) | Died of mysterious health complications |
| Amon Leopold Goeth | | December 11, 1908 | September 13, 1946 | 37 years, 276 days | Commandant of Kraków-Płaszów (1/1) | Executed by hanging |
| Dr. Josef Mengele | | March 16, 1911 | February 7, 1979 | 67 years, 328 days | Human medical experimentation, particularly children, and selection of prisoners to be gassed at Auschwitz | Escaped to Brazil; evaded arrest and died in 1979 |
| Karl Hermann Frank | | January 24, 1898 | May 22, 1946 | 48 years, 118 days | Higher SS and Police Leader (HSSPF) and State Minister for Bohemia and Moravia | Executed by hanging |
| Hanns Albin Rauter | | February 4, 1895 | March 24, 1949 | 54 years, 48 days | Higher SS and Police Leader (HSSPF) for the Netherlands | Executed by firing squad |

List of major perpetrators of the Holocaust

| | | | | | | |
|---|---|---|---|---|---|---|
| Carl Oberg | | January 27, 1897 | June 3, 1965 | 68 years, 127 days | SS and Police Leader (HSSPF) for Radom (August 1941 – May 1942) Higher SS and Police Leader (HSSPF) for France (May 1942 – November 1944). Supreme German authority in France for anti-Jewish and anti-Resistance operations | Sentenced to death – 1946, transferred to French custody and sentenced to death – 1954, commuted to life imprisonment in 1958, released November 1962 |
| Walter Rauff | File:Walter Rauff (1945).jpg | June 19, 1906 | May 14, 1984 | 77 years, 330 days | Close aide of Reinhard Heydrich. Group Leader II D of the RSHA (technical matters). Designed gas vans to poison Jews, and persons with disabilities. *Einsatzkommando* leader in North Africa (1942-1943), SS and Gestapo commander in northwest Italy (1943-1945). | Arrested in Italy in 1945; escaped in 1946, fled to Syria in 1948, to Ecuador in 1949, to Chile in 1958. Extradition request by Germany thrown out by Chile in 1963 on the grounds of expired statute of limitations. Most wanted Nazi fugitive in the 1970s and 1980s. Died of natural causes in Chile in 1984. |
| Dr. Eduard Wirths | | September 4, 1909 | September 20, 1945 | 36 years, 16 days | Human medical experimentation, and formal responsibility of medical staff at Auschwitz | Arrested; committed suicide by hanging |
| Dr. Horst Schumann | | May 1, 1906 | May 5, 1983 | 77 years, 4 days | Human medical experimentation at Auschwitz | Arrested in 1966; released on health grounds on July 29, 1972 |
| Dr. Carl Clauberg | | September 28, 1898 | August 9, 1957 | 58 years, 315 days | Human medical experimentation at Auschwitz | Sentenced to 25 years imprisonment in 1948; released in 1955; re-arrested in West Germany, but died of a heart attack before being tried |
| Viktor Hermann Brack | | November 9, 1904 | June 2, 1948 | 43 years, 206 days | Action T4; Human medical experimentation | Executed by hanging |
| Dr. Karl Franz Gebhardt | | November 23, 1897 | June 2, 1948 | 50 years, 192 days | Director of the German Red Cross and personal physician to Heinrich Himmler. Oversaw human medical experimentation of concentration camp inmates. | Executed by hanging |

# List of major perpetrators of the Holocaust

| Name | | Born | Died | Age | Role | Fate |
|---|---|---|---|---|---|---|
| Dr. Fritz Klein | | November 24, 1888 | December 13, 1945 | 57 years, 19 days | Selection of prisoners to be gassed at Auschwitz | Executed by hanging |
| Dr. Karl Brandt | | January 8, 1904 | June 2, 1948 | 44 years, 146 days | Co-director of Action T4 Conducted human medical experimentation | Executed by hanging |
| Philipp Bouhler | | September 11, 1899 | May 19, 1945 | 45 years, 250 days | Director of Action T4 | Arrested; committed suicide by cyanide poisoning |
| Josef Kramer | | November 10, 1906 | December 13, 1945 | 39 years, 33 days | Deputy commandant of Auschwitz Commandant of Bergen-Belsen | Executed by hanging |
| Hans Aumeier | | August 20, 1906 | January 28, 1948 | 41 years, 161 days | Deputy commandant of Auschwitz | Executed by hanging |
| Franz Hössler | | February 4, 1906 | December 13, 1945 | 39 years, 312 days | Deputy commandant of Auschwitz | Executed by hanging |
| Karl Fritzsch | | July 10, 1903 | May 2, 1945? | 41 years, 296 days? | Deputy commandant of Auschwitz | Disappeared in May 1945; fate uncertain |
| Maximilian Grabner | | October 2, 1905 | January 28, 1948 | 42 years, 118 days | Gestapo command (torture of prisoners) at Auschwitz | Executed by hanging |
| Heinrich Arthur Matthes | | January 11, 1902 | Deceased | | Deputy commandant of Treblinka | Arrested in 1964; sentenced to life imprisonment on September 3, 1965 |
| Josef Kaspar Oberhauser | | January 21, 1915 | November 22, 1979 | 64 years, 305 days | Deputy commandant of Bełżec | Sentenced to 15 years in prison; released early on 28 April 1956 |
| Lorenz Marie Hackenholt | | June 25, 1914 | December 31, 1945 | 31 years, 189 days | Gas chamber construction and executioner of Bełżec and other camps during Operation Reinhard | Declared legally dead |

# List of major perpetrators of the Holocaust

| Name | | Born | Died | Age | Role | Fate |
|---|---|---|---|---|---|---|
| Wilhelm Harster | | July 21, 1904 | December 25, 1991 | 87 years, 157 days | Commander of the Security Police (SiPo) and SD (Krakow, 1939-1940; Netherlands, 1940-1943; Italy, 1943-1945). Responsible for the deaths of at least 104,000 Jews. | Arrested by British forces in 1945. Transferred to Dutch custody in 1947. Tried and sentenced to 12 years imprisonment by a Dutch court in 1949; served six years and deported to West Germany in 1955. Initially classified as a "minor offender" by West Germany; arrested and tried by a Munich court in 1967, following a new investigation. Sentenced to 15 years imprisonment, but sentence subsequently commuted to time served. Released in 1969. |
| Johann Niemann | | August 4, 1913 | October 14, 1943 | 30 years, 71 days | Deputy commandant of Bełżec and Sobibór | Assassinated during Sobibór revolt |
| Gustav Franz Wagner | | July 18, 1911 | October 3, 1980 | 69 years, 77 days | Deputy commandant of Sobibór | Sentenced to death by hanging *in absentia*; evaded arrest for 35 years until found dead, believed to have committed suicide by stabbing |
| Karl August Wilhelm Frenzel | | August 28, 1911 | September 2, 1996 | 85 years, 5 days | Commandant of Camp I (forced labor camp) at Sobibór | Arrested on March 22, 1962; sentenced to life imprisonment on December 20, 1966; released on health grounds in 1982 |
| Hermann Michel | | April 23, 1912 | | | Deputy commandant of Sobibór | Evaded arrest; whereabouts unknown |
| Hermann Erich Bauer | | March 26, 1900 | February 4, 1980 | 79 years, 315 days | Gas chamber executioner of Sobibór | Sentenced to death by hanging; commuted to life imprisonment; died in prison |

| Name | | Born | Died | Age | Role | Fate |
|---|---|---|---|---|---|---|
| Heinz Kurt Bolender | | May 21, 1912 | October 10, 1966 | 54 years, 142 days | Gas chamber executioner of Sobibór | Arrested in May 1961; committed suicide by hanging |
| Jürgen Stroop | | September 26, 1895 | March 6, 1952 | 56 years, 162 days | Suppression and destruction of the Warsaw Ghetto Uprising | Executed by hanging |
| Friedrich-Wilhelm Krüger | | February 27, 1894 | May 9, 1945 | 51 years, 71 days | SS and Police Leader in occupied Poland | Committed suicide |
| Bruno Heinrich Streckenbach | | February 7, 1902 | October 28, 1977 | 75 years, 263 days | Trained the *Einsatzgruppen*; commander of *Einsatzgruppe I* in Poland | Sentenced to 25 years imprisonment in 1952; released on October 10, 1955 |
| Friedrich August Jeckeln | | February 2, 1895 | February 3, 1946 | 51 years, 1 day | Responsible for Rumbula, Babi Yar, and Kamianets-Podilskyi massacres | Executed by hanging |
| Franz Walter Stahlecker | | October 10, 1900 | March 23, 1942 | 41 years, 164 days | Commander of *Einsatzgruppe A*, Baltic states, June 22, 1941–March 23, 1942 (1/5) | Killed in action |
| Heinz Jost | | July 9, 1904 | November 12, 1964 | 60 years, 126 days | Commander of *Einsatzgruppe A*, Baltic states, March 29, 1942–September 2, 1942 (2/5) | Sentenced to life imprisonment in 1945; commuted to 10 years; released in 1951 |
| Humbert Achamer-Pifrader | | November 21, 1900 | April 25, 1945 | 44 years, 155 days | Commander of *Einsatzgruppe A*, Baltic states, September 10, 1942–September 4, 1943 (3/5) | Killed in air raid |
| Friedrich Panzinger | | February 1, 1903 | August 8, 1959 | 56 years, 188 days | Commander of *Einsatzgruppe A*, Baltic states, September 5, 1943–May 6, 1944 (4/5) Chief of the Kripo (2/2) | Arrested; committed suicide |
| Wilhelm Fuchs | | September 1, 1898 | January 24, 1947 | 48 years, 145 days | Commander of *Einsatzgruppe A*, Baltic states, May 6, 1944–October 10, 1944 (5/5); Commander of *Einsatzkommando 3*, September 15, 1943–May 27, 1944 | Executed |

# List of major perpetrators of the Holocaust

| Name | | Born | Died | Age | Role | Fate |
|---|---|---|---|---|---|---|
| Eduard Strauch | | August 17, 1906 | September 15, 1955 | 49 years, 29 days | Commander of *Einsatzkommando 2*, Latvia (Rumbula), November 4, 1941–December 2, 1941; Commander of *Sonderkommando 1b*, March 1942–August 1942 | Sentenced to death by hanging in 1948; died in prison |
| Rudolf Lange | | April 18, 1910 | February 23, 1945 | 34 years, 311 days | Commander of *Einsatzkommando 2*, Latvia, December 3, 1941–1944 | Believed to have been killed in action |
| Karl Jäger | | September 20, 1888 | June 22, 1959 | 70 years, 275 days | Commander of *Einsatzkommando 3*, Lithuania, June 1941–August 1, 1943 | Discovered and arrested in 1959; committed suicide |
| Hermann Schaper | | August 12, 1911 | deceased after 2002 | over 90 years | Commander of *Einsatzgruppe B*, Poland | Arrested in 1964; released due to insufficient evidence |
| Arthur Nebe | | November 13, 1894 | March 21, 1945 | 50 years, 128 days | Commander of *Einsatzgruppe B*, Belarus, June 1941–November 1941 (1/5) Chief of the Kripo (1/2) President of Interpol | Executed by Nazi Germany for involvement in the failed 20 July 1944 attempt to kill Adolf Hitler |
| Erich Naumann | | April 29, 1905 | June 8, 1951 | 46 years, 40 days | Commander of *Einsatzgruppe B*, Belarus, November 1941–March 1943 (2/5) | Executed by hanging |
| Horst Böhme | | August 24, 1909 | April 10, 1945 | 35 years, 229 days | Lidice Commander of *Einsatzgruppe B*, Belarus, March 12, 1943–August 28, 1943, August 12, 1944 (3/5); Commander of *Einsatzgruppe C*, north and central Ukraine, September 6, 1943–March 1944 (3/3) | Presumed killed in action in Königsberg, East Prussia; officially declared dead in 1954 |
| Erich Ehrlinger | | October 14, 1910 | July 31, 2004 | 93 years, 291 days | Commander of *Einsatzgruppe B*, Belarus, August 28, 1943–April 1944 (4/5); Commander of *Sonderkommando 1b*, June 1941–November 1941 | Arrested in December 1958; sentenced to 12 years imprisonment |

# List of major perpetrators of the Holocaust

| Name | | Born | Died | Age | Role | Fate |
|---|---|---|---|---|---|---|
| Heinrich Otto Seetzen | | June 22, 1906 | September 28, 1945 | 39 years, 98 days | Commander of *Einsatzgruppe B*, Belarus, April 28, 1944–August 1944 (5/5); Commander of *Einsatzkommando 10a*, Moldova, south Ukraine, the Crimea, and north Caucasus, June 1941–July 1942 | Arrested in September 1945; committed suicide by cyanide poisoning. |
| Otto Bradfisch | | May 10, 1903 | June 22, 1994 | 91 years, 43 days | Commander of *Einsatzkommando 8*, Belarus, June 1941–April 1, 1942 | Arrested on April 21, 1958; sentenced to 13 years imprisonment in 1963 |
| Emil Otto Rasch | | December 7, 1891 | November 1, 1948 | 56 years, 330 days | Commander of *Einsatzgruppe C*, north and central Ukraine, June 1941–October 1941 (1/3) | Arrested; removed from trial on health grounds; died in prison |
| Max Thomas | | August 4, 1891 | December 6, 1945 | 54 years, 124 days | Commander of *Einsatzgruppe C*, north and central Ukraine, October 1941–April 29, 1943 (2/3) | Committed suicide |
| Paul Blobel | | August 13, 1894 | June 8, 1951 | 56 years, 299 days | Commander of *Einsatzkommando 4a*, Ukraine (Babi Yar), June 1941–January 13, 1942; Director of Sonderaktion 1005 | Executed by hanging |
| Otto Ohlendorf | | February 4, 1907 | June 8, 1951 | 44 years, 124 days | Commander of *Einsatzgruppe D*, Moldova, south Ukraine, the Crimea, and north Caucasus, June 1941–July 1942 (1/2) | Executed by hanging |
| Walther Bierkamp | | December 17, 1901 | May 15, 1945 | 43 years, 149 days | Commander of *Einsatzgruppe D*, Moldova, south Ukraine, the Crimea, and north Caucasus, July 1942–March 1943 (2/2) | Committed suicide |
| Werner Braune | | April 11, 1909 | June 8, 1951 | 42 years, 58 days | Commander of *Einsatzkommando 11b*, south Ukraine and the Crimea, October 1941–September 1942 | Executed by hanging |
| Maria Mandel | | January 10, 1912 | January 24, 1948 | 36 years, 14 days | Commandant of female camp at Auschwitz | Executed by hanging |

| Irma Ida Ilse Grese |  | October 7, 1924 | December 13, 1945 | 21 years, 67 days | Warden of the women's section of Bergen-Belsen, and later Auschwitz | Executed by hanging |

# Aftermath of the Holocaust

Part of a series on
**The Holocaust**

Jews on selection ramp at Auschwitz, May 1944

- v
- t
- e<sup>1816</sup>

The Holocaust had a deep effect on society in both Europe and the rest of the world. Its impact has been felt in theological discussions, artistic and cultural pursuits, and political decisions.

The after effects are still evident today in children and adults whose ancestors faced this horrible scene.

## Evidence in Germany

German society largely responded to the enormity of the evidence for and the horror of the Holocaust with an attitude of self-justification and a practice of keeping quiet. Germans attempted to rewrite their own history to make it more palatable in the post-war era.[1817] For decades, West Germany and then unified Germany refused to allow access to its Holocaust-related archives in Bad Arolsen, citing privacy concerns. In May 2006, a 20-year effort by the United States Holocaust Memorial Museum led to the announcement that 30–50 million pages would be made available to survivors, historians and others.[1818]

## Survivors

### Displaced Persons and the State of Israel

The Holocaust and its aftermath left millions of refugees, including many Jews who had lost most or all of their family members and possessions, and often faced persistent antisemitism in their home countries. The original plan of the Allies was to repatriate these "displaced persons" to their countries of origin, but many refused to return, or were unable to as their homes or communities had been destroyed. As a result, more than 250,000 languished in displaced persons camps for years after the war ended.

With most displaced persons being unable or unwilling to return to their former homes in Europe, and with restrictions to immigration to many western countries remaining in place, the British Mandate of Palestine became the primary destination for many Jewish refugees. However, as local Arabs opposed their immigration, the United Kingdom refused to allow Jewish refugees into the Mandate territory. Countries in the Soviet Bloc made emigration difficult. Former Jewish partisans in Europe, along with the Haganah in British Mandate of Palestine, organized a massive effort to smuggle Jews into Palestine, called Berihah, which eventually transported 250,000 Jews (both displaced persons and those who had been in hiding during the war) to Mandate Palestine. After the State of Israel declared independence in 1948, Jews were able to emigrate to Israel legally and without restriction. By 1952, when the displaced persons camps were closed, there were more than 80,000 Jewish former displaced persons in the United States, about 136,000 in Israel, and another 10,000 in other countries, including Mexico, Japan, and countries in Africa and South America.

## Resurgence of antisemitism

The few Jews in Poland were augmented by returnees from the Soviet Union and survivors from camps in Germany. However, a resurgence of antisemitism in Poland, in such incidents as the Kraków pogrom on August 11, 1945, and the Kielce pogrom on July 4, 1946, led to the exodus of a large part of the Jewish population, which no longer felt safe in Poland.[1819] Anti-Jewish riots also broke out in several other Polish cities where many Jews were killed.[1820]

An important reason for the atrocities was a widespread Polish belief that the Jews were supporters of the new communist regime and the new oppressors of the Polish state. This belief, termed "Żydokomuna", was fuelled by the fact that two of the three Communist leaders who dominated Poland between 1948 and 1956, Jakub Berman and Hilary Minc, were of Jewish origin. The attitude of Christian Poles towards Polish Jews hardened significantly and hundreds of Jews were killed in anti-Jewish violence. Some were simply killed for financial reasons. As a result of the exodus the number of Jews in Poland decreased from 200,000 in the years immediately after the war to 50,000 in 1950 and 6,000 by the 1980s.

Lesser post-war pogroms also broke out in Hungary.

## Welfare in Israel

As of May 6, 2016 45,000 Holocaust survivors are living below the country's poverty line and need more assistance. Situations like these result in heated and dramatic protests on the part of some survivors against the Israeli government and related agencies. The average rate of cancer among survivors is nearly two and a half times the national average, while the average rate of colon cancer, attributed to the victims' experience of starvation and extreme stress, is nine times higher. The population of survivors that now live in Israel has now dwindled to 189,000.[1821,1822,1823]

## Searching for records of victims

There has been a recent resurgence of interest among descendants of survivors in researching the fates of their relatives. Yad Vashem provides a searchable database of three million names, about half of the known Jewish victims. Yad Vashem's *Central Database of Shoah Victims Names* is searchable over the internet yadvashem.org[1824] or in person at the Yad Vashem complex in Israel. Other databases and lists of victims' names, some searchable over the internet, are listed in Holocaust (resources).

## Impact on culture

### Effect on Yiddish language and culture

In the decades preceding World War II, there was a tremendous growth in the recognition of Yiddish as an official Jewish European language, even a Yiddish renaissance, in particular in Poland. On the eve of World War II, there were 11 to 13 million speakers of Yiddish in the world.[1825] The Holocaust destroyed the Eastern European bedrock of Yiddish, though the language was rapidly declining anyhow. In the 1920s and 1930s the Soviet Jewish public rejected the cultural autonomy offered to it by the regime and opted for Russification:[1826] while 70.4% of Soviet Jews declared Yiddish their mother tongue in 1926, only 39.7% did so in 1939. Even in Poland, where harsh discrimination left the Jews as a cohesive ethnic group, Yiddish was rapidly declining in favour of Polonization. 80% of the entire Jewish population declared it mother tongue in 1931, but among high school students this number fell to 53% in 1937.[1827] In the United States, the preservation of the language was always a unigenerational phenomenon, and the immigrants' children quickly abandoned it for English.[1828]

Starting with the Nazi invasion of Poland in 1939, and continuing with the destruction of Yiddish culture in Europe during the remainder of the war, Yiddish language and culture were almost completely rooted out of Europe. The Holocaust led to a dramatic decline in the use of Yiddish, as the extensive Jewish communities, both secular and religious, that used Yiddish in their day-to-day lives were largely destroyed. Around five million victims of the Holocaust, or 85% of the total, were speakers of Yiddish.[1829]

### Holocaust theology

Holocaust theology is a body of theological and philosophical debate concerning the role of God in the universe in light of the Holocaust of the late 1930s and 1940s. It is primarily found in Judaism; Jews were drastically affected by the Holocaust, in which six million Jews were murdered in a genocide by Nazi Germany and its allies.[1830] Jews were killed in higher proportions than other groups; some scholars limit the definition of the Holocaust to the Jewish victims of the Nazis as Jews alone were targeted for the Final Solution. Others include the additional five million non-Jewish victims, bringing the total to about 11 million. One third of the total worldwide Jewish population were killed during the Holocaust. The Eastern European Jewish population was particularly hard hit, being reduced by ninety percent.

Judaism, Christianity, and Islam have traditionally taught that God is omniscient (all-knowing), omnipotent (all-powerful), and omnibenevolent (all-good) in nature. However, these views are in apparent contrast with the injustice and suffering in the world. Monotheists seek to reconcile this view of God with the existence of evil and suffering. In so doing, they are confronting what is known as the problem of evil.

Within all of the monotheistic faiths many answers (theodicies) have been proposed. In light of the magnitude of depravity seen in the Holocaust, many people have also re-examined classical views on this subject. A common question raised in Holocaust theology is "How can people still have any kind of faith after the Holocaust?"

Orthodox Jews have stated that the fact that the Holocaust happened does not diminish the belief in God. For a creation will never be able to fully grasp the creator, just as a child in an operating theater can not fathom why men are cutting up a live man's body. As the grand Lubavitcher Rebbe once told Elie Weisel that after witnessing the holocaust and realising how low man can steep, who can we trust, if not God? Nevertheless, Orthodox Judaism does encourage us to pray and cry out to God, and complain to him how he lets bad things happen.

## Art and literature

Theodor Adorno commented that "writing poetry after Auschwitz is barbaric," and the Holocaust has indeed had a profound impact on art and literature, for both Jews and non-Jews. Some of the more famous works are by Holocaust survivors or victims, such as Elie Wiesel, Primo Levi, Viktor Frankl and Anne Frank, but there is a substantial body of literature and art in many languages. Indeed, Paul Celan wrote his poem *Todesfuge* as a direct response to Adorno's dictum.

The Holocaust has also been the subject of many films, including Oscar winners *Schindler's List*, *The Pianist* and *Life Is Beautiful*. With the aging population of Holocaust survivors, there has been increasing attention in recent years to preserving the memory of the Holocaust. The result has included extensive efforts to document their stories, including the Survivors of the Shoah project and Four Seasons Documentary, as well as institutions devoted to memorializing and studying the Holocaust, including Yad Vashem in Israel and the US Holocaust Museum. The historic tale of the Danish Jews fleeing to Sweden by fishing boat is recounted in an award-winning American children's novel.

## Pre-1945 European art

Huge amounts of works of art were looted by the Nazis from Jewish art collectors and dealers, either through outright theft or fire sales under extreme duress. Thus, any work of art that existed prior to 1945 has a potential provenance problem. This is a serious obstacle for anyone who currently collects pre-1945 European art. To avoid wasting thousands or even millions of dollars, they must verify (normally with the assistance of an art historian and a lawyer specializing in art law) that potential acquisitions were *not* stolen by the Nazis from a Holocaust victim. The highest-profile legal case arising from this problem is the U.S. Supreme Court decision of *Republic of Austria v. Altmann* (2006), in which the Court held that U.S. courts could retroactively apply the Foreign Sovereign Immunities Act of 1976 to Austria for torts that allegedly occurred before 1976.

# Reparations

In the immediate aftermath of the Second World War, the Jewish Agency led by Chaim Weizmann submitted to the Allies a memorandum demanding reparations to Jews by Germany but it received no answer. In March 1951, a new request was made by Israel's foreign minister Moshe Sharett which claimed global recompense to Israel of $1.5 billion based on the financial cost absorbed by Israel for the rehabilitation of 500,000 Jewish survivors. West German Chancellor Konrad Adenauer accepted these terms and declared he was ready to negotiate other reparations. A Conference on Jewish Material Claims against Germany was opened in New York City by Nahum Goldmann in order to help with individual claims. After negotiations, the claim was reduced to a sum of $845 millions direct and indirect compensations to be installed in a period of 14 years. In 1988, West Germany allocated another $125 million for reparations.[1831]

In 1999, many German industries such as Deutsche Bank, Siemens or BMW faced lawsuits for their role in the forced labour during World War II. In order to dismiss these lawsuits, Germany agreed to raise $5 billions of which Jewish forced laborers still alive could apply to receive a lump sum payment of between $2,500 and $7,500. In 2012, Germany agreed to pay a new reparation of €772 millions as a result of negotiations with Israel.[1832]

In 2014, the SNCF, the French state-owned railway company, was compelled to allocate $60 millions to American Jewish Holocaust survivors for its role in the transport of deportees to Germany. It corresponds to approximately $100,000 per survivor.[1833] Although the SNCF was forced by German authorities to cooperate in providing transport for French Jews to the border and did not make any profit from this transport, according to Serge Klarsfeld, president of the organization Sons and Daughters of Jewish Deportees from France.

These reparations were sometimes criticized in Israel where they were seen as "blood money". The American professor Norman Finkelstein wrote *The Holocaust Industry* to denounce how the American Jewish establishment exploits the memory of the Nazi Holocaust for political and financial gain, as well as to further the interests of Israel.[1834] These reparations also led to a massive scam where $57 millions were fraudulently given to thousands of people who were not eligible for the funds.[1835]

While the restitution movements of the mid-1990s reunited some families with their stolen property, Holocaust remembrance also served as an important part of the reparation and restitution movement. The main idea of Holocaust remembrance comes from Dan Diner's article "Restitution and Memory: The Holocaust in European Political Cultures" which is the idea that Europe is now bound together by a collective memory of the Holocaust. This unified memory is one of the main reasons Diner lists for the flourishing of the restitution movement of the mid-1990s, following that of the initial movement immediately after World War II. This unified memory allowed for all European countries to come together after such a tragic event to establish the Holocaust at its center as one the most damaging occurrences of the 20th century leading to a greater consciousness and awareness of this horrific event, in addition, to beginning countless discourses on the topic. Immediately after the Holocaust, countries such as the United States were preoccupied with the Cold War, whereas countries like Germany were controlled by foreign powers, and the Holocaust was not the main concern. Only as time went on did Europe begin to understand the importance of restitution and reparations. As the restoration of property increased, an increase in the memories for Holocaust survivors was found to be a direct correlation. The connection between property and memory proved to be a key in unlocking more details about the Holocaust, further adding to this collective European memory, and thereby increasing and furthering the restitution movement.

## Holocaust Memorial Days

The United Nations General Assembly voted on November 1, 2005, to designate January 27 as the "International Day of Commemoration in Memory of the Victims of the Holocaust." January 27, 1945, is the day that the former Nazi concentration and extermination camp of Auschwitz-Birkenau was liberated. The day had already been observed as Holocaust Memorial Day a number of countries. Israel and the Jewish diaspora observe Yom HaShoah Ve-Hagvora, the "Day of Remembrance of the Holocaust and the courage of the Jewish people," on the 27th day of the Hebrew month of Nisan, which generally falls in April.[1836]

## Holocaust denial

Holocaust denial is the claim that the genocide of Jews during World War II–usually referred to as the Holocaust[1837]–did not occur in the manner and to the extent described by current scholars.

Key elements of this claim are the rejection of the following: that the Nazi government had a policy of deliberately targeting Jews and people of Jewish ancestry for extermination as a people; that between five and seven million Jews were systematically killed by the Nazis and their allies; and that genocide was carried out at extermination camps using tools of mass murder, such as gas chambers.[1838,1839]

Many Holocaust deniers do not accept the term "denial" as an appropriate description of their point of view, and use the term *Holocaust revisionism* instead.[1840] Scholars, however, prefer the term "denial" to differentiate Holocaust deniers from historical revisionists, who use established historical methods.[1841]

Most Holocaust denial claims imply, or openly state, that the Holocaust is a hoax arising out of a deliberate Jewish conspiracy to advance the interest of Jews at the expense of other peoples.[1842] For this reason, Holocaust denial is generally considered to be an antisemitic[1843] conspiracy theory.[1844] The methods of Holocaust deniers are often criticized as based on a predetermined conclusion that ignores extensive historical evidence to the contrary.[1845]

## Further reading

External links, references, and other resources are listed at Holocaust (resources).

# Appendix

## References

[1] Niewyk, Donald L. and Nicosia, Francis R. *The Columbia Guide to the Holocaust* https://books.google.ca/books?id=lpDTIUklB2MC&pg=PP1&dq=Niewyk,+Donald+L.+The+Columbia+Guide+to+the+Holocaust&sig=4igufxQHRCNrkjwRuMt1if_mf5M#PPA45,M1, Columbia University Press, 2000, pp. 45-52.

[2] Donald Niewyk suggests that the broadest definition, including Soviet civilian deaths, would produce a death toll of 17 million. https://books.google.ca/books?id=lpDTIUklB2MC&pg=PP1&dq=Niewyk,+Donald+L.+The+Columbia+Guide+to+the+Holocaust&sig=4igufxQHRCNrkjwRuMt1if_mf5M#PPA45,M1 Estimates of the death toll of non-Jewish victims vary by millions, partly because the boundary between death by persecution and death by starvation and other means in a context of total war is unclear. Overall, about 5.7 million (78 percent) of the 7.3 million Jews in occupied Europe perished (Gilbert, Martin. *Atlas of the Holocaust* 1988, pp. 242-244). Compared to five to 11 million (1.4 percent to 3.0 percent) of the 360 million non-Jews in German-dominated Europe. Small, Melvin and J. David Singer. *Resort to Arms: International and civil Wars 1816-1980* and Berenbaum, Michael. *A Mosaic of Victims: Non-Jews Persecuted and Murdered by the Nazis*. New York: New York University Press, 1990

[3] //en.wikipedia.org/wiki/Names_of_the_Holocaust#endnote_shoah

[4] *Olah* (Leviticus 1:1-17) lit.: 'what goes up', ".. i.e goes up in smoke, because the entire animal, except for its hide, was burned on the altar. Other types of sacrifice were consumed in part by fire .. In English, olah has for centuries been translated "burnt offering." The olah had a high degree of sanctity, and it was regarded as the 'standard' sacrifice. . In contrast, sacrifices made by the Greeks to the Olympian gods were always shared by the worshipers; only sacrifices made to the dread underground deities to ward off evil were presented as holocausts, i.e., completely burned." W. Gunther Plaut, *The Torah - A Modern Commentary*; New York: Union of American Hebrew Congregations, 1981 and R.K. Yerkes, Sacrifice in Greek and Roman Religions and in Early Judaism; New York: Allenson, 1952, pp. 1-7.

[5] "(Amos 5:22-25. Cf. Jer. 7:22, 'When I freed your fathers from land of Egypt, I did not speak with them nor commanded them burnt offering or sacrifice'; see also I Sam. 15:22-23; Isa. 1:11-13; Hos. 6:6; Mic. 6:6-8.) .. Jewish tradition understood these utterances to be directed not against sacrifices as such, but against the substitution of ritual for morality." ibidem. (Plaut); Leviticus, Part I, Laws of Sacrifice, Introduction, p.752.

[6] Simon Schama, *A History of Britain*, episode 3, 'Dynasty'; BBC DVD, 2000

[7] John Milton quotes https://www.quotetab.com/quote/by-john-milton/like-that-self-begotten-bird-in-the-arabian-woods-embost-that-no-second-know

[8] *The Oxford English Dictionary*, Clarendon Press, 2nd ed. Oxford 1989, vol. VII p. 315 sect c.'complete destruction, esp. of a large number of persons; a great slaughter or massacre' citing examples from 1883 onwards.

[9] Colin Martin Tatz, "With Intent to Destroy: Reflecting on Genocide", Verso, 2003, σ. 18 https://books.google.gr

[10] M. Chater, "History's Greatest Trek", *National Geographic*, 1925, 533-583. In Panayiotis Diamadis, , "Aegean Eucalypts", MODERN GREEK STUDIES, Vol. 13, 2005, published by the Modern Greek Studies Association of Australia and New Zealand, p. 88 https://www.academia.edu/2368160/Aegean_Eucalypts

[11] "As for the Turkish atrocities ... helpless Armenians, men, women, and children together, whole districts blotted out in one administrative holocaust – these were beyond human redress." (Winston Churchill, *The World in Crisis, volume 4: The Aftermath*, New York, 1923, p. 158).

[12] Josh Fleet, "History And Meaning Of The Word 'Holocaust': Are We Still Comfortable With This Term?", 27-1-2012 https://www.huffingtonpost.com/2012/01/27/the-word-holocaust-history-and-meaning_n_1229043.html

[13] Petrie J., "The secular word Holocaust: scholarly myths, history, and 20th century meanings", *Journal of Genocide Research*, Volume 2, Number 1, 1 March 2000, pp. 31-63(33)

[14] Hardman, Leslie and Cecily Goodman 'The Survivors: the story of the Belsen Remnant' London: Vallentine, Mitchell,(1958)

[15] page 37, by Eliot Fremont-Smith

[16] Harnessing the Holocaust: The Politics of Memory in France, *Jewish Quarterly Review*, Volume 96, Number 2, Spring 2006, pp. 304-306

[17] Garaudy, Roger, "The Mythical Foundations of Israeli Policy", *Studies Forum International*, London 1997, p.133

[18] "It is the rejection of even the hint of such sacrificial thinking that prompts some Jews to refuse to refer to the events of the Shoah as a 'holocaust', the burnt offering with smoke wafting up to heaven". James Carroll, Constantine's Sword - The Church and the Jews; Boston: First Mariner Books, 2001. "Do Not Christianize Auschwitz and Shoah!" Władysław T. Bartoszewski, The Convent at Auschwitz; New York: George Braziller, 1991.

[19] Evans, Richard. *In Hitler's Shadow*, New York: Pantheon, 1989 page 142.

[20] Bartleby.com http://www.bartleby.com/65/ho/Holocaus.html

[21] "The Holocaust" http://www.askoxford.com/concise_oed/holocaust?view=uk, *Compact Oxford English Dictionary*: "(the Holocaust) the mass murder of Jews under the German Nazi regime in World War II."

[22] "Holocaust" http://encarta.msn.com/encyclopedia_761559508/Holocaust.html , *Encarta*: "Holocaust, the almost complete destruction of Jews in Europe by Nazi Germany and its collaborators during World War II (1939–1945). The leadership of Germany's Nazi Party ordered the extermination of 5.6 million to 5.9 million Jews (see National Socialism). Jews often refer to the Holocaust as Shoah (from the Hebrew word for "catastrophe" or "total destruction")."

[23] "Holocaust," *Encyclopædia Britannica*, 2009 http://www.britannica.com/EBchecked/topic/269548/Holocaust: "the systematic state-sponsored killing of six million Jewish men, women and children, and millions of others by Nazi Germany and its collaborators during World War II. The Nazis called this "the final solution to the Jewish question ..."

[24] *Weissman, Gary. *Fantasies of Witnessing: Postwar Attempts to Experience the Holocaust*, Cornell University Press, 2004, , p. 94: "Kren illustrates his point with his reference to the *Kommissararbefehl*. 'Should the (strikingly unreported) systematic mass starvation of Soviet prisoners of war be included in the Holocaust?' he asks. Many scholars would answer no, maintaining that 'the Holocaust' should refer strictly to those events involving the systematic killing of the Jews'." • "The Holocaust: Definition and Preliminary Discussion" http://www1.yadvashem.org/yv/en/holocaust/resource_center/the_holocaust.asp, Yad Vashem: "The Holocaust, as presented in this resource center, is defined as the sum total of all anti-Jewish actions carried out by the Nazi regime between 1933 and 1945: from stripping the German Jews of their legal and economic status in the 1930s, to segregating and starving Jews in the various occupied countries, to the murder of close to six million Jews in Europe. The Holocaust is part of a broader aggregate of acts of oppression and murder of various ethnic and political groups in Europe by the Nazis." • Niewyk, Donald L. *The Columbia Guide to the Holocaust*, Columbia University Press, 2000, p.45: "The Holocaust is commonly defined as the murder of more than 5,000,000 Jews by the Germans in World War II. Not everyone finds this a fully satisfactory definition. The Nazis also killed millions of people belonging to other groups: Gypsies, the physically and mentally handicapped, Soviet prisoners of war, Polish and Soviet civilians, political prisoners, religious dissenters, and homosexuals." • Paulsson, Steve. "A View of the Holocaust" http://www.bbc.co.uk/history/worldwars/genocide/holocaust_overview_01.shtml, BBC: "The Holocaust was the Nazis' assault on the Jews between 1933 and 1945. It culminated in what the Nazis called the 'Final Solution of the Jewish Question in Europe', in which six million Jews were murdered. The Jews were not the only victims of Nazism. It is estimated that as many as 15 million civilians were killed by this murderous and racist regime, including millions of Slavs and 'asiatics', 200,000 Gypsies and members of various other groups. Thousands of people, including Germans of African descent, were forcibly sterilised." • "The Holocaust" http://www.auschwitz.dk/, *Auschwitz.dk*: "The Holocaust was the systematic annihilation of six million Jews by the Nazis during World War II. In 1933 nine million Jews lived in the 21 countries of Europe that would be military occupied by Germany during the war. By 1945

two out of every three European Jews had been killed. 1.5 million children under the age of 12 were murdered. This figure includes more than 1.2 million Jewish children, tens of thousands of Gypsy children and thousands of handicapped children." • "Holocaust—Definition" http://www.chgs.umn.edu/Educational_Resources/Curriculum/Witness___Legacy_-_Educators__/Holocaust_-_Definition/holocaust_-_definition.html, *Encyclopedia of the Holocaust*, Center for Holocaust and Genocide Studies: "HOLOCAUST (Heb., sho'ah). In the 1950s the term came to be applied primarily to the destruction of the Jews of Europe under the Nazi regime, and it is also employed in describing the annihilation of other groups of people in World War II. The mass extermination of Jews has become the archetype of genocide, and the terms sho'ah and "holocaust" have become linked to the attempt by the Nazi German state to destroy European Jewry during World War II ... One of the first to use the term in the historical perspective was the Jerusalem historian BenZion Dinur (Dinaburg), who, in the spring of 1942, stated that the Holocaust was a "catastrophe" that symbolized the unique situation of the Jewish people among the nations of the world." • Also see the Center for Holocaust and Genocide Studies list of definitions: "Holocaust: A term for the state-sponsored, systematic persecution and annihilation of European Jewry by Nazi Germany and its collaborators between 1933 and 1945." • The 33rd Annual Scholars' Conference on the Holocaust and the Churches defines the Holocaust as "the Nazi attempt to annihilate European Jewry", cited in Hancock, Ian. "Romanies and the Holocaust: A Reevaluation and an Overview" http://www.radoc.net/radoc.php?doc=art_e_holocaust_porrajmos&lang=en , Stone, Dan. (ed.) *The Historiography of the Holocaust*. Palgrave-Macmillan, New York 2004, pp. 383–396.
• Bauer, Yehuda. *Rethinking the Holocaust*. New Haven: Yale University Press. 2001, p.10.
• Dawidowicz, Lucy. *The War Against the Jews: 1933–1945*. Bantam, 1986, p.xxxvii: "'The Holocaust' is the term that Jews themselves have chosen to describe their fate during World War II."

[25] Yehuda Bauer *A History of the Holocaust*. F. Watts, 1982 p.331; chapter 1 https://www.nytimes.com/books/first/b/bauer-rethinking.html

[26]

[27] Michael Burleigh and Wolfgang Wippermann. *The Racial State:Germany 1933–1945* Cambridge University Press 1991. This work favors a more expansive definition of the Holocaust, pointing out that Nazi Germany had a racist ideology by no means limited to anti-Semitism.

[28] *The Columbia guide to the Holocaust* by Donald L. Niewyk, Francis R. Nicosia, page 52, Columbia University Press, 2000

[29] Chapter 6 in the book *The Gypsies of Eastern Europe*, pp.81-92, ME Sharpe, London, 1991

[30] Shirer, W., *The Rise and Fall of the Third Reich* New York: 1960, Simon and Schuster, pp. 963-979

[31] A useful analysis of the terms can be found in Bartov, Omer. "Antisemitism, the Holocaust, and Reinterpretation of National Socialism", in Berenbaum, Michael & Peck, Abraham J. (eds.), *The Holocaust and History: The Known, the Unknown, the Disputed, and the Reexamined*, Bloomington: University of Indiana Press, 1998, pp. 75–98.

[32] Setbon, Jessica. "Who Beat My Father? Issues of Terminology and Translation in Teaching the Holocaust" http://www1.yadvashem.org/education/conference2006/Setbon,%20Jessica.pdf, workshop from a May 2006 conference; see Yad Vashem website. Yadvashem.org http://webcache.googleusercontent.com/search?q=cache:g1AQlb5aG44J:www1.yadvashem.org/education/conference2006/Setb

[33] Holocaust http://www1.yadvashem.org/odot_pdf/microsoft%20word%20-%206419.pdf, *Yad Vashem*

[34] "Holocaust—Definition" http://www.chgs.umn.edu/Educational_Resources/Curriculum/Witness___Legacy_-_Educators__/Holocaust_-_Definition/holocaust_-_definition.html, *Encyclopedia of the Holocaust*, Vol. II, MacMillan.

[35] Petrie, Jon. "The Secular Word 'HOLOCAUST': Scholarly Myths, History, and Twentieth Century Meanings", *Journal of Genocide Research* Vol 2, no. 1 (2000): 31–63.

[36] " "The Holocaust: Definition and Preliminary Discussion" http://www1.yadvashem.org/Odot/prog/index_before_change_table.asp?gate=0-2, Yad Vashem. Retrieved June 8, 2005.

[37] Kaufmann, Max, *Die Vernichtung des Judens Lettlands* (*The Destruction of the Jews of Latvia*), Munich, 1947, English translation by Laimdota Mazzarins available on-line as Churbn Lettland – The Destruction of the Jews of Latvia http://www.jewsoflatvia.com/
[38] Hilberg, Raul, *The Destruction of the European Jews* (3rd edition) Yale University Press, New Haven, CT 2003.
[39] //en.wikipedia.org/w/index.php?title=Template:Nazism_sidebar&action=edit
[40] "Nuremberg - Document Viewer - Table of contents for prosecution document book 8, concerning medical experiments". *nuremberg.law.harvard.edu. Retrieved 2017-04-14.*
[41] Josef Mengele and Experimentation on Human Twins at Auschwitz http://www.longwood.k12.ny.us/lhs/science/mos/twins/mengele.html , *Children of the Flames; Dr. Josef Mengele and the Untold Story of the Twins of Auschwitz*, Lucette Matalon Lagnado and Sheila Cohn Dekel, and *Mengele: the Complete Story* by Gerald Posner and John Ware.
[42] Baron, Saskia, director. *Science and the Swastika: The Deadly Experiment.* Darlow Smithson Productions, 2001.
[43] http://nuremberg.law.harvard.edu/documents/2055-deposition-concerning-medical-experiments?q=author:%22Jadwiga+Kaminska%22#p.4. *nuremberg.law.harvard.edu.* Retrieved 2017-04-14.
[44] Small, Martin; Vic Shayne. "Remember Us: My Journey from the Shtetl through the Holocaust" https://books.google.com/books?id=kaIYMRYufh0C&lpg=PA131&ots=mpeA8ZjW3q&dq=%22Dr.%20wichtmann%22&pg=PA135#v=onepage&q=%22Dr.%20wichtmann%22&f=false, Page 135, 2009.
[45] Bogod, David. "The Nazi Hypothermia Experiments: Forbidden Data?" http://www.blackwell-synergy.com/doi/full/10.1111/j.1365-2044.2004.04034.x, *Anaesthesia*, Volume 59 Issue 12 Page 1155, December 2004.
[46] "Documents Regarding Nazi Medical Experiments" http://www.jewishvirtuallibrary.org/documents-regarding-nazi-medical-experiments. *www.jewishvirtuallibrary.org.* Retrieved 2017-04-14.
[47] Neurnberg Military Tribunal, Volume I · Page 200 http://www.mazal.org/archive/nmt/01/NMT01-T200.htm
[48] Schaefer, Naomi. *The Legacy of Nazi Medicine* http://www.thenewatlantis.com/archive/5/schaefer.htm, *The New Atlantis*, Number 5, Spring 2004, pp. 54–60.
[49] "Nuremberg - Document Viewer - Affidavit concerning the seawater experiments" http://nuremberg.law.harvard.edu/documents/90-affidavit-concerning-the-seawater?q=medical+experiments#p.2. *nuremberg.law.harvard.edu.* Retrieved 2017-04-14.
[50] Gardella JE. The cost-effectiveness of killing: an overview of Nazi "euthanasia." Medical Sentinel 1999;4:132-5
[51] Dahl M. [Selection and destruction-treatment of "unworthy-to-live" children in the Third Reich and the role of child and adolescent psychiatry], Prax Kinderpsychol Kinderpsychiatr 2001;50:170-91.
[52] "Medicine and Murder in the Third Reich" http://www.jewishvirtuallibrary.org/medicine-and-murder-in-the-third-reich#2. *www.jewishvirtuallibrary.org.* Retrieved 2017-04-14.
[53] "Documents Regarding Nazi Medical Experiments". www.jewishvirtuallibrary.org. Retrieved 2017-04-14
[54] "Nuremberg - Document Viewer - Letter to Sigmund Rascher concerning the high altitude experiments" http://nuremberg.law.harvard.edu/documents/37-letter-to-sigmund-rascher?q=medical+experiement#p.1. *nuremberg.law.harvard.edu.* Retrieved 2017-04-14.
[55] Michalczyk, p. 96
[56] "Nuremberg - Document Viewer - Letter to Erhard Milch concerning the high altitude and freezing experiments" http://nuremberg.law.harvard.edu/documents/65-letter-to-erhard-milch?q=author:%22Heinrich+Himmler%22#p.1. *nuremberg.law.harvard.edu.* Retrieved 2017-04-14.
[57] https://books.google.com/books?id=4P04DuPIfAYC
[58] https://books.google.com/books?id=JUjQAAAAMAAJ
[59] http://isurvived.org/TOC-I.html#I-6_MedExp
[60] http://www.ushmm.org/research/doctors/

[61] https://web.archive.org/web/20121026014306/http://www.ushmm.org/museum/exhibit/online/deadlymedicine/
[62] http://www.ushmm.org/research/research-in-collections/search-the-collections/bibliography/medical-experiments
[63] https://www.jewishvirtuallibrary.org/jsource/Holocaust/medtoc.html
[64] https://www.ncbi.nlm.nih.gov/entrez/query.fcgi?cmd=Retrieve&db=PubMed&list_uids=11655677&dopt=Abstract
[65] http://www.medscape.com/medline/abstract/11655677
[66] http://www.garfield.library.upenn.edu/essays/v14p328y1991.pdf
[67] https://www.webcitation.org/query?url=http://www.geocities.com/pennpuab/foundations/naziresearch.html&date=2009-10-26+00:25:07
[68] http://www.garfield.library.upenn.edu/essays/v8p265y1985.pdf
[69] http://www.jlaw.com/Articles/NaziMedEx.html
[70] As many as 100,000 people may have been killed directly as part of Action T-4. Mass euthanasia killings were also carried out in the Eastern European countries and territories Nazi Germany conquered during the war. Categories are fluid, and no definitive figure can be assigned but historians put the total number of victims at around 300,000. UNIQ-ref-0-7a3479d8554a1f24-QINU
[71] Sandner 1999, p. 385.
[72] Sandner wrote that the term Aktion T4 was first used in post-war trials against doctors involved in the killings and later included in the historiography.<ref name="FOOTNOTESandner1999385">Sandner 1999, p. 385.
[73] Hojan & Munro 2015.
[74] Bialas & Fritze 2014, pp. 263, 281.
[75] Sereny 1983, p. 48.
[76] *Tiergartenstraße* 4 was the location of the Central Office and administrative headquarters of the *Gemeinnützige Stiftung für Heil- und Anstalts- pflege* (Charitable Foundation for Curative and Institutional Care).<ref name="FOOTNOTESereny198348">Sereny 1983, p. 48.
[77] Proctor 1988, p. 177.
[78] Longerich 2010, p. 477.
[79] Browning 2005, p. 193.
[80] Proctor 1988, p. 191.
[81] Notes on patient records from the archive "R 179" of the Chancellery of the Führer Main Office II b. Between 1939 and 1945, about 200,000 women, men, and children were murdered from psychiatric institutions of the German Reich in several covert actions by gas, medication or starvation. *Original:* Zwischen 1939 und 1945 wurden ca. 200.000 Frauen, Männer und Kinder aus psychiatrischen Einrichtungen des Deutschen Reichs im mehreren verdeckten Aktionen durch Vergasung, Medikamente oder unzureichende Ernährung ermordet.
[82] Evans 2009, p. 107.
[83] Burleigh 2008, p. 262.
[84] Evans 2009, p. 98.
[85] Burleigh & Wippermann 2014.
[86] Adams 1990, pp. 40, 84, 191.
[87] Ryan & Schuchman 2002, p. 25.
[88] Lifton 1986, p. 142.
[89] Ryan & Schuchman 2002, p. 62.
[90] Robert Lifton and Michael Burleigh estimated that twice the official number of T4 victims may have perished before the end of the war.<ref name="FOOTNOTEBurleigh1995">Burleigh 1995.
[91] Estimated range of 200,000 and 250,000 victims of the policy upon the arrival of Allied troops in Germany.<ref name="FOOTNOTERyanSchuchman200262">Ryan & Schuchman 2002, p. 62.
[92] Lifton 2000, p. 102.
[93] Sereny 1983, p. 54.
[94] The number of people murdered is calculated at 200,000. *Original:* "der Zahl von 200.000 Ermordungen zu rechnen ist."
[95] Hansen & King 2013, p. 141.

96 Hitler, p. 447.
97 Padfield 1990, p. 260.
98 Evans 2005, pp. 507–508.
99 Engstrom, Weber & Burgmair 2006, p. 1710.
100 Joseph 2004, p. 160.
101 Bleuler 1924, p. 214.
102 Read 2004, p. 36.
103 This was the result either of club foot or osteomyelitis. Goebbels is commonly said to have had club foot (*talipes equinovarus*), a congenital condition. William L. Shirer, who worked in Berlin as a journalist in the 1930s and was acquainted with Goebbels, wrote in *The Rise and Fall of the Third Reich* (1960) that the deformity was from a childhood attack of osteomyelitis and a failed operation to correct it.<ref name="FOOTNOTEShirer1960124">Shirer 1960, p. 124.
104 Evans 2005, p. 508.
105 Miller 2006, p. 160.
106 Breggin 1993, pp. 133–148.
107 Kershaw 2000, p. 256.
108 Friedman 2011, p. 146.
109 Robert Lifton wrote that this request was "encouraged"; the severely disabled child and the agreement of the parents to his killing were apparently genuine.<ref name="FOOTNOTELifton198650">Lifton 1986, p. 50.
110 Schmidt 2007, p. 118.
111 Cina & Perper 2012, p. 59.
112 Lifton 1986, pp. 50–51.
113 Proctor 1988, p. 10.
114 Browning 2005, p. 190.
115 Lifton 1986, p. 62.
116 Baader 2009, pp. 18–27.
117 Lifton 1986, pp. 62–63.
118 Schmitt 1965, pp. 34–35.
119 Lifton 1986, p. 47.
120 Kershaw 2000, p. 254.
121 Evans 2005, p. 444.
122 Lifton 1986, pp. 48–49.
123 Browning 2005, p. 185.
124 Kershaw 2000, p. 259.
125 Miller 2006, p. 158.
126 Torrey & Yolken 2010, pp. 26–32.
127 Local 2014.
128 Kaelber 2015.
129 Weindling 2006, p. 6.
130 Lifton 1986, p. 52.
131 Professors Werner Catel (a Leipzig psychiatrist) and Hans Heinze, head of a state institution for children with intellectual disabilities at Görden near Brandenburg; Ernst Wentzler a Berlin pediatric psychiatrist and the author Dr. Helmut Unger.<ref name="FOOTNOTELifton198652">Lifton 1986, p. 52.
132 Sereny 1983, p. 55.
133 Lifton 1986, p. 60.
134 Lifton 1986, p. 56.
135 Lifton 1986, p. 55.
136 Lifton concurs with this figure, but notes that the killing of children continued after the T4 programme was formally ended in 1941.<ref name="FOOTNOTELifton198655">Lifton 1986, p. 55.
137 Friedlander 1995, p. 163.
138 Evans 2004, p. 93.
139 Semków 2006, pp. 46–48.

[140] The second phase of Operation Tannenberg referred to as the *Unternehmen Tannenberg* by Heydrich's *Sonderreferat* began in late 1939 under the codename *Intelligenzaktion* and lasted until January 1940, in which 36,000–42,000 people, including Polish children, died before the end of 1939 in Pomerania.<ref name="FOOTNOTESemków200642–50">Semków 2006, pp. 42–50.
[141] Friedlander 1995, p. 87.
[142] Browning 2005, pp. 186–187.
[143] Browning 2005, p. 188.
[144] Kershaw 2000, p. 261.
[145] Lifton 1986, pp. 63–64.
[146] Several drafts of a formal euthanasia law were prepared but Hitler refused to authorise them. The senior participants in the programme always knew that it was not a law, even by the loose definition of legality prevailing in Nazi Germany.<ref name="FOOTNOTELifton198663–64">Lifton 1986, pp. 63–64.
[147] Padfield 1990, p. 261.
[148] Kershaw 2000, p. 253.
[149] Lifton 1986, p. 64.
[150] Lifton 1986, pp. 66–67.
[151] Browning 2005, p. 191.
[152] Padfield 1990, pp. 261, 303.
[153] Lifton 1986, p. 77.
[154] According to Lifton, most Jewish inmates of German mental institutions were dispatched to Lublin in Poland in 1940 and killed there.<ref name="FOOTNOTELifton198677">Lifton 1986, p. 77.
[155] Lifton 1986, p. 67.
[156] Annas & Grodin 1992, p. 25.
[157] Lifton 1986, pp. 71–72.
[158] Burleigh 2000, p. 54.
[159] Lifton 1986, p. 71.
[160] Lifton 1986, p. 74.
[161] These figures come from the article Aktion T4 on the German Wikipedia, which sources them to Ernst Klee.<ref name="FOOTNOTEKlee1983">Klee 1983.
[162] Sereny 1983, pp. 41–90.
[163] Hojan & Munro 2013.
[164] Klee 1985, p. 232.
[165] Jaroszewski 1993.
[166] WNSP State Hospital 2013.
[167] Beer 2015, pp. 403–417.
[168] Ringelblum 2013, p. 20.
[169] Role of T4 "Inspector" Christian Wirth in the Holocaust.<ref name="FOOTNOTESereny198354">Sereny 1983, p. 54.
[170] Joniec 2016, pp. 1–39.
[171] Sereny 1983, p. 71.
[172] Lifton 1986, p. 75.
[173] Sereny 1983, p. 58.
[174] Lifton 1986, pp. 80, 82.
[175] Lifton 1986, p. 90.
[176] NEP 2017.
[177] Lifton 1986, pp. 90–92.
[178] Padfield 1990, p. 304.
[179] Schmuhl 1987, p. 321.
[180] Burleigh 2008, p. 261.
[181] Ericksen 2012, p. 111.
[182] Evans 2009, p. 110.
[183] Lifton 1986, p. 93.
[184] Lifton 1986, p. 94.

[185] Kershaw 2000, pp. 427, 429.
[186] Lifton 1986, p. 95.
[187] Evans 2009, p. 112.
[188] Burleigh 2008, p. 26.
[189] Friedlander 1997, p. 111.
[190] Griech-Polelle 2002, p. 76.
[191] Evans 2009, pp. 529–530.
[192] Burleigh 2008, p. 263.
[193] Aly & Chroust 1994, p. 88.
[194] Lifton 1986, pp. 96–102.
[195] Hilberg 2003, p. 1,066.
[196] Hilberg 2003, p. 932.
[197] Taylor 1949.
[198] NARA 1980, pp. 1–12.
[199] Hilberg 2003, p. 1,175.
[200] Hilberg 2003, p. 1,176.
[201] Hilberg 2003, p. 1,179.
[202] Hilberg 2003, p. 1,003.
[203] Berenbaum & Peck 2002, p. 247.
[204] Hilberg 2003, p. 1,182.
[205] Totten & Parsons 2009, p. 181.
[206] Buttlar 2003.
[207] //www.worldcat.org/oclc/3755976
[208] //doi.org/10.1017%2FCBO9781139059602
[209] https://books.google.com/?id=gqLDEKVk2nMC
[210] //doi.org/10.1017%2FCBO9781139507554
[211] http://www.belzec.eu/en
[212] https://web.archive.org/web/20060903214558/http://www.holocaust-history.org/lifton/
[213] http://www.holocaust-history.org/lifton/
[214] http://www.wuw.pl/search.php?text=ringelblum
[215] //www.worldcat.org/oclc/923376286
[216] https://web.archive.org/web/20060504015049/http://www.ushmm.org/research/doctors/three.htm
[217] //www.worldcat.org/oclc/504102502
[218] http://www.ushmm.org/research/doctors/three.htm
[219] http://www.menschenfolter.de/PDF/Psychiatrie-Nationalsozialismus-Patientenmord.pdf
[220] http://breggin.com/wp-content/uploads/2008/01/psychiatrysrole.pbreggin.1993.pdf
[221] //doi.org/10.3233%2FJRS-1993-4204
[222] //www.ncbi.nlm.nih.gov/pubmed/23511221
[223] //doi.org/10.1017%2FS0960777300000886
[224] //www.worldcat.org/issn/0960-7773
[225] //doi.org/10.1176%2Fappi.ajp.163.10.1710
[226] //www.worldcat.org/issn/0002-953X
[227] //www.ncbi.nlm.nih.gov/pubmed/17012678
[228] http://www.ifz-muenchen.de/heftarchiv/1999_3.pdf
[229] //www.worldcat.org/issn/0042-5702
[230] http://www.sierpien1980.pl/download/10/15909/biuletyn8-967-68.pdf
[231] //www.worldcat.org/issn/1641-9561
[232] //www.ncbi.nlm.nih.gov/pmc/articles/PMC2800142
[233] //doi.org/10.1093%2Fschbul%2Fsbp097
[234] //www.worldcat.org/issn/0586-7614
[235] //www.ncbi.nlm.nih.gov/pubmed/19759092
[236] http://www.spiegel.de/wissenschaft/mensch/nazi-euthanasie-forscher-oeffnen-inventar-des-schreckens-a-267983.html
[237] //www.worldcat.org/issn/0038-7452
[238] http://www.thelocal.at/20141125/nazis-killed-hundreds-at-austrian-mental-hospital

[239] https://www.jewishvirtuallibrary.org/jsource/Holocaust/vans.html
[240] http://www.ushmm.org/research/research-in-collections/search-the-collections/bibliography/nazi-racial-science#h18
[241] https://web.archive.org/web/20160530184623/https://tiergartenstrasse4.org/Nazi_Euthanasia_Programme_in_Occupied_Poland_1939-1945.html
[242] https://www.scribd.com/document/348444961/Nazi-Ideology-and-Ethics
[243] https://www.worldcat.org/oclc/875635606
[244] http://tiergartenstrasse4.org/Nazi_Euthanasia_Programme_in_Occupied_Poland_1939-1945.html
[245] http://www.projectinposterum.org/docs/psychiatric_patients.htm
[246] //www.worldcat.org/oclc/68651789
[247] http//www.pomorska.pl
[248] https//archive.is
[249] http://www.szpital-psychiatryczny.swiecie.pl/mhis.html
[250] https://archive.is/20171117160852/http://www.szpital-psychiatryczny.swiecie.pl/mhis.html
[251] http://niedziela.pl/artykul/104262/nd/Psychiatrzy-w-obronie-pacjentow
[252] https://archive.is/20171117163408/http://niedziela.pl/artykul/104262/nd/Psychiatrzy-w-obronie-pacjentow
[253] https://www.uvm.edu/~lkaelber/children/amspiegelgrundwien/amspiegelgrundwien.html
[254] https://www.bundesarchiv.de/geschichte_euthanasie/Inventar_euth_doe.pdf
[255] http://www.t4-denkmal.de/eng/Alfred-Woedl
[256] https://www.archives.gov/research/captured-german-records/microfilm/m1078.pdf
[257] //www.worldcat.org/oclc/72022317
[258] //doi.org/10.1007%2Fs10991-005-5345-2
[259] //www.worldcat.org/issn/0144-932X
[260] //www.ncbi.nlm.nih.gov/pubmed/17340766
[261] https://web.archive.org/web/20110711142224/http://www.holocaustresearchproject.org/ghettos/otwock.html
[262] http://www.holocaustresearchproject.org/ghettos/otwock.html
[263] http://www.polunbi.de/pers/bouhler-01.html
[264] http://www.ushmm.org/wlc/article.php?lang=en&ModuleId=10007064
[265] http://www.ushmm.org/wlc/article.php?lang=en&ModuleId=10005200
[266] http//www.bmj.com
[267] //en.wikipedia.org/w/index.php?title=Template:The_Holocaust_sidebar&action=edit
[268] http://phdn.org/archives/holocaust-history.org/lifton/LiftonT021.shtml The Nazi Doctors: Medical Killing and the Psychology of Genocide] by Dr. Robert Jay Lifton (holocaust-history.org)
[269] The Gypsies of Eastern Europe, David Crowe, John Kolsti, Ian Hancock, Routledge, 22 Jul 2016, pg31
[270] Henry Friedlander (1995),
[271] Cover of *Die Freigabe der Vernichtung Lebensunwerten Lebens* (*Allowing the Destruction of Life Unworthy of Life*) at German Wikipedia.
[272] Dr S D Stein, "Life Unworthy of Life" and other Medical Killing Programmes. https://web.archive.org/web/20130310151949/http://www.ess.uwe.ac.uk/genocide/mord.htm UWE Faculty of Humanities, Languages, and Social Science – via Internet Archive.
[273] https://web.archive.org/web/20130310151949/http://www.ess.uwe.ac.uk/genocide/mord.htm
[274] http://lifeunworthyoflife.com
[275] http://lifeunworthyoflife.com/die-freigabe-der-vernichtung-lebensunwerten-lebens/9.htm
[276] //en.wikipedia.org/w/index.php?title=Template:Antisemitism&action=edit
[277] "'German Mobs' Vengeance on Jews", *The Daily Telegraph*, 11 November 1938, cited in Gilbert, Martin. *Kristallnacht: Prelude to Destruction*. Harper Collins, 2006, p. 42.
[278] The United States Holocaust Memorial Museum's *"Holocaust Encyclopedia"* is a more definitive reference that is similar to this Wikipedia article http://www.ushmm.org/wlc/en/article.php?ModuleId=10005201
[279] "World War II: Before the War" https://www.theatlantic.com/infocus/2011/06/world-war-ii-before-the-war/100089/, *The Atlantic*, 19 June 2011. "Windows of shops owned by Jews which

were broken during a coordinated anti-Jewish demonstration in Berlin, known as *Kristallnacht*, on Nov. 10, 1938. The Nazi authorities turned a blind eye as SA stormtroopers and civilians destroyed storefronts with hammers, leaving the streets covered in pieces of smashed windows. Some sources estimate that ninety-one Jews were killed, and 30,000 Jewish men were arrested and taken to concentration camps."

[280] Berenbaum, Michael & Kramer, Arnold (2005). *The World Must Know*. United States Holocaust Memorial Museum. p. 49.

[281] "A Black Day for Germany", *The Times*, 11 November 1938, cited in

[282] Goldstein, Joseph (1995). *Jewish History in Modern Times*. Sussex Academic Press. pp. 43–44.

[283] *Manchester Guardian*, 23 May 1936, cited in A.J. Sherman, *Island Refuge, Britain and the Refugees from the Third Reich, 1933-1939*, (London, Elek Books Ltd, 1973), p. 112, also in *The Evian Conference — Hitler's Green Light for Genocide* http://christianactionforisrael.org/antiholo/evian/evian.html , by Annette Shaw

[284] Johnson, Eric. *The Nazi Terror: Gestapo, Jews and Ordinary Germans*. United States: Basic Books, 1999, p. 117.

[285] Friedländer, Saul. *Nazi Germany and The Jews*, volume 1: *The Years of Persecution 1933-1939*, London: Phoenix, 1997, p. 270

[286] Georg Landauer to Martin Rosenbluth, 8 February 1938, cited in Friedländer, loc. cit.

[287] "Recollections of Rosalind Herzfeld," *Jewish Chronicle*, 28 September 1979, p. 80; cited in Gilbert, *The Holocaust—The Jewish Tragedy*, London: William Collins Sons & Co. Ltd, 1986.

[288] Hannah Arendt, *Eichmann in Jerusalem*, p. 228.

[289] German State Archives, Potsdam, quoted in Rita Thalmann and Emmanuel Feinermann, *Crystal night, 9-10 November 1938*, pp. 33, 42.

[290] William L. Shirer, *The Rise And Fall Of The Third Reich*, p. 430.

[291] Did gay affair provide a catalyst for Kristallnacht? https://www.theguardian.com/world/2001/oct/31/humanities.research by Kate Connolly, The Guardian, 30 October 2001,
"On November 7, 1938, Herschel Grynszpan, a Jew, walked into the German embassy in Paris and shot Ernst vom Rath, a German diplomat. Nazi propagandists condemned the shooting as a terrorist attack to further the cause of the Jewish 'world revolution' and launched the series of attacks known as Kristallnacht. Vom Rath and Grynszpan met in Le Boeuf sur le Toit bar, a popular haunt for gay men in the autumn of 1938 and became intimate."

[292] "Nazis Planning Revenge on Jews", *News Chronicle*, 9 November 1938

[293] "Nazis Smash, Loot and Burn Jewish Shops and Temples Until Goebbels Calls Halt", *New York Times*, 11 November 1938

[294] "Berlin Police Head Announces 'Disarming' of Jews – Victim of Shots in Critical State", *New York Times*, 8 November 1938

[295] Friedländer, op.cit., p. 113.

[296] Walter Buch to Goring, 13.2.1939, Michaelis and Schraepler, Ursachen, Vol.12, p. 582 as cited in Friedländer, p. 271.

[297] Graml, Anti-Semitism, p. 13 cited in Friedländer, op.cit., p 272

[298] "Heydrich's secret instructions regarding the riots in November 1938" http://motlc.wiesenthal.com/site/pp.asp?c=gvKVLcMVIuG&b=394829, (Simon Wiesenthal Center)

[299] GermanNotes, , retrieved 26 November 2007

[300] http://www.zukunft-braucht-erinnerung.de/die-kristallnacht-luege/

[301] "The deportation of Regensburg Jews to Dachau concentration camp" http://www1.yadvashem.org/exhibitions/kristallnacht/kristallnacht_photo2.html (Yad Vashem Photo Archives 57659)

[302] Lucas, Eric. "The sovereigns", Kibbutz Kfar Blum (Palestine), 1945, p. 171 cited in Gilbert, op.cit., p 67.

[303] Raul Hilberg. *The Destruction of the European Jews*, Third Edition, (Yale Univ. Press, 2003, c1961), Ch.3.

[304] Carleton Greene, Hugh. *Daily Telegraph*, 11 November 1938 cited in "The Road to World War II" http://mars.vnet.wnec.edu/~grempel/courses/berlin/lectures/17TheRoadtoWar.html , Western New England College.

[305] "The Road to World War II" http://mars.vnet.wnec.edu/~grempel/courses/berlin/lectures/17TheRoadtoWar.html , Western New England College.https://web.archive.

[305] org/web/20070930231711/http://mars.vnet.wnec.edu/~grempel/courses/berlin/lectures/17TheRoadtoWar.html

[306] Döscher, Hans-Jürgen (2000). *"Reichskristallnacht" – Die Novemberpogrome 1938* ("'Reichskristallnacht': The November pogroms of 1938"), Econ, 2000, , p. 131

[307] Conot, Robert. *Justice at Nuremberg*, New York, NY: Harper and Row, 1983, pp. 164–72.

[308] "JudenVermoegersabgabe" (The Center for Holocaust and Genocide Studies) http://www.chgs.umn.edu/Histories__Narratives__Documen/Documents_from_the_Holocaust/Post-Kristallnacht_Document/post-kristallnacht_document.html

[309] Jewish emigration from Germany http://www.ushmm.org/museum/exhibit/online/kristallnacht/frame.htm (USHMM)

[310] Scheer, Regina (1993). "I'm Revier 16 (In precinct No. 16)". Die Hackeschen Höfe. Geschichte und Geschichten Feiner Lebenswelt in der Mitte Berlins (Gesellschaft Hackesche Höfe e.V. (ed.), pp. 78 ed.). Berlin: Argon.

[311] Gilbert, op. cit., p. 70

[312] Dr. Arthur Flehinger, "Flames of Fury", *Jewish Chronicle*, 9 November 1979, p. 27, cited in Gilbert, loc. cit.

[313] "New Campaign Against Jews", *The Argus*, 11 November 1938 http://nla.gov.au/nla.news-article12062109

[314] *Daily Telegraph*, 12 November 1938. Cited in Gilbert, Martin. *Kristallnacht: Prelude to Destruction*. Harper Collins, 2006, p. 142.

[315] Eugene Davidson. The Unmaking of Adolf Hitler. Columbia: University of Missouri Press, 1996. p. 325

[316] Guardian archive image of Goebbels foreign press conference: http://static.guim.co.uk/sys-images/Guardian/Pix/pictures/2013/11/8/1383904706426/goebbels-001.jpg, retrieved 12 March 2017

[317] Bernd Nellessen, "Die schweigende Kirche: Katholiken und Judenverfolgung", in Büttner (ed) Die Deutschen und die Judenverfolgung im Dritten Reich, p. 265, cited in Daniel Goldhagen's Hitler's Willing Executioners (Vintage, 1997).

[318] Diarmaid MacCulloch, *Reformation: Europe's House Divided, 1490-1700*. New York: Penguin Books Ltd, 2004, pp. 666–67.

[319] https://www.jpost.com/Diaspora/St-Louis-Jewish-cemetery-rededicated-after-gravestones-toppled-by-vandals-501808

[320] https://www.bostonglobe.com/metro/2017/08/14/holocaust-memorial-boston-damaged-for-second-time-this-summer/ujYan70j3kXzFWS3TGcZ0J/story.html

[321] Marion A. Kaplan, "Women's Roles and Reactions during the Pogrom." in Between Dignity and Despair: Jewish Life in Nazi Germany (USA: Oxford University Press, 1998),125.

[322] Marion A. Kaplan, "Women's Roles and Reactions during the Pogrom." in Between Dignity and Despair: Jewish Life in Nazi Germany (USA: Oxford University Press, 1998),127.

[323] http://hgs.oxfordjournals.org/cgi/reprint/1/2/217.pdf

[324] https://www.telegraph.co.uk/news/worldnews/europe/germany/3235356/Hitler-led-henchmen-in-Kristallnacht-riots.html

[325] https://web.archive.org/web/20081208072954/http://www.haaretz.com/hasen/spages/1032989.html

[326] http://www.haaretz.com/hasen/spages/1032989.html

[327] http://www.aish.com/holocaust/overview/Kristallnacht.asp

[328] https://web.archive.org/web/20080225014507/http://edition.cnn.com/WORLD/europe/9811/09/germany.kristallnacht/

[329] http://edition.cnn.com/WORLD/europe/9811/09/germany.kristallnacht/

[330] https://web.archive.org/web/20080511205805/http://www.holocaust-history.org/short-essays/kristallnacht.shtml

[331] http://www.holocaust-history.org/short-essays/kristallnacht.shtml

[332] http://www.holocaustresearchproject.net/holoprelude/kristallnacht.html

[333] https://web.archive.org/web/20081210110045/http://www.chgs.umn.edu/educational/brokenThreads/kristallnacht.html

[334] http://www.chgs.umn.edu/educational/brokenThreads/kristallnacht.html

[335] http://www.nizkor.org/hweb/imt/tgmwc/tgmwc-20/tgmwc-20-194-03.shtml

[336] http://www.nps.gov/archive/elro/glossary/kristallnacht.htm
[337] http://www.ushmm.org/wlc/en/index.php?lang=en&ModuleId=10005201
[338] https://web.archive.org/web/20080517110411/http://www.ushmm.org/museum/exhibit/focus/kristallnacht_02/
[339] http://www.ushmm.org/museum/exhibit/focus/kristallnacht_02/
[340] https://archive.is/20050309221538/http://www1.yadvashem.org/exhibitions/kristallnacht/kristallnacht_home_photo.html
[341] http://www1.yadvashem.org/exhibitions/kristallnacht/kristallnacht_home_photo.html
[342] http://www.holocaustandhumanity.org/kristallnacht/events-leading-up-to-kristallnacht/
[343] https://web.archive.org/web/20130903160517/http://www.ushmm.org/museum/exhibit/focus/antisemitism/voices/transcript/?content=20080424
[344] http://www.ushmm.org/
[345] https://web.archive.org/web/20180323165208/http://ashkenazhouse.org/
[346] http://www1.yadvashem.org/yv/en/exhibitions/kristallnacht/index.asp?WT.mc_id=wiki
[347] http://www1.yadvashem.org/yv/en/education/interviews/ron.asp
[348] http://www.graceumc-stl.org/uploads/media/1/03_Track_3.mp3
[349] Ronald Headland (1992), *Messages of Murder: A Study of the Reports of the Einsatzgruppen of the Security Police and the Security Service, 1941–1943.* https://books.google.com/books?id=Mue8a5Rwyi0C&printsec=frontcover#v=onepage&q=%22Luck%2C%20Sonderkommando%22&f=false Fairleigh Dickinson Univ. Press, pp. 125–126.
[350] Kopówka & Rytel-Andrianik (2011), p. 405. https://web.archive.org/web/20161104145619/http://www.polacyizydzi.com/dam-im-imie-na-wieki.pdf [[chrome-extension://gmpljdlgcdkljlppaekciacdmdlhfeon/images/beside-link-icon.svg|link= https//docs.google.com]]
[351] [[chrome-extension://gmpljdlgcdkljlppaekciacdmdlhfeon/images/beside-link-icon.svg|link= https//docs.google.com]]
[352] Yad Vashem, *Note:* village Połonka ( or its Połonka Little Hill http://wolyn.ovh.org/opisy/gorka_polonka-07.html subdivision) is misspelled in the documentary, with testimony of eyewitness Shmuel Shilo.
[353] *Also in:*
[354] *Also in:* ;
[355] *Also in:*
[356]
[357] Kopówka & Rytel-Andrianik (2011), chapt. 3:1, p. 77.
[358]
[359] *Also in:*
[360] *Also in:*
[361] Yad Vashem Shoa Resource Center, Zegota http://www.yadvashem.org/odot_pdf/Microsoft%20Word%20-%206392.pdf [[chrome-extension://gmpljdlgcdkljlppaekciacdmdlhfeon/images/beside-link-icon.svg|link= https://docs.google.com/viewer?url=http%3A%2F%2Fwww.yadvashem.org%2Fodot_pdf%2FMicrosoft%2520Word%2520-%25206392.pdf&embedded=true&chrome=false&dov=1]] [[chrome-extension://gmpljdlgcdkljlppaekciacdmdlhfeon/images/beside-link-icon.svg|link= https//docs.google.com]] October 20, 2013, at the Wayback Machine. , page 4/34 of the Report.
[362] Hunt for the Jews https//books.google.co.il , Jan Grabowski, page 55, Indiana University Press
[363] *This last statement is based on the fact that Polish Antisemitism, even during the war, was not murderous in nature and did not speak in terms of outright liquidation except on its outermost fringes. It expressed extreme messages and unequivocal conclusions–the imperative of mass Jewish emigration from Poland–but did not advocate pogroms or genocide*Were These Ordinary Poles? Daniel Blatman
[364] Jews and the Sporting Life: Studies in Contemporary Jewry XXIII (Polish Antisemitism: A National Pshychosis?) https//books.google.co.il , Daniel Blatman in volume edited by Ezra Mendelsohn, Oxford University Press, pages 213–225
[365] ; ; ;

[366] – Recent research suggests that a million Poles were involved, but some estimates go as high as three million. Lukas, 2013 edition. https://books.google.com/books?id=_2S-ZAkAy7EC&pg=PA13 .
[367] *Also in:*
[368] //en.wikipedia.org/w/index.php?title=Template:Jewish_Polish_history&action=edit
[369] *See also:*
[370] *For the German administrative divisions of Polish kresy with prominent Jewish communities destroyed under Nazi occupation, see:*
[371] Talking with the willing executioners. https://web.archive.org/web/20090521113606/http://www.haaretz.com/hasen/spages/1086259.html Haaretz.com 18 May 2009 via Internet Archive. A horrific page of history unfolded last Monday in Ukraine. It concerned the gruesome and untold story of a spontaneous pogrom by local villagers against hundreds of Jews in a town [now suburb] south of Ternopil in 1941. Not one, but five independent witnesses recounted the tale.
[372] . *Also in:*
[373]
[374] ; *also in* .
[375] Albert Stankowski, with August Grabski and Grzegorz Berendt; *Studia z historii Żydów w Polsce po 1945 roku*, Warszawa, Żydowski Instytut Historyczny 2000, pp. 107–111.
[376] POLIN Museum of the History of Polish Jews (2014), "Core Exhibition." http://www.polin.pl/en/exhibitions/core-exhibition-grand-opening-october-28-2014
[377] https://books.google.com/books?id=YglnAAAAMAAJ
[378] https://books.google.com/books?id=nPbr0XzlTzcC
[379] https://web.archive.org/web/20120217083434/http://www1.yadvashem.org/odot_pdf/Microsoft%20Word%20-%202308.pdf
[380] https://books.google.com/books?id=d9Wg4gjtP3cC
[381] https://books.google.com/books?id=vkLTSB7NHwgC
[382] https://books.google.com/books?id=GIujK0VqWGIC&printsec=frontcover&dq=Holocaust,+Poland&sig=ACfU3U1VmbuVYbIQHPig5nbX7F6my87VgA
[383] https://books.google.com/books?id=a12WB1iknWwC&printsec=frontcover&dq=Holocaust,+Poland&sig=ACfU3U3yafRba-qKuOrPHuI3MbJab8CUcw
[384] https//books.google.com
[385] http://echomatkibozejniepokalaniepoczetej.com/embnp/pages/assets/files/2011-09/dam_ime_na_wieki.pdf
[386] https://books.google.com/books?id=lz9obsxmuW4C&pg=PA13&dq=%22The+estimates+of+Jewish+survivors+in+Poland%22
[387] https://books.google.com/books?id=Lv1mAAAAMAAJ&dq=editions:IC7HhINUjXIC%20Google
[388] https://web.archive.org/web/20120331102155/http://niniwa2.cba.pl/polska_1939_1945.htm
[389] http://niniwa2.cba.pl/polska_1939_1945.htm
[390] https://books.google.com/books?id=aZTD96Upq9AC&q=Dobraczynski+Getter
[391] https://books.google.com/books?id=hC0-dk7vpM8C&pg=PA1&dq=Holocaust,+Poland
[392] //www.worldcat.org/oclc/37195289
[393] http://www.totallyjewish.com/news/special_reports/?content_id=5962
[394] http://isurvived.org/4Debates/paulsson_view.html
[395] http://www.h-net.org/reviews/showrev.cgi?path=252691081495762
[396] https://books.google.com/books?id=pMGRtebrdS8C&pg=PA1&dq=Holocaust,+Poland&sig=ACfU3U1cBAi4IfM9OuDPtn9Hy7skQXpgpg
[397] https://books.google.com/books?id=ywZG1TwqHwoC&pg=PA1&dq=Holocaust,+Poland&sig=ACfU3U3SHEY0Dt1Vt9iljEqxBuu-SeBpKg
[398] https://books.google.com/books?id=OB1nAwAAQBAJ&q=170%2C000+people+Sobib%C3%B3r
[399] //en.wikipedia.org/w/index.php?title=Template:The_Holocaust_sidebar&action=edit
[400] Yitzhak Arad, *Belzec, Sobibor, Treblinka*. Indiana University Press, Bloomington and Indianapolis, 1987.
[401] *Biuletyn Głównej Komisji Badania Zbrodni Hitlerowskich w Polsce*, Wydawnictwo Prawnicze, 1960.

[402] Michael Berenbaum, *The World Must Know*, United States Holocaust Memorial Museum, 2006, p. 114.
[403] "The War Against The Jews." http://www.holocaustchronicle.org/staticpages/176.html *The Holocaust Chronicle*, 2009. Chicago, Il. Accessed June 21, 2011.
[404] Wojciech Roszkowski, *Historia Polski 1914–1997 http://chomikuj.pl/marek5425/e-Book\*27s/Popularnonaukowe/Historia/Wojciech+Roszkowski+-+Historia+Polski+1914-2004, Warsaw 1998. PDF file, 46,0 MB (available with purchase). Chomikuj.pl, 2013.*
[405] Dwork, Deborah and Robert Jan Van Pelt, *The Construction of Crematoria at Auschwitz* https://www.jewishvirtuallibrary.org/jsource/Holocaust/auconstruct.html, W.W. Norton & Co., 1996.
[406] Jewish Virtual Library, Łódź. Overview of the Litzmannstadt Ghetto's history. https://www.jewishvirtuallibrary.org/jsource/Holocaust/lodztoc.html Accessed June 27, 2011.
[407] United States Holocaust Memorial Museum - Online Exhibition: Give Me Your Children: Voices from the Lodz Ghetto http://www.ushmm.org/museum/exhibit/online/lodz/
[408] University of Minnesota, Majdanek Death Camp http://www.chgs.umn.edu/museum/memorials/Majdanek/
[409] Kraków Ghetto including photographs http://www.krakow-poland.com/a/Krakow-Ghetto,ehc, at www.krakow-poland.com.
[410] About Kraków Ghetto with valuable historical photographs. http://www.dws-xip.pl/reich/zaglada/getto3.html
[411] "Schindler's Krakow," https://web.archive.org/web/20040815200535/http://www.silentwall.com/Schindler.html with modern-day photographs of the WWII relics. Internet Archive, saved from Silentwall.com (discontinued).
[412] The Kraków Ghetto http://www.jewishkrakow.net/en/see/krakow-ghetto/ complete with contemporary picture gallery, at JewishKrakow.net
[413] Edward Victor, "Ghettos and Other Jewish Communities." http://www.edwardvictor.com/Holocaust/ghetto_home_main.htm *Judaica Philatelic*. Accessed June 20, 2011.
[414] Richard C. Lukas, *Out of the Inferno: Poles Remember the Holocaust*, University Press of Kentucky 1989 - 201 pages. Page 13; also in Richard C. Lukas, *The Forgotten Holocaust: The Poles Under German Occupation, 1939-1944*, University Press of Kentucky, 1986, Google Print, p.13 https://books.google.ca/books?id=lz9obsxmuW4C&pg=PA13&dq=%22&sig=ACfU3U0SGgyvqSbL4bypepYoO_CbYc_N_w.
[415] Gunnar S. Paulsson, "The Rescue of Jews by Non-Jews in Nazi-Occupied Poland," *Journal of Holocaust Education*, Vol.7, Nos.1&2, 1998, pp.19-44. Published by Frank Cass, London.
[416] Types of Ghettos. United States Holocaust Memorial Museum, Washington, D.C. http://www.ushmm.org/wlc/sp/article.php?ModuleId=10007445
[417] Peter Vogelsang & Brian B. M. Larsen, "The Ghettos of Poland." http://www.holocaust-education.dk/holocaust/ghettoer.asp *The Danish Center for Holocaust and Genocide Studies*. 2002.
[418] Warsaw Ghetto http://www.ushmm.org/wlc/article.php?lang=en&ModuleId=10005069, United States Holocaust Memorial Museum (USHMM), Washington, D.C.
[419] Ghettos http://www.ushmm.org/wlc/article.php?lang=en&ModuleId=10005059, United States Holocaust Memorial Museum
[420] François Furet, *Unanswered Questions: Nazi Germany and the Genocide of the Jews* https://books.google.com/books?id=02PpAAAACAAJ. Schocken Books (1989), p. 182;
[421]
[422] Location names in other languages are available through the active links.
[423] Maciej i Ewa Szaniawscy, *"Zagłada Żydów w Będzinie w świetle relacji" (Extermination of Jews in the light of testimony)* http://jews.w.interia.pl/relacje.html. According to 1946 research by *Wojewódzka Żydowska Komisja Historyczna* in Katowice, wrote Maciej i Ewa Szaniawscy, there were around 30,000 Jews in Będzin following the invasion, including those who came in from neighbouring settlements. Between October 1940 and May 1942, the first 4,000 Jews were deported. In May 1942 additional 2,000 and in August, 5,000 more. Deportations between August 1942 and mid June 1943 amounted to additional 5,000. On 22 June 1943 the next transport of 5,000 Jews departed to Auschwitz, and finally, between 1-3 August 1943, the remaining 8,000

were sent away. The dispersed Jews who stayed, amounting to 1,000 persons, were deported between early October 1943 and July 1944. In total, about 28,000 Jews are believed to have been deported from the Będzin Ghetto. This information however, is not confirmed by the two main sources of the remaining data nor the Jewish Historical Institute, listing only 7,000 victims.

[424] Będzin in the Jewish Historical Institute community database. http://www.jhi.pl/en/gminy/miasto/613.html Warsaw.

[425] Iwona Pogorzelska, Bodzentyn od 1869 roku do niepodległości. http://bodzentyn.polska.pl/miastodawniej/article,Bodzentyn_od_1869_roku_do_niepodleglosci,id,314887.htm Polska.pl. Accessed June 16, 2011.

[426] "Getto w Łowiczu," at Miejsca martyrologii, Wirtualny Sztetl. http://www.sztetl.org.pl/pl/article/lowicz/13,miejsca-martyrologii/12946,getto-w-lowiczu/ Instytut Adama Mickiewicza.

[427] "Cmentarz żydowski w Mogielnicy (Jewish cemetery in Mogielnica)," at Kirkuty.xip.pl. http://www.kirkuty.xip.pl/mogielnica.htm

[428] Piotrków Trybunalski – Getto w Piotrkowie Trybunalskim. http://www.sztetl.org.pl/en/article/piotrkow-trybunalski/13,places-of-martyrology/3244,getto-w-piotrkowie-trybunalskim/ Virtual Shtetl. Museum of the History of the Polish Jews. Accessed July 1, 2011.

[429] Angelika Lasiewicz-Sych, "Traces of the past", Kultura Współczesna nr 4 (38), 2003. http://www.stacjamuranow.art.pl/muranow_station/places/an_essay_on_traces_of_the_past

[430] Deportations to Sobibór took place in waves: 1,300 Jews in May 1942, 5,400 in October, 2,800 in November 1942, and 2,000 in April 1943.

[431] Yitzhak Arad, Belzec, Sobibor, Treblinka: The Operation Reinhard Death Camps. https//books.google.ca Indiana University Press. "Appendix A." Page 395.

[432] "Życie za Życie" (Righteous of Ciepielów who paid the ultimate price)." http://www.ciepielow.pl/menu/aktualnosci/zycie_za_zycie.pdf Urząd Gminy w Ciepielowie. . Accessed July 6, 2011.

[433] "Ćmielów – Historia," http://www.sztetl.org.pl/pl/article/cmielow/5,historia/?action=view&page=1 Muzeum Historii Żydów Polskich Wirtualny Sztetl (Museum of the History of the Polish Jews). Accessed July 6, 2011.

[434] . Pamięć Miejsca. Retrieved April 12, 2012.

[435] The 90th session of the Senate of the Republic of Poland. Stenograph, part 2.2. http://www.senat.gov.pl/k4/DOK/sten/090/22.HTM A Report by Leon Kieres, president of the Institute of National Remembrance, for the period from July 1, 2,000 to June 30, 2001. Donald Tusk presiding. See statement by Senator Jadwiga Stokarska.

[436] Kraków – History. Page 3. http://www.sztetl.org.pl/en/article/krakow/5,history/?action=view&page=2 Virtual Shtetl, Museum of the History of Polish Jews. Accessed July 12, 2011.

[437] Niemiecki obóz tranzytowy Kiełbasin w Grodnie (wul. Sołamawaj) http://www.sztetl.org.pl/pl/article/grodno/13,miejsca-martyrologii/34493,kielbasin-ul-o-solomowoj-byly-nazistowski-oboz-tranzytowy/ (Kiełbasin transit camp), Virtual Shtetl, POLIN Muzeum Historii Żydów Polskich 2015. Accessed November 15, 2015.

[438] Jack Kugelmass, Jonathan Boyarin, Zachary M. Baker, From a ruined garden: the memorial books of Polish Jewry, https//books.google.ca United States Holocaust Memorial Museum. Accessed June 27, 2011.

[439] Jack Fischel, The Holocaust https://books.google.com/books?id=HrW-b3Q-3ewC&pg=PA58&dq=Lublin+ghetto&lr=&as_brr=3, Greenwood Publishing Group, 1998, pg. 58; in Google Books.

[440] "Treblinka Death Camp Day-by-Day," http://www.holocaustresearchproject.net/ar/treblinkadaytoday.html at Holocaust Education & Archive Research Team (www.HolocaustResearchProject.org). Accessed June 30, 2011.

[441] YIVO Encyclopedia of Jews in Eastern Europe, Lutsk. http://www.yivoencyclopedia.org/article.aspx/Lutsk "Following the Soviet liberation of Łuck in February 1944, only about 150 Jews returned. By 1959, just 600 Jews were living in Lutsk. The fortified synagogue was turned into a movie theater and later into a sports hall. A residential area was constructed on the site of the Rabbinite and Karaite cemeteries."

[442] Piotr Berghof, "Radoszyce, wspomnienie o żydowskich mieszkańcach miasteczka." http://my.opera.com/radomszczanin/albums/show.dml?id=492213 . Accessed June 27, 2011.

[443] Słonim – History. Jewish community. http://www.sztetl.org.pl/en/article/slonim/5,history/ Virtual Shtetl. Museum of the History of Polish Jews. Accessed July 7, 2011. The prewar Polish

city of Słonim was overrun by the Red Army in September 1939 and confiscated as part of Western Belarus. The influx of refugees from Nazi-occupied Poland increased its Jewish population to 27,000. Over 1,000 were deported to Siberia by the NKVD. Following German invasion of USSR, the ghetto was set up in August 1941, but mass executions began already on 17 July (1,200 men shot just outside the city). A second shooting action took place on 14 November 1941 with 9,000 killed. The ghetto was burned to the ground with all its inhabitants between 29 June and 15 July 1942 following a revolt. Only about 500 managed to escape.

[444] "Tarnobrzeg. Warto zobaczyć" (Tarnobrzeg worth seeing) http://e-przewodniki.pl/przewodnik-nowy-137-rozdzial-2057.html, Wydawnictwo Bezdroża. Accessed June 27, 2011.

[445] Wadowice – Historia. http://www.sztetl.org.pl/pl/article/wadowice/5,historia/?action=view&amp%3Bamp%3Bpage=1&print=1 *Wirtualny Sztetl*. . Accessed June 27, 2011.

[446] "Chronology of Vilna Ghetto," http://www.vilnaghetto.com/chrono.html at Vilnaghetto.com without additional confirmation of quantitative data. Accessed June 24, 2011.

[447] "The Deportation of the Zabludow Jews to Treblinka Death Camp." http://www.zabludow.com/treblinka.html 2003 Tilford Bartman, Jerusalem, Israel.

[448]

[449]

[450] "Lachwa, Polesie province, Poland." http://www.ushmm.org/wlc/en/article.php?ModuleId=1, 0007233, *The United States Holocaust Memorial Museum Encyclopedia of Camps and Ghettos, 1933–1945*

[451] "The History of Miedzyrzec Podlaski." http://www.mezritch.org.il/eng-text/eng-town.html *Association of Immigrants of Mezritch Depodalsia Area in Israel*. Accessed July 5, 2011.

[452] "Mezritch (Międzyrzec) Podlaski in the Jewish sources." http://www.mezritch.org.il/eng-text/eng-town.html *Association of Immigrants of Mezritch Depodalsia*. Accessed June 16, 2011.

[453] Przysucha, województwo Mazowieckie, Polska. http://www.wertheimer.info/family/GRAMPS/Haapalah/plc/2/9/bbffb7da76b7d7d4992.html *Haapalah* Index and Source Database. Accessed July 5, 2011.

[454] Przysucha – History. http://www.sztetl.org.pl/en/article/przysucha/5,history/ *Virtual Shtetl*. Museum of the History of Polish Jews. Accessed July 5, 2011.

[455] Gmina Sucha Beskidzka, powiat suski. http://mapa.targeo.pl/gmina/Sucha%20Beskidzka,670862?print *Targeo*. . Accessed June 27, 2011.

[456] Stefan Krakowski, Tomaszow Mazowiecki, https://www.jewishvirtuallibrary.org/jsource/judaica/ejud_0002_0020_0_19938.html *Jewish Virtual Library*. Accessed June 24, 2001.

[457] Devorah Hakohen, *Immigrants in turmoil: mass immigration to Israel and its repercussions...* https//books.google.ca Syracuse University Press, 2003 - 325 pages. Page 70.

[458] Arieh J. Kochavi, *Post-Holocaust politics: Britain, the United States & Jewish refugees, 1945-1948*. Page 15. https//books.google.ca The University of North Carolina Press.

[459] //en.wikipedia.org/w/index.php?title=Template:The_Holocaust_sidebar&action=edit

[460] Bare en detalj - Hvorfor lurer så mange på om jeg er jøde? http://www.dagbladet.no/2014/11/15/kultur/meninger/ideer/helgekommentaren/holocaust/36254653/ [Only a detail - Why do so many wonder if I am a Jew?]

[461] These numbers do not include Jewish Soviet or Polish prisoners of war that died in captivity as a result of murder or mistreatment in Norwegian camps, nor Allied Jewish soldiers killed in action in Norway. There is some evidence that prisoners of war who were found to be Jewish were singled out and were abused.

[462] Kronikk: Frontingen av «Den største forbrytelsen» gir en Holocaust-historie uten nyanser http://www.aftenposten.no/meninger/kronikker/Kronikk-Frontingen-av-Den-storste-forbrytelsen-gir-en-Holocaust-historie-uten-nyanser-7768742.html [Op-ed: To front the book *The greatest crime*, gives a history of the Holocaust—without nuances]

[463] United States Holocaust Memorial Museum, Norway, http://www.ushmm.org/wlc/en/article.php?ModuleId=10005460

[464] In August of the same year, radio confiscation orders were extended to all Norwegian civilians. According to Ringdal (see bibliography), it is thought that targeting Jews gave the authorities a "trial balloon" both for identifying Jewish individuals and confiscating radios.

[465] Reitan 2005.

[466] http://klassekampen.no/59591/article/item/null/aldri-mer--november

[467] Edgar Brichta var nazisjefens jødiske fostersønn http://www.dagbladet.no/2009/08/25/kultur/litteratur/andre_verdenskrig/holocaust/historie/7794594/

[468] Quislings hønsegård http://borre-historielag.no/onewebmedia/Quislings_h%C3%B8nseg%C3%A5rd_0505.pdf

[469] Det siste vitnet http://www.dn.no/magasinet/2015/07/03/2155/Portrettet/det-siste-vitnet

[470] Ottosen (1994)

[471] Den allvitende forteller - Etter hvert som beretningen skrider frem er det ikke lenger mulig å skille mellom det som redelig er hentet fra andre – og der annenhåndskilder tendensiøst tilpasses forfatterens eget foretrukne narrativ om krigen. http://www.aftenposten.no/meninger/debatt/Den-allvitende-forteller-7777826.html [The all-knowing narrator- As the narration proceeds, it is no longer possible to differentiate what is appropriately fetched from others - and where *annenhåndskilder* (or secondhand sources) are *tendensiøst* fitted to the author's preferred narrative about the war.]

[472] Ulstein 2006, pp. 236-69.

[473] Mendelsohn 1986, pp. 224-5.

[474] Abrahamsen 1991, pp. 137-9.

[475] Abrahamsen 1991, p. 10.

[476] Those who signed included members of the Interim Church Leadership (Den Midlertidige Kirkeledelse) – Ole Kristian Hallesby, Ludvig Hope, Henrik Hille, James Maroni, Gabriel Skagestad, Wollert Krohn-Hansen, and Andreas Fleischer (Eivind Berggrav, Bishop of Oslo, under house arrest by the Nazis, could not sign); the administration of the Faculty of Theology at the University of Oslo – Sigmund Mowinckel, Oluf Kolsrud, Einar Molland, H. Ording, and P. Marstrander; the administration of the MF Norwegian School of Theology – Olaf Moe, Karl Vold, Andreas Seierstad, and Johannes Smemo; various other Lutheran organizations, the leaders of the Baptist church, Missionary association, Sunday School union, Methodist church, Missionary alliance, and Salvation Army. The group was later driven underground when Hallesby was arrested by the Nazis in May 1943.

[477] Historiker forventer holocaust-unnskyldning http://www.tv2.no/a/3693561

[478] A telling example is the case of Per Kjølner, a member of Nasjonal Samling who bought at a heavily discounted price the Plesansky family's apparel operations in Tønsberg, which formed the basis for the chain store Adelsten. The one surviving family, Bernhard Plesansky, tried to recover his property but was unable to and emigrated to the United Kingdom. Kjølner was never convicted of any crime. See

[479] Various calculations estimate the capital depletion during the war at about 10%. In addition, scarcity in the global economy complicated import and export activity. Rationing continued in Norway until 1961.

[480] https://www.holocaustremembrance.com/member-countries/holocaust-education-remembrance-and-research-norway

[481] – Skamplett for rettsvesenet http://www.dagen.no/Nyheter/02/10/2014/%E2%80%93_Skamplett_for_rettsvesenet-120108

[482] Det angår også deg http://www.larvikmuseum.no/det-angar-ogsa-deg/ [It concerns you too]

[483] Månedens gjenstand i januar http://jodiskmuseumoslo.no/forside/manedens-gjenstand/ [Item of the month, for January]

[484] "- Så dere er bortimot alene om å drive forskning på andre verdenskrig og Holocaust? - HL-senteret utfører det meste av forskningen som foregår innen dette felt." http://klassekampen.no/59591/article/item/null

[485] Kronikk: Nye briller på Holocaust - Den kritiske undersøkelsen av jødedeportasjonene fra Norge er bare i sin spede begynnelse. http://www.aftenposten.no/meninger/kronikker/Kronikk-Nye-briller-pa-Holocaust-7772797.html [Op-ed: A new outlook on the Holocaoust - Discriminative research on the deportation of Jews from Norway, is in its infant stage]

[486] https://web.archive.org/web/20110722114334/http://www.stiftelsen-arkivet.no/Historikk_joder_fra_Agder

[487] http://www.stiftelsen-arkivet.no/Historikk_joder_fra_Agder

[488] http://www.orionforlag.no/default.aspx?ArticleID=81947&MenuID=10050

[489] http://www.jcpa.org/phas/phas-10.htm

[490] http://www.aftenposten.no/nyheter/iriks/article902260.ece

[491] http://www.regjeringen.no/nb/dep/jd/dok/NOUer/1997/NOU-1997-22.html?id=141043
[492] https://snl.no/Holocaust_i_Norge
[493] http://www.norgeshistorie.no/andre-verdenskrig/artikler/1742-deportasjonen-av-de-norske-jodene.html
[494] https://portal.ehri-project.eu/countries/no
[495] https://portal.ehri-project.eu/countries/be
[496] http://www.ushmm.org/wlc/en/article.php?ModuleId=10005432
[497] http://www.ushmm.org/wlc/en/article.php?ModuleId=10005363
[498] https://portal.ehri-project.eu/countries/lu
[499] http://memoshoah.lu/en/
[500] http://www.bbc.co.uk/history/worldwars/jewish_deportation_01.shtml
[501] Yad Vashem http://www.yad-vashem.org.il/yv/en/education/languages/dutch/pdf/article_croes.pdf
[502] Blumenkranz 1972, IV, 5, 1.
[503] Philippe 1979, p. 227.
[504] « De la haine dans l'air », par Jérôme Gautheret et Thomas Wieder, *Le Monde*, 27 juillet 2010
[505] Yahil 1990, p. 173.
[506] See report by the *Mission d'étude sur la spoliation des Juifs* http://www.ladocumentationfrancaise.fr/rapports-publics/004000897/index.shtml
[507] Philippe 1979, p. 251.
[508] Philippe 1979, chapter "La Guerre".
[509] Blumenkranz 1972, p. 404.
[510] Tal Bruttmann, « Au bureau des affaires juives. L'administration française et l'application de la législation antisémite », La Découverte, 2006
[511] Blumenkranz 1972, pp. 401-5.
[512] Jacques Cantier, *L'Algérie sous le régime de Vichy*, Odile Jacob, 2002, page 383
[513] Yad Vashem, About the Righteous, Statistics http://www1.yadvashem.org/yv/en/righteous/statistics.asp Accessed 20 September 2011.
[514] https://www.nytimes.com/1995/07/17/world/chirac-affirms-france-s-guilt-in-fate-of-jews.html
[515] https//www.washingtonpost.com
[516] https://www.theguardian.com/world/2012/jul/22/francois-hollande-wartime-roundup-jews
[517] https//books.google.com p=53
[518] https://www.theguardian.com/world/2017/jul/17/france-macron-denounces-state-role-holocaust-atrocity-paris-1942
[519] https://www.nytimes.com/2017/07/17/world/europe/macron-israel-holocaust-antisemitism.html
[520] https//www.washingtonpost.com
[521] https://www.bbc.com/news/world-europe-40622845
[522] https://www.scribd.com/doc/25713363/La-Persecution-Raciale
[523] //www.worldcat.org/oclc/417454239
[524] //www.jstor.org/stable/3685578
[525] https://portal.ehri-project.eu/countries/fr
[526] http://www.ushmm.org/wlc/en/article.php?ModuleId=10005429
[527] http://www.yadvashem.org/yv/en/holocaust/france/index.asp
[528] http://www.yadvashem.org/yv/en/exhibitions/childrens-homes/index.asp
[529] Official name of the occupied territory<ref>Hehn (1971), pp. 344–373
[530] Pavlowitch (2002), p. 141
[531] Misha Glenny. *The Balkans: Nationalism, War and the Great Powers, 1804-1999.* Page 502: "The Nazis were assisted by several thousand ethnic Germans as well as by supporters of Dimitrje Ljotic's Serbian fascist movement, Zbor, and General Milan Nedic's quisling administration. But the main Eengine of extermination was the regular army. The destruction of the Serbian Jews gives the lie to *Wehrmacht* claims that it took no part in the genocidal programmes of the Nazis. Indeed, General Bohme and his men in Serbia planned and carried out the murder of over 20,000 Jews and Gypsies without any prompting from Berlin"
[532] Misha Glenny. *The Balkans: Nationalism, War and the Great Powers 1804-1999.* Page 502

[533] Visualizing Otherness II http://chgs.umn.edu/histories/otherness/otherness2.html, Center for Holocaust and Genocide Studies, University of Minnesota.
[534] Virtual Jewish History Tour – Serbia and Montenegro https://www.jewishvirtuallibrary.org/jsource/vjw/serbia.html
[535] *Encyclopedia of the Holocaust*, Macmillan Publishing Company New York 1990
[536] Braham, R. L. (2000)The Politics of Genocide: the Holocaust of Hungary. Detroit: Wayne State University Press p. 145
[537] *Why is Israel waffling on Kosovo*?, by LARRY DERFNER, and GIL SEDAN
[538] The Righteous Among The Nations http://www.yadvashem.org/righteous/statistics Names and Numbers of Righteous Among the Nations – per Country & Ethnic Origin, as of January 1, 2017, Yad Vashem
[539] Byford 2011, p. 296.
[540] MacDonald 2002, p. 140.
[541] Ramet 2005, p. 268.
[542] https://scholar.google.com.au/scholar?hl=en&q=Gebeit+des+serbien+hehn&btnG=Search&lr=lang_en&as_sdt=0%2C5&as_ylo=&as_vis=0
[543] https//books.google.com
[544] http://www.open.ac.uk/socialsciences/semlin/en/holocaust-in-serbia.php
[545] https://www.scribd.com/doc/36949049/Notice-to-Israel-Serbian-Nazis-Killed-Jews-in-World-War-II
[546] http://www.lekket.com/data/articles/001-015-002_000.pdf
[547] Goldstein, Ivo. *Croatia: A History*, C. Hurst & Co. Ltd., London, 1999. (p. 136)
[548] Ante Pavelic: The Croat Question lhttp://chnm.gmu.edu/history/faculty/kelly/blogs/h312/wp-content/sources/pavelic.pdf
[549] Živaković-Kerže, Zlata. *Od židovskog naselja u Tenji do sabirnog logora* http://hrcak.srce.hr/file/11347
[550] Boško Zuckerman, "Prilog proučavanju antisemitizma i protužidovske propagande u vodećem zagrebačkom ustaškom tisku (1941-1943)" Zavod za hrvatsku povijest, vol 42, Zagreb (2010).
[551] Phayer 2000, p. 35.
[552] Phayer 2000, p. 34.
[553] Mojzes 2011, p. 60.
[554] Mojzes 2009, p. 160.
[555] Pavlowitch 2008, p. 34.
[556] Official website of the Jasenovac Memorial Site
[557] Never-ending story of the Sarajevo Haggadah http://www.openbook.ba/obq/no17/wsa.pdf
[558] *Nogometni leksikon*, Miroslav Krleža Lexicographical Institute, Zagreb, 2004 (p. 307)
[559] Goldstein, Ivo. *Holokaust u Zagrebu*, Novi liber, Zagreb, 2001. (p. 475)
[560] Goldstein, Ivo. *Holokaust u Zagrebu*, Novi liber, Zagreb, 2001. (p. 470)
[561] Goldstein, Ivo. *Holokaust u Zagrebu*, Novi liber, Zagreb, 2001, p. 472.
[562] Krizman, Narcisa Lengel. *Antisemitizam Holokaust Antifašizam*, Studia Iudaico-Croatica, Zagreb, 1996, p. 256.
[563] Sudbina međimurskih Židova http://povijest.net/sadrzaj/skola/radovi/116-sudbina-medimurskih-zidova.html, povijest.net; accessed 23 October 2016.
[564] Helen Fein, *Accounting for Genocide*, New York, The Free Press, 1979, pg. 79, 105
[565] http://www.ushmm.org/wlc/en/article.php?ModuleId=10005456
[566] http://www.jusp-jasenovac.hr/Default.aspx?sid=6284
[567] https://leicester.academia.edu/AlexanderKorb
[568] //en.wikipedia.org/w/index.php?title=Template:Genocide&action=edit
[569] https://hrcak.srce.hr/file/138888
[570] https://books.google.com/books?id=ihUWAQAAMAAJ
[571] https://books.google.com/books?id=CTOCAAAAIAAJ
[572] https://books.google.com/books?id=GS4_OgAACAAJ
[573] https://books.google.com/books?id=CgJnAAAAMAAJ
[574] http://www.isi.co.rs/pages/pictures/casopis/Istorija%2020.%20veka%202011-1.pdf
[575] https://books.google.com/books?id=nyDZAAAAMAAJ
[576] https://books.google.com/books?id=kseRAAAAIAAJ

[577] https://books.google.com/books?id=gkiEDAAAQBAJ
[578] https://books.google.com/books?id=wGknBwAAQBAJ
[579] https://books.google.com/books?id=GRTdAAAAQBAJ
[580] https://books.google.com/books?id=lvAhAQAAIAAJ
[581] https://books.google.com/books?id=c-t7BAAAQBAJ
[582] https://books.google.com/books?id=1gwunFdWfNsC
[583] https://books.google.com/books?id=KwW2O7v7CUcC
[584] https://books.google.rs/books?id=b1jyvQAACAAJ
[585] https://books.google.rs/books?id=vF9GMwEACAAJ
[586] https://books.google.com/books?id=KP_SAAAAMAAJ
[587] https://books.google.com/?id=dI9pAAAAMAAJ
[588] https://books.google.rs/books?id=aZTD96Upq9AC
[589] https://books.google.rs/books?id=CgTZAAAAMAAJ
[590] https://books.google.com/books?id=QwBnceJfwgUC
[591] https://books.google.com/books?id=NQtnAAAAMAAJ
[592] https://books.google.com/books?id=pwPZAAAAMAAJ
[593] https://books.google.com/books?id=fqUSGevFe5MC
[594] https://books.google.com/books?id=Yxv4-iqVe2wC
[595] http://www.ushmm.org/exhibition/jasenovac/
[596] //en.wikipedia.org/w/index.php?title=Template:The_Holocaust_sidebar&action=edit
[597] Yehouda Shenhav. Ethnicity and National Memory: The World Organization of Jews from Arab Countries (WOJAC) in the Context of the Palestinian National Struggle http://people.socsci.tau.ac.il/mu/yshenhav/files/2013/07/Ethnicity-and-National-Memory.pdf. British Journal of Middle Eastern Studies. Volume 29, Issue 1, 2002, Pages 27 - 56.
[598] Roumani 2009, p. 133 #1"As stated above, many factors influenced and strengthened the determination of the Jewish community in Libya to emigrate. Most important were the scars left from the last years of the Italian occupation and the entry of the British Military in 1943 accompanied by the Jewish Palestinian soldiers. These soldiers played an instrumental role in reviving Zionism in the community and turning it into a pragmatic program to fulfill the dream of immigrating to Israel. Moreover, the rise of nationalism and preparations for independence made many members of the community suspicious and apprehensive about their future in Libya. The difficulties raised by the British in allowing Libyan Jews to immigrate dampened the enthusiasm of many, however."
[599] Ariel 2013, p. 150.
[600] Jewish Brigade: An Army with Two Masters 1944-45 https://books.google.co.uk/books?id=0RY7AwAAQBAJ&pg=PT42, Morris Beckman, The History Press, 2010, p. 42-52
[601] Yoav Gelber, *Jewish Palestinian Volunteering in the British Army during the Second World War*, Vol. III. *The Standard Bearers - The Mission of the Volunteers to the Jewish People*, (Hebrew, Yad Izhak Ben-Zvi, Jerusalem 1983).
[602] Roumani 2009, p. 133 #2"The Jewish Agency and the Mossad Le Aliyah Bet (the illegal immigration agency) realized the potential of this immigration and decided as early as the summer of 1943 to send three clandestine emissaries — Yair Doar, Zeev (Vilo) Katz and Naftali Bar-Ghiora - to prepare the infrastructure for aliyah of the Libyan Jewish community. These emissaries played a crucial role in establishing the immigration infrastructure that would later, in a more advanced form, facilitate the mass of immigration of Libyan Jews."
[603] Stillman, 2003, p. 145.
[604] Harris, 2001, pp. 149–150.
[605] Fischbach 2008, p. 68.
[606] NARA RG 84, Libya— Tripoli, General Records 1948-49; file 800-833, Taft to Secretary of State (November 23, 1948)
[607] Goldberg, p. 156: "Immigration began when the British authorities granted permission to the Jewish Agency to set up an office in Tripoli and organize the operation. As an indication of how the causes of events can be reinterpreted in terms of their results, a number of Libyan Jews have told me that their guess is that the Jewish Agency was behind the riots, for they clearly had the effect of bringing the Jews to Israel"
[608] https://books.google.com/books?id=d7FtAAAAMAAJ

[609] https://books.google.com/books?id=bFN2ismyhEYC
[610] https://books.google.co.uk/books?id=OluNAgAAQBAJ&source=gbs_navlinks_s
[611] http://www.merip.org/mer/mer248/fischbach.html
[612] https://books.google.co.uk/books?id=1_6XgrCXoTUC
[613] http://jewishrefugees.blogspot.co.il/
[614] http://www.jpost.com/Business/Business-News/Libyan-Jews-to-get-Holocaust-benefits
[615] https://www.youtube.com/watch?v=2O2v5d7Cqgo
[616] http://jimenaexperience.org/libya/about-jimena/past-and-present/
[617] http://www.yadvashem.org/yv/en/education/interviews/doron.asp
[618] Evans 2003, pp. 344–345.
[619] Evans 2005, p. 81.
[620] Evans 2005, p. 85.
[621] Revisiting the National Socialist Legacy: Coming to Terms With Forced Labor, Expropriation, Compensation, and Restitution page 84 Oliver Rathkolb
[622] at Wayback machine.
[623] Evans 2005, pp. 87–90.
[624] Evans 2005, p. 90.
[625] Evans 2008, p. 367.
[626] McNab 2009, p. 137.
[627] Kershaw 2008, pp. 308–314.
[628] Evans 2005, pp. 31–35, 39.
[629] Weale 2012, p. 115.
[630] Browning 2004, p. 315.
[631] Snyder 2010, p. 416.
[632] *For the map of more that 1,000 locations, see:* Map of Ghettos for Jews in Eastern Europe. https://www.nytimes.com/imagepages/2013/03/03/opinion/03ghetto-map.html The New York Times. *Source:* USHMM.
[633]
[634] Marek Przybyszewski, IBH Opracowania - Działdowo jako centrum administracyjne ziemi sasińskiej (Działdowo as centre of local administration). https://web.archive.org/web/20101022004220/http://www.historia.terramail.pl/opracowania/nowozytna/zamek_centrum_administracji.html Internet Archive, 22 October 2010.
[635] Wachsmann 2015, p. 84.
[636] Wachsmann 2015, pp. 38–45 https://books.google.com/books?id=QzKdBAAAQBAJ&printsec=frontcover#v=onepage&q=wild%20camps&f=false.
[637] Wachsmann 2015, 88 https://books.google.com/books?id=QzKdBAAAQBAJ&printsec=frontcover#v=onepage&q=107%2C000&f=false.
[638] https://books.google.com/books/about/KL.html?id=QzKdBAAAQBAJ
[639] https://www.youtube.com/watch?v=QtRDt6uAB0U
[640] http://www1.yadvashem.org/yv/en/holocaust/about/06/camps.asp?WT.mc_id=wiki
[641] http://www.druhasvetovavalka.cz/
[642] http://www.yadvashem.org/
[643] https://web.archive.org/web/20060628200833/http://www.ushmm.org/museum/exhibit/online/phistories/
[644] https://web.archive.org/web/20040919010250/http://www.holocaust-history.org/
[645] https://archive.org/stream/nazi_concentration_camps/nazi_concentration_camps_256kb.mp4
[646] https://www.jewishvirtuallibrary.org/jsource/Holocaust/cc.html
[647] https://www.pbs.org/wgbh/pages/frontline/camp/view/
[648] https://web.archive.org/web/20071013163821/http://buchenwald.libsyn.com/
[649] http://www.footnote.com/page/110056803_nazi_concentration_camp_records/
[650] Bundesministerium der Justiz (2011), List of concentration camps and their outposts in alphabetical order. https://web.archive.org/web/20121103180512/http://www.gesetze-im-internet.de/begdv_6/anlage_6.html Internet Archive.
[651] *Concentration Camp Listing* https://www.jewishvirtuallibrary.org/jsource/Holocaust/cclist.html Sourced from Van Eck, Ludo *Le livre des Camps*. Belgium: Editions Kritak; and Gilbert,

Martin *Atlas of the Holocaust*. New York: William Morrow 1993. In this on-line site are the names of 149 camps and 814 subcamps, organized by country.

[652] Search Results: Mapping the SS Concentration Camp System. http://www.ushmm.org/search/results/?q=concentration+camps Alphabetical listing. United States Holocaust Memorial Museum: Further Reading. Bergen, Dawidowicz, Gilbert, Gutman, Hilberg, Yahil.

[653] *Holocaust Encyclopedia*, Nazi Camps. Introduction. http://www.ushmm.org/wlc/en/article.php?ModuleId=10005144 United States Holocaust Memorial Museum.

[654] Peter Vogelsang & Brian B. M. Larsen (2002), The difference between concentration camps and extermination camps. http://www.holocaust-education.dk/lejre/koncudd.asp The Danish Center for Holocaust and Genocide Studies.

[655]

[656] *Also in:*

[657] http://www.subbrit.org.uk/sb-sites/sites/a/alderney/lager_sylt/index.shtml

[658] http://www.kampamersfoort.nl/

[659] Franciszek Piper, Construction and Expansion of KL Auschwitz ("Budowa i rozbudowa KL Auschwitz"). http://pl.auschwitz.org.pl/h/index.php?option=com_content&task=view&id=3&Itemid=5 The Auschwitz-Birkenau State Museum in Oświęcim, Poland (Państwowe Muzeum Auschwitz-Birkenau w Oświęcimiu), 1999–2010

[660] Ramet, Sabrina P., *The Three Yugoslavias: State-Building and Legitimation: 1918–2005*. Indiana University Press, 2006. (p. 131)

[661] https://web.archive.org/web/20090820090521/http://www.belzec.org.pl/

[662] http://www.bergenbelsen.de/

[663] http://www.ushmm.org/wlc/article.php?lang=en&ModuleId=10005482

[664] https://web.archive.org/web/20160304125901/http://degob.org/index.php?showarticle=2032

[665] https://web.archive.org/web/20051230105805/http://www.breendonk.be/

[666] http://www.gedenkstaette-breitenau.de/

[667] http://www.buchenwald.de/

[668] http://www1.yadvashem.org/odot_pdf/microsoft%20word%20-%202494.pdf

[669] https://web.archive.org/web/20070205055717/http://www.holocaust-history.org/dachau-gas-chambers/

[670] http://www.ushmm.org/wlc/article.php?lang=en&ModuleId=10005215

[671] http://www.falstadsenteret.no/

[672] http://www.gedenkstaette-flossenbuerg.de/

[673] http://www.nizkor.org/hweb/imt/tgmwc/tgmwc-05/tgmwc-05-42-05.shtml

[674] https://web.archive.org/web/20140426142745/http://www.muzeumniepodleglosci.poznan.pl/index.php?module=htmlpages&func=display&pid=2

[675] http://www.gross-rosen.pl/

[676] http://www.nmkampvught.nl/

[677] http://www.hinzert.de/

[678] http://www.menemshafilms.com/forgotten-transports-to-estonia.html

[679] http://www.ushmm.org/wlc/en

[680] http://motlc.wiesenthal.com/text/x12/xr1201.html

[681] http://www.buergervereinigung-landsberg.org/english/historicalfacts/history.htm

[682] http://www.landsberger-zeitgeschichte.de/index.htm

[683] https://web.archive.org/web/20041208190151/http://www.ushmm.org/kovno/intro/intro.htm

[684] https://web.archive.org/web/20111208083454/http://www.kz-kemna.de/

[685] http://www.jewishvirtuallibrary.org/kistarcsa

[686] http://www1.yadvashem.org/odot_pdf/microsoft%20word%20-%206622.pdf

[687] http://www.mauthausen-memorial.at/

[688] http://www.dora.de/

[689] Roger Boulanger (2006), L'historique du camp de Natzweiler-Struthof https://web.archive.org/web/20071123071645/http://crdp.ac-reims.fr/memoire/enseigner/natzweiler_struthof/historique.htm via Internet Archive.

[690] http://www.kz-gedenkstaette-neuengamme.de/

[691] https://web.archive.org/web/20041216195557/http://www.wewelsburg.de/pages/startseite/willkommen.shtml

[692] https://web.archive.org/web/20101125090257/http://dzokulm.telebus.de/index1.html
[693] http://www.ravensbrueck.de/
[694] http://www.ravensbruck.nl/
[695] http://www.risierasansabba.it/
[696] http://www.gedenkstaette-sachsenhausen.de/
[697] https://web.archive.org/web/20100527092302/http://vip.latnet.lv/LPRA/salaspils.htm
[698] https://web.archive.org/web/20121130223721/http://www.smirci-krize.cz/fotky-ms-op-skrochovice-koncentracni-tabor-oboz-koncentracyjny.php
[699] http://www1.yadvashem.org/odot_pdf/microsoft%20word%20-%206030.pdf
[700] http://www.stutthof.pl/
[701] http://wek.kiev.ua/uk/%D0%A1%D0%B8%D1%80%D0%B5%D1%86%D1%8C%D0%BA%D0%B8%D0%B9_%D0%BA%D0%BE%D0%BD%D1%86%D1%82%D0%B0%D0%B1%D1%96%D1%80
[702] http://www.pamatnik-terezin.cz/
[703] http://www1.yadvashem.org/odot_pdf/microsoft%20word%20-%205886.pdf
[704] http://motlc.wiesenthal.com/text/x33/xm3355.html
[705] https://www.jewishvirtuallibrary.org/jsource/Holocaust/Vaivara.html
[706] http://www1.yadvashem.org/yv/en/holocaust/about/06/camps.asp?WT.mc_id=wiki
[707] https://web.archive.org/web/20140525232804/http://www.tauberholocaustlibrary.org/oralhistory/concentrationcamplist2011.pdf
[708] *Hitler's Ethic* By Richard Weikar, page 73.
[709]
[710]
[711] Auschwitz Museum and Raul Hilberg: *Die Vernichtung der europäischen Juden*. extended edition Frankfurt 1990. Volume 2 Page 994f
[712] Michael Zimmermann: *Kommentierende Bemerkungen – Arbeit und Vernichtung im KZ-Kosmos*. In: Ulrich Herbert et al. (Ed.): *Die nationalsozialistischen Konzentrationslager*. Frankfurt/M 2002, , Vol. 2, p. 744
[713] Dove, Nah. *Afrikan Mothers: Bearers of Culture, Makers of Social Change*. 1998, p. 240.
[714] Gunn Morris, Vivian and Morris, Curtis L. *The Price They Paid: Desegregation in an African American Community*. 2002, p. x.
[715] Tarpley, Natasha. *Testimony: Young African-Americans on Self-Discovery and Black Identity*. 1995, p. 252.
[716] Quick guide: The slave trade; Who were the slaves? http://news.bbc.co.uk/1/hi/world/africa/6445941.stm BBC News, 15 March 2007.
[717] Stannard, David. *American Holocaust*. Oxford University Press, 1993.
[718] Patrick Manning, "The Slave Trade: The Formal Dermographics of a Global System" in Joseph E. Inikori and Stanley L. Engerman (eds), *The Atlantic Slave Trade: Effects on Economies, Societies and Peoples in Africa, the Americas, and Europe* (Duke University Press, 1992), pp. 117-44, online at pp. 119-20. https://books.google.com/books?id=abvkqNGSTZ0C&pg=PA119
[719] Demanding taxation in the form of forced labour was common across colonial Africa at the time.<ref name="FOOTNOTEStengers1969267–8">Stengers 1969, pp. 267–8.
[720] Renton, Seddon & Zeilig 2007, p. 28.
[721] Stengers 1969, pp. 267–8.
[722] Van Reybrouck 2014, p. 94.
[723] Hochschild 1999, p. 315.
[724] Hochschild's estimate of a population decline of 10 million is based on early research by the historian Jan Vansina, and follows a 1919 estimate which stated that a 50 percent fall had occurred under colonial rule, which he couples with the 1924 census records.<ref name="FOOTNOTEHochschild1999233">Hochschild 1999, p. 233.
[725] Vanthemsche 2012, p. 24.
[726] Hochschild 1999, p. 233.
[727] Vansina 2010, p. 138.
[728] Renton, Seddon & Zeilig 2007, p. 30.
[729] Renton, Seddon & Zeilig 2007, pp. 30–1.

[730] Vanthemsche 2012, p. 25.
[731] Gunnar Heinsohn *Lexikon der Völkermorde*, Rowohlt rororo 1998,
[732] Joel Kotek / Pierre Rigoulot *Gefangenschaft, Zwangsarbeit, Vernichtung*, Propyläen 2001
[733] Ralf Stettner *Archipel Gulag. Stalins Zwangslager*, Schöningh 1996,
[734] Roy Medwedew *Die Wahrheit ist unsere Stärke. Geschichte und Folgen des Stalinismus* (Ed. by David Joravsky and Georges Haupt), Fischer, Frankfurt/M. 1973,
[735] Alexander Solzhenitsyn *Arkhipelag Gulag*, Vol. 2. "Novyy Mir," 1990.
[736] Alexander Nikolaevich Yakovlev. *A Century of Violence in Soviet Russia*. Yale University Press, 2002. p. 15 https//books.google.com
[737] Stephen Wheatcroft, *The Scale and Nature of German and Soviet Repression and Mass Killings, 1930–45*. https://www.researchgate.net/publication/233004050_The_scale_and_nature_of_German_and_Soviet_repression_and_mass_killings_1930451_1 Europe-Asia Studies, Vol. 48, No. 8 (Dec., 1996), pp. 1319–1353
[738] Hannah Arendt *The Origins of Totalitarianism*, Harcourt 1985 edition, at 444 - 45"
[739] "Hannah Arendt *The Origins of Totalitarianism*, Harcourt 1985 edition, at 444 - 45"
[740] A. I. Kokurin / N. V. Petrov (Ed.): *GULAG (Glavnoe Upravlenie Lagerej): 1918–1960* (Rossija. XX vek. Dokumenty). Moskva: Materik 2000, , pp. 441–2
[741] Oleg V. Khlevniuk: *The History of the Gulag: From Collectivization to the Great Terror* New Haven: Yale University Press 2004, , pp. 326–7.
[742] ibd., pp. 308–6.
[743] Ellman, Michael. *Soviet Repression Statistics: Some Comments* http://sovietinfo.tripod.com/ELM-Repression_Statistics.pdf Europe-Asia Studies. Vol 54, No. 7, 2002, 1151–1172
[744] Applebaum, Anne (2003) *Gulag: A History*. Doubleday. pg 583
[745] Pohl, *The Stalinist Penal System*, p. 131.
[746] Stephane Courtois, et al. *The Black Book of Communism*. Harvard University Press, 1999. pp. 481-482
[747] Chang, Jung and Halliday, Jon. *Mao: The Unknown Story*. Jonathan Cape, London, 2005. p. 338: "By the general estimate China's prison and labor camp population was roughly 10 million in any one year under Mao. Descriptions of camp life by inmates, which point to high mortality rates, indicate a probable annual death rate of at least 10 per cent."
[748] Dikötter (2010). pp. 298, 304.
[749] Stéphane Courtois, Jean-Louis Margolin, et al. *The Black Book of Communism: Crimes, Terror, Repression*. Harvard University Press, 1999. p. 464
[750] Rummel, R. J. *China's Bloody Century: Genocide and Mass Murder Since 1900* http://www.hawaii.edu/powerkills/NOTE2.HTM Transaction Publishers, 1991. pp. 214–215
[751] Aikman, David. " The Laogai Archipelago" http://theweeklystandard.com/Content/Public/Articles/000/000/009/039ezdcg.asp?page=2, *The Weekly Standard*, September 29, 1997.
[752] necrometrics.com/30c300k.htm#Port00
[753] necrometrics.com/20c100k.htm#Fr00
[754] Laidler (2005)
[755] Library of Congress, 1992, "Indonesia: World War II and the Struggle For Independence, 1942-50; The Japanese Occupation, 1942-45" http://lcweb2.loc.gov/cgi-bin/query/r?frd/cstdy:@field(DOCID+id0029) Access date: February 9, 2007.
[756] Christopher Reed: Japan's Dirty Secret, One Million Korean Slaves http://www.counterpunch.org/reed02022006.html
[757] Cited in: Dower, John W. *War Without Mercy: Race and Power in the Pacific War* (1986; Pantheon; ).
[758] Van der Eng, Pierre (2008) 'Food Supply in Java during War and Decolonisation, 1940–1950.' *MPRA Paper No. 8852*. pp. 35–38. http://mpra.ub.uni-muenchen.de/8852/
[759] Kiernan, Ben. "The Demography of Genocide in Southeast Asia," http://www.tandfonline.com/doi/abs/10.1080/1467271032000147041 *Critical Asian Studies*, Vol. 35, No. 4 (2003), pp. 587-588; accessed December 3, 2016; Thompson, p. 138
[760] Omestad, Thomas, "Gulag Nation" https://web.archive.org/web/20050509131122/http://www.usnews.com/usnews/news/articles/030623/23gulag.htm, U.S. News & World Report, June 23, 2003.
[761] *Black Book of Communism*, pg. 564.

[762] Leeshai Lemish (7 October 2008) "How China is Silencing Falun Gong" http://www.david-kilgour.com/2008/Oct_07_2008_03.php, National Post david-kilgour.com

[763] Amnesty International (22 May 2006) 2006 Annual Report https://www.amnesty.org/en/library/asset/POL10/001/2006/en/59ad70c9-d46f-11dd-8743-d305bea2b2c7/pol100012006en.pdf

[764] Gutmann, Ethan. "China's Gruesome Organ Harvest" http://www.weeklystandard.com/Content/Public/Articles/000/000/015/824qbcjr.asp, The Weekly Standard, 24 November 2008

[765] David Kilgour, David Matas (6 July 2006, revised 31 January 2007) An Independent Investigation into Allegations of Organ Harvesting of Falun Gong Practitioners in China http://organharvestinvestigation.net (free in 22 languages) organharvestinvestigation.net

[766] Reuters, "Argentine judge asks China arrests over Falun Gong" https://www.reuters.com/article/2009/12/23/us-argentina-china-falungong-idUSTRE5BM02B20091223, 22 Dec 2009.

[767] Genocide Prevention Network, 'Spanish Court Indicts Chinese Leaders for Persecution of Falun Gong' http://www.genocidepreventionnow.org/GPNSearchResults/tabid/64/ctl/DisplayArticle/mid/400/aid/151/Default.aspx.

[768] La Audiencia pide interrogar al ex presidente chino Jiang por genocidio http://www.elmundo.es/elmundo/2009/11/14/espana/1258230601.html, Nov 14, 2009

[769] Davis, Robert. Christian Slaves, Muslim Masters: White Slavery in the Mediterranean, the Barbary Coast and Italy, 1500–1800.

[770] The Cambridge World History of Slavery: Volume 3, AD 1420–AD 1804

[771] stern-Serie: Besiegt, befreit, besetzt - Deutschland 1945–48 http://www.stern.de/politik/ausland/537667.html?eid=537265 "Die Schätzungen über die Zahl der in Haft gestorbenen Männer schwanken zwischen 600 000 und einer Million. Nach Angaben des Suchdienstes des Deutschen Roten Kreuzes ist bis heute das Schicksal von 1,3 Millionen Kriegsgefangenen ungeklärt - sie gelten offiziell als vermisst."

[772] stern-Serie: Besiegt, befreit, besetzt - Deutschland 1945–48 http://www.stern.de/politik/ausland/537667.html?eid=537265

[773] *The Expulsion of 'German' Communities from Eastern Europe at the end of the Second World War*, Steffen Prauser and Arfon Rees, European University Institute, Florense. HEC No. 2004/1 p. 55

[774] Ethnic Germans in Poland and the Czech Republic: A Comparative Evaluation http://www.stefanwolff.com/working-papers/EthnicGermansPolandandCzechRepublic.pdf p.9

[775]

[776] Spicer, pp. 80–82

[777] Paco Ignacio Taibo II, documenta el brutal genocidio yaqui en nuestro país http://www.tukari.udg.mx/noticia/paco-ignacio-taibo-ii-documenta-el-brutal-genocidio-yaqui-en-nuestro-pais

[778] Why do they hide? http://www.survivalinternational.org/articles/3104-why-do-they-hide, Survival International:

[779] https://books.google.com/?id=eDDoDMKrzyMC&pg=PA210&lpg=PA210&dq=Vernichtung+durch+Arbeit

[780] //doi.org/10.1086%2F235291

[781] //www.jstor.org/stable/2990503

[782] https://books.google.com/?id=zkZC6bp3upsC&pg=PA370&lpg=PA370&dq=Vernichtung+durch+Arbeit

[783] http://www.dhm.de/lemo/html/nazi/antisemitismus/kz/index.html

[784] http://www.dradio.de/dlr/sendungen/buchtipp/151903/

[785] Yad Vashem, The Ghettos. The Holocaust Martyrs' and Heroes' Remembrance Authority. http://www.yadvashem.org/yv/en/holocaust/about/03/introduction.asp Overview. Retrieved 28 September 2015.

[786] Browning 2007, pp. 166, 172.

[787] Browning 2007, p. 139, Gold rush https://books.google.ca/books?id=d9Wg4gjtP3cC&printsec=frontcover#v=snippet&q=gold%2Brush&f=false.

[788] . *Yad Vashem The Holocaust Martyrs' and Heroes' Remembrance Authority.*

[789] Warsaw http://www.ushmm.org/wlc/en/article.php?ModuleId=10005069, United States Holocaust Memorial Museum

[790] Ghettos http://www.ushmm.org/wlc/en/article.php?ModuleId=10005247 , United States Holocaust Memorial Museum
[791] Types of Ghettos. United States Holocaust Memorial Museum, Washington, D.C. http://www.ushmm.org/wlc/sp/article.php?ModuleId=10007445
[792] Browning 2007, pp. 149, 167: Sanitation https://books.google.ca/books?id=d9Wg4gjtP3cC&printsec=frontcover#v=onepage&q=sanitation&f=false.
[793] Hershel Edelheit, Abraham J. Edelheit, *A world in turmoil: an integrated chronology of the Holocaust* https://books.google.com/books?id=94NvHsiyn38C&pg=PA216, 1991
[794] Gunnar S. Paulsson, "The Rescue of Jews by Non-Jews in Nazi-Occupied Poland," *The Journal of Holocaust Education*, vol. 7, nos. 1 & 2 (summer–autumn 1998), pp. 19–44.
[795] https://books.google.ca/books?id=d9Wg4gjtP3cC&printsec=frontcover#v=snippet&q=ghettoization%2Bpolicy&f=false
[796] DIETRICH EICHHOLTZ "»Generalplan Ost« zur Versklavung osteuropäischer Völker" http://www.rosalux.de/cms/fileadmin/rls_uploads/pdfs/167eichholtz.pdf
[797] Madajczyk, Czesław. "Die Besatzungssysteme der Achsenmächte. Versuch einer komparatistischen Analyse." *Studia Historiae Oeconomicae* vol. 14 (1980): pp. 105-122 https//books.google.com in *Hitler's War in the East, 1941-1945: A Critical Assessment* by Gerd R. Ueberschär and Rolf-Dieter Müller https://www.amazon.com/dp/1571810684
[798] P. 93.
[799] Berenbaum 2006, pp. 97-8.
[800] " President Putin Has Called Ukraine a Hotbed of Anti-Semites. It's Not. http://news.nationalgeographic.com/news/2014/05/140530-ukraine-jews-poroshenko-putin-pushilin-right-sector-lviv-zissels/". *National Geographic.* May 30, 2014
[801] Nazi-hunters give low grades to 13 countries, including Ukraine http://www.kyivpost.com/news/nation/detail/94616/, *Kyiv Post* (January 12, 2011)
[802] Germans must remember the truth about Ukraine – for their own sake http://www.eurozine.com/germans-must-remember-the-truth-about-ukraine-for-their-own-sake/, Eurozine (7 July 2017)
[803] " Mobile Killing Squads http://www.ushmm.org/outreach/en/article.php?ModuleId=10007710". United States Holocaust Memorial Museum (USHMM)
[804] http://www.ushmm.org/m/pdfs/20130500-holocaust-in-ukraine.pdf
[805] https//www.academia.edu
[806] Daniel Brook, "Double Genocide. Lithuania wants to erase its ugly history of Nazi collaboration—by accusing Jewish partisans who fought the Germans of war crimes." http://www.slate.com/articles/news_and_politics/history/2015/07/lithuania_and_nazis_the_country_wants_to_forget_its_collaborationist_past.html, *Slate*, July 26, 2015
[807] http://www.genocid.lt/Leidyba/anons20.htm
[808] http://www.ceeol.com/aspx/issuedetails.aspx?issueid=f93baf32-c7b1-4f70-ab53-18d60bdea652&articleId=8235896d-652e-40d3-93a4-d9776a23c67f
[809] http://hgs.oxfordjournals.org/cgi/content/abstract/7/2/247
[810] http://hgs.oxfordjournals.org/cgi/content/abstract/5/1/53
[811] http://www.genocid.lt/Leidyba/9/vytautas.htm
[812] http://www.holocaustatlas.lt/EN/
[813] http://www.ushmm.org/wlc/article.php?lang=en&ModuleId=10005444
[814] http://www.genocid.lt/centras/en/
[815] http://www.chgs.umn.edu/museum/memorials/lithPonar/index.html
[816] http://www.lituanus.org/2001/01_4_03.htm
[817] http://defendinghistory.com/how-did-lithuanians-wrong-litvaks-by-andrius-kulikauskas/71001
[818] http://holocaustinthebaltics.com/
[819] http://www.holocaustinthebaltics.com/LithuanianHolocaustReadingListDateAsOnDoc.pdf
[820] https://web.archive.org/web/20120719043753/http://www.ushmm.org/museum/exhibit/online/kovno/invade/garage.htm
[821] http://www.vilnaghetto.com/gallery2/popular?g2_albumId=2256&g2_itemId=2398
[822] http://defendinghistory.com/collaborator-dry-clean
[823] http://www.ushmm.org/wlc/en/article.php?ModuleId=10005444

[824] http://collections1.yadvashem.org/notebook_ext.asp?item=5240
[825] https://web.archive.org/web/20131005045238/http://lithuanianjews.org.il/HTMLs/article_list4.aspx?C2014=14343&BSP=14336&BSS6=13971
[826] http://www1.yadvashem.org/yv/en/about/institute/lithuanian_testimonies.asp
[827] http://www1.yadvashem.org/yv/en/exhibitions/museum_photos/children_ghetto.asp
[828] https://web.archive.org/web/20130927083057/http://lithuanianjews.org.il/HTMLs/article_list.aspx?C2003=698&BSP=690&BSS6=698
[829] https://web.archive.org/web/20120802021332/http://www.jewish.ru/history/facts/2010/06/news994286002.php
[830] http://www.genocid.lt/centras/ru/#
[831] http://www.slate.com/articles/news_and_politics/history/2015/07/lithuania_and_nazis_the_country_wants_to_forget_its_collaborationist_past.html
[832] http://defendinghistory.com/yitzhak-arad-on-the-holocaust-in-lithuania-and-its-obfuscation-in-lithuanian-sources/46252/
[833] http//defendinghistory.com
[834] Ezergailis, *The Holocaust in Latvia*, at page 245.
[835] Ezergailis, *The Holocaust in Latvia*, at page 253
[836] Ezergailis, *The Holocaust in Latvia*, at page 211
[837] Mark Paul, Polish-Jewish Relations in Wartime Northeastern Poland and the Aftermath http://www.glaukopis.pl/pdf/czytelnia/Tangled_Web_1.pdf
[838] Vestermanis M. Juden in Riga. Ein historischer Wegweiser. Bremen, 1996, S. 29.
[839] Latvia's Jewish Community: History, Tragedy, Revival http://www.am.gov.lv/en/ministry/4265/4299/
[840] Niewyk, *The Columbia Guide to the Holocaust*, at 47.
[841] Lewy, *The Nazi Persecution of the Gypsies*, at page 123.
[842] Some sources give the name Georg Jedicke.
[843] Lewy, *The Nazi Persecution of the Gypsies*, at page 124.
[844] Lewy, *The Nazi Persecution of the Gypsies*, at pages 125 to 126.
[845] Ezergailis, *The Holocaust in Latvia*, at page 100, n.5
[846] Bloxham, Genocide on Trial, at page 198
[847]
[848] Schneider, *Unfinished Road*
[849] Fleming, *Hitler and the Final Solution*, at 93n: "After 199 days of court proceedings, on 21 December 1979, the Hamburg assize court condemned the former SS-Sturmbahnführer of the Latvian Legion and former Police Major Viktor Arajs to a life term in prison. Arajs had been living in an underground existence in Frankfurt for twenty-five years after the war under a false name and was arrested in 1975."
[850] Ezergailis, *The Holocaust in Latvia*, at pages 16 and 245-248
[851] Kuenzle, Anton and Shimron, Gad, *The Execution of the Hangman of Riga: The Only Execution of a Nazi War Criminal by the Mossad*, Valentine Mitchell, London 2004 https://books.google.com/books?id=JRSOAAAACAAJ&dq=hangman+riga+shimron&as_brr=0&hl=en
[852] Einsatzgruppen judgment, at 563-567
[853] Einsatzgruppen judgment, at 589
[854] Eduard Strauch (German wikipedia)
[855] Eduard Strauch, biography and photo at Olokaustos.org http://www.olokaustos.org/bionazi/leaders/strauch.htm
[856] Edelheit, *History of the Holocaust*, at page 340: Jeckeln was " ... responsible for the murder of Jews and Communist Party officials ... convicted and hanged in the former ghetto of Riga on February 3, 1946.
[857] http://www.rumbula.org/quesans.shtml Rumbula.org: Statement of Michael Genchik
[858] Ezergailis, in *World Reacts to the Holocaust*, at 354-88, provides a comprehensive guide to the Soviet historiographical treatment of the Holocaust in Latvia.
[859] Ezergailis, in *World Reacts to the Holocaust*, at 373-374
[860] According to the Latvia Institute (an agency of the Republic of Latvia): "There was no Holocaust research during Soviet rule in Latvia (1944–91). The victims of the Holocaust were subsumed under the rubric 'Nazi murder of peaceful Soviet citizens,' usually with unsubstantiated

and highly inflated numbers. Research in the West was mainly based on accounts of survivors and court cases against Nazi criminals. Only after regaining independence in 1991, could Latvian historians begin to assess the situation and make use of documentation available locally."

[861]
[862] Republic of Latvia, Ministry of Foreign Affairs, Rumbula memorial unveiled, December 2002
[863] http://muse.jhu.edu/journals/holocaust_and_genocide_studies/v017/17.1anders.html
[864] https://web.archive.org/web/20090511003319/http://www.am.gov.lv/en/ministry/4265/4299/#1-32#1-32
[865] https://web.archive.org/web/20091026170046/http://geocities.com/~patrin/genocide.htm
[866] http://www.jewsoflatvia.com/
[867] http://www.li.lv/index.php?option=com_content&task=view&id=141&Itemid=1100&lang=en
[868] http://www.mfa.gov.lv/en/news/Newsletters/Theme-in-Focus/4169/
[869] https://books.google.ca/books?id=NOvWYblJMSUC
[870] http://www.arbeit-und-leben-hochtaunus.de/Lettland.Der_Judenmord_in_Riga.pdf
[871] https://web.archive.org/web/20030516094249/http://rumbula.org/bookexcerpt.htm
[872] http://www.nizkor.org/hweb/orgs/german/einsatzgruppen/esg/jeckeln.html
[873] https://www.loc.gov/rr/frd/Military_Law/NTs_war-criminals.html
[874] http://www.mazal.org/NMT-HOME.htm
[875] https://www.webcitation.org/query?url=http://www.geocities.com/~Patrin/lewy.htm&date=2009-10-26+00:37:05
[876] http://www.seligman.org.il/kraslava_holocaust.html
[877] http://www.holocaustinthebaltics.com
[878] https://www.youtube.com/watch?v=zeOIQvvOBRs
[879] Museum of Tolerance Multimedia Learning Center http://motlc.learningcenter.wiesenthal.org/text/x07/xr0707.html
[880] ERA.F.R-89.N.1.S.1.L.2
[881] Quoted in Eugenia Gurin-Loov, Holocaust of Estonian Jews 1941, Eesti Juudi Kogukond, Tallinn 1994: pg. 224
[882] The Holocaust in the Baltics http://depts.washington.edu/baltic/papers/holocaust.html at University of Washington
[883] De dödsdömda vittnar http://www.levandehistoria.se/default.php?tid=955&ss=&id=45 ( *Transport Be 1.9.1942* http://www.levandehistoria.se/default.php?tid=893&ss=&id=45 )
[884]
[885] Omakaitse omakohus http://iisrael.ee/js.php3?id=343 – JERUUSALEMMA SÕNUMID
[886] Birn, Ruth Bettina (2001), Collaboration with Nazi Germany in Eastern Europe: the Case of the Estonian Security Police http://journals.cambridge.org/production/action/cjoGetFulltext?fulltextid=81766 . *Contemporary European History* 10.2, 181–198. P. 190–191.
[887] Estonia at https://www.jewishvirtuallibrary.org/jsource/vjw/Estonia.html Jewish Virtual Library
[888] *Estonian State Archives of the Former Estonian KGB (State Security Committee) records relating to war crime investigations and trials in Estonia, 1940–1987* (manuscript RG-06.026) – United States Holocaust Memorial Museum – document available on-line through this query page http://www.ushmm.org/research/collections/search/finding_aid.php using document id *RG-06.026* – Also available at Axis History Forum http://forum.axishistory.com/viewtopic.php?t=15937 – This list includes the evidence presented at the trial. It list as evidence several articles by Mere in Estonian language newspapers published in London
[889]
[890] Veebruari sündmused http://www.hot.ee/vaikal/tana_02.htm
[891] https://news.err.ee/855579/holocaust-victim-memorials-vandalised-at-kalevi-liiva
[892] Andrei Hvostov, Jakobsoni komisjon Augeiase tallis http://paber.ekspress.ee/viewdoc/F756A36DCA717BB0C22571760047DC7C
[893] Pankjewitza (Pankjavitsa) by Ruth Bettina Birn, in: Der Ort des Terrors. Geschichte der nationalsozialistischen Konzentrationslager Band. 8: Riga-Kaiserwald, Warschau, Vaivara, Kauen (Kaunas), Plaszów, Kulmhof/Chelmno, Belzéc, Sobibór, Treblinka. Gebundene Ausgabe –

24. Oktober 2008 von Wolfgang Benz (Herausgeber), Barbara Distel (Herausgeber), Angelika Königseder (Bearbeitung). P. 173.

[894] Haakristi haardes.Tallinn 1979, lk 84
[895] Haakristi haardes.Tallinn 1979, lk 68
[896] Haakristi haardes.Tallinn 1979, lk 66
[897] Haakristi haardes.Tallinn 1979, lk 64
[898] Haakristi haardes.Tallinn 1979, lk 69
[899] http://journals.cambridge.org/production/action/cjoGetFulltext?fulltextid=81766
[900] http://muse.jhu.edu/journals/holocaust_and_genocide_studies/v017/17.1weiss-wendt.html#FOOT3,
[901] http://www.buero-schwimmer.de/kuldiga/Hoffmann_lecture_english
[902] //en.wikipedia.org/w/index.php?title=Template:The_Holocaust_sidebar&action=edit
[903] Northeastern territories of Poland were attached to Belastok Voblast, Hrodna Voblast, Navahrudak Voblast (soon renamed to Baranavichy Voblast), Pinsk Voblast and Vileyka (later Maladzyechna) Voblast of Byelorussian SSR
[904] Alexey Litvin (Алексей Літвін), Participation of the local police in the extermination of Jews https://translate.google.ca/translate?hl=en&sl=ru&tl=en&u=http%3A%2F%2Fmb.s5x.org%2Fhomoliber.org%2Fru%2Fxx%2Fxx020127.html&anno=2 (Участие местной полиции в уничтожении евреев, в акциях против партизан и местного населения.); (in) Местная вспомогательная полиция на территории Беларуси, июль 1941 — июль 1944 гг. (The auxiliary police in Belarus, July 1941 - July 1944).
[905] *See also:*
[906] *See:*
[907] Reidlinger 1960, p. 157, as quoted in Turonek 1989, p. 118.
[908] Interview http://www.angelfire.com/sc3/soviet_jews_exodus/English/Interview_s/InterviewRomanovsky.shtml
[909] The Kings And The Pawns: Collaboration in Byelorussia during World War II, Leonid Rein, Berghahn Books, Oct 15, 2013, pages 264-265, 285
[910] Hilberg, Raul cited in Berenbaum, Michael. *The World Must Know*. United States Holocaust Memorial Museum, Johns Hopkins University Press, 2nd edition, 2006, p. 93.
[911] Berenbaum, Michael. *The World Must Know*. United States Holocaust Memorial Museum, Johns Hopkins University Press, 2nd edition, 2006, p. 93.
[912] This is far higher than the original number of 7 million given by Stalin, and, indeed, the number has increased under various Soviet and Russian Federation leaders. See Mark Harrison, *The Economics of World War II: Six Great Powers in International Comparison*, Cambridge University Press, 1998, p. 291 (), for more information.
[913] As evidenced at the post-war Nuremberg Trials. See Ginsburg, George, *The Nuremberg Trial and International Law*, Martinus Nijhoff, 1990, p. 160.
[914] Final Compensation Pending for Former Nazi Forced Laborers http://www.dw-world.de/dw/article/0,2144,1757323,00.html
[915] Gerlach, C. «Kalkulierte Morde» Hamburger Edition, Hamburg, 1999.
[916] Россия и СССР в войнах XX века", М. "Олма- Пресс", 2001 год
[917] "Soviet Casualties and Combat Losses in the Twentieth Century", Greenhill Books, London, 1997, G. F. Krivosheev
[918] Christian Streit: Keine Kameraden: Die Wehrmacht und die Sowjetischen Kriegsgefangenen, 1941-1945, Bonn: Dietz (3. Aufl., 1. Aufl. 1978),
[919] Gilbert, Martin, Atlas of the Holocaust, New York: William Morrow and Company, Inc, 1993.
[920] Lador-Lederer, Joseph. *World War II: Jews as Prisoners of War*, Israel Yearbook on Human Rights, vol.10, Faculty of Law, Tel Aviv University, Tel Aviv, 1980, pp. 70-89, p. 75, footnote 15. http//www.jewishagency.org
[921] Adolf Burger (1989) *Akcia Bernhard: Obchod s miliónmi*. Bratislava.
[922] Max Garcia, "Befreiung des KZ-Nebenlagers Ebensee: Neue historische Details." *Zeitschrift des Zeitgeschichtemuseums Ebensee*, 1998.
[923] *A History of the Jews* by Paul Johnson, London, 1987, p.527

[924] Stalin's Secret Pogrom: The Postwar Inquisition of the Jewish Anti-Fascist Committee http://www.joshuarubenstein.com/rubenstein/stalinsecret/intro.html (introduction) by Joshua Rubenstein
[925] Yitzhak Arad (2009). "*The Holocaust in the Soviet Union*". U of Nebraska Press, p.211,
[926] //tools.wmflabs.org/geohack/geohack.php?pagename=Einsatzgruppen&params=52_30_26_N_13_22_57_E_type:landmark
[927] Singular: *Einsatzgruppe*; Official full name: *Einsatzgruppen der Sicherheitspolizei und des SD*
[928] LEO Dictionary.
[929] Encyclopædia Britannica.
[930] Rhodes 2002, p. 4.
[931] Edeiken 2000.
[932] Streim 1989, p. 436.
[933] Longerich 2012, pp. 405, 412.
[934] Nuremberg Trial, Vol. 20, Day 194.
[935] Longerich 2010, pp. 138–141.
[936] Longerich 2012, p. 425.
[937] Longerich 2010, p. 144.
[938] Rossino 2003, p. 11.
[939] Rossino 2003, pp. 11, 20.
[940] Evans 2008, p. 17.
[941] Rossino 2003, p. 14.
[942] Rossino 2003, p. 17.
[943] Rossino 2003, p. 12.
[944] Browning & Matthäus 2004, pp. 16–18.
[945] Longerich 2010, p. 143.
[946] Rossino 2003, p. 15.
[947] Rossino 2003, p. 16.
[948] Longerich 2010, pp. 144–145.
[949] Longerich 2012, p. 429.
[950] Evans 2008, p. 15.
[951] Longerich 2012, pp. 430–432.
[952] Weale 2012, p. 225.
[953] Evans 2008, p. 18.
[954] Gerwarth 2011, p. 147.
[955] Longerich 2010, p. 146.
[956] Evans 2008, pp. 25–26.
[957] Weale 2012, pp. 227–228.
[958] Weale 2012, pp. 242–245.
[959] Hillgruber 1989, p. 95.
[960] Wette 2007, p. 93.
[961] Longerich 2012, pp. 521–522.
[962] Hillgruber 1989, pp. 95–96.
[963] Rhodes 2002, pp. 14, 48.
[964] Hillgruber 1989, pp. 94–95.
[965] Hillgruber 1989, pp. 94–96.
[966] Hillgruber 1989, p. 96.
[967] Longerich 2010, p. 181.
[968] Longerich 2010, p. 185.
[969] Thomas 1987, p. 265.
[970] Rees 1997, p. 177.
[971] Rhodes 2002, p. 15.
[972] Langerbein 2003, pp. 30–31.
[973] Langerbein 2003, pp. 31–32.
[974] Browning 1998, pp. 10–12.
[975] Einsatzgruppen judgment, pp. 414–416.
[976] Browning 1998, pp. 135–136, 141–142.

[977] Robertson.
[978] Browning 1998, p. 10.
[979] Longerich 2010, p. 186.
[980] Browning & Matthäus 2004, pp. 225–226.
[981] MacLean 1999, p. 23.
[982] Museum of Tolerance.
[983] Longerich 2010, p. 419.
[984] Dams & Stolle 2012, p. 168.
[985] Conze, Frei et al. 2010.
[986] Crowe 2007, p. 267.
[987] Mallmann & Cüppers 2006, p. 97.
[988] Larsen 2008, p. xi.
[989] Shelach 1989, p. 1169.
[990] Longerich 2010, p. 197.
[991] Mallmann, Cüppers & Smith 2010, p. 130.
[992] Longerich 2012, p. 523.
[993] Longerich 2010, p. 198.
[994] Hillgruber 1989, p. 97.
[995] Hilberg 1985, p. 368.
[996] Headland 1992, pp. 62–70.
[997] Urban 2001.
[998] Longerich 2012, p. 526.
[999] Haberer 2001, p. 68.
[1000] Longerich 2010, pp. 193–195.
[1001] Longerich 2010, p. 208.
[1002] Longerich 2010, pp. 196–202.
[1003] Longerich 2010, p. 207.
[1004] Longerich 2010, p. 208, 211.
[1005] Longerich 2010, p. 211.
[1006] Longerich 2010, pp. 211–212.
[1007] Longerich 2010, pp. 212–213.
[1008] Headland 1992, pp. 57–58.
[1009] Rhodes 2002, p. 179.
[1010] Evans 2008, p. 227.
[1011] Weale 2012, p. 315.
[1012] Rhodes 2002, pp. 172–173.
[1013] Rhodes 2002, pp. 173–176.
[1014] Rhodes 2002, p. 178.
[1015] Weale 2012, p. 317.
[1016] Hillgruber 1989, p. 98.
[1017] Rhodes 2002, p. 41.
[1018] Haberer 2001, pp. 67–68.
[1019] Rees 1997, p. 179.
[1020] Haberer 2001, pp. 68–69.
[1021] Haberer 2001, p. 69.
[1022] Haberer 2001, p. 71.
[1023] Haberer 2001, pp. 69–70.
[1024] Haberer 2001, p. 70.
[1025] Rees 1997, p. 182.
[1026] Haberer 2001, p. 66.
[1027] Haberer 2001, p. 73.
[1028] Haberer 2001, pp. 74–75.
[1029] Haberer 2001, p. 76.
[1030] Haberer 2001, p. 77.
[1031] Rhodes 2002, pp. 206–209.
[1032] Rhodes 2002, pp. 208–210.

1033 Rhodes 2002, pp. 210–214.
1034 Hilberg 1985, p. 342.
1035 Longerich 2012, p. 549.
1036 Hilberg 1985, pp. 342–343.
1037 Marrus 2000, p. 64.
1038 Hilberg 1985, p. 372.
1039 Haberer 2001, p. 78.
1040 Longerich 2010, p. 353–354.
1041 Rees 1997, p. 197.
1042 Rhodes 2002, pp. 52, 124, 168.
1043 Ingrao 2013, pp. 199—200.
1044 Rhodes 2002, p. 163.
1045 Rhodes 2002, pp. 165–166.
1046 Longerich 2012, pp. 547–548.
1047 Rhodes 2002, p. 167.
1048 Longerich 2012, p. 551.
1049 Longerich 2012, p. 548.
1050 Rhodes 2002, p. 243.
1051 Longerich 2010, pp. 280–281.
1052 Longerich 2012, pp. 555–556.
1053 Longerich 2010, pp. 279–280.
1054 Rhodes 2002, p. 248.
1055 Rhodes 2002, pp. 258–260, 262.
1056 Rhodes 2002, p. 257.
1057 Evans 2008, p. 318.
1058 Mallmann, Cüppers & Smith 2010, p. 118.
1059 Mallmann, Cüppers & Smith 2010, pp. 124–125.
1060 Mallmann, Cüppers & Smith 2010, pp. 127–130.
1061 Mallmann, Cüppers & Smith 2010, pp. 103, 117–118.
1062 Krumenacker 2006.
1063 Caron 2007.
1064 Shirer 1960, pp. 783–784.
1065 Rhodes 2002, p. 215.
1066 Rhodes 2002, p. 126.
1067 Longerich 2010, p. 230.
1068 Rhodes 2002, p. 216.
1069 Rabitz 2011.
1070 Rhodes 2002, p. 276.
1071 Hillgruber 1989, p. 102.
1072 Craig 1973, p. 10.
1073 Mayer 1988, p. 250.
1074 Smelser & Davies 2008, p. 43.
1075 Hilberg 1985, p. 301.
1076 Wette 2007, p. 131.
1077 Hilberg 1985, p. 30.
1078 Marrus 2000, p. 79.
1079 Longerich 2010, p. 194.
1080 Marrus 2000, p. 88.
1081 Klee, Dressen & Riess 1991, p. xi.
1082 Wette 2007, pp. 200–201.
1083 Hillgruber 1989, pp. 102–103.
1084 Rhodes 2002, pp. 274–275.
1085 Longerich 2010, p. 187.
1086 Longerich 2010, pp. 187–189.
1087 Streim 1989, p. 439.
1088 Longerich 2010, p. 188.

[1089] Longerich 2010, p. 189–190.
[1090] Kershaw 2008, pp. 258–259.
[1091] Rhodes 2002, pp. 275–276.
[1092] Segev 2010, pp. 226, 250, 376.
[1093] http://www.spiegel.de/wissenschaft/mensch/erwin-rommel-auf-der-jagd-nach-dem-schatz-des-wuestenfuchses-a-522484-2.html
[1094] https://web.archive.org/web/20151007085553/http://www.holocaust-history.org/intro-einsatz/
[1095] http://www.holocaust-history.org/intro-einsatz/
[1096] https://www.loc.gov/rr/frd/Military_Law/pdf/NT_war-criminals_Vol-IV.pdf
[1097] https://www.loc.gov/rr/frd/Military_Law/NTs_war-criminals.html
[1098] http://www.tandfonline.com/doi/abs/10.1080/13501670108577951
[1099] //doi.org/10.1080%2F13501670108577951
[1100] //www.worldcat.org/oclc/210897979
[1101] https//rowman.com
[1102] https://web.archive.org/web/20171222052813/http://www.redorbit.com/news/international/462094/nazis_planned_holocaust_for_palestine_historians/
[1103] http://www.redorbit.com/news/international/462094/nazis_planned_holocaust_for_palestine_historians/
[1104] http://dict.leo.org/ende?lp=ende&lang=de&searchLoc=0&cmpType=relaxed&sectHdr=on&spellToler=&search=einsatzgruppe
[1105] http://avalon.law.yale.edu/imt/08-03-46.asp
[1106] http://www.dw.com/en/biography-of-nazi-criminal-meets-resistance-from-small-german-town/a-15161137
[1107] https://web.archive.org/web/20161011132536/https://kids.britannica.com/holocaust/article-215489
[1108] http://kids.britannica.com/holocaust/article-215489
[1109] https://web.archive.org/web/20080222023331/http://www1.uni-hamburg.de/rz3a035//police101.html
[1110] http://www1.uni-hamburg.de/rz3a035//police101.html
[1111] http://motlc.wiesenthal.com/site/pp.asp?c=gvKVLcMVIuG&b=395089
[1112] //www.jstor.org/stable/260933
[1113] https://web.archive.org/web/20071124014038/http://www.rzeczpospolita.pl/gazeta/wydanie_010901/publicystyka/publicystyka_a_1.html
[1114] http://www.rzeczpospolita.pl/gazeta/wydanie_010901/publicystyka/publicystyka_a_1.html
[1115] http://www.ushmm.org/wlc/article.php?lang=en&ModuleId=10005130
[1116] http://www.holocaustresearchproject.net/einsatz/index.html
[1117] Niewyk & Nicosia 2000, p. 76.
[1118] Roseman (2002), p. 87.
[1119] *Also in:*
[1120]
[1121] ; also in
[1122] Browning (2004), pp. 35–6 https://books.google.com/books?id=d9Wg4gjtP3cC&q=Lebensraum+1941.
[1123] Roseman (2002), pp. 14–15.
[1124] Hilberg (1985), p. 278.
[1125] Longerich (2012), pp. 525–33 https://books.google.ca/books?id=GBQchepZ-7EC&lpg=PA525&vq=Bialystok%2Bprinciple&pg=PA525&redir_esc=y#v=snippet&q=Bialystok%20principle&f=false.
[1126] Browning (2004), pp.352-355, 356 https://books.google.com/books?id=d9Wg4gjtP3cC&q=gas+chambers.
[1127] Longerich (2012), p. 555.
[1128] Roseman (2002), pp. 65–7.
[1129] Cesarani (2005), pp. 110–1.
[1130] Roseman (2002), pp. 1–2.
[1131] Browning (2004), p. 216.
[1132] Browning (2004), p. 224.

1133 Hilberg (1985), p. 281.
1134 Browning (2004), p. 219 https://books.google.com/books?id=d9Wg4gjtP3cC&q=worldview#v=snippet&q=worldview&f=false.
1135 Browning (2004), p. 217.
1136 Browning (2004), p. 229.
1137 Browning (1998), p. 11: On the eve of Operation Barbarossa Major Weiss disclosed to his men the directives of Hitler's 'Barbarossa Decree'. http://www.mrclancy.com/wp-content/uploads/2011/11/Barbarossa-Decree.pdf
1138 Browning (2004), p. 232.
1139 Browning (2004), p. 260.
1140 Browning (2004), p. 261.
1141 Laqueur & Baumel (2001), p. 51.
1142 Browning (2004), pp. 291–2.
1143 Browning (2004), pp. 408-9.
1144 Browning (2004), p. 244.
1145 *Also in:*
1146 Browning (1998), p. 12.
1147 and Published under the same title, but expanded in
1148 *Also in:*
1149
1150 Also in:
1151 Arad (1987), p. 640.
1152 . See also
1153 Also in: Further info:
1154 Arad (1987), pp. 300-1.
1155 Letter written by Albert Speer who attended Posen Conference.
1156 Bradley F. Smith & Agnes Peterson (1974), *Heinrich Himmler. Speeches* Frankfurt/M., p. 169 f. ; ; also (with differing translation) in
1157 Also in:
1158 Browning (1998), pp. 135-42.
1159 See also:
1160
1161 Longerich (2010), p. 380: Extermination https://books.google.ca/books?id=cxYqYIn73SgC&q=Sosnowitz..
1162
1163 Yahil (1991), p. 637.
1164 //en.wikipedia.org/w/index.php?title=Template:The_Holocaust_sidebar&action=edit
1165 [*Also in:*] [*And:*]
1166 Hilberg (1985), p. ix.
1167 Hilberg (1985), p. 56.
1168 Hilberg (1985), p. 354.
1169 Hilberg (1985), p. 1219.
1170 Hilberg (1985), pp. 998–9.
1171 Browning (2004), (2007 ed.: p. 213 https://books.google.com/books?id=d9Wg4gjtP3cC&q=scale%2Bdwarf#v=snippet&q=scale%2Bdwarf&f=false)..
1172 Browning (2004), pp. 426–427.
1173 Browning (2004), p. 354.
1174 Longerich (2010), p. 6 https://books.google.com/books?id=cxYqYIn73SgC&lpg=PA6&vq=abandon%2Bnotion&pg=PA6#v=snippet&q=abandon+notion&f=false.
1175 Adolf Hitler's Declaration of War against the United States in Wikisource.
1176 Cesarani (2016), pp. 796.
1177 Originally presented as the author's doctoral thesis at .
1178 Commenting on Gerlach, Christopher Browning writes: "What he interprets as Hitler's basic decision, I see as an official initiation of party leaders to a decision taken several months earlier."<ref name="FOOTNOTEBrowning2004540f">Browning (2004), p. 540f.
1179 Cesarani (2016), pp. 666.

[1180] https://books.google.ca/books?id=QpAgHYTPRz0C
[1181] http//hampshirehigh.com
[1182] https//web.archive.org
[1183] https://books.google.ca/books?id=d9Wg4gjtP3cC
[1184] https://books.google.ca/books?id=mimNBwAAQBAJ
[1185] http://boris.unibe.ch/74383/1/235167.pdf
[1186] //doi.org/10.1086%2F235167
[1187] https://archive.org/details/DestructionOfTheEuropeanJewsRaulHilberg
[1188] https://books.google.ca/books?id=cxYqYIn73SgC
[1189] https://books.google.ca/books?id=GBQchepZ-7EC
[1190] http://www.ghwk.de/?lang=gb
[1191] http://www1.yadvashem.org/yv/en/holocaust/insights/video/development_final_solution.asp?WT.mc_id=wiki
[1192] http://wayback.archive-it.org/all/20081001211524/http://yad-vashem.org.il/about_holocaust/studies/vol35/Mallmann-Cuppers2.pdf
[1193] http://www.defensemedianetwork.com/stories/death-decree/
[1194] https://www.worldcat.org/oclc/1265138
[1195] The editorial policy was to marginalize news of the death camps and focus on the Nazi policies and practices, which had a better chance of resonating with American audiences. Statistics about the number of victims at the death camps were questioned at the time.<ref>
[1196] https://archive.org/details/in.ernet.dli.2015.48624
[1197] https://www.jta.org/1943/12/15/archive/black-book-of-polish-jewry-estimates-1000000-polish-jews-killed-by-nazis
[1198] http://yivoarchives.org/index.php?p=collections/controlcard&id=33383
[1199] https://www.worldcat.org/oclc/82971798
[1200] https://archive.org/stream/GermanOccupationOfPoland/German%20Occupation%20of%20Poland#page/n1/mode/2up
[1201] http://www.worldcat.org/title/german-occupation-of-poland/oclc/82971798&referer=brief_results
[1202] https://www.worldcat.org/oclc/489805
[1203] http://www.worldcat.org/title/black-book-of-poland/oclc/489805?referer=di&ht=edition
[1204] http://m.neon24.pl/bd951a0a2f092fc7b46420a0db74e32d,0,0.jpg
[1205] https://archive.is/7GFjc
[1206] Raczyński (1942)
[1207] Wroński (1971)
[1208] Engel (2014)
[1209] Raczyński (1942)
[1210] Wroński (1971)
[1211] Raczyński (1942)
[1212] Wroński (1971)
[1213] Engel (2014)
[1214] Raczyński (1942)
[1215] Raczyński (1942)
[1216] Wroński (1971)
[1217] Engel (2014)
[1218] http://bolekchrobry.tripod.com/polishinformationcenter19391945/id22.html
[1219] https://www.msz.gov.pl/en/ministry/polish_diplomacy_archive/75th_anniversary_of__raczynski_s_note_
[1220] https://www.msz.gov.pl/pl/p/msz_pl/ministerstwo/historia/zbioryon-line/broszura_msz_1942
[1221] Wojciech Zawadzki (2012), Eugeniusz Bendera (1906-po 1970). https://web.archive.org/web/20131103214327/http://www.psbprzedborz.pl/index.php?option=com_content&view=article&id=50%3Abendera-eugeniusz Przedborski Słownik Biograficzny, via Internet Archive.
[1222] "Byłem Numerem: swiadectwa Z Auschwitz" by Kazimierz Piechowski, Eugenia Bozena Kodecka-Kaczynska, Michal Ziokowski, Hardcover, Wydawn. Siostr Loretanek,
[1223] https://doi.org/10.2307%2F1853043
[1224] https://www.worldcat.org/search?fq=x0:jrnl&q=n2:0002-8762

[1225] http://archive.timesonline.co.uk/tol/viewArticle.arc?articleId=ARCHIVE-The_Times-1975-02-06-08-011&pageId=ARCHIVE-The_Times-1975-02-06-08
[1226] https//web.archive.org
[1227] https://www.youtube.com/watch?v=MU5ug2eTwGc
[1228] https://archive.org/details/TheMassExterminationOfJewsInGermanOccupiedPoland
[1229] http://witoldsreport.blogspot.com/2008/05/volunteer-for-auschwitz-report-by.html
[1230] http://www.doomedsoldiers.com/volunteer-to-Auschwitz.html
[1231] http://harcerze.zhr.pl/ch/opl/bohater_pliki/Raport_Witolda_Pileckiego.rtf
[1232] http://www.polandpolska.org/dokumenty/witold/raport-witolda-1945.htm
[1233] http://www.polandpolska.org/dokumenty/witold/raporty-witolda.htm
[1234] http://www.zwoje-scrolls.com/zwoje09/text02p.htm
[1235] http://www.diapozytyw.pl/en/site/ludzie/witold_pilecki
[1236] http://www.polishresistance-ak.org/14%20Article.htm
[1237] http://www.epizodyzauschwitz.pl
[1238] https://www.npr.org/templates/story/story.php?storyId=129956107&sc=nl&cc=es-20100926
[1239] Kahan, Lazar. Chelm Yizkor Book: The Slaughter of the Jews in Chelm http://www.jewishgen.org/yizkor/chelm/che505.html, 1954. Online.
[1240] Socha, Paweł. "The Nazi Labor Camp on 7 Lipowa Street", Sztetl.org.pl. Online: http://www.sztetl.org.pl/he/article/lublin/13,-/24257,the-nazi-labor-camp-on-7-lipowa-street/?print=1
[1241] Encyclopedia Judaica, cited by Jewish Virtual Library: Hrubieszow. Online: https://www.jewishvirtuallibrary.org/jsource/judaica/ejud_0002_0009_0_09282.html
[1242] http://www.stadt-eisenberg.de/kultur/pdf/Todesmarsch.pdf
[1243] //tools.wmflabs.org/geohack/geohack.php?pagename=Death_marches_(Holocaust)&params=47_46_6.15_N_11_38_55.30_E_
[1244] [As found on Google Earth, with two photos of it taken by Ellen Haider]
[1245] https://www.jewishvirtuallibrary.org/jsource/Holocaust/marchmap.html
[1246] http://www.pogonowski.com/books/Atlas_en/page_0213.pdf
[1247] http://www.gz-tm-dachau.de/todesmaersche
[1248] https://www.ushmm.org/search/results/?q=Waakirchen
[1249] http://chelm.freeyellow.com/deathmarchvictims.html
[1250] http://www.yadvashem.org/yv/en/exhibitions/volary_death_march/index.asp
[1251] Donald L Niewyk, *The Columbia Guide to the Holocaust,* Columbia University Press, 200, p 49
[1252] Berenbaum 2005, p. 125.
[1253] Piotrowski, Tadeusz. "Project InPosterum: Poland WWII Casualties" http://www.projectinposterum.org/docs/poland_WWII_casualties.htm. Retrieved 15 March 2007
[1254] "Genocide of European Roma (Gypsies)" http://www.ushmm.org/wlc/en/article.php?ModuleId=10005219. *Holocaust Encyclopedia*. United States Holocaust Memorial Museum. Retrieved 27 September 2012. The USHMM places the scholarly estimates at 220,000–500,000. According to , "serious scholars estimate that between 90,000 and 220,000 were killed under German rule."
[1255] Hancock 2004, pp. 383–96 http://www.radoc.net/radoc.php?doc=art_e_holocaust_porrajmos&lang=en&articles=true.
[1256] *Freemasons for Dummies*, by Christopher Hodapp http://members.aol.com/brlodge/whymasons.html, Wiley Publishing Inc., Indianapolis, 2005, page 85, sec. *Hitler and the Nazis*
[1257] The number of Slovenes estimated to have died as a result of the Nazi occupation (not including those killed by Slovene collaboration forces and other Nazi allies) is estimated between 20,000 and 25,000 people. This number only includes civilians: Slovene partisan POWs who died and resistance fighters killed in action are not included (their number is estimated at 27,000). These numbers however include only Slovenes from present-day Slovenia: it does not include Carinthian Slovene victims, nor Slovene victims from areas in present-day Italy and Croatia. These numbers are result of a 10-year-long research by the Institute for Contemporary History (*Inštitut za novejšo zgodovino*) from Ljubljana, Slovenia. The partial results of the research have been released in 2008 in the volume *Žrtve vojne in revolucije v Sloveniji* (Ljubljana: Institute for Contemporary History, 2008), and officially presented at the Slovenian National Council (http://www.ds-rs.si/sites/default/files/dokumenti/zbornik_zrtve_vojne_in_revolucije.pdf

[1258] Pike, David Wingeate. Spaniards in the Holocaust: Mauthausen, the horror on the Danube; Editorial: Routledge Chapman & Hall . London, 2000.
[1259] Shulman, William L. *A State of Terror: Germany 1933–1939*. Bayside, New York: Holocaust Resource Center and Archives.
[1260] //en.wikipedia.org/w/index.php?title=Template:The_Holocaust_sidebar&action=edit
[1261] derived from https://web.archive.org/web/20020911182809/https://www.adl.org/holocaust/response.asp
[1262] See Persecution of homosexuals in Nazi Germany and the Holocaust
[1263] See Action T4
[1264] See Religion in Nazi Germany
[1265] See also Judeo-Masonic conspiracy theory
[1266] See Nazism and race
[1267] Berenbaum, Michael. "Non-Jewish victims of Nazism" http://www.britannica.com/event/Holocaust#toc215487, *Encyclopædia Britannica*.
[1268] A figure of 26.3 million is given in *Service d'Information des Crimes de Guerre: Crimes contre la Personne Humain, Camps de Concentration*. Paris, 1946, pp. 197–198. Other references: Christopher Hodapp, Freemasons for Dummies, 2005; Raul Hilberg, *The Destruction of the European Jews*, 2003; Martin Gilbert, *Atlas of the Holocaust*, 1993; Israel Gutman, *Encyclopedia of the Holocaust*, 1995.
[1269] American Jewish Committee, Harry Schneiderman and Julius B. Maller, eds. http://ajcarchives.org/AJC_DATA/Files/1946_1947_2_Formatter.pdf, *American Jewish Year Book*, Vol. 48 (1946–1947) http://ajcarchives.org/AJC_DATA/Files/1946_1947_13_Statistics.pdf, Press of Jewish Publication Society of America, Philadelphia, 1946, page 599
[1270] The institutionalisation of cosmopolitan morality: the holocaust and human rights. Levy, Sznaider; Daniel, Natan
[1271] Sebastian Haffner, *The Meaning of Hitler* , translated from Anmerkungen zu Hitler, Publishing house. Fischer Taschenbuch, Frankfurt am Main.
[1272] Leo Goldberger: *The Rescue of the Danish Jews: Moral Courage Under Stress*, NYU Press, 1987, preface pages XX-XXI https://books.google.com/books?id=m2dJ26rfqvYC&pg=PA2&source=gbs_toc_r&cad=3#v=onepage&q=%22A%20total%20of%207%2C220%20of%20these%22&f=false Linked 2014-04-29
[1273] Ian Kershaw. *Stalinism and Nazism: dictatorships in comparison* https://books.google.com/books?id=_tmGaItZ0tsC. Cambridge University Press, 1997, p.150
[1274] Craughwell, Thomas J., The Gentile Holocaust https://www.catholicculture.org/culture/library/view.cfm?recnum=472 Catholic Culture, Accessed July 18, 2008
[1275] Hans-Walter Schmuhl. The Kaiser Wilhelm Institute for Anthropology, Human Heredity, and Eugenics, 1927–1945: crossing boundaries. Volume 259 of Boston studies in the philosophy of science. Coutts MyiLibrary. SpringerLink Humanities, Social Science & LawAuthor. Springer, 2008. , p. 348-349
[1276] Robert Gellately. Reviewed works: Vom Generalplan Ost zum Generalsiedlungsplan by Czeslaw Madajczyk. Der "Generalplan Ost." Hauptlinien der nationalsozialistischen Planungs- und Vernichtungspolitik by Mechtild Rössler; Sabine Schleiermacher. *Central European History*, Vol. 29, No. 2 (1996), pp. 270–274
[1277] Case Study: Soviet Prisoners-of-War http://www.gendercide.org/case_soviet.html, Gendercide Watch.
[1278] Donald L Niewyk, *The Columbia Guide to the Holocaust*, Columbia University Press, 200, p 49
[1279] The Russian Academy of Science Rossiiskaia Akademiia nauk. Liudskie poteri SSSR v period vtoroi mirovoi voiny:sbornik statei. Sankt-Peterburg 1995
[1280] *A Mosaic of Victims: Non-Jews Persecuted and Murdered by the Nazis*. Ed. by Michael Berenbaum. New York University Press, 1990.
[1281] The Columbia guide to the Holocaust By Donald L. Niewyk, Francis R. Nicosia, pp. 50–52, Columbia University Press, 2000
[1282] Recognition for Justice http://2august.eu/the-roma-genocide/lack-of-recognition/ International Roma Youth Network
[1283] Robert B. Downs, *Books That Changed the World* (Signet Classic, 2004), p. 325.

[1284] Adolf Hitler, *Mein Kampf* (translated by James Murphy, February, 1939) http://gutenberg.net.au/ebooks02/0200601.txt Vol. I, Chapter XI (A Project Gutenberg of Australia eBook)
[1285] *The Political Testament of Adolf Hitler*, Note #5, (February - April 1945)
[1286] Heinz Heger, *Men with the Pink Triangle*, Alyson Publishing: 1994
[1287] Plant, *The Pink Triangle*.
[1288] Garbe, Detlef (2001). In Hans Hesse. Persecution and Resistance of Jehovah's Witnesses During the Nazi-Regime 1933–1945. Bremen: Edition Temmen. p.251
[1289] Theodore S. Hamerow; On the Road to the Wolf's Lair - German Resistance to Hitler; Belknap Press of Harvard University Press; 1997; ; p. 136
[1290] • Gill, Anton (1994). *An Honourable Defeat; A History of the German Resistance to Hitler*. Heinemann Mandarin. 1995 paperback , pp. 14–15: "[the Nazis planned to] de-Christianise Germany after the final victory". • Richard J. Evans; *The Third Reich at War*; Penguin Press; New York 2009, p. 547 • Ian Kershaw; Hitler a Biography; 2008 Edn; WW Norton & Company; London p661 • Ian Kershaw; *The Nazi Dictatorship: Problems and Perspectives of Interpretation*; 4th Edn; Oxford University Press; New York; 2000"; pp. 173–74 • Griffin, Roger *Fascism's relation to religion* in Blamires, Cyprian, World fascism: a historical encyclopedia, Volume 1 https://books.google.com/books?id=nvD2rZSVau4C&dq, p. 10, ABC-CLIO, 2006: "There is no doubt that in the long run Nazi leaders such as Hitler and Himmler intended to eradicate Christianity just as ruthlessly as any other rival ideology, even if in the short term they had to be content to make compromises with it." • Mosse, George Lachmann, Nazi culture: intellectual, cultural and social life in the Third Reich https://books.google.com/books?id=_cyR3QyuSdIC&dq, p. 240, Univ of Wisconsin Press, 2003: "Had the Nazis won the war their ecclesiastical policies would have gone beyond those of the German Christians, to the utter destruction of both the Protestant and the Catholic Church." • Fischel, Jack R., Historical Dictionary of the Holocaust https://books.google.com/books?id=EzBZP92xwUUC&dq , p. 123, Scarecrow Press, 2010: "The objective was to either destroy Christianity and restore the German gods of antiquity or to turn Jesus into an Aryan." • Dill, Marshall, Germany: a modern history https://books.google.com/books?id=xRrGP7L9_hEC&dq , p. 365, University of Michigan Press, 1970: "It seems no exaggeration to insist that the greatest challenge the Nazis had to face was their effort to eradicate Christianity in Germany or at least to subjugate it to their general world outlook." • Wheaton, Eliot Barculo The Nazi revolution, 1933–1935: prelude to calamity:with a background survey of the Weimar era https://books.google.com/books?ei=Nu-6TrqBLOaTiQKL5dy2Dg&ct, p. 290, 363, Doubleday 1968: The Nazis sought "to eradicate Christianity in Germany root and branch." • Bendersky, Joseph W., A concise history of Nazi Germany https://books.google.com/books?id=ATCXucbTYX0C&dq, p. 147, Rowman & Littlefield, 2007: "Consequently, it was Hitler's long range goal to eliminate the churches once he had consolidated control over his European empire."
[1291] Peter Hoffmann; The History of the German Resistance 1933–1945; 3rd Edn (First English Edn); McDonald & Jane's; London; 1977; p 25
[1292] John S. Conway; The Nazi Persecution of the Churches, 1933–1945; Regent College Publishing; 2001; (USA); p. 90–92
[1293] Lewis, Brenda Ralph (2000); *Hitler Youth: the Hitlerjugend in War and Peace 1933–1945*; MBI Publishing; ; p. 45
[1294] Shirer, William L., *Rise and Fall of the Third Reich: A History of Nazi Germany* https://books.google.com/books?id=sY8svb-MNUwC&dq, pp. 234–235, Simon and Schuster, 1990
[1295] Paul Berben; *Dachau: The Official History 1933–1945*; Norfolk Press; London; 1975; ; p.143
[1296] Paul Berben; *Dachau: The Official History 1933–1945*; Norfolk Press; London; 1975; ; pp.276–277
[1297] Kershaw 2000, pp. 210–211.
[1298] * Evans, 2008, pp. 245–246 • Shirer, 1990, pp. 234–35 • Hamerow, 1997, p. 136 • Gill, 1994, p. 57 • Kershaw, 2008, p. 332 • Paul O'Shea; *A Cross Too Heavy*; Rosenberg Publishing; p. 234–5 • Peter Hoffmann; *The History of the German Resistance 1933–1945*; 3rd ed. (first English ed.); McDonald & Jane's; London; 1977; p. 14
[1299] Fred Taylor; *The Goebbels Diaries 1939–1941*; Hamish Hamilton Ltd; London; 1982 pp. 278 & 294
[1300] Evans, Richard J. (2005). The Third Reich in Power. New York: Penguin. ; pp. 245–246

[1301] William L. Shirer; *The Rise and Fall of the Third Reich*; Secker & Warburg; London; 1960; p. 201

[1302] Mark Mazower; *Hitler's Empire - Nazi Rule in Occupied Europe*; Penguin; 2008; ; pp. 51–52

[1303] Richard J. Evans; The Third Reich at War; Penguin Press; New York 2009, p.385

[1304] Graml, Mommsen, Reichhardt & Wolf; The German Resistance to Hitler; B. T. Batsford Ltd; London; 1970; p. 225

[1305] Norman Davies; Rising '44: the Battle for Warsaw; Viking; 2003; pp. 85–6

[1306] Richard J. Evans; The Third Reich at War; Penguin Press New York; 2009; pp. 28–29

[1307] Richard J. Evans; The Third Reich at War; Penguin Press New York; 2009; p. 33–34

[1308] Craughwell, Thomas J., The Gentile Holocaust http://www.catholicculture.org/culture/library/view.cfm?recnum=472 Catholic Culture, Accessed July 18, 2008

[1309] Encyclopædia Britannica Online - *Stefan Wyszyński*; Encyclopædia Britannica Inc; 2013. Web. 14 Apr. 2013.

[1310] Martin Gilbert; The Righteous - The Unsung Heroes of the Holocaust; Doubleday; 2002; ; p.122

[1311]

[1312] Also in:

[1313] https://books.google.com/books?id=iqMWAQAAIAAJ

[1314] http://www.radoc.net/radoc.php?doc=art_e_holocaust_porrajmos&lang=en&articles=true

[1315] http://www1.yadvashem.org/yv/en/holocaust/about/01/non_jews_persecution.asp?WT.mc_id=wiki

[1316] http://db.yadvashem.org/names/search.html

[1317] https://www.youtube.com/watch?v=-w5GLwBwN-0&index=94&list=PL06DE3D4B636D50C9

[1318] https://www.youtube.com/watch?v=n_4WoQfz-N0&index=95&list=PL06DE3D4B636D50C9

[1319] https://www.youtube.com/watch?v=knCKIny5NPU&index=96&list=PL06DE3D4B636D50C9

[1320] https://www.youtube.com/watch?v=WmHR4P5FeuA&index=97&list=PL06DE3D4B636D50C9

[1321] http://www.yahadinunum.org/?lang=en

[1322] http://www.chroniclesofterror.pl/dlibra#

[1323] //en.wikipedia.org/w/index.php?title=Template:The_Holocaust_sidebar&action=edit

[1324] Confino 2011, pp. 126–128.

[1325] Traverso 2003, p. 19.

[1326] Also see:Enzo Traverso, "Nazism's roots in European culture—Production line of murder" http://mondediplo.com/2005/02/15civildiso in *Le Monde diplomatique*, February 2005

[1327] Traverso 2003, pp. 21–27, 35–41.

[1328] Traverso also describes the colonial domination during the New Imperialism period through "rational organization", which led in a number of cases to extermination. However, this argument, which insists on the industrialization and technical rationality through which the Holocaust itself was carried out (the organization of trains, technical details, etc.—see Adolf Eichmann's bureaucratic work), was in turn opposed by other people. This argument is contrasted against the fact that the 1994 Rwandan Genocide mostly used machetes.

[1329] Jacoby (2003).

[1330] Mosse 1980, pp. 1–16.

[1331] Weikart 2006, pp. 3–10, 186–206.

[1332] Not alone in the pursuit of eugenic endeavors, other national societies (especially the United States) were rife with racialist ideals. See for instance: Kühl, Stefan. *The Nazi Connection: Eugenics, American Racism, and German National Socialism*. New York: Oxford University Press, 2002.

[1333] In his works on "biopolitics" and in his lecture course at the College de France entitled, *Society Must Be defended* http://rebels-library.org/files/foucault_society_must_be_defended.pdf, French critical theorist and philosopher Michel Foucault argued that the Holocaust was a deliberate production of the modern polity's belief in the polity as a "biological" notion, where whole populations "are at war with one another" and most of the time this "war" involves clever manipulation of social phenomena such as mass persuasion and Propaganda.

[1334] Lifton 1986, pp. 63–64.
[1335] Proctor 1988, p. 177.
[1336] Proctor 1988, pp. 177–198.
[1337] Proctor 1988, p. 192.
[1338] Friedlander 1995, p. 85.
[1339] Hillgruber 1989, p. 94.
[1340] Hillgruber 1989, pp. 95–96.
[1341] Gerlach 2000, pp. 122–123.
[1342] Burleigh & Wippermann 1991, pp. 106–107.
[1343] Laqueur & Baumel 2001, pp. 1–2.
[1344] Laqueur & Baumel 2001, p. 2.
[1345] O'Neil (2005).
[1346] Shapiro 2003, p. 184.
[1347] Breitman (2001).
[1348] Wistrich 2001, p. 193.
[1349] Wistrich 2001, pp. 194–197.
[1350] Fleming 2014, pp. 156–158.
[1351] See: Polish Ministry of Foreign Affairs (10 December 1942), *The Mass Extermination of Jews in German Occupied Poland. Note to the Governments of the United Nations.*
[1352] Lemkin 2005, p. 89fn.
[1353] Laqueur & Baumel 2001, pp. 92–93.
[1354] Laqueur & Baumel 2001, pp. 75–76.
[1355] Laqueur & Baumel 2001, pp. 715–716.
[1356] Fleming 2014, p. 181.
[1357] Laqueur & Baumel 2001, pp. 14–16.
[1358] Also see: "The Holocaust: World Response" https://www.jewishvirtuallibrary.org/jsource/Holocaust/worldres.html at the JewishVirtualLibrary.org
[1359] Wistrich 2001, pp. 199–203.
[1360] Gellately 2001, pp. 256–264.
[1361] Longerich 2006, pp. 240, 325.
[1362] Stargardt 2015, pp. 82–87, 144–154, 472–475.
[1363] Stargardt 2015, pp. 244–246, 302–303.
[1364] Stargardt 2015, pp. 38–45.
[1365] Koonz 2005, p. 190.
[1366] Ingrao 2013, pp. 107–116.
[1367] Marrus 1989, pp. 381–382.
[1368] The first systematic investigations of such attitudes drew inconclusively on national summaries of the Nazi security service (*Sicherheitsdienst* or SD) reports for the war years, along with a great many memoirs, diaries, and other descriptive material. In his 1973 article, Lawrence Stokes considered the extent to which ordinary Germans grasped the essence of the Final Solution and concluded that 'much, although not all, of the terror and destruction inflicted upon the Jews of Europe by the Nazis was generally known among the German people'. Going over the wider ground of German public opinion in the Third Reich, Marliss Steinert contended rather the opposite-that 'only a few people knew about the monstrous scope of the crimes.<ref name="FOOTNOTEMarrus1989382">Marrus 1989, p. 382.
[1369] Johnson & Reuband 2005, pp. 269–272.
[1370] Johnson & Reuband 2005, pp. 315–316.
[1371] Johnson & Reuband 2005, p. 332.
[1372] Even so, special courts (*Sondergerichte*) killed 12,000 Germans for their opposition to the Nazi regime.<ref name="FOOTNOTEHoffmann1977xiii">Hoffmann 1977, p. xiii.
[1373] Johnson & Reuband 2005, p. 383.
[1374] Johnson & Reuband 2005, p. 393.
[1375] Judt 2005, p. 58.

[1376] For discussion of the psychological war campaign concerning the idea of collective guilt, see: Denazification
[1377] Gordon 1984, p. 199.
[1378] Judt 2005, pp. 56–61.
[1379] Wachsmann 2015, pp. 12–14.
[1380] Wachsmann 2015, pp. 614–615.
[1381] Wachsmann 2015, pp. 616–617.
[1382] Wachsmann 2015, p. 616.
[1383] Wachsmann 2015, p. 618.
[1384] Wachsmann 2015, p. 619.
[1385] Hilberg 1992, p. 20.
[1386] Hilberg 1992, p. 26.
[1387] Kellner (2017).
[1388] In the same entry, Kellner wrote that "ninety-nine percent of the German population is guilty, directly or indirectly."<ref name="FOOTNOTEKellner2017">Kellner (2017).
[1389] JTA—Jewish Telegraph Agency (1999).
[1390] Feig 1981, p. 13.
[1391] Niewyk & Nicosia 2000, pp. 84–87.
[1392] Also see: Browning, Christopher R. *Ordinary Men: Reserve Police Battalion 101 and the Final Solution in Poland*, New York, Harper Collins, 1992.
[1393] Niewyk & Nicosia 2000, pp. 85–86.
[1394] Niewyk & Nicosia 2000, p. 85.
[1395] Evans 2010, p. 318.
[1396] Benz 2007, pp. 204–206, 222–228.
[1397] Bartov 1999, pp. 133–150.
[1398] Bessel 2006, pp. 110–111.
[1399] Zentner & Bedürftig 1991, p. 227.
[1400] Waller 2007, p. 111.
[1401] Waller 2007, pp. 111–113.
[1402] Blass 1998, p. 51.
[1403] Hayes 2017, p. 9.
[1404] Hayes 2017, p. 10.
[1405] Hayes 2017, p. 11.
[1406] Hayes 2017, p. 12.
[1407] Wallmann 1987, pp. 72–97.
[1408] Luther 1971, pp. 267–290.
[1409] Dawidowicz 1975, p. 23.
[1410] Jones 2006, p. 148.
[1411] Bergen 2009, pp. 4–6.
[1412] Fischer 2002, pp. 47–49.
[1413] Arendt 1973, pp. 124–134, 177–187.
[1414] Langbehn & Salama 2011, pp. xii–xvi.
[1415] Arendt 1973, p. 153.
[1416] Burleigh & Wippermann 1991, pp. 27–28, 38.
[1417] Bauer 2002, pp. 14, 20, 71–76.
[1418] McWhorter 2017, pp. 282–293.
[1419] Bialas 2013, pp. 358–359.
[1420] Waite 1993, p. 122.
[1421] Dutton 2007, pp. 23–24.
[1422] Rees 2017, p. 291.
[1423] Bergen 1996, pp. 9, 22–38.
[1424] Hayes 2017, pp. 137–139.
[1425] Kershaw 2008, pp. 316–322.
[1426] Bessel 2003, p. 15.
[1427] Niewyk & Nicosia 2000, pp. 72–74.
[1428] Niewyk & Nicosia 2000, pp. 74–75.

[1429] Niewyk & Nicosia 2000, p. 72.
[1430] Kershaw 2008, p. 93.
[1431] Stackelberg 2007, pp. 60, 74.
[1432] Kershaw 2008, p. 255.
[1433] Breitman 1992, p. 203.
[1434] Stackelberg 2007, p. 67.
[1435] Petropoulos & Roth 2005, p. 4.
[1436] Kershaw 2008, pp. 92–98, 252–256.
[1437] Marrus 1987, pp. 40–49.
[1438] Dawidowicz 1975, p. 86.
[1439] Browning 2004, p. 369.
[1440] Marrus 1987, p. 42.
[1441] Ascher 2012, p. 204.
[1442] Yahil 1990, pp. 160–161.
[1443] Yahil 1990, pp. 253–254.
[1444] Burleigh 2000, pp. 590–593.
[1445] Browning 1992, pp. 86–124.
[1446] Longerich 2012, pp. 508–512.
[1447] Rees 2017, p. 230.
[1448] Bartov 2000, p. 4.
[1449] Johnson 1988, p. 492.
[1450] Wistrich 2001, pp. 90–99.
[1451] McDonough 2008, p. 38.
[1452] Gilbert 1985, p. 116.
[1453] Kershaw 2008, p. 109.
[1454] Kershaw 2008, pp. 109–110.
[1455] Kershaw 2008, p. 110.
[1456] Kershaw 2008, pp. 89–111.
[1457] NS-Archiv (2017).
[1458] Kershaw (2005).
[1459] Fleming 1994, p. 17.
[1460] Krausnick 1968, p. 44.
[1461] Gilbert 1985, p. 285.
[1462] Dawidowicz & Altshuler 1978, pp. 83, 190.
[1463] Kaes, Jay & Dimendberg 1995, pp. 133, 806.
[1464] Confino 2014, p. 151.
[1465] Hildebrand 1984, p. 149.
[1466] Welch 2001, pp. 88–89.
[1467] Fleming 1994, pp. 8n, 20–21, 53–54, 112, 148, 174, 177, 185.
[1468] Wistrich 2001, p. 113.
[1469] Welch 2001, pp. 89–90.
[1470] Hilberg 1992, pp. 3–19.
[1471] Hilberg 1985, pp. 29, 52, 151–153, 161–188, 273–281.
[1472] Hilberg 1985, pp. 48–52, 161–163.
[1473] Thacker 2010, pp. 205, 328.
[1474] Thacker 2010, pp. 326–329.
[1475] Manvell & Fraenkel 2011, pp. 259–260.
[1476] Miller 2006, p. 152.
[1477] Evans 2015, p. 133.
[1478] Benz 2007, pp. 213–233.
[1479] Rees 2017, p. 353.
[1480] Wette 2007, pp. 95–98.
[1481] The exhibit was produced by the Hamburg Institute for Social Research
[1482] Fleischhauer (2011).
[1483] Wette 2007, pp. vii–xiii.
[1484] Fritzsche 2008, pp. 200–201.

[1485] Wette 2007, pp. 95–100.
[1486] Heer 2000, pp. 329–341.
[1487] Wette 2007, pp. 125–131.
[1488] Bessel 2006, pp. 107–118.
[1489] Mallmann & Cüppers 2006, pp. 103, 117–118.
[1490] Krumenacker (2006).
[1491] Caron (2007).
[1492] Wette 2007, pp. 101–102.
[1493] Joachim Fest claims that Stauffenberg and other German officers involved in the 20 July 1944 plot to kill Hitler were aware of the Holocaust and felt their oath was dissolved by Nazi crimes. See: Fest, Joachim. *Plotting Hitler's Death: The Story of the German Resistance*. New York: Henry Holt and Company, 1997.
[1494] Evans 2010, pp. 102–105, 219–221.
[1495] Laqueur & Baumel 2001, p. 281.
[1496] Cesarani 2016, pp. 307–312, 543–554.
[1497] Niewyk & Nicosia 2000, pp. 20–41.
[1498] Niewyk & Nicosia 2000, p. 33.
[1499] Niewyk & Nicosia 2000, pp. 26–27.
[1500] Snyder 2015, p. 237.
[1501] Cesarani 2016, pp. 378–379, 411–412.
[1502] Laqueur & Baumel 2001, p. 145.
[1503] Niewyk & Nicosia 2000, pp. 27–28.
[1504] Cesarani 2016, pp. 444, 571, 573, 671.
[1505] Koehl 2004, pp. 212–219.
[1506] Cooper 1979, p. 117.
[1507] Bullock 1993, p. 752.
[1508] Spiegel Staff, *The Dark Continent* (20 May 2009).
[1509] Perry 2012, p. 131.
[1510] Stone 2010, p. 6.
[1511] Vromen 2008, p. 147.
[1512] Van Doorslaer 2007, pp. 250–368.
[1513] Van Doorslaer 2007, pp. 514–545.
[1514] Van Doorslaer 2007, pp. 763–1054.
[1515] Friedländer 2007, pp. 422–423.
[1516] Niewyk & Nicosia 2000, p. 31.
[1517] Longerich 2010, p. 367.
[1518] Cesarani 2016, p. 602.
[1519] Longerich 2010, p. 392.
[1520] Cesarani 2016, pp. 602–603.
[1521] USHMM, "Bulgaria".
[1522] Rozett & Spector 2009, p. 161.
[1523] Rees 2005, pp. 137–138.
[1524] Gilbert 1985, p. 598.
[1525] Gilbert 1985, p. 699.
[1526] Alternate spelling, Ustaše
[1527] Niewyk & Nicosia 2000, p. 27.
[1528] Cesarani 2016, p. 444.
[1529] Yahil 1990, p. 351.
[1530] *BBC News*, "Croatian Holocaust".
[1531] Dulić 2005, p. 281.
[1532] Niewyk & Nicosia 2000, p. 28.
[1533] Many Jews fled into neighboring regions while others were deported from the Nazi invasion of Yugoslavia in 1941. Croats who opposed the Nazi regime were imprisoned in concentration camps. Some Croats risked their lives during the Holocaust in order to save Jews from extermination by the Nazis. See for instance: Croatian Righteous Among the Nations
[1534] Schuman 2004, pp. 78–79.

[1535] Dwork & van Pelt 2002, p. 153.
[1536] Dwork & van Pelt 2002, pp. 153–154.
[1537] Yahil 1990, pp. 573–574.
[1538] Before the war's end, fifty-one amid the 400-plus Jews at Theresienstadt died at the camp.<ref name="FOOTNOTEDawidowicz1975374">Dawidowicz 1975, p. 374.
[1539] Yahil 1990, p. 574.
[1540] Dawidowicz 1975, p. 373.
[1541] Dawidowicz 1975, p. 400.
[1542] Gilbert 1985, p. 281.
[1543] Hiio, Maripuu & Paavle (2006).
[1544] Hilberg 1985, pp. 120–125.
[1545] Rozett & Spector 2009, p. 205.
[1546] Bauer 1982, p. 270.
[1547] Hilberg 1985, p. 153.
[1548] Laqueur & Baumel 2001, p. 164.
[1549] Gilbert 1985, p. 135.
[1550] Gilbert 1985, p. 534.
[1551] Niewyk & Nicosia 2000, p. 88.
[1552] Lubotina 2015, pp. 82–84.
[1553] Mosse 1980, pp. 140–143.
[1554] Mosse 1980, p. 150.
[1555] Dawidowicz 1975, p. 360.
[1556] Dawidowicz 1975, pp. 360–361.
[1557] Evans 2010, pp. 130–131.
[1558] Evans 2010, pp. 131–135.
[1559] Price 2005, p. 287–291.
[1560] Dawidowicz 1975, p. 361.
[1561] Cesarani 2016, p. 307.
[1562] Yahil 1990, p. 173.
[1563] Cesarani 2016, p. 526.
[1564] Yahil 1990, p. 342.
[1565] Longerich 2010, p. 329.
[1566] Longerich 2010, p. 360.
[1567] Longerich 2010, pp. 360–361.
[1568] Bauer 1982, p. 233.
[1569] According to historian Yehuda Bauer, the Vichy government was profoundly complicit in the Holocaust; he cites the example of the Vel' d'Hiv Roundup of 16 and 17 July 1942, in which 12,884 Jewish men, women, and children were arrested, including some 4,000 small children who were previously roaming the streets of Paris. They were held at the Winter Velodrome and Drancy transit camp under horrible conditions, and nearly all were eventually transported by rail to Auschwitz.<ref name="FOOTNOTEBauer1982232-233">Bauer 1982, pp. 232–233.
[1570] Rozett & Spector 2009, p. 221.
[1571] Dawidowicz 1975, p. 393.
[1572] Mazower 2001, p. 238.
[1573] Members of the EEE assisted the occupying forces in identifying Jews and collaborated on the deportation of local Jews with remarkable efficiency, either for ethnic hatred or for more prosaic reasons such as obtaining profits from the confiscation and sale of Jewish property. By the time of the German withdrawal from Greece in 1944, nearly 90% of the Jewish community in Thessaloniki had been annihilated.
[1574] Cesarani 2016, pp. 601–602.
[1575] Rozett & Spector 2009, p. 250.
[1576] Dawidowicz 1975, p. 394.
[1577] Fromjimovics 2011, p. 250.
[1578] Fromjimovics 2011, pp. 250–251.
[1579] Fromjimovics 2011, p. 251.
[1580] Fromjimovics 2011, pp. 251–252.

[1581] Laqueur & Baumel 2001, p. 316.
[1582] Fromjimovics 2011, p. 252.
[1583] Cesarani 2016, pp. 703–704.
[1584] Hilberg 1985, pp. 250–251.
[1585] Gerlach 2016, p. 103.
[1586] Gerlach 2016, pp. 114–115.
[1587] USHMM, "Budapest".
[1588] Niewyk & Nicosia 2000, p. 87.
[1589] Laqueur & Baumel 2001, p. 321.
[1590] Dawidowicz 1975, pp. 382–383.
[1591] Bloxham 2009, p. 117.
[1592] Dawidowicz 1975, p. 369.
[1593] Rozett & Spector 2009, pp. 278–279.
[1594] Dawidowicz 1975, p. 370.
[1595] Dawidowicz 1975, pp. 370–371.
[1596] Dawidowicz 1975, p. 371.
[1597] Longerich 2010, p. 400.
[1598] Longerich 2010, p. 402.
[1599] Niewyk & Nicosia 2000, p. 421.
[1600] Niewyk & Nicosia 2000, p. 32.
[1601] Dawidowicz 1975, p. 399.
[1602] Rozett & Spector 2009, p. 295.
[1603] Gilbert 1985, p. 155.
[1604] Gilbert 1985, pp. 155–157.
[1605] Gilbert 1985, pp. 157–159.
[1606] Gilbert 1985, pp. 388–389.
[1607] Snyder 2015, pp. 169–171.
[1608] Snyder 2015, p. 170.
[1609] Snyder 2015, p. 171.
[1610] According to a U.S. State Dept. report from 2012, there were only 26 Jews residing in Liechtenstein.<ref name="FOOTNOTEU.S. Dept. of State, &quot;Religious Freedom Report for 2012&quot;">U.S. Dept. of State, "Religious Freedom Report for 2012".
[1611] *BBC News*, "Nazi crimes taint Liechtenstein".
[1612] DW Staff, "Nazi Camp Labor Used in Liechtenstein".
[1613] USHMM, "Lithuania".
[1614] Dawidowicz 1975, pp. 398–399.
[1615] Rozett & Spector 2009, pp. 301–302.
[1616] Rozett & Spector 2009, p. 302.
[1617] Rees 2017, p. 206.
[1618] Bloxham 2009, p. 128.
[1619] Rozett & Spector 2009, pp. 302–303.
[1620] Rees 2017, pp. 206–207.
[1621] Rees 2017, pp. 207–208.
[1622] Cesarani 2016, p. 364–366.
[1623] Rozett & Spector 2009, p. 303.
[1624] Cesarani 2016, p. 367.
[1625] Laqueur & Baumel 2001, pp. 664–665.
[1626] Cesarani 2016, pp. 363–368, 386–394.
[1627] Gaunt 2011, p. 211.
[1628] Bubnys 2004, pp. 218–219.
[1629] Gaunt 2011, pp. 214–215, 218.
[1630] Rees 2017, p. 219.
[1631] Dwork & van Pelt 2002, p. 155.
[1632] Dawidowicz 1975, pp. 366–367.
[1633] Dawidowicz 1975, p. 367.
[1634] Black 2016, pp. 147–148.

[1635] Dwork & van Pelt 2002, p. 232.
[1636] Bauer 1982, p. 241.
[1637] Laqueur & Baumel 2001, p. 438.
[1638] Dwork & van Pelt 2002, pp. 156–158.
[1639] According to Holocaust scholar Raul Hilberg—unlike Poland, where persecution of the Jews was openly carried out, the Nazis had to pay close attention to public opinion in the Netherlands.<ref name="FOOTNOTEHilberg198520">Hilberg 1985, p. 20.
[1640] Black 2016, p. 148.
[1641] Gerlach 2016, p. 96.
[1642] Cesarani 2016, pp. 316–317.
[1643] Dwork & van Pelt 2002, p. 158.
[1644] The 80% figure is also substantiated in *The Holocaust Encyclopedia*, edited by Walter Laqueur and Judith T. Baumel.<ref name="FOOTNOTELaqueurBaumel2001442">Laqueur & Baumel 2001, p. 442.
[1645] Additional reasons that have been suggested to explain the high percentages of Jews killed in the Netherlands range from: the occupation regime in the Netherlands was formed by fanatical Austrian Nazis; the typical Dutch landscape without mountains or woods made it practically impossible to find shelter; the majority of the Dutch Jews lived in the larger cities and thus they formed relatively easy targets for persecution and segregation; the Jewish leaders chose, "in order to prevent worse", a policy of collaboration with the Nazis. See: Ad van Liempt, *A Price on Their Heads, Kopgeld, Dutch bounty hunters in search of Jews, 1943*
[1646] Bruland 2011, p. 232.
[1647] Bergen 2009, p. 137.
[1648] Dawidowicz 1975, pp. 371–372.
[1649] Bruland 2011, pp. 233–234.
[1650] Bruland 2011, p. 235.
[1651] Niewyk & Nicosia 2000, pp. 32–33.
[1652] Longerich 2010, p. 373.
[1653] Laqueur & Baumel 2001, pp. 450–451.
[1654] Laqueur & Baumel 2001, p. 505.
[1655] Motadel 2014, pp. 227, 230–231.
[1656] Motadel 2014, pp. 42–43.
[1657] Motadel 2014, p. 42.
[1658] Motadel 2014, pp. 250, 274–281.
[1659] Stein 1984, pp. 181–185.
[1660] Dawidowicz 1975, pp. 395–396.
[1661] Hilberg 1992, pp. 203–204.
[1662] Dawidowicz 1975, p. 396.
[1663] Dawidowicz 1975, pp. 396–397.
[1664] Hilberg 1992, p. 203.
[1665] Hilberg 1992, p. 204.
[1666] Dmitrów, Szarota & Machcewicz 2004, p. 85.
[1667] Snyder 2015, p. 159.
[1668] Ringelblum 1992, p. 133.
[1669] Hilberg 1992, pp. 92–93.
[1670] Piotrowski 1998, pp. 83–84, 321.
[1671] Tec 1986, p. 40.
[1672] Niewyk & Nicosia 2000, p. 113.
[1673] Yad Vashem, "Names of Righteous by Country".
[1674] Due to its European centrality, available rail networks, and proximity to Nazi avenues of control, Poland was the nation where German persecution policies against the Jews were played out in full.<ref name="FOOTNOTELongerich2010143–150">Longerich 2010, pp. 143–150.
[1675] Bergen 2009, pp. 182–191.
[1676] Rozett & Spector 2009, p. 360.
[1677] Dawidowicz 1975, p. 384.
[1678] Dawidowicz 1975, pp. 384–385.

[1679] Dwork & van Pelt 2002, p. 119.
[1680] Dwork & van Pelt 2002, pp. 119–120.
[1681] Dwork & van Pelt 2002, p. 121.
[1682] Members of Codreanu's Iron Guard killed 120 Jews on 19–20 January 1941 and hung their bodies like cattle carcasses at a slaughterhouse in Bucharest.<ref name="FOOTNOTEBauer1982306">Bauer 1982, p. 306.
[1683] Bauer 1982, p. 309.
[1684] Sivathambu (2003).
[1685] See the official report here: https://www.ushmm.org/m/pdfs/20080226-romania-commission-holocaust-history.pdf
[1686] Yahil 1990, pp. 344–348.
[1687] Yahil 1990, p. 344.
[1688] Cesarani 2016, p. 378.
[1689] Cesarani 2016, pp. 411–412.
[1690] Also see: Golbert, Rebecca L. "Holocaust Sites in Ukraine: Pechora and the Politics of Memorialization." *Holocaust and Genocide Studies* 18, no. 2 (2004): 205–233, ISSN 1476-7937
[1691] Levy (2003).
[1692] Paldiel 2007, pp. 18–21.
[1693] USHMM, "Romania: Facing Its Past".
[1694] Rozett & Spector 2009, p. 405.
[1695] Bloxham 2009, p. 90.
[1696] Bergen 2009, p. 149.
[1697] Evans 2010, p. 236.
[1698] Evans 2010, pp. 237–239.
[1699] Longerich 2010, p. 301.
[1700] Bloxham 2009, p. 199.
[1701] Retribution against the Jews was especially severe in Serbia, partly from the fact that the German forces encountered serious resistance there earlier than they had in the Soviet Union and took from the experience, lessons for future operations.<ref name="FOOTNOTESnyder2010216–217">Snyder 2010, pp. 216–217.
[1702] Longerich 2010, p. 300.
[1703] Hilberg 1985, pp. 268–269.
[1704] Black 2016, pp. 134–135.
[1705] United States Holocaust Memorial Museum 1996, p. 171.
[1706] Jewish Heritage Europe (2016) "Serbia".
[1707] Dawidowicz 1975, pp. 377–378.
[1708] Dawidowicz 1975, p. 378.
[1709] Rees 2017, p. 260.
[1710] Rees 2017, pp. 261–263.
[1711] Rees 2017, p. 261.
[1712] USHMM, "The Holocaust in Slovakia".
[1713] Niewyk & Nicosia 2000, pp. 27, 421.
[1714] Black 2016, p. 151.
[1715] Alexy 1993, p. 74.
[1716] Alexy 1993, p. 77.
[1717] Alexy 1993, pp. 164–165.
[1718] Alexy 1993, pp. 77–78.
[1719] Alexy 1993, p. 165.
[1720] Alexy 1993, p. 79.
[1721] Alexy 1993, pp. 154–155.
[1722] Shortly afterwards, Spain began giving citizenship to Sephardic Jews in Greece, Hungary, Bulgaria, and Romania; many Ashkenazic Jews also managed to be included, as did some non-Jews. The Spanish head of mission in Budapest, Ángel Sanz Briz, may have saved thousands of Ashkenazim in Hungary by granting them Spanish citizenship, placing them in safe houses, and teaching them minimal Spanish so they could pretend to be Sephardim, at least to someone who did not know Spanish. The Spanish diplomatic corps was performing a balancing act: Alexy

conjectures that the number of Jews they took in was limited by how much German hostility they were willing to engender.<ref name="FOOTNOTEAlexy1993165 et. seq.">Alexy 1993, p. 165 et. seq..

[1723] Laqueur & Baumel 2001, p. 601.
[1724] Rozett & Spector 2009, p. 417.
[1725] USHMM, "Escape from German-Occupied Europe".
[1726] Some historians argue that these facts demonstrate the Franco regime's humane attitude, others point out that Spain only permitted *transit* and did not wish to increase its own small Jewish population. After the war, Franco's regime was quite hospitable to those who had been responsible for the deportation of the Jews, notably Louis Darquier de Pellepoix, Commissioner for Jewish Affairs (May 1942 – February 1944) under the Vichy Régime in France. See: Nicholas Fraser, "Toujours Vichy: a reckoning with disgrace", *Harper's*, October 2006, p. 86–94.
[1727] Aderet (2010).
[1728] Bauer 1982, pp. 62–63.
[1729] Bauer 1982, pp. 64–65.
[1730] Cesarani 2016, p. 359.
[1731] Bloxham 2009, p. 69.
[1732] Yahil 1990, p. 38.
[1733] Rozett & Spector 2009, p. 415.
[1734] Bauer 1982, p. 196.
[1735] Hilberg 1992, pp. 250–251.
[1736] Millo, ed. *Teaching about the Shoah*.
[1737] Dwork & van Pelt 2002, p. 193.
[1738] Bloxham 2009, pp. 129–130.
[1739] Cesarani 2016, pp. 402–404.
[1740] Gerlach 2016, pp. 68–69.
[1741] Gerlach 2016, p. 69.
[1742] Longerich 2010, pp. 345–356.
[1743] Niewyk & Nicosia 2000, pp. 13–14, 24.
[1744] Bergen 2009, p. 204.
[1745] Rozett & Spector 2009, p. 429.
[1746] Black 2016, p. 150.
[1747] Laqueur & Baumel 2001, pp. 182–183.
[1748] Rozett & Spector 2009, pp. 429–430.
[1749] Rozett & Spector 2009, p. 430.
[1750] Bauer 1982, pp. 324–325.
[1751] Dwork & van Pelt 2002, pp. 317–318.
[1752] Niewyk & Nicosia 2000, p. 125.
[1753] Niewyk & Nicosia 2000, p. 126.
[1754] Black 2016, pp. 150–151.
[1755] König & Zeugin 2002, pp. 108, 499.
[1756] Hilberg 1985, p. 55.
[1757] Hilberg 1985, pp. 54–55.
[1758] Gilbert 1985, pp. 469–470.
[1759] Gilbert 1985, p. 622.
[1760] Gilbert 1985, pp. 641, 700.
[1761] Rozett & Spector 2009, p. 431.
[1762] König & Zeugin 2002, pp. 496–497.
[1763] König & Zeugin 2002, p. 501.
[1764] König & Zeugin 2002, p. 118.
[1765] The conclusions of the ICE report about refugees have been questioned, most notably by Jean-Christian Lambelet who criticises the statistical work and argues "inter alia" that there was a big gap between policy and actual practice. He believes that the figures of Jews that were sent back were overestimated. See: A Critical Evaluation of the Bergier Report on "Switzerland and Refugees during the Nazi Era", With a New Analysis of the Issue, University of Lausanne, Ecole

des HEC, Department of Econometrics and Economics (DEEP), Research Paper No 01.03 January 2001. Accessed 2007-10-12 http://www.hec.unil.ch/jlambelet/transfinale.doc

[1766] Rozett & Spector 2009, p. 452.
[1767] USHMM, "Voyage of the St. Louis".
[1768] Rozett & Spector 2009, pp. 452–453.
[1769] Rozett & Spector 2009, p. 453.
[1770] Evans 2010, pp. 741–745, 752, 756.
[1771] Bascomb 2009, pp. 153, 163, 219–229.
[1772] Arendt 1994, p. 244.
[1773] Levy 2006, pp. 4–5.
[1774] Höhne & Zolling 1972, p. 66.
[1775] Höhne & Zolling 1972, p. 248.
[1776] Cockburn 1999, p. 167.
[1777] Steinacher 2011, pp. 203–206.
[1778] http://www.haaretz.com/print-edition/news/wwii-document-reveals-general-franco-handed-nazis-list-of-spanish-jews-1.297546
[1779] http://news.bbc.co.uk/2/hi/programmes/from_our_own_correspondent/1673249.stm
[1780] http://news.bbc.co.uk/2/hi/europe/4443809.stm
[1781] http://www.public.asu.edu/~acichope/FWA_Readings/Richard%20Bessel,%20Functionalists%20vs%20Intentionalists.pdf
[1782] http://www.analyse-und-kritik.net/1998-1/AK_Blass_1998.pdf
[1783] https://www.archives.gov/iwg/research-papers/breitman-chilean-diplomats.html
[1784] http://www.spiegel.de/wissenschaft/mensch/erwin-rommel-auf-der-jagd-nach-dem-schatz-des-wuestenfuchses-a-522484-2.html
[1785] http://www.dw.com/en/nazi-camp-labor-used-in-liechtenstein/a-1552304
[1786] http://www.spiegel.de/international/germany/rape-murder-and-genocide-nazi-war-crimes-as-described-by-german-soldiers-a-755385-5.html
[1787] http://www.mnemosyne.ee/hc.ee/index_frameset.htm
[1788] https://www.thenation.com/article/savage-modernism/
[1789] http://jewish-heritage-europe.eu/serbia
[1790] http://www.jta.org/1999/03/30/archive/parisian-branch-of-british-bank-offered-to-turn-jews-in-during-war-2
[1791] https://sites.google.com/site/friedrichkellnerdiary/kellner-diary-entries
[1792] http://www.open.edu/openlearn/history-the-arts/history/ou-lecture-2005-transcript
[1793] https://www.webcitation.org/5wQoAoZDv
[1794] https://www.uek.ch/en/schlussbericht/synthesis/ueke.pdf
[1795] http://www.redorbit.com/news/international/462094/nazis_planned_holocaust_for_palestine_historians/
[1796] http://muse.jhu.edu/login?auth=0&type=summary&url=/journals/jewish_quarterly_review/v098/98.3.levy.pdf
[1797] http://www.ffhec.org/PDF/Symposium%20Guide%20Shoah.pdf
[1798] http://www.ns-archiv.de/verfolgung/antisemitismus/hitler/gutachten.php
[1799] http://www.jewishgen.org/yizkor/poland/pol001.html
[1800] https://books.google.com/books?id=I3IItIwOzCkC&pg=PA184
[1801] https://www.telegraph.co.uk/news/worldnews/europe/romania/1433017/Romania-denies-Holocaust.html
[1802] http://www.spiegel.de/international/europe/the-dark-continent-hitler-s-european-holocaust-helpers-a-625824.html
[1803] http://www.state.gov/j/drl/rls/irf/religiousfreedom/index.htm?year=2012&dlid=208334
[1804] https://www.ushmm.org/wlc/en/article.php?ModuleId=10005264
[1805] https://www.ushmm.org/wlc/en/article.php?ModuleId=10005451
[1806] http://www.ushmm.org/wlc/en/article.php?ModuleId=10005470
[1807] https://www.ushmm.org/wlc/en/article.php?ModuleId=10005444
[1808] https://www.ushmm.org/research/scholarly-presentations/symposia/holocaust-in-romania/romania-facing-its-past
[1809] https://www.ushmm.org/wlc/en/article.php?ModuleId=10007324

[1810] http://www.ushmm.org/wlc/en/article.php?ModuleId=10005267
[1811] http://www.yadvashem.org/righteous/statistics
[1812] Kershaw (2008) *Hitler: A Biography*, p. 955
[1813] Joachimsthaler (1999) [1995] *The Last Days of Hitler: The Legends, the Evidence, the Truth*, pp. 160–182
[1814] Beevor (2002) *Berlin: The Downfall 1945*, p. 383
[1815] Miller (2006) *Leaders of the SS and German Police*, Vol. 1, p. 154
[1816] //en.wikipedia.org/w/index.php?title=Template:The_Holocaust_sidebar&action=edit
[1817] Margolin, Elaine. "The Post-War West Germans' Post-Holocaust Distortions." http://www.jewishjournal.com/books/article/review_the_holocaust_and_the_west_german_historians_historical_interpretati *Jewish Journal*. 6 February 2014. 9 February 2015.
[1818] Germany to open Holocaust archives https://web.archive.org/web/20060426045101/http://english.aljazeera.net/NR/exeres/8633EA3D-1AC2-41DF-9B7B-D2C385B1E10F.htm Al-Jazeera 19 April 2006.
[1819] Columbia University release http://www.sipa.columbia.edu/ece/research/intermarium/vol1no3/kielce.html
[1820] Yad Vashem website http://www1.yadvashem.org/odot_pdf/Microsoft%20Word%20-%203128.pdf
[1821] "40% of Holocaust Survivors in Israel Live Below Poverty Line" https://www.haaretz.com/hasen/spages/663880.html, *Haaretz*, December 29, 2005.
[1822] "Social Safety Nets" (PDF) http://www.claimscon.org/forms/allocations/Social%20Safety%20Nets.pdf, In *Re Holocaust Victim Assets Litigation (Swiss Bank)*, September 11, 2000.
[1823] (https://www.usatoday.com/story/news/world/2016/05/04/holocaust-remembrance-day-israels-needy-survivors-still-suffer/83913468/)
[1824] http://www.yadvashem.org
[1825] Jacobs, Neil G. *Yiddish: A Linguistic Introduction*, Cambridge University Press, Cambridge, 2005, .
[1826] David Shneer, Yiddish and the Creation of Soviet Jewish Culture: 1918-1930, Cambridge University Press, 2004. pp 13-14.
[1827] David E. Fishman, The Rise of Modern Yiddish Culture, University of Pittsburgh Press, 2005. pp 84-85.
[1828] : Jan Schwarz, Survivors and Exiles: Yiddish Culture after the Holocaust, Wayne State University Press, 2015. עמ' 316.
[1829] Solomo Birnbaum, *Grammatik der jiddischen Sprache* (4., erg. Aufl., Hamburg: Buske, 1984), p. 3.
[1830] Further examples of this usage can be found in: Bauer 2002, Cesarani 2004, Dawidowicz 1981, Evans 2002, Gilbert 1986, Hilberg 1996, Longerich 2012, Phayer 2000, Zuccotti 1999
[1831] Jewish Virtual Library, Holocaust Restitution: German Reparations https://www.jewishvirtuallibrary.org/jsource/Holocaust/reparations.html
[1832] Der Spiegel, *Holocaust Reparations: Germany to Pay 772 Million Euros to Survivors* http://www.spiegel.de/international/germany/germany-to-pay-772-million-euros-in-reparations-to-holocaust-survivors-a-902528.html
[1833] Le Monde, *Pour le rôle de la SNCF dans la Shoah, Paris va verser 100 000 euros à chaque déporté américain* http://www.lemonde.fr/ameriques/article/2014/12/05/etats-unis-paris-va-indemniser-les-victimes-de-la-shoah-transportees-par-la-sncf_4535530_3222.html
[1834] Norman Finkelstein, *The Holocaust Industry* https://archive.org/details/HolocaustIndustry.
[1835] Haaretz, *Ringleader of $57 million Holocaust survivor fraud found guilty* http://www.haaretz.com/jewish-world/jewish-world-news/ringleader-of-57-million-holocaust-survivor-fraud-found-guilty-1.523173
[1836] Harran, Marilyn. *The Holocaust Chronicles, A History in Words and Pictures*, Louis Weber, 2000, p. 697.
[1837] Donald L Niewyk, *The Columbia Guide to the Holocaust*, Columbia University Press, 2000, p.45: "The Holocaust is commonly defined as the murder of more than 5,000,000 Jews by the Germans in World War II." Estimates by scholars range from 5.1 million to 7 million. See the appropriate section of the Holocaust article.

[1838] Key elements of Holocaust denial: • "Before discussing how Holocaust denial constitutes a conspiracy theory, and how the theory is distinctly American, it is important to understand what is meant by the term "Holocaust denial." Holocaust deniers, or "revisionists," as they call themselves, question all three major points of definition of the Nazi Holocaust. First, they contend that, while mass murders of Jews did occur (although they dispute both the intentionality of such murders as well as the supposed deservedness of these killings), there was no official Nazi policy to murder Jews. Second, and perhaps most prominently, they contend that there were no homicidal gas chambers, particularly at Auschwitz-Birkenau, where mainstream historians believe over 1 million Jews were murdered, primarily in gas chambers. And third, Holocaust deniers contend that the death toll of European Jews during World War II was well below 6 million. Deniers float numbers anywhere between 300,000 and 1.5 million, as a general rule." Mathis, Andrew E. Holocaust Denial, a Definition http://www.holocaust-history.org/denial/abc-clio/ , The Holocaust History Project, July 2, 2004. Retrieved December 18, 2006. • "In part III we directly address the three major foundations upon which Holocaust denial rests, including... the claim that gas chambers and crematoria were used not for mass extermination but rather for delousing clothing and disposing of people who died of disease and overwork; ... the claim that the six million figure is an exaggeration by an order of magnitude—that about six hundred thousand, not six million, died at the hands of the Nazis; ... the claim that there was no intention on the part of the Nazis to exterminate European Jewry and that the Holocaust was nothing more than the unfortunate by-product of the vicissitudes of war." Michael Shermer and Alex Grobman. *Denying History: : who Says the Holocaust Never Happened and why Do They Say It?*, University of California Press, 2000, , p. 3. • "Holocaust Denial: Lies that the mass extermination of the Jews by the Nazis never happened; that the number of Jewish losses has been 'greatly exaggerated'; that the Holocaust was not systematic nor a result of an official policy; or simply that the Holocaust never took place." What is Holocaust Denial https://web.archive.org/web/20020606142334/http://www.yadvashem.org/about_holocaust/faqs/answers/faq_35.html, Yad Vashem website, 2004. Retrieved December 18, 2006. • "Among the untruths routinely promoted are the claims that no gas chambers existed at Auschwitz, that only 600,000 Jews were killed rather than twelve million, and that Hitler had no murderous intentions toward Jews or other groups persecuted by his government." Holocaust Denial http://www.adl.org/hate-patrol/holocaust.asp , Anti-Defamation League, 2001. Retrieved June 28, 2007.

[1839] "The kinds of assertions made in Holocaust-denial material include the following: • Several hundred thousand rather than approximately twelve million Jews died during the war. • Scientific evidence proves that gas chambers could not have been used to kill large numbers of people. • The Nazi command had a policy of deporting Jews, not exterminating them. • Some deliberate killings of Jews did occur, but were carried out by the peoples of Eastern Europe rather than the Nazis. • Jews died in camps of various kinds, but did so as the result of hunger and disease. The Holocaust is a myth created by the Allies for propaganda purposes, and subsequently nurtured by the Jews for their own ends. • Errors and inconsistencies in survivors' testimonies point to their essential unreliability. • Alleged documentary evidence of the Holocaust, from photographs of concentration camp victims to Anne Frank's diary, is fabricated. • The confessions of former Nazis to war crimes were extracted through torture." The nature of Holocaust denial: What is Holocaust denial? http://www.jpr.org.uk/Reports/CS_Reports/no_3_2000/index.htm , JPR report #3, 2000. Retrieved December 18, 2006.

[1840] Refer to themselves as revisionists: • "Holocaust deniers often refer to themselves as 'revisionists', in an attempt to claim legitimacy for their activities." ( The nature of Holocaust denial: What is Holocaust denial? http://www.jpr.org.uk/Reports/CS_Reports/no_3_2000/index.htm , JPR report #3, 2000. Retrieved May 16, 2007) • "The deniers' selection of the name revisionist to describe themselves is indicative of their basic strategy of deceit and distortion and of their attempt to portray themselves as legitimate historians engaged in the traditional practice of illuminating the past." Deborah Lipstadt. *Denying the Holocaust—The Growing Assault on Truth and Memory*, Penguin, 1993, , p. 25. • "Dressing themselves in pseudo-academic garb, they have adopted the term "revisionism" in order to mask and legitimate their enterprise." Introduction: Denial as Anti-Semitism http://www.adl.org/holocaust/theory.asp , "Holocaust Denial:

An Online Guide to Exposing and Combating Anti-Semitic Propaganda", Anti-Defamation League, 2001. Retrieved June 12, 2007. • "Holocaust deniers often refer to themselves as 'revisionists', in an attempt to claim legitimacy for their activities." , JPR report #3, 2000. Retrieved May 16, 2007.

[1841] Denial vs. "revisionism": • "This is the phenomenon of what has come to be known as 'revisionism', 'negationism', or 'Holocaust denial,' whose main characteristic is either an outright rejection of the very veracity of the Nazi genocide of the Jews, or at least a concerted attempt to minimize both its scale and importance... It is just as crucial, however, to distinguish between the wholly objectionable politics of denial and the fully legitimate scholarly revision of previously accepted conventional interpretations of any historical event, including the Holocaust." Bartov, Omer. *The Holocaust: Origins, Implementation and Aftermath*, Routledge, pp.11-12. Bartov is John P. Birkelund Distinguished Professor of European History at the Watson Institute, and is regarded as one of the world's leading authorities on genocide ( "Omer Bartov" http://www.watsoninstitute.org/contacts_detail.cfm?id=97 , The Watson Institute for International Studies). • "The two leading critical exposés of Holocaust denial in the United States were written by historians Deborah Lipstadt (1993) and Michael Shermer and Alex Grobman (2000). These scholars make a distinction between historical revisionism and denial. Revisionism, in their view, entails a refinement of existing knowledge about an historical event, not a denial of the event itself, that comes through the examination of new empirical evidence or a reexamination or reinterpretation of existing evidence. Legitimate historical revisionism acknowledges a "certain body of irrefutable evidence" or a "convergence of evidence" that suggest that an event_like the black plague, American slavery, or the Holocaust—did in fact occur (Lipstadt 1993:21; Shermer & Grobman 200:34). Denial, on the other hand, rejects the entire foundation of historical evidence..." Ronald J. Berger. *Fathoming the Holocaust: A Social Problems Approach*, Aldine Transaction, 2002, , p. 154. • "At this time, in the mid-1970s, the specter of Holocaust Denial (masked as "revisionism") had begun to raise its head in Australia..." Bartrop, Paul R. "A Little More Understanding: The Experience of a Holocaust Educator in Australia" in Samuel Totten, Steven Leonard Jacobs, Paul R Bartrop. *Teaching about the Holocaust*, Praeger/Greenwood, 2004, p. xix. • "Pierre Vidal-Naquet urges that denial of the Holocaust should not be called 'revisionism' because 'to deny history is not to revise it'. *Les Assassins de la Memoire. Un Eichmann de papier et autres essays sur le revisionisme* (The Assassins of Memory—A Paper-Eichmann and Other Essays on Revisionism) 15 (1987)." Cited in Roth, Stephen J. "Denial of the Holocaust as an Issue of Law" in the *Israel Yearbook on Human Rights*, Volume 23, Martinus Nijhoff Publishers, 1993, , p. 215. • "This essay describes, from a methodological perspective, some of the inherent flaws in the "revisionist" approach to the history of the Holocaust. It is not intended as a polemic, nor does it attempt to ascribe motives. Rather, it seeks to explain the fundamental error in the "revisionist" approach, as well as why that approach of necessity leaves no other choice. It concludes that "revisionism" is a misnomer because the facts do not accord with the position it puts forward and, more importantly, its methodology reverses the appropriate approach to historical investigation... "Revisionism" is obliged to deviate from the standard methodology of historical pursuit, because it seeks to mold facts to fit a preconceived result; it denies events that have been objectively and empirically proved to have occurred; and because it works backward from the conclusion to the facts, thus necessitating the distortion and manipulation of those facts where they differ from the preordained conclusion (which they almost always do). In short, "revisionism" denies something that demonstrably happened, through methodological dishonesty." McFee, Gordon. "Why 'Revisionism' Isn't" http://www.holocaust-history.org/revisionism-isnt/ , The Holocaust History Project, May 15, 1999. Retrieved December 22, 2006. • "Crucial to understanding and combating Holocaust denial is a clear distinction between denial and revisionism. One of the more insidious and dangerous aspects of contemporary Holocaust denial, a la Arthur Butz, Bradley Smith and Greg Raven, is the fact that they attempt to present their work as reputable scholarship under the guise of 'historical revisionism.' The term 'revisionist' permeates their publications as descriptive of their motives, orientation and methodology. In fact, Holocaust denial is in no sense 'revisionism,' it is denial... Contemporary Holocaust deniers are not revisionists — not even neo-revisionists. They are **Deniers**. Their motivations stem from their neo-nazi political goals and their rampant antisemitism." Austin, Ben

S. "Deniers in Revisionists Clothing" http://www.mtsu.edu/~baustin/revision.htm , The Holocaust\Shoah Page, Middle Tennessee State University. Retrieved March 29, 2007. • "Holocaust denial can be a particularly insidious form of antisemitism precisely because it often tries to disguise itself as something quite different: as genuine scholarly debate (in the pages, for example, of the innocuous-sounding Journal for Historical Review). Holocaust deniers often refer to themselves as 'revisionists', in an attempt to claim legitimacy for their activities. There are, of course, a great many scholars engaged in historical debates about the Holocaust whose work should not be confused with the output of the Holocaust deniers. Debate continues about such subjects as, for example, the extent and nature of ordinary Germans' involvement in and knowledge of the policy of genocide, and the timing of orders given for the extermination of the Jews. However, the valid endeavour of historical revisionism, which involves the re-interpretation of historical knowledge in the light of newly emerging evidence, is a very different task from that of claiming that the essential facts of the Holocaust, and the evidence for those facts, are fabrications." The nature of Holocaust denial: What is Holocaust denial? http://www.jpr.org.uk/Reports/CS_Reports/no_3_2000/index.htm , JPR report #3, 2000. Retrieved May 16, 2007. • "The deniers' selection of the name revisionist to describe themselves is indicative of their basic strategy of deceit and distortion and of their attempt to portray themselves as legitimate historians engaged in the traditional practice of illuminating the past. For historians, in fact, the name revisionism has a resonance that is perfectly legitimate – it recalls the controversial historical school known as World War I "revisionists," who argued that the Germans were unjustly held responsible for the war and that consequently the Versailles treaty was a politically misguided document based on a false premise. Thus the deniers link themselves to a specific historiographic tradition of reevaluating the past. Claiming the mantle of the World War I revisionists and denying they have any objective other than the dissemination of the truth constitute a tactical attempt to acquire an intellectual credibility that would otherwise elude them." Deborah Lipstadt. *Denying the Holocaust – The Growing Assault on Truth and Memory*, Penguin, 1993, , p. 25.

[1842] A hoax designed to advance the interests of Jews: • "The title of App's major work on the Holocaust, The Six Million Swindle, is informative because it implies on its very own the existence of a conspiracy of Jews to perpetrate a hoax against non-Jews for monetary gain." Mathis, Andrew E. Holocaust Denial, a Definition http://www.holocaust-history.org/denial/abc-clio/ , The Holocaust History Project, July 2, 2004. Retrieved May 16, 2007. • "Jews are thus depicted as manipulative and powerful conspirators who have fabricated myths of their own suffering for their own ends. According to the Holocaust deniers, by forging evidence and mounting a massive propaganda effort, the Jews have established their lies as 'truth' and reaped enormous rewards from doing so: for example, in making financial claims on Germany and acquiring international support for Israel." The nature of Holocaust denial: What is Holocaust denial? http://www.jpr.org.uk/Reports/CS_Reports/no_3_2000/index.htm , JPR report #3, 2000. Retrieved May 16, 2007. • "Why, we might ask the deniers, if the Holocaust did not happen would any group concoct such a horrific story? Because, some deniers claim, there was a conspiracy by Zionists to exaggerate the plight of Jews during the war in order to finance the state of Israel through war reparations." Michael Shermer & Alex Grobman. *Denying History: : who Says the Holocaust Never Happened and why Do They Say It?*, University of California Press, 2000, , p. 106. • "Since its inception in 1979, the Institute for Historical Review (IHR), a California-based Holocaust denial organization founded by Willis Carto of Liberty Lobby, has promoted the antisemitic conspiracy theory that Jews fabricated tales of their own genocide to manipulate the sympathies of the non-Jewish world." Antisemitism and Racism Country Reports: United States http://www.tau.ac.il/Anti-Semitism/asw2000-1/usa.htm , Stephen Roth Institute, 2000. Retrieved May 17, 2007. • "The central assertion for the deniers is that Jews are not victims but victimizers. They 'stole' billions in reparations, destroyed Germany's good name by spreading the 'myth' of the Holocaust, and won international sympathy because of what they claimed had been done to them. In the paramount miscarriage of injustice, they used the world's sympathy to 'displace' another people so that the state of Israel could be established. This contention relating to the establishment of Israel is a linchpin of their argument." Deborah Lipstadt. *Denying the Holocaust – The Growing Assault onTruth and Memory*, Penguin, 1993, , p. 27. • "They [Holocaust deniers] picture a vast shadowy conspiracy that controls and manipulates the institutions of education, culture, the media and government in order to disseminate a pernicious mythology. The purpose of this Holocaust mythology, they assert, is the inculcation of a sense of guilt in the white, Western Christian world. Those who can make others feel guilty have power over them and can make them do their bidding. This power is used to advance an international Jewish agenda centered in the Zionist enterprise of the State of Israel." Introduction: Denial as Anti-Semitism http://www.adl.org/holocaust/theory.asp , "Holocaust Denial: An Online Guide to Exposing and Combating Anti-Semitic Propaganda", Anti-Defamation League, 2001. Retrieved June 12, 2007. • "Deniers argue that the manufactured guilt and shame over a mythological Holocaust led to Western, specifically United States, support for the establishment and sustenance of the Israeli state — a sustenance that costs the American taxpayer over three billion dollars per year. They assert that American taxpayers have been and continue to be swindled..." , "Holocaust Denial: An Online Guide to Exposing and Combating Anti-Semitic Propaganda", Anti-Defamation League, 2001. Retrieved June 12, 2007. • "The stress on Holocaust revisionism underscored the new anti-Semitic agenda gaining ground within the Klan movement. Holocaust denial refurbished conspiratorial anti-Semitism. Who else but the Jews had the media power to hoodwink unsuspecting masses with one of the greatest hoaxes in history? And for what motive? To promote the claims of the illegitimate state of Israel by making non-Jews feel guilty, of course." Lawrence N. Powell, *Troubled Memory: Anne Levy, the Holocaust, and David Duke's Louisiana*, University of North Carolina Press, 2000, , p. 445.

[1843] Antisemitic: • "Denying the fact, scope, mechanisms (e.g. gas chambers) or intentionality of the genocide of the Jewish people at the hands of National Socialist Germany and its supporters and accomplices during World War II (the Holocaust)." EUMC Working Definition of Antisemitism. EUMC. Contemporary examples of antisemitism • "It would elevate their antisemitic ideology — which is what Holocaust denial is — to the level of responsible historiography — which it is not." Deborah Lipstadt, *Denying the Holocaust*, , p. 11. • "The denial of the Holocaust is among the most insidious forms of anti-Semitism..." Roth, Stephen J. "Denial of the Holocaust as an Issue of Law" in the *Israel Yearbook on Human Rights*, Volume 23, Martinus Nijhoff Publishers, 1993, , p. 215. • "Contemporary Holocaust deniers are not revisionists — not even neo-revisionists. They are **Deniers**. Their motivations stem from their neo-nazi political goals and their rampant antisemitism." Austin, Ben S. "Deniers in Revisionists Clothing" http://www.mtsu.edu/~baustin/revision.htm , The Holocaust\Shoah Page, Middle Tennessee State University. Retrieved March 29, 2007. • "Holocaust denial can be a particularly insidious form of antisemitism precisely because it often tries to disguise itself as something quite different: as genuine scholarly debate (in the pages, for example, of the innocuous-sounding Journal for Historical Review)." The nature of Holocaust denial: What is Holocaust denial? http://www.jpr.org.uk/Reports/CS_Reports/no_3_2000/index.htm , JPR report #3, 2000. Retrieved May 16, 2007. • "This books treats several of the myths that have made antisemitism so lethal... In addition to these historic myths, we also treat the new, maliciously manufactured myth of Holocaust denial, another groundless belief that is used to stir up Jew-hatred." Schweitzer, Frederick M. & Perry, Marvin. *Anti-Semitism: myth and hate from antiquity to the present*, Palgrave Macmillan, 2002, , p. 3. • "One predictable strand of Arab Islamic antisemitism is Holocaust denial..." Schweitzer, Frederick M. & Perry, Marvin. *Anti-Semitism: myth and hate from antiquity to the present*, Palgrave Macmillan, 2002, , p. 10. • "Anti-Semitism, in the form of Holocaust denial, had been experienced by just one teacher when working in a Catholic school with large numbers of Polish and Croatian students." Geoffrey Short, Carole Ann Reed. *Issues in Holocaust Education*, Ashgate Publishing, 2004, , p. 71. • "Indeed, the task of organized antisemitism in the last decade of the century has been the establishment of Holocaust Revisionism – the denial that the Holocaust occurred." Stephen Trombley, "antisemitism", *The Norton Dictionary of Modern Thought*, W. W. Norton & Company, 1999, , p. 40. • "After the Yom Kippur War an apparent reappearance of antisemitism in France troubled the tranquility of the community; there were several notorious terrorist attacks on synagogues, Holocaust revisionism appeared, and a new antisemitic political right tried to achieve respectability." Howard K. Wettstein, *Diasporas and Exiles: Varieties of Jewish Identity*, University of California Press, 2002, , p. 169. • "Holocaust denial is a contemporary form of the classic anti-Semitic doctrine of the evil, manipulative and threatening world Jewish conspiracy." Introduction: Denial as Anti-Semitism http://www.adl.org/holocaust/theory.asp , "Holocaust Denial: An Online Guide to Exposing and Combating Anti-Semitic Propaganda", Anti-Defamation League, 2001. Retrieved June 12, 2007. • "In a number of countries, in Europe as well as in the United States, the negation or gross minimization of the Nazi genocide of Jews has been the subject of books, essay and articles. Should their authors be protected by freedom of speech? The European answer has been in the negative: such writings are not only a perverse form of anti-semitism but also an aggression against the dead, their families, the survivors and society at large." Roger Errera, "Freedom of speech in Europe", in Georg Nolte, *European and US Constitutionalism*, Cambridge University Press, 2005, , pp. 39-40. • "Particularly popular in Syria is Holocaust denial, another staple of Arab anti-Semitism that is sometimes coupled with overt sympathy for Nazi Germany." Efraim Karsh, *Rethinking the Middle East*, Routledge, 2003, , p. 104. • "Holocaust denial is a new form of anti-Semitism, but one that hinges on age-old motifs." Dinah Shelton, *Encyclopedia of Genocide and Crimes Against Humanity*, Macmillan Reference, 2005, p. 45. • "The stress on Holocaust revisionism underscored the new anti-Semitic agenda gaining ground within the Klan movement. Holocaust denial refurbished conspiratorial anti-Semitism. Who else but the Jews had the media power to hoodwink unsuspecting masses with one of the greatest hoaxes in history? And for what motive? To promote the claims of the illegitimate state of Israel by making non-Jews feel guilty, of course." Lawrence N. Powell, *Troubled Memory: Anne Levy, the Holocaust, and David Duke's Louisiana*, University of North Carolina Press, 2000, , p. 445. • "Since its inception in 1979, the Institute for Historical Review (IHR), a California-based Holocaust denial organization founded by Willis Carto of Liberty Lobby, has promoted the antisemitic conspiracy theory that Jews fabricated tales of their own genocide to manipulate the sympathies of the non-Jewish world." Antisemitism and Racism Country Reports: United States http://www.tau.ac.il/Anti-Semitism/asw2000-1/usa.htm , Stephen Roth Institute, 2000. Retrieved May 17, 2007 . • "There is now a creeping, nasty wave of anti-Semitism ... insinuating itself into our political thought and rhetoric ... The history of the Arab world ... is disfigured ... by a whole series of outmoded and discredited ideas, of which the notion that the Jews never suffered and that the Holocaust is an obfuscatory confection created by the elders of Zion is one that is acquiring too much, far too much, currency." Edward Said, "A Desolation, and They Called it Peace" in *Those who forget the past*, Ron Rosenbaum (ed), Random House 2004, p. 518.

[1844] Conspiracy theory: • "While appearing on the surface as a rather arcane pseudo-scholarly challenge to the well-established record of Nazi genocide during the Second World War, Holocaust denial serves as a powerful conspiracy theory uniting otherwise disparate fringe groups..." Introduction: Denial as Anti-Semitism http://www.adl.org/holocaust/theory.asp , "Holocaust Denial: An Online Guide to Exposing and Combating Anti-Semitic Propaganda", Anti-Defamation League, 2001. Retrieved June 12, 2007. • "Before discussing how Holocaust denial constitutes a conspiracy theory, and how the theory is distinctly American, it is important to understand what is meant by the term 'Holocaust denial.'" Mathis, Andrew E. Holocaust Denial, a Definition http://www.holocaust-history.org/denial/abc-clio/ , The Holocaust History Project, July 2, 2004. Retrieved December 18, 2006. • "Since its inception in 1979, the Institute for Historical Review (IHR), a California-based Holocaust denial organization founded by Willis Carto of Liberty Lobby, has promoted the antisemitic conspiracy theory that Jews fabricated tales of their own genocide to manipulate the sympathies of the non-Jewish world." Antisemitism and Racism Country Reports: United States http://www.tau.ac.il/Anti-Semitism/asw2000-1/usa.htm , Stephen Roth Institute, 2000. Retrieved May 17, 2007 .

[1845] • "'Revisionism' is obliged to deviate from the standard method of historical pursuit because it seeks to mold facts to fit a preconceived result, it denies events that have been objectively and empirically proved to have occurred, and because it works backward from the conclusion to the facts, thus necessitating the distortion and manipulation of those facts where they differ from the preordained conclusion (which they almost always do). In short, "revisionism" denies something that demonstrably happened, through methodical dishonesty." McFee, Gordon. "Why 'Revisionism' Isn't" http://www.holocaust-history.org/revisionism-isnt/ , The Holocaust History Project, May 15, 1999. Retrieved December 22, 2006. • Alan L. Berger, "Holocaust

Denial: Tempest in a Teapot, or Storm on the Horizon?", in Zev Garber and Richard Libowitz (eds), *Peace, in Deed: Essays in Honor of Harry James Cargas*, Atlanta: Scholars Press, 1998, p. 154.

# Article Sources and Contributors

## The sources listed for each article provide more detailed licensing information including the copyright status, the copyright owner, and the license conditions.

**Names of the Holocaust** *Source:* https://en.wikipedia.org/w/index.php?oldid=860464844 *License:* Creative Commons Attribution-Share Alike 3.0 *Contributors:* A.S. Brown, Abce2, AlanM1, AndyTheGrump, Angusmclellan, Anthony Appleyard, Anyep, Argento Surfer, Arminden, Awen23, BD2412, Biosketch, Brickhobo, CAPTAIN RAJU, Citizen Canine, ClueBot NG, Codrinb, CorbieVreccan, Cosus, Courcelles, Dalai lama ding dong, Dbachmann, Deborahjay, Debouch, Desiphral, Edonovan, El C, Epbr123, Ethdhelwen, Foetusized, Gilliam, Goodoldpolonius2, Gökhan, Hagyan, Henia Perlman, Hmains, Icallitvera, Ixfd64, J04n, Jayjg, Jeepday, Jordjweb, Joshmaul, Jsl83, Julia langlois46290, Keraunos, Khazar2, Kits2, LFaraone, Lawrence King, LilHelpa, MC10, Magioladitis, Malcolmxl5, Malik Shabazz, Maqsarian, Materialscientist, Mcferran, Mtsmallwood, Mystichumwipe, Nederlandse Leeuw, Neelix, Nick Number, Ninarosa, NotYak, Ori, Otto4711, Paul Barlow, Pharos, Rich Farmbrough, Rodhullandemu, Samuel Blanning, Shankarsivarajan, Shellwood, Skylax30, SlimVirgin, Squiddy, SuperSha, The Anonymouse, Tkynerd, Tom harrison, Vanished user lt94ma34le12, Vchimpanzee, Wallie, Whatever404, Wikipelli, דויד ,שי' 88 anonymous edits ........ 3

**Nazi human experimentation** *Source:* https://en.wikipedia.org/w/index.php?oldid=861781315 *License:* Creative Commons Attribution-Share Alike 3.0 *Contributors:* 7mike5000, 93sandra, Acroterion, Adrian Tofei, Altaïr, Anastrophe, AniMate, Anthony Appleyard, Apclass123, Apokrif, Arigoldberg, Arno789, Arthur Rubin, Assayer, BD2412, Ben Ben, Bender235, BobEnyart, Bongwarrior, Boundarylayer, Brandmeister, Ceradon, Cleopatran Apocalypse, Cloudz679, ClueBot NG, CommonsDelinker, CowboySpartan, DARTH SIDIOUS 2, DRAGON BOOSTER, Dan Atkinson, Danielpublic, Davejohnsan, Devourer09, Diannaa, Dixtosa, Dl2000, Doctorkaufman, Doug Weller, Douglas R. Skopp, Dr bab, DrStrauss, DuLithgow, Ducknish, Duivelwaan, DybrarH, EduardoFernandez, Equilibrial, Esrever, Falcon8765, Fifelfoo, FreeKnowledgeCreator, Froid, Gabriel syme, Gamnamu, Gilderien, Gilo1969, Gohnarch, GorillaWarfare, Groyolo, HJ Mitchell, Hamiltonstone, HappyValleyEditor, Harizotoh9, Headbomb, His Ryanness, Hmains, Ich, IdreamofJeanie, Implied-Fibre, Improve∼enwiki, InverseHypercube, IronGargoyle, Jackfork, Jesanj, Jess Riedel, Joanvarsek, John, Joseph A. Spadaro, Juan.Villabona001, K kisses, KNHaw, Kamots, Karl 334, Kierzek, Kintetsubuffalo, Lear's Fool, Lizard the Wizard, Logan, Marek69, Martin.Jares, Maxmizerski2000, Mertimer, Metalhead94, Mifter, MikeLynch, Monochrome Monitor, MoogleUK, Mrand, Nabokov, Nasnema, Neelix, NickGarvey, Nihiltres, Nono64, Nonstopmaximum, Nsaum75, Ohconfucius, Ost316, Peterlewis, Pincrete, Pointillist, Porterhse, Prinsgezinde, Protestnt, Proxima Centauri, RashersTierney, Redrose64, RhinoMind, Rjwilmsi, Rlegends, Royalcourtier, Schmausschmaus, Seanette, Skysmith, Socrates2008, Some jerk on the Internet, Spy007au, Squiddy, Steeletrap, Stickee, StillTrill, TRM001, Tbhotch, Thane, The Anome, The Celestial City, The PIPE, TheFreeWorld, Theopolisme, TomCat4680, Tpbradbury, Uhbooh, Ujaanthiny, VanishedUser sdu9aya9fasdsopa, Varlaam, Vinayaraj, Vrenator, Wall Screamer, Wasell, Whoistheroach, Wiki3Languages, WikiTryHardDieHard, William Case Morris, Wingman417, Wknight94, Yatzhek, Ylee, Zeklandia, 185 anonymous edits ........ 13

**Aktion T4** *Source:* https://en.wikipedia.org/w/index.php?oldid=865130821 *License:* Creative Commons Attribution-Share Alike 3.0 *Contributors:* Alexb102072, Arjayay, Askari Mark, BananaCarrot152, Beadbop, BeŻet, Blinkfan, Carlotm, Chris the speller, ChrisTakey, Clayalc, ClueBot NG, Coffeeandcrumbs, Curly Turkey, Dilidor, Drmies, DuncanHill, Elessell, Esrever, FlyingAce, Freshacconci, Gaia Octavia Agrippa, Hanbush, Hebrides, Hmains, Howcheng, Hugginsian, Hux, Ifny, Iridescent, Joel B. Lewis, Jon Kolbert, Keith-264, Kierzek, LahmacunKebab, LilyKitty, Magioladitis, Maskettaman, Me, Myself, and I are Here, Milo44, MinorEnglishMajor, Mortense, Naraht, Newzild, PeteGaughan, Plastikspork, Poeticbent, PriceDL, Pwolit iets, Quebec99, Rathfelder, ScrapIronIV, SemiHypercube, Seraphim System, Shellwood, Signedzzz, Simon Adler, Sunnya343, Taras, The Banner, The Rambling Man, Trappist the monk, TreebeardTheEnt, Viennamusik, Vivexdino, Vycl1994, Wbm1058, Wingman417, Woogie10w, 82 anonymous edits ........ 25

**Life unworthy of life** *Source:* https://en.wikipedia.org/w/index.php?oldid=852094918 *License:* Creative Commons Attribution-Share Alike 3.0 *Contributors:* 'Merikan, After Midnight, Alexb102072, Ante Aikio, Austinlawdog, BDD, Big Adamsky, Bossanoven, Causa sui, Cjwright79, Cold Light, CommonsDelinker, CopperKettle, Cramyourspam, Cybercobra, DanMS, Davidcpearce, Davidwr, Ddoomdoom, Delos∼enwiki, Dobermanji, Dogface, Dom Kaos, Dr Gangrene, EastTN, Edward321, Ernest, Faithlessthewonderboy, Fastfission, Flarkins, Fobizan, Gareth Griffith-Jones, Gasta220, Guest2625, Guns of brixham, Hairy Dude, Humus sapiens, Imroy, J04n, Jacqui M, Jarble, JasonAQuest, Jickyincognito, Kintetsubuffalo, Lapaz, Magnet For Knowledge, Magus732, Malick78, Marcocapelle, Mark v1.0, Matthew Fennell, Melaen, Mengela, Monochrome Monitor, Mtsmallwood, NSH002, Nneonneo, Octopus-Hands, Omiya17, Omnipaedista, Paulus Caesar∼enwiki, Peterlewis, PianoKeys, Poeticbent, Portillo, Proxima Centauri, Pwjb, RashersTierney, RayAYang, Robin klein, RockMFR, Sam Spade, Sergelapelle, Sherurcij, Soman, Squiddy, Stuffybunbun, Suthnoli, TallNapoleon, Tatarian, Tazmaniacs, The Banner, Trep26, Treybien, Trfs, Trinitrix, User2004, Uthican, Vivexdino, Werieth, Wingman417, Woohookitty, Wwiikkiippeeddiiaaaccount, 81 anonymous edits ........ 61

**Kristallnacht** *Source:* https://en.wikipedia.org/w/index.php?oldid=864926407 *License:* Creative Commons Attribution-Share Alike 3.0 *Contributors:* A Quest For Knowledge, Abardill, Ad Orientem, African man69, Al-Andalus, Alexb102072, Alghenius, Aloysius the Gaul, Andy Dingley, Antique Rose, Arzewski, Aspening, Astrid999, AustralianRupert, Ax13x, Axiomus, Bender235, Bentogoa, Berg22, BokicaK, Brenont, Bus stop, C.Fred, CAPTAIN RAJU, Callanecc, CapLiber, CataracticPlanets, Charles01, ClueBot NG, DVdm, Dale Arnett, Dbrodbeck, Dcirovic, Deor, Dina-Fram, Dirkbb, DisillusionedBitterAndKnackered, Dl2000, Donner60, DrStrauss, Droffroad, DybrarH, Edelseider, Elisa.rolle, EmmaRB1, Eoriigngrhionr, Equinox, Erionne12, Ernio48, Error, Feminist, FoCuSandLeArN, Frankenab, Furchild, GeneralizationsAreBad, Gianttrombone, Giftpflanze, Gilliam, Gluons12, Gob Lofa, Graham87, Gruzinim, HJS1234, HMSLavender, Harizotoh9, Headhitter, Hedidnothingwrong34, Historian932, Historynerd1933, Hmains, Home Lander, Hubon, I dream of horses, IronGargoyle, Isefant, J 1982, JakArdington, Jandalhandler, Jeuwre, Jim1138, Jon Van Kreuger Svenson, Joshmaul, Jpgordon, Keelie.oberlies, Keith-264, Kennethaw88, Kerry Raymond, Kielbasa1, Kierzek, Kind Tennis Fan, Kirbanzo, Lentower, Leoger, Lovkal, Lucius Winslow, Lutzv, MagicatthemovieS, Mandruss, Marcocapelle, Marek69, Marioc15, Mariolis MG, Markbenjamin, Mary Mark Ockerbloom, Materialscientist, Mean as custard, Meatmaster69, Midnightblueowl, Mojo Hand, Mx. Granger, Mystichumwipe, Nathan buck1, Nillurcheier, Nthep, Nusaybah, OUR-BOY-FLYNN, Obotlig, Omnipaedista, Oof62, Oshwah, Palmtree23, Permstrump, Philroc, Pleiotrop3, Pulsarwind, RA0808, Radnompieceofgarbage, Redpumpkin28, Riddleness, Riscnotcisc, Rodericksilly, Rrburke, Seraphim System, Serols, Shellwood, Simplexity22, Spicemix, Stuartjmoore, Teresacurl, The Anomebot2, The PIPE, The Rambling Man, The-, TheFrog001, Thegreatluigi, Toploftical, Twinsday, Tyler mcgaw, Verbcatcher, Vinayaraj, Volunteer Marek, Wesleyjenkins112, Wikimandia, Yerevantsi, Zaenon, ZelyaV, Zupotachyon, Zzuuzz, ינ'ב ,הורון ,סידנ'יל 190 anonymous edits ........ 64

**The Holocaust in Poland** *Source:* https://en.wikipedia.org/w/index.php?oldid=862533449 *License:* Creative Commons Attribution-Share Alike 3.0 *Contributors:* Acroterion, Baerentp, Barteos, Bgwhite, Billjhunt, Brenont, CLCStudent, Carlotm, Catrìona, Chester Leszek, Classicwiki, ClueBot NG, Cotton2, Courcelles, DHeyward, Davemck, DisillusionedBitterAndKnackered, Dixie Cotton, Donnaa85, Ealdgyth, Firefly, Fixer88, François Robere, Freshacconci, Frietjes, GizzyCatBella, GreenC, Headbomb, Hmains, Icewhiz, Ira Leviton, Jaro7788, John of Reading, K.e.coffman, Kablammo, Kind Tennis Fan, LcawteHuggle, Lotje, MShabazz, Malik Shabazz, Mat0018, MeanMotherJr, Metoody, Missvain, Mjasfca, Mr Stephen, MyMoloboaccount, Nihil novi, Onceinawhile, Paulinho28, Pernambuko, Pharos, Piotrus, Poeticbent, Prinsgezinde, Quondum, R9tgokunks, Seraphim System, Shellwood, Swazoo, Terrek, Vanamonde93, Volunteer Marek, WereSpielChequers, Wiedzosław, Willondon, Wyspianski, X1\, Xx236, ינ'ב ,הורון 90 anonymous edits ........ 87

**Jewish ghettos in German-occupied Poland** *Source:* https://en.wikipedia.org/w/index.php?oldid=863506792 *License:* Creative Commons Attribution-Share Alike 3.0 *Contributors:* Alepik, Azzifeldman, Barteos, Bender235, Bgwhite, Bossanoven, Brenont, Carlotm, Catrìona, Dcirovic, DrKay, Drichter53, Enthusiast01, Ericoides, Genealogykid82, George Ponderevo, Hmains, IRISZOOM, Jmertel23, John of Reading, K.e.coffman, K9re11, Kpalion, Magioladitis, Matalea, Mgiganteus1, Midas02, NSH002, Niceguyedc, Piotrus, Poeticbent, Rodw, Rohith goura, Romuald Wróblewski, The Banner, Xx236, 4 anonymous edits ........ 120

**The Holocaust in Norway** *Source:* https://en.wikipedia.org/w/index.php?oldid=863805226 *License:* Creative Commons Attribution-Share Alike 3.0 *Contributors:* –peter.josvai, 4ing, Aeleen, Alansohn, Alpinu, Aqwis, Arcandam, AuthorAuthor, Brettrade, Brigade Piron, Carlotm, Carsten R D, Chris the speller, Creambreek, Dalai lama ding dong, Danzeneu, Dewritech, Dig.log, Doncram, Doremo, Drichter53, Erik9, ExRat, Futurist110, Geschichte, GrahamHardy, Guy355, Hmains, IRISZOOM, Iselilja, J.delanoy, JDDJS, John of Reading, JohnI, Jonesey95, Kenatipo, Keraunos, Kevin12xd, Leifern, Louisedoverbl, Magioladitis, Mais oui!, Manxruler, Monopoly31121993, NSH002, Netsilo, Nick Number, No Swan So Fine, Oceanh, OnWikiNo, Pessimist2006, Poodlecrudoil, QueenofBattle, Rettetast, Rich Farmbrough, Rjwilmsi, Rodw, Sardanaphalus, ScottyNolan, Sfan00 IMG, Shadowytwed, SolarWind, Sparviere, Stiangutten, Trappist the monk, Ulflarsen, Viscosyryp, Vwanweb, Wakuran, Wallnot, Wiae, ZappaOMati, Île flottante, 43 anonymous edits ........ 137

**The Holocaust in Belgium** *Source:* https://en.wikipedia.org/w/index.php?oldid=846976233 *License:* Creative Commons Attribution-Share Alike 3.0 *Contributors:* Brigade Piron, Carlotm, David Fuchs, Diannaa, Dig.log, Donner60, Frietjes, Futurist110, Hillbillyholiday, Jasonanaggie, JoJan, Khazar2, Kierzek, Madelgarius, Mathglot, Mr Stephen, NSH002, OttRider, Rjwilmsi, SchreiberBike, Trappist the monk, Vwanweb, 10 anonymous edits ........ 162

**The Holocaust in Luxembourg** *Source:* https://en.wikipedia.org/w/index.php?oldid=851985188 *License:* Creative Commons Attribution-Share Alike 3.0 *Contributors:* Brigade Piron, Carlotm, DadaNeem, Dig.log, Dr Gangrene, IZAK, Jwh, Madelgarius, NSH002, 1 anonymous edits ........ 176

**The Holocaust in France** *Source:* https://en.wikipedia.org/w/index.php?oldid=854668981 *License:* Creative Commons Attribution-Share Alike 3.0 *Contributors:* Anders Feder, Bender235, Blaue Max, Bossanoven, Brigade Piron, Carlotm, Certes, Cuber 08, Dig.log, Edithlbarzel, Ehud Amir, Erisie, GrahamHardy, Ground Zero, Hamish59, Henia Perlman, Hmains, Jllm06, Joel Mc, Jonesey95, Joriki, JoshuaWKnight, Liam987, LouisAlain, Magioladitis, Mathglot, MisterPatitucci, Monopoly31121993, NSH002, OnBeyondZebrax, Peter K Burian, Rachelle Perlman, Ralphhalgas, ReneLafoy, Rich Smith, Smalljim, Sparky091601, Uglemat, Volunteer Marek, 25 anonymous edits ........ 178

**The Holocaust in Serbia** *Source:* https://en.wikipedia.org/w/index.php?oldid=862282075 *License:* Creative Commons Attribution-Share Alike 3.0 *Contributors:* 1SongManyVoices, 23 editor, A-ciha, ABehrens, Alf.laylah.wa.laylah, Anastan, Antidiskriminator, Arjayay, Avaya1, Balkan-historian,

Bender235, Bossanoven, Brigade Piron, Buttons, Calthinus, ChrisGualtieri, Croq, Damir Marinovic, Davidcannon, Dewritech, Donner60, Every-leaf-that-trembles, Fayenatic london, FkpCascais, GrahamHardy, Hmains, Iehutin, Imersion, Ira Leviton, Jenks24, Jim1138, John of Reading, Kalinthos, KanteP, Ktrimi991, Lt firebird, Maesterial, Michaeldsuarez, Narky Blert, Neelix, Niceguyedc, Nikola910, No such user, NottNott, OlEnglish, Peacemaker67, Pessimist2006, Santasa99, Sjö, Sorabino, Tabletop, Tassedethe, Thhhommmasss, Trappist the monk, Vwanweb, WereSpielChequers, Zoupan, 11 anonymous edits .......... 187

**The Holocaust in the Independent State of Croatia** *Source:* https://en.wikipedia.org/w/index.php?oldid=854669002 *License:* Creative Commons Attribution-Share Alike 3.0 *Contributors:* Alexb102072, Alf.laylah.wa.laylah, Anonimski, Antidiskriminator, Bender235, Bgwhite, Brigade Piron, CommonsDelinker, Davidcannon, Demoniccathandler, Drmies, Fayenatic london, Fschoepf, Gob Lofa, Good Olfactory, GrahamHardy, GregorB, Hmains, IZAK, Jnestorius, John of Reading, Jonesey95, Joy, Kebeta, Kubura, Laurinavicius, LilHelpa, Macofe, Magioladitis, Miranche, Mogism, Nbanic, Peacemaker67, Prophet of Truth and Knowledge, Quinton Feldberg, Rich Farmbrough, Rms125a@hotmail.com, Robby, Romanm, Sorabino, Spellcast, Thewanderer, Thhhommmasss, Timbouctou, Tomislav101, TwoTwoHello, Tzowu, Tátótát, Urchu, Valoem, Vulokoko, Vwanweb, Wiae, Zoupan, 35 anonymous edits .......... 194

**Jews of Libya during the Holocaust** *Source:* https://en.wikipedia.org/w/index.php?oldid=854823448 *License:* Creative Commons Attribution-Share Alike 3.0 *Contributors:* 5glogger, Altered Walter, Batzion94, Bender235, BiggestSataniaFanboy89, Born2bgratis, Brigade Piron, Brutaldeluxe, Capt Jim, Carlotm, DagosNavy, Davidcannon, Dewritech, Drpickem, Giordanobucca, Greyshark09, Ground Zero, Gruzinim, Henia Perlman, Hmains, IRISZOOM, IceKarma, Irabarbanel, Jacob D, LilHelpa, Lokalkosmopolit, Lquilter, Materialscientist, Mccapra, MeanMotherJr, Mediran, Metron, Mjasfca, NSH002, Naraht, Onceinawhile, Quisqualis, Rachelle Perlman, Rcbutcher, Srnec, TheFreeWorld, Turismond, Vieque, WOSlinker, Yambaram, 23 anonymous edits 207

**Nazi concentration camps** *Source:* https://en.wikipedia.org/w/index.php?oldid=863103604 *License:* Creative Commons Attribution-Share Alike 3.0 *Contributors:* Abhinav, Acroterion, Alastair B. Campbell, Alexb102072, Altenmann, Anaxial, Andrew Gray, BBar, Bdatruthwriter, Bear-rings, Bender235, Bentogoa, Beyond My Ken, Bobby H. Heffley, Bonadea, Bongwarrior, Bossanoven, Brain696, Brenont, Brigade Piron, Bus stop, CLCStudent, Caliburn, Cambalachero, Cannonmc, Capitalist Christian, Carlotm, Catrìona, Chefallen, ClueBot NG, Cncmaster, Crystallizedcarbon, DDRowiec, Dadadadadadadadada, Dazedbythebell, Dcirovic, DeBellorum, Diannaa, Discospinster, DocWatson42, Donner60, Editor2020, Editør, Enterprisey, Excirial, Ezequiel Matias Acosta, Felixkrater, Feminist, Flyer22 Reborn, Froggy25, General Ization, GeneralizationsAreBad, Gilliam, Hairy Dude, Hashi0707, Hemanth r 21, Hgrosser, Hinmanbing, Hmains, Hohum, Hotspur23, Intensity254, JJARichardson, Jarble, Jbaranao, Jdb204, Jimw338, Johnuniq, Jpgordon, K.e.coffman, Kelvin, Keri, Kierzek, Kintetsubuffalo, Koopatrev, L235, Laszlo Panaflex, Lechia, Loganxpert, Look2See1, Lumos3, Mandruss, Mark v1.0, Materialscientist, Maximajorian Viridio, Mean as custard, Monochrome Monitor, Monopoly31121993, My Chemistry romantic, NSH002, Neelix, Niceguyedc, Nick Cooper, Nyttend, O.Koslowski, Obenritter, Patient Zero, Peter238, Pgallert, Pinethicket, Pleiotrop3, Poeticbent, Pratyya Ghosh, Prhartcom, R'n'B, Rachel Helps (BYU), Ri hwa won, Rich Farmbrough, Richard Yin, Rivertorch, Rjwilmsi, Sca, Scholar792, Scottloug, Sehund, Serols, Shlishke, Shrekisgod, Shrekisgodd, Simonl7, Sjö, Spirit of Eagle, Stefan2, Steve03Mills, Sundays evening, Svoi Perez, Tobby72, TracyMcClark, Uglemat, Waters.Justin, Webysther, What cat?, Widr, Witan, Writeonk, Y2kcrazyjoker4, Yamaguchi先生 , Yatzhek, Yogesh Khandke, Zppix, Гатерас, 135 anonymous edits .......... 217

**List of Nazi concentration camps** *Source:* https://en.wikipedia.org/w/index.php?oldid=865151773 *License:* Creative Commons Attribution-Share Alike 3.0 *Contributors:* 23 editor, A.amitkumar, Abcdukil, Abhinav, Abrahamic Faiths, Afernand74, AlejandroR1990, Aleksandr Grigoryev, Alexb102072, Amaury, Anna Frodesiak, Archicathedra, Atani, Awer123, BenAriAtMicrosoft, Bender235, Bermicourt, Bgwhite, Bobrayner, Bossanoven, Brewcrewer, Bwitiye, Bürgervereinigung, Calabe1992, CanadianLinuxUser, Carlotm, Chefallen, ClueBot NG, Colonies Chris, Compfreak7, Corusant, CowboySpartan, Creambreek, Curb Chain, Dannynewman77, Dimadick, DocWatson42, Donner60, DrDevilFX, DrTPo, Drewmutt, Dukurs, Dw122339, EDWI1972, Editor2020, Eliyahu S, Entranced98, Equilibrial, Er-vet-en, Ethangent, ExRat, Excirial, Fatidiot1234, Fifelfoo, Fraggle81, GCZPN3, Gilliam, GizzyCatBella, Gorthian, GünniX, Heyjoesoap, Hmains, Homoatrox, Hoonho97, Hugo999, Igreen997, Ikan Kekek, Jim1138, JoelDick, Joshuapm2015, Juantheman96, K.e.coffman, Keith D, Kevin12xd, Khajidha, Kingking789789, Kuifje007, L Kensington, LilHelpa, Lotje, LuK3, Lugosy, Marcocapelle, Marrante, Matalea, Materialscientist, Meltdown627, MikeAtari, Mild Bill Hiccup, Mm.12310, Molly-in-md, Monochrome Monitor, Mr Stephen, Msaynevirta, NSH002, Nahal Oz, Neufund, Niceguyedc, Ninja Diannaa, Nnemo, Ondewelle, Oshwah, Paaskynen, Paulinho28, Pharos, Poeticbent, Prairieplant, Retardednamingpolicy, Robin klein, Rybec, Samuel Clemmons, Santr00, Scholar792, Shellwood, Shunpiker, Smalljim, Smallman12q, Smasongarrison, Sorabino, Srich32977, Stuntguy3000, Tabletop, Tassedethe, TheFreeWorld, Vanstrat, Viniciusmc, Virago250, Wiae, Widr, Wikipelli, William Avery, Wingman417, Wizardking76, Wkeithvan, Yamaguchi先生 , Yehiel.M.5, Zdravko mk, Zikking, Zugspitze2962, Ânes-pur-sàng, 208 anonymous edits .......... 231

**Extermination through labour** *Source:* https://en.wikipedia.org/w/index.php?oldid=857669725 *License:* Creative Commons Attribution-Share Alike 3.0 *Contributors:* A876, Acroterion, Adam9007, Aenus, Agnostihuck, Alexb102072, Altenmann, Amerul, Archon 2488, Audaciter, BagInACampfire, Barts1a, Bear-rings, Bender235, Bgwhite, Bishonen, Bobanni, Bossanoven, C.J. Griffin, Calliopejen1, Cantdecideifimgonnacollidewithhopeormakemybridetheropeorjusthideinthedope, Catlemur, Causa sui, Ceosad, Chris the speller, Ck4829, CommonsDelinker, Cookingbythebook, Dakinijones, Diannaa, Disembodied Soul, Dodj33, Duttler, EamonnPKeane, EronMain, Gerrit, Gonzalo84, Graham87, Grant65, Greyhood, Halibutt, Harfarhs, Headbomb, Hmains, Hodja Nasreddin, Hotspur23, Hubon, Humus sapiens, I dream of horses, Ich, Ingolfson, Iohannes Animosus, Izno, Jarble, K.e.coffman, Kane5187, Khajidha, Kind Tennis Fan, Kirisutogomen, LilHelpa, Luokehao, MCTales, MathFacts, Melodiouschaos, Miacek, Mohamed CJ, Mojo Hand, Monochrome Monitor, Morrister, MyMoloboaccount, Nabokov, NewEnglandYankee, OnBeyondZebrax, Overwroughtwashingmachinescaughtwatchingmemeslosingselfesteem, Paul Siebert, Pgarret, Piotrus, Poeticbent, Quinton Feldberg, R'n'B, R3venans, Randomusername123, RashersTierney, Rjwilmsi, Saebvn, Seelefant, Shintaraguru, Smith2006, Staszek Lem, Stumink, TAnthony, Tavix, Terryn3, ThatPeskyCommoner, The Umbrage, TheDJ, Themightyquill, Twinsday, Venona, Vidor, WereSpielChequers, Windows66, WolfmanSF, Woohookitty, Woovee, Writeonk, 92 anonymous edits .......... 238

**Nazi ghettos** *Source:* https://en.wikipedia.org/w/index.php?oldid=861476472 *License:* Creative Commons Attribution-Share Alike 3.0 *Contributors:* 72, AGentleServant, AdventurousSquirrel, Ahadland1234, Allstarecho, Andrew Dorsons, Andropod, Arch dude, Arfade, Arjayay, Badagnani, Barry Kent∼enwiki, Bender235, Bossanoven, Brigade Piron, BryanG, Calabraxthis, Capricorn42, Cautiuos2, Chefallen, Ckruschke, Closedmouth, ClueBot NG, DA BLOB 2009, DARTH SIDIOUS 2, David Kernow, Dbfirs, Deor, EWikist, El cid, el campeador, Eliashc, Enthusiast01, Everyone Dies In the End, Excirial, Eyesnore, Feminist, Fisel, Flyer22 Reborn, Fogster, GCarty, Gene Nygaard, Ghoongta, Gilliam, GizzyCatBella, GreenC, Gtg204y, Hamtechperson, HanzoHattori, HarryHenryGebel, Historian932, Hmains, Hohum, Homer slips., Hsinnreich, Humus sapiens, IZAK, Iamunknown, Icewhiz, J04n, Jacurek, Jauerback, Jeffrd10, JohnCD, Jonathan.s.kt, Jossi, Jprg1966, K.e.coffman, Kloth∼enwiki, Knightflyte, KnowledgeOfSelf, Knyzna1, Leandrod, LeaveSleaves, LieutenantLatvia, Liftarn, LittleOldMe, Lugia2453, Mahagaja, Marcocapelle, Matalea, Matthew Fennell, Mike Rosoft, MikeLynch, Mjasfca, Mongoose666, Msginsberg, Mynamejesus, NSH002, NawlinWiki, Nihil novi, North Shoreman, Oshwah, PL290, Pablothepenguin, Palmtree23, Pewwer42, Pharos, Pi, Piotrus, Poeticbent, Poldy Bloom, Quantumobserver, RA0808, Renata3, Resoru, Rodw, Rrburke, ST47, Simplexity22, Sirenofthesea, Skeezix1000, Skizzik, Snow Blizzard, Snowolf, Solarra, Squiddy, Swimmer1300, TU-nor, Tamwin, The Thing That Should Not Be, Tresiden, Tyrol5, Ubiquity, Usalof3, VoABot II, Widr, WikHead, William Avery, Winner 42, Writeonk, Wzap, XVreturns, Xx236, £, Раціональне анархіст, חורין, יניב 192 anonymous edits .......... 253

**The Holocaust in Ukraine** *Source:* https://en.wikipedia.org/w/index.php?oldid=863962234 *License:* Creative Commons Attribution-Share Alike 3.0 *Contributors:* Alf.laylah.wa.laylah, Antique Rose, Atrix20, Auntof6, Black Falcon, Black Future, Bobanni, Bossanoven, Bri, Brigade Piron, Carlotm, Catrìona, Cloudz679, ClueBot NG, CommonsDelinker, Cornelius89, DadaNeem, Dale Arnett, Eetoast, Emptycrowd1, Eumolpo, Falcon8765, Fartherred, Fogelstrom, Frietjes, Galassi, GazaHaza, Gilliam, GizzyCatBella, GoingBatty, Goldfritha, Grzesiu199425, Hashi0707, Hmains, IRISZOOM, Jacurek, James James Morrison Morrison, Jayjg, Jolly gym socks, Joy, K.e.coffman, Karl.i.biased, L Kensington, LM2000, Look2See1, Lute88, Lvivske, Magioladitis, Meltdown627, Miacek, Mtsmallwood, Mwehle, NewEnglandYankee, Noclador, Pais, PamD, Partisan1, Petri Krohn, Piotrus, Poeticbent, Polyenetian, Qzd, RABIALEJAHU, Raquel Baranow, RevelationDirect, Richard David Ramsey, Senor Freebie, Shotgun pete, Sluzzelin, Tavrian, Tobby72, Trappist the monk, Velella, Volunteer Marek, Vwanweb, Wikidemon, WillA54456, Xx236, Yann, Yelizandpaul, Ynhockey, Yulia Romero, Δ, 76 anonymous edits ..... 258

**The Holocaust in Lithuania** *Source:* https://en.wikipedia.org/w/index.php?oldid=854668992 *License:* Creative Commons Attribution-Share Alike 3.0 *Contributors:* 7mike5000, Alexb102072, Altenmann, Amortias, AndriusKulikauskas, Angusmclellan, Ardfern, Bearas, Bender235, Biruitorul, Black Falcon, Bogomolov.PL, Boodlesthecat, Bosihiov, Bossanoven, Brigade Piron, Bruce1314, CLCStudent, Carlotm, Catherine2∼enwiki, Chefallen, Chorvitch, Citation bot 1, ClueBot NG, Codswallower, Colonies Chris, CommonsDelinker, Cyborg Ninja, D645550, Daniel Case, Darwinek, Deacon of Pndapetzim, Doopdoop, Dr. Dan, Fainites, Gadget850, Gaius Cornelius, GiW, Gilliam, GizzyCatBella, GrahamHardy, Grumpy otter, GünniX, H Padleckas, H-JAM, H1nkles, Halibutt, Hmains, Huehnerpo, IRISZOOM, IZAK, Imperial Monarch, Incnis Mrsi, Irpen, Iulius, IvanStepaniuk, Jacurek, JohnI, K.e.coffman, Knife-in-the-drawer, Koavf, Legobot II, Lokyz, Lysy, M.K, Maximilian Schönherr, MeanMotherJr, Mhym, Miacek, Minkmink, Molobo, Motacilla, Mtsmallwood, Nrgullapalli, Nug, Nwbeeson, Paul Siebert, Peltimikko, Pharos, Piotrus, Plastikspork, Poeticbent, R'n'B, Renata3, Rjwilmsi, Sabbatino, Safehaven86, Sca, SchreiberBike, Sidoroff-B, Srednuas Lenoroc, Staszek Lem, Stubbleboy, Themadmannn, Tobby72, Uziel302, Vecrumba, Vidor, Vwanweb, Welsh, Žemėpatis, 84 anonymous edits .......... 265

**The Holocaust in Latvia** *Source:* https://en.wikipedia.org/w/index.php?oldid=855412483 *License:* Creative Commons Attribution-Share Alike 3.0 *Contributors:* Abune, Adavidb, Alex Bakharev, Aliotra, Arrivisto, Auntof6, BD2412, Bejnar, Bender235, Bgwhite, Black Falcon, BlackcurrantTea, Bossanoven, Brigade Piron, Carlotm, Catlemur, Chris the speller, Cloptonson, CommonsDelinker, Dukurs, Eisbaer4419, EoGuy, Fogelstrom, Frietjes, GizzyCatBella, Grafen, Hellknowz, Hmains, Icewhiz, Ingarix, Khazar2, LilHelpa, Mack2, Marcocapelle, MeanMotherJr, Mtsmallwood, Nick Number, Ondewelle, Partisan1, Pashute, Philaweb, PigFlu Oink, Piotrus, R'n'B, Rjwilmsi, Robevans123, SchreiberBike, Serioussam909, Vecrumba, Wikielwikingo, Woohookitty, YUL89YYZ, Zygezint, 19 anonymous edits .......... 277

**The Holocaust in Estonia** *Source:* https://en.wikipedia.org/w/index.php?oldid=858128887 *License:* Creative Commons Attribution-Share Alike 3.0 *Contributors:* Alcherin, Amire80, Atrix20, Aurora2698, Bender235, Black Falcon, Brewcrewer, Brigade Piron, Carlotm, Chez alexito, Colchicum, CommonsDelinker, DJ Sturm, Davidcannon, Debresser, Digwuren, Dodo19∼enwiki, ExRat, Felix Folio Secundus, Flying Saucer, Future Perfect at Sunrise, Fylbecatulous, Gilo1969, GrahamHardy, Gugus15, HarDNox, Hmains, JaGa, Jaan, Jim Sweeney, John of Reading, JustAGal, K.e.coffman, Kaltenmeyer, Kbdank71, Khazar2, Miacek, Mikedelsol, Mjasfca, Monopoly31121993, Mtsmallwood, Mukadderat, Nedrutland, Nug, Ohconfucius, Oop, Petri Krohn,

Piotrus, Quibik, R'n'B, Renata3, Sander Säde, Shadowjams, SheriffIsInTown, Soojus, Staberinde, Supavollcheckabunny, Telaviv1, Thecheesykid, Timurite, Toddst1, Vihelik, Wbm1058, Welsh, WereSpielChequers, Wilson44691, Woohookitty, YUL89YYZ, Ânes-pur-sàng, 36 anonymous edits .......... 296

**The Holocaust in Belarus** *Source:* https://en.wikipedia.org/w/index.php?oldid=855411396 *License:* Creative Commons Attribution-Share Alike 3.0 *Contributors:* Anastrophe, BD2412, Baiji, Bender235, Black Falcon, Brigade Piron, Carlotm, Catrìona, Clivemacd, Czalex, Derek R Bullamore, Dewritech, DocWatson42, Dshugar, Faizhaider, Finnusertop, Froid, Galassi, Ghirlandajo, Giraffedata, Gladkyandrey, H-JAM, Hmains, I dream of horses, JaGa, Jacurek, Jauhienij, Jim Sweeney, Jonashtand, K.e.coffman, Koavf, Ladnadruk, Look2See1, Lotje, MisterBee1966, Monochrome Monitor, Mtsmallwood, NSH002, Nikthestunned, Partisan1, Pessimist2006, Piotrus, Poeticbent, Prince Ludwig, Qzd, Satani, Skeezix1000, Staszek Lem, TaBOT-zerem, Thoughtmonkey, Transity, Urchu, Vwanweb, Welsh, Whoop whoop pull up, Woohookitty, Xx234∼enwiki, Xx236, Yoninah, Zbase4, Zygezint, 27 anonymous edits .......... 308

**The Holocaust in Russia** *Source:* https://en.wikipedia.org/w/index.php?oldid=859398090 *License:* Creative Commons Attribution-Share Alike 3.0 *Contributors:* Alex Bakharev, Alf.laylah.wa.laylah, Altenmann, Bellerophon5685, Black Falcon, Bossanoven, Brigade Piron, Carlotm, ClueBot NG, CommonsDelinker, Cornelius89, Cramyourspam, Delusion23, Discospinster, Dixie Cotton, Dodo19∼enwiki, DonaldDuck, EagleFan, Fagboybeiber, Galassi, GrahamHardy, Ground Zero, HHubi, Hmains, Hugo999, IRISZOOM, Iloveandrea, Jamesx12345, Jmcgnh, John of Reading, JohnCD, Jonesey95, K.e.coffman, Kierzek, Lute88, Magioladitis, Marcocapelle, Mervyn, Muhandes, Olegwiki, Partisan1, Piotrus, Poeticbent, R'n'B, Renata3, Richard David Ramsey, Ron Ritzman, Rsloch, Tad Lincoln, Tassedethe, Theopolisme, Tobby72, Tomas62, Trueabbie, Vwanweb, Wikipelli, Winner 42, Woohookitty, Zundark, 23 anonymous edits .......... 320

**Einsatzgruppen** *Source:* https://en.wikipedia.org/w/index.php?oldid=853499005 *License:* Creative Commons Attribution-Share Alike 3.0 *Contributors:* 2fletch, A.S. Brown, A2soup, Adel.M.Radwan, Adelson Velsky Landis, Alex1011, Alexb102072, Antique Rose, Arminden, Bender235, Birdie, Bongoramsey, Bossanoven, Br'er Rabbit, Caroline Sanford, Catrìona, Chas. Caltrop, Chris the speller, Clivemacd, CommonsDelinker, Cortagravatas, Cwkmail, Dchris1990, Deamonpen, Degen Earthfast, Diannaa, Dick Shane, EoGuy, EpicDream86, EtienneDolet, Gaussgauss, GeneralizationsAreBad, Gob Lofa, Gohnarch, GoingBatty, Hairy Dude, Harizotoh9, Helsned, Hibernian, Hohum, Huddyhuddy, I dream of horses, Illegitimate Barrister, Joel Mc, K.e.coffman, Khazar2, Kierzek, LahmacunKebab, Lesser Cartographies, LilHelpa, Marcocapelle, MattRay6, Mauro Lanari, MisterBee1966, MosheA, Mr. Someguy, NSH002, Neufund, Nthep, Obenritter, Omnipaedista, OnBeyondZebrax, Onceinawhile, PMLawrence, Pernambuko, Piantanida31, Piotrus, Poeticbent, R'n'B, Retal, Rich Farmbrough, Robert Lindsay, Seraphim System, Squawk7500, Sun Creator, Thalassathalassa, The PIPE, Tomobe03, TreebeardTheEnt, Vihelik, Volunteer Marek, WallyWyatt, Wavelength, Xyzzyva, Yohananw, Zealander, ÄDA - DÄP .......... 329

**Final Solution** *Source:* https://en.wikipedia.org/w/index.php?oldid=863770586 *License:* Creative Commons Attribution-Share Alike 3.0 *Contributors:* -glove-, 0xF8E8, 2PercentTruth, 72, AjaxSmack, Alexb102072, AntiCompositeNumber, Antique Rose, Arminden, Avoided, Baxter4173, Bender235, Bgwhite, Bomb319, Bongwarrior, CLCStudent, Carlotm, Chianti, Chrisf., ClueBot NG, Contentnotyetrated, Courtney.alexis, CubeSat4U, Ddcm8991, DferDaisy, Diabetes123, Eeeeeeeeeeeeeeeeeeeeeeeeeeeeeeeeeeeeee, El C, Famspear, Flyer22 Reborn, Frmorrison, GSS, GeneralizationsAreBad, Gestrid, Gilburrito, Gilliam, Gilo1969, GizzyCatBella, Guns of brixham, Hannolans, Headbomb, HeilAnning, Henia Perlman, Hmains, Hohum, HolyT, Hubon, IZAK, Ilikepeanutbutter1000, Imzadi1979, JMilty, Jacksonderner, Jim1138, Joel Mc, John of Reading, JohnGDallman, Jsharpminor, Jusdafax, K.e.coffman, KTo288, Keith-264, Laberkiste, Laoris, LiamKasbar, Lordtobi, Magioladitis, Marcocapelle, Marek69, MarginalCost, Mattster3517, Mick gold, MonkeyMensch, Natg 19, Nemo bis, Neufund, Nick Moyes, Nquinn91, Nxavar, Obenritter, Oshwah, PRRfan, Paulinho28, Peaksnary, Philip Cross, PlyrStar93, Poeticbent, Quebec99, Raquel Baranow, Raymondjharari, Rich Farmbrough, RickinBaltimore, Rjwilmsi, Rrburke, Sendreply, Seraphim System, Simon Adler, SoWhy, Staszek Lem, Stesmo, Tarun2394, Thalia42, TheFinalSolition, TheFreeWorld, TheFrog001, Tullyvallin, Urchu, UserDe, VQuakr, Viewmont Viking, Waggers, WhisperToMe, Whiterice603, XenoMyte, חורון, יניב □, 150 anonymous edits .......... 357

**The Black Book of Polish Jewry** *Source:* https://en.wikipedia.org/w/index.php?oldid=842506737 *License:* Creative Commons Attribution-Share Alike 3.0 *Contributors:* Bellerophon5685, Curly Turkey, Cwmhiraeth, Ealdgyth, Murchison-Eye, Nikkimaria, Onel5969, Piotrus, Pisucki, Poeticbent, StartTerminal, The Rambling Man, Yoninah, 1 anonymous edits .......... 377

**The Polish White Book** *Source:* https://en.wikipedia.org/w/index.php?oldid=850187100 *License:* Creative Commons Attribution-Share Alike 3.0 *Contributors:* Graeme Bartlett, Kudpung, Metoody, Piotrus, Pisucki, Poeticbent, 1 anonymous edits .......... 380

**The Black Book of Poland** *Source:* https://en.wikipedia.org/w/index.php?oldid=850187328 *License:* Creative Commons Attribution-Share Alike 3.0 *Contributors:* Metoody, Piotrus, Pisucki, Poeticbent, 7 anonymous edits .......... 383

**Raczyński's Note** *Source:* https://en.wikipedia.org/w/index.php?oldid=864013850 *License:* Creative Commons Attribution-Share Alike 3.0 *Contributors:* Angelwriter9, Esrever, François Robere, GoingBatty, HitroMilanese, Metoody, Packer1028, Pernambuko, Staszek Lem, 1 anonymous edits .. 385

**Witold's Report** *Source:* https://en.wikipedia.org/w/index.php?oldid=864014034 *License:* Creative Commons Attribution-Share Alike 3.0 *Contributors:* 1Rabid Monkey, Andkore, AndriusKulikauskas, ApolloLV, Bellerophon5685, Bender235, BjKa, Boing! said Zebedee, Bossanoven, CasualObserver'48, Chris the speller, ClueBot NG, CommonsDelinker, Darwinek, Davidcannon, Fhdjdjdjdjdjdjsnhqoobdvwixbdv, François Robere, Fred927, Froid, Halibutt, Hatlessness, Hergilei, Hmains, In ictu oculi, J Milburn, Jaro7788, Jimp, John of Reading, K.e.coffman, KLBot2, Lugia2453, Metalello, Metoody, Mild Bill Hiccup, Misterhistory, Mr. Guye, No Swan So Fine, Ok18879, One Night In Hackney, Pernambuko, Poeticbent, RashersTierney, RichardMills65, Rjwilmsi, Shakko, Sjam2004, SlimVirgin, Staszek Lem, ToBeFree, Tourorist, Tradereddy, Wingman417, Zelenilav, 27 anonymous edits .......... 391

**Death marches (Holocaust)** *Source:* https://en.wikipedia.org/w/index.php?oldid=861267285 *License:* Creative Commons Attribution-Share Alike 3.0 *Contributors:* 7mike5000, A.amitkumar, Adel.M.Radwan, AdmiralGT, Altaïr, Altenmann, Andnomoresorrow, Andreasmperu, Antandrus, Antiqueight, Archon 2488, Avoided, B14709, Bender235, BigDunc, Biruitorul, Bongwarrior, CapitalR, Captain Fantasy, Catrìona, Charvex, Chorrall, ClueBot NG, Cmichael, CommonsDelinker, Courcelles, Cramyourspam, Damiens.rf, Danieltiger45, Dawn Bard, Dcirovic, Dewritech, Diannaa, DorisAntony, Ehud Amir, El C, Epbr123, Epicgenius, Flyer22 Reborn, Froid, Funnyfarmofdoom, Fusion7, Gadfium, Gaius Cornelius, Gavinken, Genealogykid82, Gerson Nunes Pereira, GizzyCatBella, Goplibertycaucus, GünniX, Hamiltonstone, Hippo43, Hugo999, Ikt123, Interswd, Jacky.che0ng, JaconaFrere, Jacurek, Jake Wartenberg, Jamesx12345, Jarble, Jbrzow, Jillium, Jj137, Josve05a, Jéské Couriano, Katieh5584, Khazar2, Klenot, LeaveSleaves, Lihagen, Lklundin, Luis1970, Mark3k, Materialscientist, MeanMotherJr, Miquonranger03, Moe Epsilon, NSH002, Nabokov, Narky Blert, Nazgul02, NicoScribe, Niteshift, O.Koslowski, Ocrasaroon, Ondewelle, Osarius, Patar knight, Patrick, Pessimist2006, Philaweb, Philip Trueman, Pinethicket, Poeticbent, Prüm, QuiteUnusual, Quondum, Qxz, RASAM, RenamedUser01302013, Renatokeshet, Rich Farmbrough, Rkmlai, Robert A West, Robin klein, RomanK79, Saforrest, Shellwood, SheriffIsInTown, SlimVirgin, Smalljim, Smasongarrison, Snowheatmiser1092, Some jerk on the Internet, Squiddy, Swd, TaBOT-zerem, Tatarian, Tedder, The Myotis, The PIPE, Theopolisme, Tomas62, Tphi, Tyrol5, Uncle Dick, Vrenator, WayfaringWanderer, Wiae, Widr, Wikisucks10, Will2102, Wingman417, Wzwz, XPTO, Xous, Xx236, Yelir55, Ywis, ∼riley, 218 anonymous edits .......... 397

**Holocaust victims** *Source:* https://en.wikipedia.org/w/index.php?oldid=864768057 *License:* Creative Commons Attribution-Share Alike 3.0 *Contributors:* 23 editor, 97198, Adalfuns8237832, AddWittyNameHere, Adolf Schutzstaffel, Alephb, Alex Cohn, Alexb102072, Alt lys er svunnet hen, Antidiskriminator, Arjayay, Barteos, Bathory Motives, Bender235, Beyond My Ken, Boneyard90, Borinquen122617, Buddyschreder, CAPTAIN RAJU, Capt Jim, Carlotm, CataracticPlanets, Catrìona, Ceosad, Chris the speller, ClueBot NG, Continentaleurope, Cortagravatas, Dcirovic, Der Golem, Dixie Cotton, DocWatson42, DoctorJoeE, Doczilla, Ernio48, Ethangent, Etothepi, Eurodyne, Excirial, Finnusertop, Flooded with them hundreds, Fustos, GRM Al, Gilliam, Givibidou, GizzyCatBella, Gluons12, Grayfell, Henrimitterand, Hillbillyholiday, Hume42, IronGargoyle, IvanGulev, JJMC89, Jefft18, Jiten D, Jonesey95, Jonney2000, Jusdafax, KAP03, KGirlTrucker81, Kamperman2017, Keith D, Kierzek, Kranix, LilHelpa, Magioladitis, Mardus, Materialscientist, Mcc1789, Mean as custard, Michipedian, Miniapolis, MisterRandomized, Mr Stephen, Muboshgu, Music1201, N3hima, Name goes here, NewEnglandYankee, Nihiltres, OcarinaOfTime, Oshwah, Overt covert, Pharexia, PohranicniStraze, Raquel Baranow, RetroCraft314, Rich Farmbrough, Salopian, Sasha Divine, Saucy, ScratchMarshall, Serols, Shellwood, Sjrct, SkyWarrior, Taddah, The Voidwalker, The boss of editing, Tnacomics14, Tomeatstheworld, TouchOfFruit, Velella, Vexations, Volunteer Marek, Vycl1994, Wiki841, Wikishovel, WizWheatly, Yatzhek, Zumoarirodoka, חורון, יניב 199 anonymous edits .......... 405

**Responsibility for the Holocaust** *Source:* https://en.wikipedia.org/w/index.php?oldid=863114088 *License:* Creative Commons Attribution-Share Alike 3.0 *Contributors:* Alexb102072, Anthonydemesa, Arjayay, BD2412, Bobstone1111, Bukanowski, Catrìona, Citizen Canine, ClueBot NG, CommanderOzEvolved, CoolieCoolster, Coretheapple, Dicklyon, Dl2000, Editor2020, GizzyCatBella, Hmains, Iridescent, Jodosma, JohnGDallman, JosephusOfJerusalem, K.e.coffman, Kierzek, LMSchmitt, Malik Shabazz, Materialscientist, Mdavids, Metoody, Mvaldemar, Obenritter, Oshwah, Packer1028, Pernambuko, Poeticbent, Qwirkle, Reallycooldude32, Scaleshombre, Sein und Zeit, SlimVirgin, Slobodan Grasic, Titore, WereSpielChequers, Xx236, Yoshi24517, חורון, יניב 25 anonymous edits .......... 425

**List of major perpetrators of the Holocaust** *Source:* https://en.wikipedia.org/w/index.php?oldid=863111649 *License:* Creative Commons Attribution-Share Alike 3.0 *Contributors:* AlejandroR1990, Aumnamahashiva, Binksternet, Blue Edits, Bossanoven, Citizen Canine, Classicwiki, ClueBot NG, Colonies Chris, CommonsDelinker, Darkwind, Deor, DerBorg, Diannaa, Frietjes, Ganesh.rao, Gilliam, Head, Hmains, Hullaballoo Wolfowitz, J Milburn, JJMC89, Jim1138, Johnuniq, KaiMartin, Kierzek, LahmacunKebab, Lquilter, Magog the Ogre, Marcus Cyron, Materialscientist, Monopoly31121993, NSH002, Natg 19, Nazgul02, Obenritter, P. S. Burton, Pburka, Poeticbent, Preston North End Dan, SamuelDWilkerson, Skier Dude, Smsarmad, SpacedOut84, Stefanomione, Steven J. Anderson, TLSuda, Wallie, Wbm1058, Werieth, Ww2censor, Yabti, 36 anonymous edits .......... 481

**Aftermath of the Holocaust** *Source:* https://en.wikipedia.org/w/index.php?oldid=863218830 *License:* Creative Commons Attribution-Share Alike 3.0 *Contributors:* 90djdfgf, AddMore-III, Alansohn, Atrix20, Avoided, BD2412, Bender235, Bilal5836, Biosketch, Black Falcon, Blaue Max, Bmirman94, Bnovack, Bobfrombrockley, Bobo192, Bosed11212121212, CAPTAIN RAJU, CLCStudent, Catrìona, Ccollins2, Charles Essie, ChrisCork, Closedmouth, ClueBot NG, Coolcaesar, Cornellrockey, DVdm, Deror avi, Donner60, Drewmutt, Drivopenmcj, Editor2020, Edkollin, Enviroboy, Esprit15d, FlightTime, Funandtrvl, GHcool, Galorr, Glane23, Great big kcid, GreenC, Hebrides, Hemlock Martinis, Hmains, Iammargi, Igoldste, Iridescent, J991, Jacurek, Jayjg, Jennica, Jim1138, Jimhoward72, Jniech, John "Hannibal" Smith, Jonund, K kisses, K.e.coffman, Lightmouse, LilYachty666, Lugia2453, M4c∼enwiki, MPerel, MaNeMeBasat, Master Thief Garrett, Materialscientist, Mediran, Melonkelon, Meters, Microchip08, Moe Epsilon, Mogism, Molestash, Mthson, Mtsmallwood, Necronaut, Neils51, NerdyScienceDude, NoAmCom, Oshwah, Penbat, Pratyya Ghosh, R'n'B, Reaper Eternal, Rjwilmsi, Rositasaul, Rsrikanth05, Rupert loup, Ruyter, Ryan Postlethwaite, Signalhead, Skäpperöd, SlimVirgin, Smalljim, Stephenb, Stor stark7, Strongbrow, Sue Rangell, The Utahraptor, TheFreeWorld, Thehelpfulone, Thingg, Tide rolls, Tiggerjay, Trappist the monk, WadeSimMiser, Webclient101, Welsh, Whistlemethis, Yintan, Yodin, 176 anonymous edits .......... 493

# Image Sources, Licenses and Contributors

The sources listed for each image provide more detailed licensing information including the copyright status, the copyright owner, and the license conditions.

**Figure 1** *Source:* https://en.wikipedia.org/w/index.php?title=File:WWII-HolocaustDeaths-Pie-All.svg *License:* Public Domain *Contributors:* WWII-HolocaustDeaths-Pie-All.png: User:Dna-Dennis derivative work: Pedroca cerebral Talk-Up ............ 6
**Image** *Source:* https://en.wikipedia.org/w/index.php?title=File:Padlock-silver.svg *Contributors:* AzaToth, BotMultichill, BotMultichillT, Gurch, Jarekt, Kallerna, Multichill, Perhelion, Rd232, Riana, Sarang, Siebrand, Steinsplitter, 4 anonymous edits ............ 13
**Image** *Source:* https://en.wikipedia.org/w/index.php?title=File:Flag_of_the_NSDAP_(1920–1945).svg *License:* Public Domain *Contributors:* User:Guanaco, User:Rotemliss ............ 13
**Image** *Source:* https://en.wikipedia.org/w/index.php?title=File:Folder_Hexagonal_Icon.svg *License:* GNU Free Documentation License *Contributors:* Anomie, Jo-Jo Eumerus, Mifter ............ 13
**Image** *Source:* https://en.wikipedia.org/w/index.php?title=File:Flag_of_German_Reich_(1935–1945).svg *Contributors:* ............ 13
**Figure 2** *Source:* https://en.wikipedia.org/w/index.php?title=File:Aktion_Marcel.jpeg *License:* Public Domain *Contributors:* Marcel ............ 25
**Image** *Source:* https://en.wikipedia.org/w/index.php?title=File:EuthanasiePropaganda.jpg *Contributors:* Ansbachdragoner, Avraham, Beyond My Ken, BotMultichill, Cenarium, DagosNavy, Davidvr, Fourdee, Green Squares, Hozro, Mtsmallwood, Narkstraws, Nikodemos, Pilatus, Quadell, Qwerty Binary, Rjensen, Ronhjones, SlimVirgin, Stefan2, Tauwasser, Túrelio, Unused0029, Xiaopo, 9 anonymous edits ............ 27
**Figure 3** *Source:* https://en.wikipedia.org/w/index.php?title=File:Bundesarchiv_Bild_183-H13374,_Philipp_Bouhler.jpg *License:* Creative Commons Attribution-Sharealike 3.0 Germany *Contributors:* BotMultichill, Bundesarchiv-B6, Drdoht, Mtsmallwood, Ras67 ............ 29
**Figure 4** *Source:* https://en.wikipedia.org/w/index.php?title=File:Karl_Brandt_SS-Arzt.jpg *License:* Public Domain *Contributors:* USHMM .. 30
**Figure 5** *Source:* https://en.wikipedia.org/w/index.php?title=File:Bundesarchiv_Bild_152-04-28,_Heilanstalt_Schönbrunn,_Kinder.jpg *License:* Creative Commons Attribution-Sharealike 3.0 Germany *Contributors:* ABrocke, Blackcat, BotMultichill, Lupo, Mtsmallwood, Ras67, Stilfehler, 7 anonymous edits ............ 31
**Figure 6** *Source:* https://en.wikipedia.org/w/index.php?title=File:Viktor_Brack_Nürnberg_2.jpg *License:* Public Domain *Contributors:* USHMM, courtesy of Hedwig Wachenheimer Epstein ............ 32
**Figure 7** *Source:* https://en.wikipedia.org/w/index.php?title=File:Bundesarchiv_Bild_183-1989-0309-501,_Leonardo_Conti.jpg *License:* Creative Commons Attribution-Sharealike 3.0 Germany *Contributors:* BotMultichill, PDD, Ras67 ............ 34
**Figure 8** *Source:* https://en.wikipedia.org/w/index.php?title=File:Fort_VII_Poznań_RB8.JPG *License:* GNU Free Documentation License *Contributors:* Radomil ............ 35
**Figure 9** *Source:* https://en.wikipedia.org/w/index.php?title=File:Alkoven_Schloss_Hartheim_2005-08-18_3589.jpg *License:* Creative Commons Attribution-Sharealike 2.5 *Contributors:* Dralon ............ 37
**Figure 10** *Source:* https://en.wikipedia.org/w/index.php?title=File:Jan_Kowalski-arcybiskup_(1926-27).jpg *Contributors:* File Upload Bot (Magnus Manske), Hoixum, Masur, Mateusz Szymkiewicz, OgreBot 2, Tomasz Wachowski ............ 38
**Figure 11** *Source:* https://en.wikipedia.org/w/index.php?title=File:Hadamar_012.JPG *License:* Creative Commons Attribution 3.0 *Contributors:* Frank Winkelmann ............ 42
**Figure 12** *Source:* https://en.wikipedia.org/w/index.php?title=File:Hans_Gerhard_Creutzfeldt_(ca._1920).jpg *License:* anonymous-EU *Contributors:* Didym, DragonflySixtyseven, Filip em, Kresspahl, Llecco ............ 43
**Figure 13** *Source:* https://en.wikipedia.org/w/index.php?title=File:CAvGalenBAMS200612.jpg *License:* Creative Commons Attribution 2.5 *Contributors:* Domkapitular Gustav Albers († 1957) ............ 45
**Figure 14** *Source:* https://en.wikipedia.org/w/index.php?title=File:A_plaque_set_in_the_pavement_at_No_4_Tiergartenstrasse.JPG *License:* Public Domain *Contributors:* 1989, AndreasPraefcke, Beria, BotAdventures, Petrusbarbygere, Ulf Heinsohn ............ 46
**Figure 15** *Source:* https://en.wikipedia.org/w/index.php?title=File:Fort_VII_Poznań_RB7.JPG *License:* GNU Free Documentation License *Contributors:* Radomil ............ 46
**Figure 16** *Source:* https://en.wikipedia.org/w/index.php?title=File:Gedenkstele_Tiergartenstr_4_(Tierg)_Aktion_T4.JPG *License:* Creative Commons Attribution-Sharealike 3.0,2.5,2.0,1.0 *Contributors:* OTFW, Berlin ............ 49
**Figure 17** *Source:* https://en.wikipedia.org/w/index.php?title=File:T4_Memorial.JPG *License:* Public Domain *Contributors:* Drrss15 ............ 51
**Image** *Source:* https://en.wikipedia.org/w/index.php?title=File:Commons-logo.svg *License:* logo *Contributors:* Anomie, Callanecc, CambridgeBayWeather, Jo-Jo Eumerus, RHaworth ............ 60
**Image** *Source:* https://en.wikipedia.org/w/index.php?title=File:Bundesarchiv_Bild_183-N0827-318,_KZ_Auschwitz,_Ankunft_ungarischer_Juden.jpg *License:* Creative Commons Attribution-Sharealike 3.0 Germany *Contributors:* AdamBMorgan, BotMultichill, Catsmeat, Davidplan66, Gertsam, Goesseln, Hannolans, Jarekt, LudwigSebastianMicheler, Man vyi, Mtsmallwood, Rowanwindwhistler, SlimVirgin, Svajcr, Tom5551, Yarl, 5 anonymous edits ............ 61
**Figure 18** *Source:* https://en.wikipedia.org/w/index.php?title=File:EuthanasiePropaganda.jpg *Contributors:* Ansbachdragoner, Avraham, Beyond My Ken, BotMultichill, Cenarium, DagosNavy, Davidvr, Fourdee, Green Squares, Hozro, Mtsmallwood, Narkstraws, Nikodemos, Pilatus, Quadell, Qwerty Binary, Rjensen, Ronhjones, SlimVirgin, Stefan2, Tauwasser, Túrelio, Unused0029, Xiaopo, 9 anonymous edits ............ 63
**Image** *Source:* https://en.wikipedia.org/w/index.php?title=File:Flag_of_the_Free_City_of_Danzig.svg *License:* Public Domain *Contributors:* Mnmazur ............ 64
**Image** *Source:* https://en.wikipedia.org/w/index.php?title=File:Yellowbadge_logo.svg *License:* Public Domain *Contributors:* Self made, based on a photograph ............ 64
**Image** *Source:* https://en.wikipedia.org/w/index.php?title=File:Loudspeaker.svg *License:* Public Domain *Contributors:* User:Dbenbenn, User:Optimager, User:Tsca, User:Dbenbenn, User:Optimager, User:Tsca, User:Dbenbenn, User:Optimager, User:Tsca ............ 64
**Figure 19** *Source:* https://en.wikipedia.org/w/index.php?title=File:Bundesarchiv_Bild_102-14182-174-27,_Nürnberg,_Ausweisung_polnischer_Juden.jpg *License:* Creative Commons Attribution-Sharealike 3.0 Germany *Contributors:* Balcer~commonswiki, Bernd Schwabe in Hannover, BotMultichill, Janericloebe, Mogelzahn, Netanel h, Ras67, Thgoiter, 1 anonymous edits ............ 67
**Figure 20** *Source:* https://en.wikipedia.org/w/index.php?title=File:Herschel_Grynszpan_nov_7_1938.jpg *License:* anonymous-EU *Contributors:* Jdsteakley, Jonkerz, Lupo, SchroCat, Tasja~commonswiki, Themightyquill ............ 69
**Figure 21** *Source:* https://en.wikipedia.org/w/index.php?title=File:Ernst-vom-Rath.jpg *License:* anonymous-EU *Contributors:* Thesupermat, 2 anonymous edits ............ 69
**Figure 22** *Source:* https://en.wikipedia.org/w/index.php?title=File:Kristallnacht_rh_telegram_pg1.png *License:* Public Domain *Contributors:* Reinhard Heydrich ............ 71
**Figure 23** *Source:* https://en.wikipedia.org/w/index.php?title=File:Bundesarchiv_Bild_146-1970-083-42,_Magdeburg,_zerstörtes_jüdisches_Geschäft.jpg *License:* Creative Commons Attribution-Sharealike 3.0 Germany *Contributors:* Bernd Schwabe in Hannover, BlackIceNRW, BotMultichill, Goesseln, Hic et nunc, Marcric, Tsui ............ 73
**Figure 24** *Source:* https://en.wikipedia.org/w/index.php?title=File:Destroyed_Ohel_Yaaqov_Synagogue.jpeg *License:* Creative Commons Attribution 3.0 *Contributors:* ידרע אל / Unknown ............ 73
**Figure 25** *Source:* https://en.wikipedia.org/w/index.php?title=File:Synagogue_Eisenach_burning-_Nov_1938.jpg *License:* Public Domain *Contributors:* Apdency, Chefallen, FLLL, Jaybear, Jonund, Stefan Knauf ............ 74
**Figure 26** *Source:* https://en.wikipedia.org/w/index.php?title=File:0254_HM_Monson_Collection_Vienna_1938_01_49_45_00.webm *License:* Creative Commons Zero *Contributors:* M0tty, Pristurus, Reguyla, Tokfo, Wikieditoroftoday ............ 74
**Figure 27** *Source:* https://en.wikipedia.org/w/index.php?title=File:Paul_Ehrlich_by_Franz_Wilhelm_Voigt_2014.031.jpg *License:* Public Domain *Contributors:* BotAdventures, Mary Mark Ockerbloom ............ 76
**Figure 28** *Source:* https://en.wikipedia.org/w/index.php?title=File:Plaque_on_the_New_Synagogue.JPG *License:* GNU Free Documentation License *Contributors:* GeorgHH, Leit, MB-one, MGA73bot2, Man vyi, Narsamson~commonswiki, Ulf Heinsohn, 5 anonymous edits ............ 79
**Image** *Source:* https://en.wikipedia.org/w/index.php?title=File:Warsaw-Gdansk_railway_station_with_Warsaw_Ghetto_burning,_1943.jpg *License:* anonymous-EU *Contributors:* User:Poeticbent ............ 88
**Image** *Source:* https://en.wikipedia.org/w/index.php?title=File:Lodz_Ghetto_children_deportation_to_Chelmno.jpg *License:* anonymous-EU *Contributors:* User:Poeticbent ............ 88
**Image** *Source:* https://en.wikipedia.org/w/index.php?title=File:Einsatzgruppe_shooting.jpg *License:* Public Domain *Contributors:* Gustav Hille 88
**Image** *Source:* https://en.wikipedia.org/w/index.php?title=File:Stroop_Report_-_Warsaw_Ghetto_Uprising_10.jpg *License:* Public Domain *Contributors:* BotMultichill, Faigl.ladislav, Gkml, Jarekt, M11rtinb, Mtsmallwood, Yann, 1 anonymous edits ............ 88
**Image** *Source:* https://en.wikipedia.org/w/index.php?title=File:Selection_Birkenau_ramp.jpg *Contributors:* Unknown. Several sources believe the photographer to have been Ernst Hoffmann or Bernhard Walter of the SS ............ 88

**Image** *Source:* https://en.wikipedia.org/w/index.php?title=File:WW2-Holocaust-Poland.PNG *License:* Creative Commons Attribution 3.0 *Contributors:* En:User:Poeticbent (new original map) partly inspired by WW2-Holocaust-Europe.png by User:Dna-Dennis ... 88

**Figure 29** *Source:* https://en.wikipedia.org/w/index.php?title=File:Nazi_Holocaust_by_bullets_-_Jewish_mass_grave_near_Zolochiv,_west_Ukraine.jpg *License:* Public Domain *Contributors:* Butko, Figure19, JHistory, Poeticbent, Roman Z, Ruff tuff cream puff, Yann, יעל, 1 anonymous edits ... 92

**Figure 30** *Source:* https://en.wikipedia.org/w/index.php?title=File:The_Black_Book_of_Poland_(21–24).jpg *License:* Public Domain *Contributors:* Ministry of Information of the Polish government-in-exile ... 93

**Figure 31** *Source:* https://en.wikipedia.org/w/index.php?title=File:Auschwitz_e_Birkenau_con_neve.JPG *License:* Creative Commons Attribution-Sharealike 3.0 *Contributors:* Dawid Skalec ... 94

**Figure 32** *Source:* https://en.wikipedia.org/w/index.php?title=File:Krakow_Ghetto_06694.jpg *License:* Public Domain *Contributors:* NN ... 95

**Figure 33** *Source:* https://en.wikipedia.org/w/index.php?title=File:Chełmno_(Kulmhof)_1942_(Koło).jpg *License:* Public Domain *Contributors:* SS ... 97

**Figure 34** *Source:* https://en.wikipedia.org/w/index.php?title=File:Birkenau_Inmates_heading_towards_the_barracks_in_the_camp.jpg *Contributors:* Hannolans, Jeff G. ... 98

**Figure 35** *Source:* https://en.wikipedia.org/w/index.php?title=File:Treblinka_uprising_(Ząbecki_1943).jpg *License:* Public Domain *Contributors:* Franciszek Ząbecki ... 100

**Figure 36** *Source:* https://en.wikipedia.org/w/index.php?title=File:Belzec_-_SS_staff_(1942).jpg *License:* Public Domain *Contributors:* Antonkurt, Dd1495, Gkml, Mzungu, Poeticbent ... 101

**Figure 37** *Source:* https://en.wikipedia.org/w/index.php?title=File:Hoefletelegram.jpg *License:* Public Domain *Contributors:* Hermann Höfle (1911–1962) ... 102

**Figure 38** *Source:* https://en.wikipedia.org/w/index.php?title=File:Lublin_-_Majdanek_-_014_-_Ovens.jpg *License:* Public Domain *Contributors:* Roland Geider (Ogre) ... 103

**Figure 39** *Source:* https://en.wikipedia.org/w/index.php?title=File:Stroop_Report_-_Warsaw_Ghetto_Uprising_13.jpg *License:* Public Domain *Contributors:* Andros64, BomBom, BotMultichill, Catrìona, Howcheng, Jarekt, Lotje, Movieevery, Nizzan Cohen, Pieter Kuiper, Poeticbent, 1 anonymous edits ... 104

**Figure 40** *Source:* https://en.wikipedia.org/w/index.php?title=File:Protest-inc-w-ghetcie-warszawskim-za-murem-odcinajacym-od-swiata-kilkaset-tysiecy-0.jpg *License:* Public Domain *Contributors:* Ankry, OgreBot 2, Pernambuko, Piotrus ... 105

**Figure 41** *Source:* https://en.wikipedia.org/w/index.php?title=File:Bundesarchiv_Bild_101I-134-0771A-39,_Polen,_Ghetto_Warschau,_Kind_in_Lumpen_cropped.jpg *License:* Creative Commons Attribution-Sharealike 3.0 Germany *Contributors:* Carlotm, Jarekt, Kürschner, OCNative ... 106

**Figure 42** *Source:* https://en.wikipedia.org/w/index.php?title=File:Michal_Kruk_1943_execution(2).jpg *License:* Public Domain *Contributors:* Dreamcatcher25, Poeticbent, Zoupan, 1 anonymous edits ... 107

**Figure 43** *Source:* https://en.wikipedia.org/w/index.php?title=File:Żegota_ulotka_1943.JPG *License:* Public Domain *Contributors:* Achim55, Cathy Richards, Grottger, Gungir1983, JHistory, Poeticbent ... 108

**Image** *Source:* https://en.wikipedia.org/w/index.php?title=File:Star_of_David.svg *License:* Public Domain *Contributors:* ABF, Aamsse, CMBJ, Cathy Richards, Cirt, Dbc334, DenisKrivosheev, Ekeb, Erin Silversmith, Fibonacci, Fs, Gjyaj, Huhsunqu, Humus sapiens∼commonswiki, Knochen, Korg, Madden, Margriet, Mormegil, Nagy, Nickjbor∼commonswiki, Ogre, Pd4u, Penguins Are Animals 5327, Pessimist2006, Ricordisamoa, Rocket000, Rugby471, Sarang, Shalom, Stratford490, The Evil IP address, Thivierr, Tom-L, Waldir, Wildfeuer, Zscout370, 46 anonymous edits ... 110

**Image** *Source:* https://en.wikipedia.org/w/index.php?title=File:Herb_Polski.svg *License:* Public Domain *Contributors:* pl:User:Follow by white rabbit ... 110

**Figure 44** *Source:* https://en.wikipedia.org/w/index.php?title=File:Lviv_pogrom_(June_-_July_1941).jpg *License:* Public Domain *Contributors:* Butko, Darekm135, Dd1495, Poeticbent ... 112

**Figure 45** *Source:* https://en.wikipedia.org/w/index.php?title=File:Słonim_Ghetto_burning_(1942-06-29).jpg *License:* Public Domain *Contributors:* Kazimier Lachnovič, Poeticbent ... 114

**Figure 46** *Source:* https://en.wikipedia.org/w/index.php?title=File:Zegota(Rada_Pomocy_Zydom)1946.jpg *License:* Public Domain *Contributors:* Polska Agencja Prasowa ... 115

**Figure 47** *Source:* https://en.wikipedia.org/w/index.php?title=File:Jüdisches_historisches_Museum_Warschau,_IMG_2806.JPG *License:* Creative Commons Attribution-Sharealike 3.0 *Contributors:* User:Wistula ... 117

**Figure 48** *Source:* https://en.wikipedia.org/w/index.php?title=File:Bundesarchiv_Bild_101I-134-0771A-39,_Polen,_Ghetto_Warschau,_Kind_in_Lumpen.jpg *License:* Creative Commons Attribution-Sharealike 3.0 Germany *Contributors:* Balcer∼commonswiki, BotMultichill, Jarekt, PaulBommel 122

**Figure 49** *Source:* https://en.wikipedia.org/w/index.php?title=File:Bialystok_Ghetto_15-20_August_1943_(liquidation).jpg *License:* Public Domain *Contributors:* Unknown. Published in Dr. Szymon Datner, The Fight and the Destruction of Ghetto Białystok, December 1945, Yehud. ... 123

**Figure 50** *Source:* https://en.wikipedia.org/w/index.php?title=File:Stroop_Report_-_Warsaw_Ghetto_Uprising_BW.jpg *License:* Public Domain *Contributors:* Beyond My Ken, Blackcat, Catrìona, Jarekt, Mtsmallwood, Paris 16, Pkbwcgs, Yann, 1 anonymous edits ... 137

**Figure 51** *Source:* https://en.wikipedia.org/w/index.php?title=File:Hvem_er_Hvem_i_Jødeverden,_3._udgave.jpg *Contributors:* User:Danzeneu 139

**Figure 52** *Source:* https://en.wikipedia.org/w/index.php?title=File:WannseeList.jpg *License:* Public Domain *Contributors:* BotMultichill, Daczor, Hannolans, Mogelzahn, Mtsmallwood, Russian Rocky, Vidor, 2 anonymous edits ... 140

**Figure 53** *Source:* https://en.wikipedia.org/w/index.php?title=File:Anti-Semite_graffiti_Oslo_1941.jpg *License:* Public Domain *Contributors:* Anders Beer Wilse (1865–1949) ... 141

**Figure 54** *Source:* https://en.wikipedia.org/w/index.php?title=File:Memorial_plaque_at_Stabekk_skole_over_murdered_Jewish_children.jpg *License:* Creative Commons Attribution-Sharealike 3.0 *Contributors:* Leifern ... 142

**Figure 55** *Source:* https://en.wikipedia.org/w/index.php?title=File:Backpack_from_WWII_at_border_bw_Sweden_and_Norway.jpg *License:* Creative Commons Attribution-Sharealike 3.0 *Contributors:* Leifern ... 145

**Figure 56** *Source:* https://en.wikipedia.org/w/index.php?title=File:Bundesarchiv_Bild_121-1386,_Skeikampen,_deutsche_Offiziere,_Terboven.jpg *License:* Creative Commons Attribution-Sharealike 3.0 Germany *Contributors:* Anne-Sophie Ofrim, BotMultichill, Catsmeat, Drdoht, Jörg Zägel, Kåre-Olav, Manxruler, Melanom, Ras67, Wolfmann ... 147

**Figure 57** *Source:* https://en.wikipedia.org/w/index.php?title=File:Holocaust_memorial_in_Trondheim.jpg *License:* Creative Commons Attribution-Sharealike 3.0 *Contributors:* Leifern ... 150

**Figure 58** *Source:* https://en.wikipedia.org/w/index.php?title=File:Villa_grande_oslo.jpg *License:* Creative Commons Attribution-Sharealike 3.0,2.5,2.0,1.0 *Contributors:* Espen Solberg ... 156

**Figure 59** *Source:* https://en.wikipedia.org/w/index.php?title=File:Proclamation_about_Jews_in_German-occupied_Belgium.jpg *License:* Public Domain *Contributors:* User:Brigade Piron ... 163

**Figure 60** *Source:* https://en.wikipedia.org/w/index.php?title=File:Synagogue_de_Bruxelles.jpg *License:* Public Domain *Contributors:* Jpcuvelier 164

**Figure 61** *Source:* https://en.wikipedia.org/w/index.php?title=File:Poster_denoting_Jewish-owned_business_from_occupied_Belgium.jpg *License:* Public Domain *Contributors:* User:Brigade Piron ... 165

**Figure 62** *Source:* https://en.wikipedia.org/w/index.php?title=File:Jodenster_van_kledij.jpg *Contributors:* User:DRG-fan ... 167

**Figure 63** *Source:* https://en.wikipedia.org/w/index.php?title=File:Dossin_2.JPG *License:* Creative Commons Zero *Contributors:* Wasily ... 168

**Figure 64** *Source:* https://en.wikipedia.org/w/index.php?title=File:Circular_describing_the_Belgian_anti-jewish_laws_of_October_1940.jpg *License:* Public Domain *Contributors:* Anvilaquarius, Brigade Piron ... 170

**Figure 65** *Source:* https://en.wikipedia.org/w/index.php?title=File:Breendonk071.jpg *License:* Creative Commons Attribution-ShareAlike 3.0 Unported *Contributors:* JoJan ... 172

**Figure 66** *Source:* https://en.wikipedia.org/w/index.php?title=File:Schaerbeek_41_rue_de_la_Chaumière_-_Pavé_de_la_mémoire_Haja_Roter-Tenenbaum.JPG *License:* Creative Commons Attribution-Sharealike 3.0 *Contributors:* User:Odonacc ... 174

**Image** *Source:* https://en.wikipedia.org/w/index.php?title=File:Symbol_support_vote.svg *License:* Public Domain *Contributors:* Anomie, Fastily, Jo-Jo Eumerus ... 175

**Figure 67** *Source:* https://en.wikipedia.org/w/index.php?title=File:Al_SynagogueLux_Nazidefile.jpg *License:* anonymous-EU *Contributors:* user:Jwh ... 177

**Figure 68** *Source:* https://en.wikipedia.org/w/index.php?title=File:Recensement_des_Juifs.JPG *License:* Creative Commons Attribution-Sharealike 3.0,2.5,2.0,1.0 *Contributors:* Olevy ... 179

**Figure 69** *Source:* https://en.wikipedia.org/w/index.php?title=File:Bundesarchiv_Bild_146-1975-041-07,_Paris,_Propaganda_gegen_Juden.jpg *License:* Creative Commons Attribution-Sharealike 3.0 Germany *Contributors:* Bohème, BotMultichill, Brigade Piron, DIREKTOR, Dezidor, Mogelzahn, Para, Ras67, Tangopaso ... 180

**Figure 70** *Source:* https://en.wikipedia.org/w/index.php?title=File:Bundesarchiv_Bild_183-N0619-506,_Paris,_Jüdische_Frauen_mit_Stern.jpg *License:* Creative Commons Attribution-Sharealike 3.0 Germany *Contributors:* BotMultichill, Duesentrieb, GodefroyParis, Infrogmation, Mtsmallwood, Olybrius, Renamed user akdllvjbhlnbjfl, Yarnalgo ... 181

**Figure 71** *Source:* https://en.wikipedia.org/w/index.php?title=File:Juif.JPG *License:* Creative Commons Attribution-Sharealike 3.0 *Contributors:* Edited version of original photo by Rama ... 181

**Figure 72** *Source:* https://en.wikipedia.org/w/index.php?title=File:Bundesarchiv_Bild_101I-027-1476-20A,_Marseille,_Gare_d'Arenc._Deportation_von_Juden.jpg *License:* Creative Commons Attribution-Sharealike 3.0 Germany *Contributors:* Artix Kreiger 2, BotMultichill, Groupsixty, Lucarelli, Martin H., Melanom ..... 183

**Figure 73** *Source:* https://en.wikipedia.org/w/index.php?title=File:Fascist_concentration_camps_in_yugoslavia.png *License:* Public Domain *Contributors:* PANONIAN ..... 188

**Figure 74** *Source:* https://en.wikipedia.org/w/index.php?title=File:Bundesarchiv_Bild_101I-185-0112-28,_Belgrad,_Erfassung_von_Juden.jpg *License:* Creative Commons Attribution-Sharealike 3.0 Germany *Contributors:* BotMultichill, Fezz5555, Martin H., Melanom, Mtsmallwood ..... 188

**Figure 75** *Source:* https://en.wikipedia.org/w/index.php?title=File:Bundesarchiv_Bild_101I-185-0112-35,_Belgrad,_Erfassung_von_Juden.jpg *License:* Creative Commons Attribution-Sharealike 3.0 Germany *Contributors:* BotMultichill, Fezz5555, Flor!an, GT1976, Johnbod, Martin H., Melanom, Mtsmallwood, Nikola Smolenski, Olybrius, Tiefkuehlfan, Wolfmann, 1 anonymous edits ..... 189

**Figure 76** *Source:* https://en.wikipedia.org/w/index.php?title=File:Fascist_concentration_camps_in_yugoslavia.png *License:* Public Domain *Contributors:* PANONIAN ..... 195

**Figure 77** *Source:* https://en.wikipedia.org/w/index.php?title=File:Jewish_prisoner_in_Jasenovac.jpg *License:* Public Domain *Contributors:* Assayas, Slowking4, Spellcast ..... 196

**Figure 78** *Source:* https://en.wikipedia.org/w/index.php?title=File:Ustaše_militia_execute_prisoners_near_the_Jasenovac_concentration_camp.jpg *License:* Public Domain *Contributors:* Bojovnik, DIREKTOR, Ex13, Jdx, Madmax32, Mladifilozof, Mtsmallwood, R-41～commonswiki, Strike Eagle, Veliki Kategorizator, Zoupan, 2 anonymous edits ..... 197

**Figure 79** *Source:* https://en.wikipedia.org/w/index.php?title=File:Ustaše_order_for_Jews_and_Serbs_to_leave-1941.jpg *License:* Public Domain *Contributors:* Ustasa government ..... 200

**Figure 80** *Source:* https://en.wikipedia.org/w/index.php?title=File:GreaterItalia.jpg *License:* Public Domain *Contributors:* Brunodambrosio ..... 208

**Figure 81** *Source:* https://en.wikipedia.org/w/index.php?title=File:Jewish_Holocaust_survivors_return_to_Libya_from_Concentration_Camp_Bergen-Belsen_1945.jpg *Contributors:* Yad Vashem ..... 213

**Image** *Source:* https://en.wikipedia.org/w/index.php?title=File:NaziConcentrationCamp.gif *License:* Public Domain *Contributors:* Walter Chichersky, U.S. Signal Corps ..... 217

**Figure 82** *Source:* https://en.wikipedia.org/w/index.php?title=File:Bundesarchiv_Bild_183-R96361,_Dachau,_Konzentrationslager.jpg *License:* Creative Commons Attribution-Sharealike 3.0 Germany *Contributors:* Hydro, Mbdortmund, Mtsmallwood, Ruff tuff cream puff, 2 anonymous edits 219

**Figure 83** *Source:* https://en.wikipedia.org/w/index.php?title=File:Bundesarchiv_Bild_152-11-12,_Dachau,_Konzentrationslager,_Besuch_Himmlers.jpg *License:* Creative Commons Attribution-Sharealike 3.0 Germany *Contributors:* A1B2C3D4, ABrocke, Bossanoven, BotMultichill, Gödeke, Lupo, Mtsmallwood, 1 anonymous edits ..... 220

**Figure 84** *Source:* https://en.wikipedia.org/w/index.php?title=File:Bundesarchiv_Bild_101III-Duerr-053-29,_Lettland,_KZ_Salaspils,_Essensausgabe.jpg *License:* Creative Commons Attribution-Sharealike 3.0 Germany *Contributors:* Alonso de Mendoza, BotMultichill, Melanom, Tsui, 1 anonymous edits ..... 221

**Figure 85** *Source:* https://en.wikipedia.org/w/index.php?title=File:Buchenwald_Corpses_07511.jpg *License:* Public Domain *Contributors:* Aschroet, Pieter Kuiper, Ruff tuff cream puff, Slowking4, Surya Prakash.S.A., USHMM, Wolfmann, יעל ' ..... 223

**Figure 86** *Source:* https://en.wikipedia.org/w/index.php?title=File:Eines_von_3_Massengräbern_in_Bergen-Belsen,_so_wie_es_von_den_Befreiern_vorgefunden_wurde,_1945.jpg *License:* Public Domain *Contributors:* Lieutenant (Lt) Alan Moore ..... 224

**Figure 87** *Source:* https://en.wikipedia.org/w/index.php?title=File:Gen_Eisenhower_at_death_camp_report_crop.jpg *License:* Public Domain *Contributors:* cropped by Before My Ken 0918, 12 April 2009 (UTC) ..... 225

**Figure 88** *Source:* https://en.wikipedia.org/w/index.php?title=File:Ebensee_concentration_camp_prisoners_1945.jpg *License:* Public Domain *Contributors:* Lt. Arnold E. Samuelson ..... 226

**Figure 89** *Source:* https://en.wikipedia.org/w/index.php?title=File:MajorConcentrationCamps.png *License:* Public Domain *Contributors:* Charmbook, Leyo, Ludde23, OgreBot 2, Piotrus, Poeticbent, QuiteUnusual, TUBS ..... 227

**Figure 90** *Source:* https://en.wikipedia.org/w/index.php?title=File:Concentration_camp_SS.jpg *License:* Public Domain *Contributors:* "Illustrations are from Department of Defense files, with the exception of photographs on pages 199 and 229 which are re ..... 229

**Figure 91** *Source:* https://en.wikipedia.org/w/index.php?title=File:Birkenau_gate.JPG *License:* Creative Commons Attribution-Sharealike 2.5 *Contributors:* Michel Zacharz AKA Grippenn ..... 232

**Figure 92** *Source:* https://en.wikipedia.org/w/index.php?title=File:Bundesarchiv_Bild_192-269,_KZ_Mauthausen,_Häftlinge_im_Steinbruch.jpg *License:* Creative Commons Attribution-Sharealike 3.0 Germany *Contributors:* Alonso de Mendoza, Daniel Baránek, Diannaa, Herzi Pinki, John commons, Lechthaler, Mtsmallwood, Tm, Tom5551, 1 anonymous edits ..... 239

**Figure 93** *Source:* https://en.wikipedia.org/w/index.php?title=File:Ortsamt_Süderelbe_Gedenktafel.jpg *License:* Public Domain *Contributors:* GeorgHH ..... 240

**Figure 94** *Source:* https://en.wikipedia.org/w/index.php?title=File:Bundesarchiv_Bild_101I-138-1083-30,_Russland,_Mogilew,_Zwangsarbeit_von_Juden.jpg *License:* Creative Commons Attribution-Sharealike 3.0 Germany *Contributors:* BotMultichill, Christian Ganzer, EugeneZelenko, Martin H., Mtsmallwood, Origamiemensch, Red Winged Duck, Vadim Akopyan, Чаховіч Уладзіслаў ..... 241

**Figure 95** *Source:* https://en.wikipedia.org/w/index.php?title=File:Arbeitmachtfrei.JPG *License:* GNU Free Documentation License *Contributors:* MGA73bot2, MichaelFrey, Rudolph Buch, Wikitour ..... 242

**Figure 96** *Source:* https://en.wikipedia.org/w/index.php?title=File:Hardenburgamazonindians.jpeg *License:* Public Domain *Contributors:* Rhododendrites, Turn685, 1 anonymous edits ..... 249

**Image** *Source:* https://en.wikipedia.org/w/index.php?title=File:WW2-Holocaust-Europe.png *License:* Creative Commons Attribution 3.0 *Contributors:* User:Dna-Dennis ..... 253

**Figure 97** *Source:* https://en.wikipedia.org/w/index.php?title=File:Ringelblum_collection_-_Ghetto_in_Grodno_in_occupied_Poland.jpg *License:* Public Domain *Contributors:* An unknown onlooker (Polish or Jewish) in an adjacent building ..... 254

**Figure 98** *Source:* https://en.wikipedia.org/w/index.php?title=File:The_Wall_of_ghetto_in_Warsaw_-_Building_on_Nazi-German_order_August_1940.jpg *License:* Public Domain *Contributors:* Andros64, Bulwersator, Daczor, Jarekt, Mtsmallwood, Starscream, Tom5551, 1 anonymous edits 255

**Figure 99** *Source:* https://en.wikipedia.org/w/index.php?title=File:Biala_Podlaska_-_likwidacja_getta_-_1942.jpg *License:* Public Domain *Contributors:* OgreBot 2, Poeticbent ..... 257

**Image** *Source:* https://en.wikipedia.org/w/index.php?title=File:Einsatzgruppen_murder_Jews_in_Ivanhorod,_Ukraine,_1942.jpg *License:* Public Domain *Contributors:* Ajraddatz, Akim Dubrow, Andy Dingley, Billinghurst, Butko, Catrìona, Christian Ganzer, Daniel*D, Foroa, Fraulein HH, Gungir1983, Haditudósító, Herbythyme, Jarekt, Joostik, KiloByte, Kramer Associates, Lklundin, Macesito, Marcus Cyron, Movieevery, Mtsmallwood, Niridya, Paterm, Poeticbent, R-41～commonswiki, SKas, Sanya3, Silar, Starscream, Túrelio, Yann, 16 anonymous edits ..... 258

**Figure 100** *Source:* https://en.wikipedia.org/w/index.php?title=File:WW2-Holocaust-Ukraine_big_legend.PNG *License:* Creative Commons Attribution 3.0 *Contributors:* WW2-Holocaust-Europe.png: User:Dna-Dennis ..... 259

**Figure 101** *Source:* https://en.wikipedia.org/w/index.php?title=File:The_last_Jew_in_Vinnitsa,_1941.jpg *License:* anonymous-EU *Contributors:* DragonflySixtyseven, Yann, 8 anonymous edits ..... 260

**Figure 102** *Source:* https://en.wikipedia.org/w/index.php?title=File:Bundesarchiv_Bild_183-A0706-0018-029,_Sowjetunion,_Storow,_Juden_vor_Exekution.jpg *License:* Creative Commons Attribution-Sharealike 3.0 Germany *Contributors:* Butko, Figure19, Melanom, Mtsmallwood, PaulBommel, Sanya3, Thgoiter, Ykvach, ŠJů, Микола Василечко, 1 anonymous edits ..... 261

**Figure 103** *Source:* https://en.wikipedia.org/w/index.php?title=File:Lwow_Ghetto_(spring_1942).jpg *License:* Public Domain *Contributors:* AlikFr, Butko, Jayjg, Matalea, Ykvach, 2 anonymous edits ..... 263

**Image** *Source:* https://en.wikipedia.org/w/index.php?title=File:Reichskommissariat_Ostland_Administrative.png *License:* Creative Commons Attribution-ShareAlike 3.0 Unported *Contributors:* XrysD ..... 265

**Image** *Source:* https://en.wikipedia.org/w/index.php?title=File:WW2-Holocaust-ROstland_big_legend.PNG *License:* Creative Commons Attribution 3.0 *Contributors:* WW2-Holocaust-Europe.png: User:Dna-Dennis ..... 265

**Figure 104** *Source:* https://en.wikipedia.org/w/index.php?title=File:Map_used_to_illustrate_Stahlecker's_report_to_Heydrich_on_January_31,_1942.jpg *License:* Public Domain *Contributors:* Franz Walter Stahlecker (1900–1942) ..... 267

**Figure 105** *Source:* https://en.wikipedia.org/w/index.php?title=File:9thFort.jpg *License:* Attribution *Contributors:* Andrius.v, Creativelt, OgreBot 2, Thomas Reid ..... 268

**Figure 106** *Source:* https://en.wikipedia.org/w/index.php?title=File:Bundesarchiv_Bild_183-L19427,_Litauen,_brennende_Synagoge.jpg *License:* Creative Commons Attribution-Sharealike 3.0 Germany *Contributors:* BotMultichill, Chefallen, Dezidor, Melanom, Origamiemensch, Ras67, 2 anonymous edits ..... 269

**Figure 107** *Source:* https://en.wikipedia.org/w/index.php?title=File:Jonavos_holokausto_kapai.jpg *License:* Creative Commons Attribution-Sharealike 3.0 *Contributors:* Bearas ..... 270

**Figure 108** *Source:* https//en.wikipedia.org *License:* Creative Commons Attribution-Sharealike 2.0 *Contributors:* Adam Jones from Kelowna, BC, Canada ..... 272

**Figure 109** *Source:* https://en.wikipedia.org/w/index.php?title=File:WW2-Holocaust-ROstland_big_legend.PNG *License:* Creative Commons Attribution 3.0 *Contributors:* WW2-Holocaust-Europe.png: User:Dna-Dennis ..... 278

**Figure 110** *Source:* https://en.wikipedia.org/w/index.php?title=File:Dünaburg_Juli_1941.jpg *License:* Public Domain *Contributors:* User GregorHelms on de.wikipedia ... 278

**Figure 111** *Source:* https://en.wikipedia.org/w/index.php?title=File:LiepajaLatvia1941.jpg *License:* Creative Commons Attribution-Share Alike 3.0 Germany *Contributors:* Carl Strott ... 280

**Figure 112** *Source:* https://en.wikipedia.org/w/index.php?title=File:Bundesarchiv_Bild_101I-765-0596-24,_Lettland,_deutsche_Propagandatafel.jpg *License:* Creative Commons Attribution-Sharealike 3.0 Germany *Contributors:* ALE!, BotMultichill, Butko, Martin H., Mattes, Mtsmallwood, Ras67 ... 281

**Figure 113** *Source:* https://en.wikipedia.org/w/index.php?title=File:Bundesarchiv_Bild_183-B11441,_Libau,_Zusammengetriebene_Juden.jpg *License:* Creative Commons Attribution-Sharealike 3.0 Germany *Contributors:* BotMultichill, Innotata, Melanom ... 282

**Figure 114** *Source:* https//en.wikipedia.org *License:* Creative Commons Attribution-Sharealike 3.0 Germany *Contributors:* Bundesarchiv-B6, Diannaa, Drdoht, Gkml, Graphium, Kalnroze, Kresspahl, Krinkle, M2545, Metilsteiner, Mtsmallwood, Nemo5576, Philaweb, Uacs451, Wknight94, Wolfmann, 5 anonymous edits ... 284

**Figure 115** *Source:* https://en.wikipedia.org/w/index.php?title=File:Bundesarchiv_Bild_183-N1212-319,_Riga,_Juden_müssen_aus_dem_Fahrdamm_gehen..jpg *License:* Creative Commons Attribution-Sharealike 3.0 Germany *Contributors:* Bernd Schwabe in Hannover, BotMultichill, Infrogmation, M2545, Marrante, Melanom, Metilsteiner, Mtsmallwood, Philaweb, 1 anonymous edits ... 285

**Figure 116** *Source:* https://en.wikipedia.org/w/index.php?title=File:Bundesarchiv_Bild_183-N1212-326,_Riga,_Judenghetto.jpg *License:* Creative Commons Attribution-Sharealike 3.0 Germany *Contributors:* BotMultichill, Bundesarchiv-B6, Melanom, Mogelzahn, Raymond ... 285

**Figure 117** *Source:* https://en.wikipedia.org/w/index.php?title=File:Bundesarchiv_Bild_101III-Duerr-056-04A,_Lettland,_KZ_Salaspils,_jüdische_Häftlinge.jpg *License:* Creative Commons Attribution-Sharealike 3.0 Germany *Contributors:* BotMultichill, Melanom, Tsui, 1 anonymous edits ... 286

**Figure 118** *Source:* https://en.wikipedia.org/w/index.php?title=File:Bundesarchiv_Bild_183-B23740,_Lettland,_Freijäger_im_Einsatz_gegen_Partisanen.jpg *License:* Creative Commons Attribution-Sharealike 3.0 Germany *Contributors:* BotMultichill, Dezidor, Mtsmallwood, Ras67, 1 anonymous edits ... 286

**Image** *Source:* https://en.wikipedia.org/w/index.php?title=File:Wikisource-logo.svg *License:* Creative Commons Attribution-Sharealike 3.0 *Contributors:* ChrisiPK, Guillom, INeverCry, Jarekt, JuTa, Leyo, Lokal Profil, MichaelMaggs, NielsF, Rei-artur, Rocket000, Romaine, Steinsplitter ... 284

**Figure 119** *Source:* https://en.wikipedia.org/w/index.php?title=File:Bundesarchiv_Bild_183-R53525,_Hans_Prützmann.jpg *License:* Creative Commons Attribution-Sharealike 3.0 Germany *Contributors:* Hic et nunc, Jarekt, Jörg Zägel, Kigsz, Lupo, Mtsmallwood, Themightyquill, Wolfmann, 2 anonymous edits ... 290

**Figure 120** *Source:* https://en.wikipedia.org/w/index.php?title=File:Map_used_to_illustrate_Stahlecker's_report_to_Heydrich_on_January_31,_1942.jpg *License:* Public Domain *Contributors:* Franz Walter Stahlecker (1900–1942) ... 297

**Figure 121** *Source:* https://en.wikipedia.org/w/index.php?title=File:WW2-Holocaust-ROstland_big_legend.PNG *License:* Creative Commons Attribution 3.0 *Contributors:* WW2-Holocaust-Europe.png: User:Dna-Dennis ... 299

**Figure 122** *Source:* https://en.wikipedia.org/w/index.php?title=File:Holocaust_Memorial_in_Estonia.jpg *License:* Creative Commons Attribution 2.5 *Contributors:* Billinghurst, Cathy Richards, Christian Ganzer, Flying Saucer, MGA73bot2, Mtsmallwood, Raul6, Renessaince, 1 anonymous edits . 303

**Figure 123** *Source:* https://en.wikipedia.org/w/index.php?title=File:Kivioli_Concentration_Camp_Holocaust_Memorial.jpg *License:* Creative Commons Zero *Contributors:* User:Wilson44691 ... 304

**Figure 124** *Source:* https://en.wikipedia.org/w/index.php?title=File:Bundesarchiv_Bild_146-1972-026-43,_Minsk,_Widerstandskämpfer_vor_Hinrichtung.jpg *License:* Creative Commons Attribution-Sharealike 3.0 Germany *Contributors:* BotMultichill, Christian Ganzer, EugeneZelenko, Fastboy, Gobonobo, Kazimier Lachnovič, Leit, Lomita, Neolexx, Pessimist2006, Torsch, Zedlik, 2 anonymous edits ... 309

**Figure 125** *Source:* https://en.wikipedia.org/w/index.php?title=File:Bundesarchiv_Bild_183-B07892,_Minsk,_Juden_beim_Schneeräumen_auf_Bahnhof.jpg *License:* Creative Commons Attribution-Sharealike 3.0 Germany *Contributors:* BotMultichill, Botaurus-stellaris, Christian Ganzer, EugeneZelenko, Kazimier Lachnovič, Monopoly31121993, Vadim Akopyan, Wieralee, Zedlik ... 310

**Figure 126** *Source:* https://en.wikipedia.org/w/index.php?title=File:WW2-Holocaust-ROstland_big_legend.PNG *License:* Creative Commons Attribution 3.0 *Contributors:* WW2-Holocaust-Europe.png: User:Dna-Dennis ... 311

**Image** *Source:* https://en.wikipedia.org/w/index.php?title=File:Map_Stahlecker's_Report_1941-1943.jpg *License:* Public Domain *Contributors:* Franz Walter Stahlecker (1900–1942) / Франц Вальтер Шталекер (1900–1942) ... 312

**Image** *Source:* https://en.wikipedia.org/w/index.php?title=File:Belorussian_SSR_in_1940_after_annexation_of_eastern_Poland.jpg *License:* Public Domain *Contributors:* Soviet government ... 312

**Figure 127** *Source:* https://en.wikipedia.org/w/index.php?title=File:Bundesarchiv_Bild_121-1847,_Russland-Mitte,_Kampfgruppe_Schimana.jpg *License:* Creative Commons Attribution-Sharealike 3.0 Germany *Contributors:* BotMultichill, Fastboy, Mtsmallwood ... 315

**Figure 128** *Source:* https://en.wikipedia.org/w/index.php?title=File:Bundesarchiv_Bild_101I-280-1075-10A,_Russland,_Borislaw_Kaminski.jpg *License:* Creative Commons Attribution-Sharealike 3.0 Germany *Contributors:* Balcer~commonswiki, BotMultichill, Catsmeat, Dezidor, Hohum, K.e.coffman, Martin H., Parsecboy, Ras67, Well-Informed Optimist, 2 anonymous edits ... 316

**Figure 129** *Source:* https://en.wikipedia.org/w/index.php?title=File:Belarus-Minsk-Memorial_Pit-2.jpg *License:* Creative Commons Attribution-Share Alike *Contributors:* Hanna Zelenko ... 318

**Figure 130** *Source:* https://en.wikipedia.org/w/index.php?title=File:WW2-Holocaust-ROstland_big_legend.PNG *License:* Creative Commons Attribution 3.0 *Contributors:* WW2-Holocaust-Europe.png: User:Dna-Dennis ... 321

**Figure 131** *Source:* https://en.wikipedia.org/w/index.php?title=File:Bundesarchiv_B_145_Bild-F016206-0003,_Russland,_Deportation_von_Juden.jpg *License:* Creative Commons Attribution-Sharealike 3.0 Germany *Contributors:* Fredy.00, Mtsmallwood, Renamed user akdllvjbhlnbjfl, Thib Phil, 1 anonymous edits ... 321

**Figure 132** *Source:* https://en.wikipedia.org/w/index.php?title=File:Map_used_to_illustrate_Stahlecker's_report_to_Heydrich_on_January_31,_1942.jpg *License:* Public Domain *Contributors:* Franz Walter Stahlecker (1900–1942) ... 322

**Figure 133** *Source:* https://en.wikipedia.org/w/index.php?title=File:Soviet_Jews_participation_in_WW2.png *License:* Public Domain *Contributors:* Ashashyou, Butko, Off-shell, Wheeke, יעקב ... 324

**Figure 134** *Source:* https://en.wikipedia.org/w/index.php?title=File:Bundesarchiv_Bild_147-0483,_Berlin,_Besuch_Amin_el_Husseini.jpg *License:* Creative Commons Attribution-Sharealike 3.0 Germany *Contributors:* Balcer~commonswiki, BotMultichill, Bürgerentscheid, Common Good, FunkMonk, Kaganer, Mutter Erde, N. Wadid, Stewi101015, Takabeg, 1 anonymous edits ... 325

**Image** *Source:* https://en.wikipedia.org/w/index.php?title=File:Flag_Schutzstaffel.svg *Contributors:* - ... 329

**Image** *Source:* https://en.wikipedia.org/w/index.php?title=File:Jew_Killings_in_Ivangorod_(1942).jpg *Contributors:* - ... 329

**Figure 135** *Source:* https://en.wikipedia.org/w/index.php?title=File:Bundesarchiv_Bild_146-1968-034-19A,_Exekution_von_polnischen_Geiseln.jpg *License:* Creative Commons Attribution-Sharealike 3.0 Germany *Contributors:* Alonso de Mendoza, Bohème, BotMultichill, Carlotm, Cucumber, Dreamcatcher25, Pibwl, Silar, 4 anonymous edits ... 332

**Figure 136** *Source:* https://en.wikipedia.org/w/index.php?title=File:Otto_Rasch_at_the_Nuremberg_Trials.jpg *License:* Public Domain *Contributors:* US Army photographers on behalf of the OCCWC ... 336

**Figure 137** *Source:* https://en.wikipedia.org/w/index.php?title=File:Bundesarchiv_Bild_183-A0706-0018-030,_Ukraine,_ermordete_Familie.jpg *License:* Creative Commons Attribution-Sharealike 3.0 Germany *Contributors:* BotMultichill, Butko, Diannaa, Ds02006, GeisterPirat, Gkml, Groupsixty, Kintetsubuffalo, Mtsmallwood, Noclador, Pjacobi, Ras67, Schreiben, Silar, Thgoiter, Ykvach, Микола Василечко, 1 anonymous edits ... 338

**Figure 138** *Source:* https://en.wikipedia.org/w/index.php?title=File:Einsatzgruppen_SD_issued_and_used_dog-tag.jpg *Contributors:* User:Huddyhuddy ... 342

**Figure 139** *Source:* https://en.wikipedia.org/w/index.php?title=File:Chelmno_Gas_Van.jpg *Contributors:* - ... 344

**Figure 140** *Source:* https://en.wikipedia.org/w/index.php?title=File:Bundesarchiv_Bild_183-B0716-0005-007,_Oberstes_Gericht,_Globke-Prozess,_Beweisstück.jpg *License:* Creative Commons Attribution-Sharealike 3.0 Germany *Contributors:* BotMultichill, Jörg Zägel, Minderbinder 347

**Figure 141** *Source:* https://en.wikipedia.org/w/index.php?title=File:Bundesarchiv_Bild_183-J08517,_Otto_Ohlendorf.jpg *License:* Creative Commons Attribution-Sharealike 3.0 Germany *Contributors:* BotMultichill, Dezidor, Minderbinder, Ras67, Uaauaa ... 350

**Image** *Source:* https://en.wikipedia.org/w/index.php?title=File:Heydrich-Endlosung.jpg *License:* Public Domain *Contributors:* Reinhard Heydrich 357

**Figure 142** *Source:* https://en.wikipedia.org/w/index.php?title=File:Haus_der_Wannsee-Konferenz_02-2014.jpg *Contributors:* A.Savin ... 360

**Figure 143** *Source:* https://en.wikipedia.org/w/index.php?title=File:Himmler_note_18_december_1941.jpg *License:* Public Domain *Contributors:* Hannolans, Wolfmann ... 361

**Figure 144** *Source:* https://en.wikipedia.org/w/index.php?title=File:WW2-Holocaust-Poland.PNG *License:* Creative Commons Attribution 3.0 *Contributors:* En:User:Poeticbent (new original map) partly inspired by WW2-Holocaust-Europe.png by User:Dna-Dennis ... 366

**Figure 145** *Source:* https://en.wikipedia.org/w/index.php?title=File:Bundesarchiv_Bild_183-B06275A,_Berlin,_Reichstagssitzung,_Rede_Adolf_Hitler.jpg *License:* Creative Commons Attribution-Sharealike 3.0 Germany *Contributors:* A1B2C3D4, BotMultichill, Drdoht, Felix Stember, Henristosch, Jarekt, Jörg Zägel, Manxruler, Morio, Mtsmallwood, Neelix, 3 anonymous edits ... 373

**Image** *Source:* https://en.wikipedia.org/w/index.php?title=File:The_Black_Book_of_Polish_Jewry_(1943).jpg *License:* Public Domain *Contributors:* American Federation for Polish Jews ... 377

**Figure 146** *Source:* https://en.wikipedia.org/w/index.php?title=File:Edward_Raczynski.jpg *License:* Public Domain *Contributors:* Andros64, Fastily, Halibutt, Jarekt, Kocio, Niki K, Poeticbent, Serdelll, Someone not using his real name, 2 anonymous edits ... 386

**Figure 147** *Source:* https://en.wikipedia.org/w/index.php?title=File:2_Nota_1.jpg *Contributors:* Pernambuko ... 386

**Figure 148** *Source:* https://en.wikipedia.org/w/index.php?title=File:2_Nota_2.jpg *Contributors:* Pernambuko ... 387

**Figure 149** *Source:* https://en.wikipedia.org/w/index.php?title=File:2_Nota_3.jpg *Contributors:* Pernambuko ... 387

**Figure 150** *Source:* https://en.wikipedia.org/w/index.php?title=File:2_Nota_4.jpg *Contributors:* Pernambuko ... 387

**Figure 151** *Source:* https://en.wikipedia.org/w/index.php?title=File:2_Nota_5.jpg *Contributors:* Pernambuko ... 388

**Figure 152** *Source:* https://en.wikipedia.org/w/index.php?title=File:2_Nota_6.jpg *Contributors:* Pernambuko ... 388

**Figure 153** *Source:* https://en.wikipedia.org/w/index.php?title=File:2_Nota_8.jpg *Contributors:* Pernambuko ... 389

**Figure 154** *Source:* https://en.wikipedia.org/w/index.php?title=File:2_Nota_9.jpg *Contributors:* Pernambuko ... 390

**Figure 155** *Source:* https://en.wikipedia.org/w/index.php?title=File:2_Nota_10.jpg *Contributors:* Pernambuko ... 390

**Figure 156** *Source:* https://en.wikipedia.org/w/index.php?title=File:Witold_Pilecki_in_color.jpg *License:* Public Domain *Contributors:* Lomita, Materialscientist, Michał Sobkowski, OgreBot 2, Oldphotosincolor ... 392

**Image** *Source:* https://en.wikipedia.org/w/index.php?title=File:Wikiquote-logo.svg *License:* Public Domain *Contributors:* Rei-artur ... 395

**Figure 157** *Source:* https://en.wikipedia.org/w/index.php?title=File:VolarydeadJews.jpg *License:* Public Domain *Contributors:* US Army Signal Corps ... 398

**Figure 158** *Source:* https://en.wikipedia.org/w/index.php?title=File:Jena_Gedenktafel_Todesmarsch_Buchenwald.jpg *License:* Creative Commons Attribution 3.0 *Contributors:* Photo: Andreas Praefcke ... 401

**Figure 159** *Source:* https://en.wikipedia.org/w/index.php?title=File:Pomnik_mogila_ofiar_marszu_smierci_Wodzislaw_Slaski.JPG *License:* Creative Commons Attribution-Sharealike 3.0 *Contributors:* Piotrhojka, Swd, Zero0000, 4 anonymous edits ... 401

**Figure 160** *Source:* https://en.wikipedia.org/w/index.php?title=File:Blievenstorf_Denkmal_Todesmarsch.jpg *License:* Public Domain *Contributors:* Niteshift (talk) ... 402

**Figure 161** *Source:* https://en.wikipedia.org/w/index.php?title=File:Putlitz_Todesmarsch_Gedenktafel.jpg *License:* Creative Commons Attribution-Share Alike *Contributors:* Doris Antony, Berlin ... 402

**Figure 162** *Source:* https://en.wikipedia.org/w/index.php?title=File:Cmentarz_ofiar_nawcz.jpg *License:* Creative Commons Attribution-Sharealike 3.0 *Contributors:* User:SzymSzy ... 403

**Figure 163** *Source:* https://en.wikipedia.org/w/index.php?title=File:Chełmno_(Kulmhof)_1942_(Koło).jpg *License:* Public Domain *Contributors:* SS ... 408

**Figure 164** *Source:* https://en.wikipedia.org/w/index.php?title=File:Stroop_Report_-_Warsaw_Ghetto_Uprising_BW.jpg *License:* Public Domain *Contributors:* Beyond My Ken, Blackcat, Catrìona, Jarekt, Mtsmallwood, Paris 16, Pkbwcgs, Yann, 1 anonymous edits ... 409

**Figure 165** *Source:* https://en.wikipedia.org/w/index.php?title=File:Bydgoszcz_1939_Polish_priests_and_civilians_at_the_Old_Market.jpg *License:* Public Domain *Contributors:* Cucumber, Dd1495, Dreamcatcher25, INeverCry, Micione ... 410

**Figure 166** *Source:* https://en.wikipedia.org/w/index.php?title=File:Bundesarchiv_Bild_192-208,_KZ_Mauthausen,_Sowjetische_Kriegsgefangene.jpg *License:* Creative Commons Attribution-Sharealike 3.0 Germany *Contributors:* Auric, Bdell555, BotMultichill, Bundesarchiv-B6, Lechthaler, Monopoly31121993, Mtsmallwood, Quibik, Ruff tuff cream puff, SunOfErat, XenonX3, 4 anonymous edits ... 412

**Figure 167** *Source:* https://en.wikipedia.org/w/index.php?title=File:Bundesarchiv_R_165_Bild-244-52,_Asperg,_Deportation_von_Sinti_und_Roma.jpg *License:* Creative Commons Attribution-Sharealike 3.0 Germany *Contributors:* BotMultichill, Bundesarchiv-B6, Greenshed, Hohum, Kjetil r, Mogelzahn, Mtsmallwood, Olahus, Wikig ... 413

**Figure 168** *Source:* https://en.wikipedia.org/w/index.php?title=File:EuthanasiePropaganda.jpg *Contributors:* Ansbachdragoner, Avraham, Beyond My Ken, BotMultichill, Cenarium, DagosNavy, Davidwr, Fourdee, Green Squares, Hozro, Mtsmallwood, Narkstraws, Nikodemos, Pilatus, Quadell, Qwerty Binary, Rjensen, Ronhjones, SlimVirgin, Stefan2, Tauwasser, Túrelio, Unused0029, Xiaopo, 9 anonymous edits ... 414

**Figure 169** *Source:* https://en.wikipedia.org/w/index.php?title=File:German_nazi_rasist_propaganda.jpg *License:* Public Domain *Contributors:* Hoa binh, OgreBot 2 ... 415

**Figure 170** *Source:* https://en.wikipedia.org/w/index.php?title=File:Saint_Edith_Stein.jpg *License:* Public Domain *Contributors:* AlexanderRahm, AndreasPraefcke, Aschroet, Bennó, Ecummenic, Jianhui67, Olybrius, Pe-Jo, Shakko, Tanja5, Turris Davidica, 1 anonymous edits ... 418

**Figure 171** *Source:* https://en.wikipedia.org/w/index.php?title=File:KZ_Dachau_Todesangst-Christi-Kapelle.jpg *License:* Creative Commons Attribution-ShareAlike 3.0 Unported *Contributors:* Tafkas uploaded with Commonist ... 420

**Figure 172** *Source:* https://en.wikipedia.org/w/index.php?title=File:Fr.Maximilian_Kolbe_1939.jpg *License:* Public Domain *Contributors:* http://www.v-like-vintage.net/uploads/images/Cropped700/00130919.jpg ... 421

**Figure 173** *Source:* https://en.wikipedia.org/w/index.php?title=File:Protest-inc-w-ghetcie-warszawskim-za-murem-odcinajacym-od-swiata-kilkaset-tysiecy-0.jpg *License:* Public Domain *Contributors:* Ankry, OgreBot 2, Pernambuko, Piotrus ... 428

**Figure 174** *Source:* https://en.wikipedia.org/w/index.php?title=File:2_Nota_10.jpg *Contributors:* Pernambuko ... 429

**Figure 175** *Source:* https//en.wikipedia.org *License:* Public Domain *Contributors:* Photographer: Pfc. W. Chichersky. (Army) ... 436

**Figure 176** *Source:* https://en.wikipedia.org/w/index.php?title=File:Mein_Kampf_-_Kongreszhalle,_Nuernberg.jpg *License:* Public Domain *Contributors:* Ralf Roletschek (talk) - Infos über Fahrräder auf fahrradmonteur.de ... 438

**Figure 177** *Source:* https://en.wikipedia.org/w/index.php?title=File:Bundesarchiv_Bild_101I-680-8285A-08,_Budapest,_Festnahme_von_Juden.jpg *License:* Creative Commons Attribution-Sharealike 3.0 Germany *Contributors:* Antissimo, BotMultichill, Dezidor, Globetrotter19, Martin H., Melanom, Noclador, Pessimist2006, Ras67, 1 anonymous edits ... 450

**Image** *Source:* https://en.wikipedia.org/w/index.php?title=File:Bundesarchiv_Bild_183-S33882,_Adolf_Hitler_retouched.jpg *License:* Creative Commons Attribution-Sharealike 3.0 Germany *Contributors:* User:AlMare ... 481

**Image** *Source:* https://en.wikipedia.org/w/index.php?title=File:Bundesarchiv_Bild_183-S72707,_Heinrich_Himmler.jpg *License:* Creative Commons Attribution-Sharealike 3.0 Germany *Contributors:* A1B2C3D4, AlMare, Bossanoven, BotMultichill, ChrisiPK, DIREKTOR, Foroa, Fridolin freudenfett, GT1976, Gungir1983, Lupo, Mtsmallwood, Parsacj930, Robert Weemeyer, Uaauaa, Wieralee, Wolfmann, ثعلب شبه الجزيره, 2 anonymous edits ... 481

**Image** *Source:* https://en.wikipedia.org/w/index.php?title=File:Bundesarchiv_Bild_146-1969-054-16,_Reinhard_Heydrich.jpg *License:* Creative Commons Attribution-Sharealike 3.0 Germany *Contributors:* Appaloosa, Bossanoven, BotMultichill, Bundesarchiv-B6, Foroa, GT1976, Gkml, Hohum, Jacek Halicki, K.e.coffman, Kierzek, Notwist, Ozhistory, Radek Rassel, Ruffneck'88, Uaauaa, 1 anonymous edits ... 481

**Image** *Source:* https://en.wikipedia.org/w/index.php?title=File:Adolf_Eichmann_at_Trial1961.jpg *License:* Public Domain *Contributors:* Israel Government Press Office ... 481

**Image** *Source:* https://en.wikipedia.org/w/index.php?title=File:Hermann_Goering_-_Nuremberg2.jpg *License:* Public Domain *Contributors:* Beyond My Ken, DIREKTOR, Dove, Eintagsfliege2017, Felix Stember, Frank C. Müller, Friedolf, G.dallorto, GT1976, Jörg Zägel, O (bot), R-41～commonswiki, 1 anonymous edits ... 481

**Image** *Source:* https://en.wikipedia.org/w/index.php?title=File:Bundesarchiv_Bild_146-2007-0188,_Odilo_Globocnik.jpg *License:* Creative Commons Attribution-Sharealike 3.0 Germany *Contributors:* Blackcat, Disembodied Soul, G.dallorto, Gkml, Lechthaler, Mtsmallwood, Wolfmann ... 482

**Image** *Source:* https://en.wikipedia.org/w/index.php?title=File:Bundesarchiv_Bild_146-1974-160-13A,_Theodor_Eicke.jpg *License:* Creative Commons Attribution-Sharealike 3.0 Germany *Contributors:* Florival fr, Lazar Karoll, Macesito, Trijnstel, Uaauaa ... 482

**Image** *Source:* https://en.wikipedia.org/w/index.php?title=File:Richard_Glücks.jpg *Contributors:* Articseahorse, Bossanoven, DerBorg, K.e.coffman, OgreBot 2, Reguyla ... 482

**Image** *Source:* https://en.wikipedia.org/w/index.php?title=File:ErnstKaltenbrunner1944.jpg *Contributors:* Lt.Specht, Martin H., Sfan00 IMG ... 482

**Image** *Source:* https://en.wikipedia.org/w/index.php?title=File:Bundesarchiv_Bild_146-1968-101-20A,_Joseph_Goebbels.jpg *License:* Creative Commons Attribution-Sharealike 3.0 Germany *Contributors:* A1B2C3D4, BotMultichill, DIREKTOR, Ellin Beltz, Lupo, Ralf Roletschek, Tekstman, VanKleinen ... 482

**Image** *Source:* https://en.wikipedia.org/w/index.php?title=File:Bundesarchiv_Bild_146-1989-011-13,_Hans_Frank.jpg *License:* Creative Commons Attribution-Sharealike 3.0 Germany *Contributors:* A1B2C3D4, Andros64, BotMultichill, Jarekt ... 482

**Image** *Source:* https://en.wikipedia.org/w/index.php?title=File:Inquart_crop.jpg *License:* Public Domain *Contributors:* Foroa, Hanhil, Kilom691, MachoCarioca, Mtsmallwood, R-41～commonswiki, Soerfm, 1 anonymous edits ... 482

**Image** *Source:* https://en.wikipedia.org/w/index.php?title=File:Bundesarchiv_Bild_146-1985-054-07,_Kurt_Daluege.jpg *License:* Creative Commons Attribution-Sharealike 3.0 Germany *Contributors:* BotMultichill, Drdoht, Eugene van der Pijll, P. S. Burton ... 482

**Image** *Source:* https://en.wikipedia.org/w/index.php?title=File:Rolf_Gunther.jpg *License:* anonymous-EU *Contributors:* Bossanoven, Kigsz, Martin H., Rudolph Buch ... 483

**Image** *Source:* https://en.wikipedia.org/w/index.php?title=File:Pohl,_Oswald.JPG *License:* Public Domain *Contributors:* US Army photographers on behalf of the OUSCCPAC or its successor organisation, the OCCWC ... 483

**Image** *Source:* https://en.wikipedia.org/w/index.php?title=File:Bundesarchiv_Bild_183-E05455,_Arthur_Greiser_(2).jpg *License:* Creative Commons Attribution-Sharealike 3.0 Germany *Contributors:* Drdoht, Poeticbent, Wolfmann ... 483

**Image** *Source:* https://en.wikipedia.org/w/index.php?title=File:Bundesarchiv_Bild_183-R14128A,_Martin_Bormann.jpg *License:* Creative Commons Attribution-Sharealike 3.0 Germany *Contributors:* A1B2C3D4, DIREKTOR, Duch, Ecummenic, J.-H. Janßen, Jarekt, Lupo, Mogelzahn, Mtsmallwood, Ozhistory, TheVovaNik ... 484

**Image** *Source:* https://en.wikipedia.org/w/index.php?title=File:Bundesarchiv_Bild_146-2005-0168,_Alfred_Rosenberg.jpg *License:* Creative Commons Attribution-Sharealike 3.0 Germany *Contributors:* 1970gemini, BotMultichill, Christian Ganzer, DIREKTOR, Dezidor, Movieevery, Quibik, YMS 484

**Image** *Source:* https://en.wikipedia.org/w/index.php?title=File:Rudolf_Brandt_(SS-Mitglied).jpg *License:* Public Domain *Contributors:* USHMM, courtesy of Hedwig Wachenheimer Epstein ... 484
**Image** *Source:* https://en.wikipedia.org/w/index.php?title=File:Bundesarchiv_Bild_183-J03238,_Roland_Freisler.jpg *License:* Creative Commons Attribution-Sharealike 3.0 Germany *Contributors:* AlMare, BotMultichill, Botaurus, Common Good, Duch, Groupsixty, 2 anonymous edits ... 484
**Image** *Source:* https://en.wikipedia.org/w/index.php?title=File:Bundesarchiv_Bild_183-H30220,_Wilhelm_Keitel.jpg *License:* Creative Commons Attribution-Sharealike 3.0 Germany *Contributors:* A1B2C3D4, BotMultichill, DIREKTOR, Drdoht, Felix Stember, Foroa, GT1976, Gungir1983, K.e.coffman, Parsecboy, Uaauaa ... 484
**Image** *Source:* https://en.wikipedia.org/w/index.php?title=File:Hermann_Julius_Hoefle.jpg *Contributors:* Bossanoven, Lotje, Magog the Ogre 484
**Image** *Source:* https://en.wikipedia.org/w/index.php?title=File:Richard_Thomalla.jpg *License:* Public Domain *Contributors:* Bossanoven, DerBorg, Leyo, Mtsmallwood, Torvindus~commonswiki, 2 anonymous edits ... 485
**Image** *Source:* https://en.wikipedia.org/w/index.php?title=File:Lambert,_Erwin.jpg *Contributors:* Bossanoven, Magog the Ogre, Matanya, OgreBot 2 ... 485
**Image** *Source:* https://en.wikipedia.org/w/index.php?title=File:Wirth,_Christian.jpg *License:* Creative Commons Attribution-Sharealike 3.0,2.5,2.0,1.0 *Contributors:* User:Poeticbent, crop from upload by OTFW, Berlin ... 485
**Image** *Source:* https://en.wikipedia.org/w/index.php?title=File:Rudolf_Höß.jpg *License:* Public Domain *Contributors:* Polska Agencja Prasowa (PAP) ... 485
**Image** *Source:* https://en.wikipedia.org/w/index.php?title=File:Liebehenschel,_Arthur.jpg *Contributors:* Unknown (SS official portrait) ... 485
**Image** *Source:* https://en.wikipedia.org/w/index.php?title=File:Martin_Gottfried_Weiss.jpg *License:* Public Domain *Contributors:* Member of War Crimes Branch: Origin: Dr. Victor L. Wegard ... 485
**Image** *Source:* https://en.wikipedia.org/w/index.php?title=File:Irmfried_Eberl.jpg *Contributors:* Disembodied Soul, Jeff G., Magog the Ogre, OgreBot 2 ... 485
**Image** *Source:* https://en.wikipedia.org/w/index.php?title=File:Hans_Bothmann_(1911_-_1946).jpg *License:* Public Domain *Contributors:* Unknown (Public domain) ... 485
**Image** *Source:* https://en.wikipedia.org/w/index.php?title=File:Franz_Reichleitner.jpg *Contributors:* Bossanoven, CommonSupporter, Lotje, OgreBot 2, Svensson1, Zyperkux ... 486
**Image** *Source:* https://en.wikipedia.org/w/index.php?title=File:Amon_goeth_1946.jpg *License:* Public Domain *Contributors:* ChristophT, Diannaa, HenkvD, Jarekt, Malo, Mtsmallwood, Wiggum, 1 anonymous edits ... 486
**Image** *Source:* https://en.wikipedia.org/w/index.php?title=File:WP_Josef_Mengele_1956.jpg *License:* Public Domain *Contributors:* Anonymous photographer, not identified anywhere ... 486
**Image** *Source:* https://en.wikipedia.org/w/index.php?title=File:Karl_Hermann_Frank.jpg *License:* Creative Commons Attribution-Sharealike 3.0 Germany *Contributors:* Diannaa, Drdoht ... 486
**Image** *Source:* https://en.wikipedia.org/w/index.php?title=File:Bundesarchiv_Bild_183-1982-1021-509,_Hanns_Rauter-edit.jpg *License:* Creative Commons Attribution-Sharealike 3.0 Germany *Contributors:* Drdoht, P. S. Burton ... 486
**Image** *Source:* https://en.wikipedia.org/w/index.php?title=File:Pierre_Laval_and_Carl_Oberg_in_Paris.png *License:* Creative Commons Attribution-Share Alike 3.0 Germany *Contributors:* -revi, AnRo0002, Duch, Gorgo, Minderbinder, Para, ~Pyb ... 487
**Image** *Source:* https://en.wikipedia.org/w/index.php?title=File:Eduard_Wirths.jpg *Contributors:* Athaenara, Bossanoven, Lotje, Magog the Ogre, OgreBot 2, Paralacre ... 487
**Image** *Source:* https://en.wikipedia.org/w/index.php?title=File:Schumann,_Horst.jpg *Contributors:* Bossanoven, Uziel302 ... 487
**Image** *Source:* https://en.wikipedia.org/w/index.php?title=File:Karl_Gebhardt,_SS-Arzt.jpg *License:* Public Domain *Contributors:* Duch, Frank C. Müller, Maiplatz, Mtsmallwood, 3 anonymous edits ... 487
**Image** *Source:* https://en.wikipedia.org/w/index.php?title=File:Fritz_Klein.jpg *License:* Public Domain *Contributors:* An Errant Knight, Huntster, Jahobr, Mtsmallwood, Rocket000, Torvindus~commonswiki ... 488
**Image** *Source:* https://en.wikipedia.org/w/index.php?title=File:Bundesarchiv_Bild_146-1983-094-01,_Phillip_Bouhler.jpg *License:* Creative Commons Attribution-Sharealike 3.0 Germany *Contributors:* Drdoht, Kintetsubuffalo, Mtsmallwood, Orca2014, Tresckow, 1 anonymous edits ... 488
**Image** *Source:* https://en.wikipedia.org/w/index.php?title=File:Kramer_Josef.jpeg *License:* Public Domain *Contributors:* Silverside (Sgt) No 5 Army Film & Photographic Unit ... 488
**Image** *Source:* https://en.wikipedia.org/w/index.php?title=File:Aumeier,_Hans.jpg *Contributors:* official mug shot ... 488
**Image** *Source:* https://en.wikipedia.org/w/index.php?title=File:Franz_Hoessler.jpeg *License:* Public Domain *Contributors:* Silverside (Sgt) No 5 Army Film & Photographic Unit ... 488
**Image** *Source:* https://en.wikipedia.org/w/index.php?title=File:Karl_Fritzsch_at_Auschwitz.jpg *License:* Creative Commons Attribution-Sharealike 2.5 *Contributors:* Bossanoven, BotMultichill, Deadstar, File Upload Bot (Magnus Manske), Kintetsubuffalo, Mbdortmund, Mtsmallwood, OgreBot 2, Rudolph Buch, Väsk, Yarl ... 488
**Image** *Source:* https://en.wikipedia.org/w/index.php?title=File:Grabner,_Maximilian.jpg *Contributors:* Bossanoven ... 488
**Image** *Source:* https://en.wikipedia.org/w/index.php?title=File:Matthes,_Heinrich.jpg *Contributors:* Modern Sciences, OgreBot 2 ... 488
**Image** *Source:* https://en.wikipedia.org/w/index.php?title=File:Johann_Niemann.jpg *Contributors:* Bossanoven, Magog the Ogre, Uziel302 ... 489
**Image** *Source:* https://en.wikipedia.org/w/index.php?title=File:Hermann_Michel_2.jpg *Contributors:* Bossanoven, Magog the Ogre, Sfan00 IMG, Uziel302 ... 489
**Image** *Source:* https://en.wikipedia.org/w/index.php?title=File:Heinz_Kurt_Bolender.jpg *Contributors:* Matanya, OgreBot 2 ... 490
**Image** *Source:* https://en.wikipedia.org/w/index.php?title=File:Jürgen_Stroop.jpg *License:* Public Domain *Contributors:* An Errant Knight, Conscious, Jarekt, Jastrow, Kintetsubuffalo, Madmax32, Mahagaja, Materialscientist, Mattes, Minderbinder, Mtsmallwood, PFHLai, Pharos, Poeticbent, Quibik, Rocket000, Schimmelreiter, Sir Gawain, Túrelio, とある白い猫, 3 anonymous edits ... 490
**Image** *Source:* https://en.wikipedia.org/w/index.php?title=File:Bruno_Streckenbach.jpg *Contributors:* Bossanoven, Magog the Ogre ... 490
**Image** *Source:* https://en.wikipedia.org/w/index.php?title=File:Friedrich_Jeckeln.jpg *License:* Creative Commons Attribution-Sharealike 3.0 Germany *Contributors:* Diannaa, Drdoht, Metilsteiner, Pessimist2006 ... 490
**Image** *Source:* https://en.wikipedia.org/w/index.php?title=File:Franz_Walter_Stahlecker01.jpg *License:* Public Domain *Contributors:* unknown / неизвестно ... 490
**Image** *Source:* https://en.wikipedia.org/w/index.php?title=File:Heinz_Jost_09936.jpg *License:* Public Domain *Contributors:* Unknown U.S. signal corps photographer ... 490
**Image** *Source:* https://en.wikipedia.org/w/index.php?title=File:Eduard_Strauch.jpg *License:* Public Domain *Contributors:* Unknown U.S. signal corps photographer ... 491
**Image** *Source:* https://en.wikipedia.org/w/index.php?title=File:Bundesarchiv_Bild_101III-Alber-096-34,_Arthur_Nebe.jpg *License:* Creative Commons Attribution-Sharealike 3.0 Germany *Contributors:* ABrocke, BotMultichill, LMK3, Ras67, Ukas, 2 anonymous edits ... 491
**Image** *Source:* https://en.wikipedia.org/w/index.php?title=File:Erich_Naumann_at_the_Nuremberg_Trials.PNG *License:* Public Domain *Contributors:* US Army photographers on behalf of the OCCWC ... 491
**Image** *Source:* https://en.wikipedia.org/w/index.php?title=File:Paul-Blobel.jpg *License:* Public Domain *Contributors:* Aotake, FA2010, Minderbinder, Mtsmallwood, Revolus, Schreiben, TommyBee, Wolley~commonswiki ... 492
**Image** *Source:* https://en.wikipedia.org/w/index.php?title=File:Otto_Ohlendorf_at_the_Nuremberg_Trials.PNG *License:* Public Domain *Contributors:* US Army photographers on behalf of the OCCWC ... 492
**Image** *Source:* https://en.wikipedia.org/w/index.php?title=File:Braune_Werner.jpg *License:* Public Domain *Contributors:* US Army photographers on behalf of the OCCWC ... 492
**Image** *Source:* https://en.wikipedia.org/w/index.php?title=File:Maria_Mandel.jpg *License:* Public Domain *Contributors:* Unknown, probably an U.S. Army soldier ... 492
**Image** *Source:* https://en.wikipedia.org/w/index.php?title=File:Irma_Grese.jpg *License:* Public Domain *Contributors:* FSII, Huntster, Juiced lemon, Mtsmallwood, OgreBot 2, Stanmar, Túrelio, 1 anonymous edits ... 493

# License

Creative Commons Attribution-Share Alike 3.0
//creativecommons.org/licenses/by-sa/3.0/

# Index

Abraham Joshua Heschel, 68
Absberg, 43
Absorption, 215
A Child of Our Time, 80
Action 14f13, 48, 62, 223
Action T4, 3, 61, 95, 97, 223, 331, 371, 426, 485, 487, 488, 537
Activist, 417
Adam Daniel Rotfeld, 263
Address (geography), 298
Adelsten, 517
Ad hoc, 365
Admiral, 222
Adolf Burger, 529
Adolf Eichmann, 68, 147, 166, 372, 427, 466, 481, 539
Adolf Hitler, 26, 53, 61, 65, 218, 222, 320, 330, 331, 359, 425, 426, 481
Adrian Weale, 355
Africa, 414
African Holocaust, 243
Afrika Korps, 346, 444
Afro-Germans, 407
Aftermath of the Holocaust, **493**
Aftermath of the Soviet invasion of Poland, 457
Agder, 157
Ain-Ervin Mere, 297, 300, 302, 304
Aizsargi, 341
A Jewish boy surrenders in Warsaw, 409
A. J. P. Taylor, 426
Aktion Erntefest, 102, 368
Aktion Reinhard, 367
Aktion Reinhardt, 112
Aktion T4, **25**
Alan Bullock, 445
Alan Levy, 474
Albert Bormann, 238
Albert Einstein, 378, 379
Albert Löffler, 325
Albert Moll (German psychiatrist), 21
Albert Neisser, 21
Albert Speer, 534
Albert Widmann, 35
Alcoholism, 423

Alderney camps, 233
Aleksander Laak, 302, 304
Aleksandrów Łódzki, 124
Alexander B. Rossino, 354
Alexander Nikolaevich Yakovlev, 244, 524
Alexander Solzhenitsyn, 244, 524
Alexander von Falkenhausen, 173
Alfonsas Eidintas, 272, 273
Alfred Becu, 280
Alfred Hoche, 30, 62
Alfred Jodl, 361, 443
Alfred Rosenberg, 484
Alfrēds Dikmanis, 281
Algemeene-SS Vlaanderen, 167
Algirdas Brazauskas, 272
Algirdas Klimaitis, 269
Aliyah, 116, 136
Al-Jazeera, 550
Allach (concentration camp), 404
Allgemeine SS, 330
Allies, 391
Allies of World War II, 101, 107, 151, 162, 222, 247, 323, 360, 397, 417
Alois Brunner, 483
Alsace, 178
Alsace-Lorraine, 182
Altenburg, 400
Amalie Christie, 145
Amazon rubber boom, 250
American Federation for Polish Jews, 377
American Jewish Joint Distribution Committee, 116, 462
American Jews, 499
Americans, 247
American Zone of Occupation, 49
Amersfoort concentration camp, 233
Amiel Shomrony, 204
Amon Goeth, 486
Am Spiegelgrund, 32
Am Spiegelgrund clinic, 50
Anarchist, 407
Andreas Fleischer, 517
Andreas Hillgruber, 334, 352, 438, 472
Andreas Seierstad, 517

569

Andrew Conway Ivy, 21
Andrew Ezergailis, 293
Andrievs Ezergailis, 282
Andrija Artuković, 199
Andrychów, 134
Andrzej Krzysztof Kunert, 119
An Essay on the Inequality of the Human Races, 436
Anesthesia, 15
Anfal genocide, 202

Ángel Sanz Briz, 547

Annamaria Orla-Bukowska, 118
Anne Applebaum, 524
Anne Frank, 497
Annopol, 134
Anschluss, 66, 331, 358, 427
Ante Pavelić, 196, 199
Anthony Eden, 386, 387, 429
Anti-communist, 281
Anti-communist mass killings, 203
Anti-Defamation League, 551, 552, 554, 555
Anti-Jewish legislation in prewar Nazi Germany, 66
Anti-Jewish pogroms in the Russian Empire, 79
Anti-Jewish violence in Poland, 1944-1946, 495
Anti-partisan operation, 286
Anti-partisan operations, 315
Antisemites, 324
Anti-Semitic, 31, 66, 281
Antisemitism, 6, 64, 138, 222, 266, 323, 379, 409, 426, 437, 450, 500
Anti-Semitism, 163, 211, 282
Antisemitism (authors), 64
Anti-Zionism, 320
Anti-Zionist, 323
Anton Gill, 538
Anton Korošec, 187
Antopal, 96, 318
Antwerp, 162, 163
Apolda, 400
Appendicitis, 42
Arab nationalism, 456
Arab slave trade, 243, 248
Arajs Commando, 289, 453
Arajs Kommando, 277, 281, 341
Arbeit macht frei, 94, 243
Arbeitsdorf, 233
Arbeitseinsatz, 168
Arbeitskommandos, 228
Arbeitslager, 102, 124, 125, 228, 233
Ardennes offensive, 336
Area bombardment, 430
Argentina, 466

Aribert Heim, 14
Arlon, 173
Armenian Genocide, 4, 202
Armenian quote, 411
Armia Krajowa, 393
Armistice between Italy and Allied armed forces, 417
Armistice of 22 June 1940, 178
Arms industry, 240
Army Group Centre, 335
Army Group North, 335
Army Group South, 335
Arno J. Mayer, 354, 438
Arnold Jacoby, 159
Arnold Schoenberg, 80
Arrest, 281
Arrested, 481
Arrow Cross, 192
Arrow Cross coup, 451
Arson, 64
Arthur de Gobineau, 436
Arthur Greiser, 372, 483
Arthur Liebehenschel, 485
Arthur Nebe, 491
Arthur Seyss-Inquart, 482
Artur Hojan, 57
Arūnas Bubnys, 273
Aryan, 36, 287
Aryanization (Nazism), 166
Aryan race, 143, 407, 410, 435
Aseri, 305
Ashkenazi, 406
Ashkenazic Jews, 547
Asia, 414
Asīte, 280
Assassinated, 481
Assassination, 65
Association football, 75
Assyrian genocide, 202
Athens, 346
Atlantic slave trade, 243
Atlantic Wall, 168
Atomic bombings of Hiroshima and Nagasaki, 4
Atonality, 80
August Becker, 36, 49
Augustinas Voldemaras, 274
Augustów, 128
August von Galen, 45
Auschwitz, 16, 94–96, 108, 124–126, 128, 130–135, 183, 192, 345, 366, 372, 391, 393, 399, 430, 485–488, 492, 493, 514, 544
Auschwitz Album, 369
Auschwitz-Birkenau, 88, 98, 104, 117, 218, 365, 393, 398

Auschwitz-Birkenau State Museum, 117, 233, 522
Auschwitz concentration camp, 14, 94, 98, 134, 143, 162, 168, 176, 199, 224, 226, 228, 232, 233, 242, 359, 367, 402, 407, 408, 497
Auschwitz II, 143, 369, 391
Auschwitz II-Birkenau, 368, 485
Auschwitz Protocols, 391
Australia, 538
Australian Aboriginal League, 79
Australians, 247
Austria, 64, 66, 80, 236, 331, 498
Austria-Hungary, 435
Authoritarianism, 426
Autopsy, 19
Auvere, 305
Auxiliary police, 300
Auxiliary Police Battalions, 92
Avant-garde, 80
Axis forces, 323
Axis occupation of Vojvodina, 192
Axis powers, 187, 195, 411

Babi Yar, 260, 264, 330, 335, 362, 364, 490, 492
Bačka, 192
Background, 92
Bacterium, 18
Bad Arolsen, 494
Bad date, 158
Baden-Baden, 148
Bad Köstritz, 400
Bad Tölz, 401
Baháí Faith, 422
Balkans, 456
Ballistic trauma, 481, 482
Baltic Sea, 277, 398
Baltic states, 138, 287, 288, 299, 340, 364
Banat, 187, 192
Banderites, 113
Banja Luka, 336
Banjica concentration camp, 189, 233, 460
BAP (German band), 80
Baranavichy Voblast, 529
Baranja, 192
Baranowicze, 15
Baranów Sandomierski, 134
Barclays Bank, 433
Bardufoss concentration camp, 233, 235
Barracks, 14, 307
Basic Books, 54, 82, 475
Baton (law enforcement), 287
Battalions, 366
Battery (crime), 281
Battle of Belgium, 162, 164

Battle of Berlin, 486
Battle of Białystok–Minsk, 313
Battle of Britain, 359
Battle of El Agheila, 214
Battle of Stalingrad, 346
Battle of the Bulge, 423
Bauska, 289
Bavaria, 33
Beatification, 420
Beaune-la-Rolande internment camp, 182
Będzin Ghetto, 99, 124, 133, 515
Beer Hall Putsch, 70
Beet, 20
Beit HaMikdash, 3
Belarus, 235, 236, 287, 411
Belarusian Auxiliary Police, 97, 113, 310, 313, 364, 367
Belarusian Home Defence, 97
Belarusian partisans, 323
Belarusians, 317
Belastok Voblast, 529
Bełchatów, 128
Belgian Anti-Racism Law, 173
Belgian Army, 164
Belgian Holocaust denial law, 173
Belgians, 407
Belgium, 234, 236, 290, 408
Belgrade, 188, 189
Belz, 399
Belzec, 218, 345
Bełżec death camp, 127, 128
Belzec extermination camp, 94, 228, 408
Bełżec extermination camp, 41, 88, 100, 101, 124–136, 226, 232, 234, 365, 367, 378, 485, 486, 488, 489
Belzyce, 124
Bełżyce, 124
Bendzin Ghetto, 369
Benghazi, 207, 214
Benito Mussolini, 209, 452
Benjamin Bild, 141
Berazino, 318
Berga concentration camp, 423
Berg concentration camp, 143
Bergen-Belsen concentration camp, 4, 214, 218, 224, 226, 234, 300, 464, 488, 493
Bergen, Norway, 159
Bergier commission, 464
Berihah, 494
Berit Reisel, 153
Berlin, 95, 123, 134, 279, 287, 358
Berlin Jazz Festival, 80
Berlin-Marzahn concentration camp, 234
Berlin Sportpalast, 441
Berlin Wall, 80
Bermuda Conference, 429

Bernburg Euthanasia Centre, 32, 37, 40, 97, 234
Bernhard Lichtenberg, 420
Bessarabia, 459
Bestiality, 416
Bethel Institution, 44
Beuthen Ghetto, 99
Bezirk Bialystok, 40, 109, 123, 254, 363
Biała Podlaska, 128, 257, 399
Biała Rawska, 128
Białystok, 134, 359
Bialystok Ghetto, 130, 131
Białystok Ghetto, 96, 123, 128, 130, 362, 363
Białystok Ghetto uprising, 89, 103, 121
Białystok Voivodeship (1919–1939), 362
Bicycle, 282
Biecz, 128, 134
Bielefeld, 44
Bielski partisans, 314, 323
Bielsk Podlaski, 129
Bikernieki Memorial, 291
Biķernieku Forest, 281
Biłgoraj, 128
Biological warfare, 22
Biomedical research, 22
Biopolitics, 436, 539
Birkenau, 88, 378
Birkenau revolt, 89
Bisexual, 407
Bishop, 420
Bishop of Münster, 45
Bjarte Bruland, 153
Bjørn Westlie, 152, 153
Black Book of Communism, 524
Black Death, 435
Black Sea, 458
Black triangle (badge), 223
Blievenstorf, 402
Blockade, 439
Blockade of Germany (1939–45), 358, 359
Błonie, 124
Blood libel, 435
Bloody Sunday massacre, 92, 112
Bloomington, Indiana, 374
Blue Police, 457
BMW, 498
Bobowa, 128
Bobruisk, 318
Bochnia, 128
Bodzentyn, 124
Bogdan Musiał, 119
Bogdanovka, 234, 459
Bogusze, Bielsk County, 129
Bogusze, Warmian-Masurian Voivodeship, 132, 133
Bohemia, 408

Bolków, 116
Bolshevik, 410
Bolsheviks, 370
Bolshevism, 361
Bolzano Transit Camp, 234
Bombing of Dresden in World War II, 4
Bone, 15
Boris Kinsler, 281
Boris Smyslovsky, 325
Bor, Serbia, 234
Bosnia and Herzegovina, 194
Bosniaks, 456
Bosnian genocide, 202
Boxcar, 223
Brage Prize, 157
Branch line, 99
Brandenburg, 75
Brandenburg Euthanasia Centre, 32, 40
Branko Lustig, 204
Bransk, 129
Brazil, 290
Breakup of Yugoslavia, 193
Bredtveit prison, 143
Bredtvet concentration camp, 234
Breitenau concentration camp, 234
Bremen, 422
Bremerhaven, 435
Breslauer Bahnhof, 143
Brigadeführer, 269, 332, 333
British Army, 485
British people, 247, 323
Bronislav Kaminski, 316, 326
Bronislaw Kaminski, 325
Bronna Góra, 88, 96, 128, 135, 318
Brumovice (Opava District), 237
Bruno Jedicke, 288
Bruno Streckenbach, 332, 490
Brussels, 162, 163
Brześć Ghetto, 92, 96, 128, 378
Brześć Kujawski, 124
Brzeziny, 124
Brzozów, 124
Buchenwald, 124, 358, 399
Buchenwald concentration camp, 19, 72, 169, 217, 218, 223, 226, 229, 234, 243, 400, 423, 436, 449
Budapest, 450, 547
Budzyń, Opole Lubelskie County, 124, 134
Bukovina, 459
Bulgaria, 446, 547
Bulgarian Orthodox Church, 446
Bundesnachrichtendienst, 466
Burma Railway, 247
Burning of the synagogue, 280
Burundian genocides, 202
Business, 66

Business sector, 65
Busko Zdrój, 128
Byaroza, 96
Bychawa, 124
Byelorussian Home Defence, 89
Byelorussian Soviet Socialist Republic, 123, 309, 363
Byelorussian SSR, 114, 529

California Genocide, 202
Calorie, 255
Cambodia, 5
Cambodian genocide, 202, 247
Cambridge University Press, 59
Campaign to Suppress Counterrevolutionaries, 246
Camp de Rivesaltes, 182
Camp des Milles, 182
Canada, 27
Cancer, 495
Cand.philol., 153
Capitalist, 407
Capital punishment, 104, 426
Captain (naval), 222
Captured Hehalutz fighters photograph, 104
Carbon monoxide, 34, 62
Carbon monoxide poisoning, 367
Cargo ship, 143
Carinthian Slovene, 536
Caritas Internationalis, 44
Carl Clauberg, 19, 487
Carl Fredriksens Transport, 147
Carl Oberg, 487
Carl Schneider, 36, 50
Casablanca, 461
Case Anton, 183
Castration, 416
Category:Antisemitism, 64
Category:Genocide, 201, 203
Category:Holocaust trials, 434
Category:Jewish Polish history, 110
Category:Nazism, 13
Category:The Holocaust, 61, 120, 137, 209, 308, 369, 405, 425, 493
Catholic, 163
Catholic Church, 187
Catholicism, 419, 435
Catholic Party (Belgium), 163
Catholic resistance to Nazi Germany, 419
Catholic University of Leuven (1834–1968), 171
Caucasus, 259
Cemetery, 261
Center of Contemporary Jewish Documentation, 323
Central African genocide, 202

Central Committee of Polish Jews, 116, 136
Central Europe, 397, 410
Central Labour Camp in Potulice, 229
Central Labour Camp Jaworzno, 229
Centre for Equal Opportunities and Opposition to Racism, 173
Centre for Historical Research and Documentation on War and Contemporary Society, 173
Cerebral palsy, 32
Chaim Weizmann, 8, 66, 498
Chancellor of Germany, 65, 481
Channel Islands, 446
Charitable Ambulance, 38
Charleroi, 162, 163
Charles Darwin, 426
Charles de Gaulle, 184, 449
Chavusy, 318
Chechersk, 313
Chęciny, 124
Chełm, 40, 128, 399
Chełmno, 372
Chelmno concentration camp, 408
Chełmno death camp, 97, 124, 126
Chełmno extermination camp, 228, 485, 486
Chełmno extermination camp, 41, 88, 93, 97, 124–131, 133–135, 218, 234, 344, 365, 367
Chełmno nad Nerem, 118
Chełmno Trials, 98
Chemical burn, 17
Chernihiv, 364
Chief of Police, 220
China, 75
Chmielnik, 128, 135
Chodel, 128
Choroszcz, 40
Christian cross, 422
Christian Gerlach, 373, 375, 451, 471
Christianity, 419, 426, 497
Christian Wirth, 37, 485
Christofascism, 164
Christoph Diehm, 325
Christopher Browning, 118, 191, 229, 257, 293, 335, 351, 358, 371, 375, 438
Chronological items, 27, 193
Chrzanów, 128
Church of Norway, 152
CIA, 466
Ciechanów, 99, 124
Ciechanowiec, 128
Ciepielów, Masovian Voivodeship, 128
Cieszyn Silesia, 333
Circassian genocide, 202
Cissi Klein, 155
CITEREFAbrahamsen1991, 151, 156, 517

CITEREFAdams1990, 505
CITEREFAderet2010, 548
CITEREFAlexy1993, 547, 548
CITEREFAlyChroust1994, 508
CITEREFAnnasGrodin1992, 507
CITEREFArad1987, 534
CITEREFArendt1973, 541
CITEREFArendt1994, 549
CITEREFAriel2013, 520
CITEREFAscher2012, 542
CITEREFBaader2009, 506
CITEREFBartov1999, 541
CITEREFBartov2000, 542
CITEREFBascomb2009, 549
CITEREFBauer1982, 544, 546–548
CITEREFBauer2002, 541, 550
CITEREFBBC News, Croatian Holocaust, 543
CITEREFBBC News, Nazi crimes taint Liechtenstein, 545
CITEREFBeer2015, 507
CITEREFBenz2007, 541, 542
CITEREFBerenbaum2005, 536
CITEREFBerenbaum2006, 526
CITEREFBerenbaumPeck2002, 508
CITEREFBergen1996, 541
CITEREFBergen2009, 541, 546–548
CITEREFBessel2003, 541
CITEREFBessel2006, 541, 543
CITEREFBialas2013, 541
CITEREFBialasFritze2014, 505
CITEREFBlack2016, 545–548
CITEREFBlass1998, 541
CITEREFBleuler1924, 506
CITEREFBloxham2009, 545, 547, 548
CITEREFBlumenkranz1972, 518
CITEREFBreggin1993, 506
CITEREFBreitman1992, 542
CITEREFBreitman2001, 540
CITEREFBrowning1992, 542
CITEREFBrowning1998, 530, 531, 534
CITEREFBrowning2004, 521, 533, 534, 542
CITEREFBrowning2005, 505–507
CITEREFBrowning2007, 525, 526
CITEREFBrowningMatthäus2004, 530, 531
CITEREFBruland2011, 546
CITEREFBubnys2004, 545
CITEREFBullock1993, 543
CITEREFBurleigh1995, 505
CITEREFBurleigh2000, 507, 542
CITEREFBurleigh2008, 505, 507, 508
CITEREFBurleighWippermann1991, 540, 541
CITEREFBurleighWippermann2014, 505
CITEREFButtlar2003, 508
CITEREFByford2011, 519
CITEREFCaron2007, 532, 543
CITEREFCesarani2004, 550

CITEREFCesarani2005, 533
CITEREFCesarani2016, 534, 543–548
CITEREFCinaPerper2012, 506
CITEREFCockburn1999, 549
CITEREFConfino2011, 539
CITEREFConfino2014, 542
CITEREFConze, Frei et al.2010, 531
CITEREFCooper1979, 543
CITEREFCraig1973, 532
CITEREFCrowe2007, 531
CITEREFDamsStolle2012, 531
CITEREFDawidowicz1975, 541, 542, 544–547
CITEREFDawidowicz1981, 550
CITEREFDawidowiczAltshuler1978, 542
CITEREFDmitrówSzarotaMachcewicz2004, 546
CITEREFDulić2005, 543
CITEREFDutton2007, 541
CITEREFDworkvan Pelt2002, 544–548
CITEREFDW Staff, Nazi Camp Labor Used in Liechtenstein, 545
CITEREFEdeiken2000, 530
CITEREFEinsatzgruppen judgment, 530
CITEREFEncyclopædia Britannica, 530
CITEREFEngstromWeberBurgmair2006, 506
CITEREFEricksen2012, 507
CITEREFEvans2002, 550
CITEREFEvans2003, 521
CITEREFEvans2004, 506
CITEREFEvans2005, 506, 521
CITEREFEvans2008, 521, 530–532
CITEREFEvans2009, 505, 507, 508
CITEREFEvans2010, 541, 543, 544, 547, 549
CITEREFEvans2015, 542
CITEREFFeig1981, 541
CITEREFFischbach2008, 520
CITEREFFischer2002, 541
CITEREFFleischhauer2011, 542
CITEREFFleming1994, 542
CITEREFFleming2014, 540
CITEREFFriedlander1995, 506, 507, 540
CITEREFFriedlander1997, 508
CITEREFFriedländer2007, 543
CITEREFFriedman2011, 506
CITEREFFritzsche2008, 542
CITEREFFromjimovics2011, 544, 545
CITEREFGaunt2011, 545
CITEREFGellately2001, 540
CITEREFGerlach2000, 540
CITEREFGerlach2016, 545, 546, 548
CITEREFGerwarth2011, 530
CITEREFGilbert1985, 542–545, 548
CITEREFGilbert1986, 550
CITEREFGoldberg, 520
CITEREFGordon1984, 541

CITEREFGriech-Polelle2002, 508
CITEREFHaberer2001, 531, 532
CITEREFHancock2004, 536
CITEREFHansenKing2013, 505
CITEREFHayes2017, 541
CITEREFHeadland1992, 531
CITEREFHeer2000, 543
CITEREFHiioMaripuuPaavle2006, 544
CITEREFHilberg1985, 531–534, 542, 544–548
CITEREFHilberg1992, 541, 542, 546, 548
CITEREFHilberg1996, 550
CITEREFHilberg2003, 508
CITEREFHildebrand1984, 542
CITEREFHillgruber1989, 530–532, 540
CITEREFHitler, 506
CITEREFHochschild1999, 523
CITEREFHoffmann1977, 540
CITEREFHöhneZolling1972, 549
CITEREFHojanMunro2013, 507
CITEREFHojanMunro2015, 505
CITEREFIngrao2013, 532, 540
CITEREFJacoby2003, 539
CITEREFJaroszewski1993, 507
CITEREFJewish Heritage Europe (2016) Serbia, 547
CITEREFJohnson1988, 542
CITEREFJohnsonReuband2005, 540
CITEREFJones2006, 541
CITEREFJoniec2016, 507
CITEREFJoseph2004, 506
CITEREFJTA—Jewish Telegraph Agency1999, 541
CITEREFJudt2005, 540, 541
CITEREFKaelber2015, 506
CITEREFKaesJayDimendberg1995, 542
CITEREFKellner2017, 541
CITEREFKershaw2000, 506–508, 538
CITEREFKershaw2005, 542
CITEREFKershaw2008, 521, 533, 541, 542
CITEREFKlee1983, 507
CITEREFKlee1985, 507
CITEREFKleeDressenRiess1991, 532
CITEREFKoehl2004, 543
CITEREFKönigZeugin2002, 548
CITEREFKoonz2005, 540
CITEREFKrausnick1968, 542
CITEREFKrumenacker2006, 532, 543
CITEREFLangbehnSalama2011, 541
CITEREFLangerbein2003, 530
CITEREFLaqueurBaumel2001, 534, 540, 543–546, 548
CITEREFLarsen2008, 531
CITEREFLemkin2005, 540
CITEREFLEO Dictionary, 530
CITEREFLevy2003, 547
CITEREFLevy2006, 549
CITEREFLifton1986, 505–508, 540
CITEREFLifton2000, 505
CITEREFLocal2014, 506
CITEREFLongerich2006, 540
CITEREFLongerich2010, 505, 530–534, 543–548
CITEREFLongerich2012, 530–533, 542, 550
CITEREFLubotina2015, 544
CITEREFLuther1971, 541
CITEREFMacDonald2002, 519
CITEREFMacLean1999, 531
CITEREFMallmannCüppers2006, 531, 543
CITEREFMallmannCüppersSmith2010, 531, 532
CITEREFManvellFraenkel2011, 542
CITEREFMarrus1987, 542
CITEREFMarrus1989, 540
CITEREFMarrus2000, 532
CITEREFMayer1988, 532
CITEREFMazower2001, 544
CITEREFMcDonough2008, 542
CITEREFMcNab2009, 521
CITEREFMcWhorter2017, 541
CITEREFMendelsohn1986, 156, 517
CITEREFMiller2006, 506, 542
CITEREFMillo, ed. Teaching about the Shoah, 548
CITEREFMojzes2009, 519
CITEREFMojzes2011, 519
CITEREFMosse1980, 539, 544
CITEREFMotadel2014, 546
CITEREFMuseum of Tolerance, 531
CITEREFNARA1980, 508
CITEREFNEP2017, 507
CITEREFNiewykNicosia2000, 533, 541–548
CITEREFNS-Archiv2017, 542
CITEREFNuremberg Trial, Vol. 20, Day 194, 530
CITEREFONeil2005, 540
CITEREFPadfield1990, 506, 507
CITEREFPaldiel2007, 547
CITEREFPavlowitch2008, 519
CITEREFPerry2012, 543
CITEREFPetropoulosRoth2005, 542
CITEREFPhayer2000, 519, 550
CITEREFPhilippe1979, 518
CITEREFPiotrowski1998, 546
CITEREFPrice2005, 544
CITEREFProctor1988, 505, 506, 540
CITEREFRabitz2011, 532
CITEREFRamet2005, 519
CITEREFRead2004, 506
CITEREFRees1997, 530–532
CITEREFRees2005, 543
CITEREFRees2017, 541, 542, 545, 547

CITEREFReitan2005, 516
CITEREFRentonSeddonZeilig2007, 523
CITEREFRhodes2002, 530–533
CITEREFRingelblum1992, 546
CITEREFRingelblum2013, 507
CITEREFRobertson, 531
CITEREFRoseman2002, 533
CITEREFRossino2003, 530
CITEREFRoumani2009, 520
CITEREFRozettSpector2009, 543–549
CITEREFRyanSchuchman2002, 505
CITEREFSandner1999, 505
CITEREFSchmidt2007, 506
CITEREFSchmitt1965, 506
CITEREFSchmuhl1987, 507
CITEREFSchuman2004, 543
CITEREFSegev2010, 533
CITEREFSemków2006, 506, 507
CITEREFSereny1983, 505–507
CITEREFShapiro2003, 540
CITEREFShelach1989, 531
CITEREFShirer1960, 506, 532
CITEREFSivathambu2003, 547
CITEREFSmelserDavies2008, 532
CITEREFSnyder2010, 521, 547
CITEREFSnyder2015, 543, 545, 546
CITEREFSpiegel Staff, The Dark Continent (20 May 2009), 543
CITEREFStackelberg2007, 542
CITEREFStargardt2015, 540
CITEREFStein1984, 546
CITEREFSteinacher2011, 549
CITEREFStengers1969, 523
CITEREFStone2010, 543
CITEREFStreim1989, 530, 532
CITEREFTaylor1949, 508
CITEREFTec1986, 546
CITEREFThacker2010, 542
CITEREFThomas1987, 530
CITEREFTorreyYolken2010, 506
CITEREFTottenParsons2009, 508
CITEREFTraverso2003, 539
CITEREFUlstein2006, 156, 517
CITEREFUnited States Holocaust Memorial Museum1996, 547
CITEREFUrban2001, 531
CITEREFU.S. Dept. of State, Religious Freedom Report for 2012, 545
CITEREFUSHMM, Budapest, 545
CITEREFUSHMM, Bulgaria, 543
CITEREFUSHMM, Escape from German-Occupied Europe, 548
CITEREFUSHMM, Lithuania, 545
CITEREFUSHMM, Romania: Facing Its Past, 547

CITEREFUSHMM, The Holocaust in Slovakia, 547
CITEREFUSHMM, Voyage of the St. Louis, 549
CITEREFVan Doorslaer2007, 543
CITEREFVan Reybrouck2014, 523
CITEREFVansina2010, 523
CITEREFVanthemsche2012, 523, 524
CITEREFVromen2008, 543
CITEREFWachsmann2015, 521, 541
CITEREFWaite1993, 541
CITEREFWaller2007, 541
CITEREFWallmann1987, 541
CITEREFWeale2012, 521, 530, 531
CITEREFWeikart2006, 539
CITEREFWeindling2006, 506
CITEREFWelch2001, 542
CITEREFWette2007, 530, 532, 542, 543
CITEREFWistrich2001, 540, 542
CITEREFWNSP State Hospital2013, 507
CITEREFYad Vashem, Names of Righteous by Country, 546
CITEREFYahil1990, 518, 542–544, 547, 548
CITEREFYahil1991, 534
CITEREFZentnerBedürftig1991, 541
CITEREFZuccotti1999, 550
Civilian, 229
Civil war (1943–1945), 417
Claims Conference, 498
Clemens August Graf von Galen, 26
Clergy, 418
Clostridium perfringens, 18
Clostridium tetani, 18
Club foot, 506

Ćmielów, 129

Coagulate, 20
Coal mining, 224
Code name, 357
Coerced sterilisation, 27
Coin, 282
Cold War, 202
Collaboration during World War II, 108
Collaborationist, 280, 425
Collaborationist auxiliary police, 92, 96
Collaboration with the Axis Powers during World War II, 256
Cologne, 81
Colognian dialect, 81
Colon cancer, 495
Colonialism, 243, 436
Colonial war, 426
Columbia Encyclopedia, 5
Columbia University, 550
Columbia University Press, 501, 502

Comintern, 337
Comité de Défense des Juifs, 162, 170
Command post, 317
Commissar, 337
Commissar Order, 417
Committee of Secretary-Generals, 162
Commons:Category:Action T4, 60
Commons:Category:Einsatzgruppen, 356
Commons:Category:Germany concentration camps, 238
Commons:Category:Kristallnacht, 86
Commons:Category:Nazi concentration camps, 231
Commons:Category:The Holocaust in Belgium, 175
Commons:Category:The Holocaust in Croatia, 207
Commons:Category:The Holocaust in France, 186
Commons:Category:The Holocaust in Latvia, 296
Commons:Category:The Holocaust in Luxembourg, 177
Commons:Category:The Holocaust in Romania, 458
Commons:Category:The Holocaust in Serbia, 194
Communism, 170, 222, 239, 417
Communist, 407
Communist party, 406
Communist Party of Byelorussia, 319
Communist Party of the Soviet Union, 337
Compact Oxford English Dictionary of Current English, 5
Component reports, 391
Compulsory sterilisation, 27
Compulsory sterilization, 19, 406, 413
Concentration camp, 38, 72, 178, 219, 257, 298, 407
Concentration camps, 218, 241
Concentration camps in France, 169
Concentration Camps Inspectorate, 218
Concentration camps in the Independent State of Croatia, 195
Confessing Church, 41, 422
Confiscate, 298
Confiscation, 282
Congo Free State, 243
Conjoined twins, 14
Conscientious objector, 239
Conscription, 423
Conspiracy theory, 500
Constantin Heldmann, 325
Constantin Karadja, 459
Constantinople, 378
Constitution of Belarus, 319

Contemporary European History, 307, 528
Convoy, 283
Córdoba, Veracruz, 250
Corneliu Zelea Codreanu, 458
Cornell University Press, 502
Coronation and anti-Jewish violence, 3
Country neutrality (international relations), 409
Courland, 281
Courts-martial, 221
Crawler excavator, 367
Crematorium, 103
Crime, 218, 423
Crimea, 259
Crimean Tatars, 326
Crimes against humanity, 48, 248, 330, 349, 397, 465, 466
Criminology, 157
Croatia, 194, 444, 447
Croatian Righteous among the Nations, 204, 543
Crowd psychology, 436
Crveni Krst concentration camp, 234
Cuba, 219
Cultural genocide, 201
Curt von Gottberg, 315, 316
Curzon Line, 116
Cyanide poisoning, 481, 482, 488
Cynicism (contemporary), 243
Cyrenaica, 207, 211, 215
Czech lands, 419
Czechoslovak government-in-exile, 347
Czechoslovakia, 302
Czechoslovakian Jews, 300
Czech Republic, 237
Czechs, 71
Czeladź, 128
Czesław Madajczyk, 114
Częstochowa Ghetto, 96, 129
Częstochowa Ghetto Uprising, 89
Czortków, 134

Dąbie, Greater Poland Voivodeship, 129
Dąbrowa Górnicza, 99, 124
Dąbrowa Tarnowska, 134
Dachau, 214, 407
Dachau concentration camp, 16, 72, 218–220, 225, 226, 229, 234, 242, 358, 400, 404, 417, 485
Dagens Næringsliv, 153
Dagsavisen, 155
Daily Telegraph, 428
Danes, 150
Daniel Brook, 526
Daniel Goldhagen, 404, 426, 437
Daniel Romanovsky, 319
Danish resistance movement, 409

Danube-Black Sea Canal, 249
Danube River, 451
Danube Swabian, 192
Darfur genocide, 202
Darmstadt, 422
Das Erbe, 31
Das Schwarze Korps, 80
Daugavpils, 279
Daugavpils Ghetto, 288
David Bergelson, 324
David Cesarani, 360, 372, 375
David Engel (historian), 114, 119
David Hofstein, 324
David Irving, 440
David J. Landau, 113
David Kilgour, 248, 525
David Matas, 248, 525
Davyd-Haradok, 318
De:Aktion T4, 507
Death camp, 37, 88, 94, 137, 257
Death camps, 121, 184, 381
Death certificate, 298
Death factory, 94
Death march, 232, 249
Death marches (Holocaust), **397**, 411, 451
Death penalty, 408
Death sentence, 417
Death squad, 330, 335
Dębica, 133, 134
Dęblin, 124
De:Blutsonntag von Stanislau, 365
Deborah Lipstadt, 551–554
Declaration by United Nations, 386
De:Datei:BindingHoche FreigabeCover-Aufl22.jpg, 509
De:Eduard Strauch, 527
De:Friedrich Mennecke, 50
De:Fritz Cropp, 50
Degesch, 101
De:Herbert Fischer (Polizeibeamter), 333
De:Herbert Linden, 50
Dehomag, 96
Dehydration, 223
De jure, 184
Delvidek, 187
D. Elyashev, 287
Democide, 201, 246, 249
Democracy, 239
Democratic Party of Serbia, 193
Democratic Republic of the Congo, 243
Denazification, 49, 289, 541
Denmark, 27
Den Midlertidige Kirkeledelse, 517
Denunciation, 108
Deportation of the Chechens and Ingush, 202
Deportation of the Crimean Tatars, 202

Der Spiegel, 550
Detention facility, 221
Deutsche Bank, 498
Deutsche Welle, 354
Deutschland Über Alles, 80
Developmental disability, 407
Development of resistance, 121
Devisenschutzkommando, 168
Diana Budisavljević, 204
Diarmaid MacCulloch, 78, 511
Dieter Pohl, 262
Dieter Pohl (historian), 262
Digital object identifier, 394
Dimitrije Ljotić, 187, 191
Dina Porat, 273, 364
Disability, 14
Disabled people, 218
Discrimination, 412
Disease, 240
Disfigurement, 14
Displaced persons camp, 494
Dissident, 407
Dissolution of the Soviet Union, 314
Distrikt Galizien, 366
Dnepropetrovsk, 343
Dnipropetrovsk, 364
Dobre, Masovian Voivodeship, 129
Dobrush, 313
Doctors Trial, 14, 21
Domanevka, 459
Donald Niewyk, 110
Donald Tusk, 515
Donbass, 248
Doubleday (publisher), 524
Dovid Katz, 275
Down syndrome, 32
DP camp, 116
Drancy internment camp, 182, 234, 483, 544
Dresden, 48
Dreyfus Affair, 448
Dr. Hilda Wernicke, 47
Drohiczyn, 119, 129
Drohobycz Ghetto, 134, 379
Drug addiction, 423
Drzewica, 129
Dubienka, 129
Dubno, Podlaskie Voivodeship, 134
Durbe, 280
Duress, 498
Dušan Simović, 195
Düsseldorf, 39
Dutch language, 163
Dutch people, 247, 407
Dvigatel, 306
Dwight D. Eisenhower, 225
Dysentery, 256

Działdowo, 40, 126
Działoszyce, 124
Dzungar genocide, 202
Dzyatlava massacre, 318

Eastern Bloc, 116, 136
Eastern Europe, 163, 255, 323, 397, 410, 481
Eastern Front of World War II, 346
Eastern Front (World War II), 16, 91, 371, 397, 411
East Germany, 229, 249
East Prussia, 35, 269, 397, 491
East Timorese genocide, 202
Ebensee, 323
Ebensee concentration camp, 218, 226
EBook, 538
Economy of Nazi Germany, 268
Edgar Faure, 323
Edith Stein, 418, 420
Edmond Paris, 206
Eduard Strauch, 290, 491
Eduard Wagner, 334
Eduard Wirths, 14, 487
Edward Bernard Raczyński, 385
Edward Kopówka, 119, 512
Edward Said, 555
Edwin Fuller Torrey, 57
Eesti Vabadusliit, 303
Effects of genocide on youth, 203
Efraim Karsh, 555
Efraim Zuroff, 272
EG B. Einsatzkommando 9, 112
Eggert Reeder, 173
Eichmann, 367
Eichmann in Jerusalem, 466
Einar Molland, 517
Einsatzgruppe, 88, 267, 280, 283
Einsatzgruppe A, 296, 297, 305, 322, 448
Einsatzgruppe B, 109
Einsatzgruppe C, 259
Einsatzgruppe D, 259, 260
Einsatzgruppe Dirlewanger, 317
Einsatzgruppe Egypt, 346
Einsatzgruppen, 89, 92, 258, 259, 263, 265, 267, 277, 279, 312, 313, 320, 323, 325, **329**, 358, 359, 361, 411, 427, 433, 457, 490
Einsatzgruppen reports, 93, 309, 338, 360, 362, 364
Einsatzgruppen Trial, 259, 290, 321, 330, 349
Einsatzkommando, 34, 128, 263, 279, 297, 325, 331, 490–492
Einsatzkommando 1b, 283
Einsatzkommando Tilsit, 337
Eisenach, 74
Eisenberg, Thuringia, 400

Eivind Berggrav, 517
Ejection seat, 20
Eleanor Roosevelt, 85, 378, 379
Elections to the Peoples Assemblies of Western Ukraine and Western Belarus, 90, 123, 309
Elie Weisel, 497
Elie Wiesel, 399, 459, 497
Eli Fure, 153
Elisabeth of Bavaria, Queen of Belgium, 168
Ellamaa, 306
Emanuel Ringelblum, 91
Emanuel Schäfer, 191, 332, 336
Emil Kraepelin, 28
Emmanuel Macron, 185
Empire of Japan, 247
Enabling Act of 1933, 65, 417
Encephalitis, 36
Encyclopædia Britannica, 5, 422, 537
Encyclopedia of Camps and Ghettos, 1933–1945, 225, 237, 516
En:Digital object identifier, 52, 53, 56, 57, 60, 251, 352, 375
Endnote anone, 265
Endnote bnone, 265
Endnote cnone, 268
Endnote dnone, 271
End of World War II in Europe, 97
En:International Standard Serial Number, 56, 57, 60
En:JSTOR, 186, 251, 355
En:OCLC, 52, 55, 58, 59, 120, 185, 352
En:PubMed Central, 57
Enzo Traverso, 426, 539
Epidemic typhus, 102
Epilepsy, 27
Ereda, 305
Erfurt, 94
Erhard Grauel, 283
Erich Bauer, 489
Erich Ehrlinger, 279, 283, 491
Erich Hoepner, 349, 443
Erich Koch, 35, 50, 258
Erich Naumann, 333, 491
Erich von dem Bach-Zelewski, 316
Erich von Manstein, 348, 443
Ernst Damzog, 333
Ernst Illing, 50
Ernst Kaltenbrunner, 330, 335, 442, 482
Ernst Klee, 353
Ernst-Robert Grawitz, 36, 50
Ernst vom Rath, 65, 68, 69
Ervin Viks, 302, 304
Erwin Lambert, 50, 485
Erwin Rommel, 346, 444
Erzgebirge, 249

Esperanto, 423
Essu, 306
Estate (law), 154
Esther Gitman, 204
Estonia, 235, 237, 297, 340, 409, 447
Estonian Auxiliary Police, 301, 305
Estonian Jews, 296, 303
Estonian Legion, 301
Estonians, 296
Estonian Self-Administration, 302
Estonian Soviet Socialist Republic, 302
Estonian SSR, 301
Estonian war crimes trials, 1961, 302
Ethnic cleansing, 110, 201
Ethnic group, 406
Ethnic hatred, 544
Ethnic persecution, 426
Ethnic relations, 201
Ethnocide, 201
Ethnoreligious group, 409
Et:Pankjavitsa, 305
Ettore Bastico, 211
Eugen Bleuler, 28
Eugenia Gurin-Loov, 528
Eugenics, 225, 413, 426
Eugenic sterilization, 28
EUMC Working Definition of Antisemitism, 554
Euphemism, 221, 279, 358
Eurasburg, 400
Europe, 9, 79, 207
European colonization of the Americas, 202
European Monitoring Centre on Racism and Xenophobia, 554
Europeans, 415
Eurozine, 526
Euthanasia, 28, 406
Evangelicalism, 263
Evangelical Lutheran Church in Thuringia, 78
Evangelical-Lutheran Church in Württemberg, 44
Evgenia Goorin-Loov, 303

Évian Conference, 66, 178


Executor, 280
Expropriation, 180
Expulsion of Poles by Nazi Germany, 121, 254
Extermination camp, 39, 88, 94, 203, 218, 221, 222, 228, 231–233, 256, 257, 345, 358, 359, 367, 408, 500
Extermination camps, 62, 121, 253, 378, 481
Extermination of Soviet prisoners of war by Nazi Germany, 3
Extermination through labor, 345
Extermination through labour, 232, **238**

External links, 495
Extraordinary State Commission, 319, 412

Falk Pingel, 238
Fall of France, 358
Fall of the Fascist regime in Italy, 183
False premise, 553
Falstad Center, 156
Falstad concentration camp, 141, 157, 234
Falun Gong, 248
Famine, 322
Fannrem concentration camp, 235
Fasanenstrasse Synagogue, 64
Fascist, 164, 270
Fehrbelliner Platz (Berlin U-Bahn), 326
Feldmann case, 149
Felix Nussbaum, 169
Field marshal, 333
File:StLouisHavana.jpg, 358
File:The Mass Extermination of Jews in German Occupied.pdf, 540
File:Walter Rauff (1945).jpg, 487
Final Solution, 5, 6, 37, 65, 80, 88–90, 93, 95, 121, 123, 162, 202, 239, 258, 271, 330, 345, **357**, 378, 383, 407, 461, 462, 496
Final solution to the Jewish question, 47, 427
Fire sale, 498
Firing squad, 486
First Battle of El Alamein, 346, 444
First World War, 4
Fischer Taschenbuch Verlag, 54
Flag of Europe, 173
Flak, 317
Flemish Brabant, 171
Flemish National Union, 164
Florencio Durán, 80
Flossenbürg concentration camp, 218, 234, 358, 400
Food ration, 282
Forced labor, 406
Forced labor in Nazi Germany, 268
Forced labor of Germans in the Soviet Union, 248
Forced labor of Hungarians in the Soviet Union, 249
Forced labour, 238, 247
Forced labour under German rule during World War II, 91, 99, 121, 232, 314, 319, 498
Forced sterilization, 19
Foreign Office (Germany), 172
Foreign Sovereign Immunities Act, 498
Forget-me-not, 422
Form letter, 113
Fort Breendonk, 169, 172, 234
Fort de Romainville, 235
Fortress of Ulm, 236

580

Fort VII, 34, 35, 46, 235
Fossoli di Carpi, 235
France, 151, 178, 234–236, 409, 417
Franciscan, 421
Franciscan Sisters of the Family of Mary, 114
Francisco Franco, 461
Francisco Gómez-Jordana, 461
Francis Nicosia, 110
Franciszek Piper, 119
Franciszek Ząbecki, 100
François Englert, 173
François Furet, 514
François Hollande, 184
François Mitterrand, 184
Franconia, 43
Fr:André Baur, 182
Frank Dikötter, 246
Frankel, 461
Frankfurt, 48
Franklin D. Roosevelt, 379
Franklin Roosevelt, 427
František Chvalkovský, 441
Franz Abromeit, 199
Franz Gürtner, 42
Franz Halder, 334
Franz Henningfeld, 325
Franz Hössler, 488
Franz Novak, 483
Franz Reichleitner, 486
Franz Schwede, 50
Franz Schwede-Coburg, 35
Franz Six, 422
Franz Stangl, 39, 486
Franz Walter Stahlecker, 269, 277, 295, 312, 338, 363, 490
Franz Xaver Schwarz, 66
Fr:Commissariat Général aux Questions juives, 182
Frederick Winslow Taylor, 426
Frederic Rzewski, 81
Frederik Pohl, 22
Fredric Wertham, 60
Free City of Danzig, 64
Freedom Square, Tallinn, 298
Free French Forces, 449
Freemasonry, 422, 462
Freemasons, 407
Free State of Saxony, 37
Freezing, 16
Freikorps, 331
Freiwilligen-Stamm-Regiment 3, 326
Freiwilligen-Stamm-Regiment 4, 326
Freiwillige SS reg. Warager, 326
French Algeria, 179, 184
French language, 163
French people, 407

French Republic, 184
French Resistance, 449
French State, 179
French Third Republic, 448
Fr:Gare de Bobigny, 184
Frieda S. Miller, 85
Friedrich Franz Bauer, 31
Friedrich Jahnke, 290
Friedrich Jeckeln, 258, 261, 277, 288, 291, 295, 339, 362, 490
Friedrich Kellner, 433
Friedrich Kurg, 304
Friedrich Panzinger, 490
Friedrich von Bodelschwingh, 44
Friedrich-Wilhelm Krüger, 490
Fritz Dietrich (Nazi official), 288
Fritz Klein, 488
Fritz Lusting, 145
Fritz Sauckel, 442
Front de lIndépendance, 171
Frontline (U.S. TV series), 231
Fr:René-Raoul Lambert, 182
Frysztak, 134
Führer, 75, 364, 481
Fulda, 44
Functionalism versus intentionalism, 370, 425
Furniture, 282

Gąbin, 124
Gabriel González Videla, 80
Gabriel Skagestad, 517
Galaxy Science Fiction, 22
Gallaudet University Press, 55
Gamma radiation, 19
Gargždai, 362
Gary Lucas, 80
Gas chamber, 35, 62, 218, 331, 359, 391, 414, 500
Gas chambers, 98
Gas gangrene, 18
Gas van, 98, 190, 332, 344
Gas vans, 367
Gatchinsky District, 305
Gauleiter, 35, 66, 111, 287, 373, 419, 443, 461, 483
Gay, 407
Gdańsk, 34, 398
Gdynia, 34
Gehlen Organisation, 466
Generalbezirk Weißruthenien, 313
General Government, 40, 41, 89–91, 94, 162, 169, 222, 254, 362, 365, 366, 368, 378, 397, 408, 482, 490
General Government administration, 111
General Jewish Labour Bund in Poland, 428
Generaloberst, 333

Generalplan Ost, 3, 110, 224, 258, 269, 297, 411
Genetic disorder, 27, 63, 414
Genetics, 14
Geneva Conventions, 333
Genocidal rape, 201
Genocide, 5, 80, 89, 201, 222, 248, 357, 406, 426, 500, 552
Genocide and Resistance Research Centre of Lithuania, 274
Genocide of Christians by ISIL, 202
Genocide of indigenous peoples, 202
Genocide of Poles in the Soviet Union (1937–1938), 123
Genocide of Shias by ISIL, 202
Genocides in history, 203, 436
Gentile, 107, 162
Geoff Eley, 5
Geoffrey P. Megargee, 225, 237, 257
George Lachmann Mosse, 538
George Mosse, 426
Georg Ferdinand Duckwitz, 150
Georgy Zhukov, 323
Gera, 400
Gerald Reitlinger, 294
Gerd R. Ueberschär, 526
Gerd von Rundstedt, 348
Gerhard Kretschmar, 29
Gerhard Wagner (Nazi physician), 28
Gerhard Weinberg, 73, 438
German Army (Wehrmacht), 334, 433
German camps in occupied Poland during World War II, 110
German Christians, 78, 422
German citizen, 300
German concentration camps, 233
German empire, 435
German Federal Archives, 39
German–Soviet Frontier Treaty, 88, 93, 128, 337
Germanic peoples, 415
Germanic-SS, 142, 143, 151
German Instrument of Surrender, 115
Germanization, 90
German Jews, 111, 302
German Labor Service, 260
German language, 7, 61, 97, 218, 224, 253, 315, 357
German military administration in occupied France during World War II, 178
German Ministry of Justice, 221, 231
German mistreatment of Soviet prisoners of war, 13, 296
German occupation of Belgium during World War II, 162

German occupation of Byelorussia during World War II, 308
German occupation of Lithuania during World War II, 265
German occupation of Luxembourg during World War II, 176
German-occupied Europe, 25, 221, 231, 253, 357, 406, 429
German Red Cross, 487
German Reunification, 50, 80
Germans, 172
German South-West Africa, 219
German-Soviet Frontier Treaty, 309, 359, 362, 366
German-Soviet War, 245
Germany, 218, 233–236, 239, 266, 313, 407, 419
Gerstein Report, 101
Gesellschaft für deutsche Sprache, 5
Gestapo, 68, 139, 199, 331, 357, 361, 393, 481, 483
Gestapo–NKVD Conferences, 123, 358
Ghent, 173
Ghetto, 166, 253, 268
Ghetto resistance, 89, 104
Ghetto resistance and liquidation, 89, 104
Ghettos, 481
Ghettos in Nazi-occupied Europe, 91, 96, 121, 218, 233, 313, 333, 357, 407
Ghetto uprising, 89, 103, 110, 121, 253, 257, 364, 367
Gitta Sereny, 39, 55
Głogów Małopolski, 129
Głowno, 124
Gniewoszów, Masovian Voivodeship, 129
Gniezno, 40
God in Abrahamic religions, 496
Gold, 282
Gomel Region, 311
Goniądz, 129
Goods wagon, 95
Google Books, 515
Góra Kalwaria, 125
Gorlice, 124, 128, 129
Gorlice Ghetto, 124
Gostynin, 129
Gottlieb Hering, 486
Götz Aly, 438
Government of Israel, 495
Government of National Salvation, 187
Government of the Republic of Estonia, 303
G.P. Putnams Sons, 380, 381, 384
Grafeneck Castle, 37
Grafeneck Euthanasia Centre, 32, 40
Graffiti, 141
Grajewo, 129

Grand Duchy of Moscow, 248
Grand Mufti, 456
Grand Mufti of Jerusalem, 325, 346
Graz, 48
Great Depression, 30
Great Depression in Central Europe, 66
Greater Netherlands, 164
Greater Poland, 90
Great Leap Forward, 246
Great Synagogue of Brussels, 164
Greece, 408, 450, 547
Greek genocide, 202
Greek Language, 3
Greeks, 407
Greenwood Publishing Group, 83
Grini concentration camp, 235
Grīva, 283
Grobiņa, 280
Grodno, 130, 318
Grodno Ghetto, 254, 319, 378
Grodzisk Mazowiecki, 125
Grójec, 125
Gross Aktion, 103
Grossaktion Warsaw (1942), 99, 369
Gross Rosen, 142
Gross-Rosen, 218
Gross-Rosen concentration camp, 225, 235
Group 13, 109
Groupe Flammarion, 381
Gruppenführer, 325, 333
Guangxi, 246
Guard Corps Brigade of ROA, 326
Guatemalan genocide, 202
Guaymas, 250
Guenter Lewy, 294
Gugging, 32
Guillotine, 426
Gulag, 244, 248–250
Gulag: A History, 524
Gunnar Heinsohn, 524
Gunnar S. Paulsson, 104, 105, 114, 120, 502, 514
Günther Herrmann (SS commander), 336
Guri Sunde, 153
Gurs internment camp, 180, 182
Gustave Le Bon, 437
Gustav Lombard, 325
Gustav Wagner, 489
Gypsy (term), 407

Haacht, 171
Haapsalu, 306
Haaretz, 550
Haavara Agreement, 239
Hacienda, 249, 250
Hadamar, 42

Hadamar Euthanasia Centre, 32, 38, 40, 97
Hadamar killing centre, 48
Haganah, 116, 494
Haj Amin al-Husseini, 325, 346, 456
Halldis Neegaard Østbye, 138
Halvor Hegtun, 141
Hamburger Edition, 529
Hamburg Institute for Social Research, 542
Hanging, 482–485, 487, 490
Hannah Arendt, 244, 436, 466
Hannes Heer, 472
Hanns Albin Rauter, 486
Hanover, 68
Hans-Adolf Prützmann, 290
Hans Aumeier, 488
Hans Bothmann, 485
Hans Eppinger, 18
Hans Frank, 104, 111, 362, 439, 440, 442, 482
Hans Gerhard Creutzfeldt, 43
Hans Günther (SS officer), 483
Hans Hedtoft, 150
Hans Heinze, 506
Hans-Joachim Tesmer, 331
Hans-Jürgen Döscher, 70, 83
Hans Lammers, 28
Hans Mommsen, 66, 438
Harald Riipalu, 303
Harald Turner, 191
Hardcover, 380, 383
Harku, 298, 306
Harry Wu, 246
Hartheim Euthanasia Centre, 32, 37, 38, 40
Harvard College, 54
Harvard University Press, 524
Hatikvah, 80
Haugesund, 142
H. Barth, 281
Health care, 240
Hebrew, 106
Hebrew language, 3, 7, 8
Hehn 1971, 518
Heim ins Reich, 111
Heinrich Bergmann, 300
Heinrich Fehlis, 148
Heinrich Fraenkel, 475
Heinrich Gross, 33, 50
Heinrich Himmler, 16, 35, 70, 95, 173, 199, 218, 220, 238, 257, 314, 320, 330, 333, 359, 381, 411, 422, 427, 481
Heinrich Matthes, 488
Heinrich Müller (Gestapo), 361, 442, 481
Heinrich Seetzen, 492
Heinz Heger, 416
Heinz Jost, 490
Hellmuth Reinhard, 148
Helmut Krausnick, 356, 474

Henri Giraud, 184
Henrik Hille, 517
Henry Friedlander, 47, 471, 509
Henry Rinnan, 144
Herbert Lange, 39, 486
Herberts Cukurs, 281, 290
Hereditary Health Court, 28
Herero and Namaqua genocide, 202, 219
Hermann Göring, 44, 67, 80, 218, 224, 359, 417, 442, 481
Hermann Höfle, 484
Hermann Kaienburg, 238
Hermann Michel, 489
Hermann Schaper, 109, 457, 491
Herrenvolk, 407
Herschel Grynszpan, 65, 68, 69
Herzogenbusch concentration camp, 235
Hesse-Nassau, 50
Hilary Minc, 495
Himmler, 92, 359
Hinrich Lohse, 284, 287–289
Hinzert concentration camp, 235
Hirden, 143
Historical revisionism, 500
Historiography, 273
History, 264, 358
History of antisemitism, 64
History of Blacks in Nazi Germany and the Holocaust, 414
History of children in the Holocaust, 287
History of Germany, 426
History of Lithuania, 265
History of Poland (1939–1945), 108, 109
History of Poland (1939–45), 371
History of the Jews in 20th-century Poland, 110
History of the Jews in Algeria, 409
History of the Jews in Belarus, 308
History of the Jews in China, 409
History of the Jews in Iraq, 409
History of the Jews in Japan, 409
History of the Jews in Latvia, 283
History of the Jews in Liechtenstein, 453
History of the Jews in Morocco, 409
History of the Jews in Poland, 68, 89, 110, 121, 122, 222, 265, 314
History of the Jews in Tunisia, 409
History of The Kingdom of Yugoslavia, 191
History of the Netherlands (1939–1945), 482
Hitler, 30, 260
Hitlers War in the East 1941–1945, 526
Hitlers Willing Executioners, 426, 437
Hitlers Willing Executioners: Ordinary Germans and the Holocaust, 404
Hitler Youth, 260
Hiwi (volunteer), 326
Hjalmar Mäe, 304

Hlinka Guard, 460
Hoax, 500
Höfle Telegram, 102, 367
Holocaust, 8, 94, 95, 136, 194, 218, 231, 303, 323, 367, 391, 393, 539
Holocaust Center of Northern California, 238
Holocaust (disambiguation), 406
Holocaust in Lithuania, 113
Holocaust memorials, 497
Holocaust (miniseries), 5
Holocaust Remembrance Day, 155
Holocaust (resources), 500
Holocaust (sacrifice), 3
Holocaust train, 89, 91, 94–96, 99, 102, 121, 162, 253, 358, 544
Holocaust trains, 98, 223, 359, 367, 378
Holocaust trials in Soviet Estonia, 300, 302, 303
Holocaust trivialization, 244
Holocaust uniqueness debate, 201
Holocaust victims, 3, **405**
Holodomor, 202, 251
Holodomor genocide question, 203
Holt, Rinehart and Winston, 375
Holy Cross Mountains Brigade, 109
Holy Orders, 222
Holy See, 26, 419
Holýšov, 109
Home Army, 109, 256, 262, 393
Homel, 313
Homosexuality, 222, 416
Homo Sovieticus, 319
Honorary Aryan, 415
Hordaland, 159
H. Ording, 517
Horst Böhme (SS officer), 491
Horst Schumann, 487
Horthy, 192
Hospital, 287
Hotel Polski, 113
Hot spring, 249
House of Commons of the United Kingdom, 429
Houston Stewart Chamberlain, 435
Hrodna Voblast, 529
Hrubieszów, 129, 134, 399
HSSPF, 362
Hubes Pocket, 317
Hugh Greene, 72
Hugh Trevor-Roper, 349
Human experimentation, 13
Humbert Achamer-Pifrader, 490
Humiliate, 282
Hungary, 235, 256, 277, 336, 408
Hunting Eichmann, 467
Huntingtons chorea, 36

Huntingtons disease, 27
Hutchinson & Co, 380, 381
Hutchinson (publisher), 384
Hutu Power, 203
Hydrocephaly, 32
Hygiene, 240
Hypothermia, 15, 22

Ian Hancock, 9, 293, 295, 424
Ian Kershaw, 350, 352, 410, 439, 474
Iași pogrom, 459
Ich klage an, 31
Identifiers and linked data, 377, 380, 383
Ideology, 61
IG Farben, 224, 242
Ignacy Schwarzbart, 378
Iliya Yevelson, 287
Il Kal Grande, 199
Ilūkste, 281
Iłża, 129
Imam, 456
Imperial German Army, 219
Imperial Japanese Army, 22
Incendiary bomb, 20
Independent State of Croatia, 190, 192, 194, 195, 197, 200, 336
Indiana University, 252
Indiana University Press, 513, 515
Indian Removal, 202
Indochina, 179
Indonesian genocide, 202
Industrialization in practice, 320
Industrial Revolution, 426
Inflation in the Weimar Republic, 66
Informed consent, 21, 61
Injustice, 497
Innsbruck-Reichenau camp, 214
Inowłódz, 129
Inspector of Concentration Camps, 220
Institute of National Remembrance, 56, 109, 119
Institut für Zeitgeschichte, 56
Instytut Adama Mickiewicza, 515
Intellectual disability, 32
Intelligentsia, 222, 330, 411
Intelligenzaktion, 90, 507
International Holocaust Remembrance Alliance, 155
International law, 465
International Standard Book Number, 22, 23, 51–57, 59, 60, 82–84, 118–120, 158–161, 174, 175, 177, 185, 186, 194, 205, 216, 229, 230, 237, 251, 252, 257, 274, 275, 292–295, 351–356, 374–376, 391, 394, 395, 404, 424, 466–481
International Standard Serial Number, 394

Interpol, 482, 491
Interrogation, 241, 417
Interwar, 320
Interwar period, 164, 178
Introduction, 1
Invasion of Poland, 29, 90, 92, 124, 253, 266, 273, 308, 330, 331, 380, 383, 392
Invasion of the Soviet Union, 330
Invasion of Yugoslavia, 195
Involuntary euthanasia, 25, 61
Iodine, 19
Ion Antonescu, 444, 458
IPN Gdańsk, 56
Irena Sendler, 108
Irena Sendlerowa, 422
Irene Runge, 84
Irma Grese, 493
Irmfried Eberl, 41, 485
Irmgard Huber, 49
Iron Guard, 458
Iron Wolf (organization), 270
Irsee, 33
Isaaq genocide, 202
Isak Samokovlija, 204
Islam, 497
Islamic State of Iraq and the Levant, 202
Israel, 8, 80, 89, 174, 271, 495, 498, 499
Israel Defense Forces, 117
Israel Gutman, 113
Israeli declaration of independence, 494
Italian Libya, 207
Italian occupation of France, 183
Italian resistance movement, 417
Italians, 407, 417
Italian Social Republic, 183, 452
Italo Balbo, 208
Italy, 234–236, 409
Itzik Feffer, 324
Ivanava, 96
Ivanhorod, 258, 329
Ivano-Frankivsk, 112
Ivan the Terrible (Treblinka guard), 262
Ivan Yermachenka, 310
Ivatsevichy, 129
Ivo Goldstein, 519
Iwo Cyprian Pogonowski, 404
Iwye, 319
Izbica concentration camp, 101
Izbica Ghetto, 111, 128, 129
Izbica Kujawska, 125

Jaan Viik, 302, 304
Jack Fischel, 538
Jacques Chirac, 184
Jado concentration camp, 211
Jadovno concentration camp, 198, 203

Jägala, 300–302
Jägala concentration camp, 235, 300, 306
Jäger Report, 347
Jahn Otto Johansen, 157
Jakub Berman, 495
James Maroni, 517
James Waller, 434
Jan Karski, 108, 222, 385, 429
Jan Maria Michał Kowalski, 38
Janowska concentration camp, 96, 130, 135, 218, 235, 365
Janusz Kurtyka, 119
Jan Włodarkiewicz, 392
Japanese American, 401
Japanese American internment, 401
Japanese occupation of the Dutch East Indies, 247
Japanese people, 415
Japanese war crimes, 247
Järvakandi, 306
Jasenovac concentration camp, 192, 194, 196, 198, 199, 201, 203, 447
Jasenovac Memorial Site, 519
Jasienica Rosielna, 134
Jasło, 129, 134
Jean Ancel, 459
Jedem das Seine, 243
Jędrzejów, 125, 133
Jedwabne, 109, 129
Jedwabne pogrom, 106, 109, 457
Jehovahs Witnesses, 222, 406, 407
Jelgava, 280
Jena, 400
Jens-Christian Wagner, 238
Jens Stoltenberg, 155
Jerusalem, 456
Jerzy Tabeau, 391
Jesuit, 45
Jesus, 435
Jew, 3, 138, 323, 330, 500
Jewelry, 282
Jewish, 267
Jewish Agency, 215
Jewish Agency for Israel, 498
Jewish Anti-Fascist Committee, 324
Jewish assimilation, 406
Jewish Bolshevism, 274, 309, 334
Jewish Brigade, 215
Jewish cemetery, 150
Jewish Communists, 111
Jewish communities, 207
Jewish Community, 102
Jewish diaspora, 499
Jewish exodus from Arab and Muslim countries, 207
JewishGen, 284
Jewish Ghetto Police, 255
Jewish ghettos in German-occupied Poland, 91, 96, 110, **120**, 357, 359
Jewish history, 64
Jewish life in Mezhirichi, 264
Jewish Museum in Oslo, 157
Jewish-Polish history (1989–present), 110
Jewish population of Luxembourg, 176
Jewish presence, 264
Jewish Quarter (diaspora), 122, 253
Jewish question, 287, 330, 345, 357, 359
Jewish resistance during the Holocaust, 108, 257
Jewish resistance under Nazi rule, 110
Jewish Star, 298
Jewish uprising and the ghetto liquidation, 89, 104
Jewish Virtual Library, 221, 231, 271, 550
Jews, 5, 7, 13, 64, 162, 178, 187, 188, 194, 200, 253, 308, 320, 357, 385, 406, 425, 496
Jews in Kraśnik, 96
Jews in Nazi Germany, 218
Jews of Libya, 207, 214
Jews of Libya during the Holocaust, **207**
Jews outside Europe under Axis occupation, 409
Jeżów, Lublin Voivodeship, 125
Joachim Fest, 543
Joachim Hamann, 283
Joachim von Ribbentrop, 182
Jødeproblemet og dets løsning, 138
Johannes Blaskowitz, 333, 444
Johannes de Jong, 420
Johannes Smemo, 517
Johann Niemann, 489
John Connelly (historian), 109
John Milton, 4
Johns Hopkins University Press, 424
John S. Schuchman, 55
John Zorn, 80
Jõhvi, 305
Joint Declaration by Members of the United Nations, 429
Jonas Lie (government minister), 148
Jonathan Cape, 524
Jonava, 270
Jon Halliday, 246
Jörg Echternkamp, 251
Josef Bühler, 93, 407
Josef Bürckel, 182
Josef Kramer, 488
Josef Kreuzer, 336
Josef Mengele, 14, 486
Josef Oberhauser, 488
Josef Terboven, 139, 456

Jose Maria Finat y Escriva de Romani, 462
Joseph Goebbels, 28, 70, 238, 373, 442, 482
Joseph Stalin, 5, 244, 320, 323
Joseph Van De Meulebroeck, 173
Joshua Rubenstein, 530
Journal of Modern History, 251
Józef and Wiktoria Ulma, 105
Jozef-Ernest van Roey, 172
Jozef Garlinski, 394
Jozef Tiso, 461
Jozo Tomasevich, 207
Jpost, 216
Judaism, 496
Judenfrei, 93, 97, 176, 191, 283, 297, 339, 362, 364, 460
Judenrat, 91, 162, 166
Judeo-Masonic conspiracy theory, 537
Juhan Jüriste, 302, 304
Jules Schelvis, 120
Julian Grobelny, 108
Jung Chang, 246
Jürgen Förster, 356
Jürgen Matthäus, 351, 375
Jürgen Stroop, 490

Kaddish, 291
Kaiserwald concentration camp, 218, 235, 398
Kalevi-Liiva, 300, 302, 304
Kalinkovichi, 313
Kalisz, 129
Kálmán Darányi, 451
Kalmi Baruh, 204
Kalmyk deportations of 1943, 202
Kałusz, 129
Kamianets-Podilskyi massacre, 362, 364, 490
Kampfgruppe Schimana, 315
Kapo (concentration camp), 423
Karczew, 129
Karl Binding, 30, 62
Karl Bischoff, 485
Karl Brandt, 26, 30, 488
Karl Dietrich Bracher, 438
Karl Frenzel, 489
Karl Fritzsch, 488
Karl Gebhardt, 487
Karl Hermann Frank, 486
Karl Jäger, 347, 491
Karl Linnas, 302, 304, 306
Karl Marthinsen, 148
Karl Steubl, 485
Karl Vold, 517
Károly Bartha (Minister of Defence), 451
Karstala, 305
Katowice, 514
Kattowitz (region), 40
Kaufbeuren, 33

Kaufering concentration camp, 235, 404
Kaunas, 269, 338, 340, 365
Kaunas Ghetto, 235, 274
Kaunas pogrom, 270, 272, 454
Kazakhstan famine of 1932–1933, 202
Kazerne Dossin – Memorial, 173
Kazimierz Dolny, 125
Kazimierz Piechowski, 393
Kaziņu Forest, 283
Keene State College, 434
Kemna concentration camp, 235
Kharkiv, 365
Khatyn, 423
Khatyn massacre, 319
Khmer Rouge, 5
Khmer Rouge Killing Fields, 203
Khrushchev Thaw, 116
Kiel, 43
Kiełbasin, 132
Kielce Ghetto, 130
Kielce pogrom, 106, 116, 495
Kiev, 260, 339, 362
Kilgour-Matas report, 248
Killed in action, 482, 486
Killings by Einsatzgruppe, 92
Kilojoule, 255
Kindertransport, 79
Kingdom of Hungary (1920–1946), 200
Kingdom of Italy (1861–1946), 415
Kingdom of Yugoslavia, 187, 195
Kirchenkampf, 419
Kistarcsa, 235
Kiviõli, 304, 305
Kjersti Dybvig, 153
Kjesäter, 146
Klaipėda, 267
Klaus Barbie, 466
Klaus Hildebrand, 438
Klaus-Michael Mallmann, 346, 353
Klaus Naumann (historian), 472
Klaus von Stauffenberg, 543
KLB Club, 423
Kłobuck, 130
Klooga concentration camp, 235, 301, 303, 305
KMSB, 73
Knesset, 8, 272
Knin, 336
Knokke, 173
Knut Rød, 148
Knyszyn, 130
Kobryn, 96, 130
Kobyłka, 125
Kock, 130
Kodeń, 130
Kohtla, 305

Kolbuszowa, 130
Kołdichevo, 235
Koło, 125
Kolomyia, 135
Koluszki, 130
Kolyma, 244, 249
Komarówka, Lublin Voivodeship, 96
Komorg, 144
Konev, 323
Koniecpol, 125
Königsberg, 491
Konin, 125
Konrad Adenauer, 498
Konrad Kwiet, 273
Końskie, 130
Końskowola, 96, 101
Konstantin Rodzaevsky, 327
Konstantīns Kaķis, 281
Koprzywnica, 135
Korban Olah, 3
Korczyn, 130
Kórnik, 332
Kościan, 40
Kovno, 341
Kowale Pańskie, 127, 135
Kowel, 135
Kozienice, 125
Koźminek, 125
Kraków, 98, 111
Kraków District, 111
Kraków Ghetto, 91, 95, 96, 99, 102, 130, 132
Kraków-Płaszów concentration camp, 124, 130, 218, 236, 486
Kraków pogrom, 495
Kraśnik, 129, 130, 134, 135
Krasnystaw, 125
Kresy, 90, 91, 111, 308, 309, 312, 318, 341, 363, 379
Kriegsmarine, 277
Kriminalpolitiet, 143
Kriminalpolizei, 96, 335, 357, 361, 490, 491
Kripo, 37
Kristallnacht, **64**, 164, 253, 271
Kristallnacht (album), 80
Kristian Ottosen, 159, 161
Krośniewice, 125
Krosno, 135
Krupki, 317
Kruščica concentration camp, 198
Krynki, 130
Kryvyi Rih, 365
Książ Wielki, 130
Kukruse, 305
Kuldīga, 283
Kulmhof extermination camp, 367
Kunda, Estonia, 305

Kunów, 130
Kuremäe, 305
Kuressaare, 306
Kurt Bolender, 490
Kurt Daluege, 361, 482
Kurt Franz, 486
Kurt Gerstein, 101
Kutno, 125
Kvænangen concentration camp, 235
Kyiv Post, 526

Labor Zionism, 170
Labour camps, 238
Labour force, 287

Łachwa Ghetto, 103, 135, 319

Lademoen, 150
Lagedi, 301, 305
Lager Borkum, 233
Lager Helgoland, 233
Lager Norderney, 233
Lager Sylt, 233
Laitse, 306
Lake Starnberg, 400
Lakhva, 319
La Libre Belgique during World War II, 172
Lalleri, 412

Łańcut, 125

Laogai, 245

Łapanka, 392

Lapel, 423

Łapy, 130
Łask, 125
Łaskarzew, 130

Lasnamäe, 306
László Teleki (1959), 7
Latgale, 283
Latin, 3
Latin America, 415
Latrine, 96
Latvia, 235, 237, 277, 280, 281, 338, 408
Latvian Auxiliary Police, 277, 280, 282, 283
Latvian Police, 280
Laubach, 433
Lauenburg, 400
Laundry, 287
Laurence Rees, 354
Lavassaare, 306

Law for the Prevention of Genetically Defective Progeny, 18
Law for the Restoration of the Professional Civil Service, 66
Lea Deutsch, 204
Lebensraum, 90, 258, 359, 410
Le Boeuf sur le Toit (cabaret), 70

Łęczna, 135
Łęczyca, 130

Leftist, 407
Left-wing, 170
Legal purge in Norway after World War II, 157, 161, 456
Legionowo, 125
Lehtse, 306
Leib Kvitko, 324
Leipzig, 29
Leitch Ritchie, 3
Lelle, 306
Le Monde, 550
Le Monde diplomatique, 539
Leningrad, 320, 323
Leo Alexander, 21
Leo Eitinger, 145
Leonardo Conti, 29, 34, 49
Leon Feiner, 428
Leon Kieres, 515
Léon Poliakov, 323
Leopold III of Belgium, 164
Leopold II of Belgium, 243
Lesbian, 407, 416
Lesko, 135
Leslie Hardman, 4
Leszek Gondek, 109
Levanger, 141
Levetzowstrasse Synagogue, 144
Lewisite, 17
Ležáky, 482
LGBT, 407
Liberalism, 426
Libyan Jews, 207
Lida, 319
Lída Baarová, 71
Lidice, 482, 491
Lidice massacre, 423
Liechtenstein, 545
Liège, 162, 163
Liepāja, 280, 282, 283
Lietuvos gyventojų genocido ir rezistencijos tyrimo centras, 275
Life Is Beautiful, 497
Life unworthy of life, 29, **61**, 426
Limanowa, 130
Linen, 282

Linz, 37
Lipowa 7, 399
Lipsk, 130
Lise Børsum, 145
List of Einsatzgruppen, 262
List of genocides by death toll, 203
List of major perpetrators of the Holocaust, **481**
List of Nazi concentration camps, **231**
List of Nazi doctors, 14, 223, 226
List of Nazi-era ghettos, 233, 253
List of Polish Jews, 110
List of political ideologies, 406
List of subcamps of Auschwitz, 225, 233
List of subcamps of Buchenwald, 234, 358
List of subcamps of Dachau, 234
List of subcamps of Flossenbürg, 234
List of subcamps of Gross-Rosen, 235
List of subcamps of Kraków-Płaszów, 236
List of subcamps of KZ Herzogenbusch, 235
List of subcamps of Mauthausen, 236
List of subcamps of Mittelbau, 236
List of subcamps of Natzweiler-Struthof, 236
List of subcamps of Neuengamme, 236
List of subcamps of Ravensbrück, 236
List of subcamps of Sachsenhausen, 236
List of subcamps of Stutthof, 237
List of wars and anthropogenic disasters by death toll, 203
Literal translation, 64
Lithuania, 235, 256, 279, 281, 338, 365, 408
Lithuanian Activist Front, 266
Lithuanian Auxiliary Police Battalions, 112, 113, 362
Lithuanian Jews, 265, 305, 454
Lithuanian language, 112
Lithuanian Provisional Government, 266, 273
Lithuanian Security Police, 270
Lithuanian SSR, 265
Lithuanian TDA Battalions, 89
L. L. Zamenhof, 423
Lobor concentration camp, 203

Łódź, 40, 90, 97, 118, 369, 371
Łódź Ghetto, 88, 90, 91, 97–99, 121, 122, 124–126, 131, 176, 254, 366, 408

Loiret, 182
Lokot Republic, 326
Lolium, 419

Łomazy, 96
Łomża Ghetto, 99, 129, 130

Looting, 64
Lorenz Hackenholt, 50, 488

Łosice, 131

Loslau, 398, 399
Lothar Beutel, 332, 333
Lothar Kreyssig, 41
Louis Darquier de Pellepoix, 548
Louis VII of France, 4
Lower Silesia, 116

Łowicz, 124, 125

Lubaczów, 135
Lubartów Ghetto, 130
Lubavitcher Rebbe, 497
Lübeck martyrs, 420
Lublin, 101, 439
Lublin Ghetto, 96, 130, 378
Lubliniec, 40
Lublin-Majdanek, 368
Lublin Reservation, 94, 95, 100, 397
Lucjan Dobroszycki, 118

Łuck Ghetto, 88, 96, 111, 131, 364

Lucy Dawidowicz, 231, 308, 323, 375, 425, 435, 437, 503
Lüderitz, 219
Ludvig Hope, 517
Ludwig Hahn, 336
Ludwig Teichmann, 336
Luftwaffe, 15
Luís Carrero Blanco, 461
Luis García Meza Tejada, 466

Łuków, 96, 131

Luniniec, 319
Lutheranism, 222, 435
Luxembourg, 176, 409
Luxembourg (city), 177
Lviv, 112, 365
Lviv pogroms, 112, 264, 349, 365
Lvov Ghetto, 96, 263
Lwów Ghetto, 96, 101, 102, 112, 130, 379
Lyon, France, 466
Lyubavichi, 319

Maafa, 5, 243
Machete, 539
Macroregion, 90, 112
Madagascar, 247, 439
Madagascar Plan, 239, 358, 439
Magdeburg, 72
Magirus-Deutz, 344
Majdanek, 88, 94, 96, 102, 126–128, 130, 132, 218, 228, 229, 398, 408, 485

Majdanek concentration camp, 124, 226, 236, 367, 368, 449
Majdanek State Museum, 103, 117
Major General, 317
Maków Mazowiecki, 131
Malaria, 17
Malchow concentration camp, 236
Malmö, Sweden, 400
Maly Trostenets extermination camp, 228, 236, 319, 408
Manchukuo, 327
Mandate Palestine, 67
Mandatory Palestine, 116, 346, 378, 494
Manifest Destiny, 202
Manifesto of Race, 207
Mao: The Unknown Story, 246, 524
Mao Zedong, 245, 246
Marcel Reich-Ranicki, 68
March of the Living, 117
Marco Aurelio Rivelli, 206
Marģers Vestermanis, 287
Marginalized, 238
Maria Mandel, 492
Marian Spychalski, 116
Marine Le Pen, 184
Marki, 125
Mark Mazower, 539
Mark Roseman, 358, 372, 376
Marmaduke Grove, 80
Marseilles, 179
Marszałkowska Street, Warsaw, 255
Marte Michelet, 157, 159
Martial law in Trondheim in 1942, 142
Martin Bormann, 95, 442, 484
Martin Broszat, 438
Martin Gilbert, 65, 76, 313, 323, 501, 509
Martin Gottfried Weiss, 485
Martin Luther, 78, 435
Martin Luther (diplomat), 357
Martin Niemöller, 222
Martin Sandberger, 297, 303
Mārtiņš Vagulāns, 280
Martyrs of Nowogródek, 318, 420
Marxist, 437
Masha Bruskina, 309
Massacre of Lviv professors, 264
Massacres of Poles in Volhynia, 113
Massacres of Poles in Volhynia and Eastern Galicia, 113
Mass (Catholic Church), 116
Mass killings under Communist regimes, 203
Mass murder, 64, 500
Masterplan (band), 80
Masterplan (Masterplan album), 80
Mate Ujević, 204
Mauthausen concentration camp, 226, 455

Mauthausen-Gusen, 218, 413
Mauthausen-Gusen concentration camp, 14, 226, 236, 239, 358
Max de Crinis, 36
Max Garcia, 529
Maximilian Grabner, 488
Maximilian Kolbe, 420
Maximillian Kolbe, 421
Max Thomas (SS officer), 492
Max von Schenckendorff, 316
Mayn Yngele, 81
Mazyr, 313
McFarland & Company, 120
Mechelen, 168
Mechelen transit camp, 162, 168, 236
Media:De-Reichskristallnacht.ogg, 64
Media:Novemberpogrome.ogg, 64
Media:Pogromnacht.ogg, 64
Medical ethics, 14, 22
Medical law, 21
Medical torture, 14
Medication, 19
Međimurje, 200
Mein Kampf, 27, 414, 419, 438
Memorial, 229, 418
Mental illness, 407, 414
Meryl Streep, 5
Mestizo, 415
Methodology, 500
Metropolitan France, 178
Mexico, 249, 417
Mezuzot, 75
MF Norwegian School of Theology, 517
MI5, 466
Michael Berenbaum, 322, 424, 501, 510, 514, 529
Michael Burleigh, 7, 44, 52, 503
Michael Fleming (historian), 378, 379
Michael Marrus, 354, 355, 439
Michael Müller-Claudius, 77
Michael Musmanno, 290
Michael Phayer, 206
Michael Shermer, 552
Michael Tippett, 80
Michałowo, 131
Michel Foucault, 436, 539
Microcephaly, 32
Microsoft Encarta, 5
Middle Ages, 7, 426, 435
Middle East, 323
Middle East Report, 216
Middle Tennessee State University, 553, 554
Miechow, 130
Miechów, 131
Międzyrzec Podlaski, 96
Międzyrzec Podlaski Ghetto, 130

Międzyrzec Podlaski Ghetto, 135
Mielec, 124, 125
Miklós Horthy, 444
Milan Bulajić, 204, 205
Milan Nedic, 187
Milan Nedić, 187, 460
Milgram experiment, 434
Milice, 184
Military Administration in Belgium and Northern France, 162, 165, 367
Military decorations, 324
Military occupation, 165
Military service, 324
Milorg, 144, 147, 152, 157
Mina Rosner, 263
Mine clearance, 317
Ministry of Public Enlightenment and Propaganda, 482
Ministry of Public Security of Poland, 109
Minsk, 309, 315, 319, 345
Minsk Ghetto, 310, 311, 313, 319
Mińsk Mazowiecki Ghetto, 111, 126
Minsk Voblast, 319
Miroslav Kárný, 238
Miroslav Šalom Freiberger, 199
Mischling, 407
Misha Movshenson, 288
Mit brennender Sorge, 419
Mittelbau-Dora, 218, 236, 398
Mizoch, 264
Mizocz Ghetto, 88, 103
Mława, 124, 126
M. Mintz, 287
Modris Eksteins, 341
Mogielnica, 126
Mogilev, 241
Moldova, 320
Molotov–Ribbentrop Pact, 90, 320, 363
Monarchist Party, 327
Monotheism, 497
Monowitz, 144
Monowitz concentration camp, 224
Monument to the Ghetto Heroes, 117
Moral Theology, 41
Mordechai Rokeach, 263
Mordy, 126
Moritz Rabinowitz, 142
Moscow, 320
Moselle, 178
Moshe Sharett, 498
Mosquitoes, 17
Mossad, 290
Mossad LeAliyah Bet, 215
Motal, 319
Movie theater, 282
MS Gotenland, 143

MS Monte Rosa (1930), 143
MS St. Louis, 164, 358, 465
Mucous gland, 17
Mühldorf subcamp, 404
Mullah, 456
Munich, 73, 358
Munich Agreement, 331
Münster, 44
Muranów, 127
Murder operations, 457
Murnau am Staffelsee, 393
Muscle, 15
Museum, 282
Museum of the History of Polish Jews, 515, 516
Museum of the History of the Polish Jews, 117, 515
Muslim, 407, 456
Muszyna, 124
Muteness, 220
Mykolaiv, 260
My Opposition, 433
Myślenice, 126
Mystici corporis Christi, 47

Nachtigall Battalion, 263
Nacht und Nebel, 236, 422
Nagykanizsa, 200
Nahum Goldmann, 498
Names of the Holocaust, **3**
Namibia, 219
Nansenhjelpen, 138
Nansen International Office for Refugees, 145
Narva, 305, 306
Narva-Jõesuu, 306
Nasjonal Samling, 138, 147, 456
National Archival Services of Norway, 153
National Armed Forces, 109
National Coalition Supporting Soviet Jewry, 272
National Congress of Chile, 80
National Council of Poland, 378
National Front (France), 184
National Geographic (magazine), 262, 526
Nationalism, 426
Nationalist, 450
National Museum of Bosnia and Herzegovina, 199
National Socialist Peoples Welfare, 422
National Union of Greece, 450
Nation-state, 115
Native Americans in the United States, 219
Natural rubber, 243
Natzweiler, 17, 161, 358
Natzweiler-Struthof, 218, 236
Navahrudak, 313

Navahrudak Voblast, 529
Nawcz, 403
Nazi, 138, 499
Nazi camps, 103, 397
Nazi concentration camp, 94, 300, 397
Nazi concentration camp badge, 402, 422
Nazi concentration camp badges, 222
Nazi concentration camps, 13, 62, 65, 71, 89, 130, 162, 184, **217**, 231, 268, 371, 397, 482
Nazi crime, 296, 308, 320
Nazi crimes against ethnic Poles, 3, 202
Nazi crimes against Soviet POWs, 202
Nazi crimes against the Polish nation, 381, 384
Nazi death camps, 443
Nazi eugenics, 62
Nazi extermination camp, 62
Nazi–Soviet Pact, 90
Nazi German, 124, 269, 357
Nazi Germany, 3, 5, 13, 25, 64, 65, 89, 111, 121, 163, 176, 182, 187, 195, 210, 218, 223, 238, 253, 257, 258, 265, 296, 308, 320, 323, 329, 330, 357, 371, 385, 397, 406, 413, 491, 496
Nazi ghetto, 378
Nazi ghettos, 91, **253**, 381
Nazi human experimentation, **13**, 62, 225, 406
Nazi Party, 27, 63, 65, 165, 218, 220, 359, 370, 373, 409, 414, 425, 481, 500
Nazi persecution of the Catholic Church in Germany, 419
Nazi persecution of the Catholic Church in Poland, 330, 332, 410
Nazi propaganda, 66
Nazis, 7, 181
Nazism, 13, 61, 65, 218, 253, 313, 409, 416, 422, 426
Nazism and race, 14, 537
Nazi-Soviet Pact, 115, 308
Nazi term, 61
Neal Bascomb, 467
Negro, 414
Nerve, 15
Netherlands, 151, 233, 235, 237, 408, 455
Neuengamme concentration camp, 218, 236, 400, 485
Neues Volk, 27, 63, 414
New Order (Nazism), 164
New Scientist, 23
New Synagogue, Berlin, 76
New World, 243
New York City, 498
Niederhagen concentration camp, 236
Niederkirchnerstraße, 329
Nieśwież, 103
Night (book), 399

Night of the Long Knives, 419
Night of the Murdered Poets, 324
Nikolaev massacre, 260, 264
Nikolaus Wachsmann, 230
Nils Johan Ringdal, 161
Ninth Fort, 268
Nisan, 500
NKVD, 90, 111, 229, 292, 485
Nobel Peace Prize, 399
Nobel Prize in Physics, 173
Non-heterosexual, 416
Non-Jewish, 407
Nora Levin, 4
Nora Lustig, 145
Nordland Line, 155
Nord-Pas-de-Calais, 165
Norman Davies, 420
Norman Finkelstein, 499
Norm (social), 282
North Africa, 414
North America, 79
North Korea, 238
Northwestern University Press, 294
Nortraship, 151
Norway, 138, 157, 233–235, 409
Norwegian apology, 154
Norwegian Armed Forces in exile, 151
Norwegian Center for Studies of Holocaust and Religious Minorities, 156, 157, 159
Norwegian resistance movement, 138, 456
Norwegian State Railways, 141, 152, 155
Notary, 298
November 9 in German history, 80
Novgorod, 411
Novi Sad, 187, 192
Nowe Miasto nad Pilicą, 131
Nowogródek, 131
Nowogródek Voivodeship (1919–1939), 313
Nowogródek Voivodeship (1919–39), 114
Nowy Dwór Mazowiecki, 126
Nowy Korczyn, 126
Nowy Sącz Ghetto, 131
Nowy Targ, 131
Nowy Żmigród, 131
NSDAP, 29
Nuclear holocaust, 4
Number of deaths in Buchenwald, 234
Nuremberg, 48
Nuremberg Code, 14, 21
Nuremberg Defense, 466
Nuremberg Laws, 66, 165, 176, 298, 337, 358
Nuremberg Trial, 323, 360
Nuremberg trials, 238, 240, 336, 360, 397, 417, 438, 465, 529
Nutrition, 240

Obech, Belarus, 319
Obedience (human behavior), 434
Oberer Kuhberg concentration camp, 236
Oberführer, 31, 333
Obergruppenführer, 224, 312, 330
Oberkommando der Wehrmacht, 484
Oberkommando des Heeres, 320
Obersturmbannführer, 166, 303, 332
Oblast, 309
Occupation of East Poland by Soviet Union, 128
Occupation of Estonia by Nazi Germany, 296
Occupation of Latvia by Nazi Germany, 277
Occupation of Lithuania by Nazi Germany, 265
Occupation of Norway by Nazi Germany, 139
Occupation of Poland, 256
Occupation of Poland (1939–1945), 89, 104, 121, 134
Occupation of Poland (1939–45), 90, 399
Occupied Europe, 329
Occupied Poland, 39, 89, 121, 253, 256, 257, 359, 378, 381, 383
OCLC, 57
Octavian Goga, 458
Odd-Bjørn Fure, 157
Odd Reidar Humlegård, 155
Odilo Globocnik, 94, 95, 368, 419, 442, 482
Odrzywół, Przysucha County, 255
Office of Censorship, 379
Office of Racial Policy, 27, 63, 414
Office of Strategic Services, 391
Oflag, 228
Ohrdruf concentration camp, 225
Oil shale, 300
Ojārs Vācietis, 291
Olaf Moe, 517
Ole Berg, 147
Oleg Khlevniuk, 245
Ole Hallesby, 517
Ole Jacob Malm, 145
Ole Kristian Grimnes, 153
Olkusz, 99, 131
Oluf Kolsrud, 517
Oluf Skarpnes, 153
Omakaitse, 301, 305
Omer Bartov, 503, 552
Omnibenevolence, 497
Omnipotence, 497
Omniscience, 497
On the Jews and Their Lies, 78, 435
Opatów Ghetto, 131
Operational Zone Adriatic Coast, 200
Operation Anthropoid, 481
Operation Barbarossa, 41, 88, 91, 97, 109, 123, 128, 141, 265, 266, 309, 313, 320, 333,

359, 361, 364, 371, 383, 411, 427, 448, 457
Operation Blumenpflücken, 149
Operation Cottbus, 317
Operation Heinrich, 316
Operation Last Chance, 272
Operation Reinhard, 26, 94, 136, 228, 232, 256, 367, 383, 482, 484, 485, 488
Operation Reinhardt, 95
Operation Sea Lion, 346
Operation Tannenberg, 34, 507
Operation Weserübung, 139
Opfer der Vergangenheit, 31
Opoczno, 126, 132
Opole Lubelskie, 126, 131
Oradour-sur-Glane massacre, 423
Oranienburg concentration camp, 236
Ordnungspolizei, 253, 258, 277, 283, 288, 305, 331, 482
Organisation Todt, 168
Organization of Ukrainian Nationalists, 112, 258, 349
Orpo battalions, 254, 312, 313, 359, 361, 363
Orsza, 317
Orthodox Christianity, 407
Osiek, Świętokrzyskie Voivodeship, 131
Oskar Dirlewanger, 97, 317
Oskar Mendelsohn, 160
Oskars Baltmanis, 281
Oskar Schindlers Enamel Factory, 118
Oslo, 140, 141
Ostarbeiters, 319
Osteomyelitis, 506
Osthofen, 236
Ostland, 287, 362
Ostlegionen, 326
Ostpreussen, 40
Ostrowiec Świętokrzyski, 131
Oswald Pohl, 222, 241, 442, 483
Oświęcim, 117, 522
Otdelniy Russkiy Korpus, 326
Otto Abetz, 180
Otto Bradfisch, 492
Otto Brautigam, 325
Otto Bräutigam, 295
Otto Georg Thierack, 238
Otto-Heinrich Drechsler, 298
Ottoman Empire, 208
Ottoman Slave Trade, 248
Otto Ohlendorf, 258, 259, 290, 321, 325, 345, 350, 492
Otto Rasch, 259, 333, 336, 492
Otwock, 99, 126
OUN-UPA, 113
Oven, 103
Overthrow of Slobodan Milošević, 193

Owińska, 40
Oxford English Dictionary, 3, 501
Oxford University, 430
Oxford University Press, 83, 251
Ożarów, 131, 135
Ozorków, 131

Pabianice, 126
Pacification actions in German-occupied Poland, 113
Pacification of Libya, 202
Pacifism, 423
Paganism, 3
Pajęczno, 131
Pale of Settlement, 111, 320
Palestine Regiment, 215
Palestine (region), 358, 430
Palestinian people, 456
Palgrave Macmillan, 56
Palgrave-Macmillan, 424
Pan-Serbism, 191
Pansexual, 407
Papal nuncio, 461
Paragraph 175, 416
Paralysis, 36
Parczew, 96, 131, 399
Paris, 449
Park, 282
Pärnu, 306
Parson, 78
Partisan (military), 315, 330
Partisans Armés, 171
Party Chancellery, 484
Passover, 259
Pastoral letter, 78
Patriotism, 324
Paul Blobel, 258, 290, 336, 346, 364, 492
Paul Celan, 497
Paul de Lagarde, 435
Paul Ehrlich, 76
Paul Johnson (writer), 440, 529
Paul M. G. Lévy, 173
Paul Nitsche, 36, 50
Pavlowitch 2002, 518
Peace of Riga, 103
Pechory, 306
Pectin, 20
People of color, 407
Peoples Army of Poland, 114
Peoples commissar, 337
Peoples Court (German), 417
Peoples Republic of Poland, 229
Peretz Markish, 324
Pērkonkrusts, 280, 341
Persecution of Falun Gong, 248

Persecution of homosexuals in Nazi Germany and the Holocaust, 3, 537
Persecution of Jehovahs Witnesses, 418
Pertinent, 298
Peter Breggin, 56
Peter Hansen (SS officer), 325
Peter Hayes (historian), 435, 472
Peter II of Yugoslavia, 195
Peter Longerich, 114, 349, 353, 372, 376, 430, 475
Peter Padfield, 54
Pharmacies, 282
Pharmacist, 280
Pharmacy, 287
Phase one: killing squads of Operation Barbarossa, 379
Phenol, 33
Philipp Bouhler, 26, 29, 49, 488
Philippe Pétain, 178, 184, 449
Philipp, Landgrave of Hesse, 50
Philosophy, 496
Phosgene, 22
Phosphorus, 20
Physical abuse, 241
Physical disability, 407
Physician, 282
Piaseczno, 126
Piaski, 126
Piątek, 131
Pierre Vidal-Naquet, 552
Pilzno, 131
Pińczów, 131
Pinsk, 319
Pińsk Ghetto, 135, 319, 364, 367
Pinsk Voblast, 529
Pionki, 131
Piotrków Trybunalski, 124, 254
Piotrków Trybunalski Ghetto, 124, 126, 254
Piryatin, 259
Pithiviers internment camp, 182
Planned destruction of Warsaw, 411
Pl:Grupy marszowe OUN, 111
Pl:Grzegorz Berendt, 114
Pl:Horodec, 96
Pl:Natalia Aleksiun, 116
Płock, 126
Płońsk, 126
P. Marstrander, 517
Pneumonia, 33
Poddębice, 126
Pogledi, 193
Pogrom, 64, 65, 67, 167, 280, 335
Pogroms, 138, 269, 435
Poland, 68, 122, 124, 233–237, 413, 417, 439, 461, 496, 522
Poland occupied by Germany, 385
Połaniec, 131
Polenaktion, 68
Poles, 6, 13, 89, 108, 218, 222, 407, 410
Police Battalions, 89, 92, 96, 109, 112, 255, 330
Police station, 298
POLIN Museum of the History of Polish Jews, 90, 117, 513
POLIN Muzeum Historii Żydów Polskich, 515
Polish 1st Independent Parachute Brigade, 393
Polish areas annexed by Nazi Germany, 39, 90, 365, 368, 421
Polish census of 1931, 314
Polish death camp controversy, 94
Polish–Lithuanian Commonwealth, 248
Polish government-in-exile, 93, 115, 378, 380, 381, 383, 385, 428, 429
Polish Government in Exile, 107, 393
Polish Jew, 411
Polish Jews, 41, 89, 90, 254, 273, 309, 313, 318, 363, 381, 406, 456
Polish minority in Lithuania, 271
Polish peoples referendum, 1946, 116
Polish population transfers (1944–1946), 115, 116
Polish resistance movement in World War II, 104, 391
Polish Righteous among the Nations, 89, 105, 109, 110, 119
Polish Second Republic, 253
Polish September Campaign, 411
Polish Theatre in Warsaw, 115
Polish Underground State, 109
Polish Workers Party, 116
Political Catholicism, 419
Political commissar, 330
Political economy of Nazi Germany, 225
Political neutrality, 164
Political prisoner, 109, 222, 417
Polotsk, 319
Pomerania, 35
Pomerelia, 90
Pomiechówek, 126
Ponary Forest, 268
Ponary massacre, 88, 92, 112, 113, 270, 319, 454
Poniatowa, 131
Poniatowa concentration camp, 96, 127
Pope Pius XI, 419
Population transfer in the Soviet Union, 202
Porajmos, 3, 194, 202, 358
Portal:Nazism, 13
Posen Conference, 368
Posen speeches, 368, 374
Positive Christianity, 422
Postimees, 298

Post-mortem examination, 21
Post-Soviet, 272
Potsdam, 510
Poverty, 287
POW, 99, 407
POW camp, 228
Power metal, 80
Poznań, 34, 35
Prague, 145
Prague Uprising, 483
Praszka, 131
Prenatal development, 22
President of Serbia and Montenegro, 193
Pressure vessel, 20
Pretzsch, Wittenberg, 334
Priekule, Latvia, 280
Priest Barracks of Dachau Concentration Camp, 419
Primo Levi, 497
Prince Paul of Yugoslavia, 187, 195
Prisoner of war, 222, 232, 397
Prisoner of war camp, 411
Prisoner-of-war camp, 302
Prisoners of war, 6, 247, 323
Prisoner suicide, 481
Prisons in North Korea, 247
Problem of evil, 497
Profession, 298
Professor, 287
Progreso, Yucatán, 250
Project Gutenberg, 538
Project Muse, 475
Prokocim, 95
Propaganda, 281, 439, 540
Property, 298
Prostitution, 423
Protectorate, 310
Protectorate of Bohemia and Moravia, 26, 481–483
Protest, 105, 428
Protestant, 407, 422
Provenance, 498
Provinz Oberschlesien, 40, 365, 366
Provinz Ostpreußen, 123
Provisional Committee to Aid Jews, 108
Prussic acid, 428
Pruszków, 126
Przedbórz, 126
Przemyśl, 107, 135
Przeworsk, 135
Przysucha, 135
Pskov, 301, 411
Psychiatrist, 62
Psychological manipulation, 553
Public bathing, 282
Public holiday, 80

Public order crime, 224
Public relations, 155
PubMed Identifier, 56, 57, 60
Pula, 200
Puławy, 126
Puppet government, 456
Pursuit of Nazi collaborators, 466
Pustków, Podkarpackie Voivodeship, 97
Putlitz, 403
Putrefaction, 100
Pyetrykaw, 313
Pyotr Masherov, 319

Quisling, 108, 187
Q:Witold Pilecki, 395

Raasiku, 300, 301
Rabbi, 162, 167
Rabka-Zdrój, 131
Race (classification of human beings), 320
Race (human categorization), 435
Racial hygiene, 26, 95, 412, 426
Racial policies of the Third Reich, 62
Racial policy of Nazi Germany, 61, 65, 66, 334
Racism, 414, 426, 435
Raczyńskis Note, **385**, 429
Radama I, 247
Radegast train station, 118
Radiation burns, 19
Radio, 282
Radium, 249
Radom Ghetto, 96, 132
Radomsko, 126
Radomyśl Wielki, 132
Radoszyce, Podkarpackie Voivodeship, 132
Radzymin, 126
Radzyn Podlaski, 132
Radzyń Podlaski, 96
Rafi Eitan, 466
Ragnar Ulstein, 160
Rail transport in Latvia, 284
Railway station, 99
Rajgród, 132
Ralf Gerrets, 302
Ralph L. Braham, 192
Ranavalona I, 247
Randi Eckhoff, 145
Raoul Wallenberg, 463
Raphaël Alibert, 180
Rashid Ali al-Gaylani, 346
Ratusz, 118
Raul Hilberg, 8, 53, 293, 321, 330, 343, 352, 358, 359, 370, 375, 391, 425, 438, 504, 510, 523, 529
Raul Hillberg, 262
Ravensbruck, 358

Ravensbrück, 161, 218
Ravensbrück concentration camp, 15, 169, 226, 236
Rawa Mazowiecka, 132
R. Batz, 281
Red Army, 266, 305, 313, 314, 316, 323, 337, 397, 411, 457
Red Cross, 143
Ref anone, 273
Ref bnone, 271, 273
Ref cnone, 274
Ref dnone, 274
Reformation, 435
Reformation: Europes House Divided, 1490-1700, 511
Refugee, 323, 417
Refugee camps, 68
Refusenik, 319
Regeneration (biology), 15
Reich, 282
Reich Chancellery meeting of 12 December 1941, 427
Reich Main Security Office, 224, 359, 367, 422, 481, 482
Reich Ministry for the Occupied Eastern Territories, 484
Reichsbanner Schwarz-Rot-Gold, 220
Reichsdeutsche, 111
Reichsführer-SS, 16, 35, 173, 330, 333, 359, 427, 481
Reichsgau, 40, 90
Reichsgau Danzig-West Prussia, 34, 40, 90
Reichsgaue, 397
Reichsgau Wartheland, 90, 93, 254, 365, 421
Reichskomissariat Ostland, 310
Reichskommissar, 287, 456
Reichskommissariat of Belgium and Northern France, 165
Reichskommissariat Ostland, 96, 123, 265, 278, 297–299, 311–313, 321, 343
Reichskommissariat Ukraine, 258, 310, 397
Reichskonkordat, 419
Reichsleiter, 29, 373
Reichsmark, 27, 63, 414
Reichsmarschall, 359
Reichssicherheitshauptamt, 279, 331
Reichstag fire, 65
Reichstag (German Empire), 441
Reichstag (Nazi Germany), 373
Reinhard Gehlen, 466
Reinhard Heydrich, 34, 71, 93, 111, 134, 224, 312, 321, 330, 331, 357, 359, 408, 427, 481, 487
Rejowiec, Lublin Voivodeship, 132
Religion, 406
Religion in Nazi Germany, 537
Religious persecution, 426
Renzo De Felice, 215
Republicanism in Spain, 407
Republic of Austria v. Altmann, 498
Republic of Užice, 187
Rescue of Jews by Poles during the Holocaust, 110, 122, 128
Rescue of the Danish Jews, 149
Reserve Police Battalion 101, 96, 257, 368
Resistance, 89, 104
Resistance during World War II, 417
Responsibility for the Holocaust, **425**
Rexism, 164
Rēzekne, 283
Rhineland, 414
Rhineland Bastard, 407
Richard Breitman, 375
Richard C. Lukas, 107, 119, 514
Richard Glücks, 482
Richard J. Evans, 8, 26, 45, 53, 65, 230, 352, 421, 538
Richard of Devizes, 3
Richard Rhodes, 354
Richard Thomalla, 485
Richert, 317
Riegner Telegram, 428
Riga, 277, 280, 284, 285, 287, 340
Riga Ghetto, 290, 342
Righteous Among the Nations, 104, 174, 184, 204, 263, 271, 314, 323, 458
Righteous Gentiles, 460
Right to life, 61
Rijeka, 200
Risiera di San Sabba, 236
Rivne, 96
R. J. Rummel, 524
R.J. Rummel, 246
Road surface, 282
Roald Hoffmann, 263
Robert D. Cherry, 118
Robert F. Wagner, 378, 379
Robert Gellately, 430
Robert Gerwarth, 352
Robert Heinrich Wagner, 182
Robert Jay Lifton, 54, 62, 475
Robert Ley, 442
Robert Lifton, 30
Robert Riefling, 145
Roberts Blūzmanis, 283
Rocket propellant, 224
Roela, 307
Roger Griffin, 538
Roger Manvell, 475
Roger of Howden, 3
Rohingya people, 203
Rokiškis, 347

Roland Freisler, 484
Rolf Eckhoff, 145
Rolf Günther, 483
Rollkommando Hamann, 341
Roman Catholicism in Poland, 420
Roman Catholics, 407
Romania, 336, 409, 547
Romani people, 6, 7, 9, 13, 18, 41, 66, 187, 190, 194, 218, 234, 253, 279, 288, 296, 302, 306, 330, 332, 358, 407, 412
Romani (people), 162, 178
Romusha, 247
Ronald Smelser, 355
Ropczyce, 132
Rostov, 320
Rotmistrz, 395
Roundup (history), 313, 358
Routledge, 52, 53
Rovno Ghetto, 379
Royal Air Force, 45
Roy Medvedev, 244
RSHA, 41, 99, 139, 147, 329, 360, 372
Rubber, 287
Rubin Teitelbaum, 298
Rudolf Batz, 280
Rudolf Brandt, 484
Rudolf Höss, 393, 485
Rudolf Lange, 277, 281, 491
Rudolph Rummel, 249
Rumbula massacre, 330, 335, 490, 491
Rummu, 306
Russell Jacoby, 426
Russia, 138
Russian Academy of Sciences, 412
Russian Corps, 326
Russian Fascist Party, 327
Russian National Socialist Party, 326
Russians, 407, 410
Russian Soviet Federative Socialist Republic, 320, 321
Russification, 496
Rwandan Genocide, 5, 201, 202, 539
Rybnik, 40
Ryki, 132
Rymanów, 132
Rzeczpospolita (newspaper), 355
Rzeszów, 129, 133

Sachsenhausen concentration camp, 17, 72, 142, 161, 218, 229, 236, 323, 402, 403
S:Adolf Hitlers Declaration of War against the United States, 534
Saint Petersburg, 320, 323
Sajmište concentration camp, 190, 192, 204, 237, 460
Saka, Estonia, 306
Salaspils concentration camp, 221, 237, 286
Salomon Smolianoff, 323
Salvador Allende, 80
Sambor Ghetto, 135, 379
Samson Agonistes, 4
San Blas, Nayarit, 250
San Marcos, Jalisco, 250
SantAnna di Stazzema massacre, 423
Sarajevo, 199, 336
Sarajevo Haggadah, 199
Satellite camps, 401
Saul Friedländer, 8, 70, 293, 438
Sava Šumanović, 204
Schaerbeek, 174
Schindlers List, 497
Schizophrenia, 28
Schizophrenia Bulletin, 57
Schleswig-Holstein, 287
Schloss Hartheim, 37
School, 282
Schuma, 92
Schutzmannschaft, 113, 256, 261, 263, 310, 313, 335, 341, 367
Schutzmannschaft-Brigade Siegling, 325, 326
Schutzmannschaften, 313
Schutzstaffel, 16, 25, 31, 80, 94, 165, 218, 222, 232, 238, 241, 253, 279, 288, 329–331, 357, 359, 425, 433
Schutztruppe, 219
Scientific consensus, 500
Scientific racism, 426, 436
Scripture, 283
SD Security Service, 15
Sea water, 18
Sebastian Haffner, 408
Second Battle of El Alamein, 346, 444
Second Boer War, 219
Second Polish Republic, 67, 89, 90, 122–124, 308, 309, 313, 314, 363
Second World War, 22
Secretary of State, 407
Secret Polish Army, 392
Security Police in Estonia (1942-1944), 297, 300, 305
Sędziszów Małopolski, 132
Sefer Torah, 167
Seimas, 272
Selbstschutz, 34, 281, 299
Selective breeding, 412
Selektion, 300, 391
Selknam genocide, 202
Senate (Belgium), 173
Senile dementia, 36
Sentenced to death, 481
Sephardi, 450
Sephardic Jews, 547

Sephardi Jews, 199
Sepp Janko, 192
Serbia, 187, 194, 233, 234, 237
Serbian Academy of Sciences and Arts, 193
Serbian Volunteer Corps (World War II), 191
Serbs, 194, 200, 218, 222, 407, 410
Serge and Beate Klarsfeld, 499
Serock, 126
Severity Order, 348
Sexually assaulting children, 416
Sexual orientation, 406
Sexual slavery, 406
Shanghai ghetto, 75
Shanxi, 246
Shark Island Concentration Camp, 219
Shavli Ghetto, 274
Shevah Weiss, 263
Shkloŭ, 319
Sh:Laura Papo Bohoreta, 204
Shmuel Shilo, 512
Shtetl, 106, 320
Shtundists, 263
Shwoveh, 192
Shwovish, 192
Siberia, 89, 296, 358
Sicherheitsdienst, 44, 96, 139, 166, 269, 279, 301, 313, 331, 357, 361
Sicherheitspolizei, 71, 112, 166, 269, 298, 301, 302, 331, 357, 361
Sidewalk, 298
Siedlce, 118
Siedlce Ghetto, 118, 132
Siege of Jerusalem (70), 8
Siege of Leningrad, 411
Siemens, 498
Siemiatycze, 132
Sieniawa, 132
Siennica, 132
Sieradz, 126
Sierpc, 127
Sigmund Mowinckel, 517
Sigmund Rascher, 16, 20, 225
Signage, 253
Silesians, 229
Silver, 282
Silver nitrate, 19
Simferopol, 326
Simon & Schuster, 83
Simon Wiesenthal, 263, 466
Simon Wiesenthal Center, 272, 304, 355, 510
Sinti, 13, 412
SiPo, 92
Sisak childrens concentration camp, 203
Sisters of the Holy Family of Nazareth, 314
Sitsi, 307
Sivorg, 144, 147, 152

Skaryszew, 127
Skarżysko-Kamienna, 132
Skeikampen, 147
Skierniewice, 127
Skrzynno, 132
Slantsy, Leningrad Oblast, 306
Slate (magazine), 526
Slav, 258
Slave labor, 322
Slavery, 411
Slavko Goldstein, 203
Slavs, 248, 407, 410
Slobodan Milošević, 193
Slonim, 319
Słonim Ghetto, 114, 129, 132, 319, 379
Slovakia, 336, 408
Slovak Republic (1939–1945), 266
Slovenes, 536
Slovenia, 187, 536
Słuck, 132
Slutsk Affair, 319
Smallpox, 250
SNCF, 498

Śniadowo, Podlaskie Voivodeship, 133

Sobibor, 124–129, 131, 132, 135, 218
Sobibór, 88, 367, 486, 489, 490
Sobibor extermination camp, 39, 129, 323, 345, 399
Sobibór extermination camp, 94, 101, 102, 124, 226, 228, 232, 237, 367, 368, 378, 408, 449, 515
Sobibór Museum, 118
Sochaczew, 127
Social class, 417
Social democracy, 239
Social democrat, 407
Social Democratic, 220
Socialism, 323
Socialist, 407
Social status, 320
Social stigma, 426
Sokal, 399
Sokółka, 132
Sokołów Małopolski, 132
Sokołów Podlaski, 132
Soldau concentration camp, 41, 97, 237
Solec nad Wisłą, 132
Solomon Birnbaum, 550
Solomons Temple, 8
Sonda, Estonia, 306
Sonderabteilung Lola, 144
Sonderaktion 1005, 98, 346, 492
Sonderbehandlung, 38, 224
Sonderdienst, 111

Sonderfahndungsbuch Polen, 332
Sonderführer, 325
Sondergerichte, 219, 221, 540
Sonderheadquarters R, 326
Sonderkommando, 101, 103, 283, 297, 369
Sonderkommando 1a, 305
Sonnenstein Euthanasia Centre, 32, 37, 40, 97
Sons and Daughters of Jewish Deportees from France, 499
Sosnowiec Ghetto, 99, 135, 369
South African, 415
Southeast Asia, 247
Southern Bug, 459
Southern Europe, 248
Soviet administration zone, 333
Soviet atomic bomb project, 249
Soviet Belarus, 308
Soviet bloc, 272
Soviet era, 308
Soviet famine of 1932–33, 202
Soviet–Lithuanian Mutual Assistance Treaty, 266
Soviet historiography, 273
Soviet invasion of Poland, 109, 114, 308, 309, 312, 314, 359, 363
Soviet invasion of Poland (1939), 111
Soviet occupation of Estonia, 296
Soviet occupation of the Baltic states (1940), 266
Soviet partisans, 315, 323
Soviet repressions of Polish citizens (1939–1946), 109
Soviet Ukraine, 258, 308
Soviet Union, 6, 122, 202, 238, 254, 266, 296, 315, 320, 323, 407, 409, 417
Sozh Floating Bridge, 313
Spanish Civil War, 417
Spartacist uprising, 417
Special Courts, 109
Special division R, 326
Special Prosecution Book-Poland, 383
Spiritual Assembly, 422
Srebrenica massacre, 202
SS, 31, 91, 112, 121, 269, 280, 300, 305, 397
SS and Police Leader, 315, 335, 359, 372, 482, 486, 487, 490
SS Cavalry Brigade, 364
SS Division Totenkopf, 482
SS Donau (1929), 143
SS-Obergruppenführer, 290, 357
SS-Obersturmführer, 109
SS-Reichssicherheitshauptamt, 173, 433
SS-Totenkopfverbände, 89, 101, 218, 433
SS-Truppenübungsplatz Heidelager, 97
SS-Wirtschafts-Verwaltungshauptamt, 218, 222, 242, 433, 482

Stabbing, 489
Stabekk, 142
Stalinism, 320
Stalowa Wola, 127
Standard German, 25, 64, 330, 357
Standartenführer, 332
Stanford University, 185
Stanisławów Ghetto, 112, 132, 365, 379
Stanley Milgram, 434
Starachowice, 132, 135, 136
Stara Gradiška concentration camp, 198, 203
Star of David, 75, 88, 167, 282, 298
Starogard Gdański, 40
Starvation, 411
Starvation in other German-occupied territories, 92
Stary Sącz, 132
Stasi, 50
Staszów, 132
Statelessness, 168
State of Israel, 136, 494
State racism, 436
State terrorism, 64
Statspolitiet, 143
Statute on Jews, 180
Stefan Korboński, 109
Stefan Petelycky, 263
Stefan Wyszyński, 539
Stephane Courtois, 524
Stéphane Courtois, 524
Stephen Roth Institute, 553, 555
Stephen Wise, 428
Stepinac, 199
Sterilization and fertility experiments, 391
Stettin, 143
Stevan K. Pavlowitch, 206
Steyr automobile, 393
Stolperstein, 155, 174
Stopnica, 133
Store norske leksikon, 161
Strappado, 241
Strasshof, 192
Street hawker, 298
Streptococcus, 18
Stroop Report, 96, 104
Stroud, 376
Stryj, Lublin Voivodeship, 127, 135
Strzemieszyce Wielkie, 133
Strzyżów, 133
Sturmabteilung, 65, 71
Sturmbannführer, 281
Stutthof, 218
Stutthof concentration camp, 225, 237, 398, 400, 403
Subcamp (SS), 221, 224
Submachine gun, 261

Sub-Sahara, 414
Subsequent Nuremberg Trials, 14, 349, 360
Subversion, 221
Sucha Beskidzka, 135
Suchedniów, 124, 133
Sudetenland, 64, 331
Sudetenland Crisis, 71
Sudra Holocaust, 5
Suffering, 497
Suicide, 49, 429, 481
Sulejów, 133
Sulfonamide (medicine), 18
Sulfur mustard, 17
Summary execution, 411
Surazh, 362
Surgeon, 287
Sussex Academic Press, 510
Suum cuique, 243
Sven Lindqvist, 436
Sverre Riisnæs, 148
Swastika, 422
Sweden during World War II, 409

Świecie, 40
Świętokrzyska Street, Warsaw, 255

Switzerland, 27
Sybirak, 111
Synagogue, 65, 71, 167, 177, 199
Synne Corell, 157
Synthetic rubber, 224
Syphilis, 36
Syrets concentration camp, 237
Syrmia, 187, 192, 194
Szadek, 127
Szczebrzeszyn, 127
Szczuczyn, 133
Szebnie concentration camp, 96, 128
Szmalcownik, 106, 457
Szmul Zygielbojm, 429
Szydłów, 135
Szydlowiec, 127

T-4 Euthanasia Program, 413
Tadeusz Piotrowski (sociologist), 120
Taiwan, 417
Tal Bruttmann, 518
Tallinn, 298, 300, 306, 307, 341
Tamil Malaysians, 247
Tapa, Estonia, 298
Tarczyn, 133
Tarlow, 132
Tarnobrzeg, 133
Tarnogród, 133, 135
Tarnopol Ghetto, 112, 133, 379
Tarnopol Voivodeship, 92, 112, 379

Tarnów, 133
Tartu, 298, 302, 306
Tartu concentration camp, 302
Task force, 330
Tautinio Darbo Apsaugos Batalionas, 113, 454
Tautiška giesmė, 340
Taylorism, 426
Tegernsee (lake), 400
Tehran Conference, 115
Telavåg, 142
Telegram, 80
Telford Taylor, 55, 360
Template:Antisemitism, 64
Template:Genocide, 203
Template:Jewish Polish history, 110
Template:Nazism sidebar, 13
Template talk:Antisemitism, 64
Template talk:Genocide, 203
Template talk:Jewish Polish history, 110
Template talk:Nazism sidebar, 13
Template talk:The Holocaust sidebar, 61, 121, 138, 209, 308, 370, 406, 425, 493
Template:The Holocaust sidebar, 61, 121, 138, 209, 308, 370, 406, 425, 493
Tenja, 199
Terebovl, 264
Terezin, 300
Ternopil, 112
Territorial changes of Poland immediately after World War II, 115
Territories of Poland annexed by the Soviet Union, 89, 123, 308, 309, 312, 318, 363, 365
Territory of the Military Commander in Serbia, 187
Tetanus, 18
The 100 most prominent Serbs, 193
The American Journal of Psychiatry, 56
The Black Book, 346
The Black Book of Communism, 246, 524
The Black Book of Poland, 93, 380, 381, **383**
The Black Book of Polish Jewry, **377**
The Coming of the Third Reich, 230
The Daily Telegraph, 509
The Destruction of the European Jews, 262, 352, 370
The Encyclopedia of the Third Reich, 481
The Eternal Jew (1940 film), 167
The final solution of the Jewish question, 134
Theft, 498
The Great Patriotic War, 1941-1945, 202
The Gulag Archipelago, 244
The Holocaust, 3, 13, 26, 61, 64, 65, 80, 89, 96, 120, 137, 144, 162, 176, 178, 202, 207, 209, 221, 253, 265, 266, 280, 303,

308, 320, 323, 330, 357, 360, 369, 385, 397, 405–407, 425, 429, 437, 493, 496
The Holocaust History Project, 551–553, 555
The Holocaust in Belarus, 89, 113, **308**, 491, 492
The Holocaust in Belgium, **162**, 445
The Holocaust Industry, 499
The Holocaust in Estonia, **296**, 490
The Holocaust in France, **178**
The Holocaust in Italian Libya, 409
The Holocaust in Latvia, **277**, 490, 491
The Holocaust in Lithuania, 104, **265**, 364, 490, 491
The Holocaust in Luxembourg, **176**
The Holocaust in Norway, **137**
The Holocaust in occupied Poland, 110
The Holocaust in Poland, **87**, 121, 357, 358, 377, 491
The Holocaust in Russia, **320**, 492
The Holocaust in Serbia, **187**
The Holocaust in the Independent State of Croatia, **194**
The Holocaust in Ukraine, 89, **258**, 491, 492
The Holocaust Museum, 118
The Jewish Chronicle, 296
The Jewish world domination conspiracy theory, 500
The Journal of Modern History, 375
The Myth of the Eastern Front, 355
The New York Times, 408
Theodicy, 497
Theodor Dannecker, 446, 484
Theodor Eicke, 219, 220, 482
Theodor Steltzer, 145
Theodosia again, 264
Theology, 496
Theophil Wurm, 44
The Origins of Totalitarianism, 436, 524
The Pianist (2002 film), 497
The Polish White Book, **380**, 383
Theresienstadt, 369
Theresienstadt concentration camp, 149, 176, 218, 226, 237, 300, 400, 447, 464
The revolt, 367
The Rise and Fall of the Third Reich, 7, 55, 83, 355, 506
The Second World War (The Great Patriotic War), 411
The Seventeen Principles, 195
The Simon Wiesenthal Center, 262
Thessaloniki, 450
The Third Reich at War, 352
The Times, 65
The uprising, 89, 102–104
The War Against the Jews, 231, 308, 375, 435
The Weekly Standard, 524, 525

The Wehrmacht: History, Myth, Reality, 355, 480
The Years of Extermination, 293
Third Reich, 89, 309, 371, 481
Thomas Blass, 434
Thor Falkanger, 153
Tiergarten, Berlin, 25
Tiergarten park, 51
Tiergartenstraße, 25
Timeline of antisemitism, 64
Timeline of Jewish-Polish history, 110
Timothy D. Snyder, 230, 258, 356
Timothy Mason, 437
Timothy Snyder, 262, 372
Titus Brandsma, 420
Tobruk, 346, 444
Tomaszów Lubelski, 133
Tomaszow Mazowiecki, 129
Tomaszów Mazowiecki, 127, 136
Tomasz Szarota, 119
Tom Segev, 355
Tõnismägi, 299
Tønsberg, 517
Topf and Sons, 94
Torfinn Vollan, 153
Torture, 15, 241
Totalitarianism, 426
Total war, 501
Totenkopf, 279
Tove Filseth, 145
Trade union, 417
Trade unionist, 407
Train, 282
Tram, 282
Transaction Publishers, 524
Transgender, 407
Transition from emigration to deportation, 358
Transnistria, 256, 459
Trauma (medicine), 14
Trawniki concentration camp, 96, 126, 127
Trawniki men, 96, 368
Trawnikis, 89, 94
Treblinka, 88, 118, 124–135, 218, 257, 262, 345, 367, 372, 485, 486, 488
Treblinka extermination camp, 39, 94, 99, 125–127, 129, 132, 134, 226, 228, 232, 237, 359, 367, 378, 408, 446
Treblinka II, 96, 100
Treblinka prisoner uprising, 89, 96, 100, 103
Trial in absentia, 302, 484, 489
Trieste, 236
Tripartite Pact, 187, 195, 415
Tripoli, 207
Tripolitania, 207, 211, 215
Troisvierges, 176
Trondheim, 141, 150

Trondheim Synagogue, 142
Trygve Lie, 146, 151
Tübingen, 48
Tuchów, 136
Tukums, 289
Tuliszków, 127, 254
Tunis, 337
Tunisia, 211
Turba, Estonia, 306
Turek, 127
Turkic, Caucasian, Cossack, and Crimean collaborationism with the Axis powers, 263
Twentieth convoy, 162
Tyczyn, 133
Types of ghettos and the living conditions, 129, 134
Typhus, 227, 256
Tyszowce, 127

U-boat, 222
Uchanie, 127
Udo von Woyrsch, 333
Ugunsdzēsēju Square, 283
Ujvidek, 187
Ukraine, 234, 235, 237, 256, 258–260, 329, 336, 338, 411
Ukrainian Auxiliary Police, 112, 261, 362, 365
Ukrainian collaborationism with the Axis powers, 258
Ukrainian Genocide, 5
Ukrainian Insurgent Army, 89, 262
Ukrainian Peoples Militia, 112, 364
Ukrainians, 229, 407, 410, 411
Ukrainian Soviet Socialist Republic, 123
Ukrainian SSR, 258
Ukrainische Hilfspolizei, 263
Ulanów, 127

Ülemiste, 306
Ülenurme, 306

Umbrella organization, 422
Umschlagplatz, 88, 118
Underground railroad, 144
Underworld, 3
Unfree labour, 241
Uniejów, 127
Unit 731, 22
United Grand Lodges of Germany, 423
United Kingdom, 79, 138, 233, 323
United Nations, 385, 499
United States, 27, 79, 80
United States Holocaust Memorial Museum, 57, 59, 175, 178, 186, 198, 231, 232, 254, 259, 264, 406, 424, 494, 497, 510, 514, 515, 525, 526, 528, 536

University of Bergen, 158
University of Bielefeld, 55
University of California Press, 375
University of Cologne, 171
University of Freiburg, 62
University of Kiel, 49
University of Leipzig, 62
University of North Carolina, 516
University of North Carolina Press, 59
University of Oslo, 161, 517
University of Paderborn, 41
University of the West of England, 63
University of Wisconsin Press, 82, 83
University Press of Kentucky, 119
Untermensch, 61, 406
Untersturmführer, 305
Upper Austria, 239
Upper Silesia, 333, 399
Uppsala, 146
Uprising, 89
Uprising and massacre, 89
Uprising and mass killings, 89
Uprising in Serbia (1941), 187
Urban population, 320
Uruguay, 290
US Army, 323
USHMM, 122, 364, 521
U.S. News & World Report, 524
U.S. Supreme Court, 498
Ustaše, 195–199, 437, 447
Ustasha, 192
Ustashe, 194
Utilitarian genocide, 201

Vagrancy (people), 423
Vaira Vīķe-Freiberga, 292
Vaivara concentration camp, 237, 300, 301, 305
Valentinas Brandišauskas, 273
Valeriano Weyler, 219
Valga, Estonia, 306
Valmiera, 289
Vandenhoeck & Ruprecht, 55
Varaklani, 284
Vasalemma, 307
Vasknarva, 306
Vaste, 307
VDM Publishing, 84
Vel dHiv Roundup, 183, 544
Ventspils, 283
Veracruz, Veracruz, 250
Verdinaso, 164
Verklärte Nacht, 80
Vernichtungskrieg, 258
Vesicant, 17
Vest Agder, 153

Vichy, 179
Vichy France, 176, 178, 180, 185, 444, 449
Vichy laws on the status of Jews, 165
Vichy Régime, 548
Victims and death toll, 550
Victims of Nazism, 407
Victor Martin, 171
Victors Arajs, 289
Vidkun Quisling, 456
Vidzeme, 281
Vienna, 358, 419
Viivikonna, 306
Viktor Brack, 31, 32, 487
Viktor Frankl, 497
Viktor Novak, 206
Viktors Arājs, 277, 280, 281, 341
Vileyka, 362
Vileyka Voblast, 529
Vilna Gaon Jewish State Museum, 272
Vilna Ghetto, 274
Vilnius, 112, 268, 365
Vingåker Municipality, 146
Vinkovci, 336
Vinnytsia, 260, 364
Vintage Books, 55
Virtual Shtetl, 515, 516
Visa (document), 164
Vistula River, 323
Vitebsk, 319
Vitebsk Ghetto, 319
Vitry-le-François, 4
Vivisection, 20
Vladimir Dedijer, 205
Vladimir Lenin, 462
Vladimir Mintz, 287
Vladimir Žerjavić, 200
Vojislav Koštunica, 193
Vojvodina, 187, 192
Volhynia, 366
Völkisch movement, 435
Volksdeutsche, 111, 457
Volksdeutsche in German-occupied western Poland, 34
Volksdeutscher Selbstschutz, 111, 332
Võru, 306

Waakirchen, 401
Wadowice, 133
Waffen SS, 88, 301, 411
Waffen-SS, 92, 101, 335, 357, 361, 433, 444
Wallonia, 164
Walter Buch, 70
Walter Laqueur, 5, 118
Walter Rauff, 337, 346, 487
Walter Schellenberg, 335
Walter Schimana, 325

Walter Stahlecker, 280, 287, 297, 303
Walther Bierkamp, 492
Walther Rauff, 346, 444
Walther von Brauchitsch, 334
Walther von Reichenau, 348, 443
Wannsee conference, 41, 93, 123, 134, 140, 147, 166, 239, 277, 297, 345, 357, 359, 360, 407, 427, 448, 460
Wannsee Protocol, 240
War crimes, 330, 349, 381, 482
War crimes in occupied Poland during World War II, 381, 384
Warka, 127
Warsaw, 99, 108, 127, 255, 393, 411, 461, 515
Warsaw concentration camp, 237
Warsaw Ghetto, 88, 91, 99, 102, 103, 106, 122, 124–129, 254, 255, 257, 369, 378, 381, 430
Warsaw Ghetto Uprising, 88, 89, 96, 103, 104, 115, 121, 137, 367, 409, 430, 490
Warta, 98, 127
Warta, Poland, 40
Warthegau, 40, 366
Wartheland, 34, 97, 483
Warzyce, 134
Washington, D.C., 514
Waterloo, Belgium, 173
Wąwolnica, Lublin Voivodeship, 133
Wayback Machine, 293, 512, 521
Węgrów, 133
Wehrmacht, 90, 165, 187, 260, 277, 279, 309, 317, 330, 332, 361, 370, 411, 425
Weimar, 217
Wendy Lower, 262
Werner Best, 331
Werner Blankenburg, 32, 49
Werner Braune, 492
Werner Catel, 49, 506
Werner Heyde, 34, 50
West Belarus, 123
Westerbork, 358
Westerbork concentration camp, 237
Westerbork transit camp, 218
Western Belorussia, 312
Western culture, 426
West Germany, 289, 413, 466, 498
White Buses, 153
White people, 415
White Sea-Baltic Canal, 244
White supremacy, 426
Whitworth College, 434
Wieliczka, 133
Wielkopolska, 333
Wielun, 133
Wieruszów, 133
Wiesel Commission, 458

Wikipedia:Citation needed, 21, 105, 141–144, 154, 183, 198, 201, 212, 245, 259, 270, 315, 393, 394, 417
Wikipedia:Citing sources, 26
Wikipedia:Identifying reliable sources, 406, 415
Wikipedia:Please clarify, 142, 144, 208, 210, 211, 315
Wikipedia:Vagueness, 271
Wikipedia:Verifiability, 301
Wikisource, 284, 356
Wikisource:Comprehensive report of Einsatzgruppe A up to 15 October 1941, 284, 356
Wikt:deprive, 282
Wikt:massacre, 407
Wikt:rob, 281
Wilhelm Canaris, 222
Wilhelm Frick, 28, 218, 442
Wilhelm Fuchs, 336, 337, 490
Wilhelm Harster, 489
Wilhelm Keitel, 443, 484
Wilhelm Kube, 313, 314
Wilhelm Werle, 305
William Cooper (Aboriginal Australian), 79
William Craig (author), 351
William L. Shirer, 55, 83, 355, 506, 538
William Shirer, 7
William W. Hagen, 258
Wilno Ghetto, 111, 133, 379
Wilno Voivodeship (1926–1939), 92, 112, 362, 378
Wilno Voivodeship (1926–39), 364
Winston Churchill, 4
Winterhilfswerk, 422
Winter Velodrome, 544
Wiślica, 133
Witold Pilecki, 108, 391, 392, 428
Witolds Report, 108, **391**, 428
Władysław Bartoszewski, 502
Włocławek, 127
Włodawa, 127
Włoszczowa, 127
Wodzisław, 127
Wodzisław Śląski, 399, 402
WOJAC, 214
Wola massacre, 423
Wolbrom, 133
Wolfgang Geldmacher, 145
Wolfram Wette, 355, 480
Wollert Krohn-Hansen, 517
Wołomin, 127
Wołyń Voivodeship (1921–1939), 96
Word of the year (Germany), 5
World Jewish Congress, 151, 428
World war, 8

World War I, 66, 163, 422, 441
World War II, 3, 4, 13, 89, 98, 121, 162, 176, 178, 187, 194, 207, 218, 221, 253, 265, 308, 322, 323, 330, 331, 357, 377, 397, 406, 407, 414, 496, 500
World War II and its violence, 358
World War II casualties of Poland, 107
World War II evacuation and expulsion, 367
World War II persecution of Serbs, 194, 202
World War Two, 157, 358
Wound ballistics, 20
WP:NOTRS, 247, 352, 423
Wysokie Mazowieckie, 134
Wyszogród, 127

Xenophobia, 414
X-ray, 19

Yad Vashem, 6, 8, 104, 105, 186, 231, 238, 314, 324, 376, 404, 424, 458, 495, 497, 502, 503, 510, 512, 518, 525, 550, 551
Yale University Press, 503, 524
Yalta Conference, 115, 116, 136
Yanchang, 246
Yaqui genocide, 249
Yaquis, 250
Yaron Svoray, 75
Yazidi genocide, 202
Yehuda Bauer, 6, 362, 439, 503
Yellow badge, 162, 167, 176, 181, 182, 285, 310
Yezhovshchina, 123
Yiddish, 106, 324, 496
Yiddish language, 8, 170
Yiddish renaissance, 496
Yitzhak Arad, 118, 262, 326, 374, 513, 515
Yivo, 118
Yoav Gelber, 520
Yom HaShoah, 3, 8, 499
YouTube, 216, 231, 395
Ypatingasis būrys, 89, 113, 265, 270
Yugoslavia, 408

Zabłudów, 134
Zagórów, 125, 128
Zagreb, 200, 336, 447
Zagreb Synagogue, 199
Zambrow, 133, 134
Zambrów, 134
Zamość, 128

Żarki, 134
Žarko Dolinar, 204

Zawiercie, 134
Zbor, 187, 191

Zboriv, 338
Zduńska Wola, 128
Zdzięcioł Ghetto, 136, 319
Zdzięcioł massacres, 136

Żegota, 104, 108, 115, 422
Żelechów, 134

Zelów, 134
Zemgale, 280, 281
Zemun, 190

ŽGiŠK Makabi Zagreb, 199

Zgoda labour camp, 229
Zhitkovichi, 313
Zhlobin, 313
Zhytomyr, 311, 364
Zionism, 324, 439, 462
Zionist, 67
Zionist Action Committee, 8
Złoczów, 92
Zloty, 108

ŻOB, 108

Zofia Kossak-Szczucka, 105, 108, 428
Zofjówka, 365

ŽŠK Makabi Osijek, 199

Związek Organizacji Wojskowej, 393
Zwoleń, 129, 131, 134

Żychlin, 128
Żydokomuna, 105, 495
Żydowski Instytut Historyczny, 513

Zyklon B, 94, 98, 101, 345, 367, 368

Żyrardów, 128
ŻZW, 108

www.ingramcontent.com/pod-product-compliance
Lightning Source LLC
Chambersburg PA
CBHW030512230426
43665CB00010B/599